E PLURIBUS UNUM
New Mexico Southeast

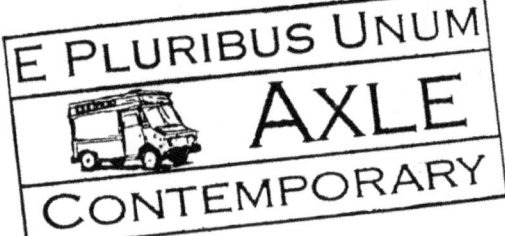

E PLURIBUS UNUM
New Mexico Southeast

October 1-24, 2018

Axle Contemporary, Santa Fe, New Mexico

Published by Axle Contemporary
P.O. Box 22095
Santa Fe, New Mexico 87502
www.axlecontemporarypress.com

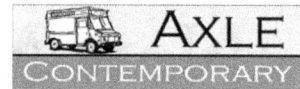

ISBN: 978-0-9963991-5-9

Axle Contemporary would like to thank The Anderson Museum of Contemporary Art, Nancy Fleming and the Roswell Artist-in-Residence Foundation, Roswell Museum and Arts Center, Lovington Mainstreet, New Mexico Junior College, Western Heritage Museum & Lea County Cowboy Hall of Fame, NMSU Alamogordo, Alamogordo Mainstreet, MoMAZoZo, Donna Stern at Mescalero, Carlsbad Creative Arts Council, NMSU Carlsbad, Artesia Arts and Cultural District, Artesia Mainstreet, Artesia Arts Council, Artesia Historical Museum and Art Center, Artesia Public Library, Portales Mainstreet, ENMU Portales, and Clovis Mainstreet.

This project is supported in part by an award from the National Endowment for the Arts, This project is made possible in part by New Mexico Arts, a division of the Department of Cultural Affairs, and the National Endowment for the Arts. Support also provided by the FUNd of the Albuquerque Community Foundation, and the PY Foundation.

Food for the artists generously provided in part by Lowe's Signature Market in Alamogordo, Alamogordo Mainstreet, Lovington Mainstreet, MoMAZoZo, Sacred Grounds in Ruidoso, Larry Bob Phillips and Tamara Zibners, Stellar Coffee in Roswell, David Morgan at the Carlsbad Museum and Art Center, Red Arrow in Clovis, Clovis Mainstreet, and Lina & Ally's Tea Shoppe in Clovis.

Lodging provided in part by The Roswell Artist-in-Residence Foundation, Lovington Mainstreet, The Western Heritage Museum & Lea County Cowboy Hall of Fame in Hobbs, Country Inn and Suites in Hobbs, Alamogordo Mainstreet, MoMAZoZo, Holiday Inn Portales, Comfort Inn Clovis, and Clovis Mainstreet.

Special thanks to towing services provided by The City of Lovington, Crystal Ball, New Mexico Junior College, and The Western Heritage Museum & Lea County Cowboy Hall of Fame.

Nina Mastrangelo and Carol Cooper came to Roswell and worked hard with us for the big days at the Fair there. Thank you both!

And our greatest thanks goes to the more than 900 people who came by, were photographed, and participated to make the project possible.

The photographs from E Pluribus Unum: New Mexico Southeast are presented as an exhibition at The Western Heritage Museum & Lea County Cowboy Hall of Fame in Hobbs New Mexico, from August 22–November 3, 2019; and at the Roswell Museum and Art Center in Roswell, New Mexico, from November 16, 2019–April 12, 2020.

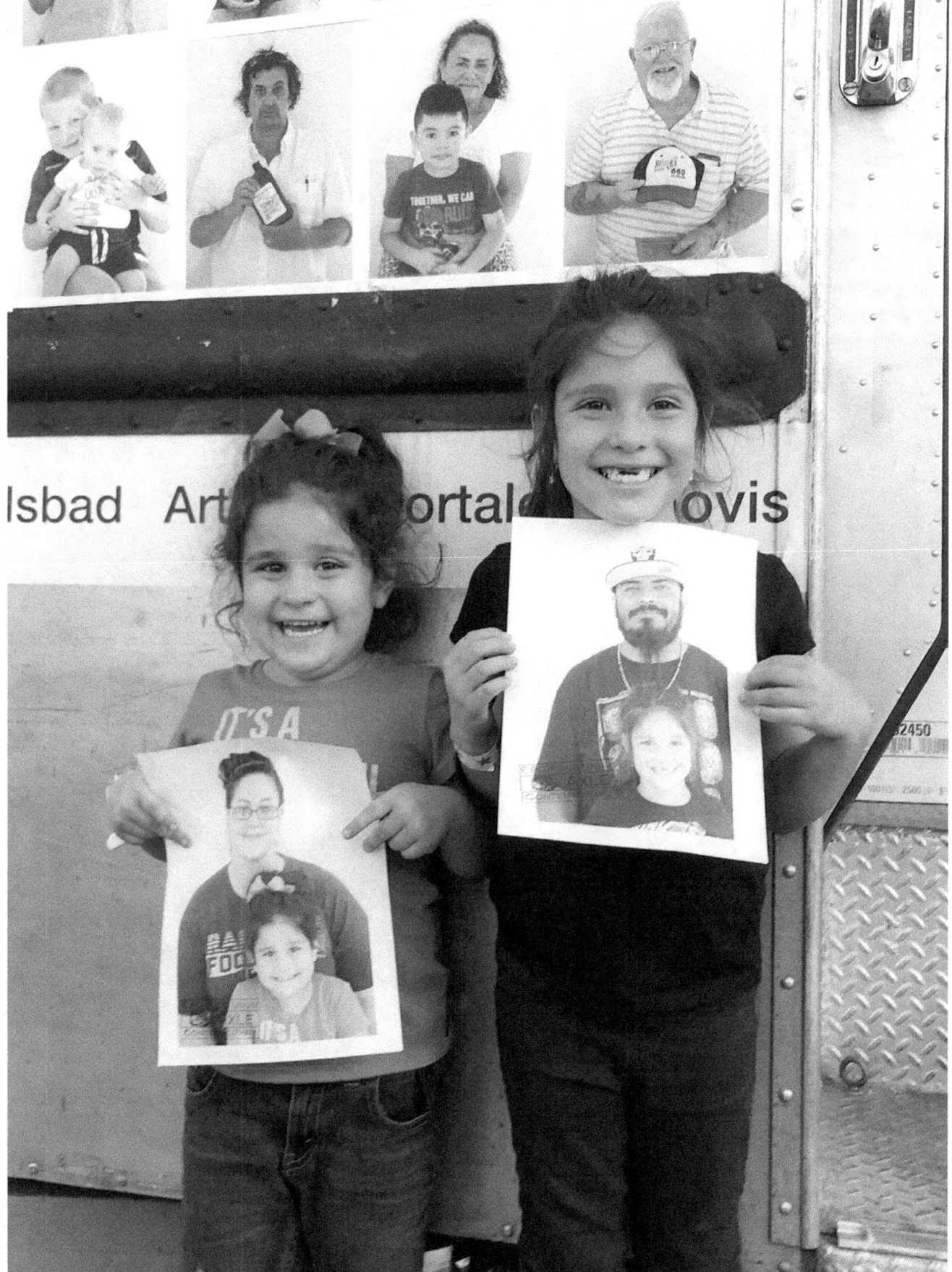

Table of Contents

The Photographs

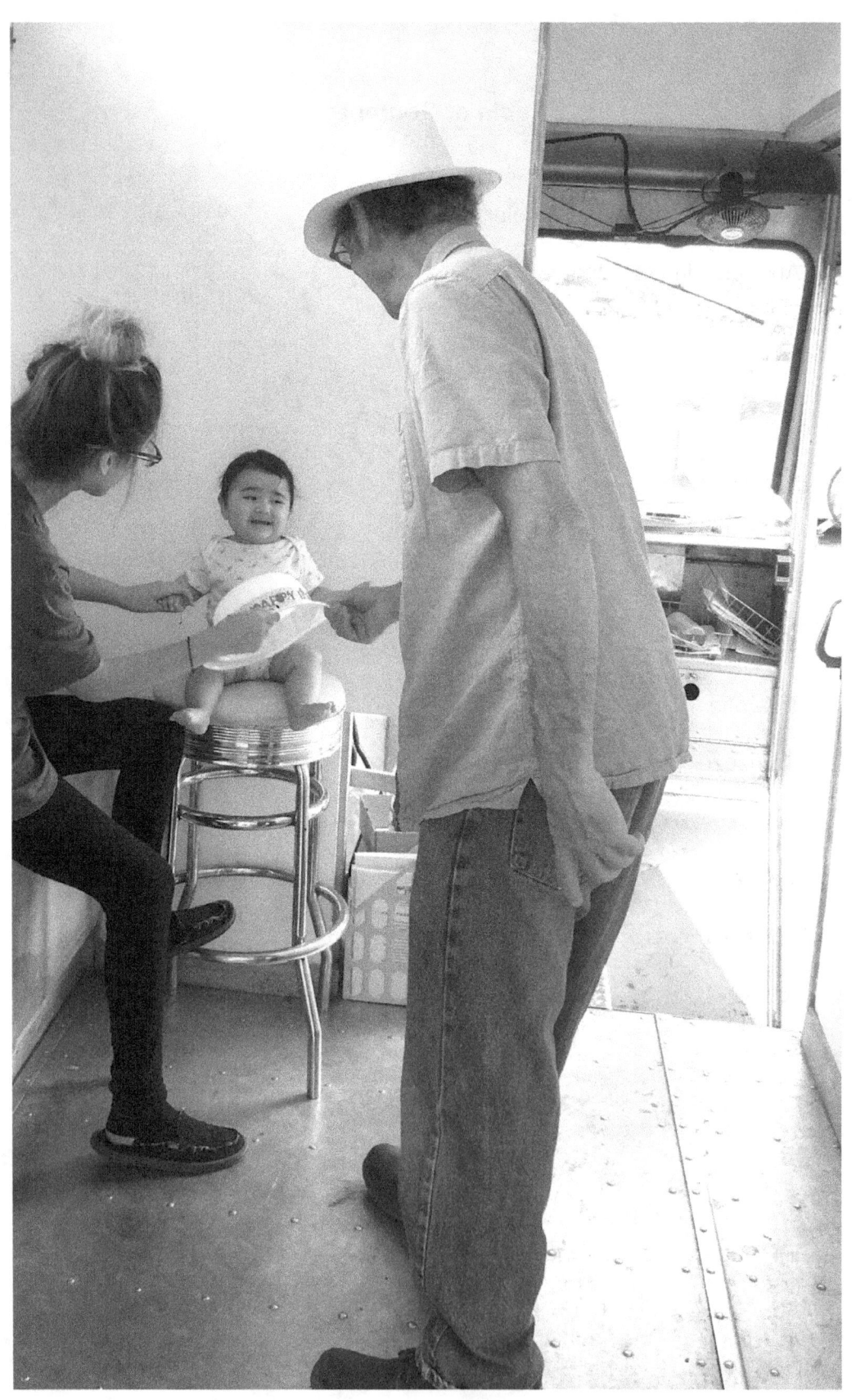

Axle Contemporary's *E Pluribus Unum: New Mexico Southeast*

Even I sometimes lapse again into the bad habit of calling Southern New Mexico a desert. It's easy to talk about the region that way because it does indeed contain a desert—Chihuahua—and because anybody not from there almost always has some notion of the place—half impossibly desolate and half impossibly romantic—so they can fill in the picture for themselves without asking me a whole slew of annoying questions. Never mind that the picture they get isn't entirely accurate. Sometimes I'm not interested in portraying an accurate picture. For instance, when the Texans found out Southern New Mexico contained some of the most picaresque mountain life south of the Rockies, complete with skiing and great barbeque, Cloudcroft and Ruidoso got overrun with terribly driven diesel trucks sporting steer horns mounted above one bumper and nuts hanging below the other. So when folks like myself, whose whole histories are intertwined with Southern New Mexico, say the place is a desert, we're not so much discounting the diversity of the landscape—vast plains in the east, snowcapped mountains down the middle, the whole magical Gila wilderness in the west—it's more like we're trying to protect it from Texans, or just keep it to ourselves.

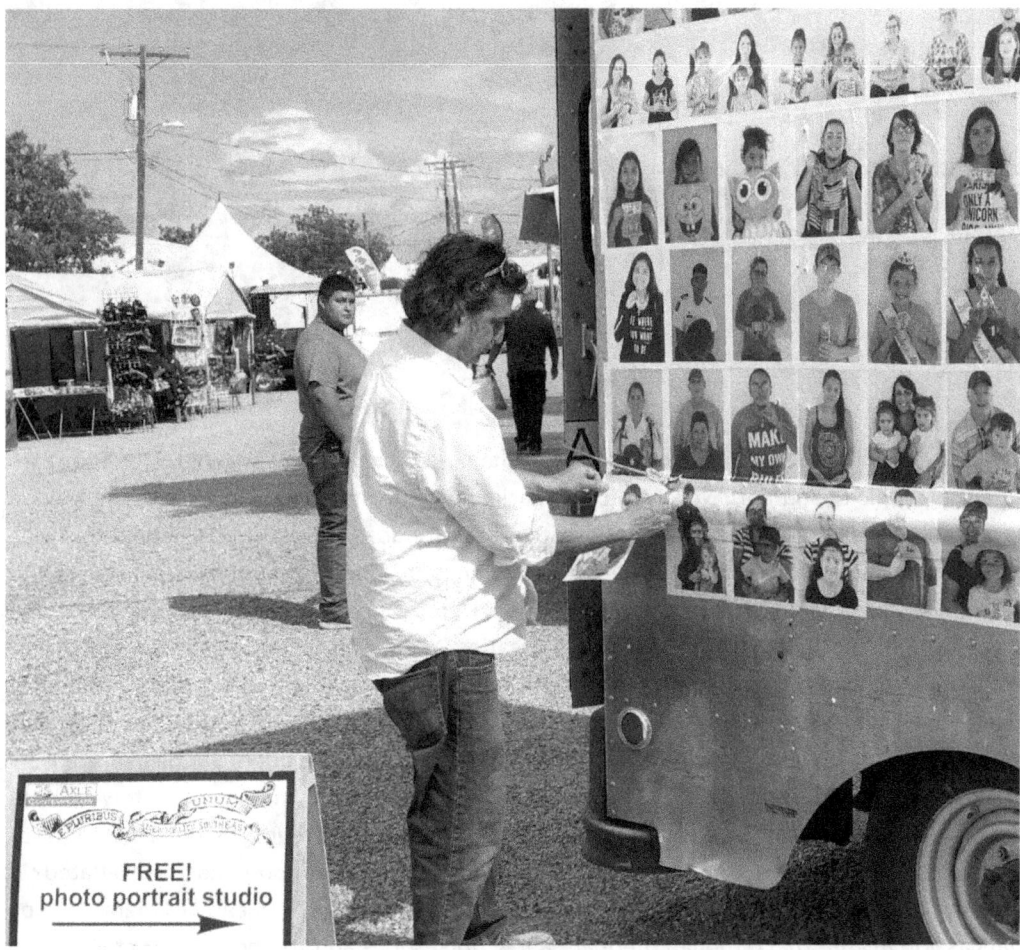

But, of course, that's not very generous of us. In fact, it's downright mean. It puts me in mind of the portraits fashion photographer Richard Avedon did in the early 80s, collected in his book *In the American West*. The project was to capture something of the people in the West and so he stripped the iconic landscapes out of his pictures. He put his subjects against a white background and snapped away at their faces, not a one of them smiling. The portraits, while arresting, make me grumpy. The people, mostly impoverished laborers, look grumpy and Avedon maybe means to say something about the harsh life on the Western frontier, but to my eye the people in those portraits don't read as dissatisfied with life generally, just dissatisfied with this moment in their lives when a fancy East Coast photographer is fussing at them from behind his giant camera. Avedon doesn't seek to portray the people of this Western region with generosity and they don't seem to have any generosity saved for him. Their looks say *Get out* and I do suspect Avedon didn't linger.

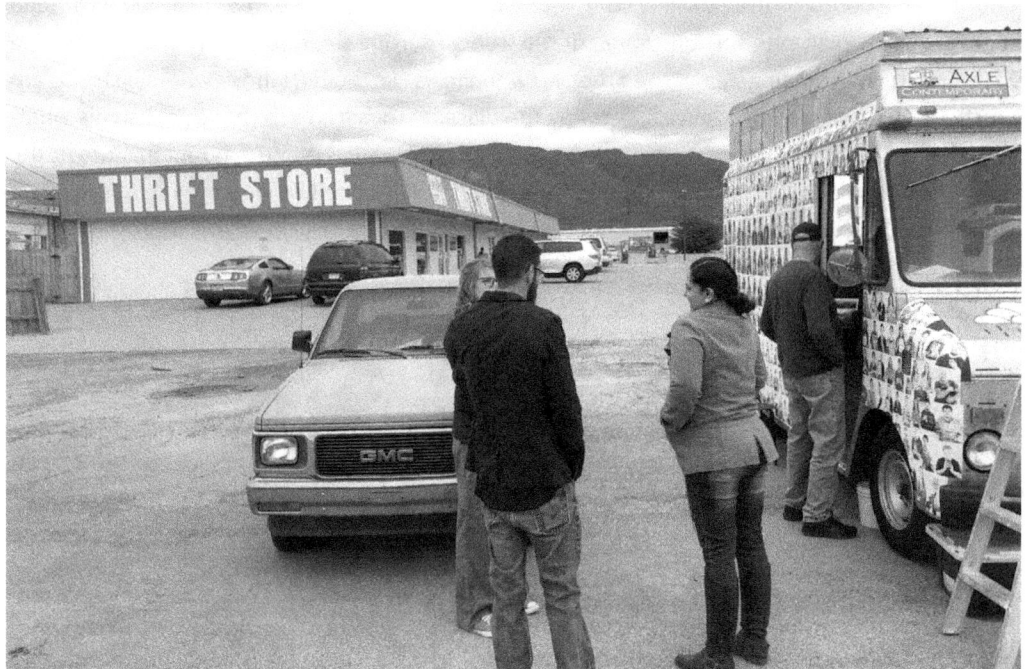

The portraits in this book, on the other hand, contain no such shortage of generosity. They capture the people of Southern New Mexico in black and white against a blank canvas, as Avedon captured his westerners. But here that artistic simplicity does not cause the people to shrink into their misery. Instead, it magnifies their magnanimity, which is, if you ask me, one of the great natural resources in Southern New Mexico. Here, everyone shares something. Flipping through these portraits you'll find a dozen rosaries. You'll find hula-hoops and beer cozies. You'll find Bibles and smartphones and figurines of aliens. You'll find a surprising number of skulls, both human and animal, and a surprising number of children with toy guns. There's a woman who looks charmingly like her poodle and prophetic figure offering a pair of sneakers like the messiah evaporated out of them only moments ago. In Lovington, an oil town whose ambitious name might seem a trick until you get to know the folks there, we see a woman with a hand scrawled menu for Angie's Gorditas. How many grumpy laborers has she satiated? If only she'd been hawking her wares near Avedon's outfit. There are not nearly as many cowboy hats as you might expect, though there are a few horseshoes and sombreros and at least one top hat in good condition. Not everyone smiles but there is not, save one small child afraid to lose her blankey, a single grumpy face in the bunch.

Though Southern New Mexico's vast landscapes of plains, mountains, and deserts are not visible, there is a largeness in these Axle Contemporary portraits that tells you all you need to know about the region, the hearts and eyes as wide open as the terrain. In this book my fellow New Mexicans are depicted in all their complexity, as artists and writers and adherents, as firefighters and truckers and farmers, as soda drinkers and phone talkers and movie watchers, as widows and sons and friends. In this, one of the poorest states in the union, their diverse lives no doubt share the quality of often being, more often than not, extraordinarily difficult. But in these portraits it's the resilience that shines through. That, and something else: these Southern New Mexicans are relaxed, and in the Land of Mañana, that's maybe the most accurate thing a photographer could ever capture.

-Joshua Wheeler

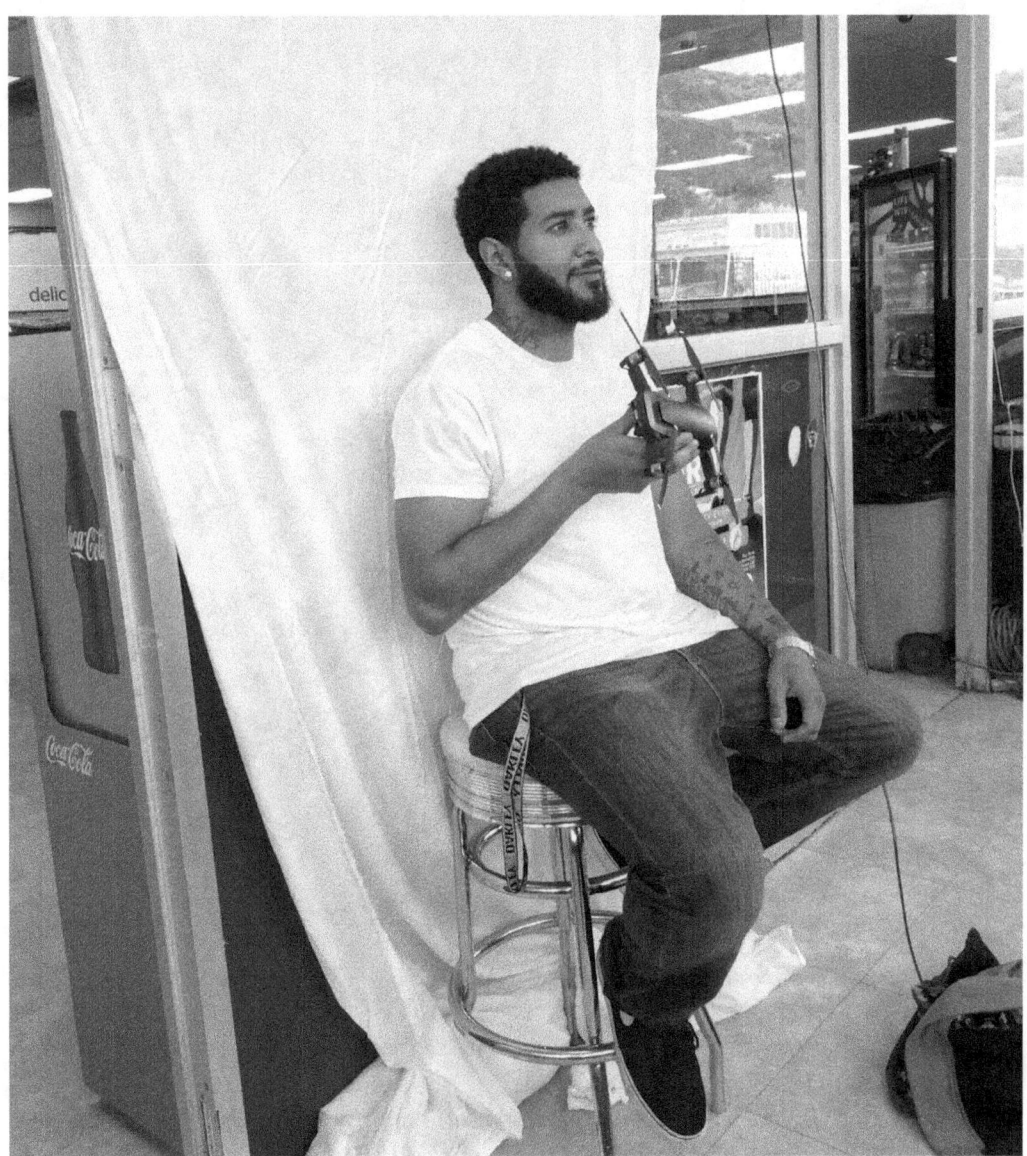

Joshua Wheeler is from Alamogordo, New Mexico. He teaches at Louisiana State University. He's the author of Acid West, a collection of essays about Southern New Mexico.

During the month of October, 2018, artists Matthew Chase-Daniel and Jerry Wellman traveled to communities throughout Southeastern New Mexico, offering free portraits and participation in E Pluribus Unum: New Mexico Southeast. Over the course of their travels, they created over 900 portraits. Communities visited were: Roswell, Lovington, Hobbs, Alamogordo, Tularosa, Carrizozo, Ruidoso, Mescalero, Carlsbad, Artesia, Portales, and Clovis.

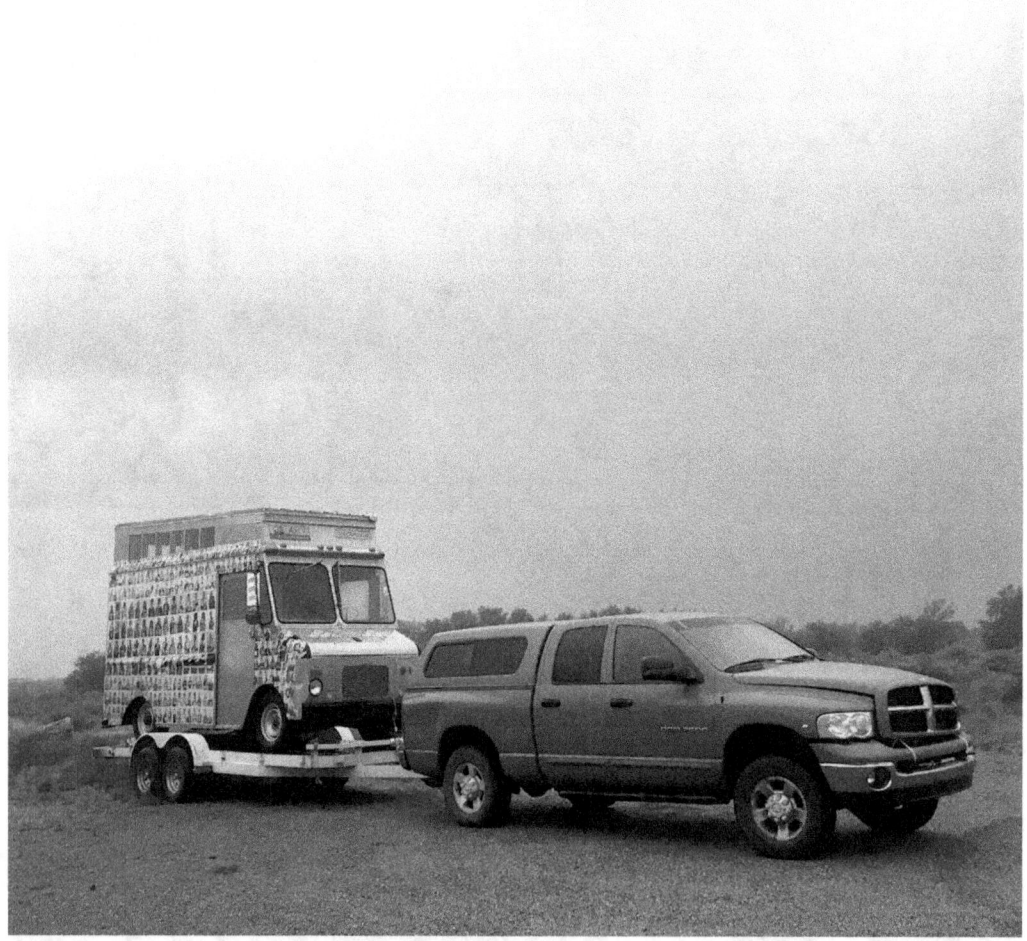

For these *E Pluribus Unum* projects, the artists outfit the Axle Contemporary mobile artspace as a natural light photographic portrait studio. People sit for a portrait while holding a small personally significant object. Prints are immediately distributed to the participants and also wheat-pasted to the exterior of the studio-gallery. Later, an image is created by overlaying all the portraits to create one face that includes equal portions of all the participants. Each project is published in its entirety as a book.

Since 2012 we've made E Pluribus Unum projects in New Mexico every two years. This has gradually become a portrait of New Mexico in our time. We've set up in Santa Fe, Albuquerque, on the Navajo Nation, and now in the small cities and towns of Southeastern New Mexico. The enthusiasm that we were met with throughout our travels to rural areas of the Navajo Nation gave us the desire and confidence to take this project to the equally remote Southeastern New Mexico.

Before we even left on our journey we were met with great support from community organizations, local colleges, museums, and local MainStreet organizations. Generosity is fundamental to this project and was consistently demonstrated by co-organizers, participants and the communities that we visited. We also were honored with dedicated funding for this project from the National Endowment for the Arts and the Albuquerque Community Foundation.

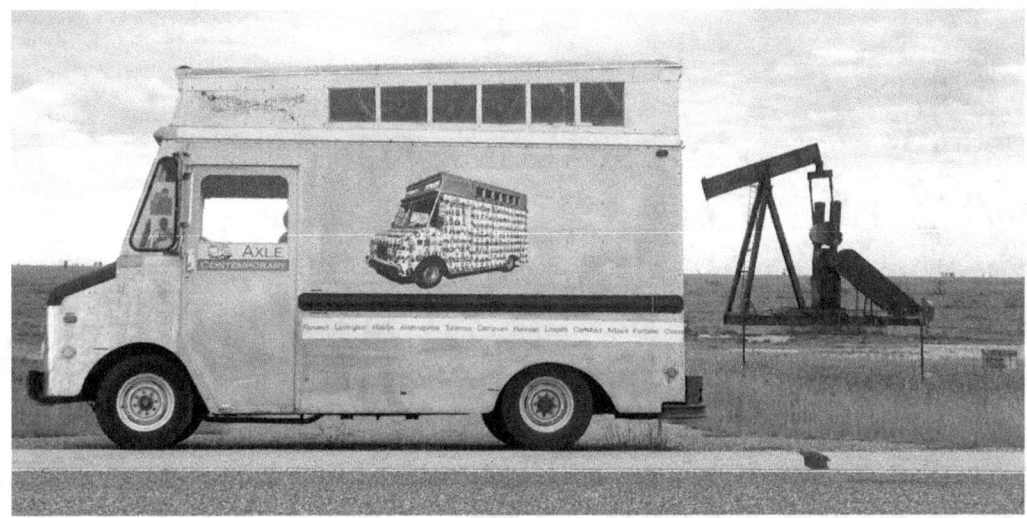

We left Santa Fe with a newly rebuilt engine that was for some reason burning entirely too much oil. But our month's schedule was set, and since we would be visiting the oil producing capital of New Mexico, burning oil seemed somehow appropriate. Heading down to do our project in Southeastern New Mexico we were expecting to feel out of place. This part of New Mexico has a reputation for being very different than where we live in Santa Fe. Santa Fe is a liberal progressive town, standing deep in our tourism and government based economy. Down south, the politics are more conservative, the churches are more numerous, and the economy is driven by resource extraction and feedlot dairies.

We began our expedition in Roswell. Downtown was densely populated by large and small green alien statues, but the people we encountered seemed much more grounded. Our first day we joined the Eastern New Mexico State Fair parade. Our van followed costumed kids encouraging recycling, Shriners, rodeo queens, and floats and a monster truck promoting a political candidate for the upcoming November election. The Parade ended at the fairgrounds where we parked by a reptile handler and a funnel cake maker, not far from the 4H demonstration tent. We finished up our Roswell stay by visiting a downtown coffee shop, a local bank headquarters, and a contemporary art museum.

Exhilarated from our time in Roswell, we headed to Lovington, 95 miles away and seperated by only one tiny village. As we left Roswell we passed through miles of alfalfa fields, irrigated from the waters of the Pecos. As we crossed the river, the vegetation grew sparse and we moved into an area populated by oil rigs. Nearing Lovington, our stepvan erupted in loud clanging, as coincidence would have it, right in front of a pumpjack. The engine was severely compromised, and clearly would not bring us to that day's destination.

We gave our coordinator in Lovington a call to say we would be a little late and attempted to tow the stepvan with our auxiliary vehicle. That worked for a while, but not quite all the way to Lovington. Another apologetic phone call was met with "No problem, we'll send one of our city workers to tow you in." He took us to Bob's Thriftway where we were scheduled to park. Only 45 minutes late, we were set up and making photographs.

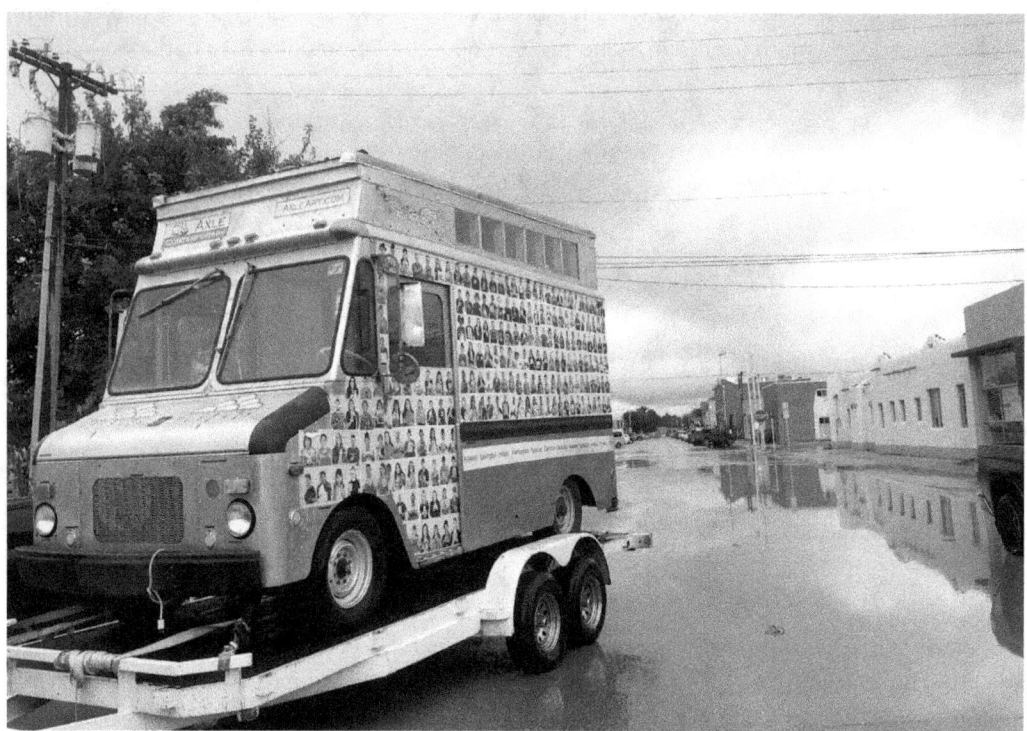

That evening, exhausted, we accepted an invitation for a beer at the local microbrewery and then went straight to our hotel, knowing that our wonderful Lovington host had arranged for us to get a twenty mile tow to our next stop, Hobbs.

The director of the Western Heritage Museum and Lea County Cowboy Hall of Fame arranged our accommodations and personally towed the Axle stepvan-studio around town for the next couple of days. At the end of our Hobbs stay, we left the van in front of the museum, a unique combination of celebration of local cowboy history, and revolving exhibitions of international interest. We hustled back to Santa Fe to pick up Matthew's truck and a car-hauler trailer, lent to us by our mechanic.

We resumed our Southeastern New Mexico adventure with the trailer, a hand made ramp, and a stepvan with a failing engine. We only needed that van to go up 10 feet onto the trailer, but every time we started it up, we knew it may be the last time. We bought a winch as a type of insurance so no matter what, we could get the van up on the trailer. Five hours and a mountain pass later, we arrived in Alamogordo.

Alamogordo has it's own UFO stories. It is close to the Trinity nuclear bomb test site, and the spectacular White Sands National Monument. Visitors to our mobile photo studio included retired military personnel from the nearby Holloman Air Force base and the director of the New Mexico Museum of Space History. Once again we were met with generous hosts and a home-cooked meal in the nearby mountain town of High Rolls.

From Alamogordo we headed north to the villages of Tularosa and Carrizozo. We were accompanied by a huge temperature drop and some monumentally strong winds. Our hosts in Carrizozo got out the word and despite some unseasonably cold weather we were met with a large contingent outside the old Lyric Theatre. Carrizozo was once a busy railroad town, but later fell into disrepair and was nearly abandoned to the ravages of time. In recent years there has been an influx of artists and writers from around New Mexico and around the country. The community is small but cohesive and energetic. Our hosts there are the creators of a dynamic local hub of activity, the MoMaZoZo.

From Carizozo we drove through the rain and up the Sacramento Mountains to Ruidoso and Mescalero. Ruidoso is a tourist town (the closest mountain town to all of Texas) founded on skiing, horse racing, and outdoor recreation. Only a few miles away, Mescalero is the home of Mescalero Apache tribe.

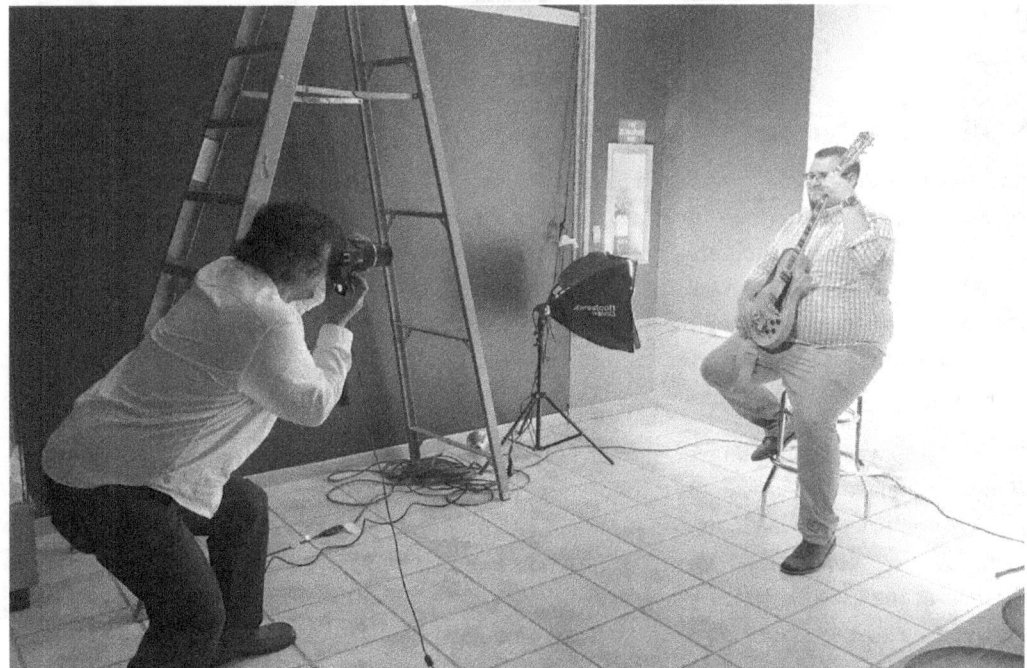

Our usual photo studio arrangement couldn't work in the driving rain. We didn't feel comfortable driving the truck down the slippery wooden ramp so we improvised a studio, old-school, using a white sheet as a backdrop. In Ruidoso we set up right in the middle of the Sacred Grounds coffee shop, creating a new tangent of conversation for locals. In Mescalero, we hung our backdrop and set up our tripod in the small glass-walled entryway to the Mescalero Tribal Store. The bustling activity in the small space, through which everyone passed on their way to buy their groceries, added an element of curiosity that definitely worked in our favor to attract participants.

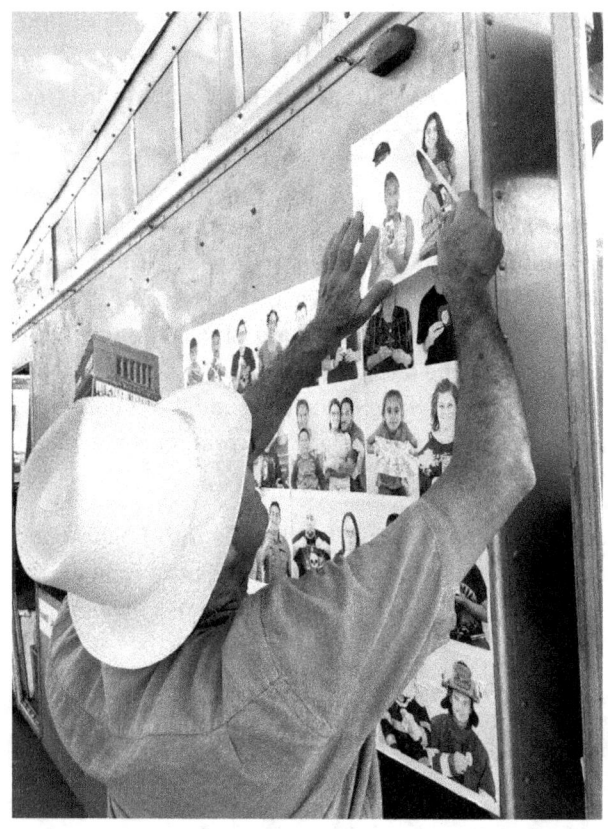

Back over to the eastern side of the mountains, we rolled into Carlsbad the next morning and were warmly welcomed to an art class at New Mexico State University there. After that we drove through the flooded streets of Carlsbad and set up at the museum downtown. We created a makeshift studio in the room next to their charming mechanized miniature historical Carlsbad model train display.

We spent two days in Artesia, first at the very modern and busy public library, and then at the well attended annual Art-in-the-Park festival, complete with art, school bands, food vendors, and a strong sense of community pride.

Early in the morning we drove a long and lonely road to make it to the Portales Peanut Valley Festival by 10 am. A contingent of strong and enthusiastic volunteers jumped in to help us push the stepvan through a huge roll-up door into our allotted space inside the large festival hall. Many of the vendors came to be photographed holding their paintings, sculptures, and assorted products, including local dill-flavored peanuts. A convincing top-hatted Mr. Peanut strolled the exhibition hall and posed for us, peering out through his monocle. Later we visited Eastern New Mexico University. Art students came out to be seen with skulls, paintings, skateboards, speakers, and other varied objects from their college lives.

Our last stop was Clovis, home of Norman Petty studios, the original recording studio for Buddy Holly and many more early Rock 'n Roll stars. Drawing on Clovis' Rock 'n Roll fame, is Red Arrow Entertainment, a video arcade, coffee shop, restaurant, and bingo parlor. We parked right out front by the bronze buffalo. We ended our stay in Clovis and the E Pluribus Unum: Southeast project at the Clovis Carver Library, in the heart of the historic downtown. When it was time for us to leave, it was cold and raining again. Our engine finally gave out, so we unsheathed our come-along winch. In a much appreciated final act of generosity a local participant jumped in to help. We took turns, each cracking the winch until exhausted, then passing the handle off to the other. A neighbor with a tea shop came by with hot tea and pastries for our trip home. We strapped Axle to the trailer one last time and headed West toward Santa Fe.

A couple of hours later, still 90 miles from home, we experienced one final travail. Our borrowed trailer blew a tire. We pulled to the side of the highway as the sun set, removed the wheel and drove in the dark back to Santa Fe. The next day we returned with a new tire and soon were home safe and whole, with a project accomplished and a new engine soon to be installed.

On reflection, we feel that despite the initial visual onslaught of franchise restaurants, auto parts outlets, and dollar stores, closer engagement reveals that each of these Southeastern New Mexico communities has its own unique flavor. Our project isn't so different down here. Yes, the politics and the landscape and the culture and the economy are very different than up north, but in E Pluribus Unum we are engaging with individuals, not with groups of people or caricatures and presuppositions. It seems that when the interaction is pared down to a one-on-one, we are all so much more alike than we are different. Our concerns, our desires, and our motivations are direct, understandable, kind, human.

In our little studio there is only space for the photographer and that one other person, and both are working together to make the photo. It is a brief collaboration and the communication and connection is often unspoken, but the depth of meaning in this moment can be profound.

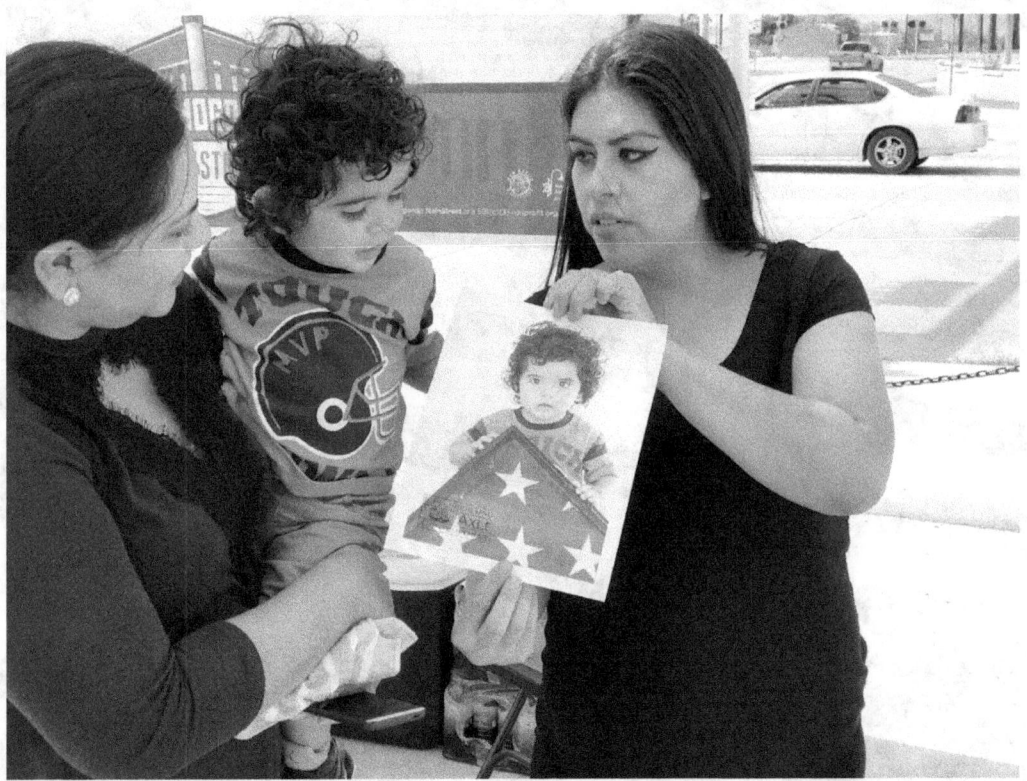

We've now made about 3,000 of these E Pluribus Unum portraits around New Mexico. Each one is unique, alive, full of spirit, and also they are all so very similar. The variations in each face are so slight and subtle, we could never describe in words the differences, but when we see them they are clear and resonant and seeing this, we are changed every time.

This is humanity, striving, clashing, loving, talking, smiling, worried. When we mediate our connection with others with electronics and economics, political parties and war and fear, we so often lose the direct connection that can happen when two people look at each other and are made whole as one, momentarily. This is the heart of our E Pluribus Unum project. We are unique and we are all together as one.

-Jerry Wellman and Matthew Chase-Daniel

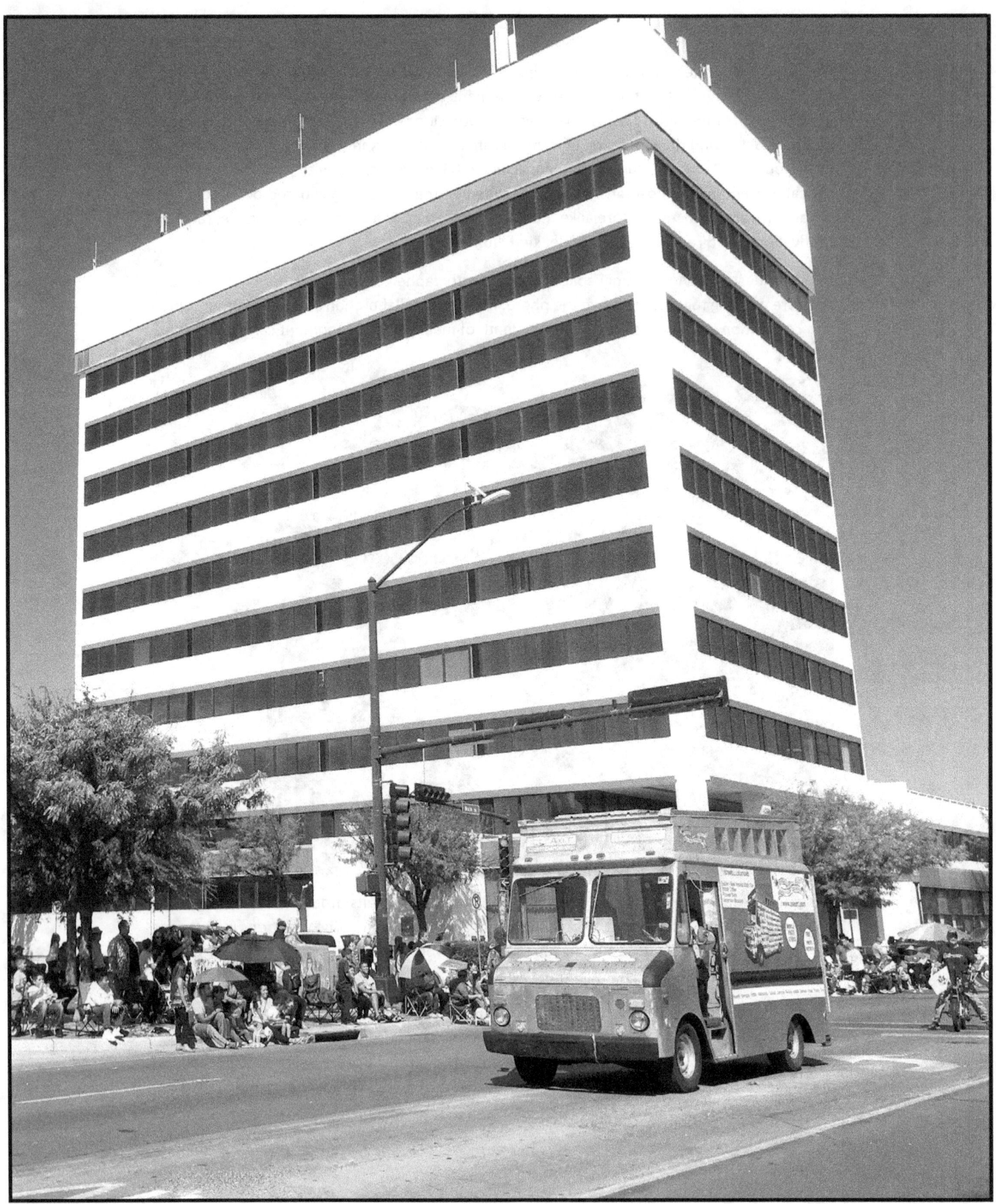

Roswell

October 1-3, 2019

Eastern New Mexico State Fair
Stellar Coffee
Pioneer Bank
Anderson Museum

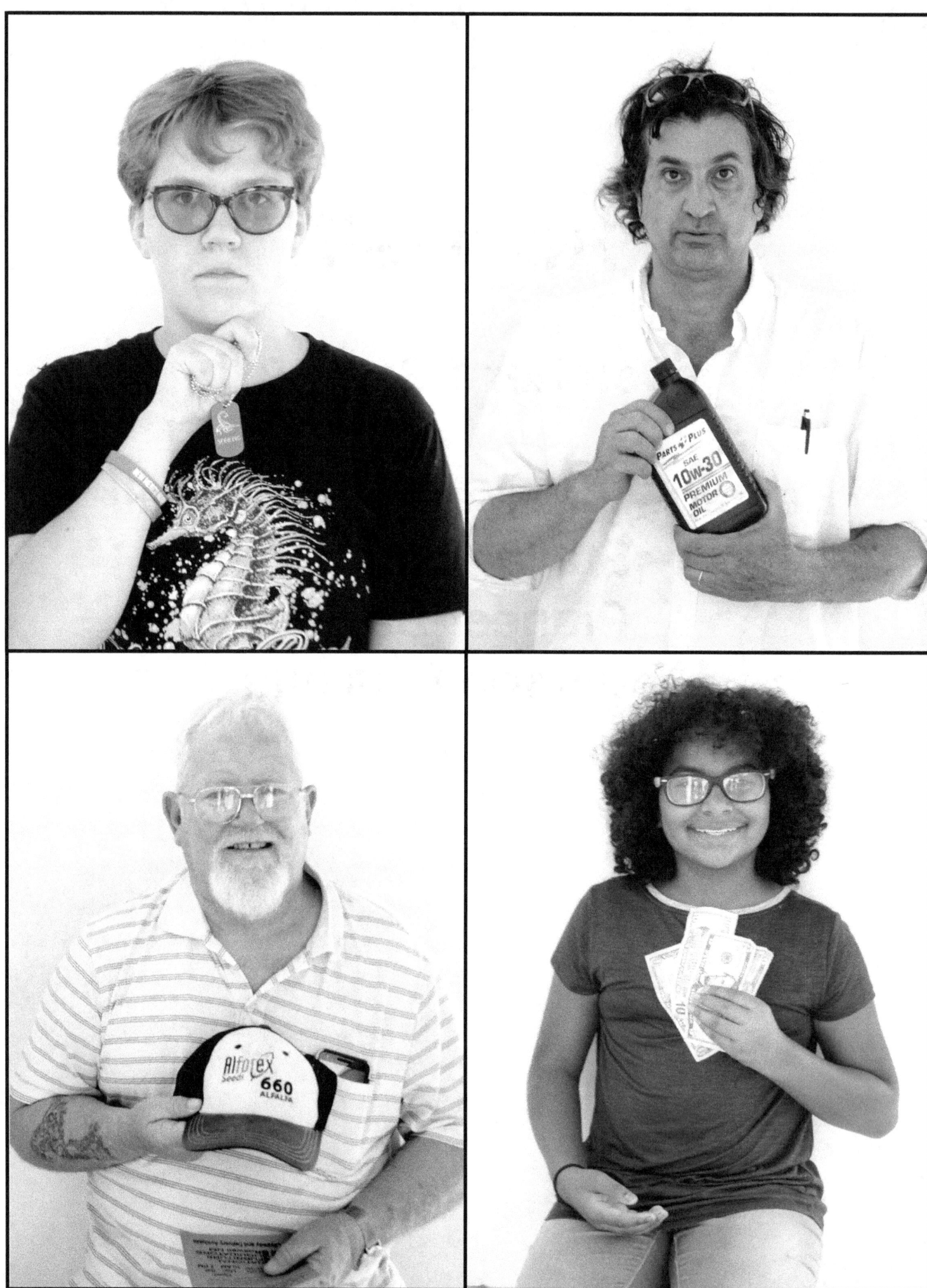

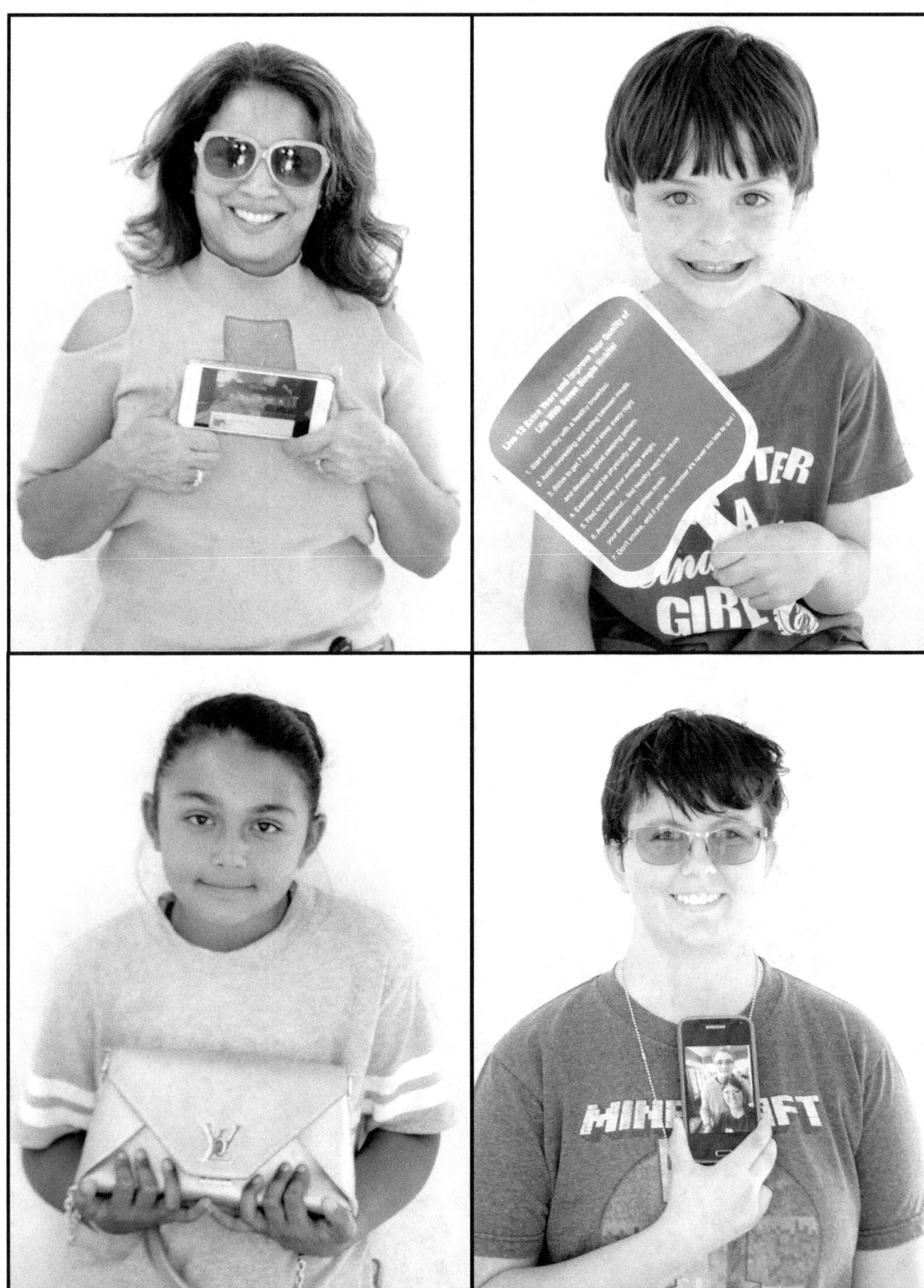

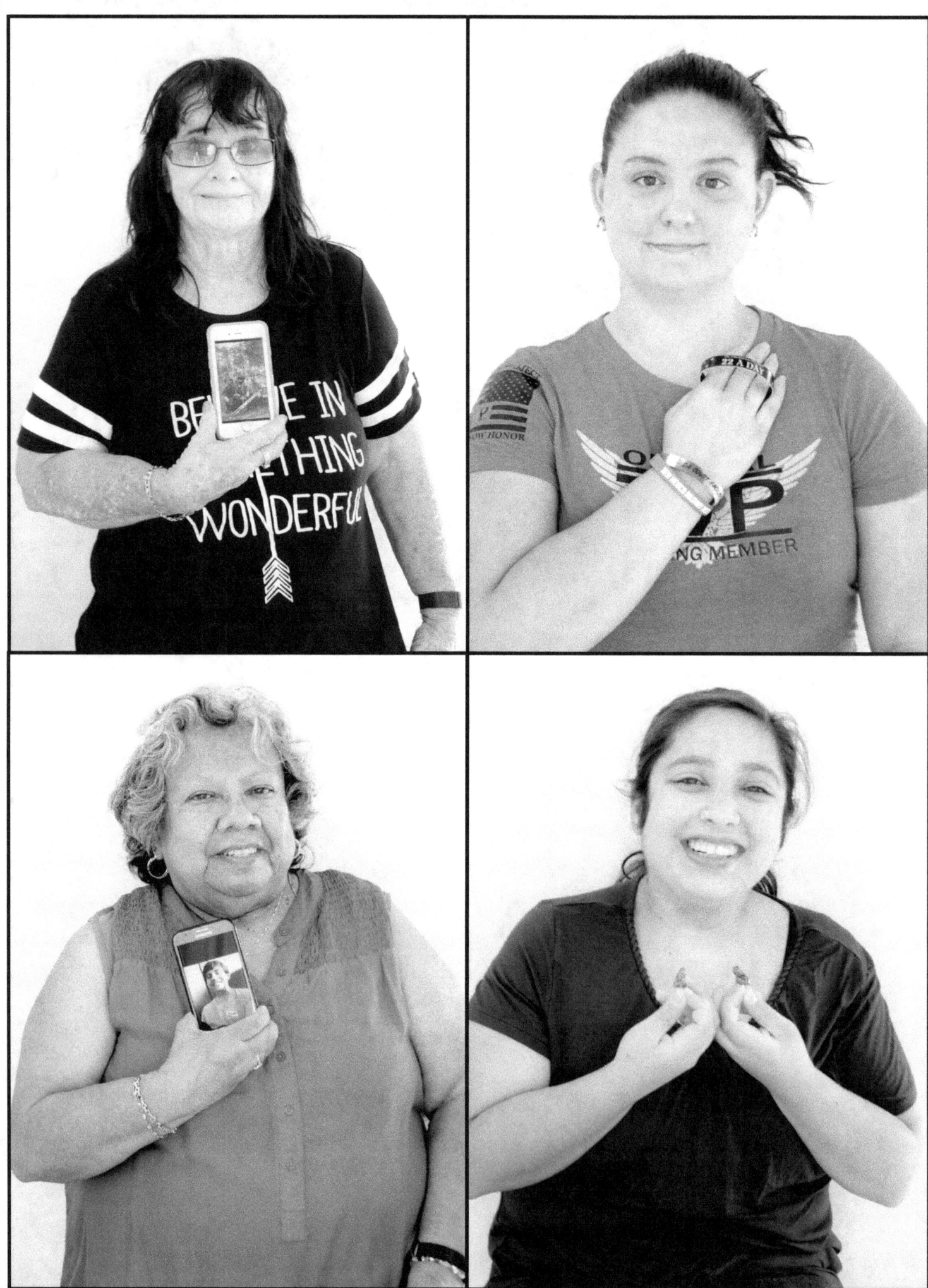

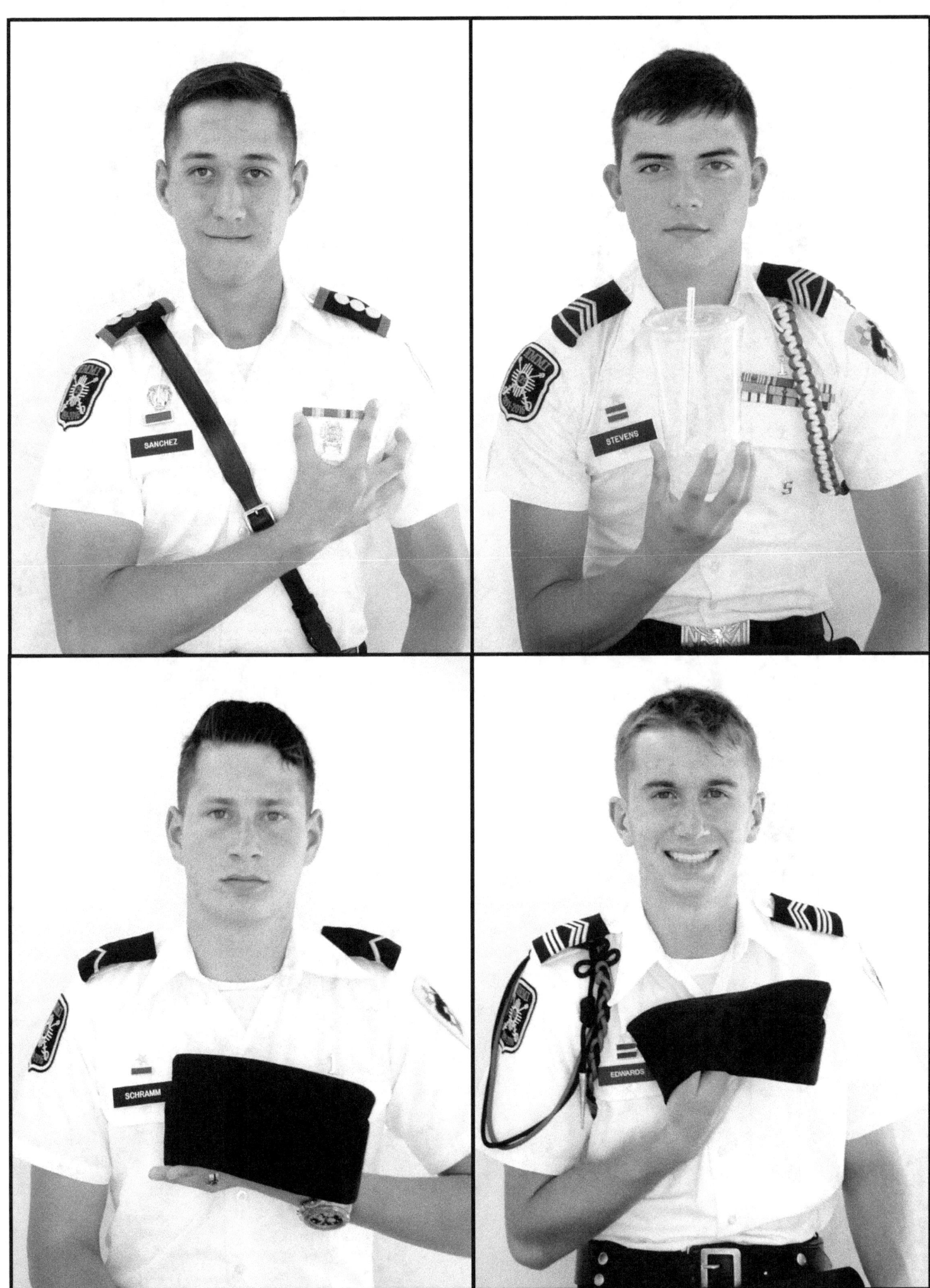

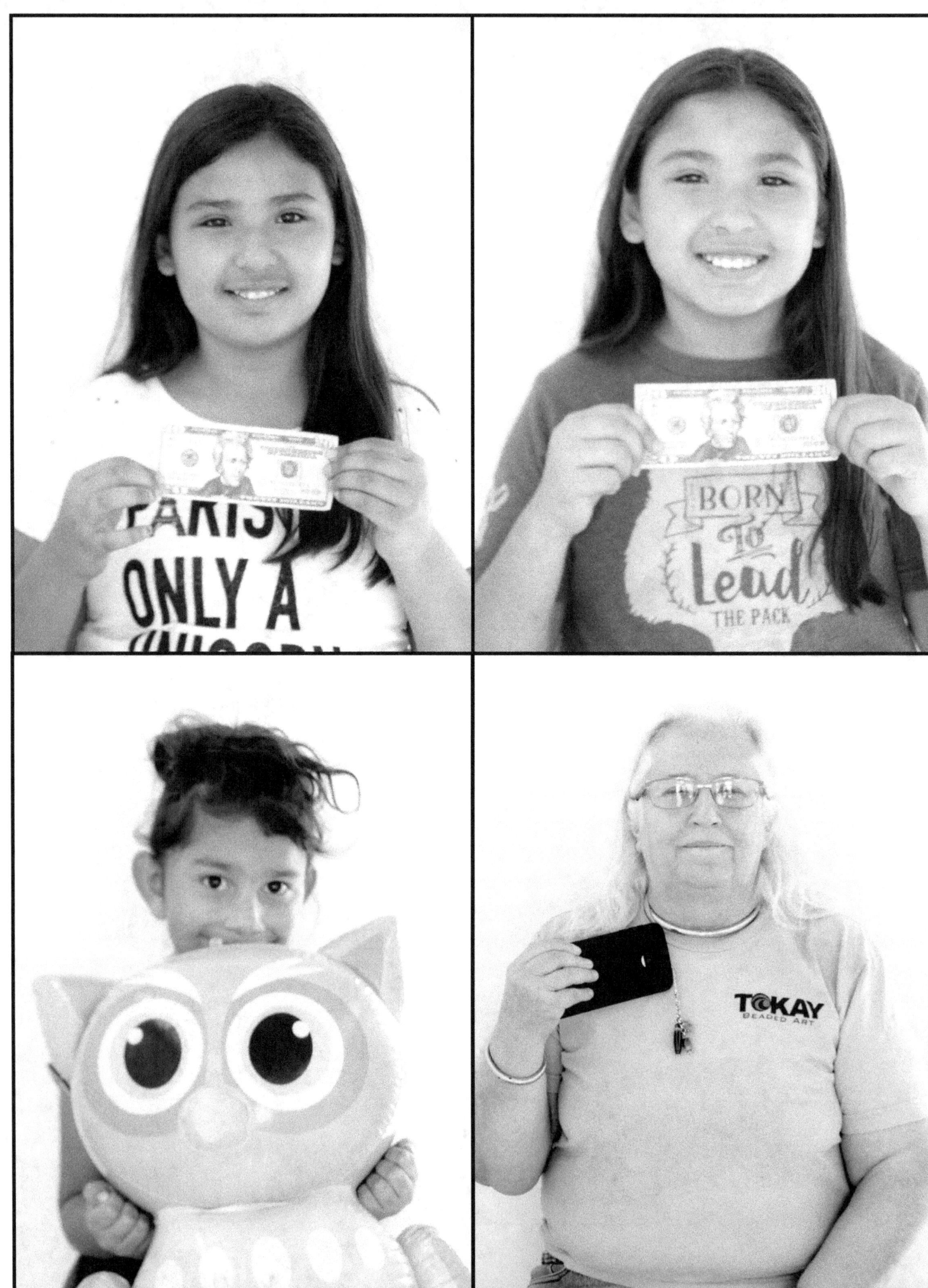

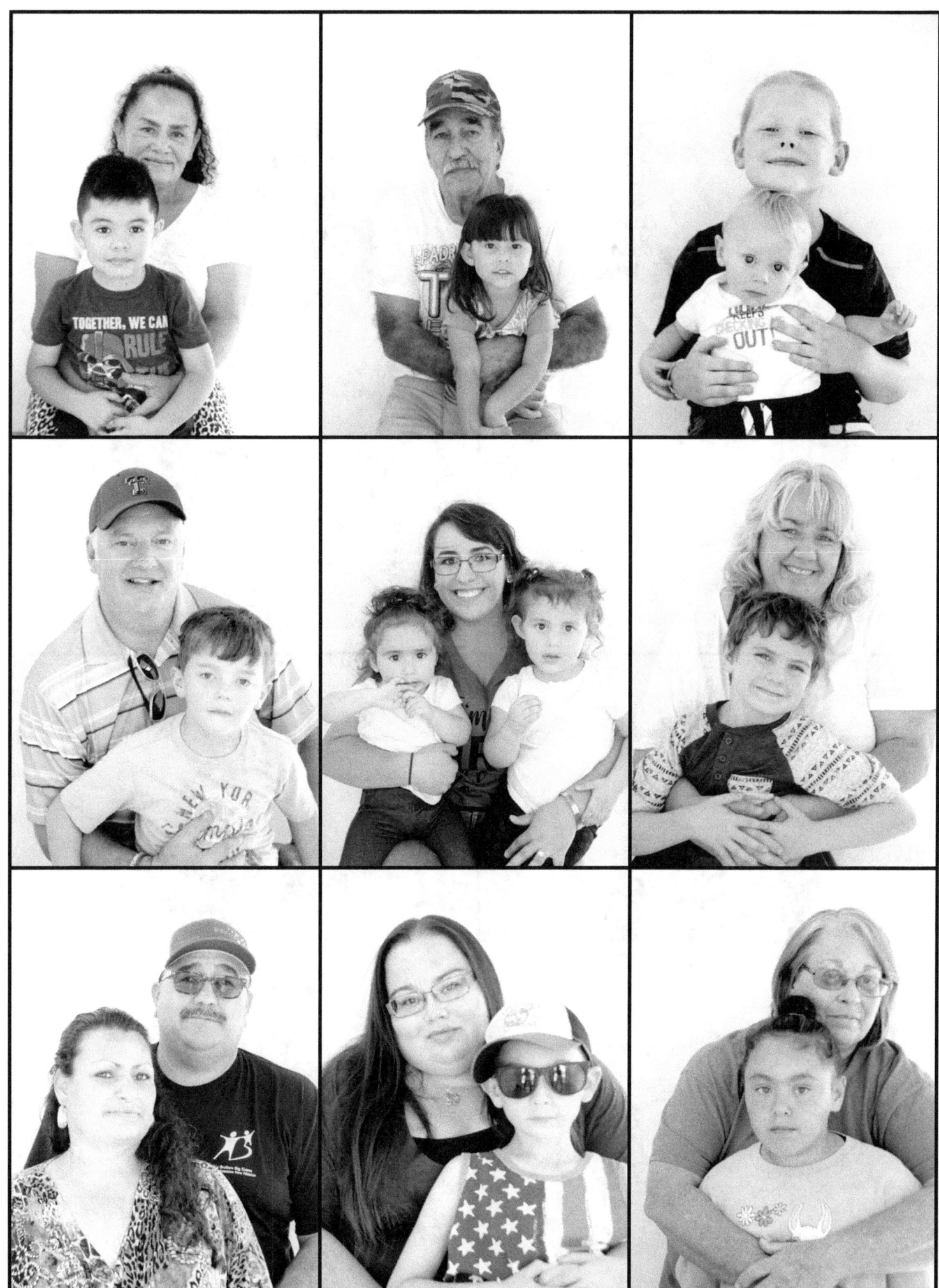

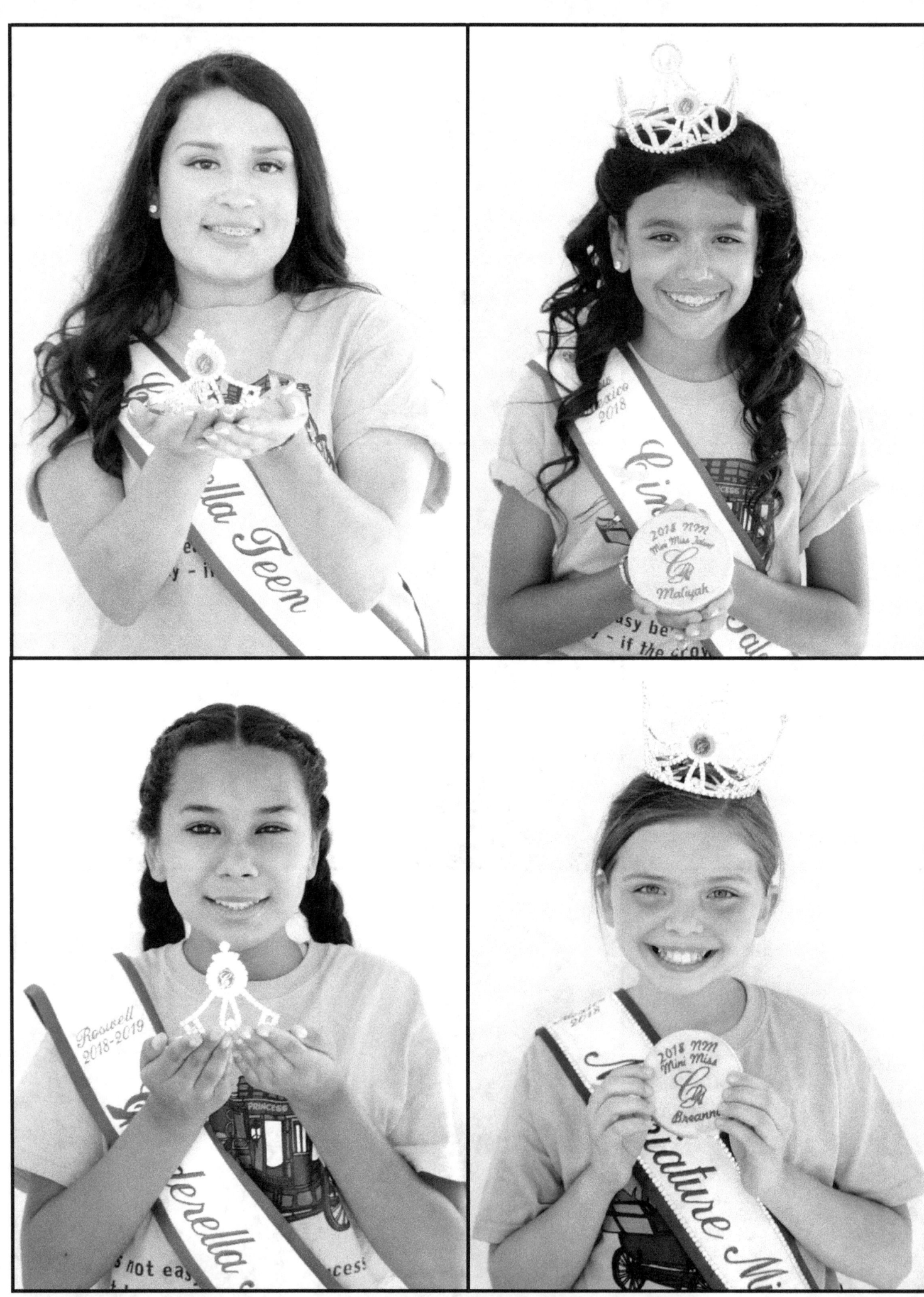

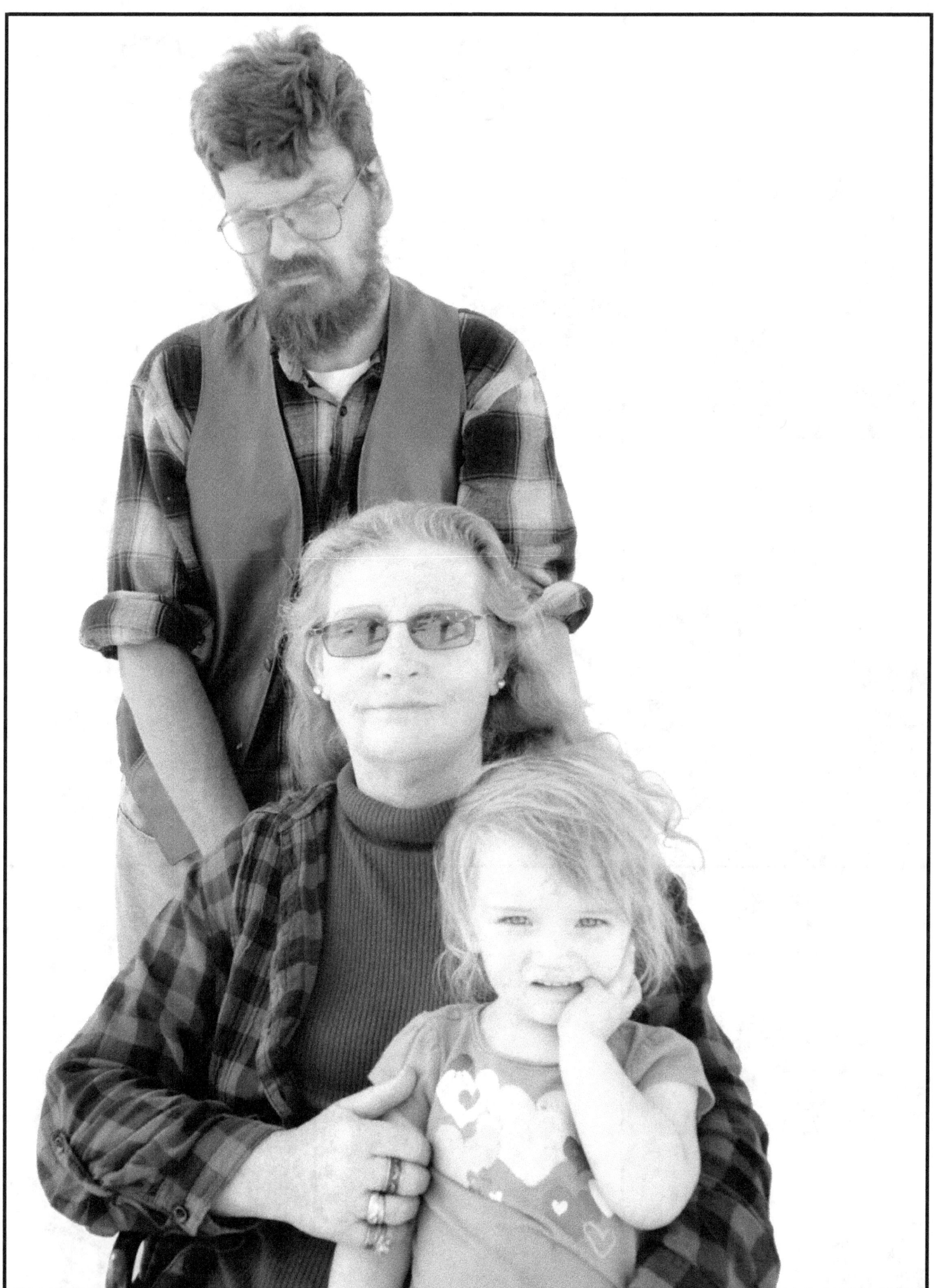

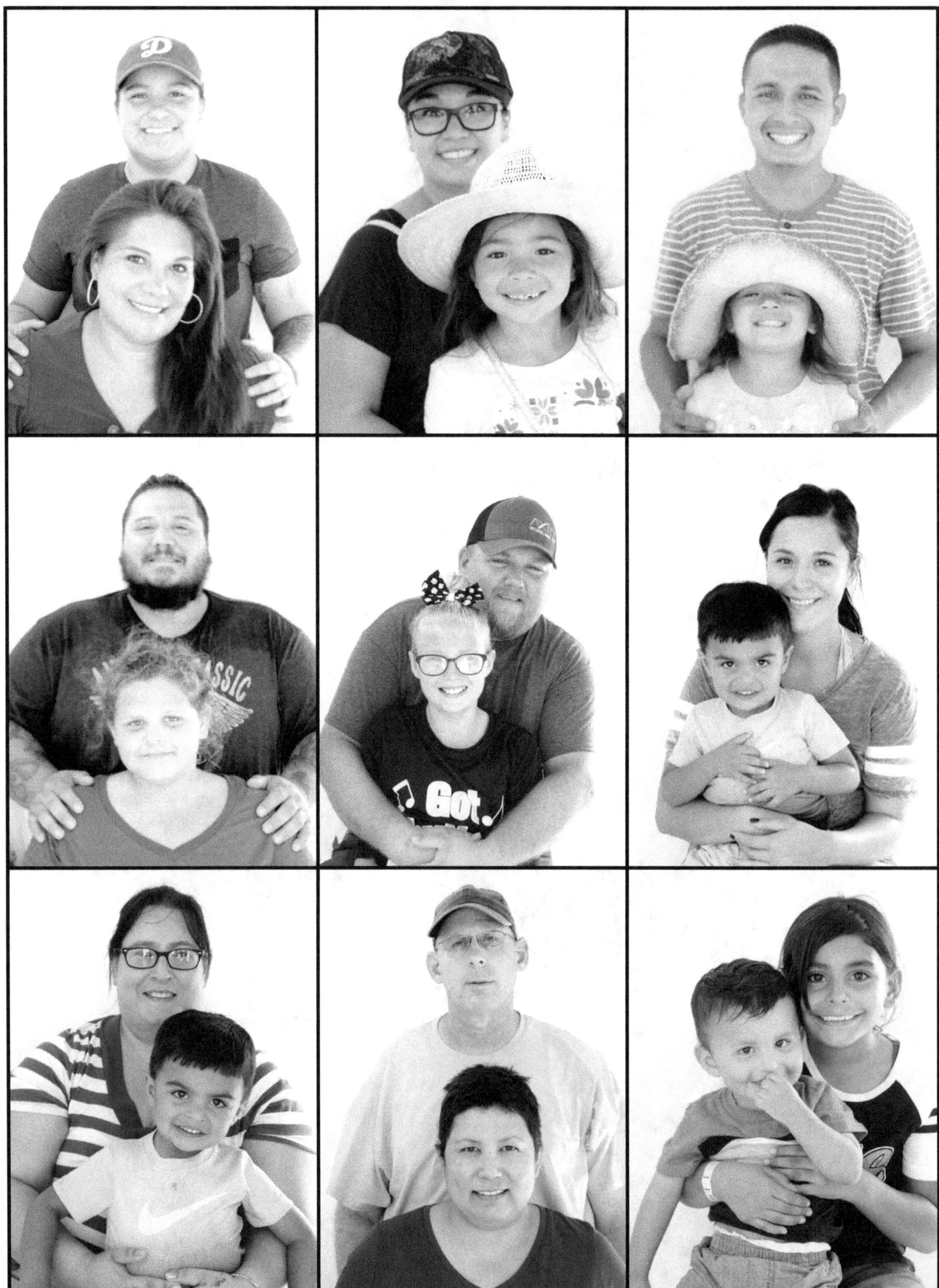

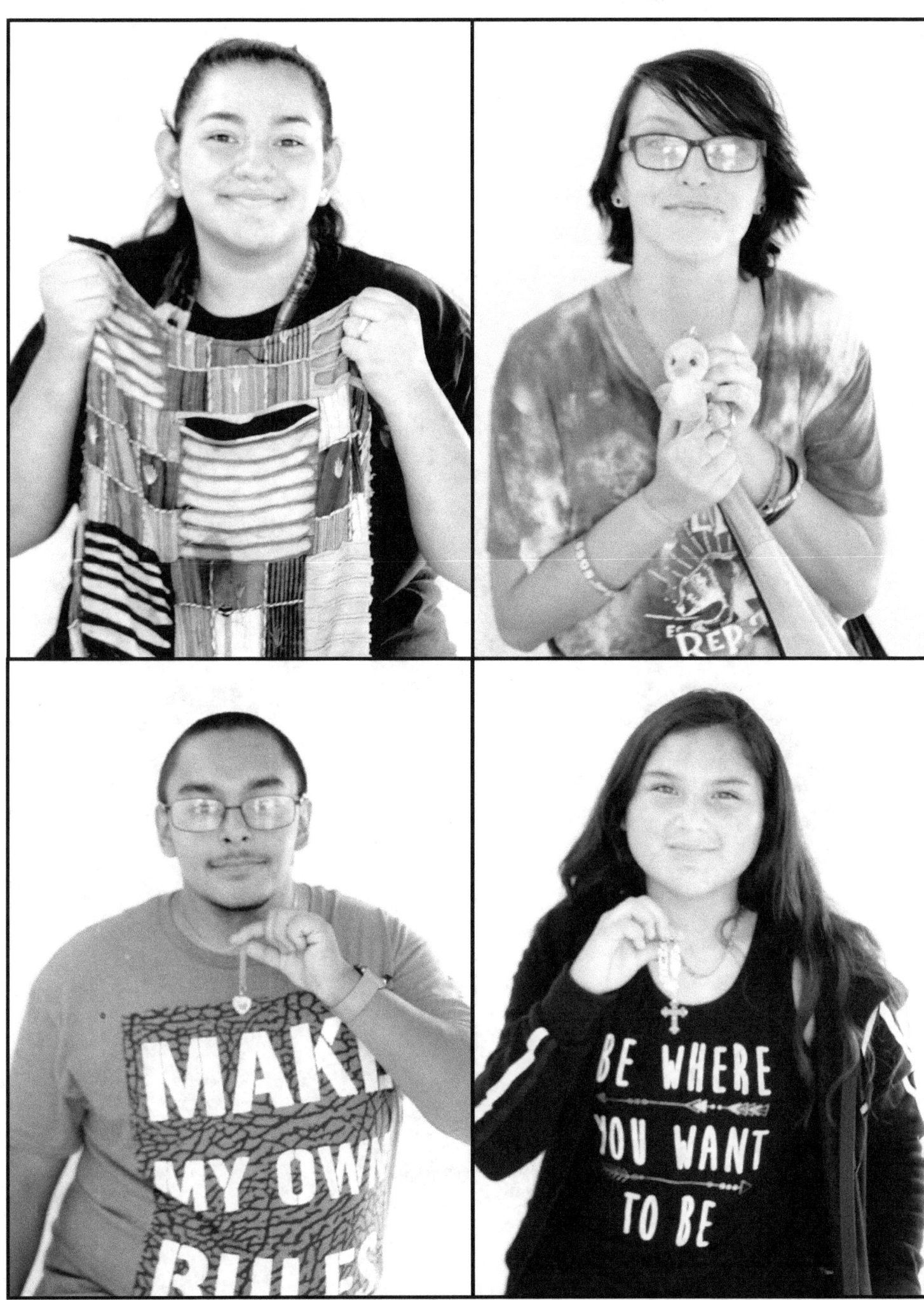

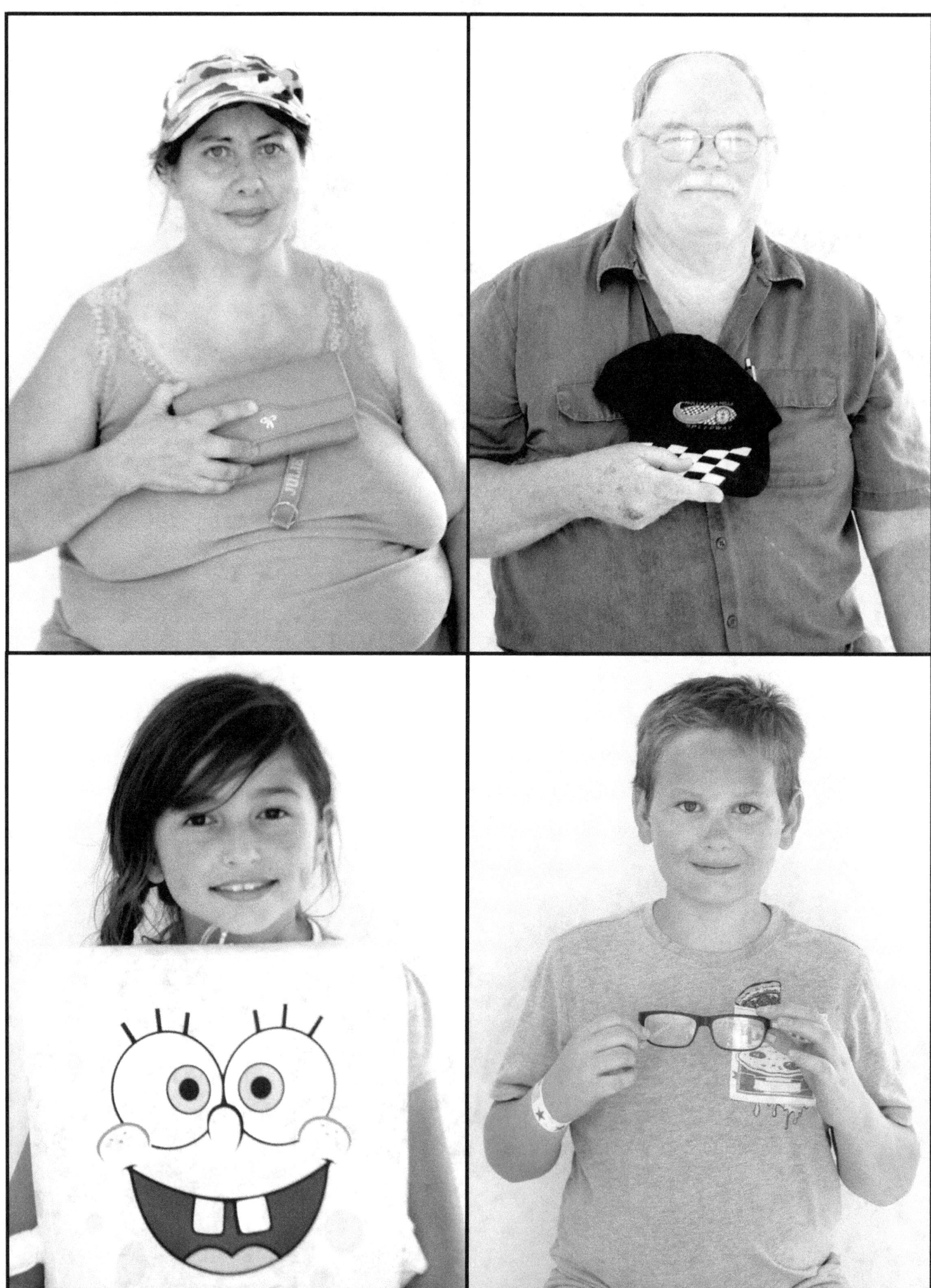

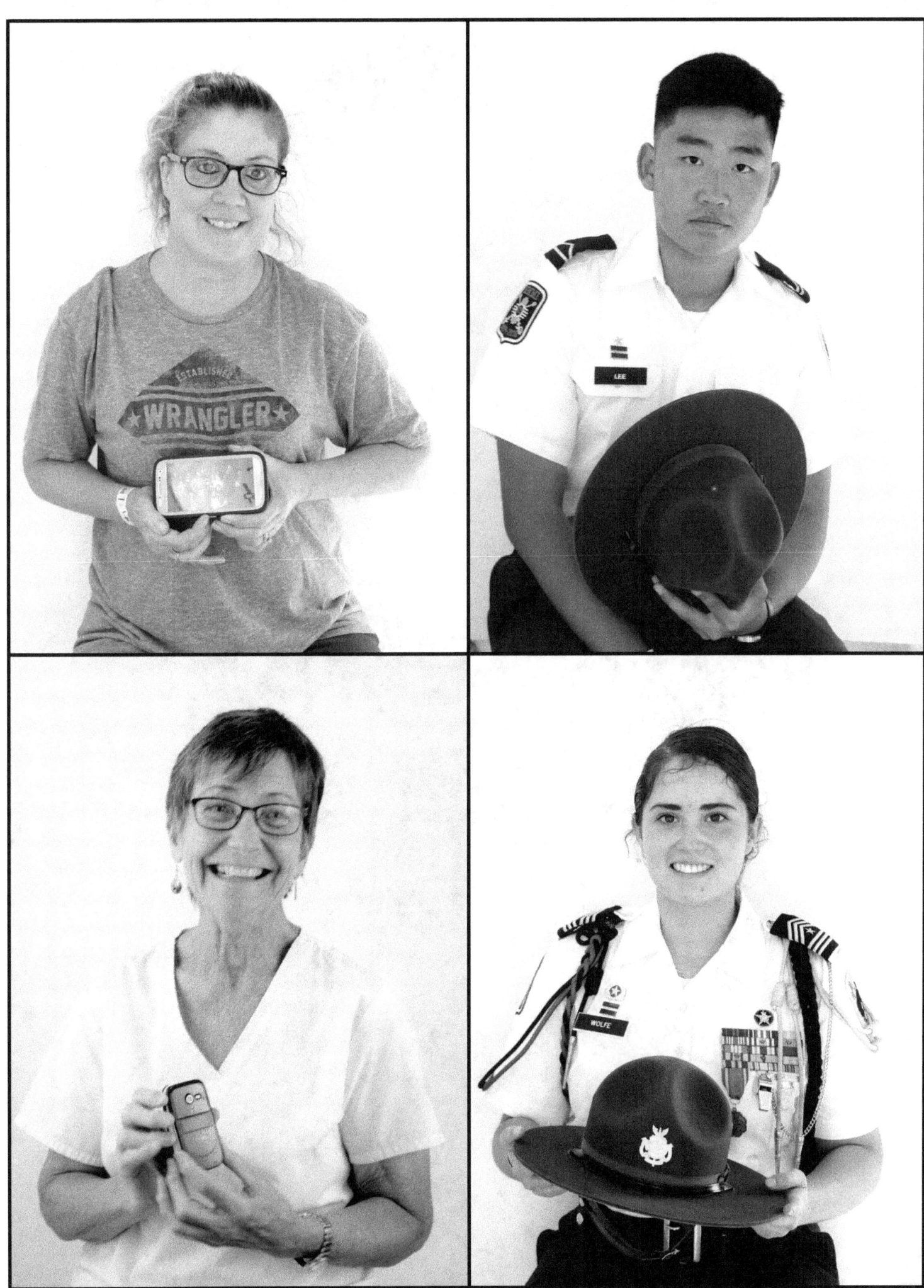

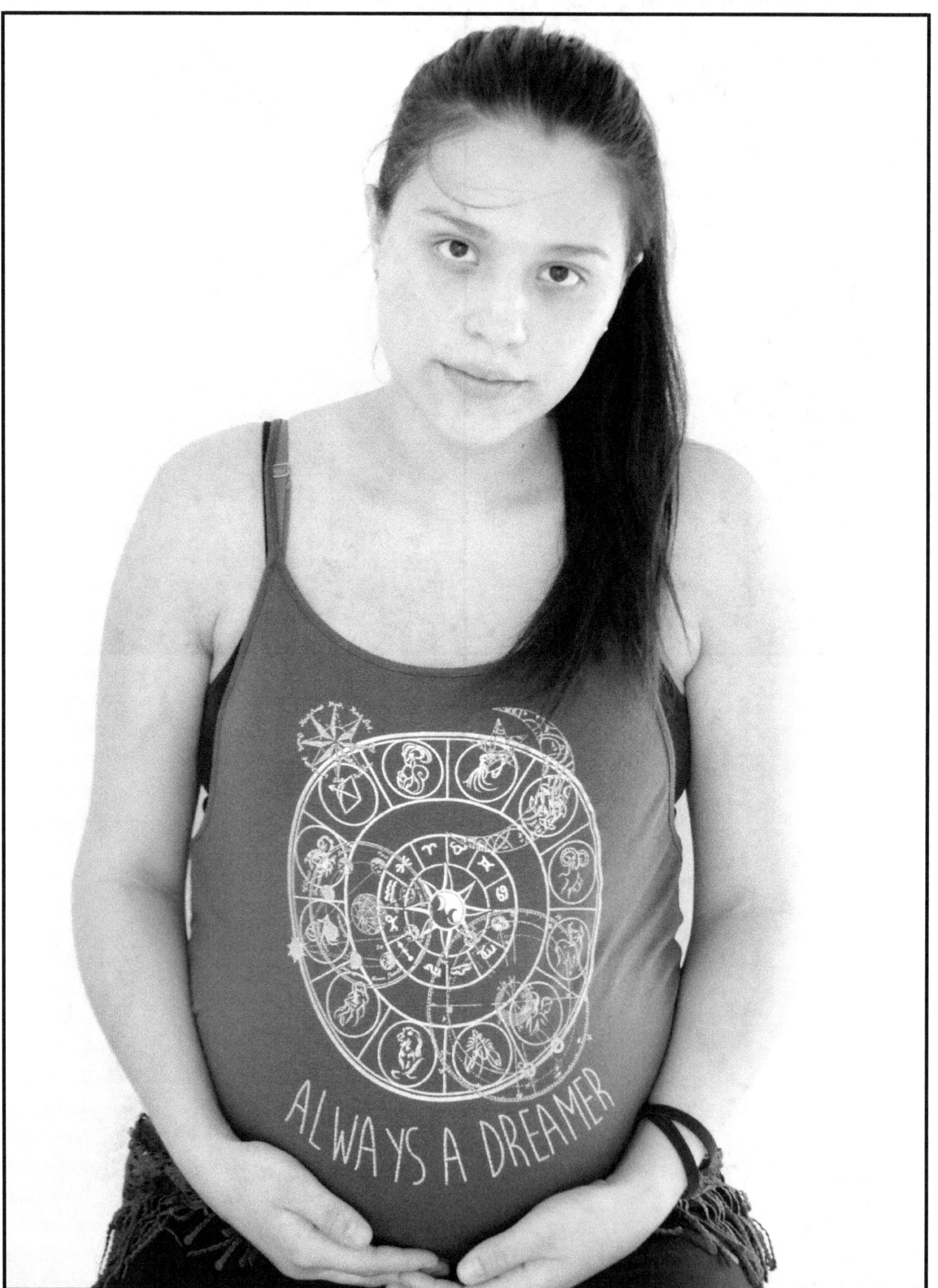

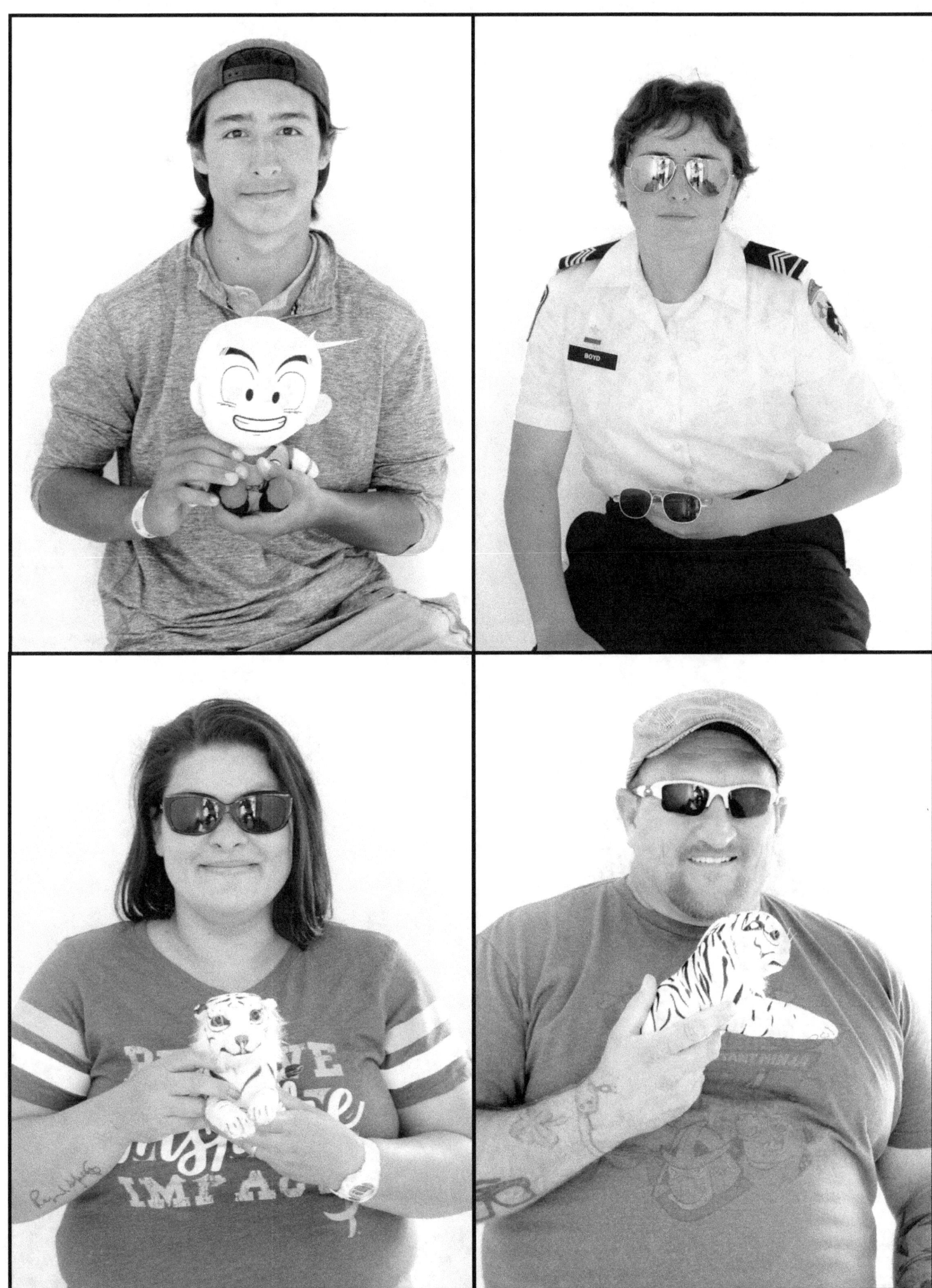

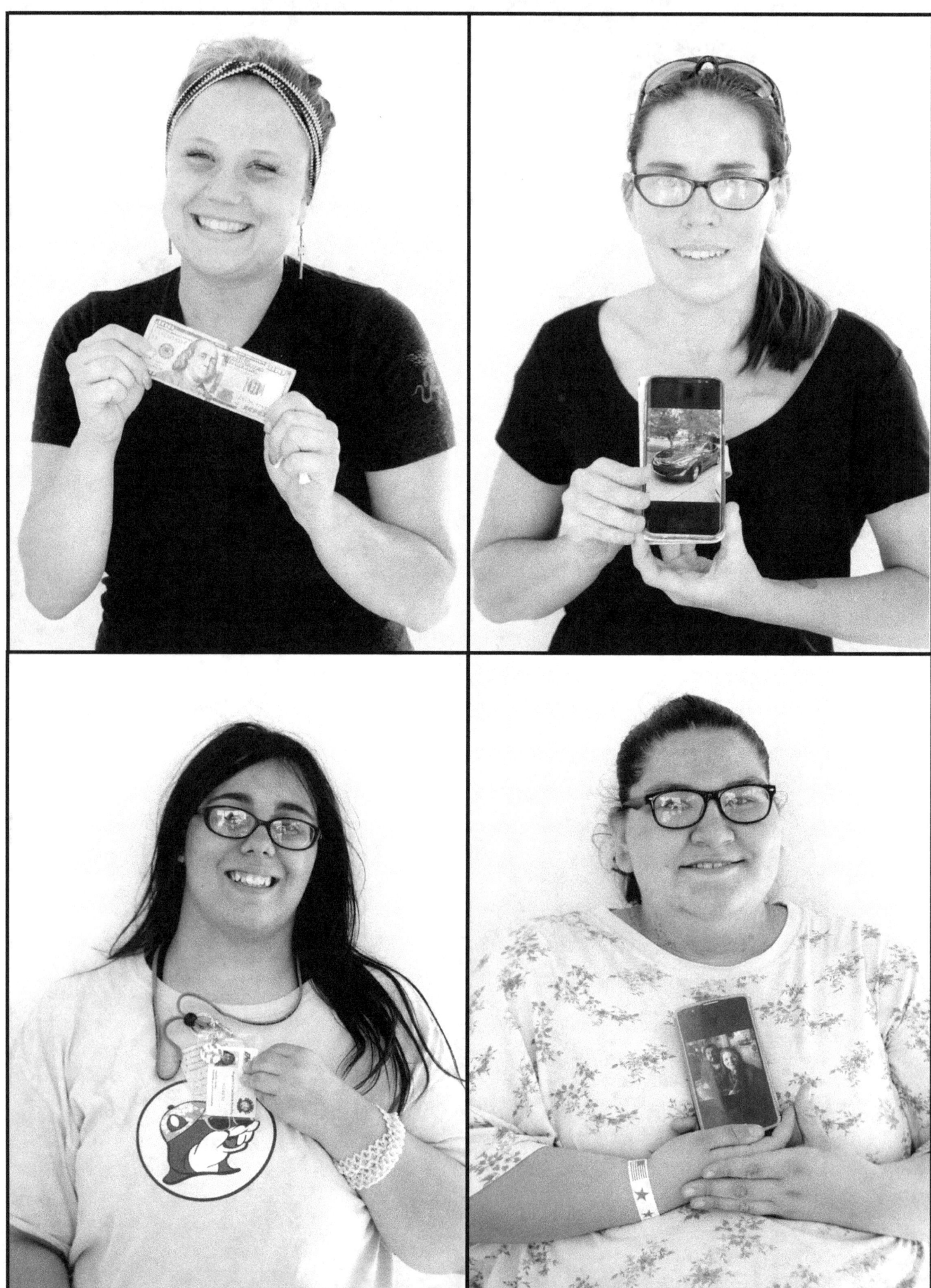

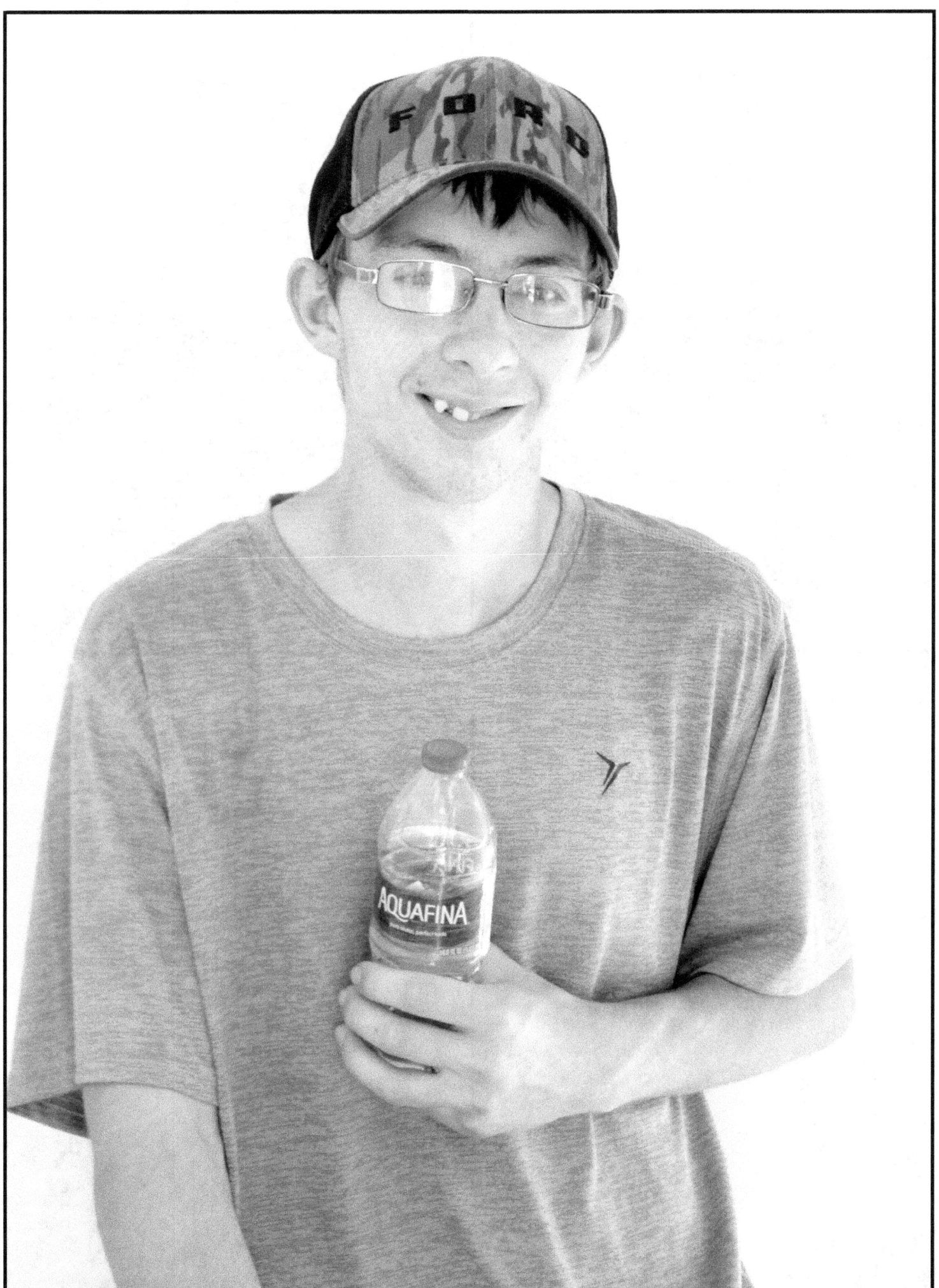

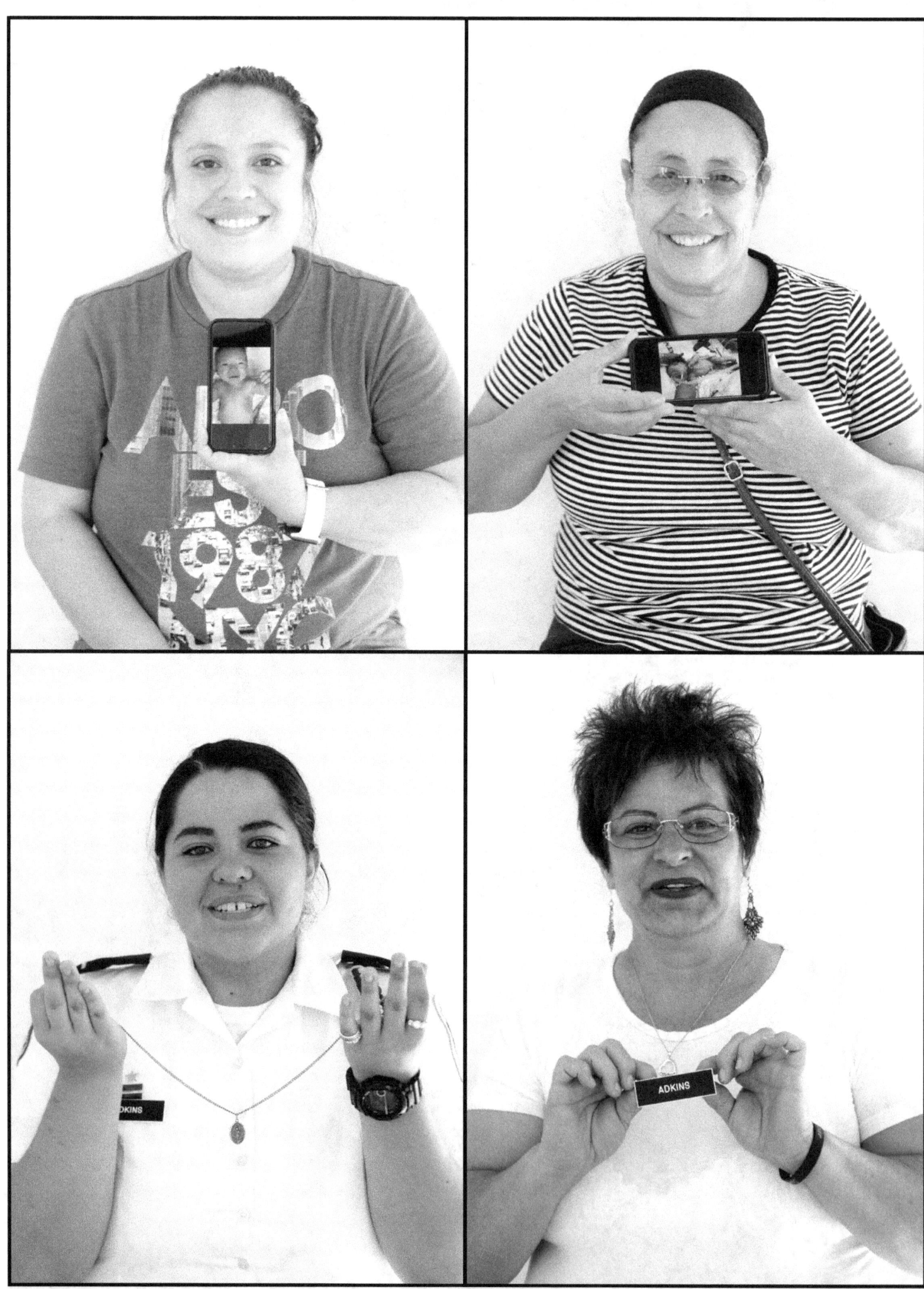

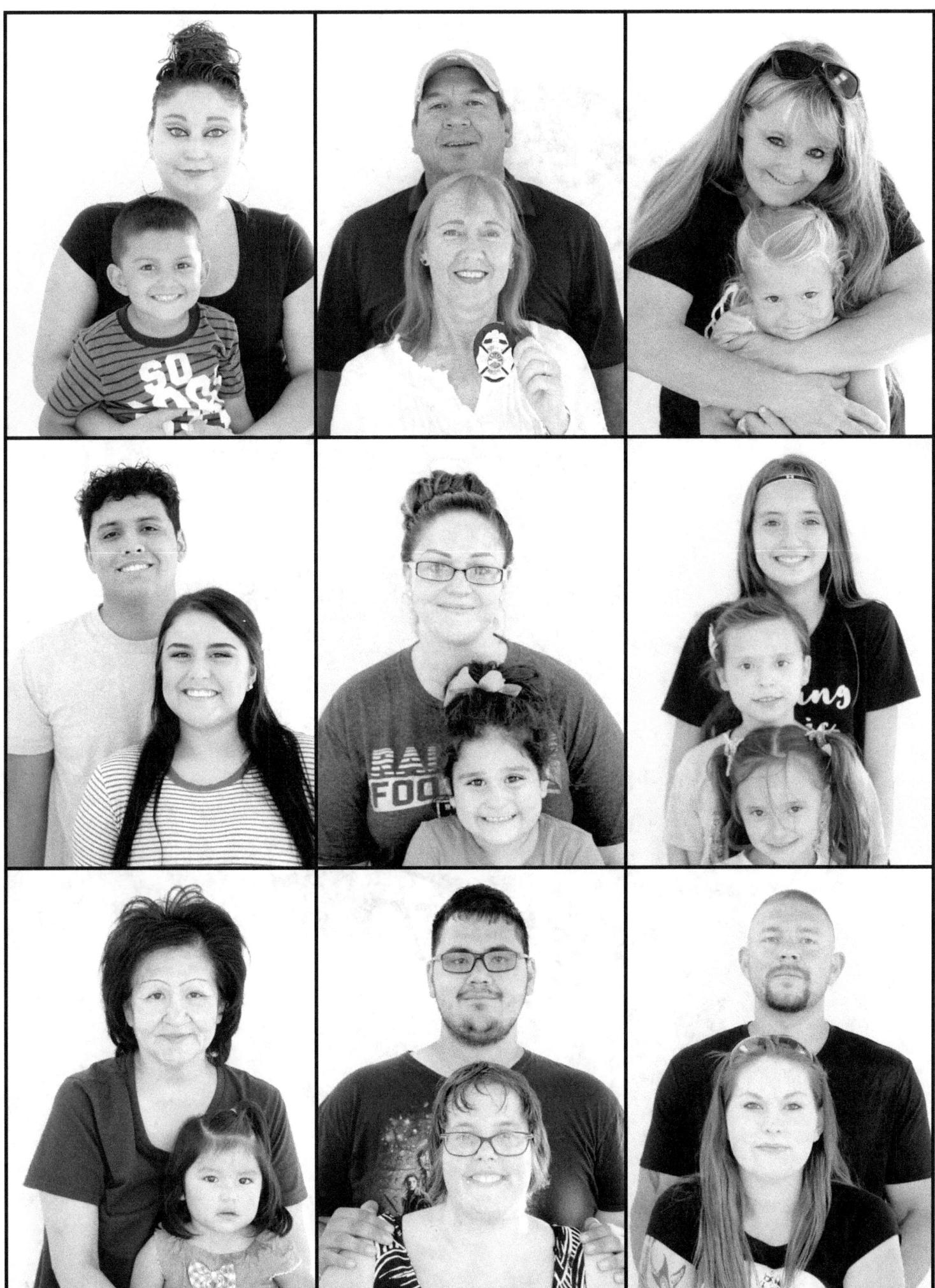

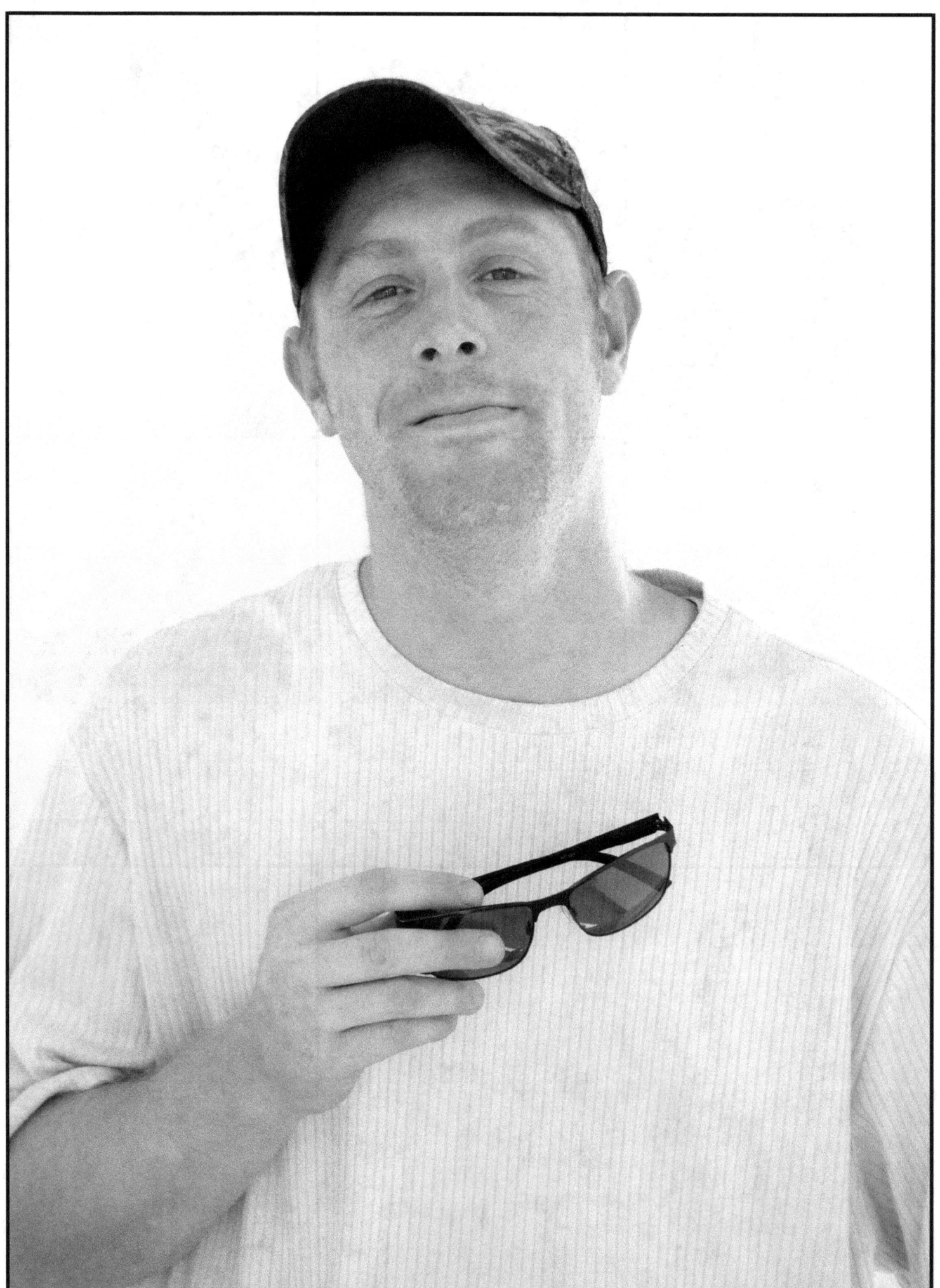

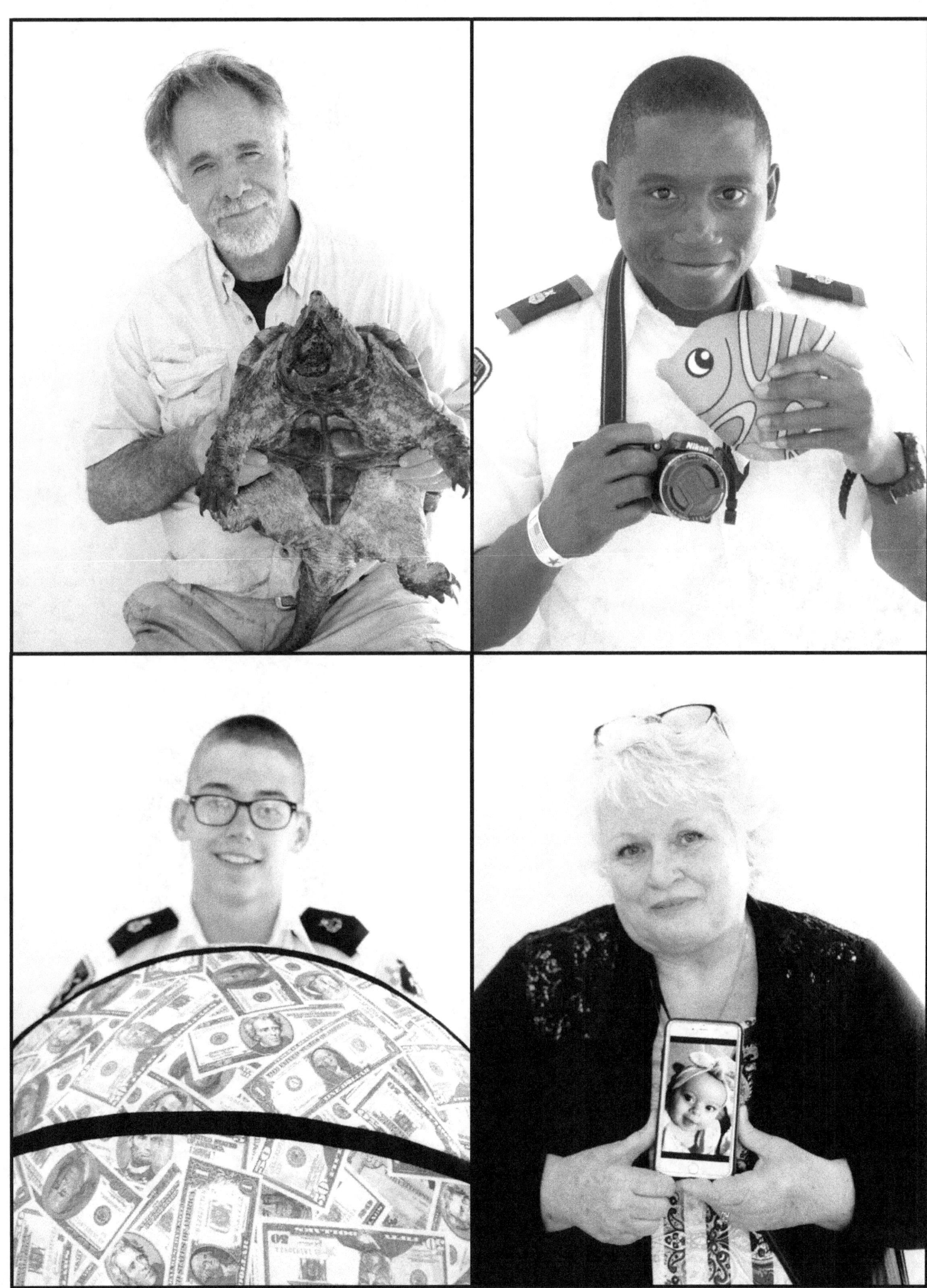

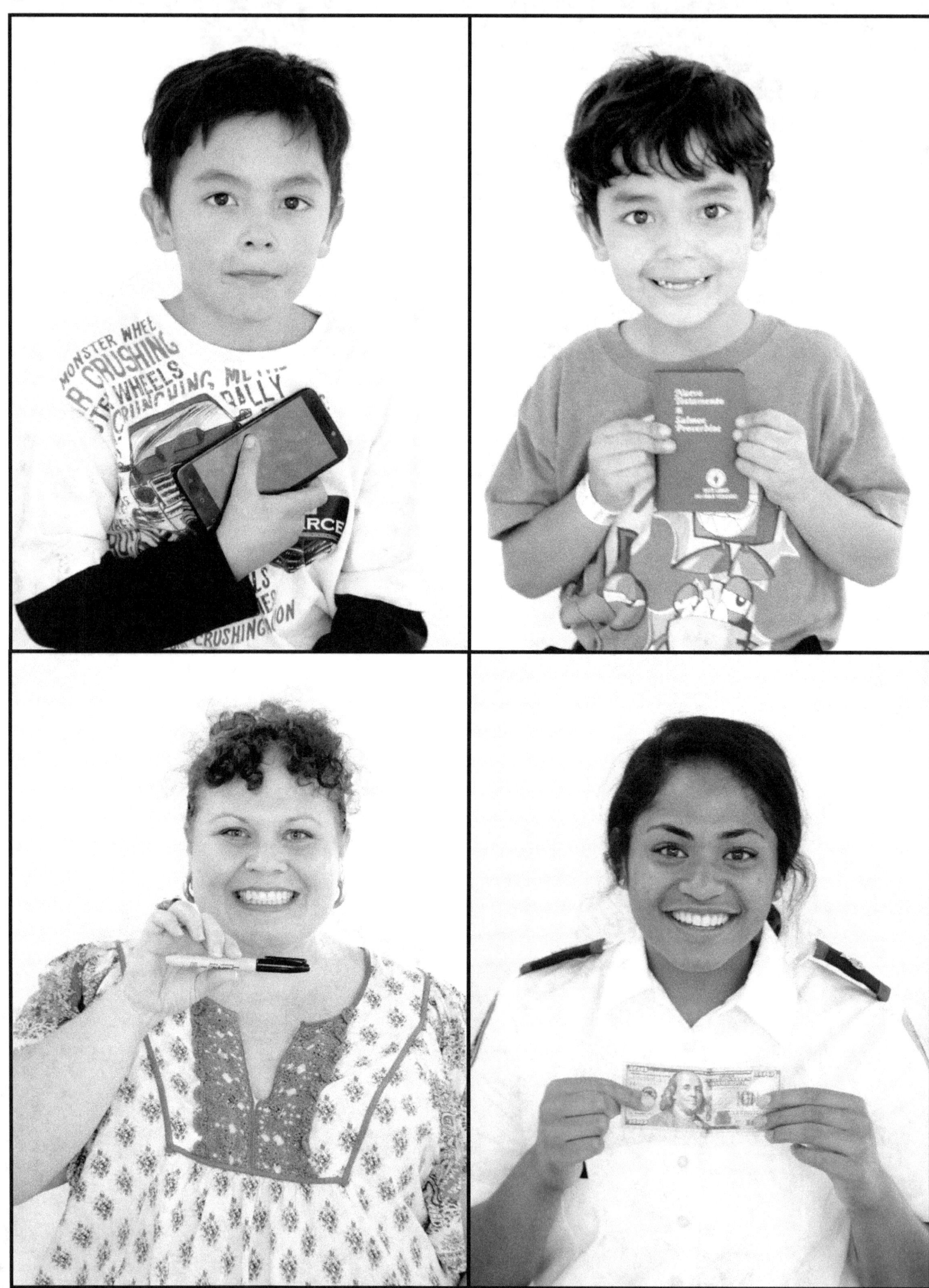

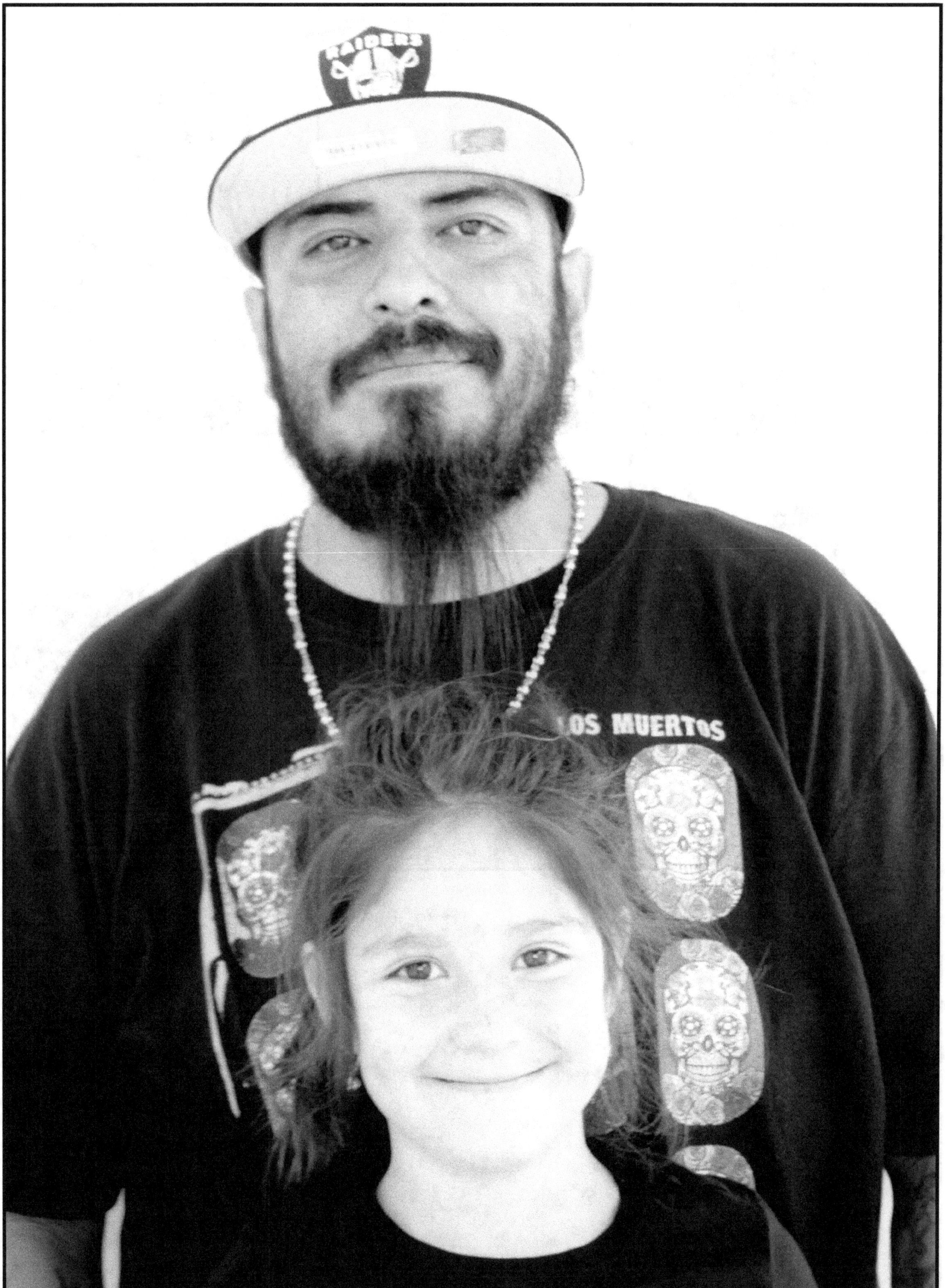
RAIDERS
MUERTOS

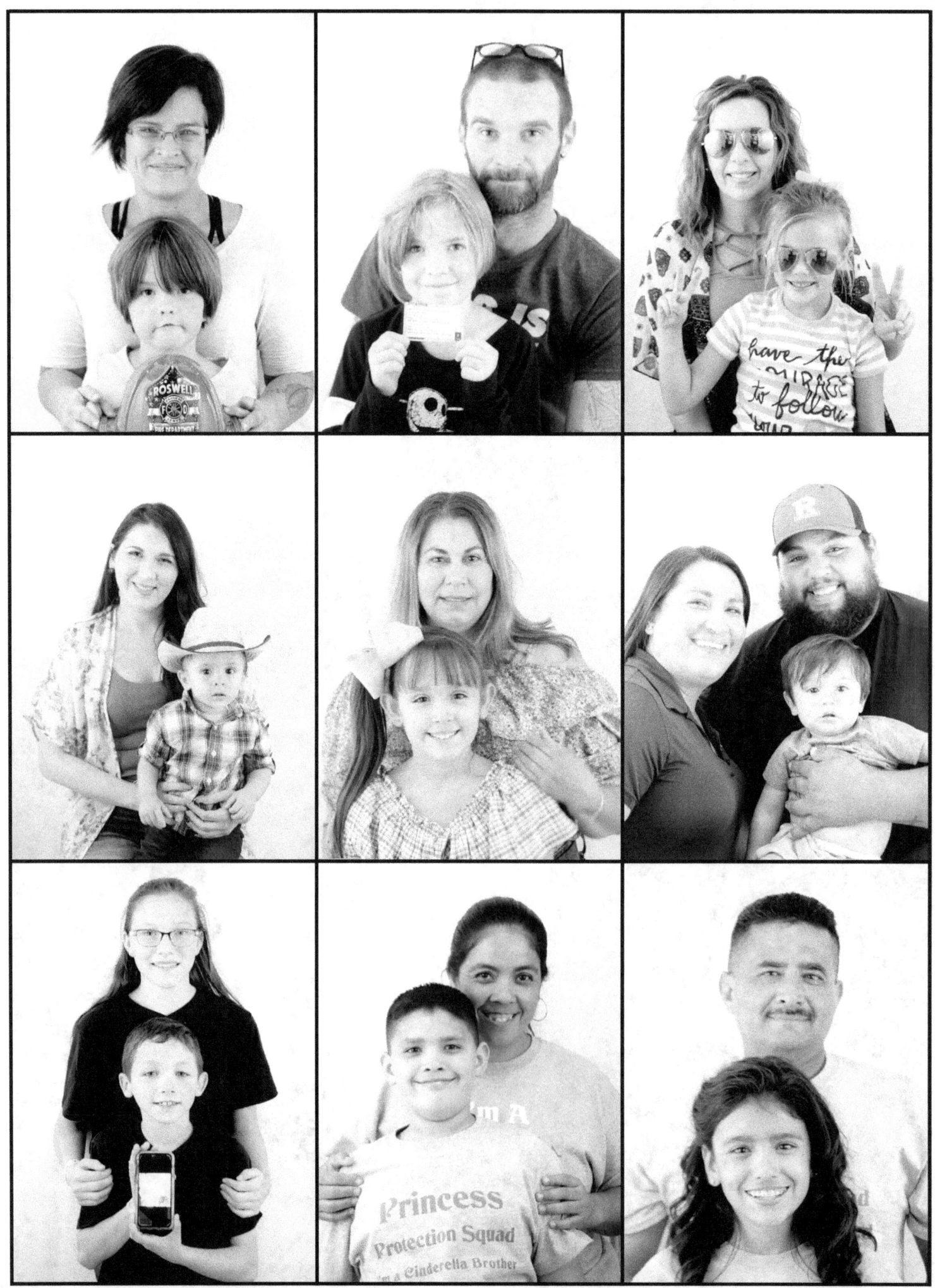

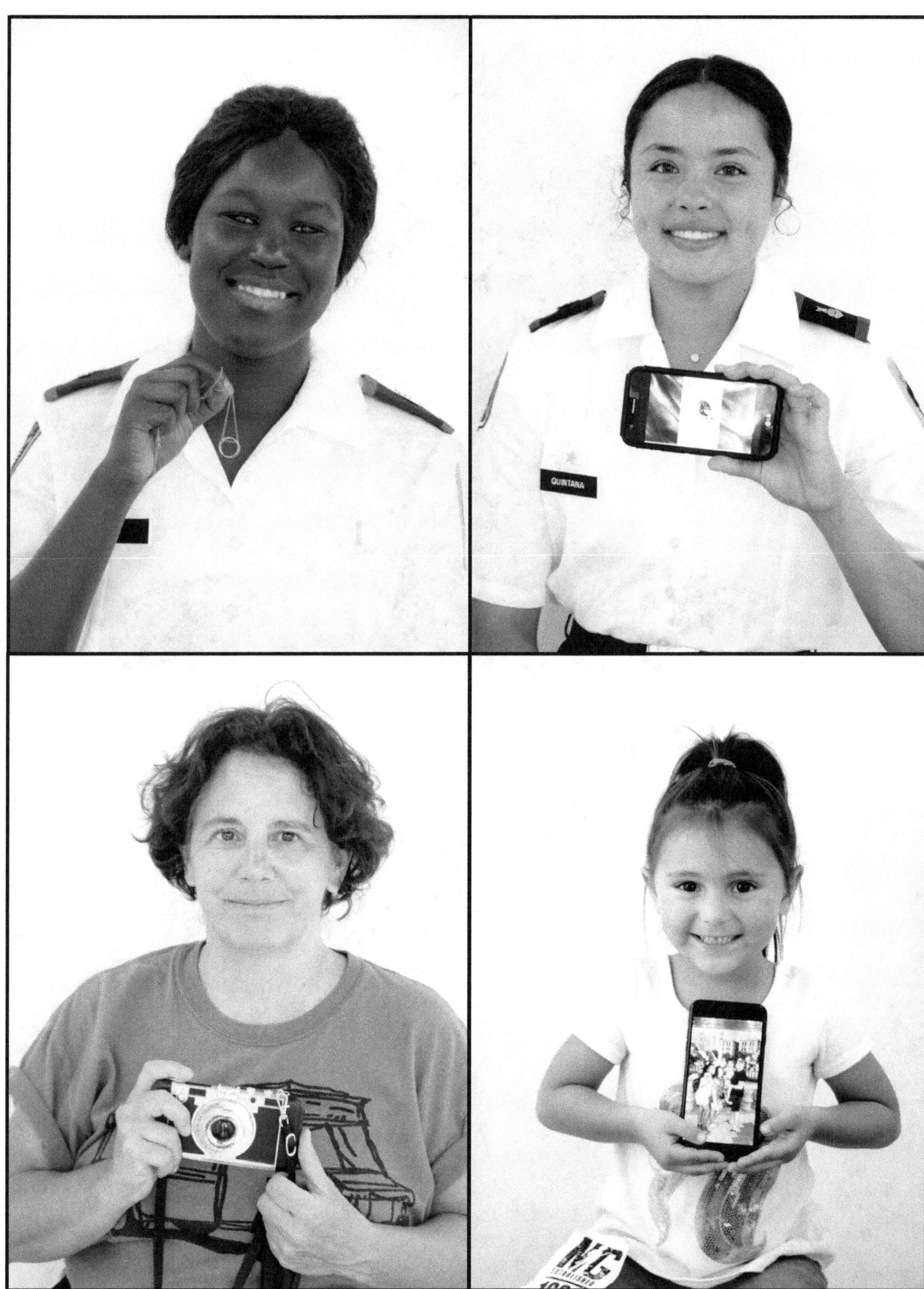

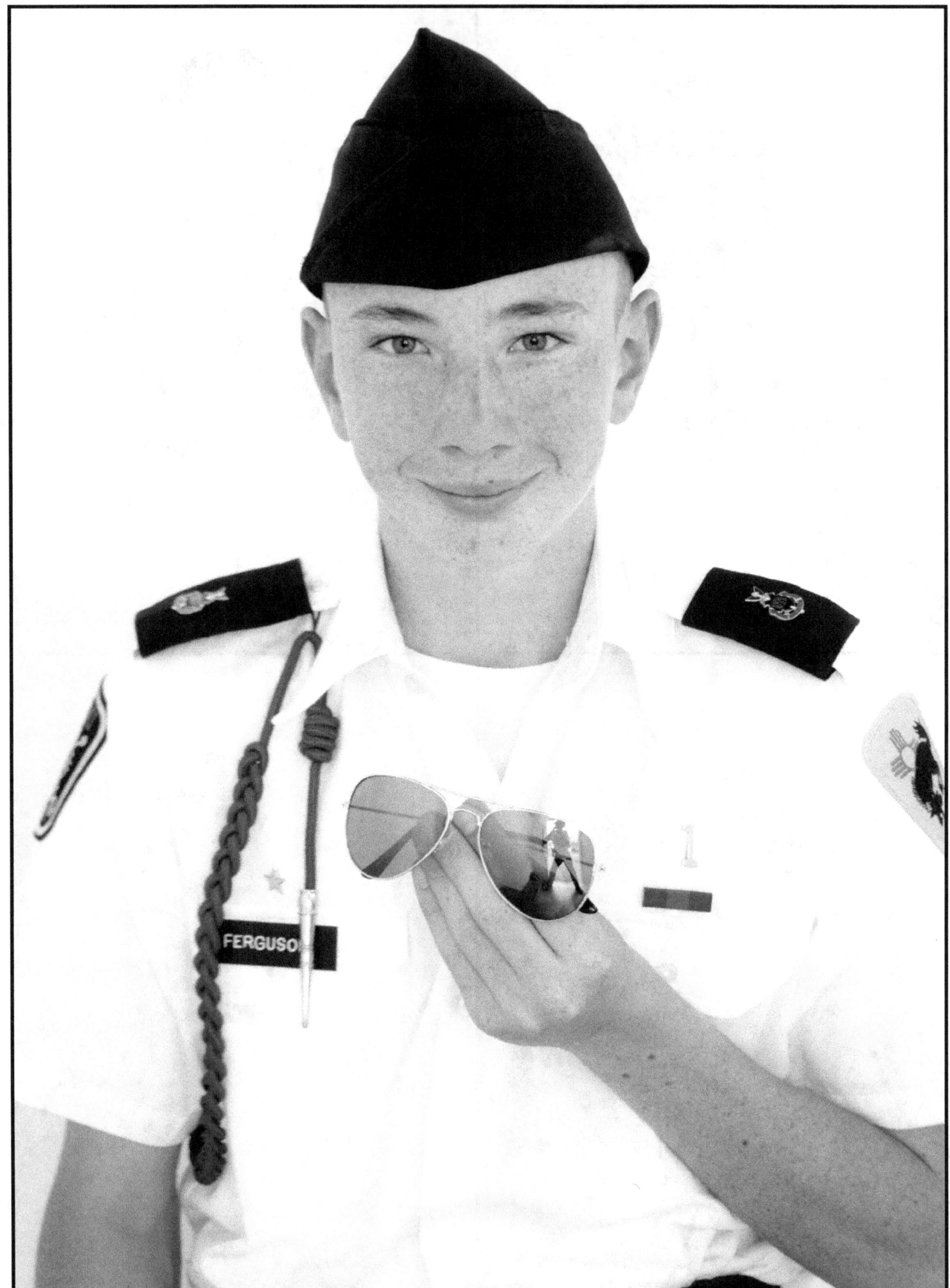

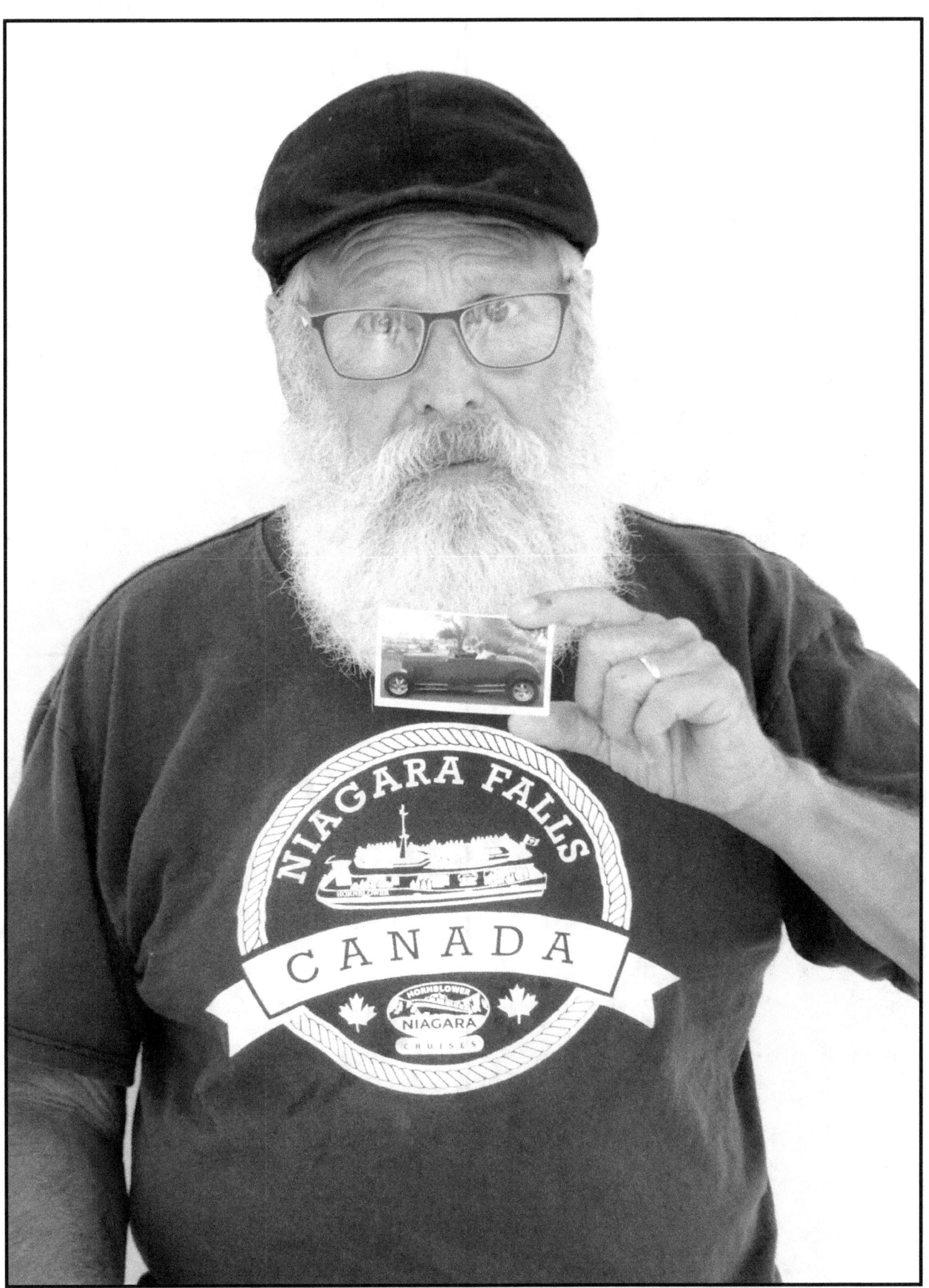

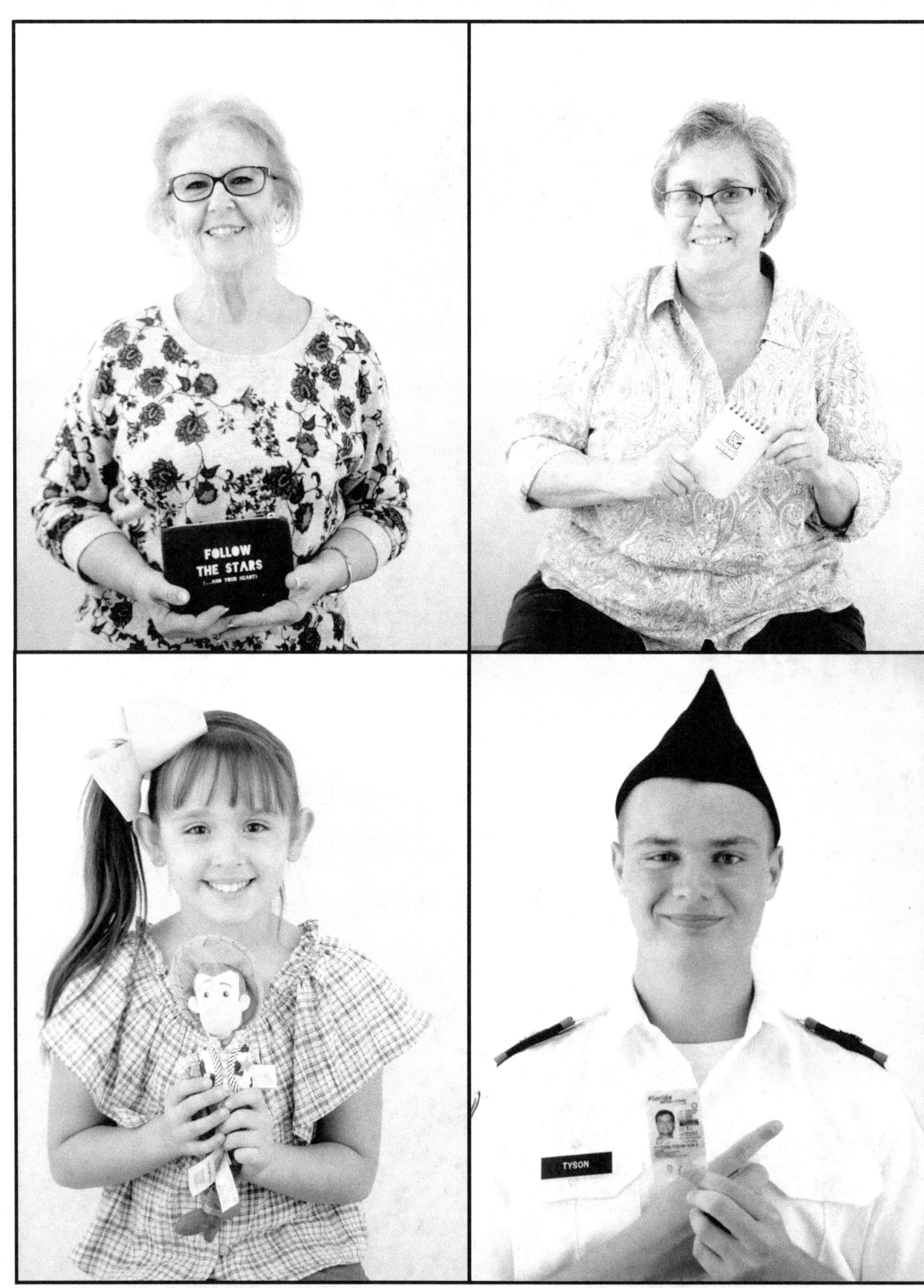

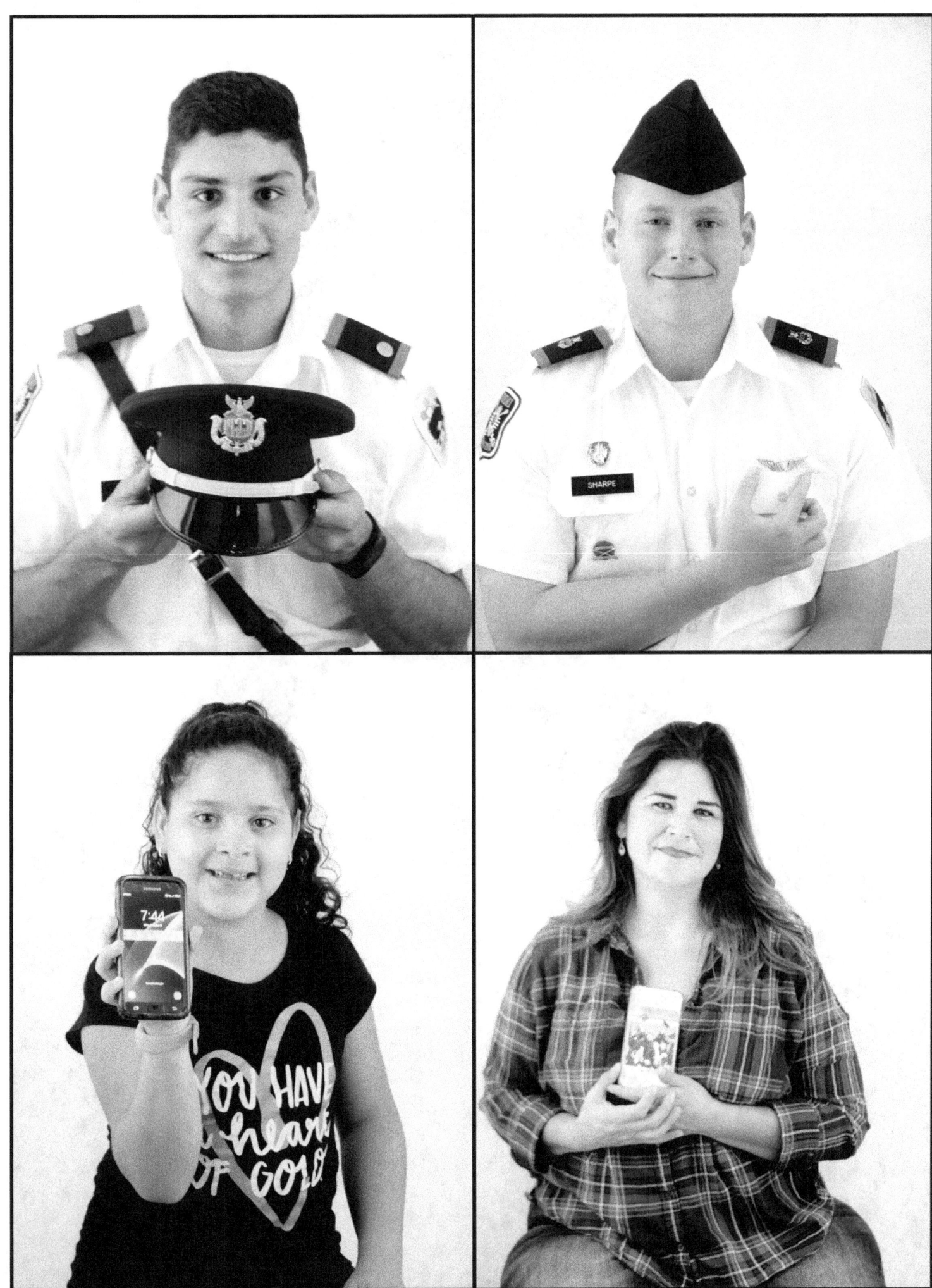

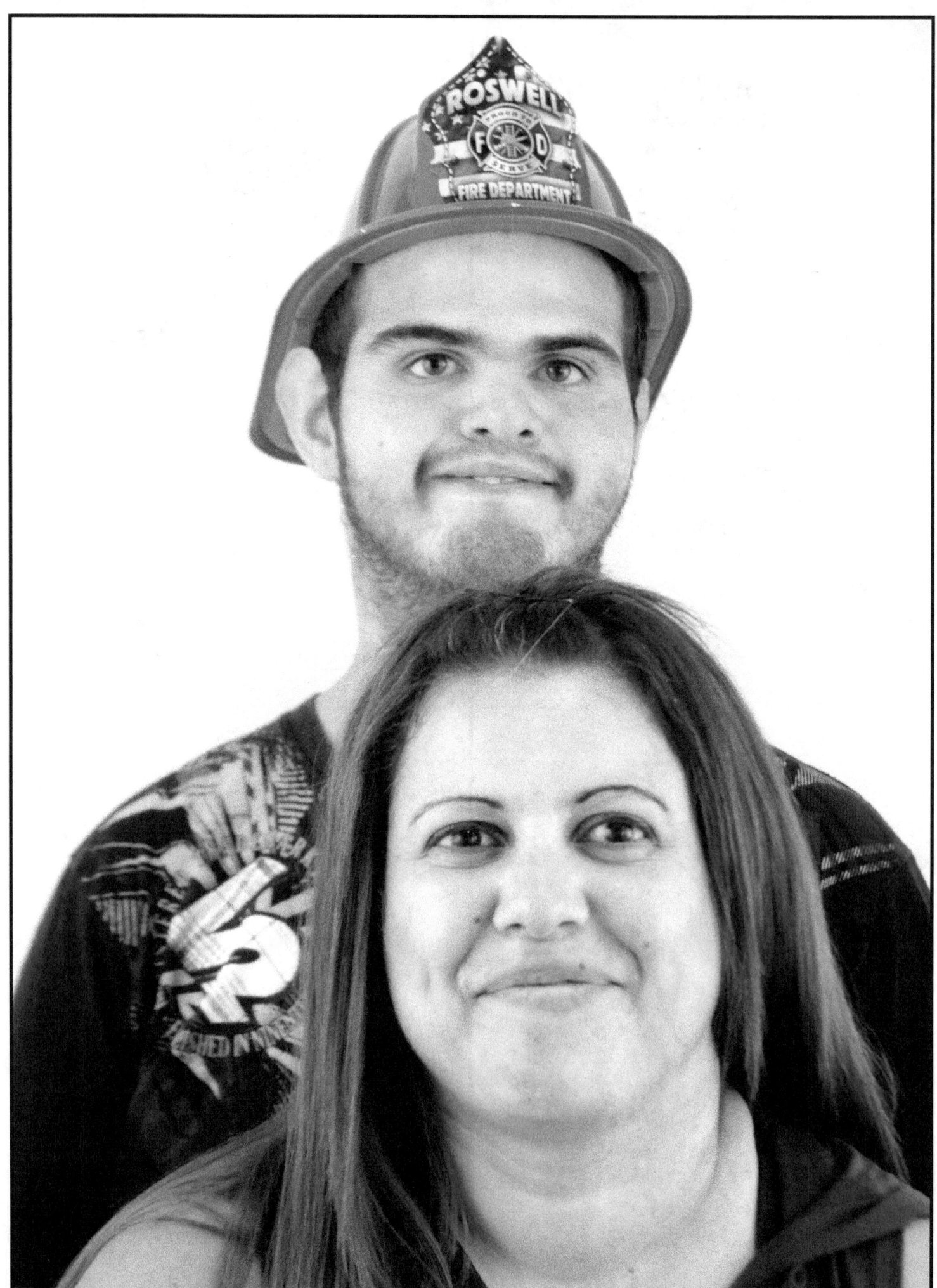

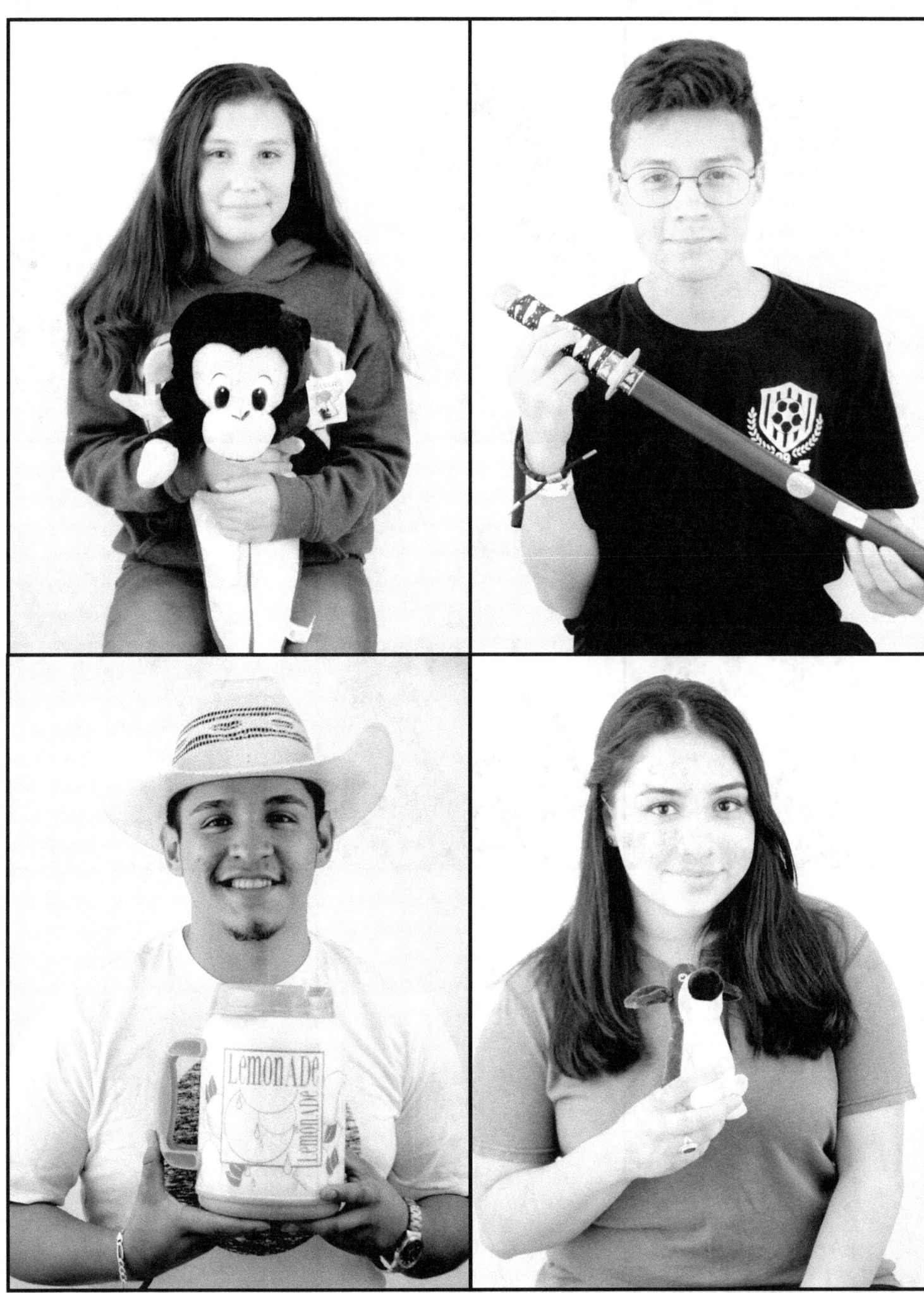

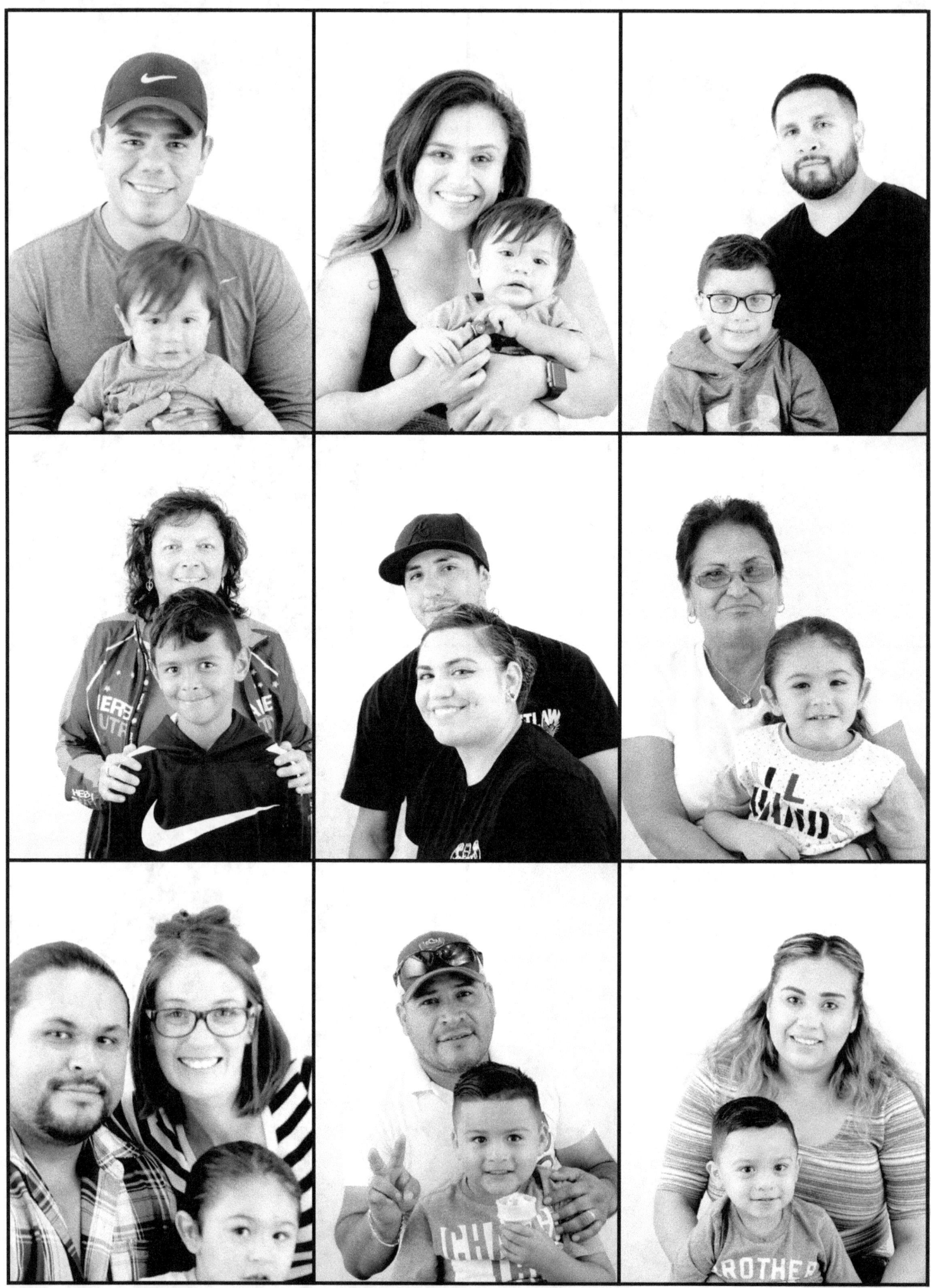

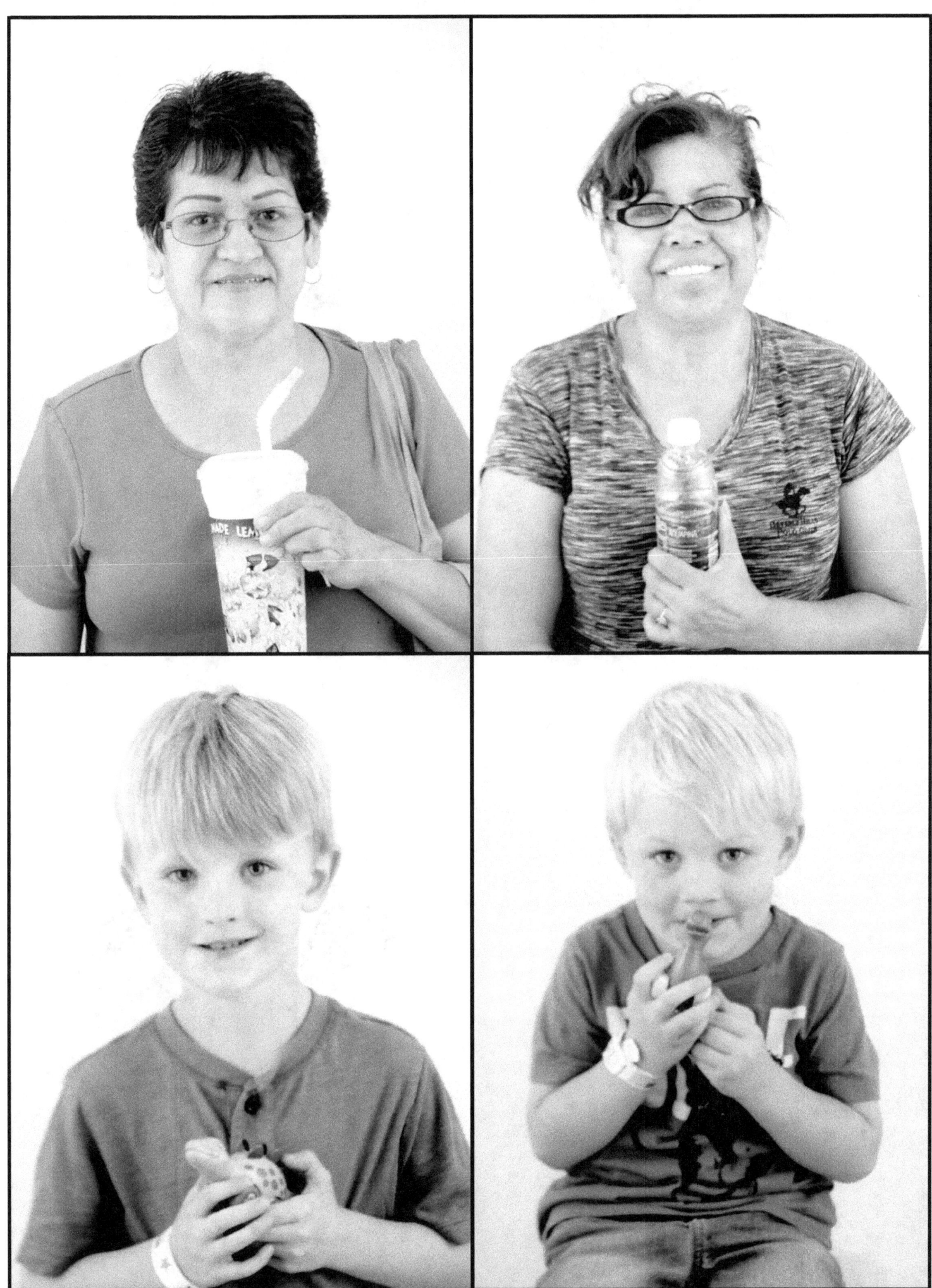

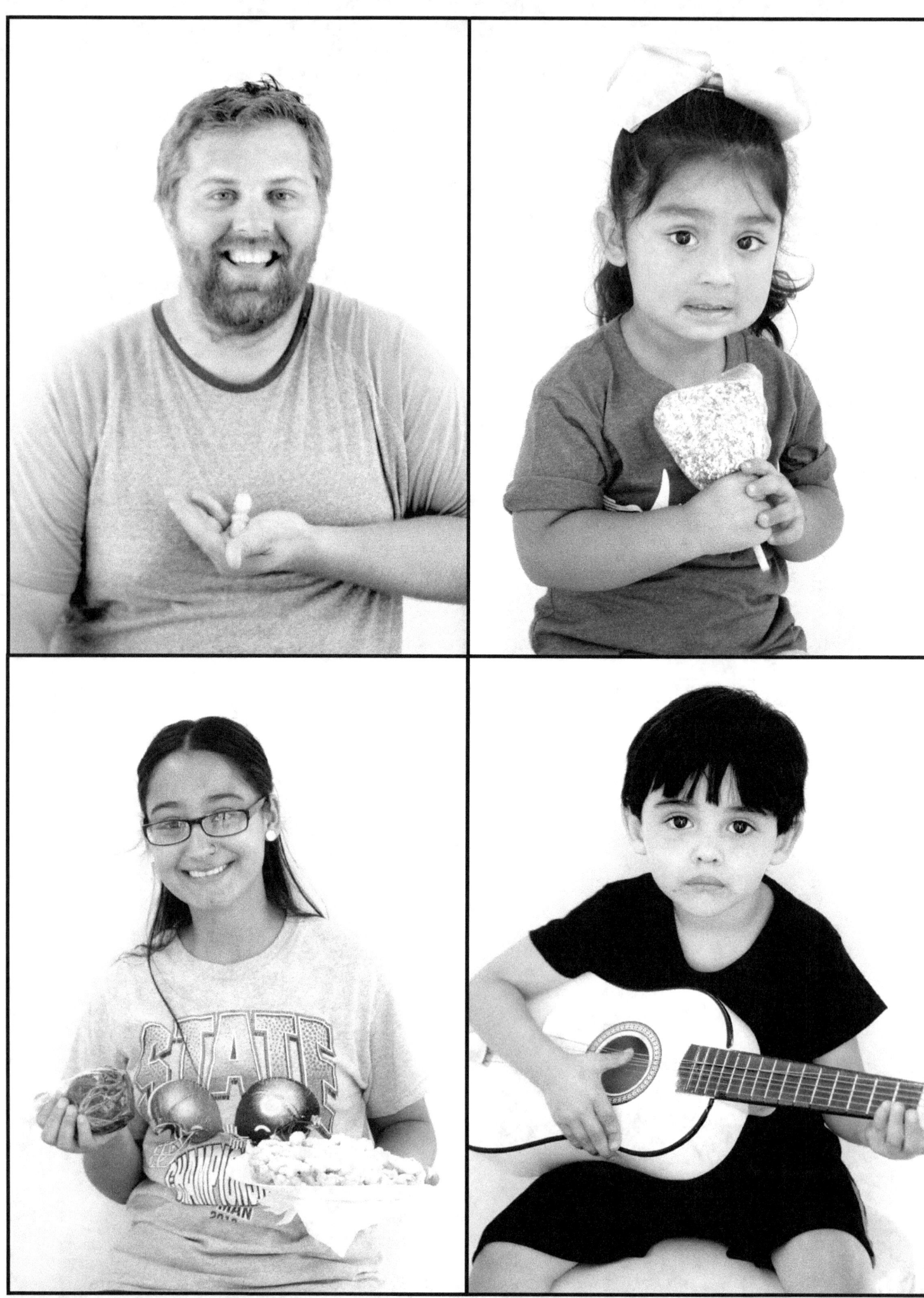

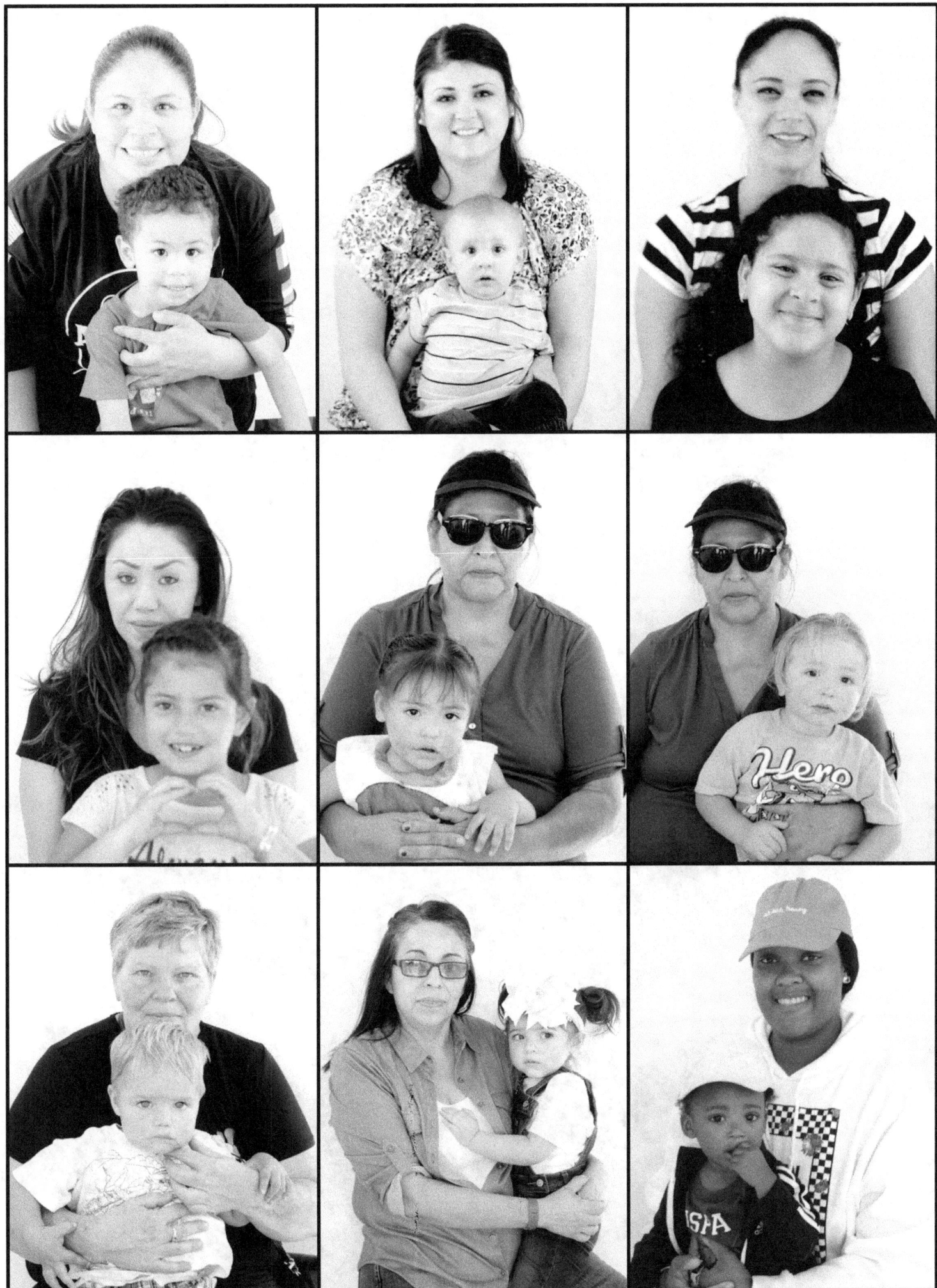

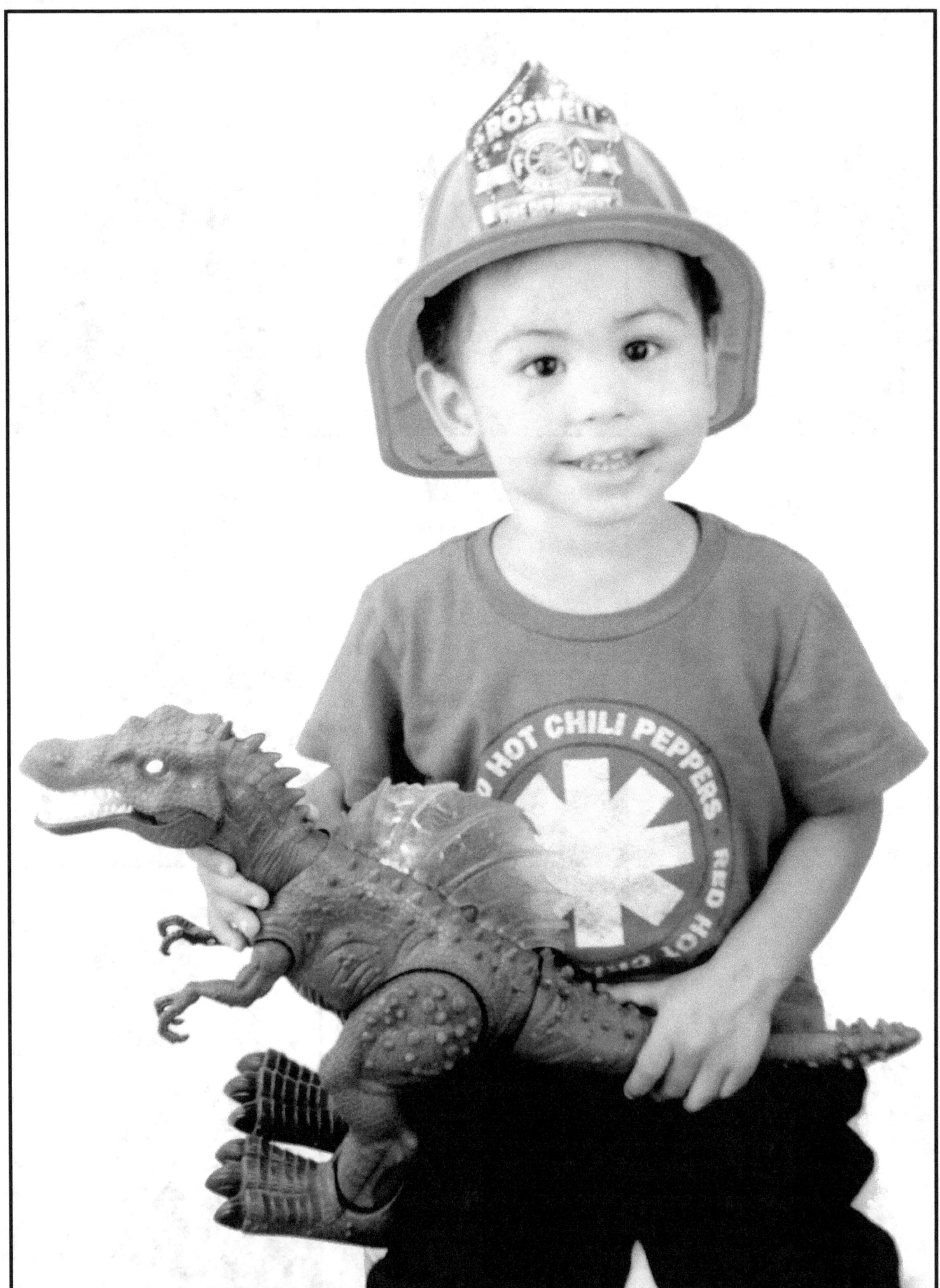

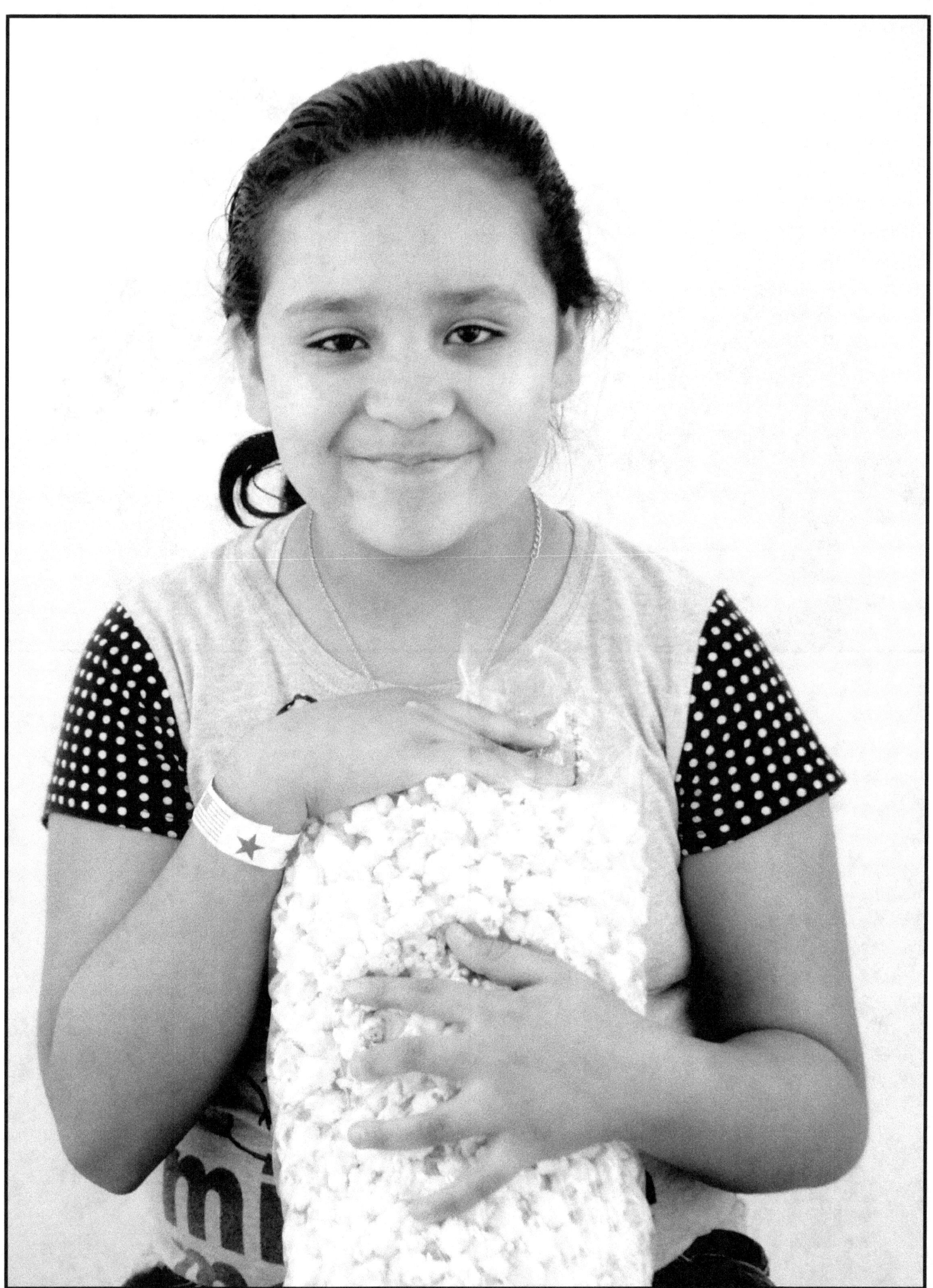

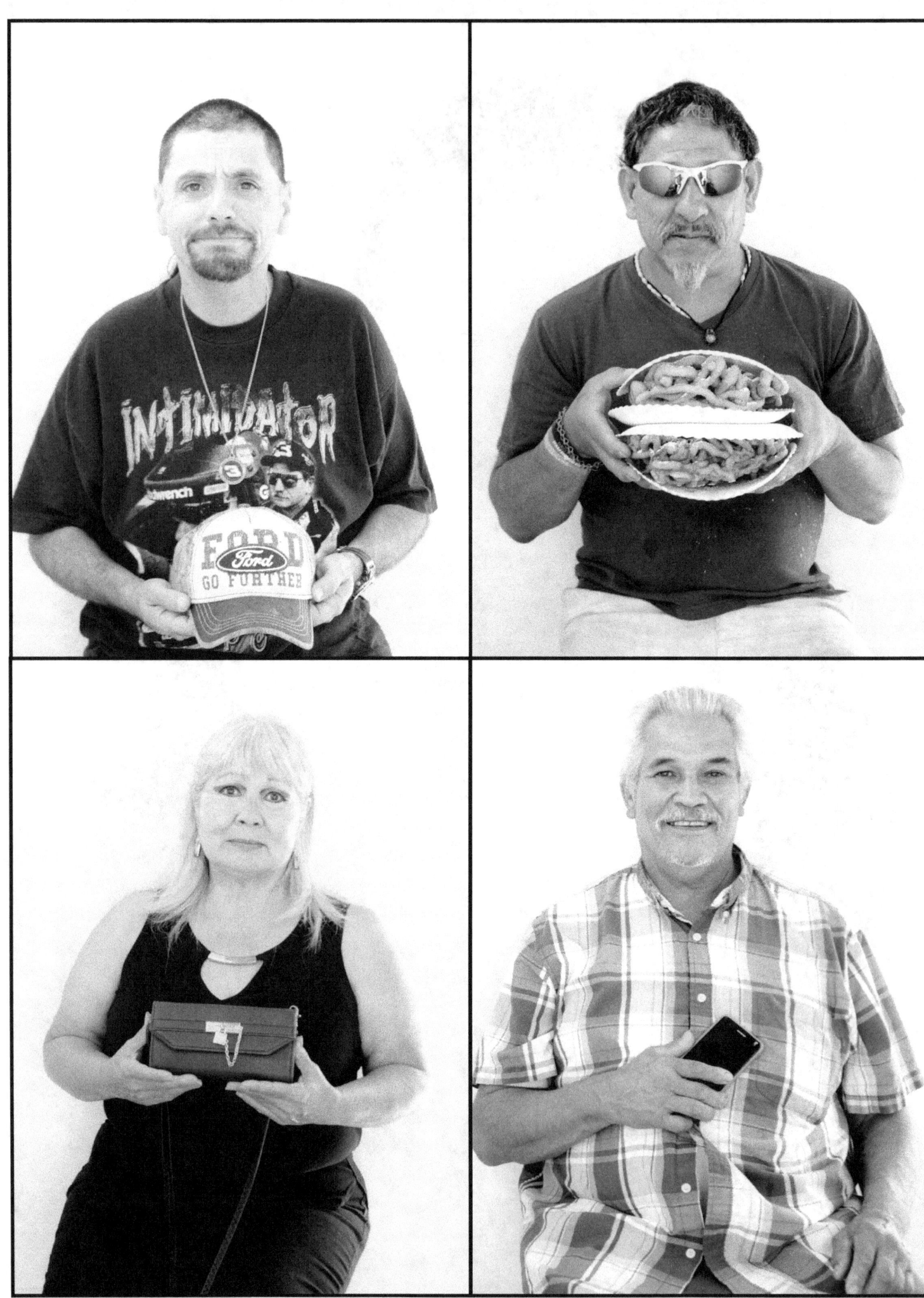

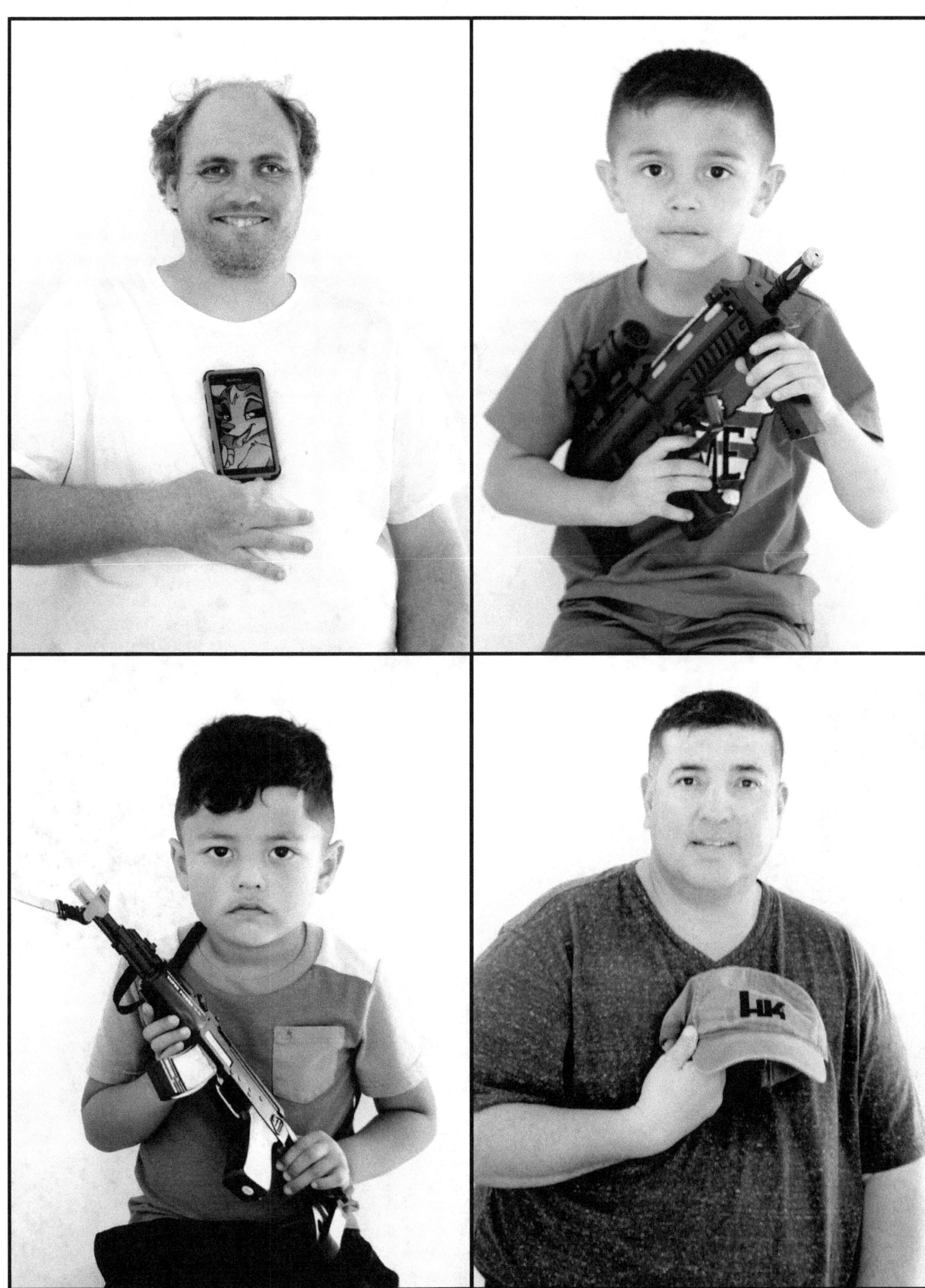

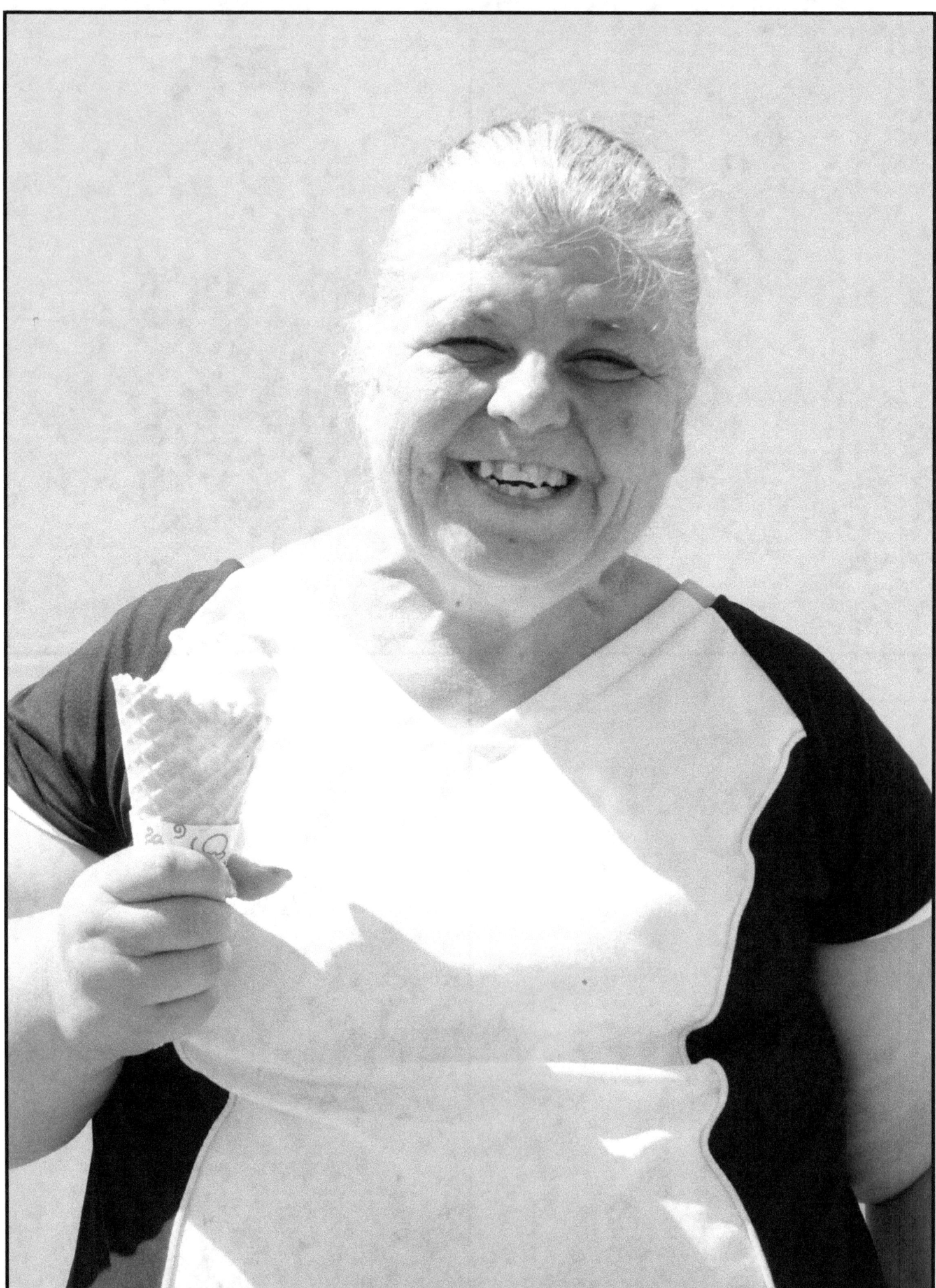

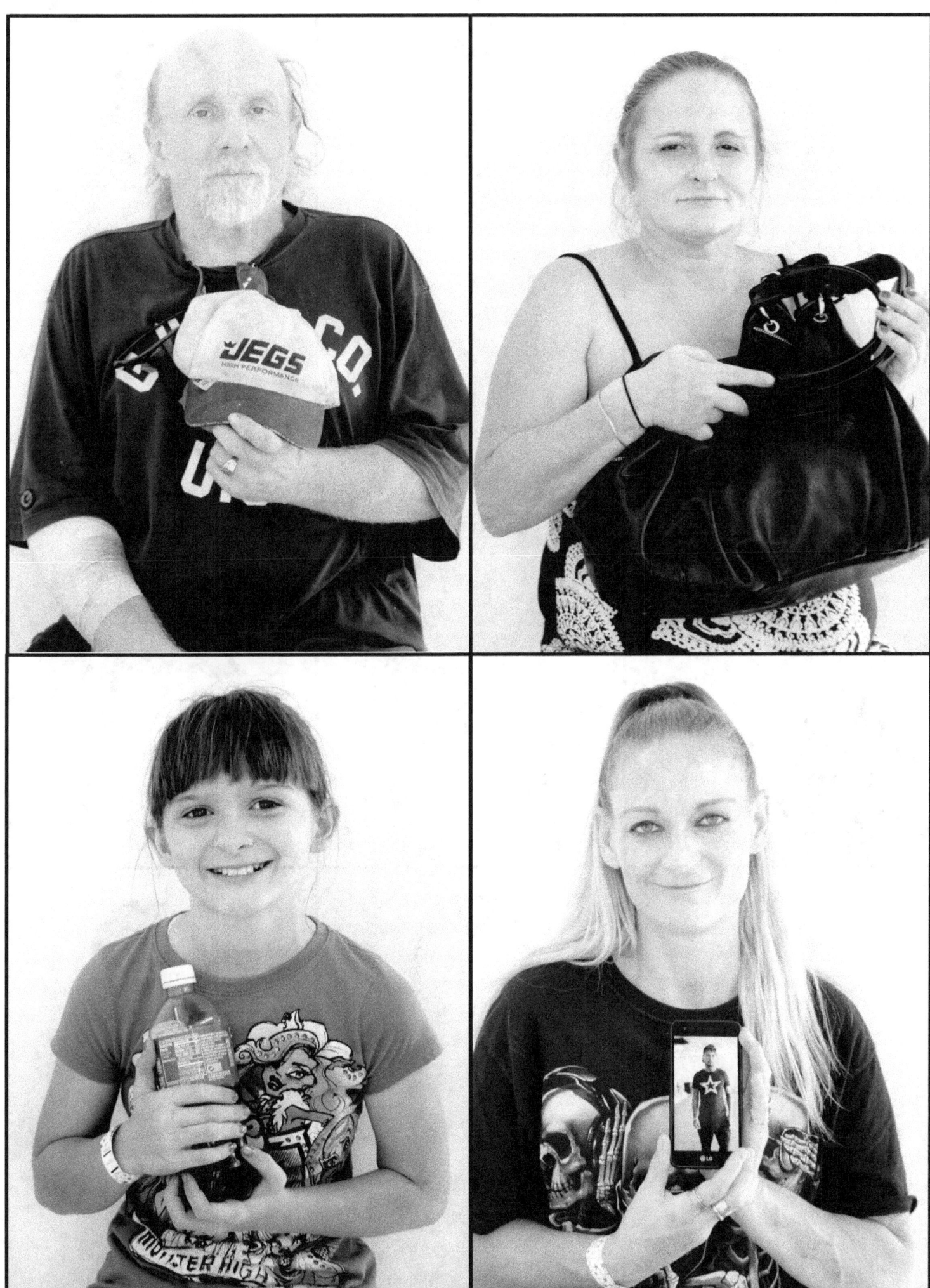

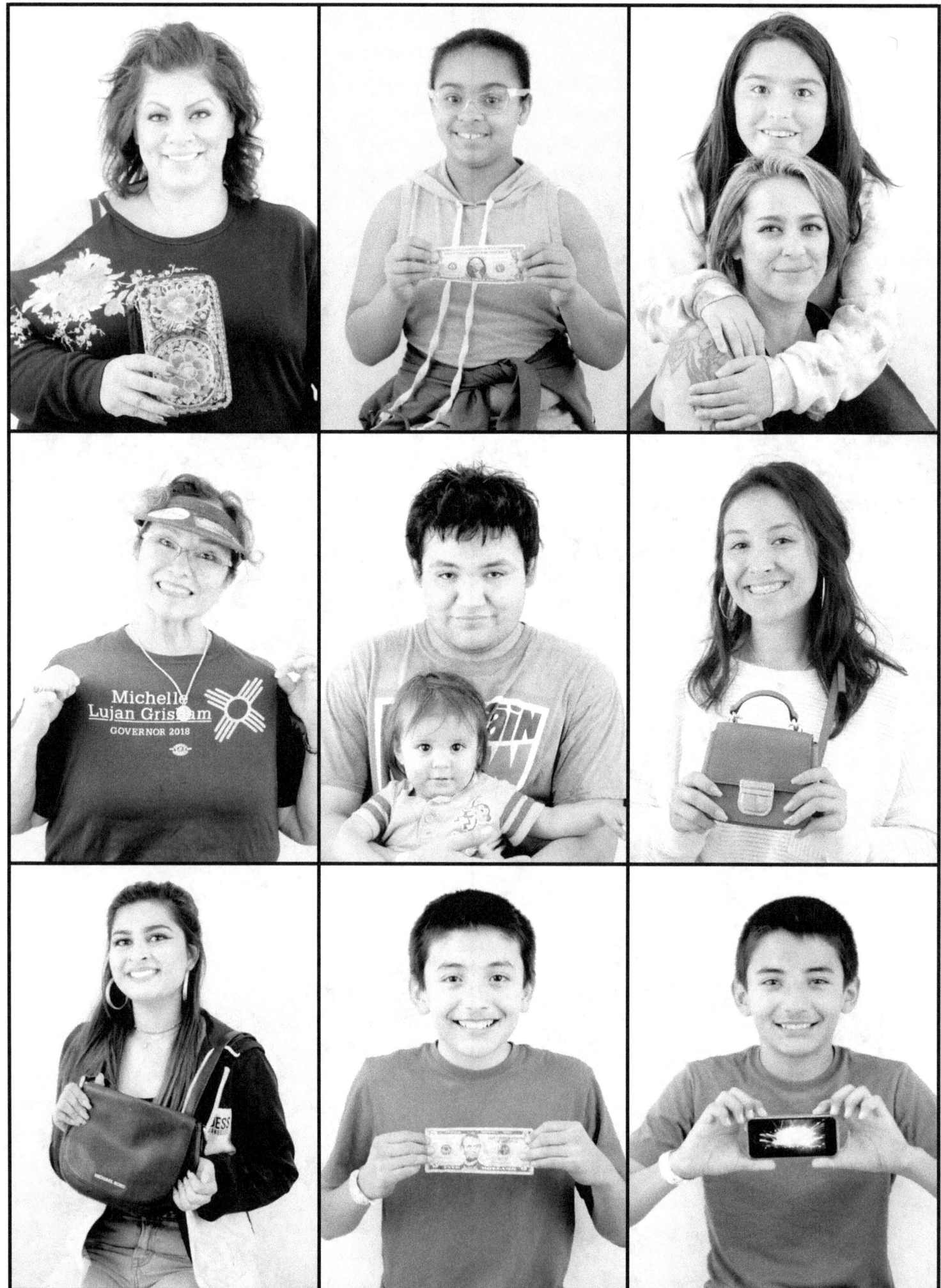

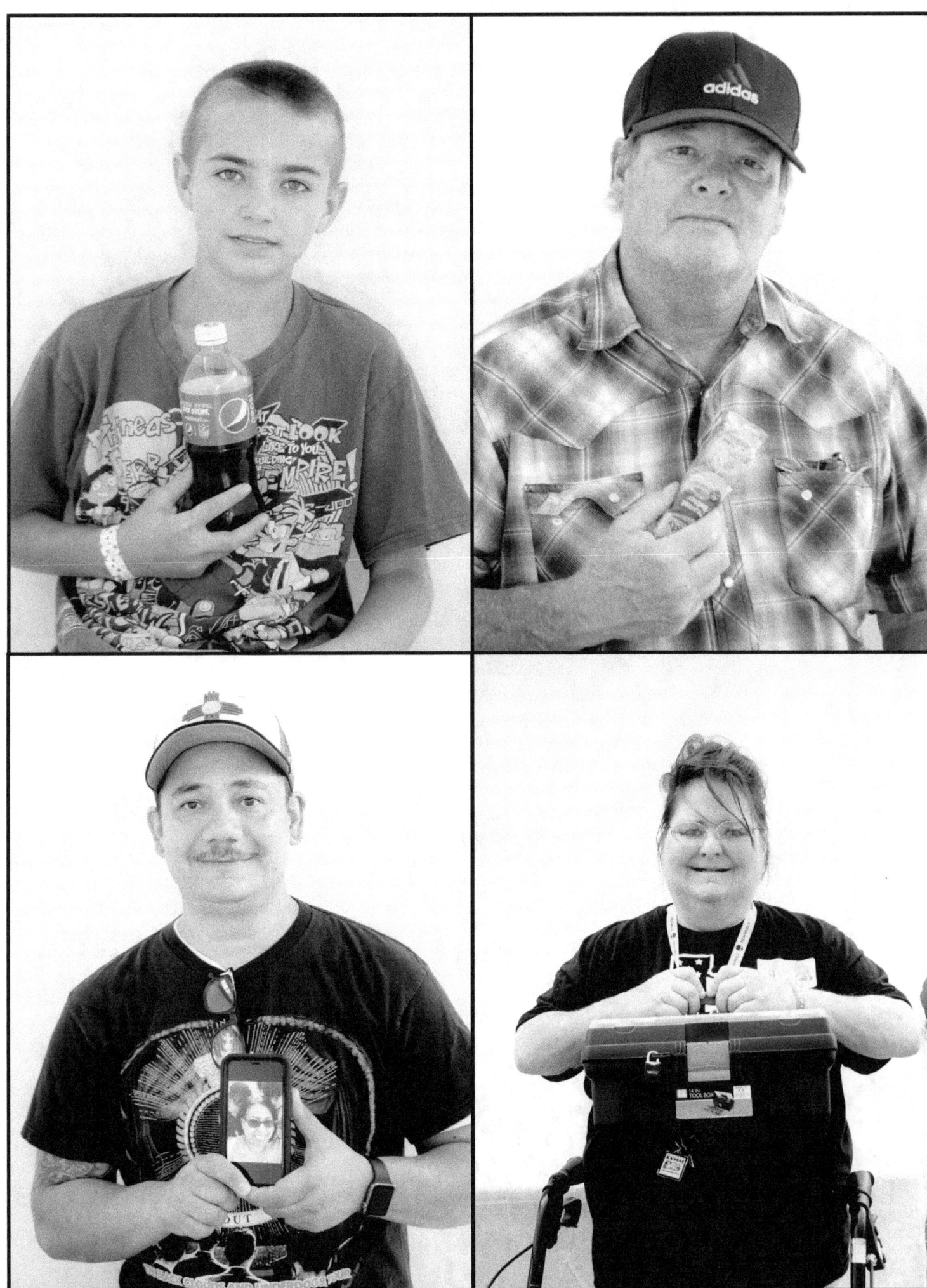

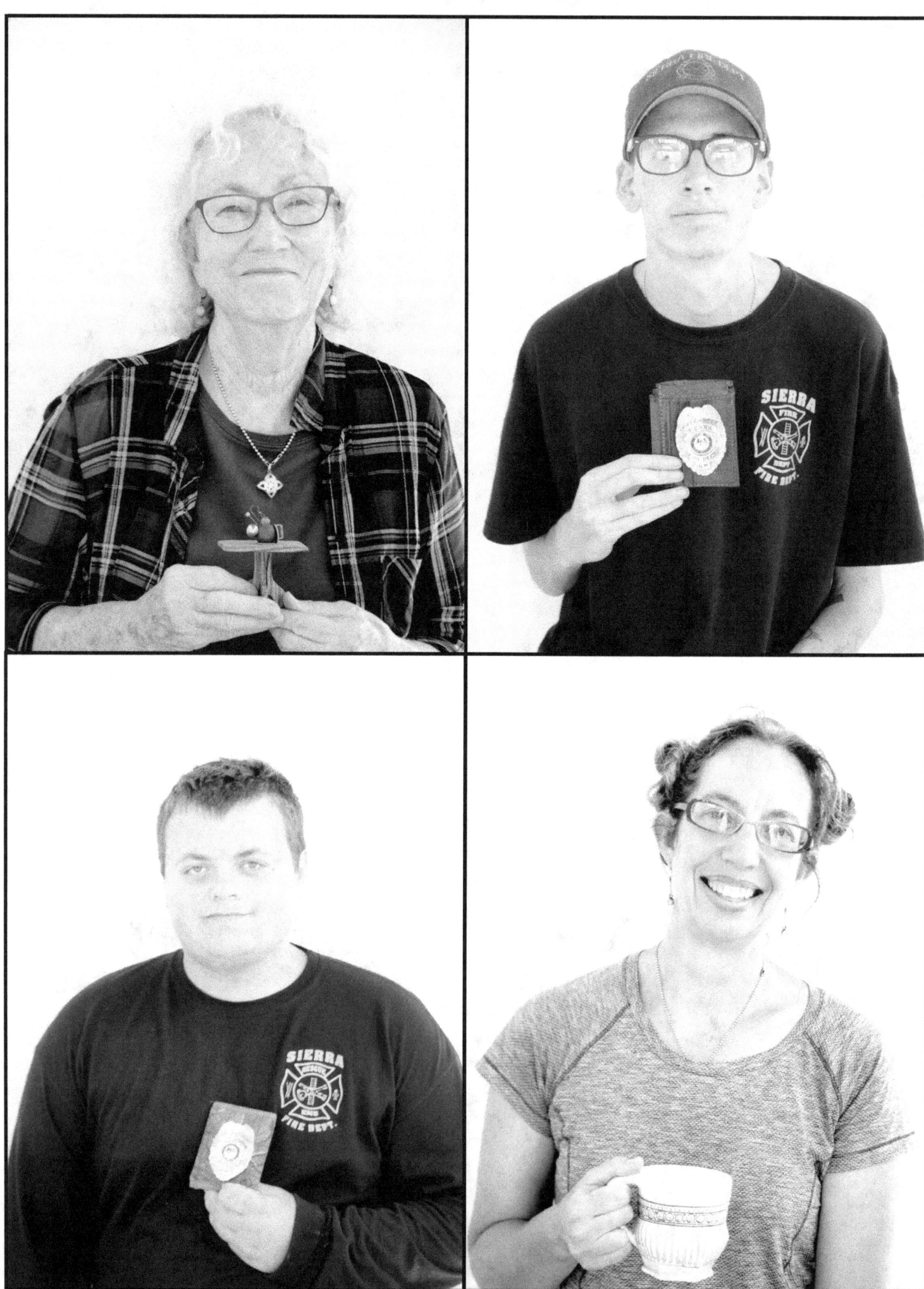

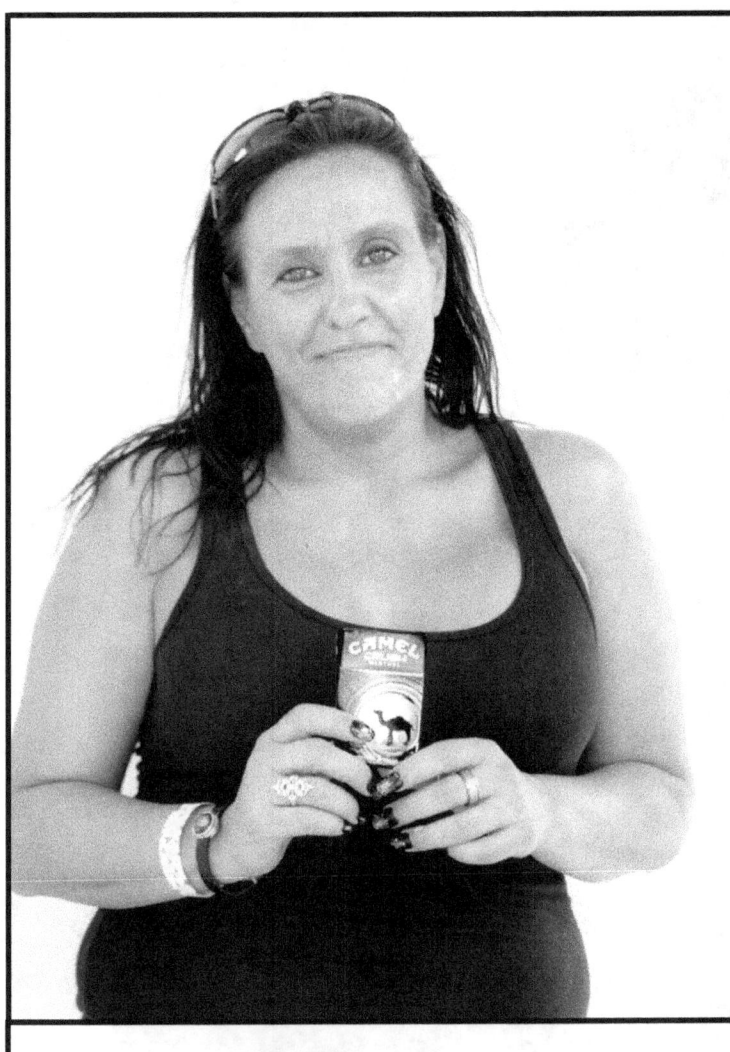

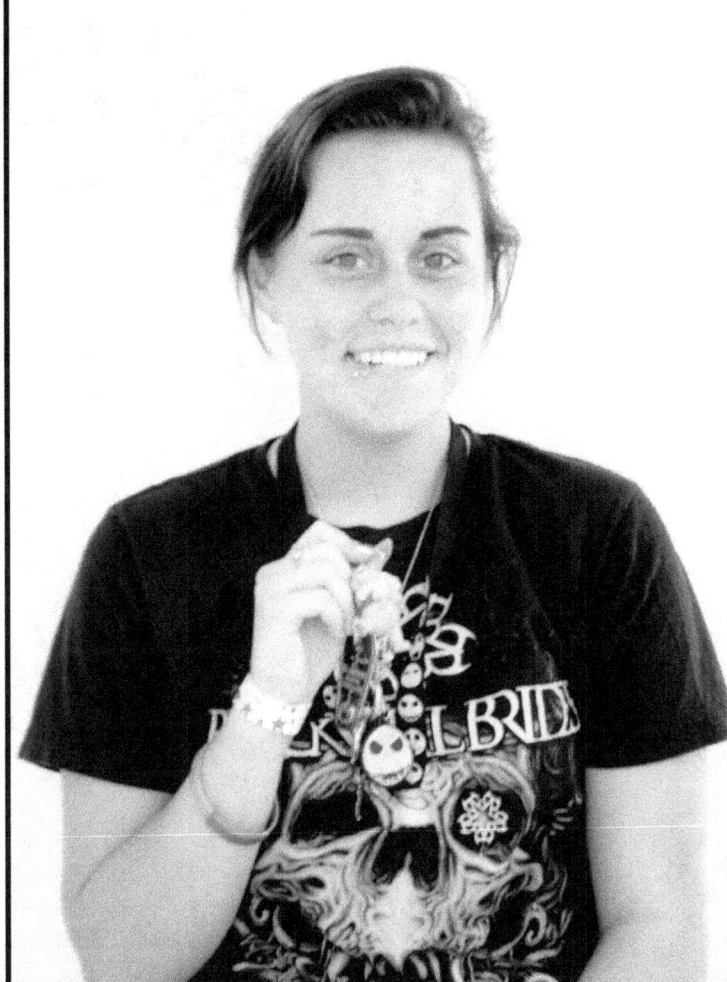

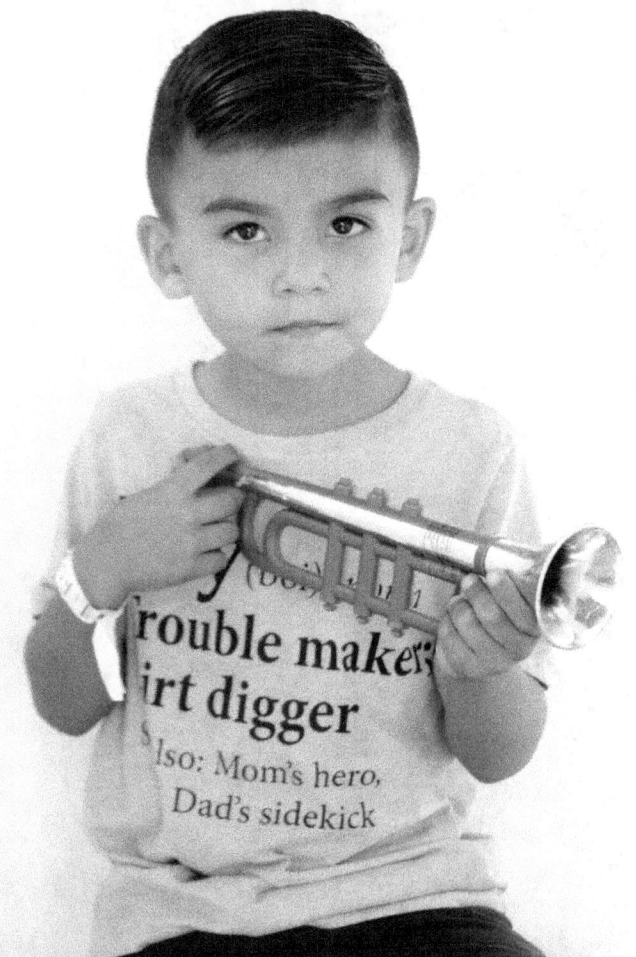

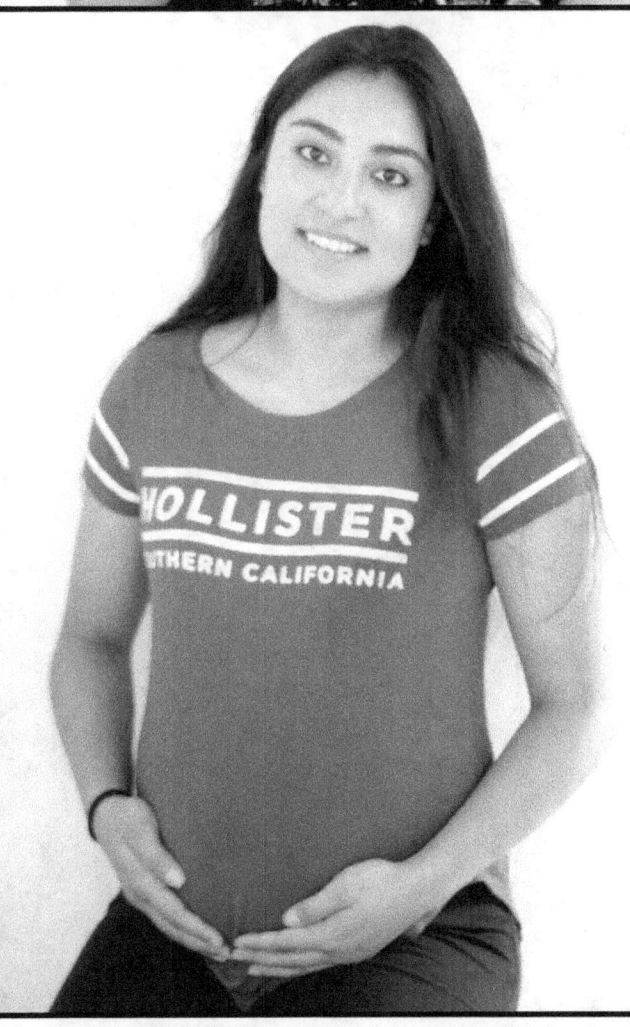

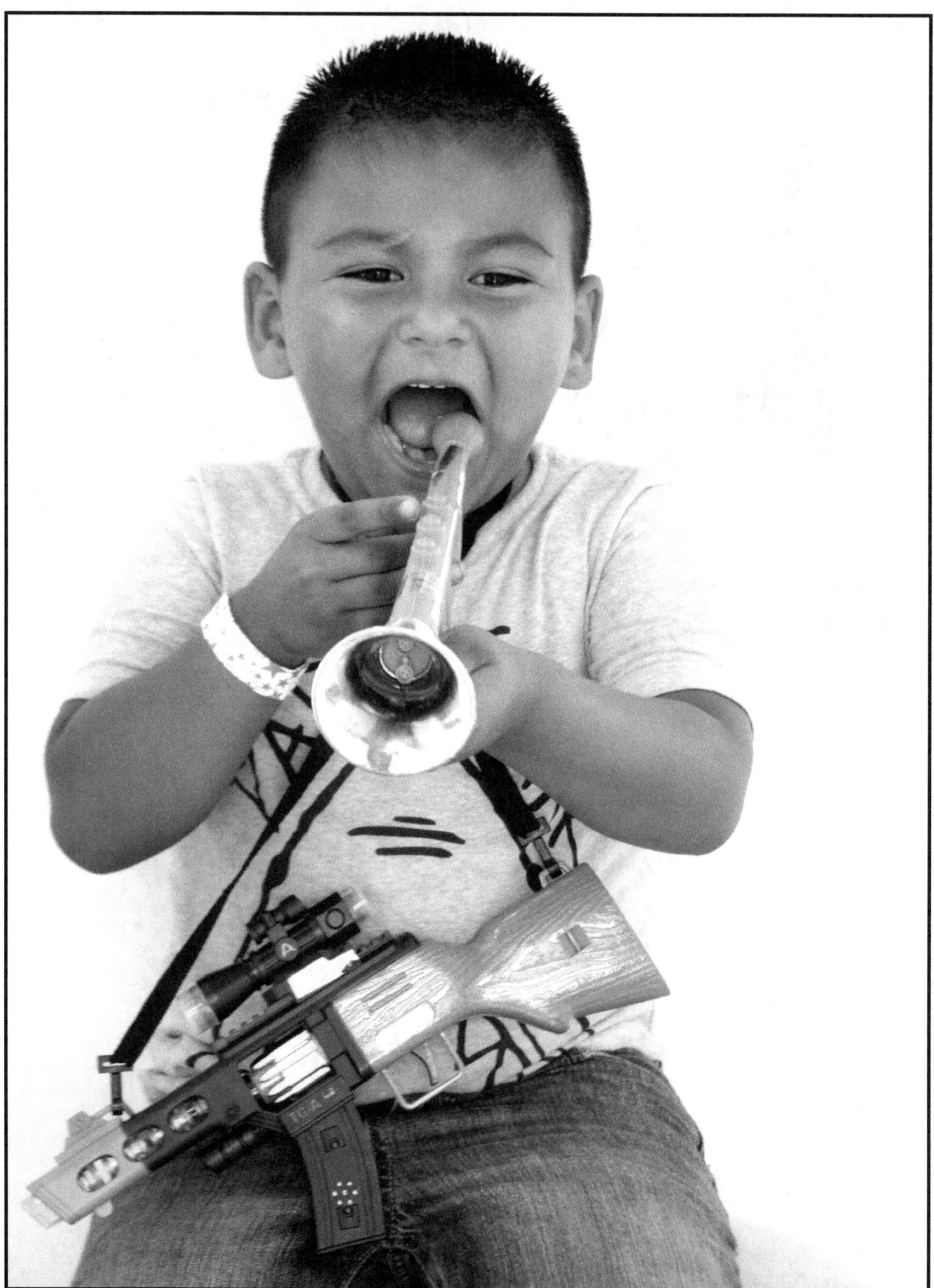

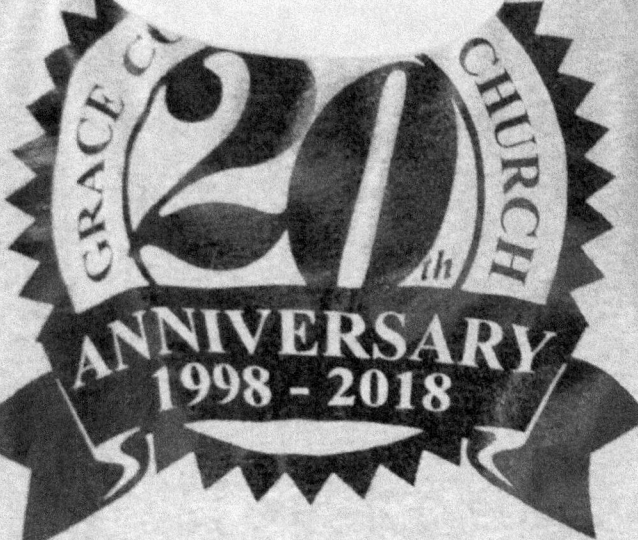

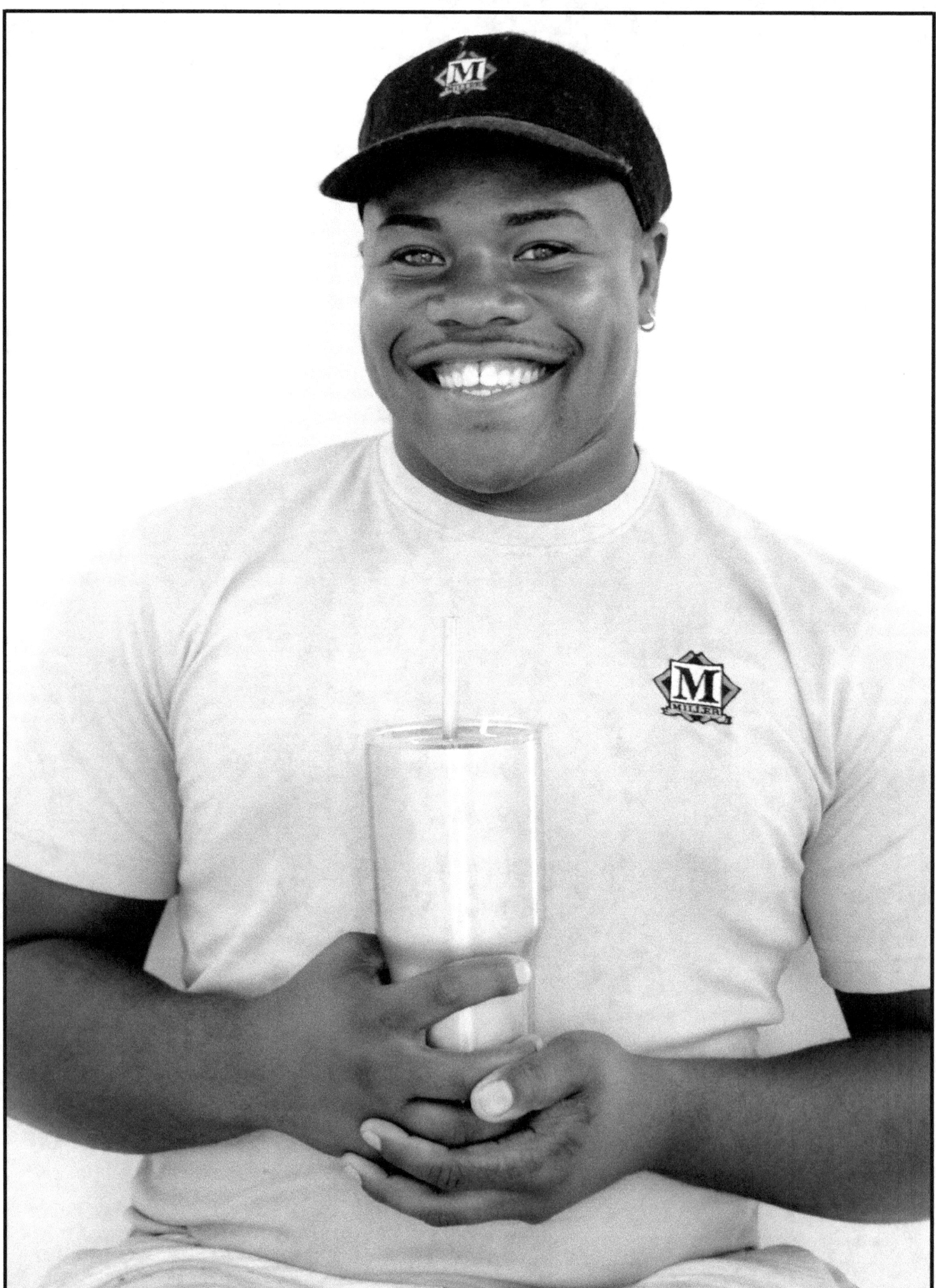

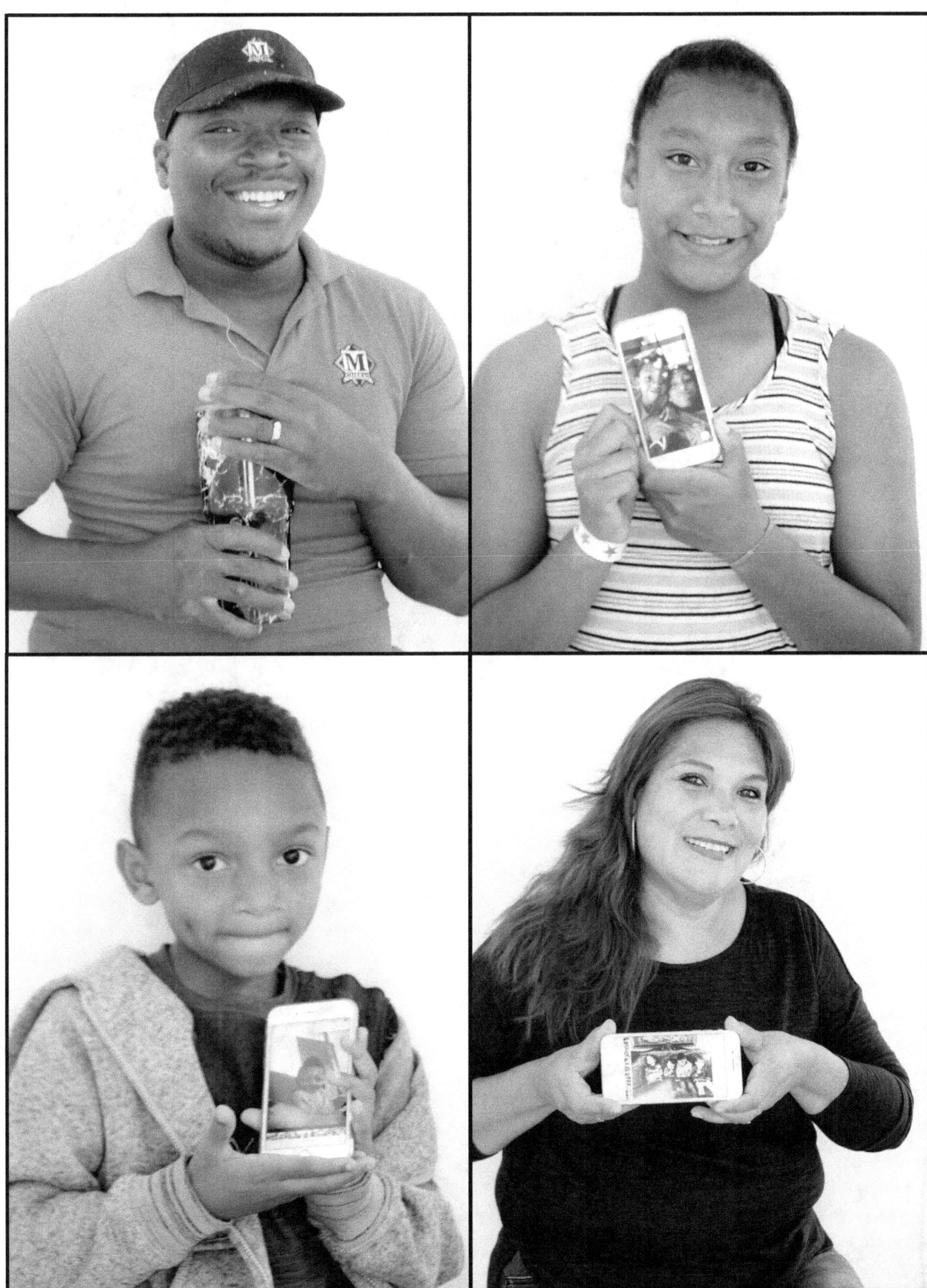

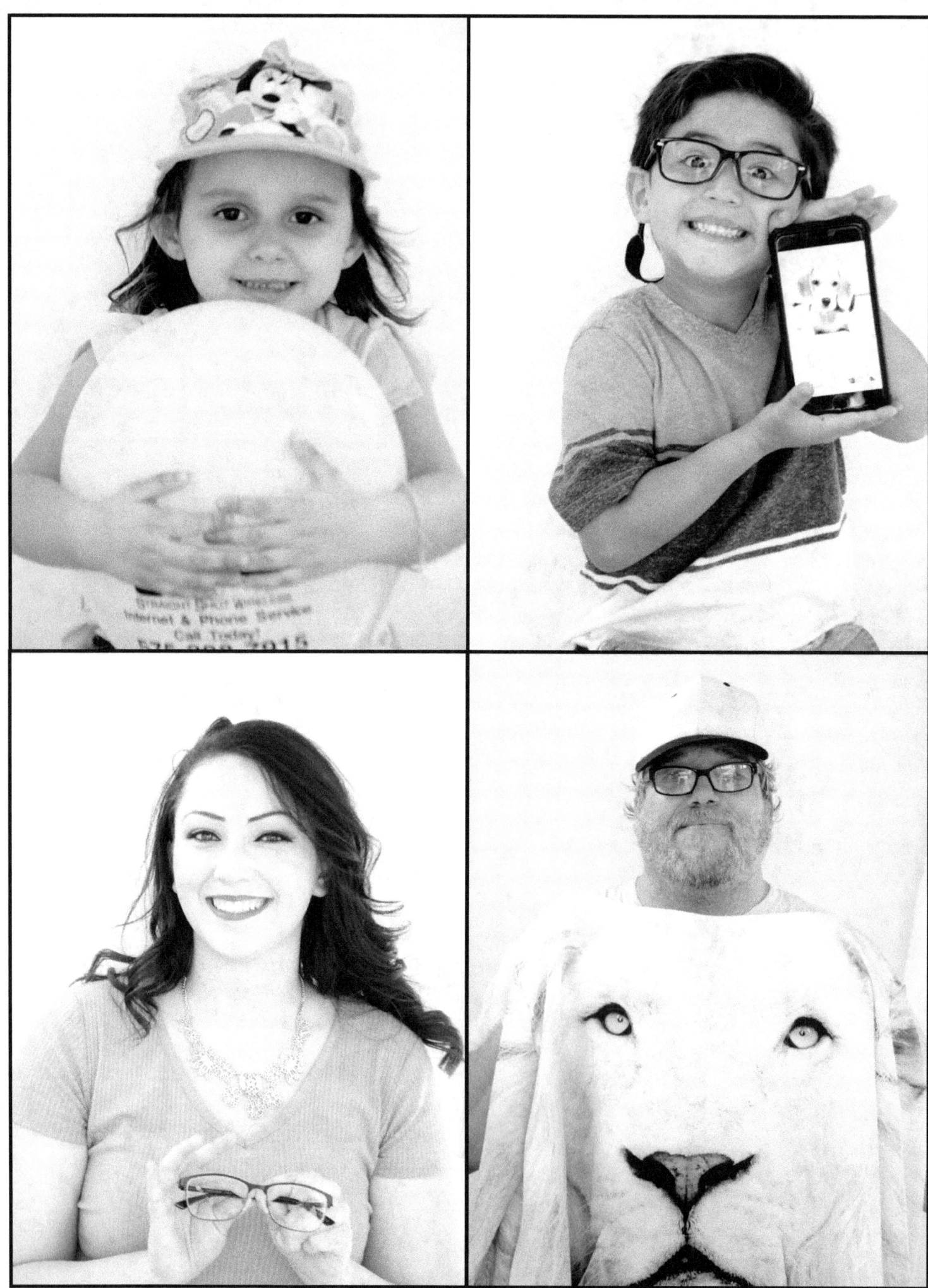

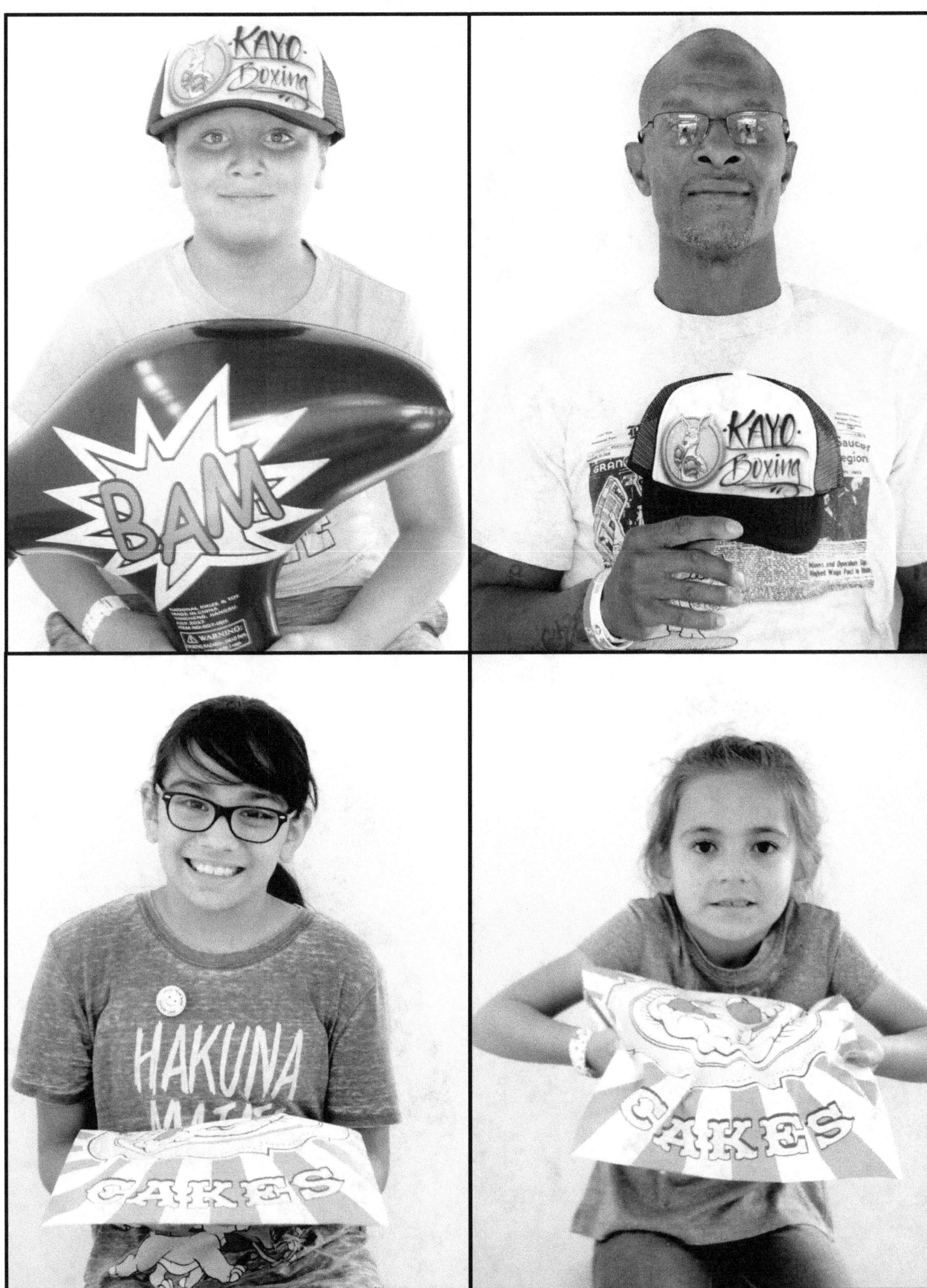

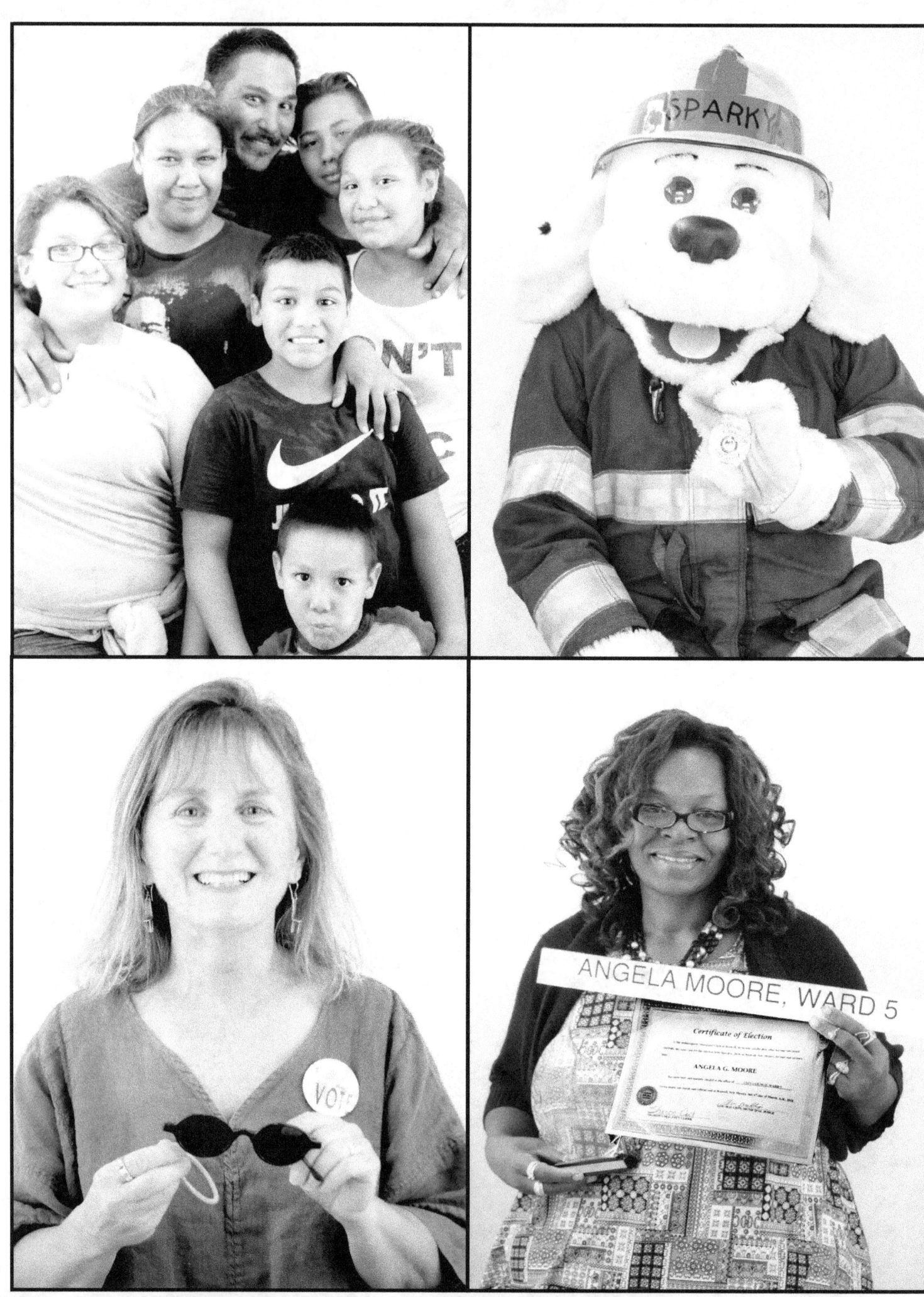

ANGELA MOORE, WARD 5

Certificate of Election

ANGELA G. MOORE

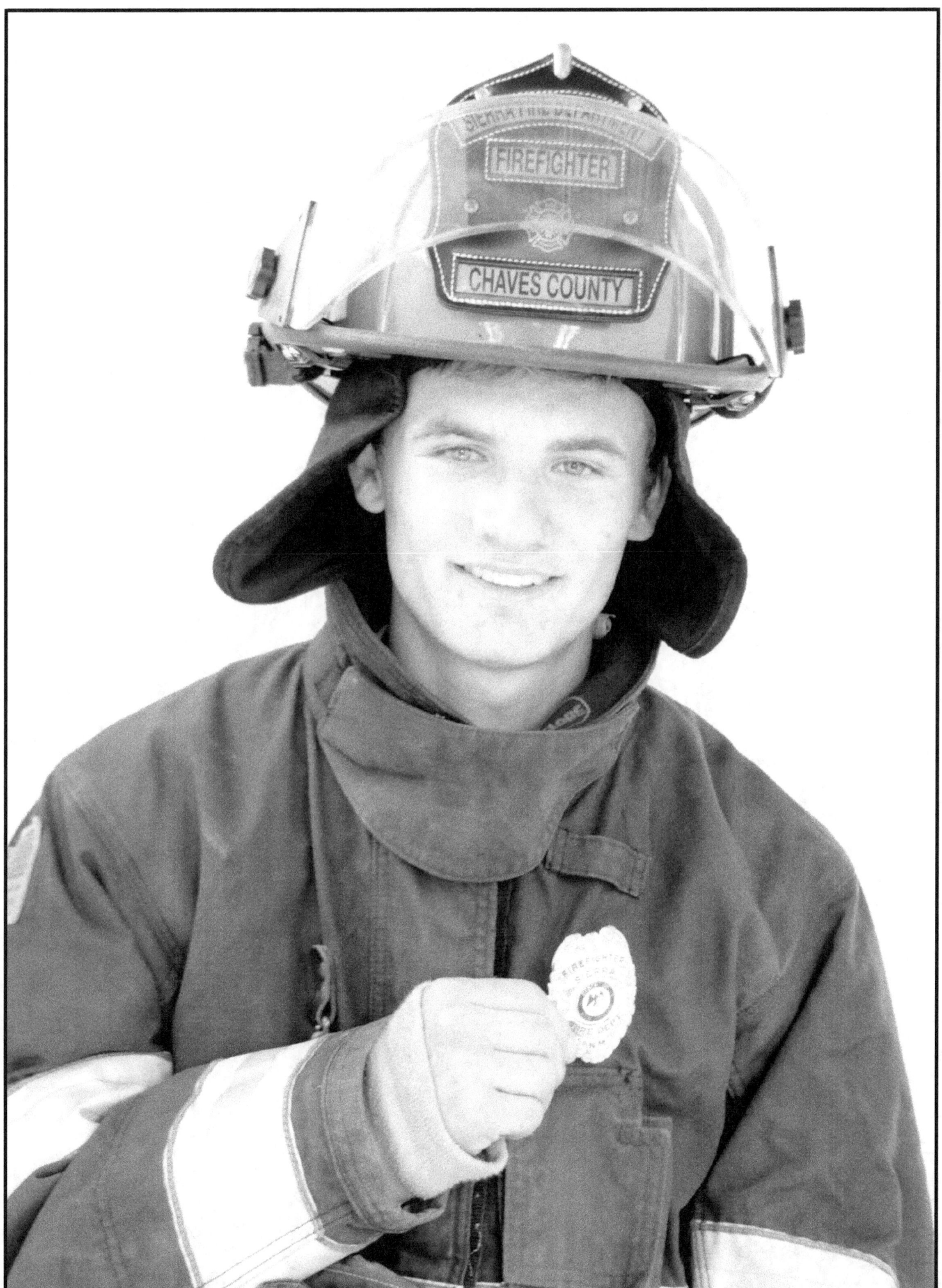

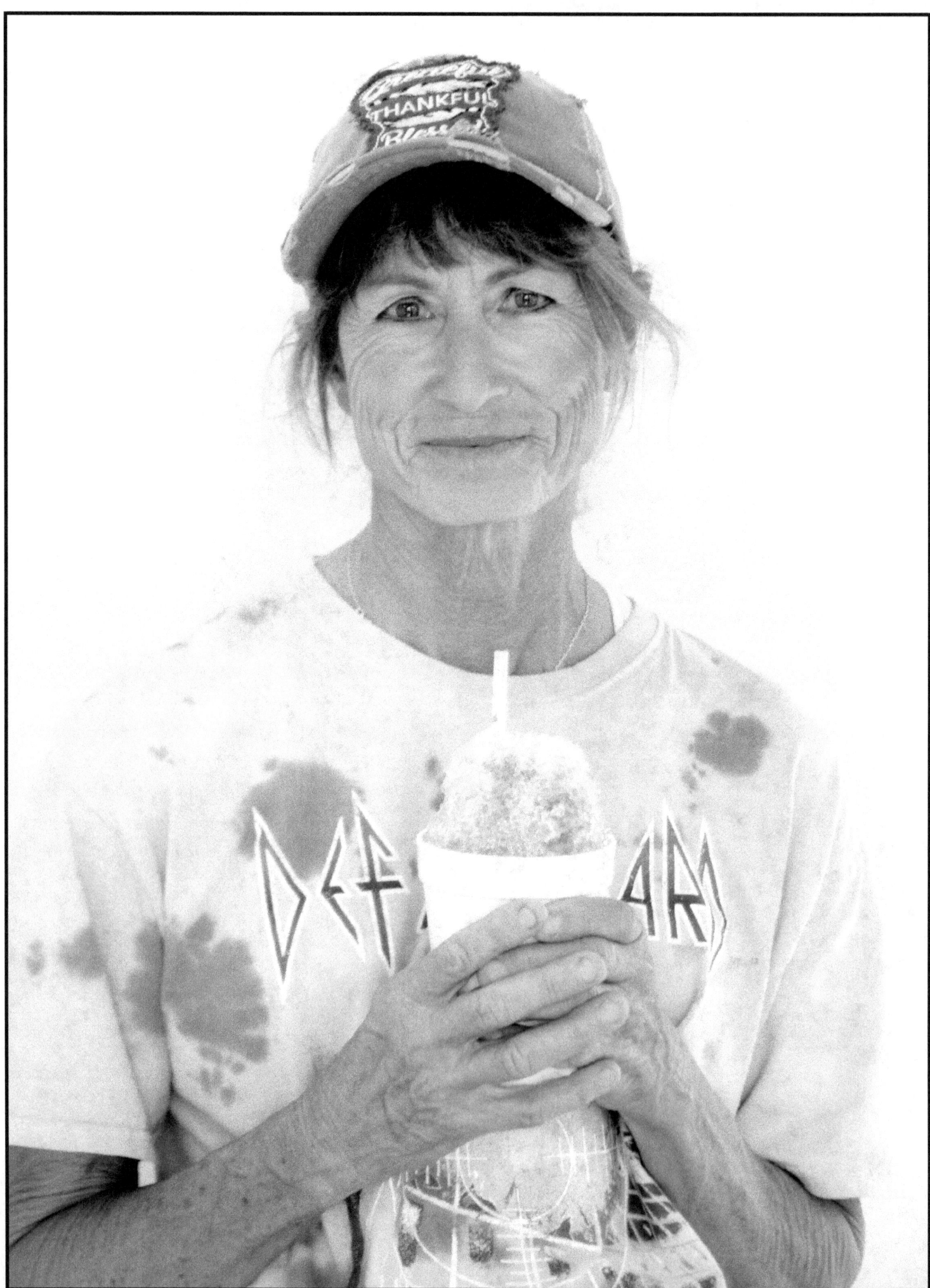

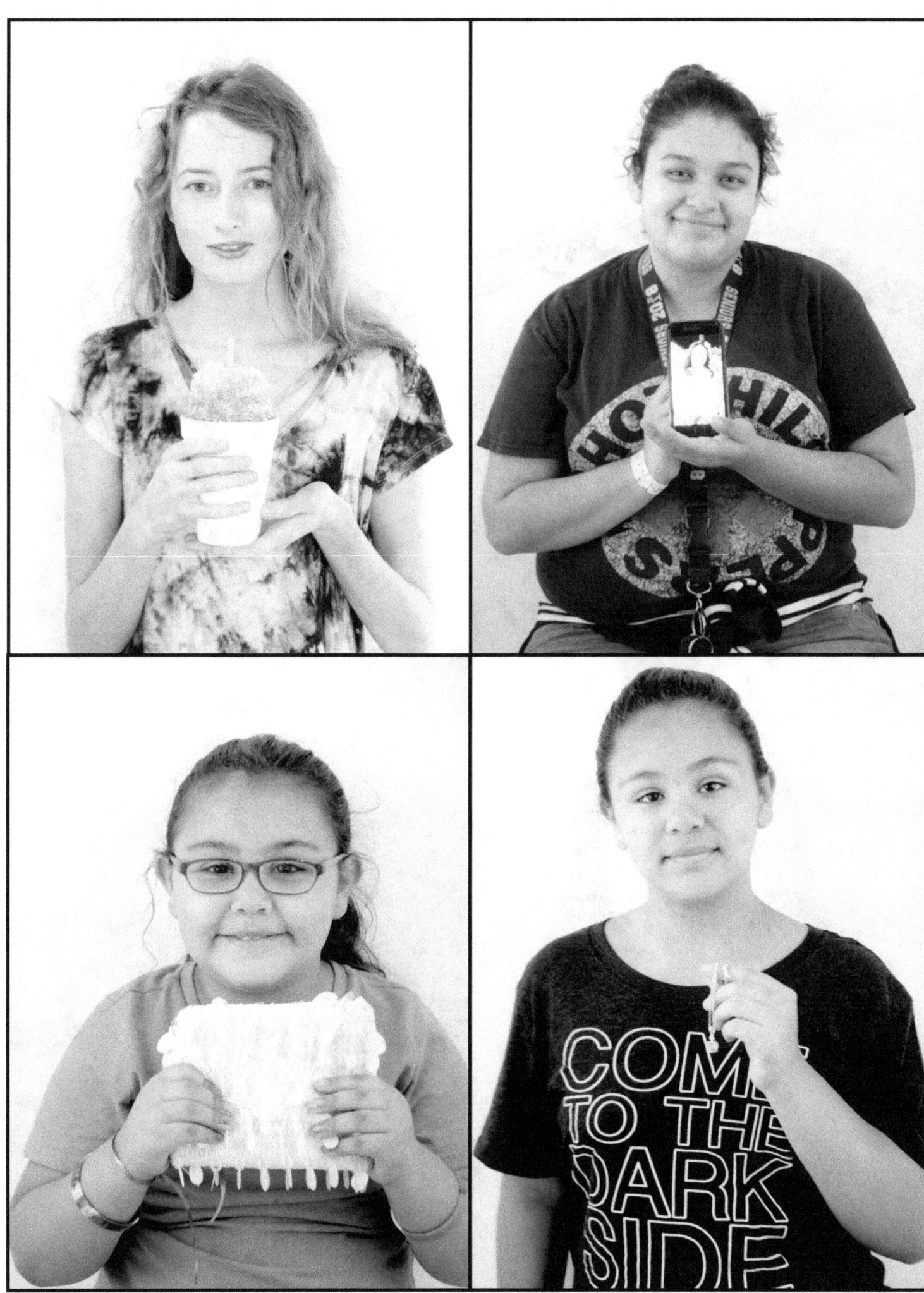

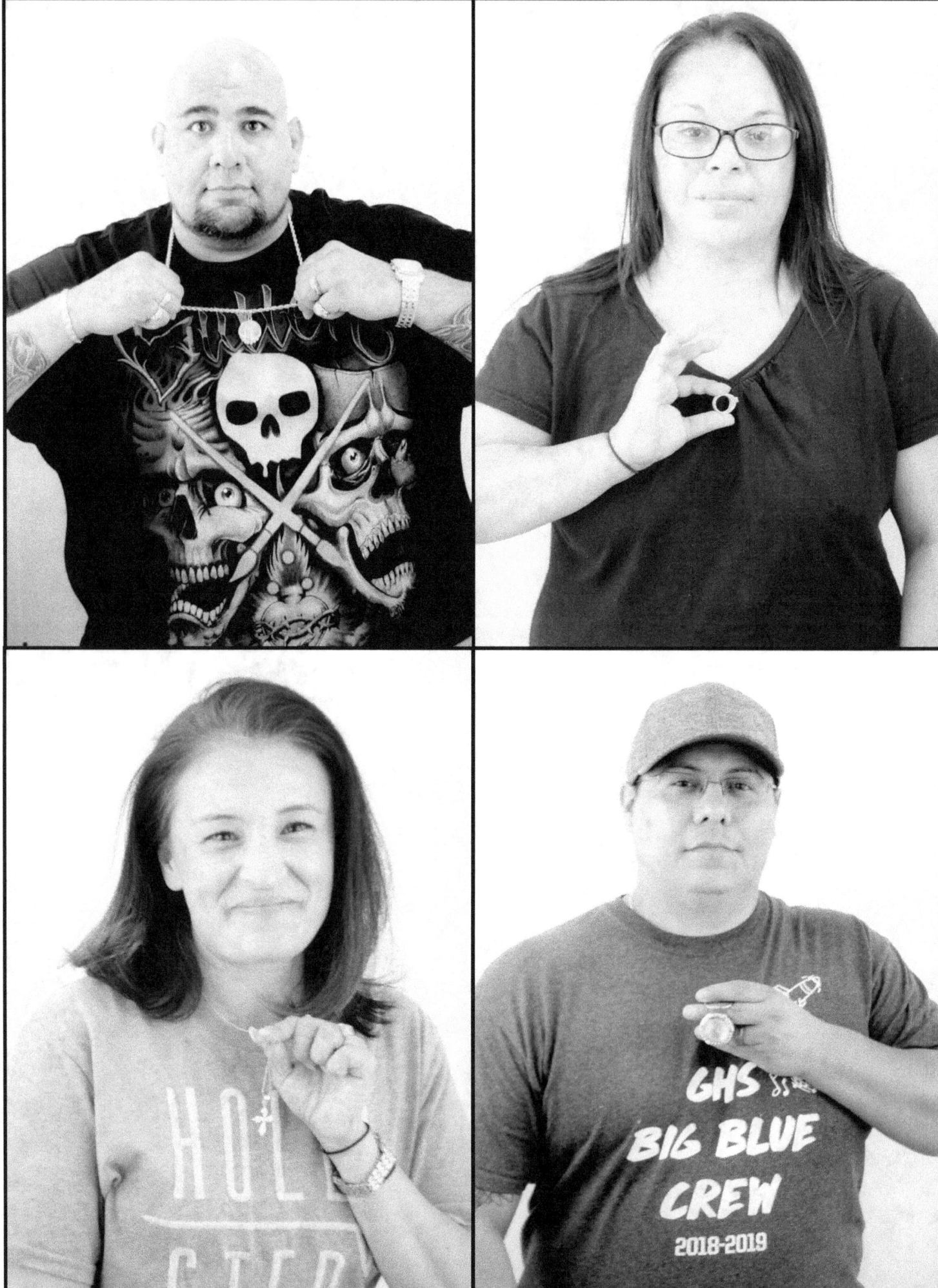

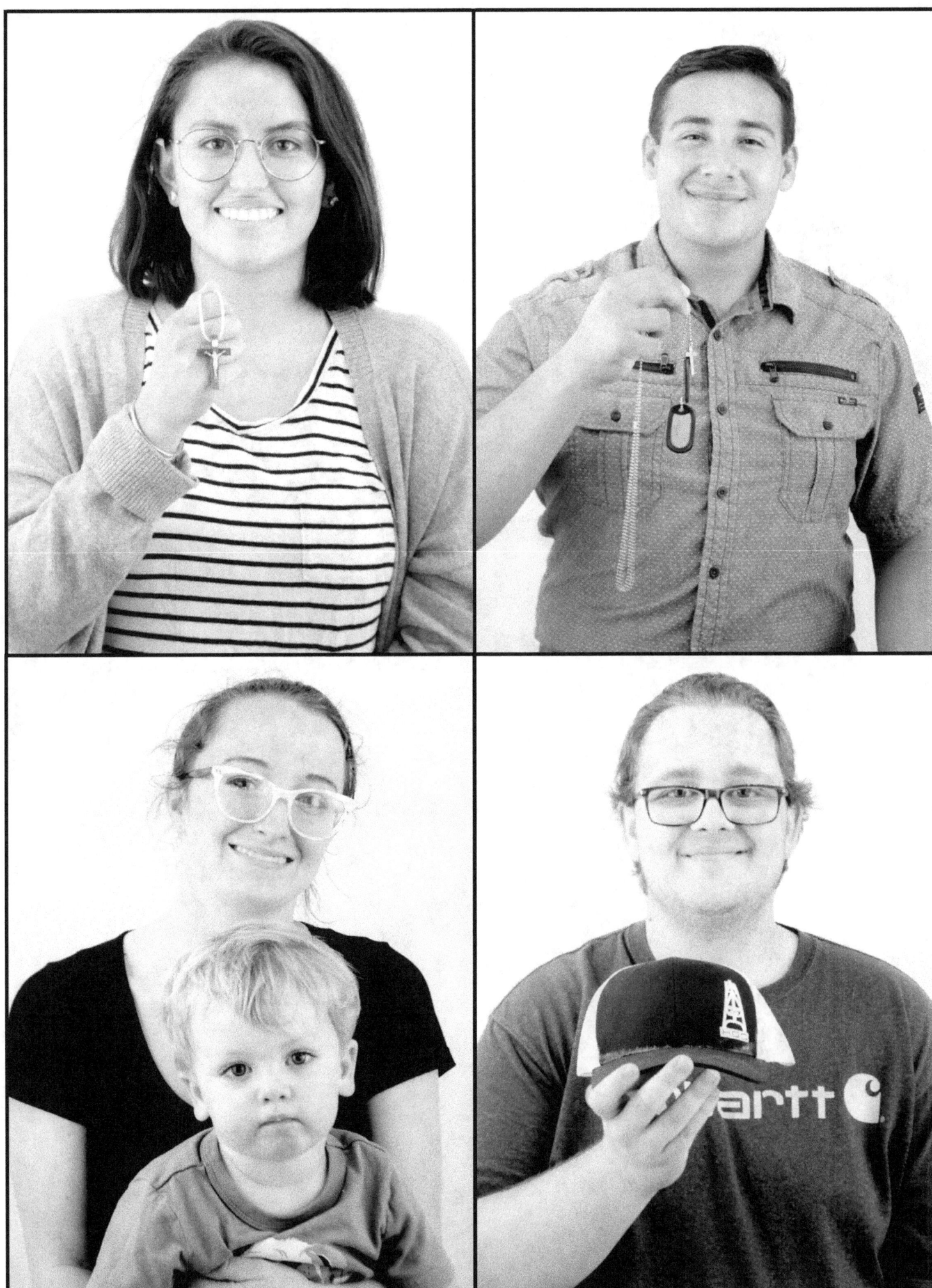

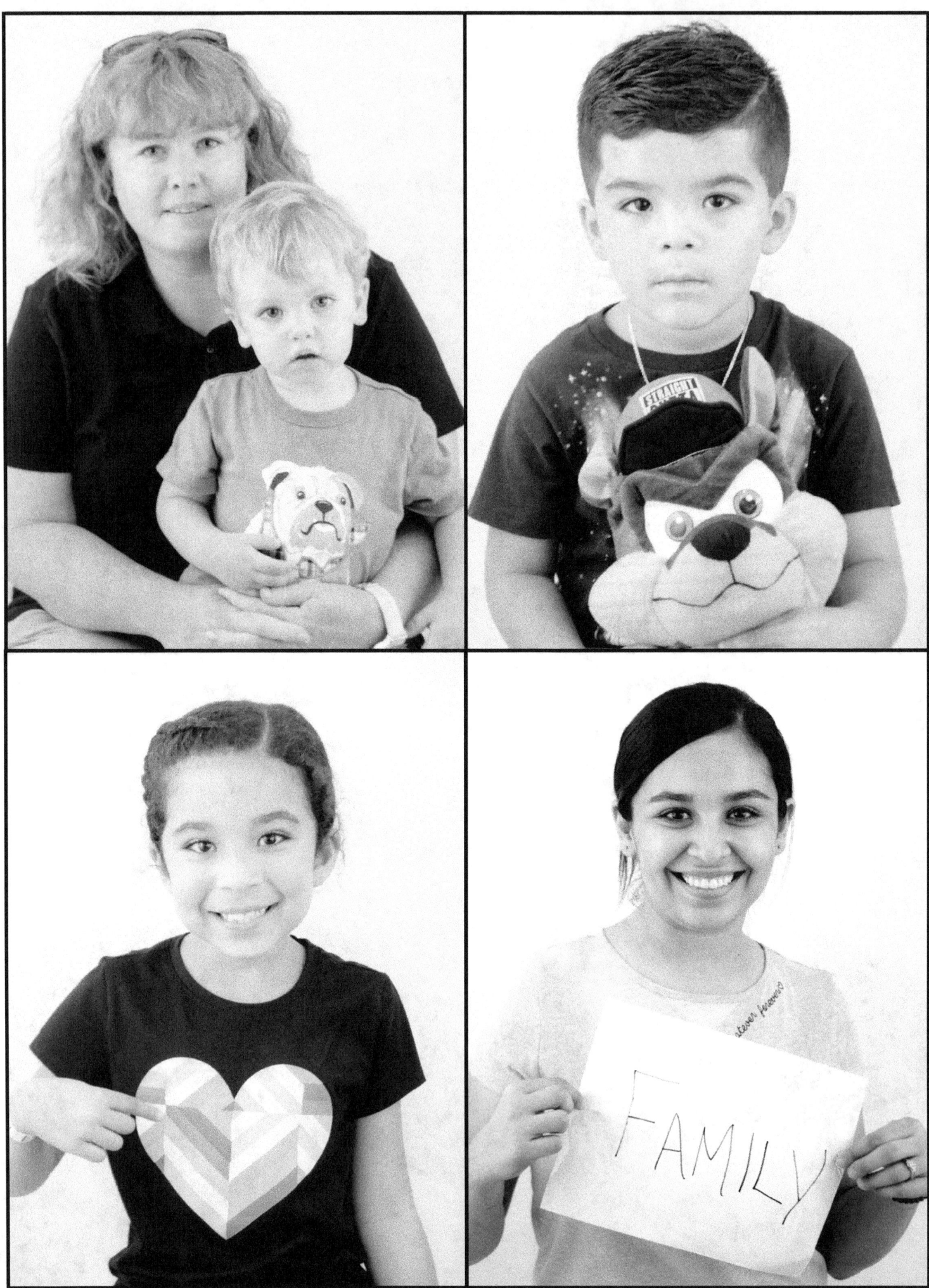

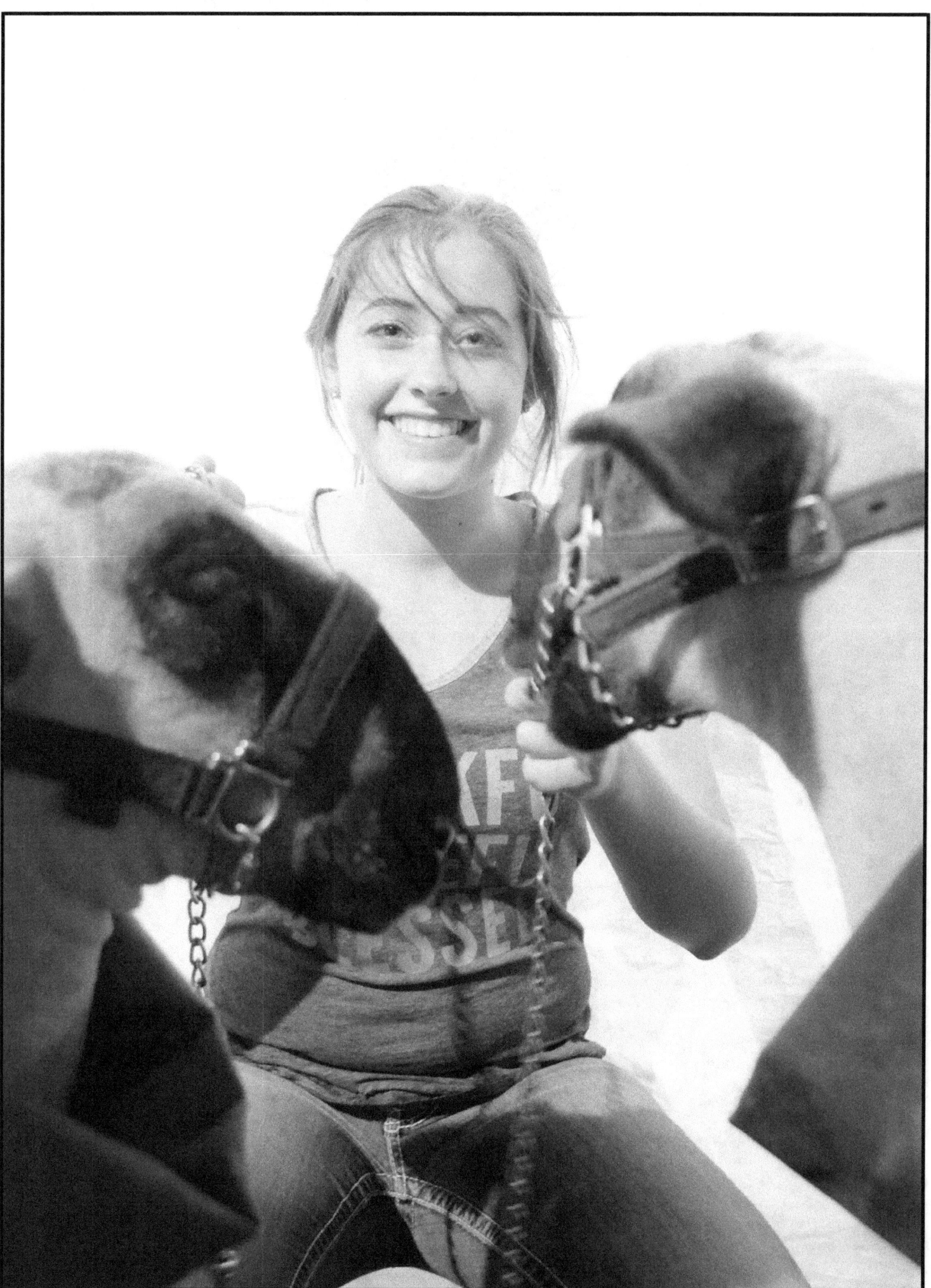

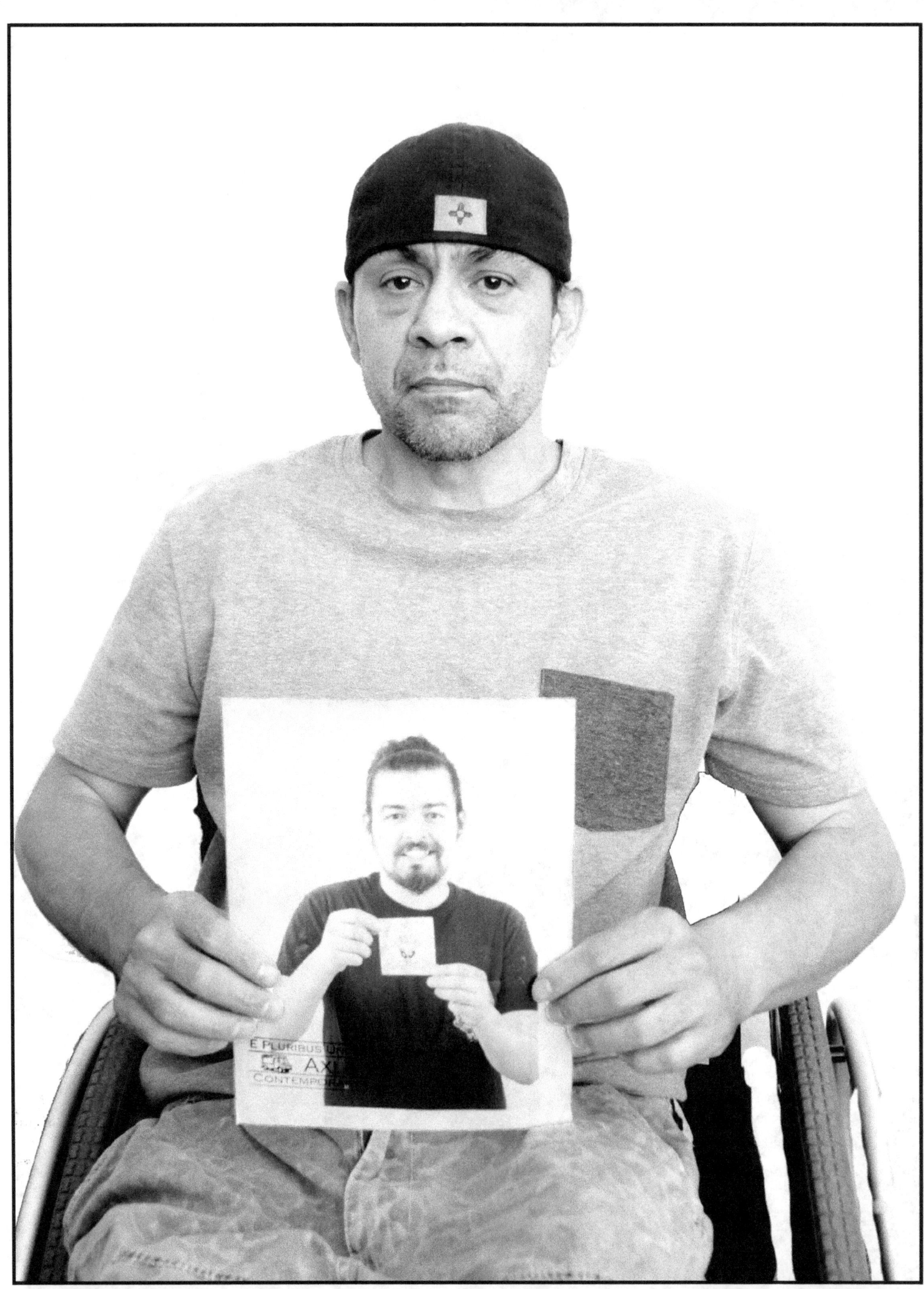

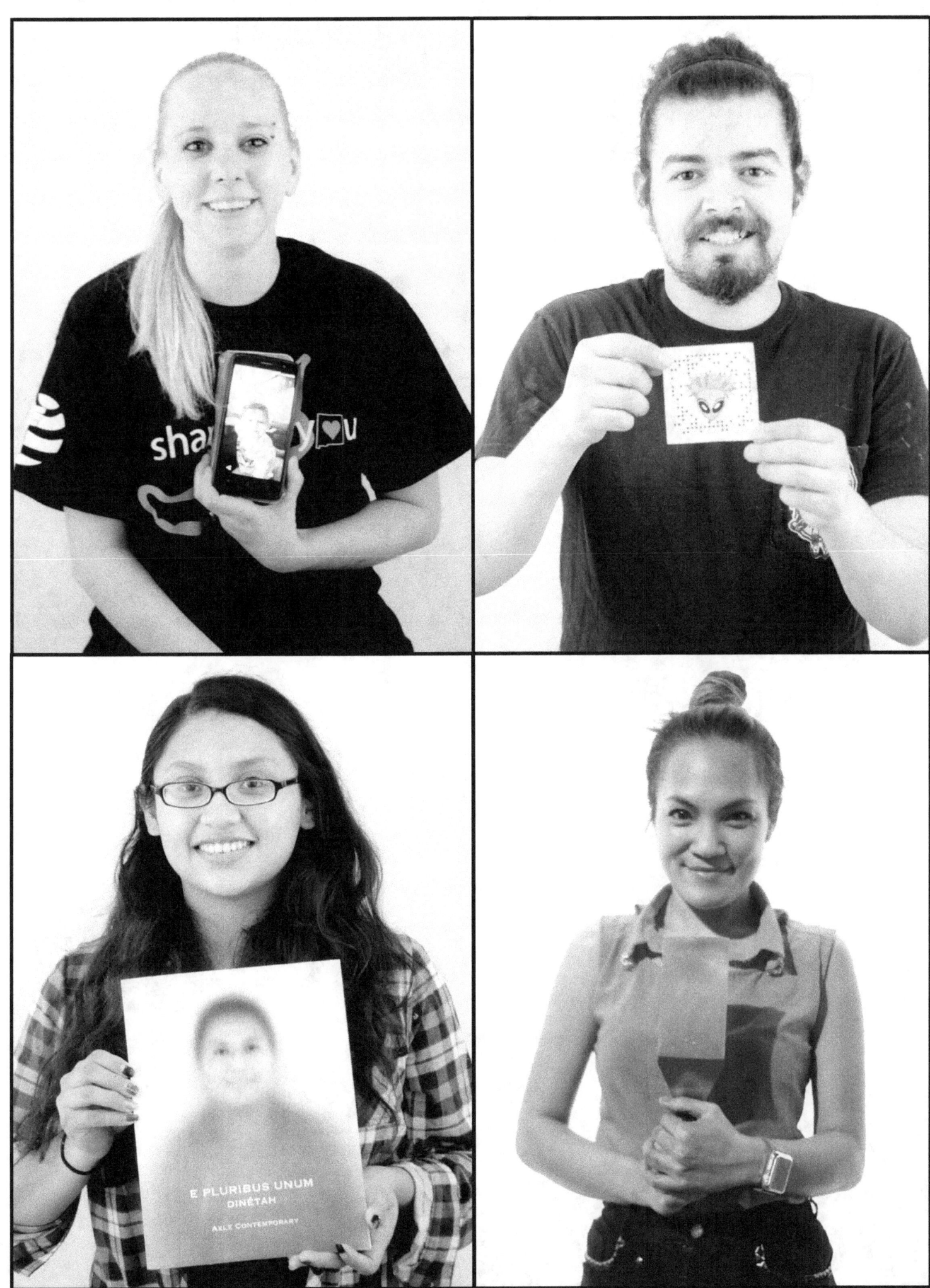

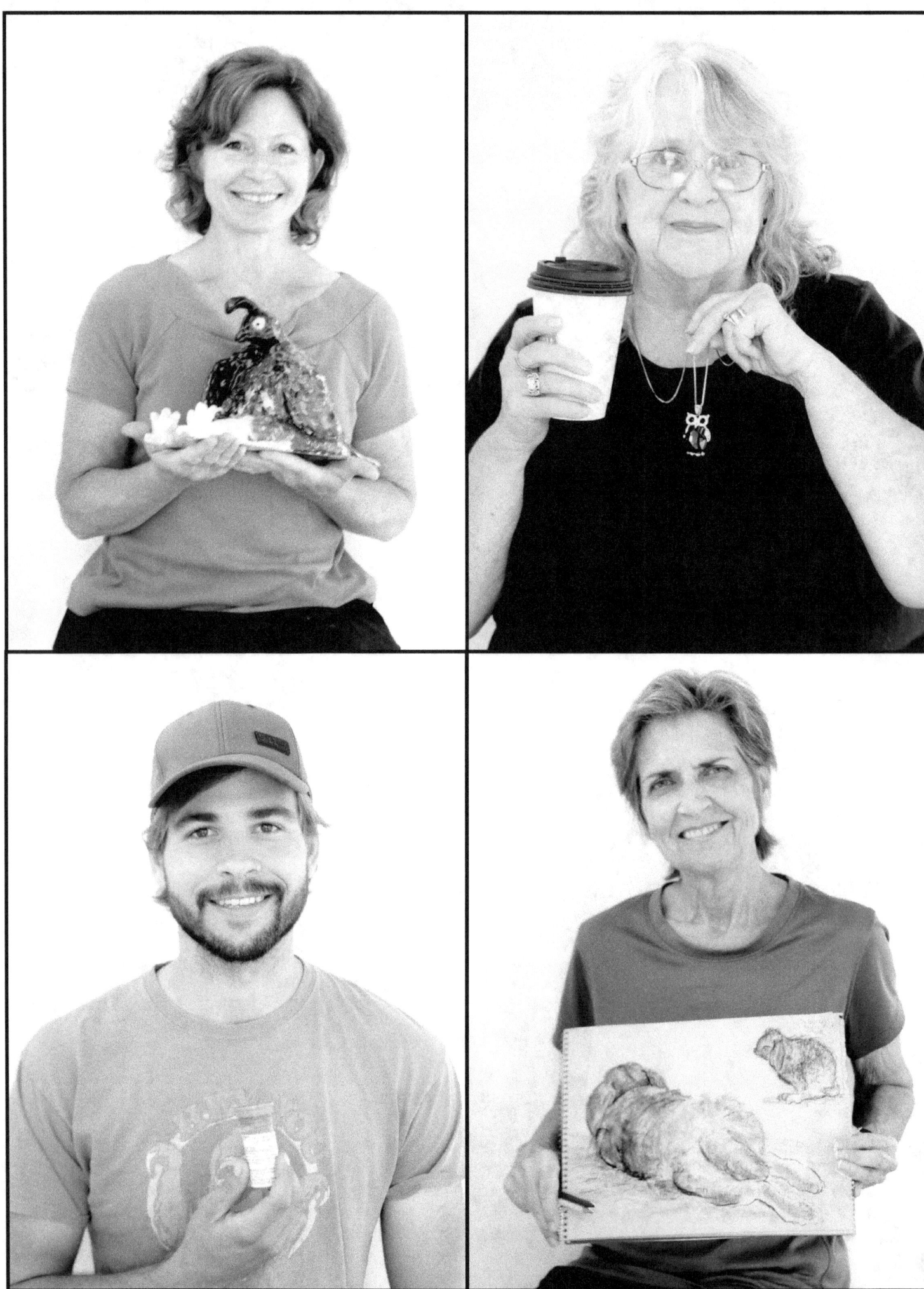

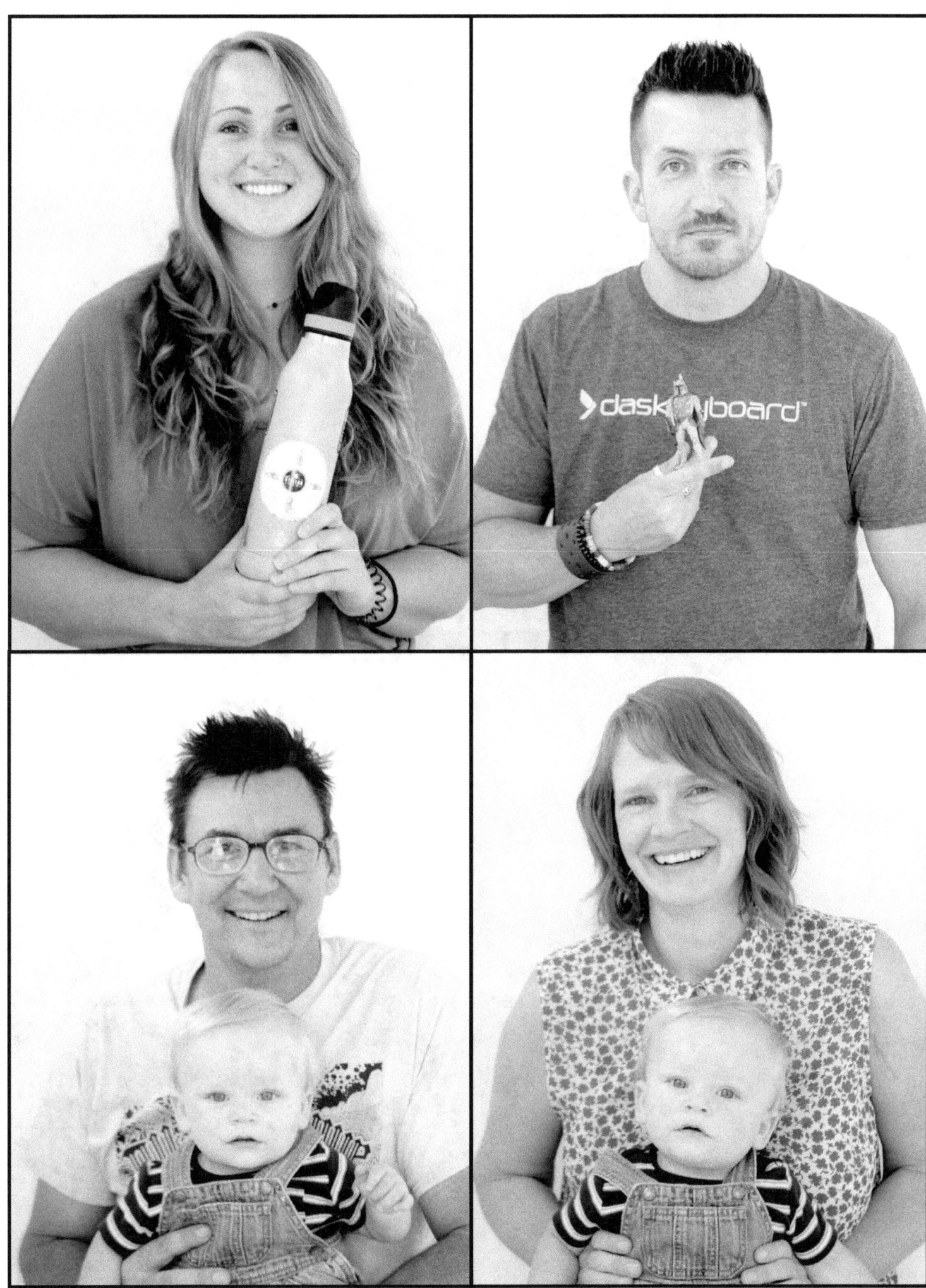

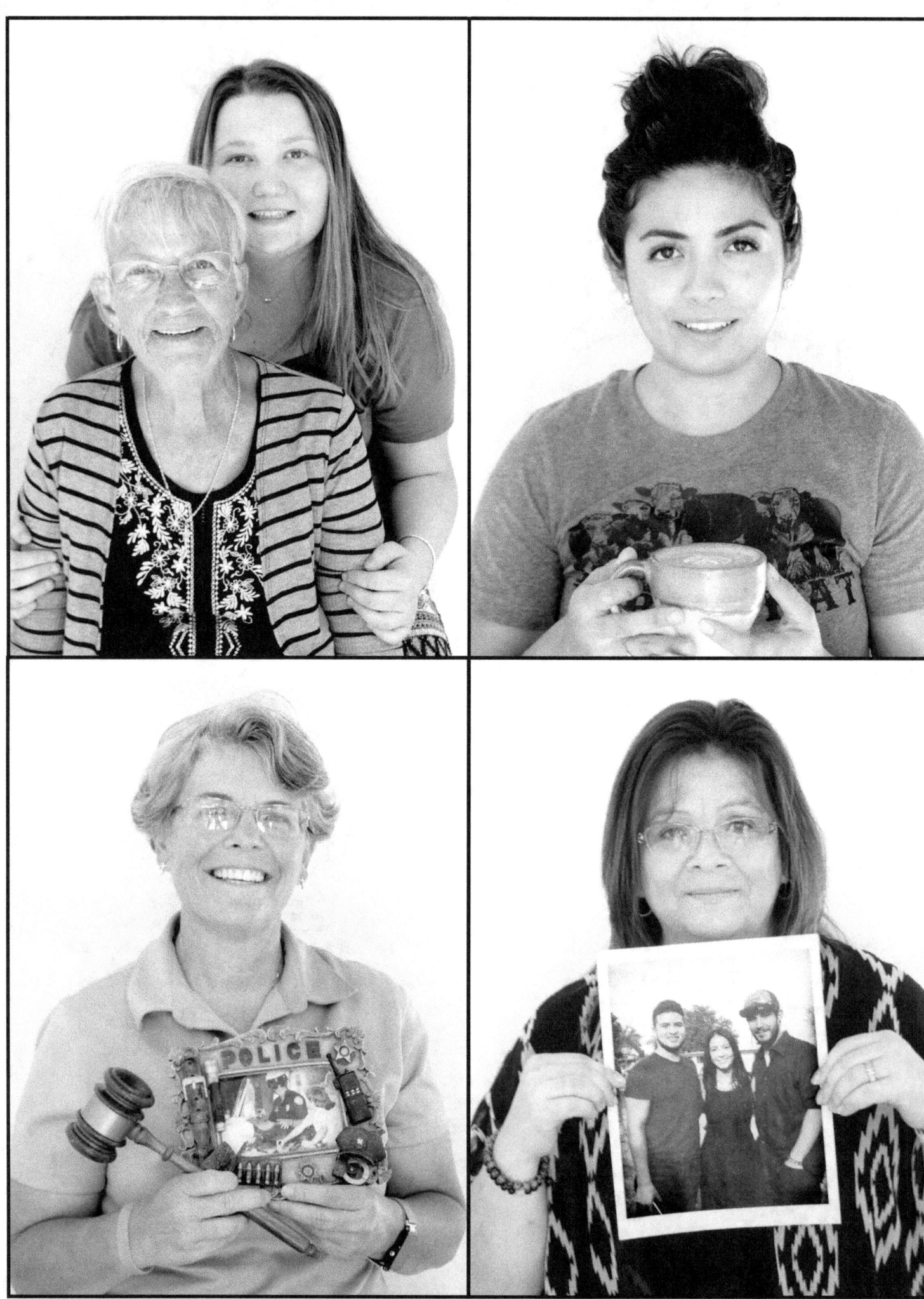

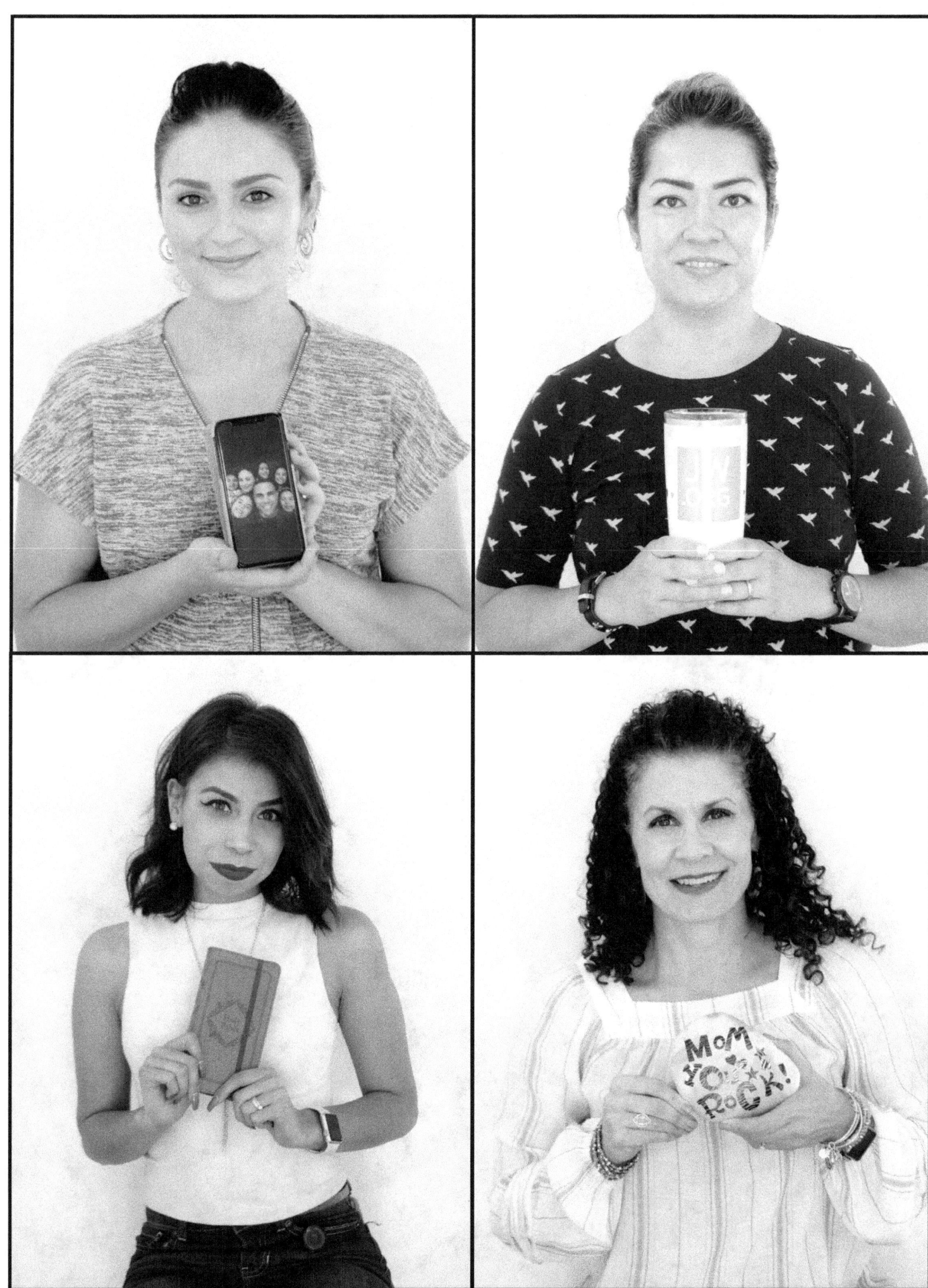

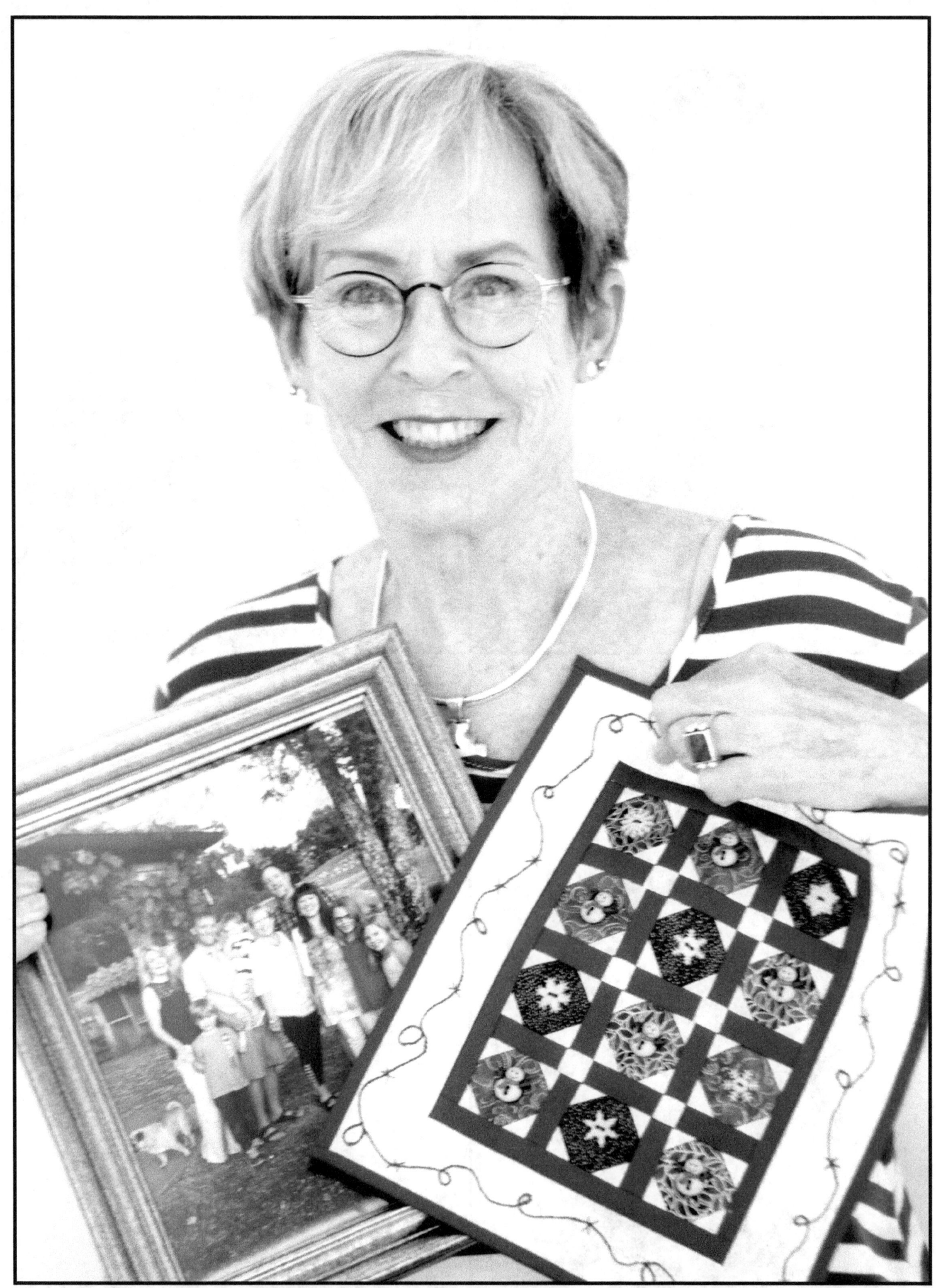

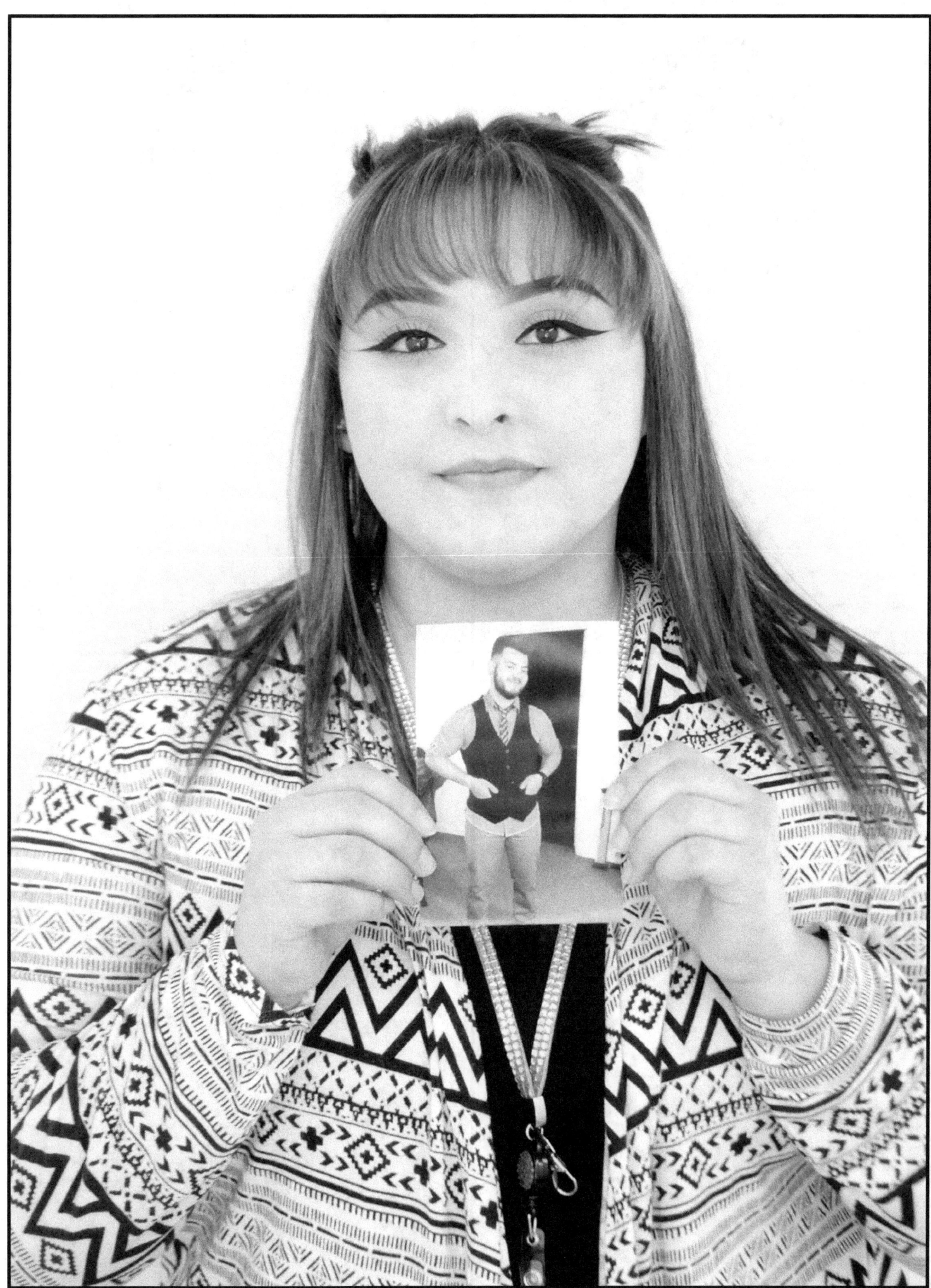

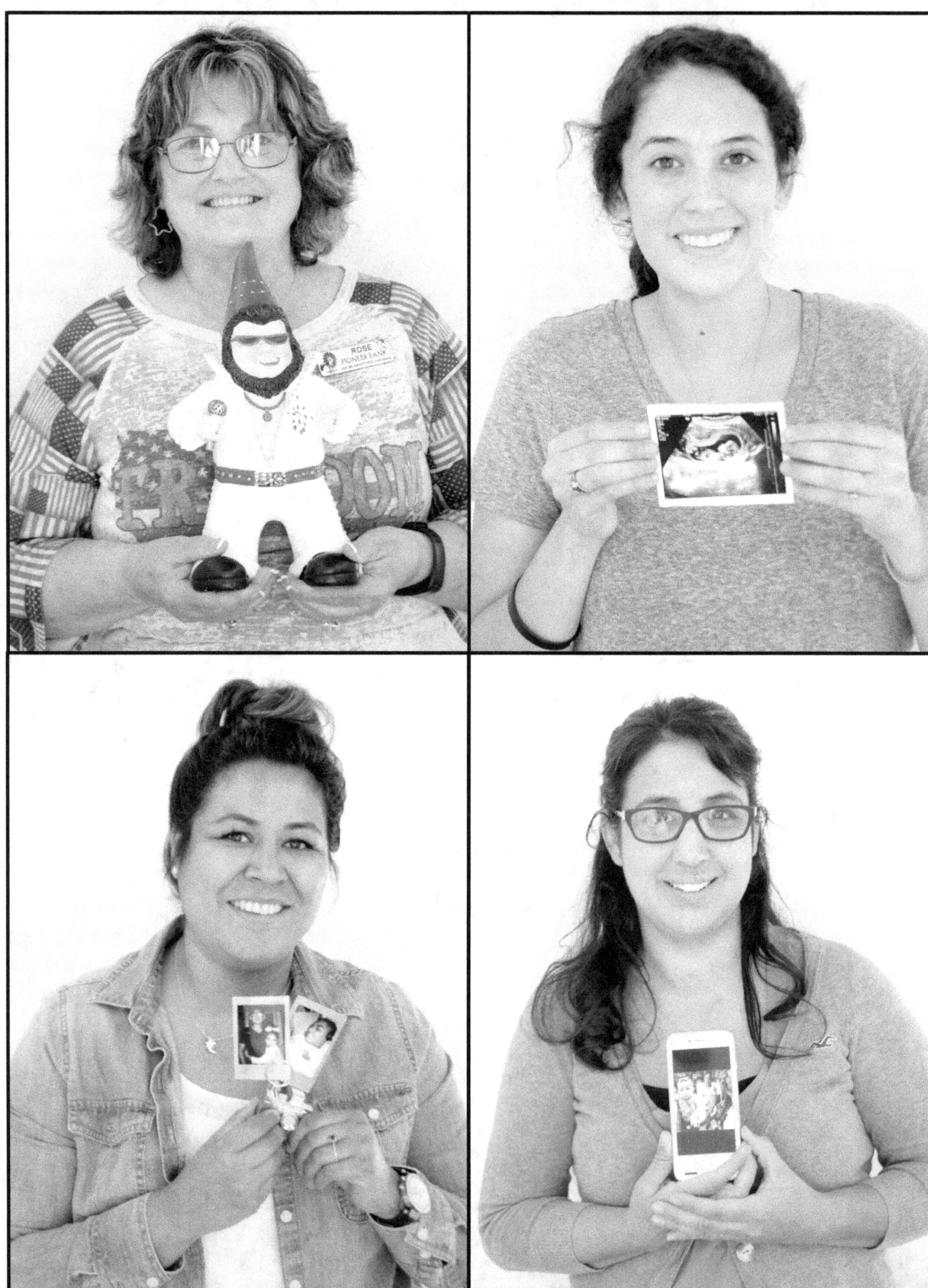

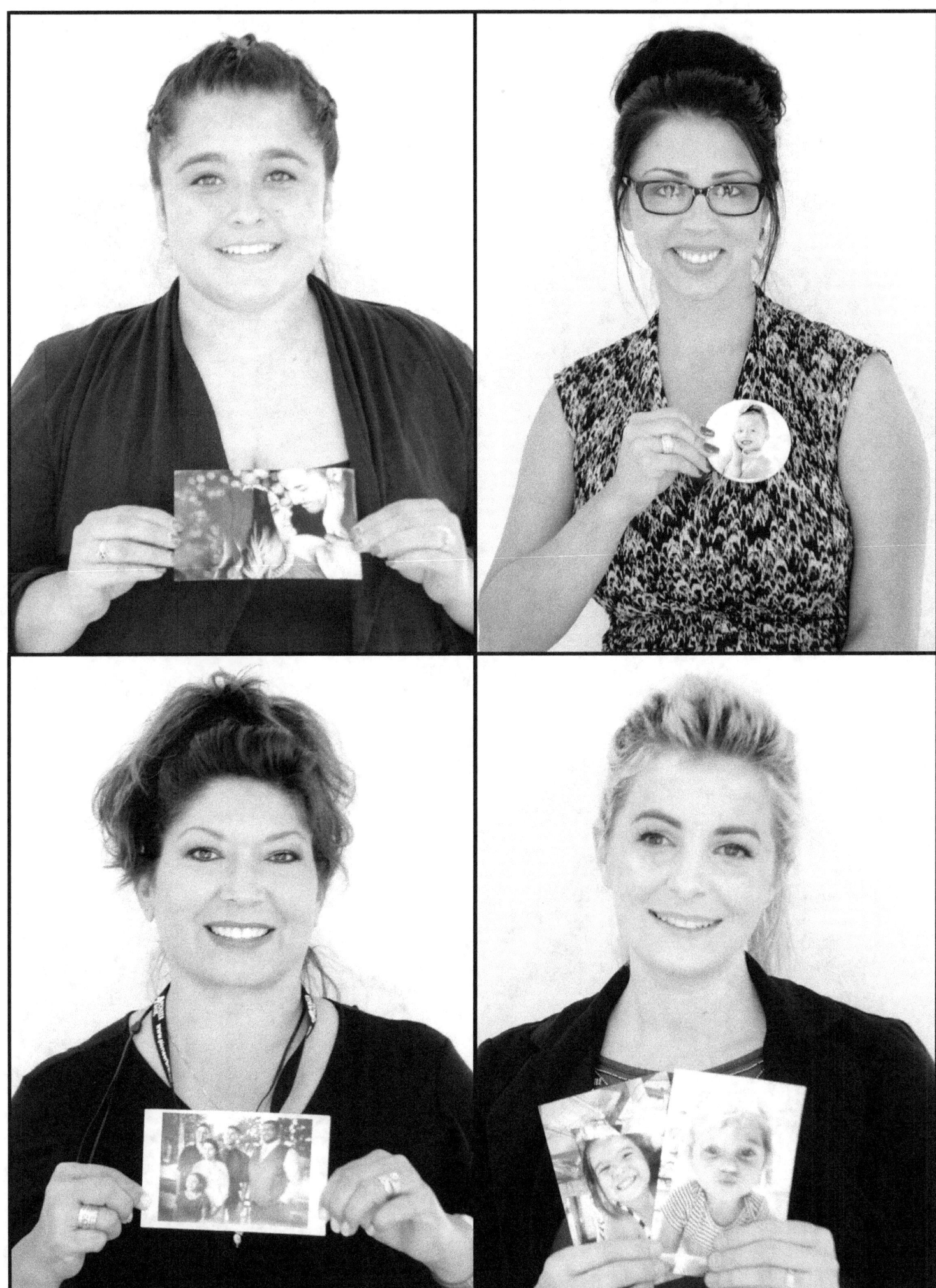

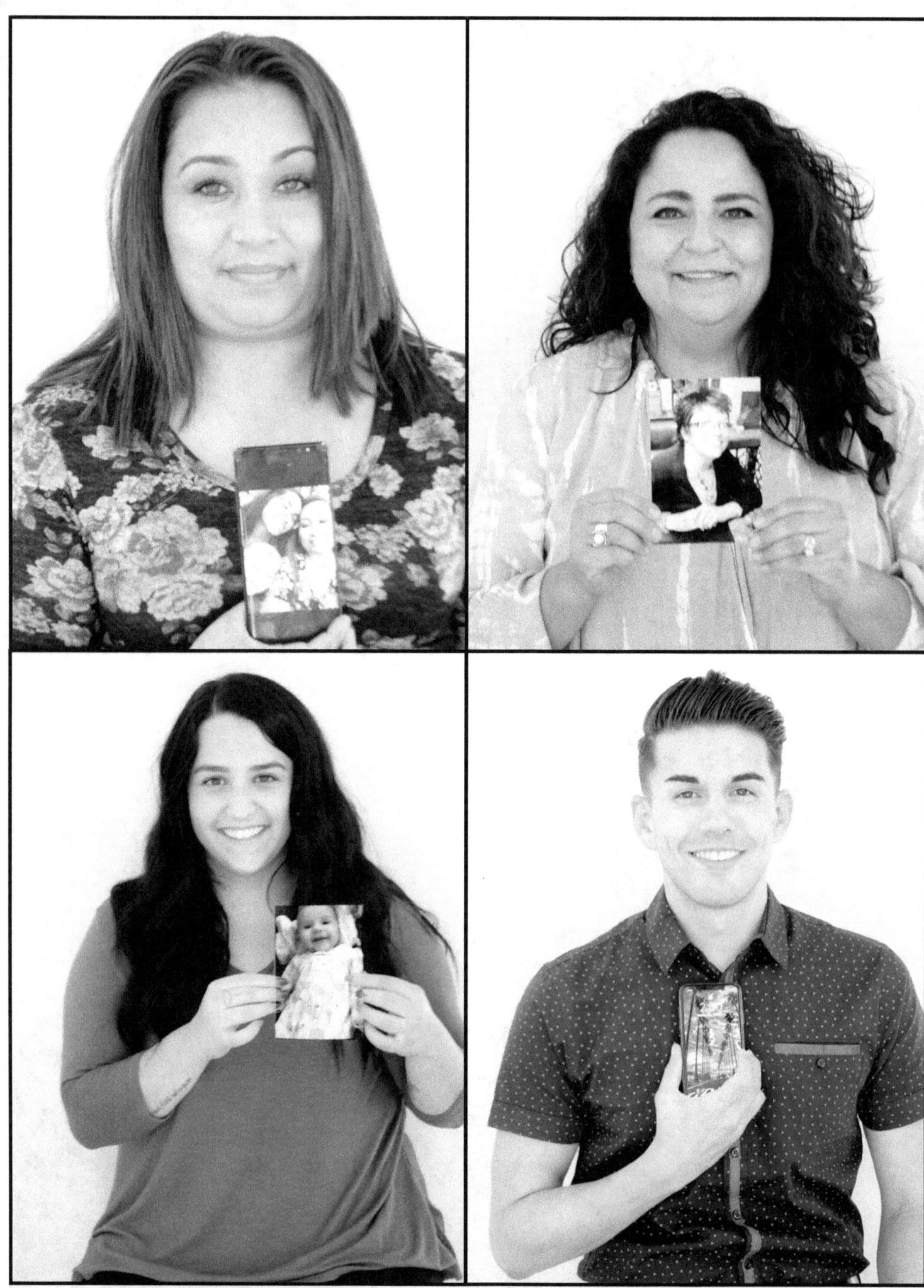

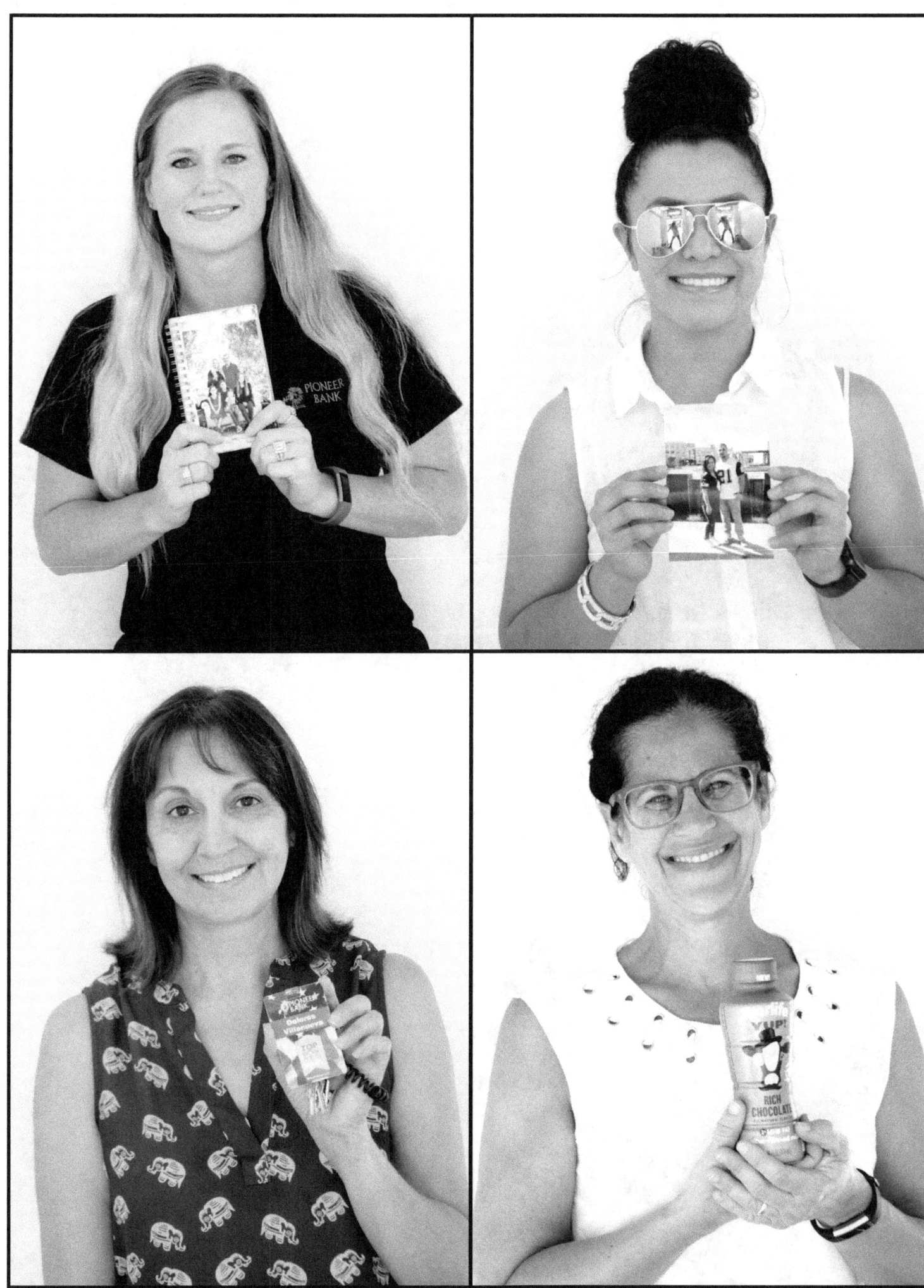

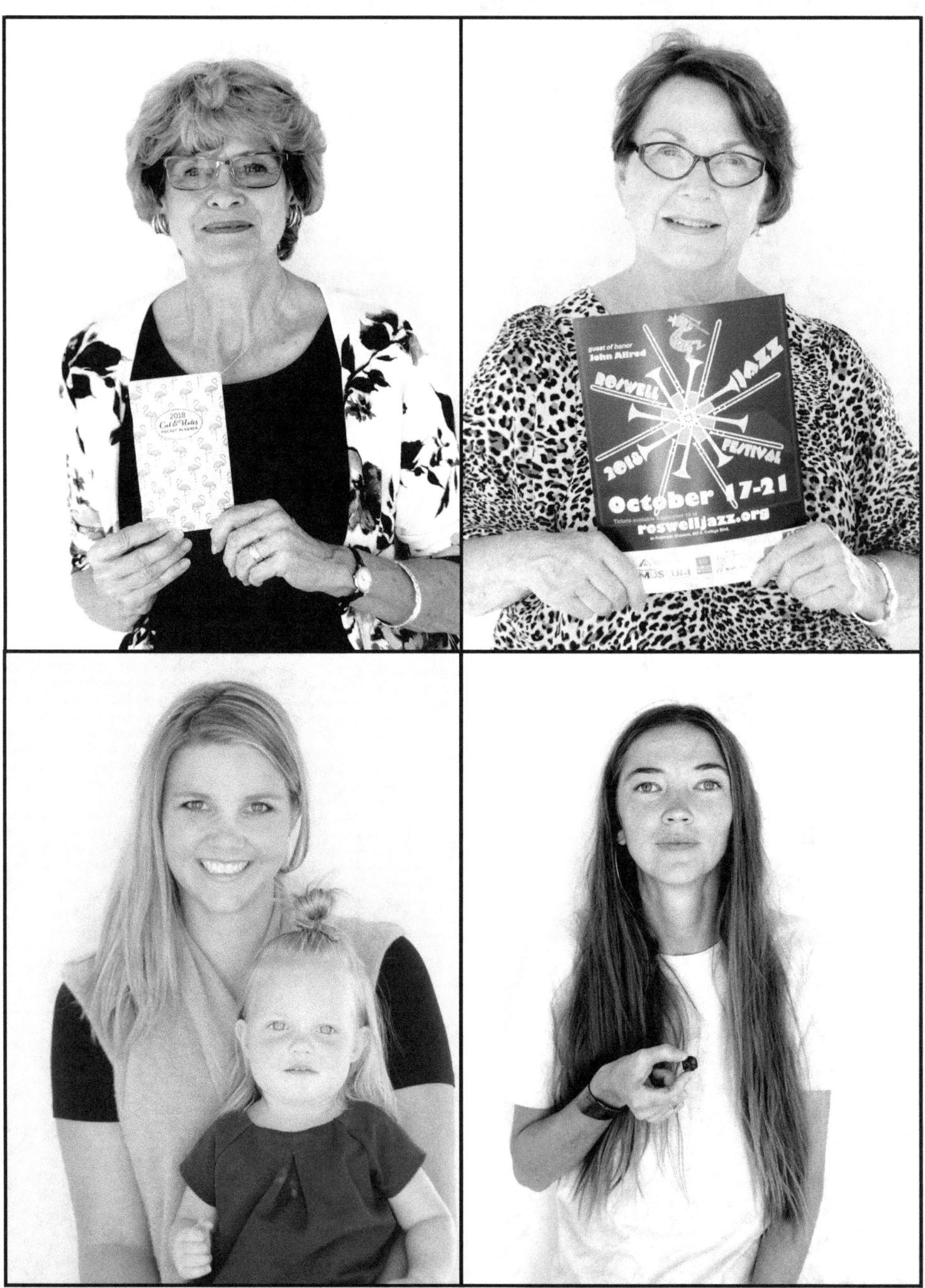

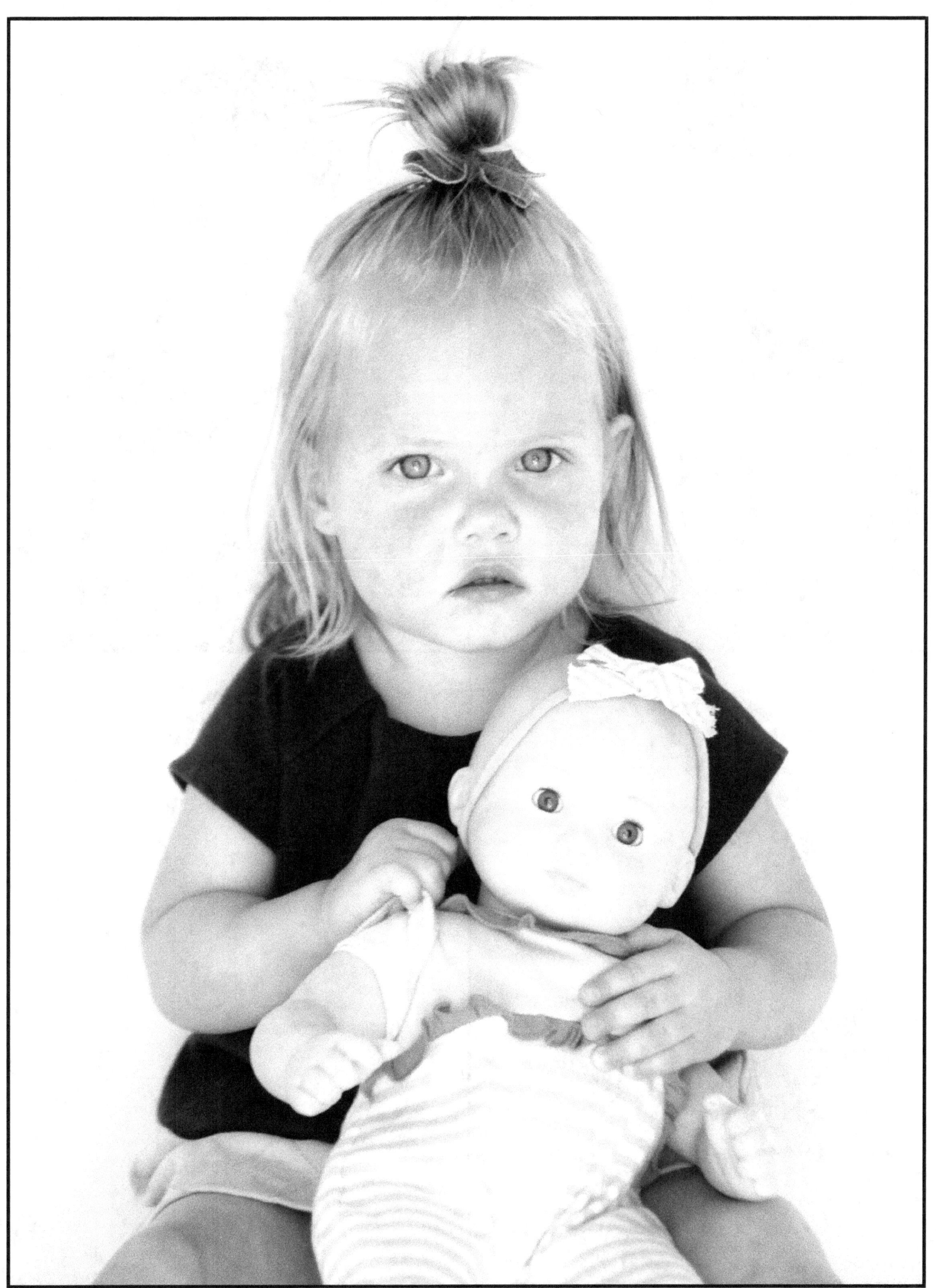

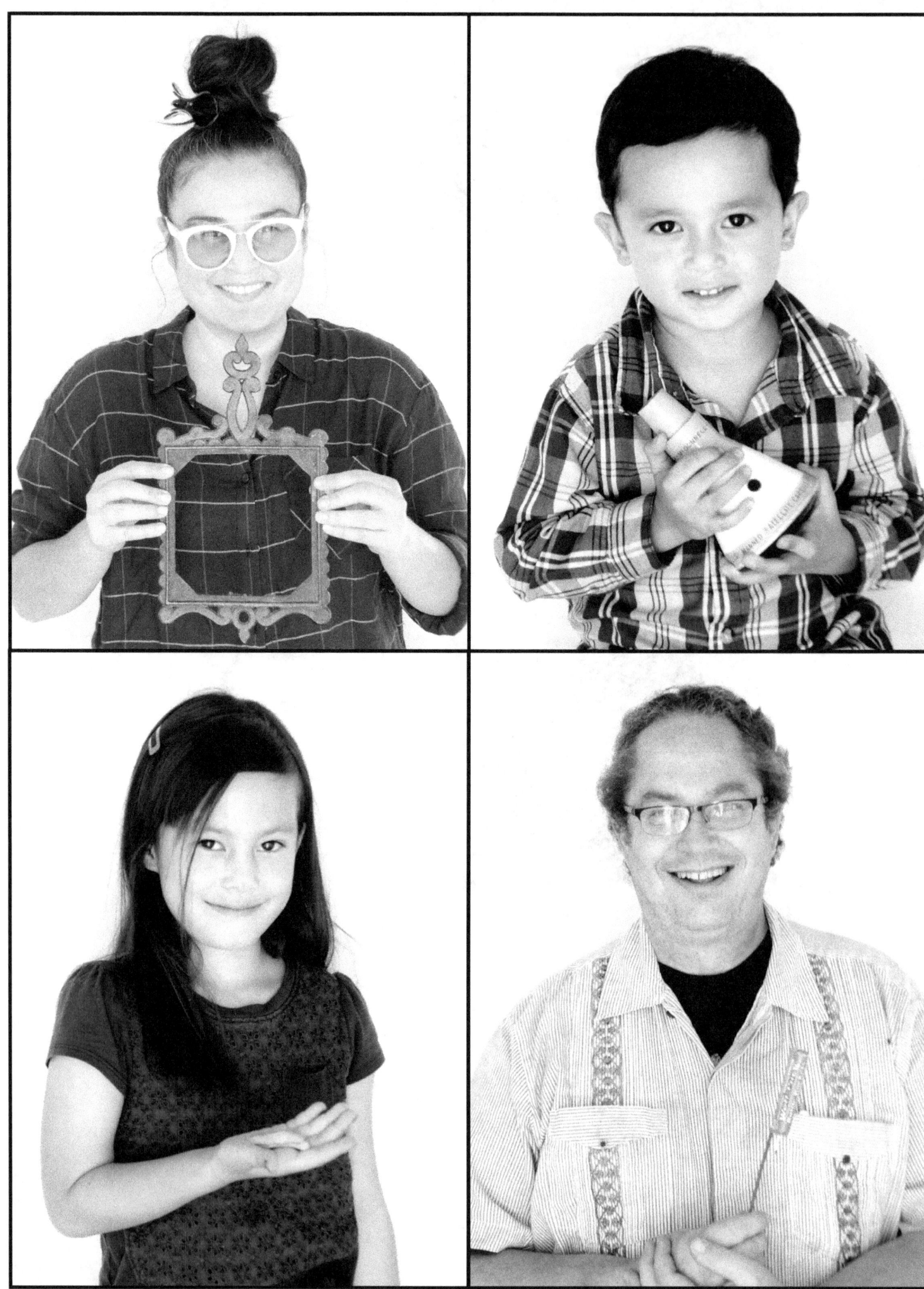

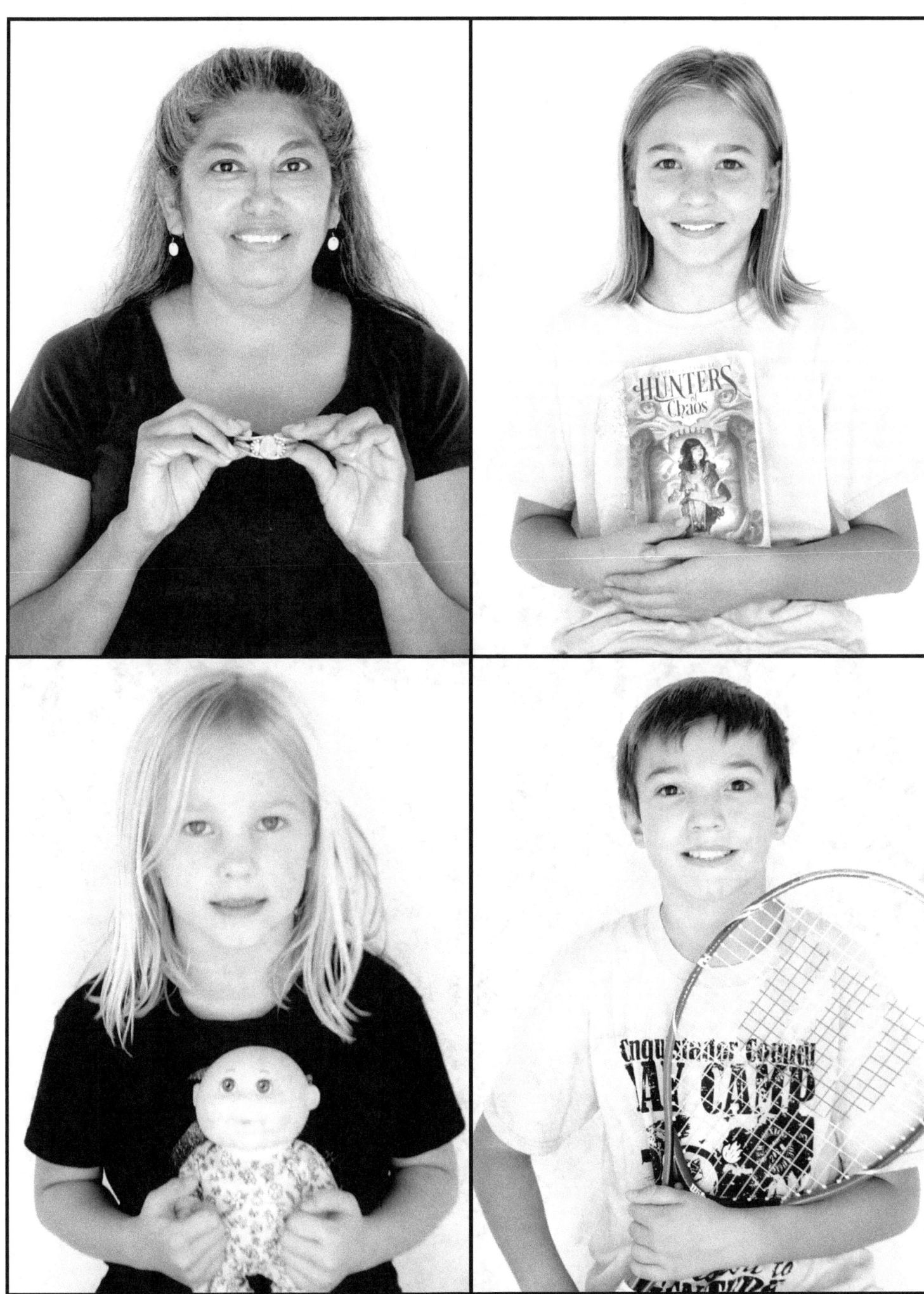

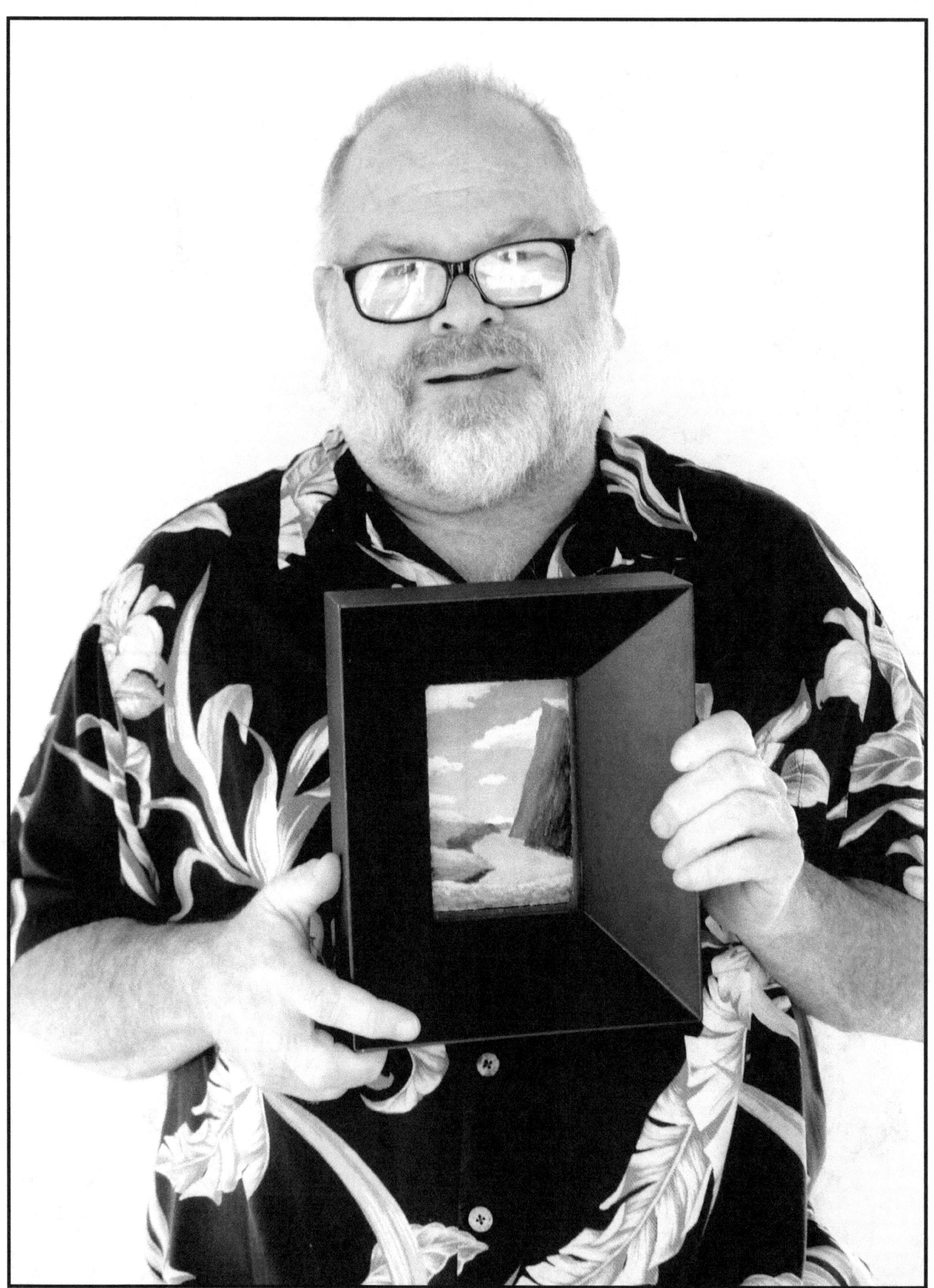

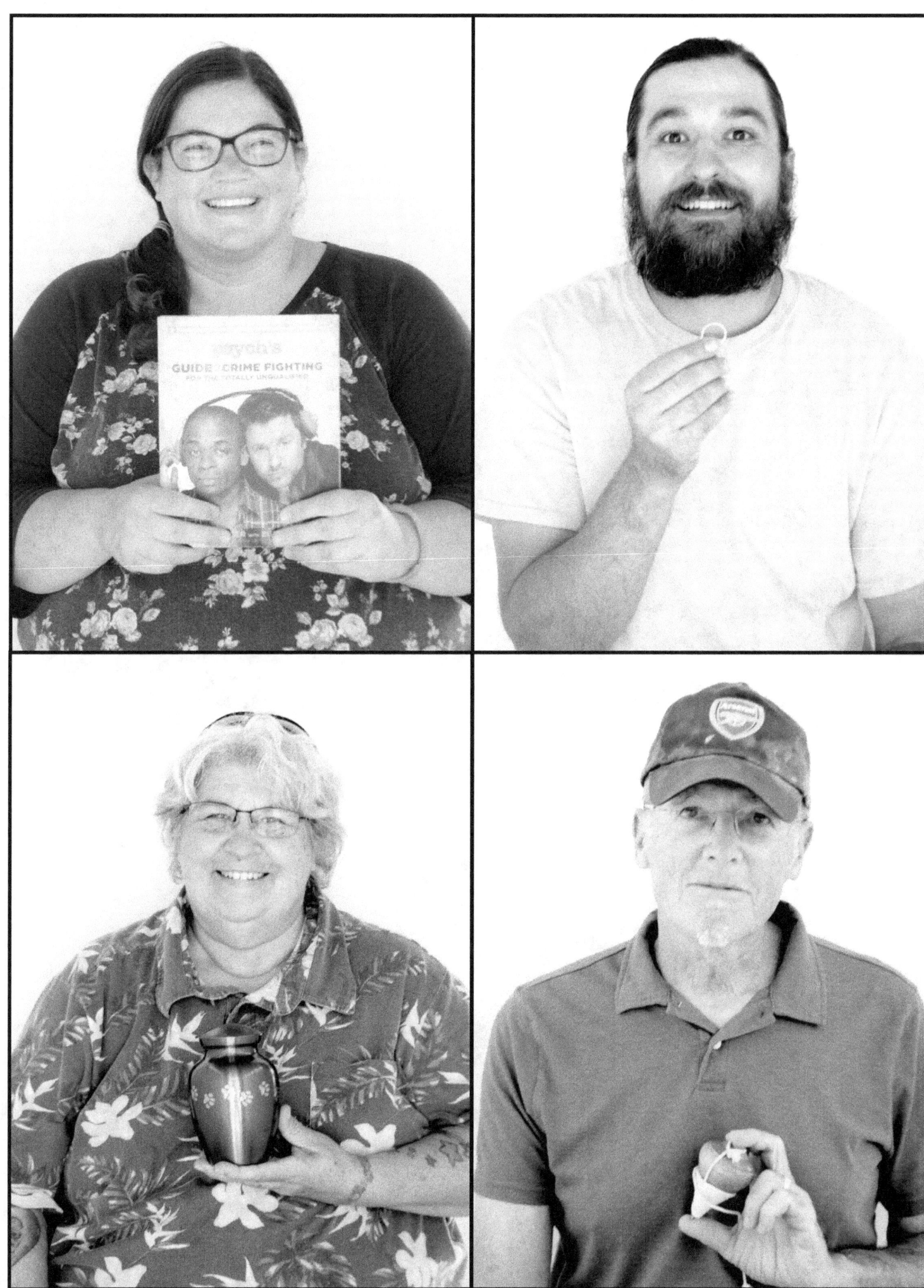

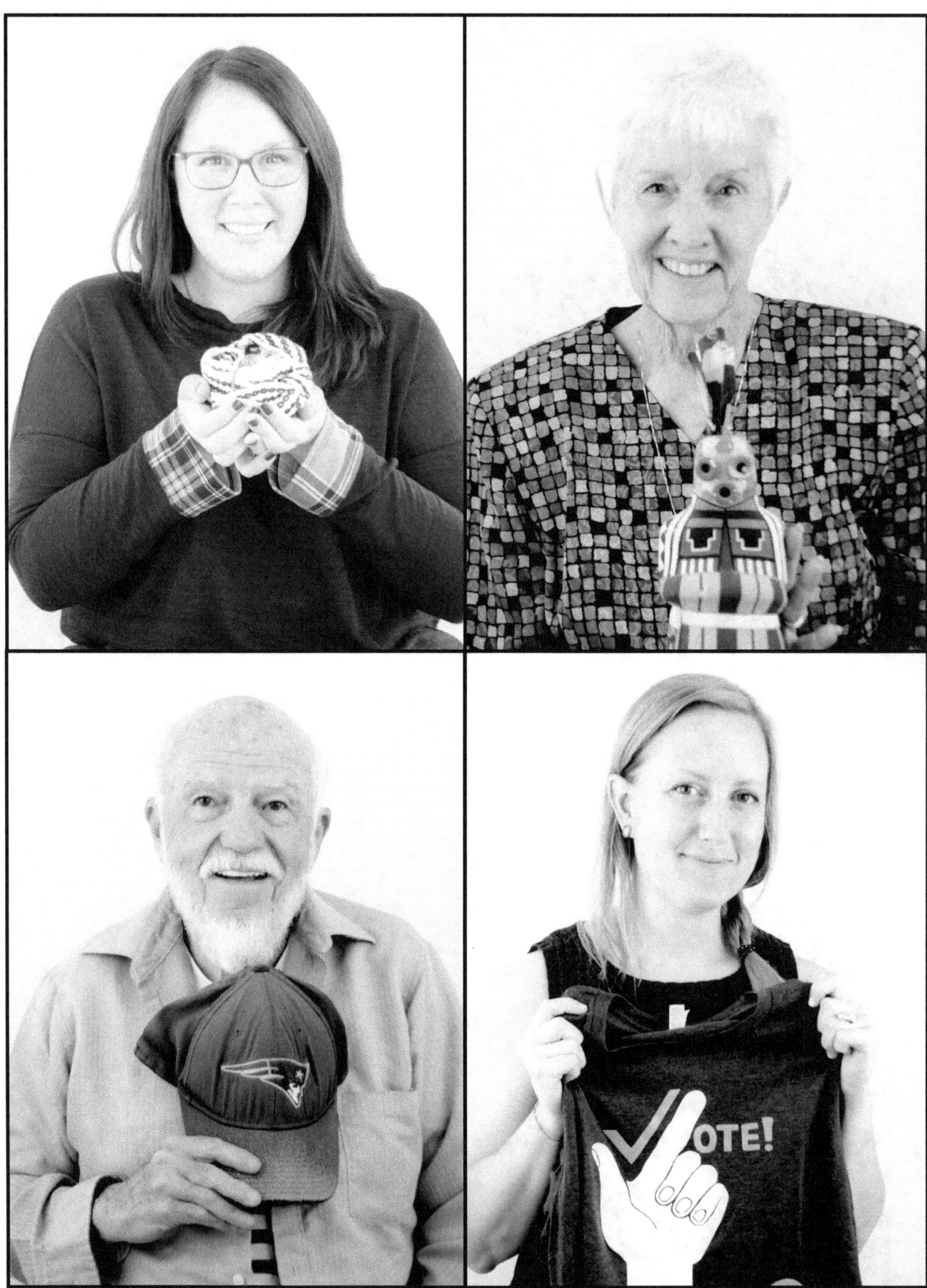

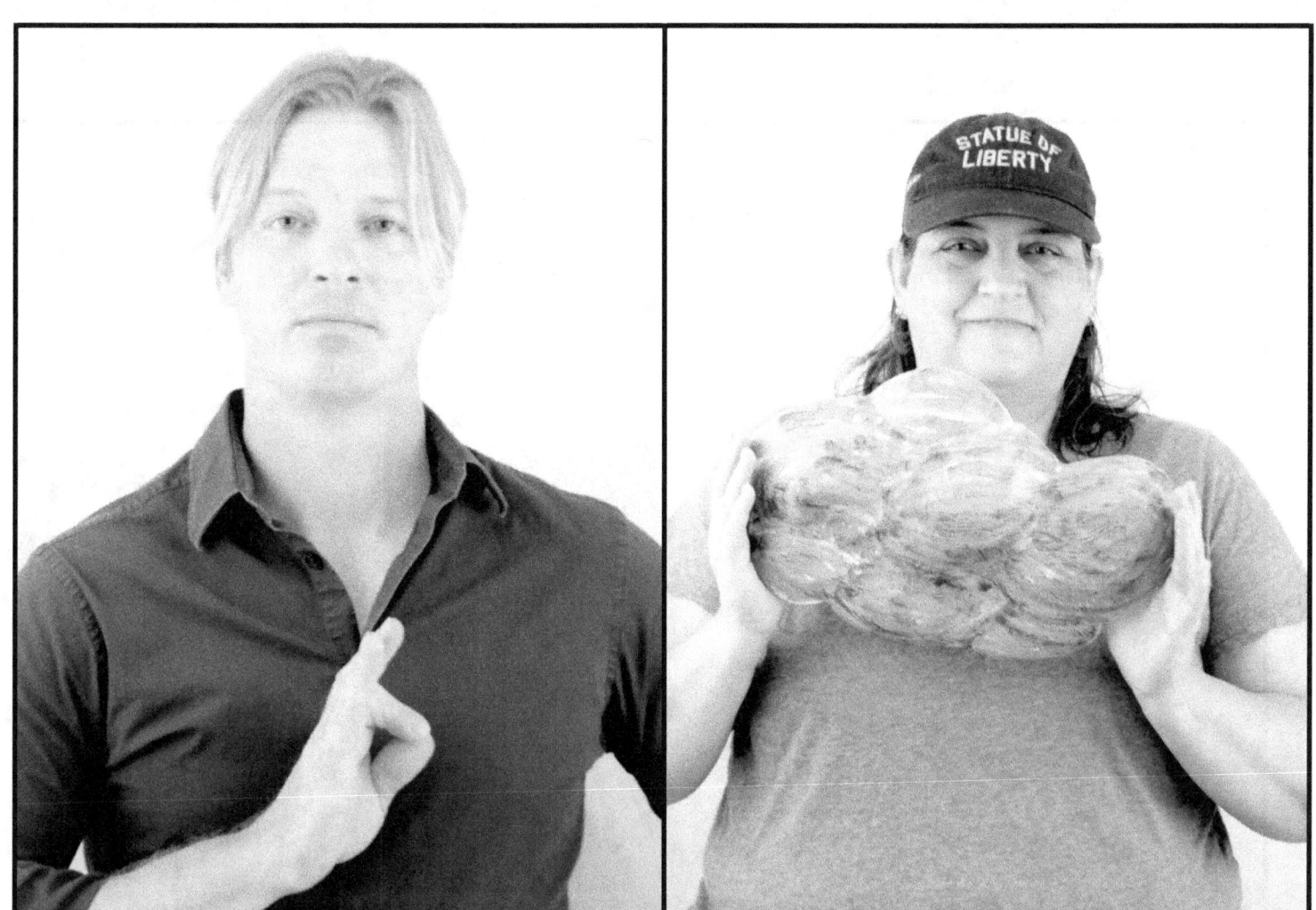

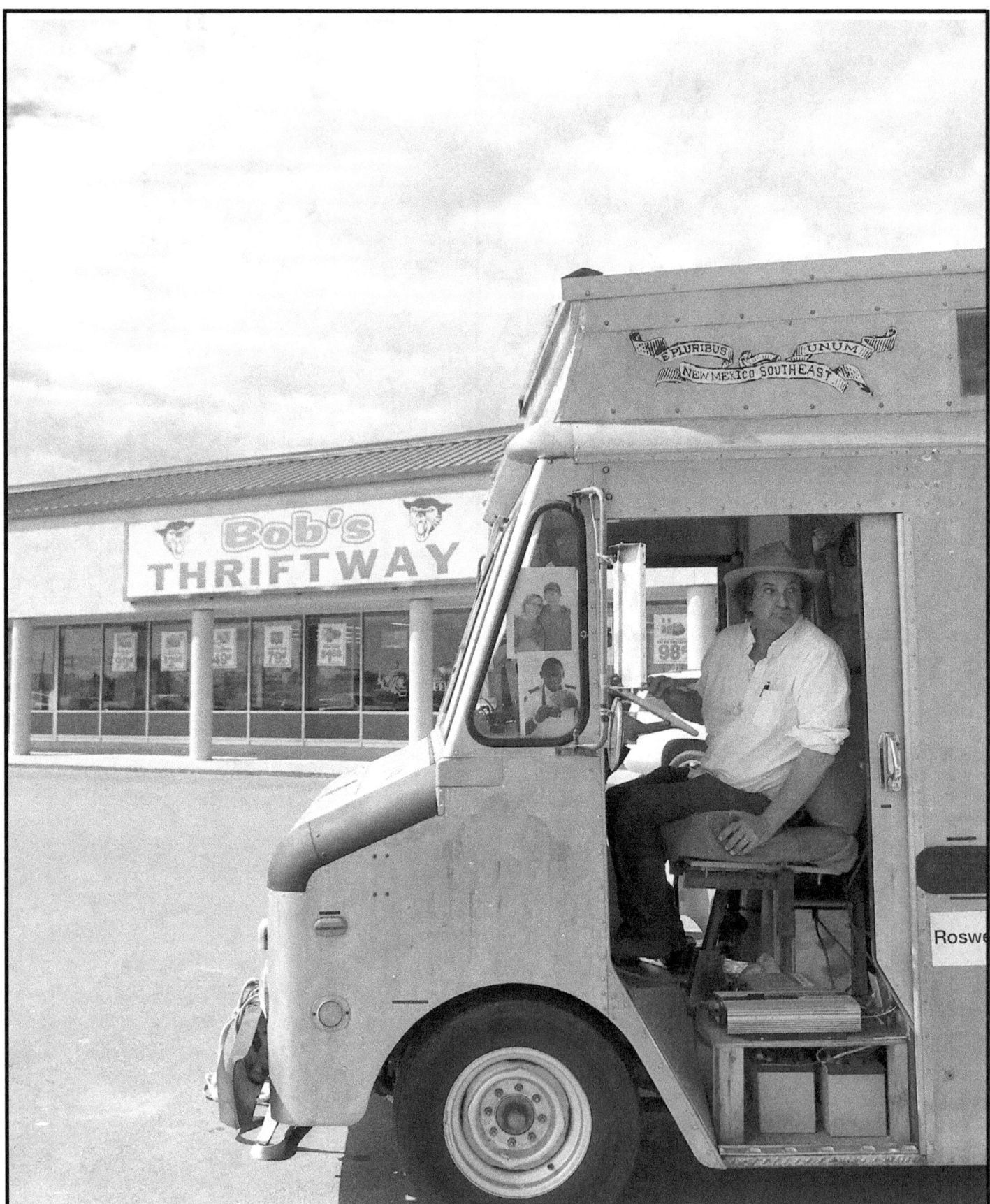

Lovington

October 4, 2019

Bob's Thriftway

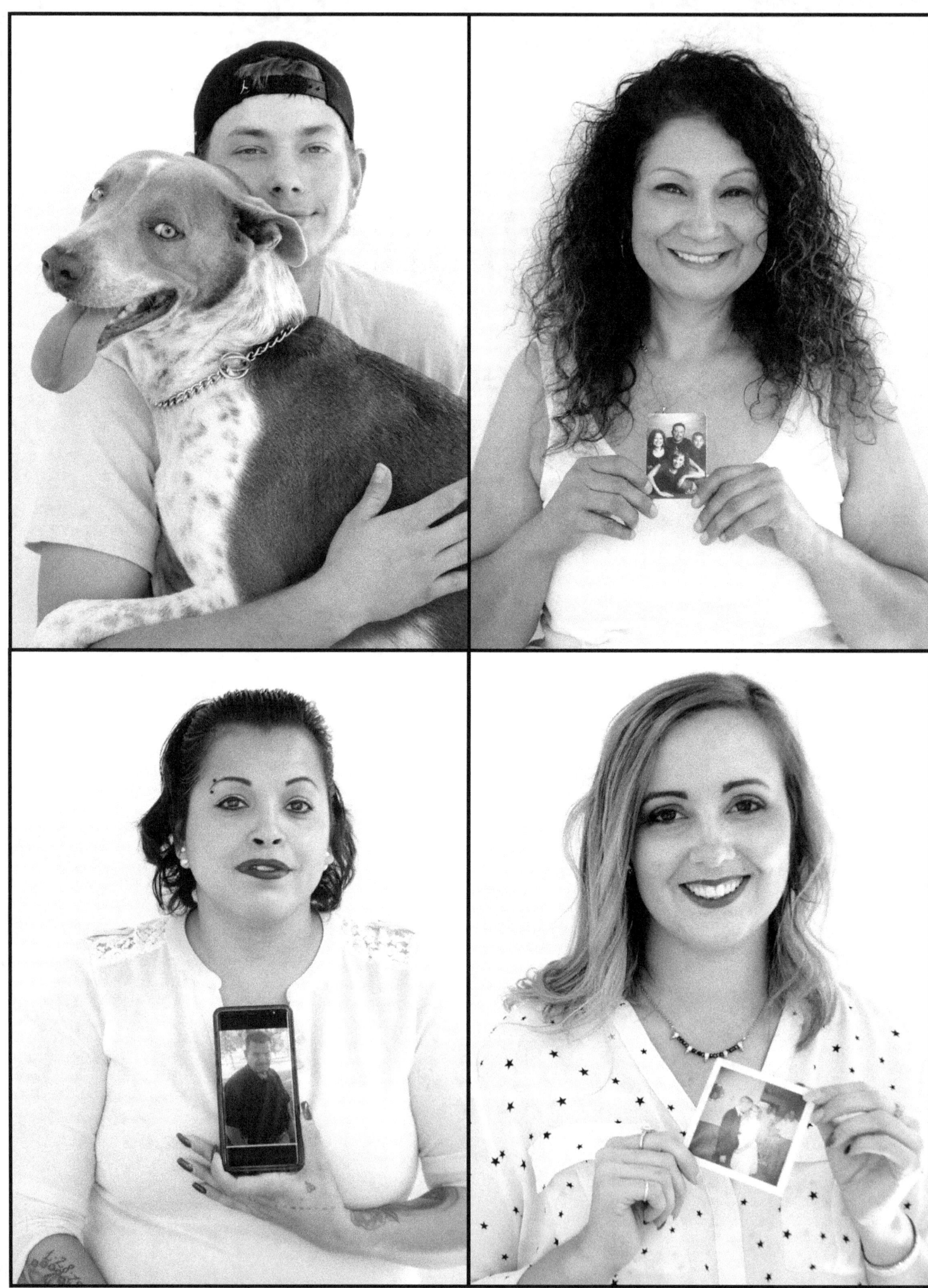

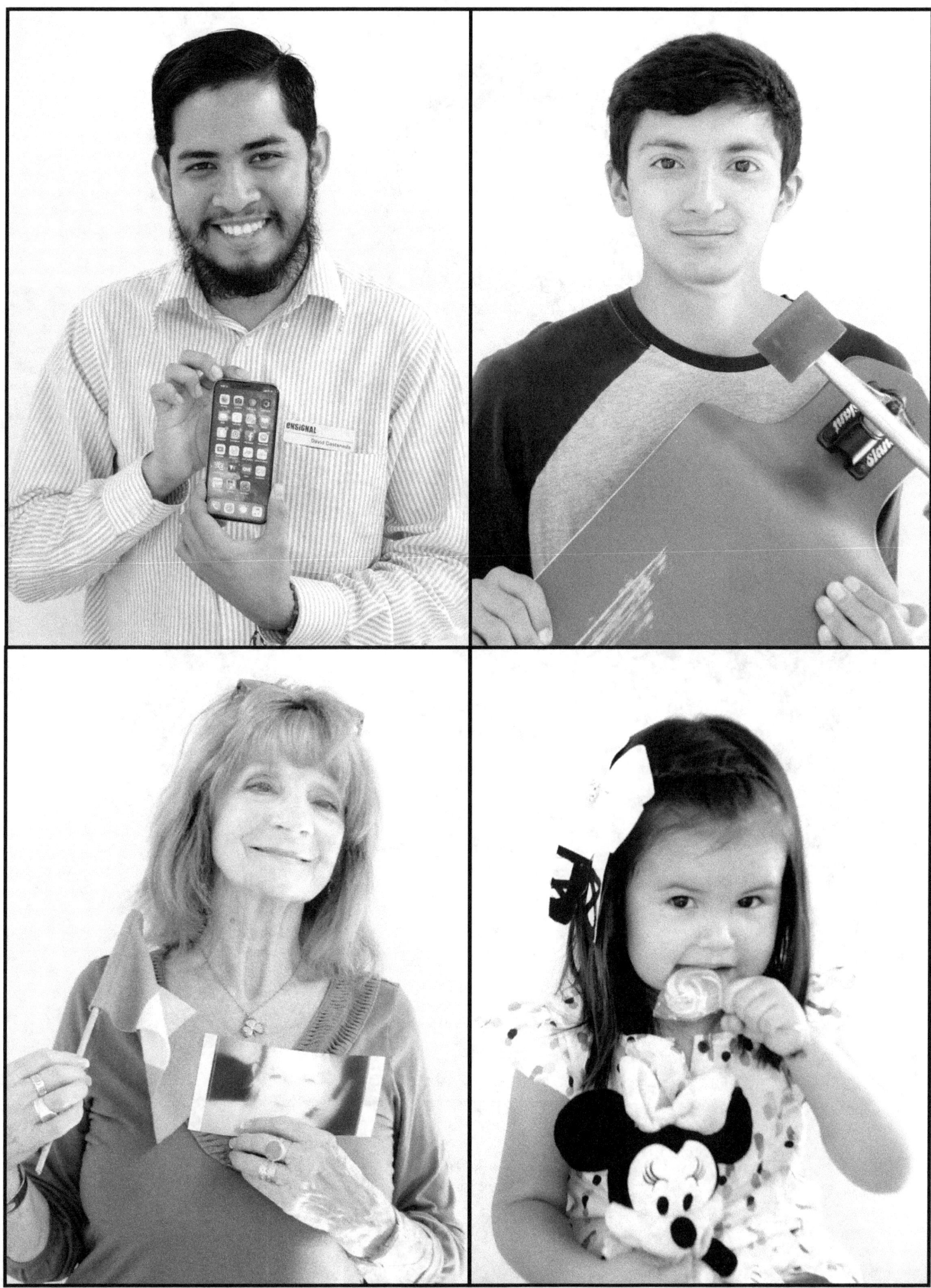

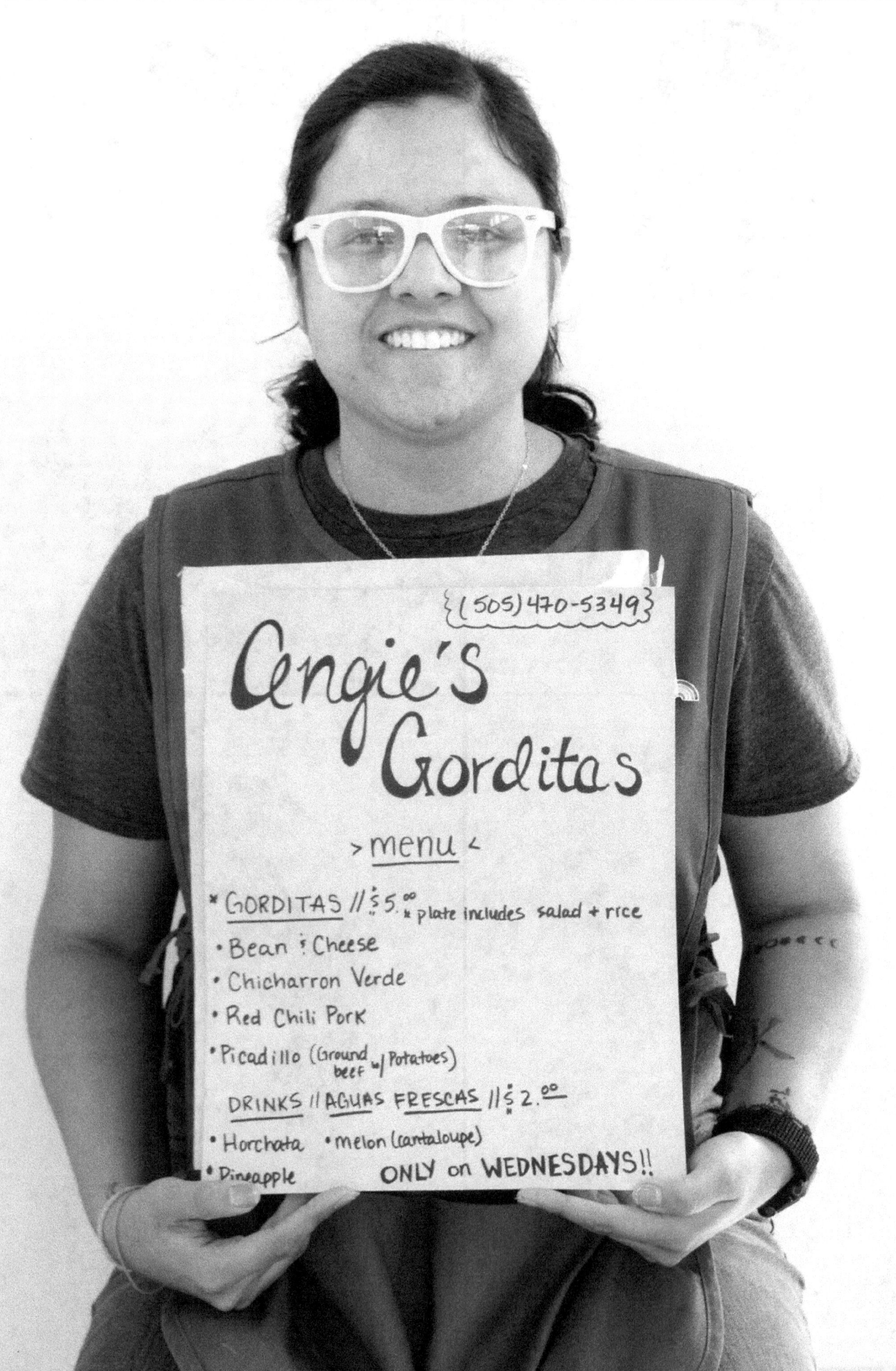

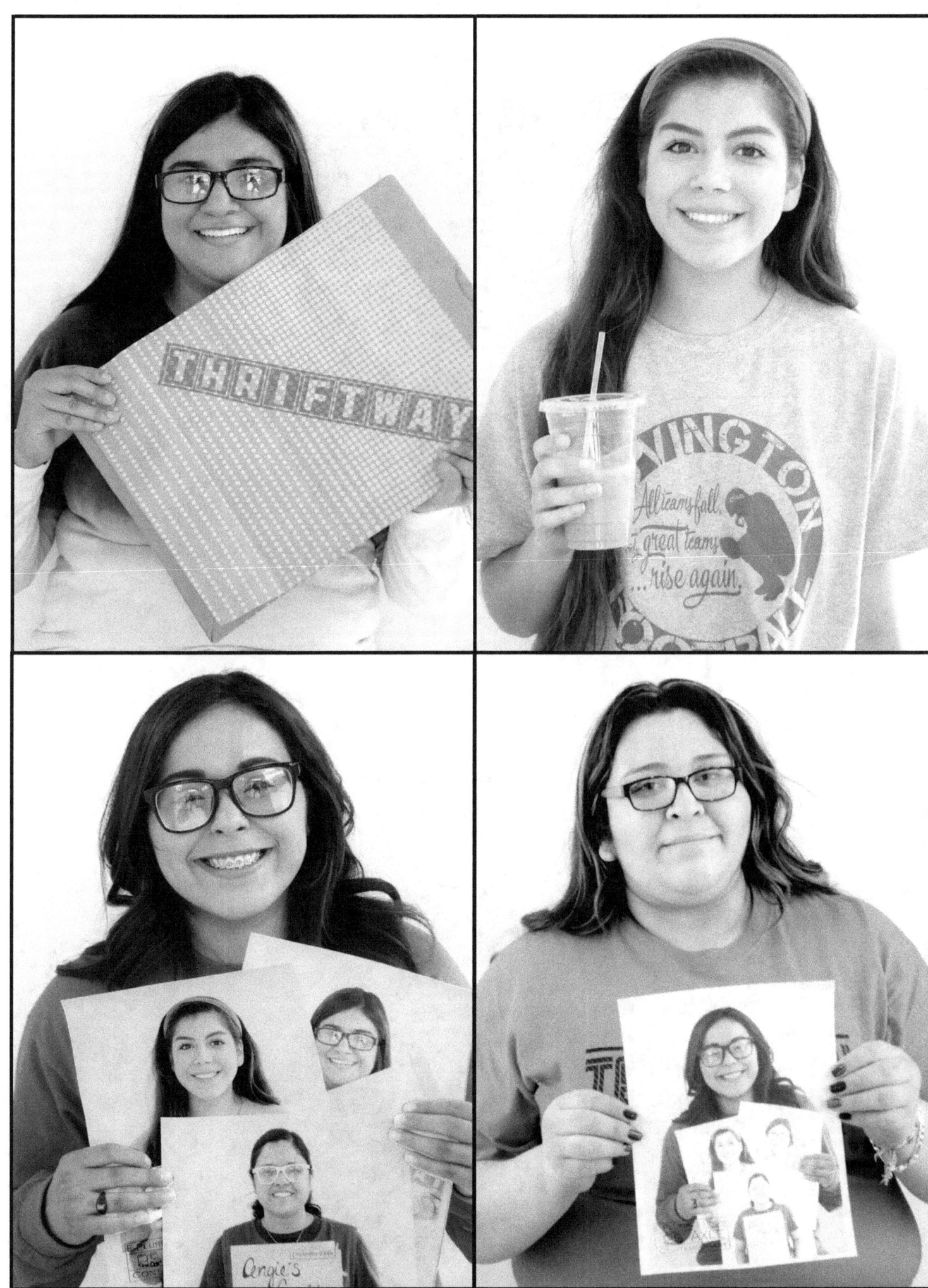

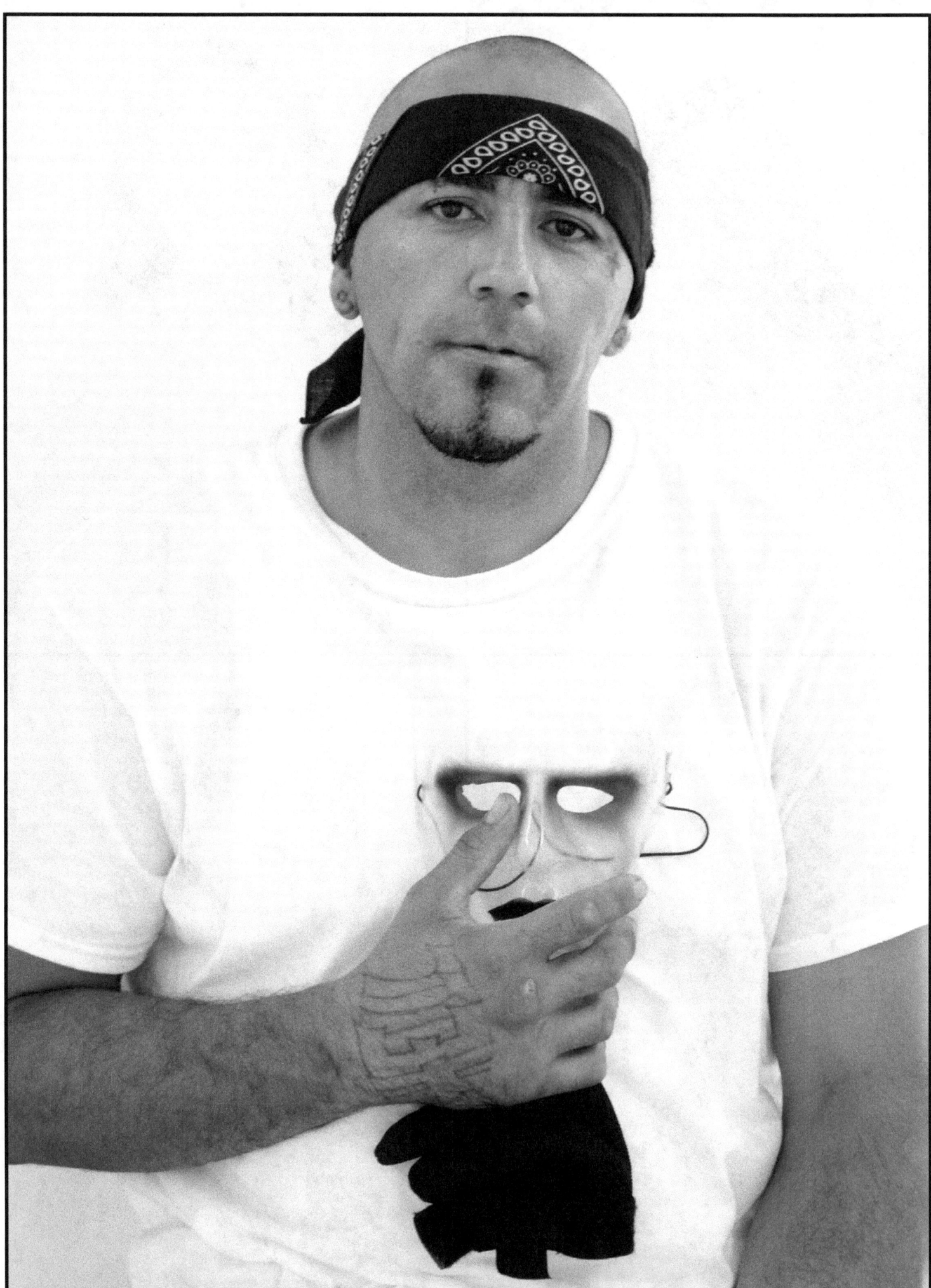

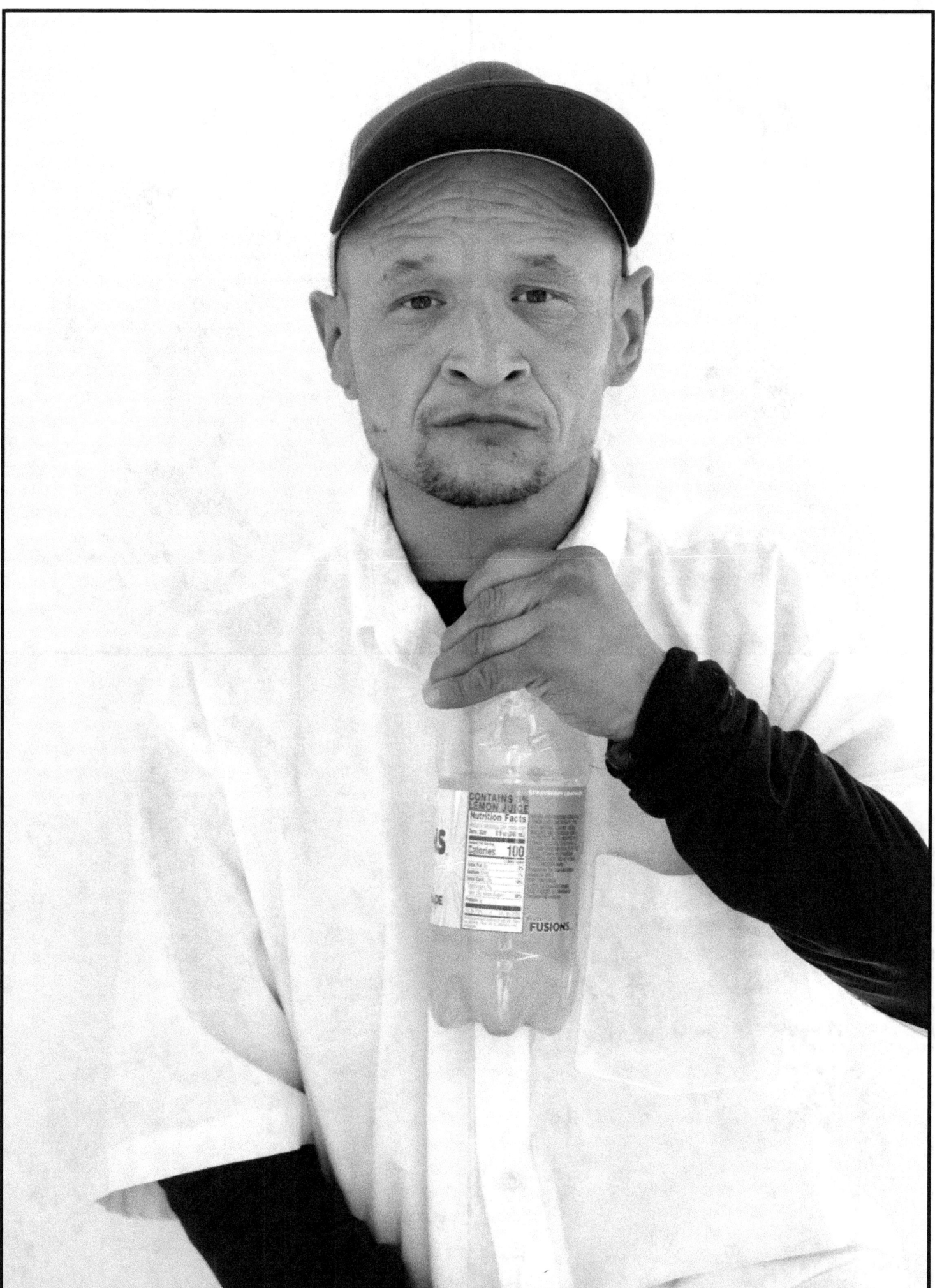

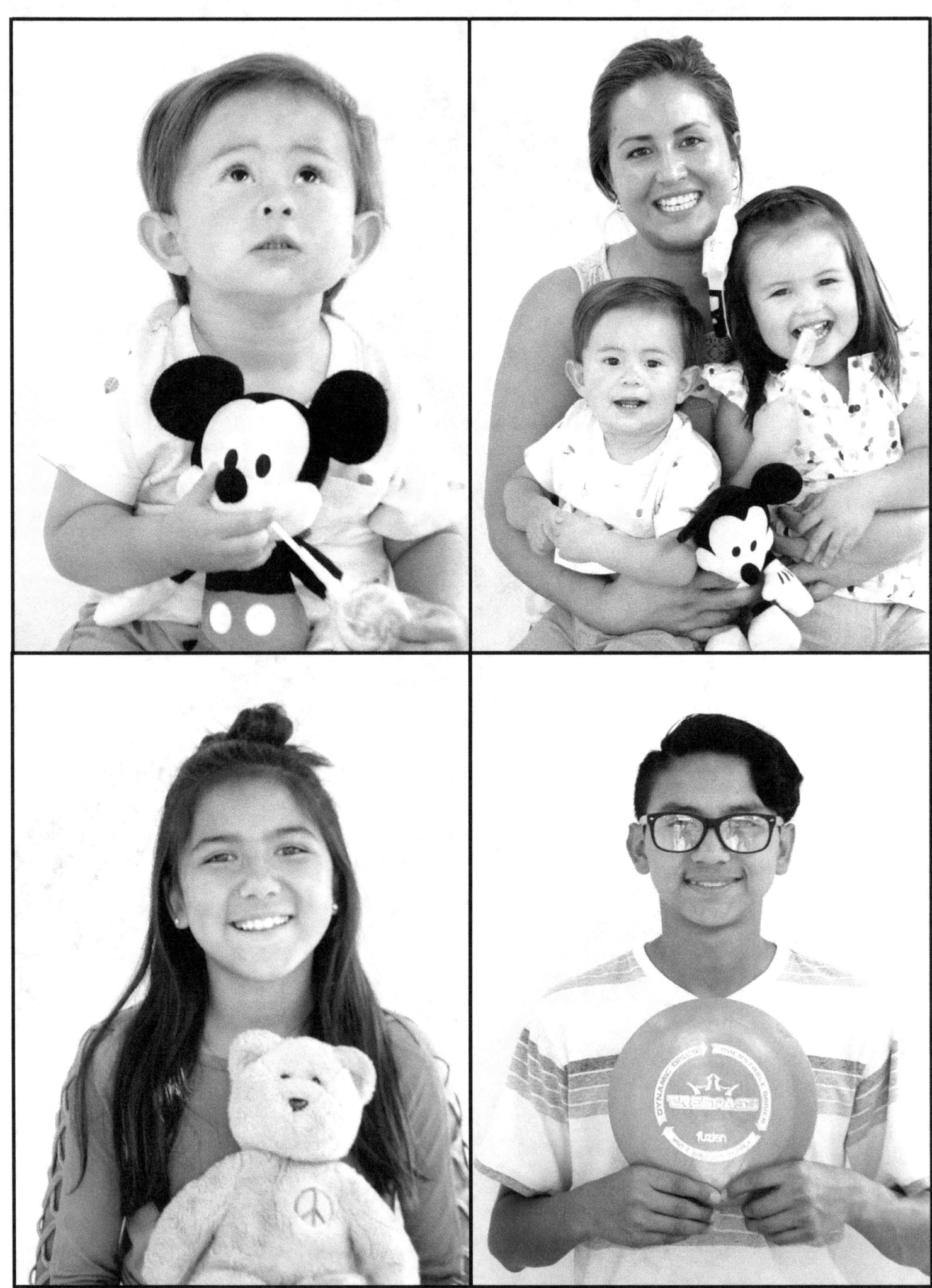

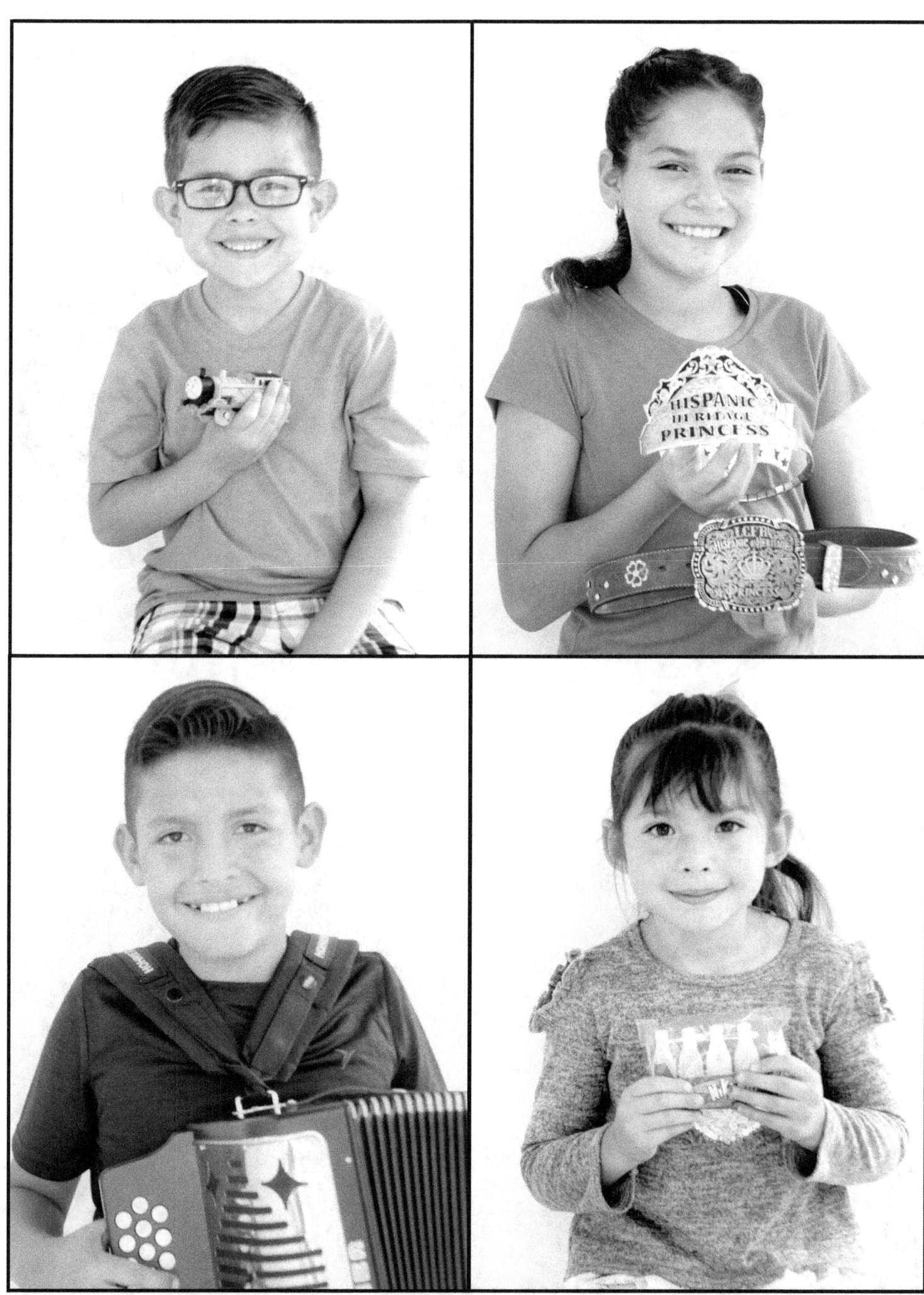

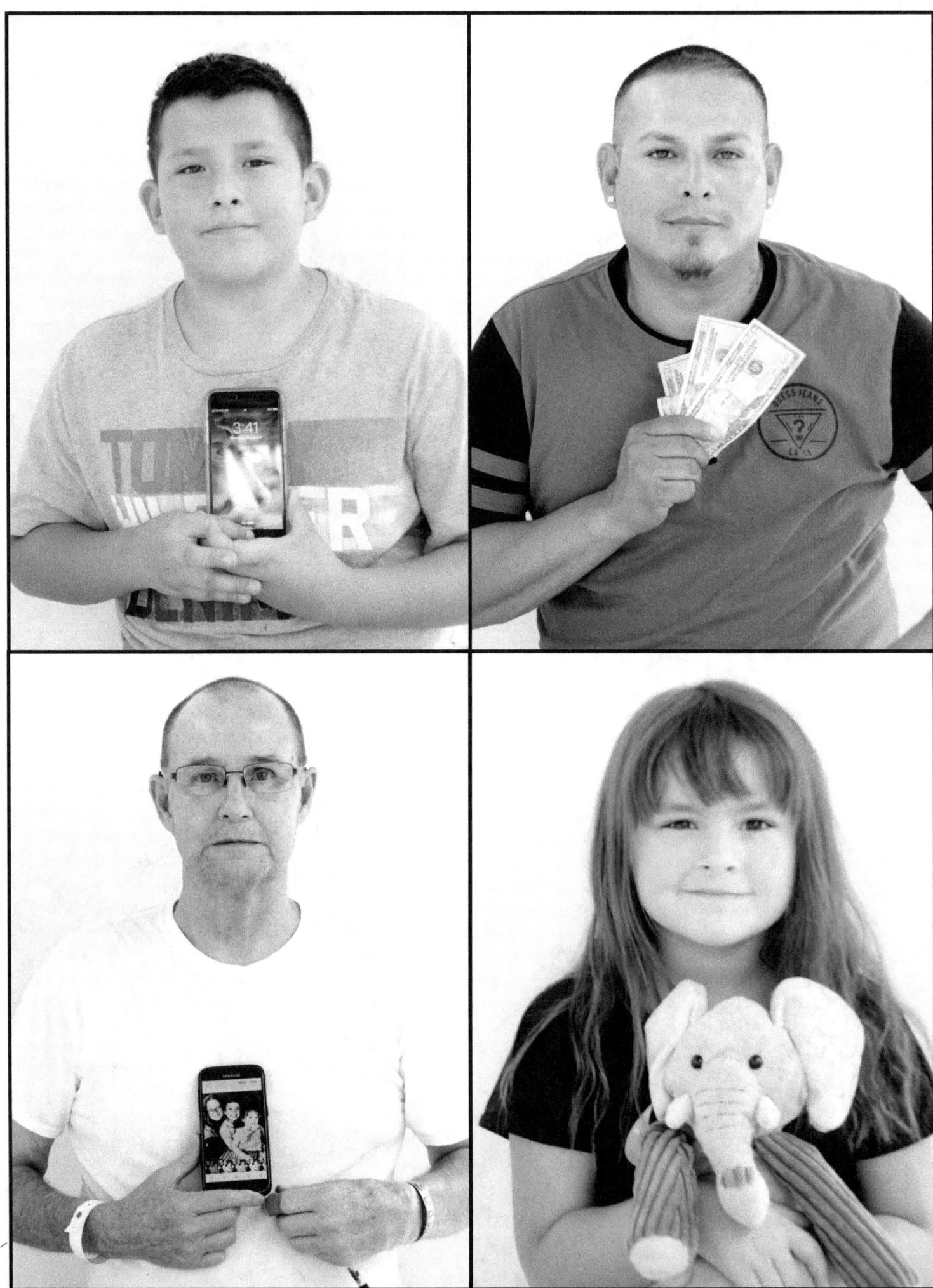

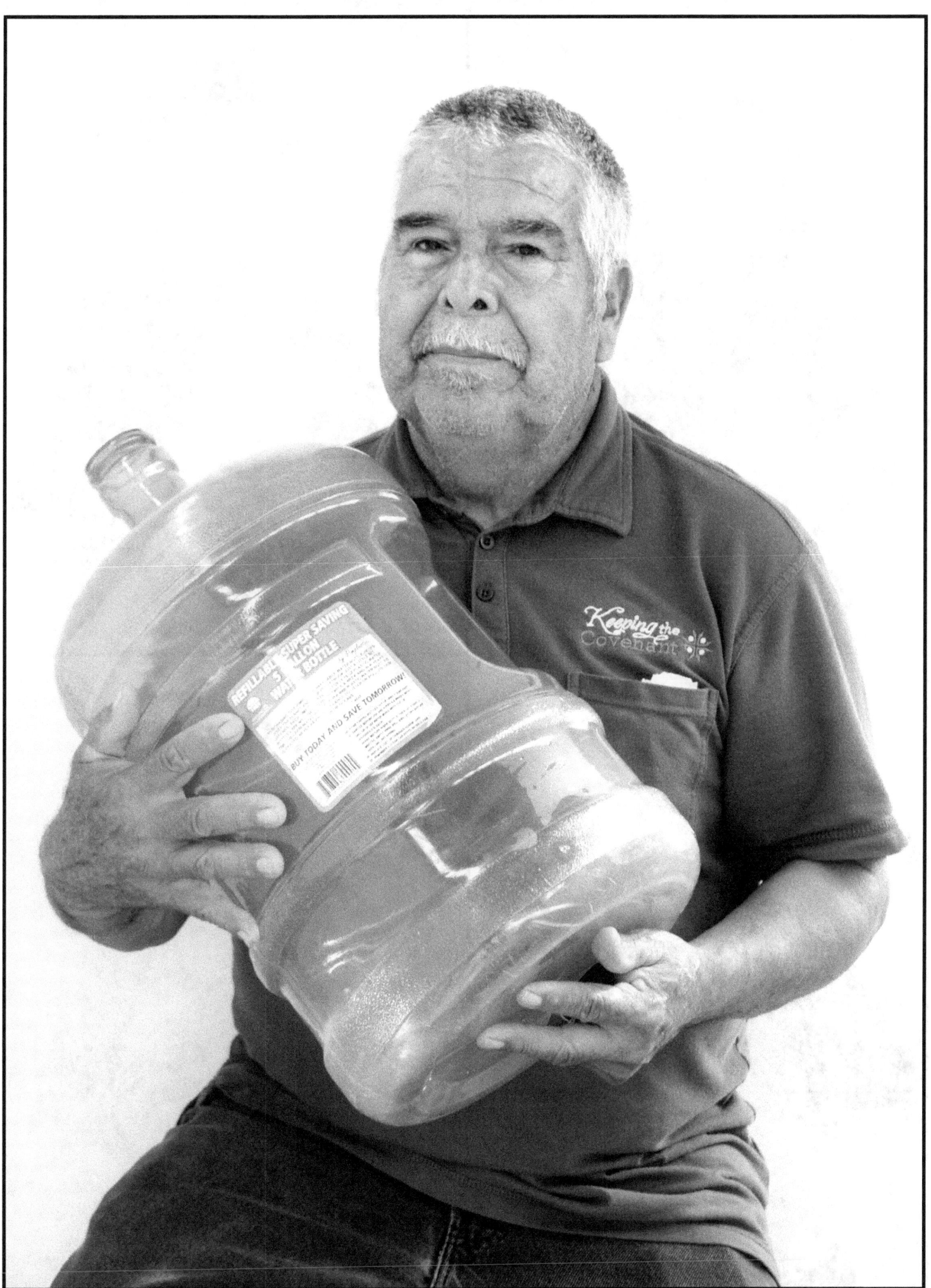

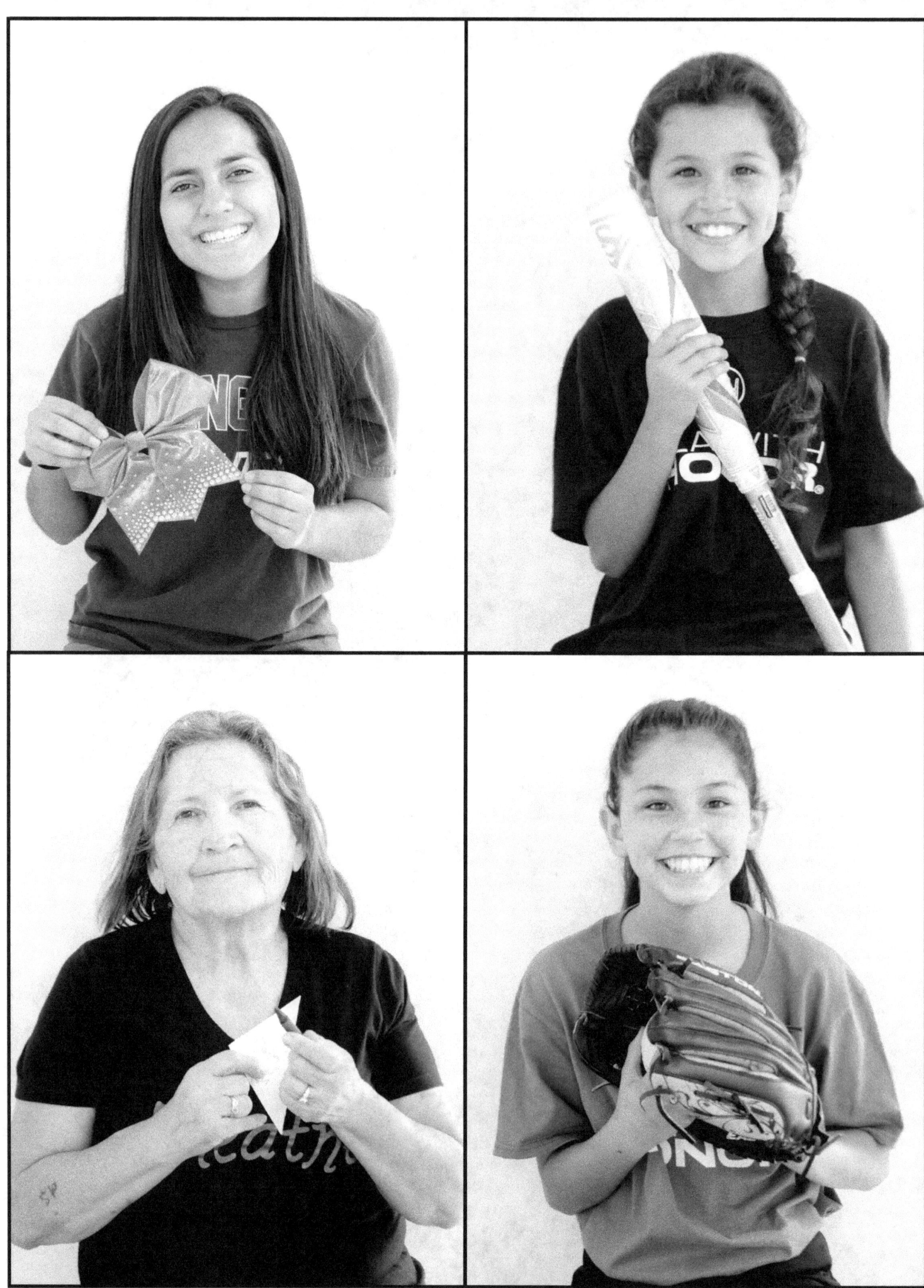

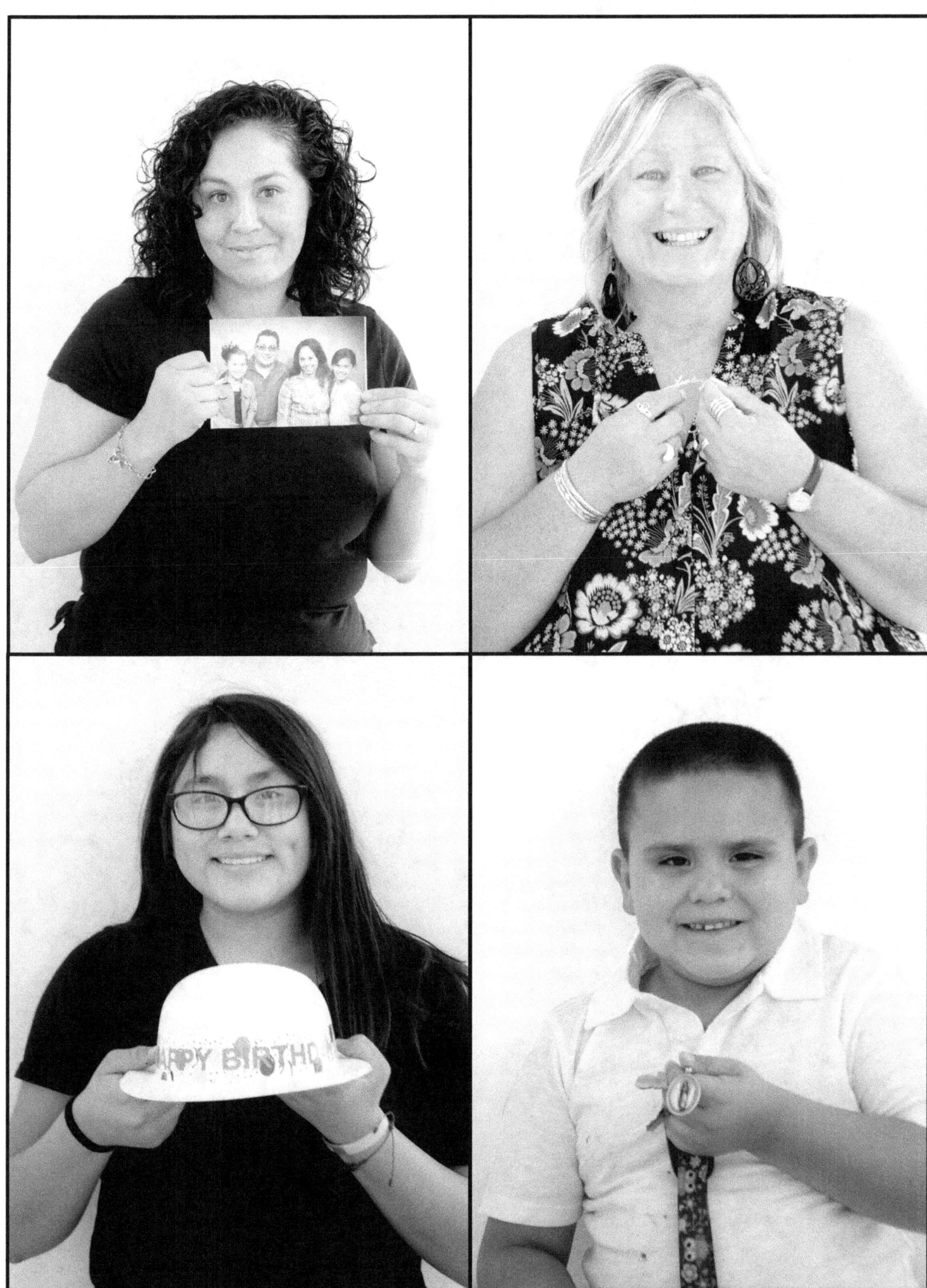

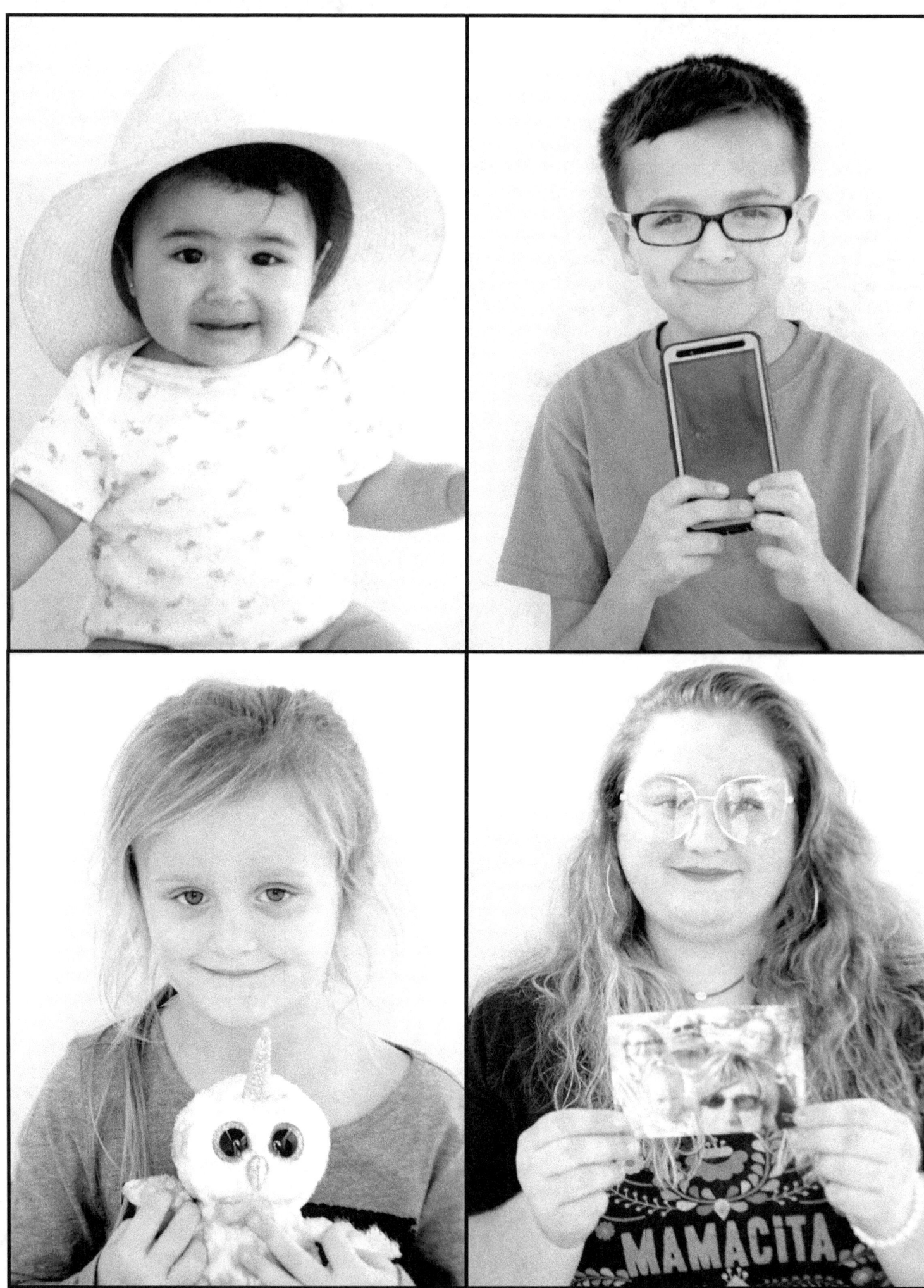

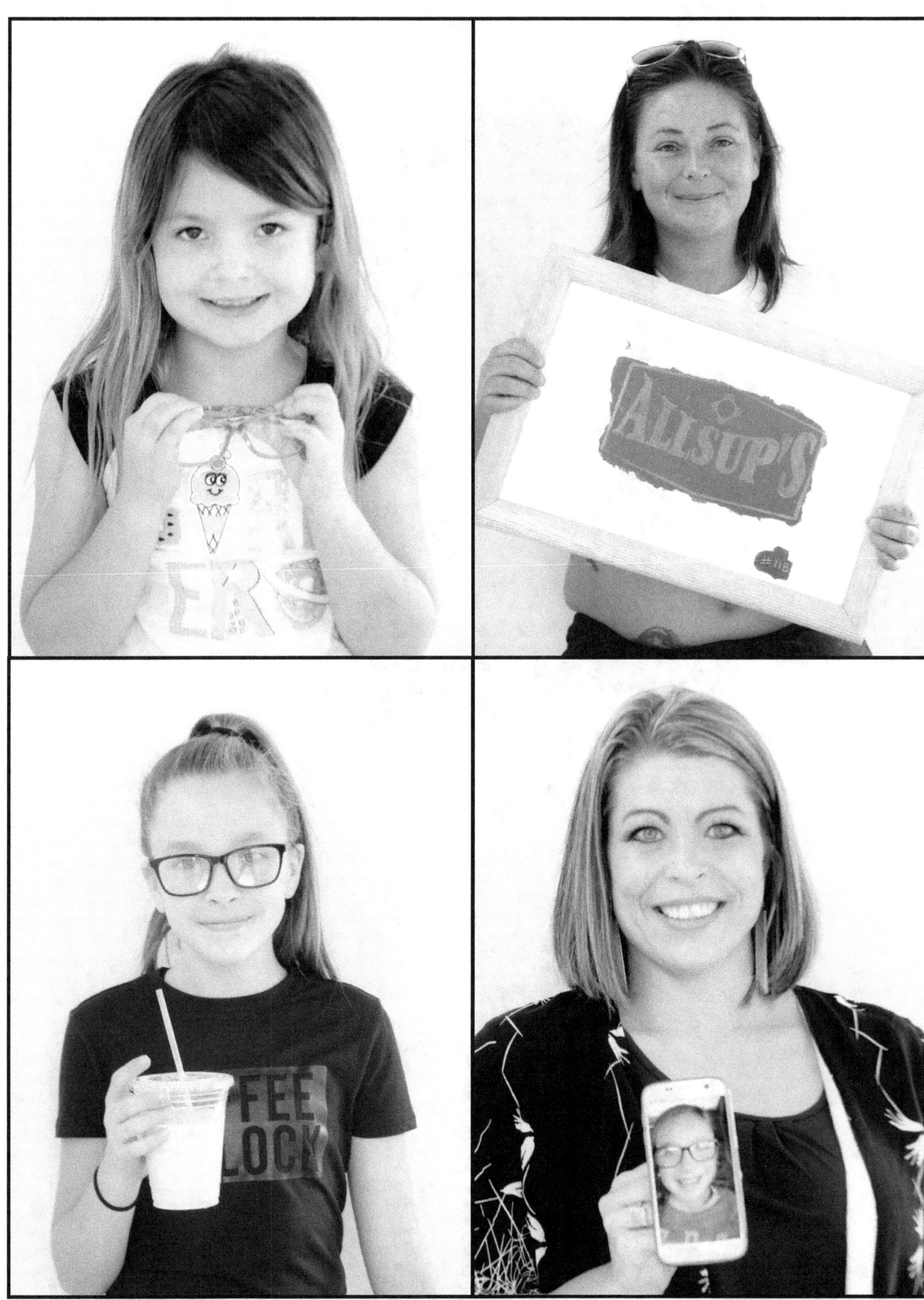

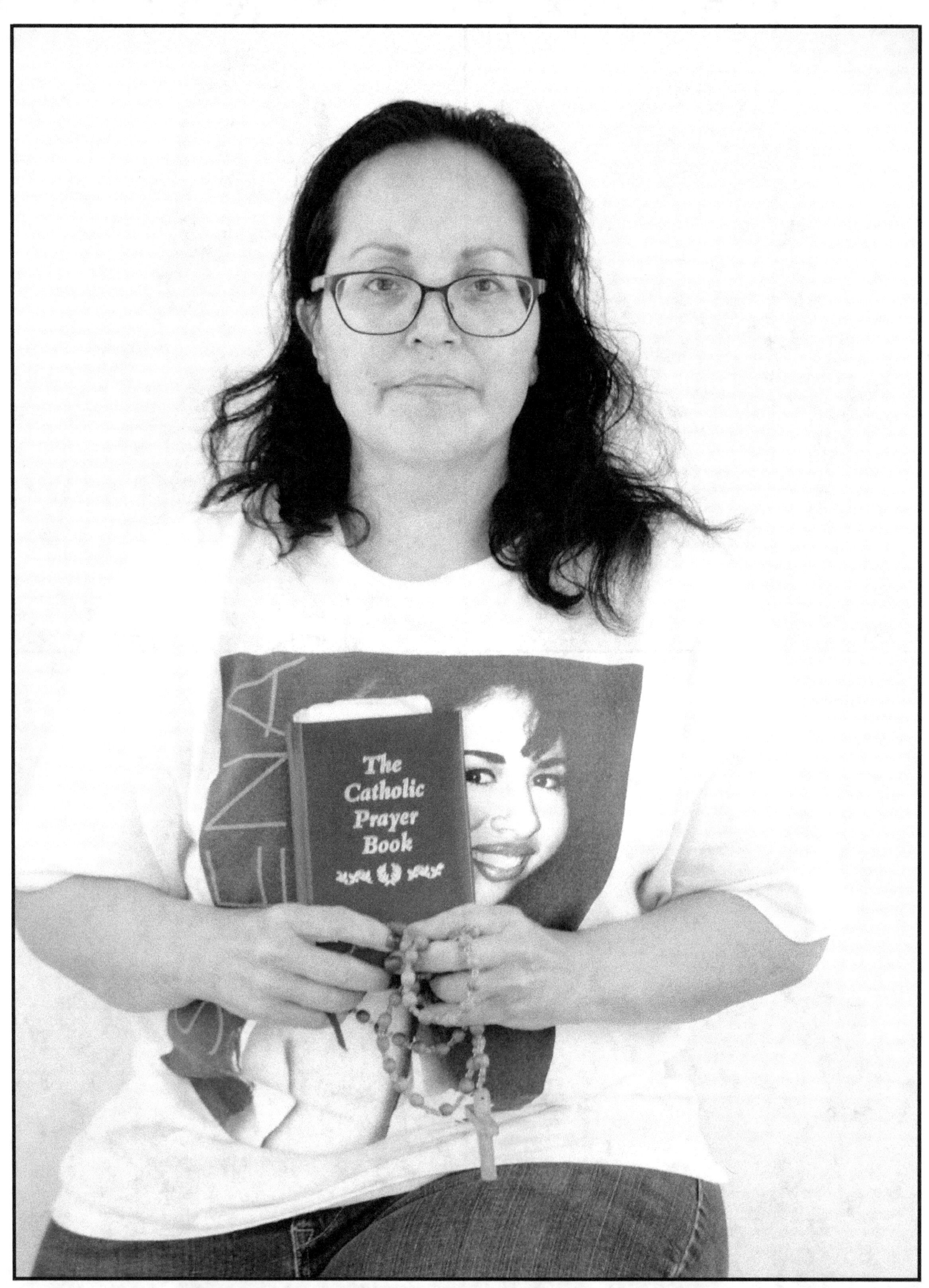

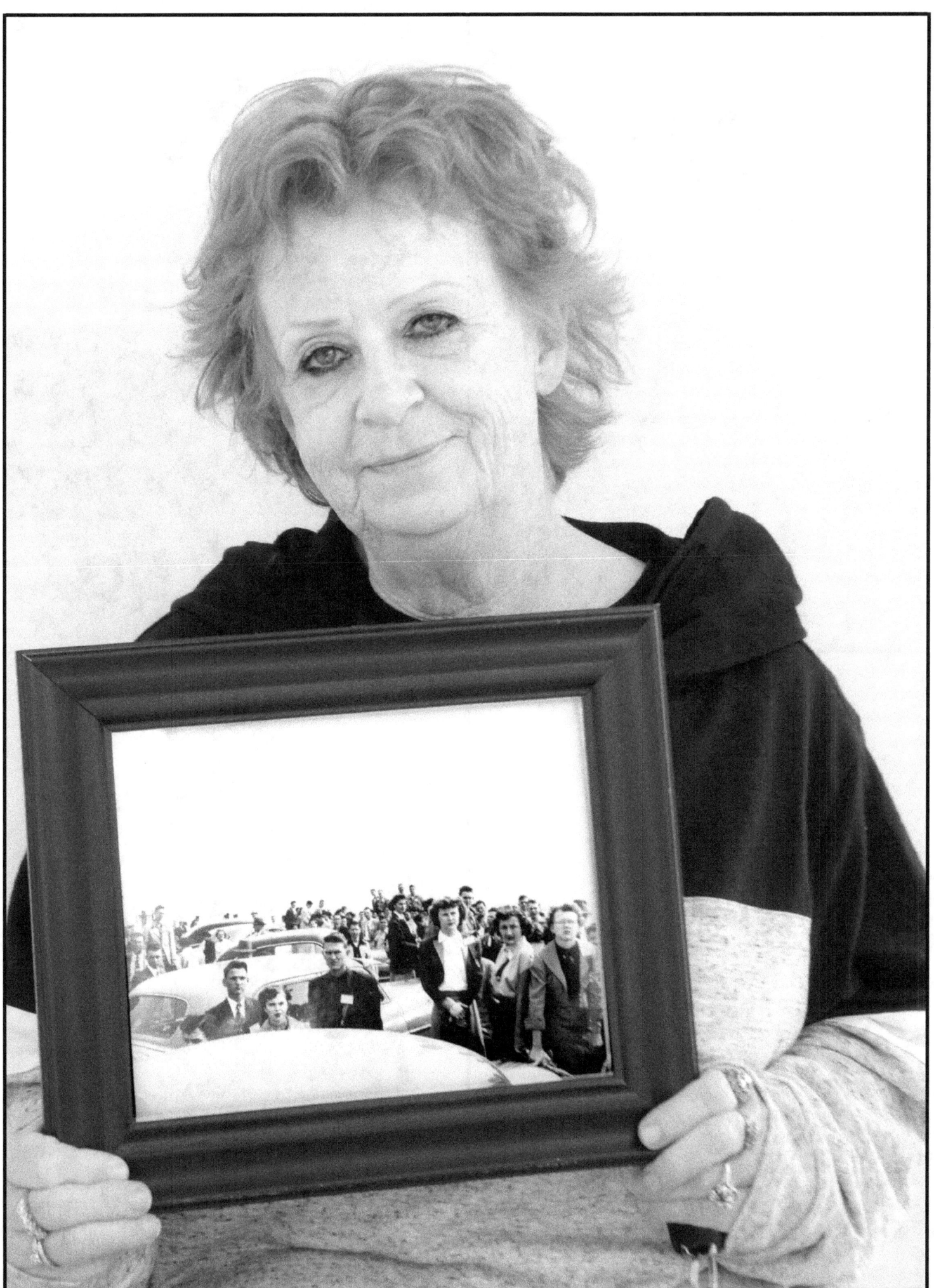

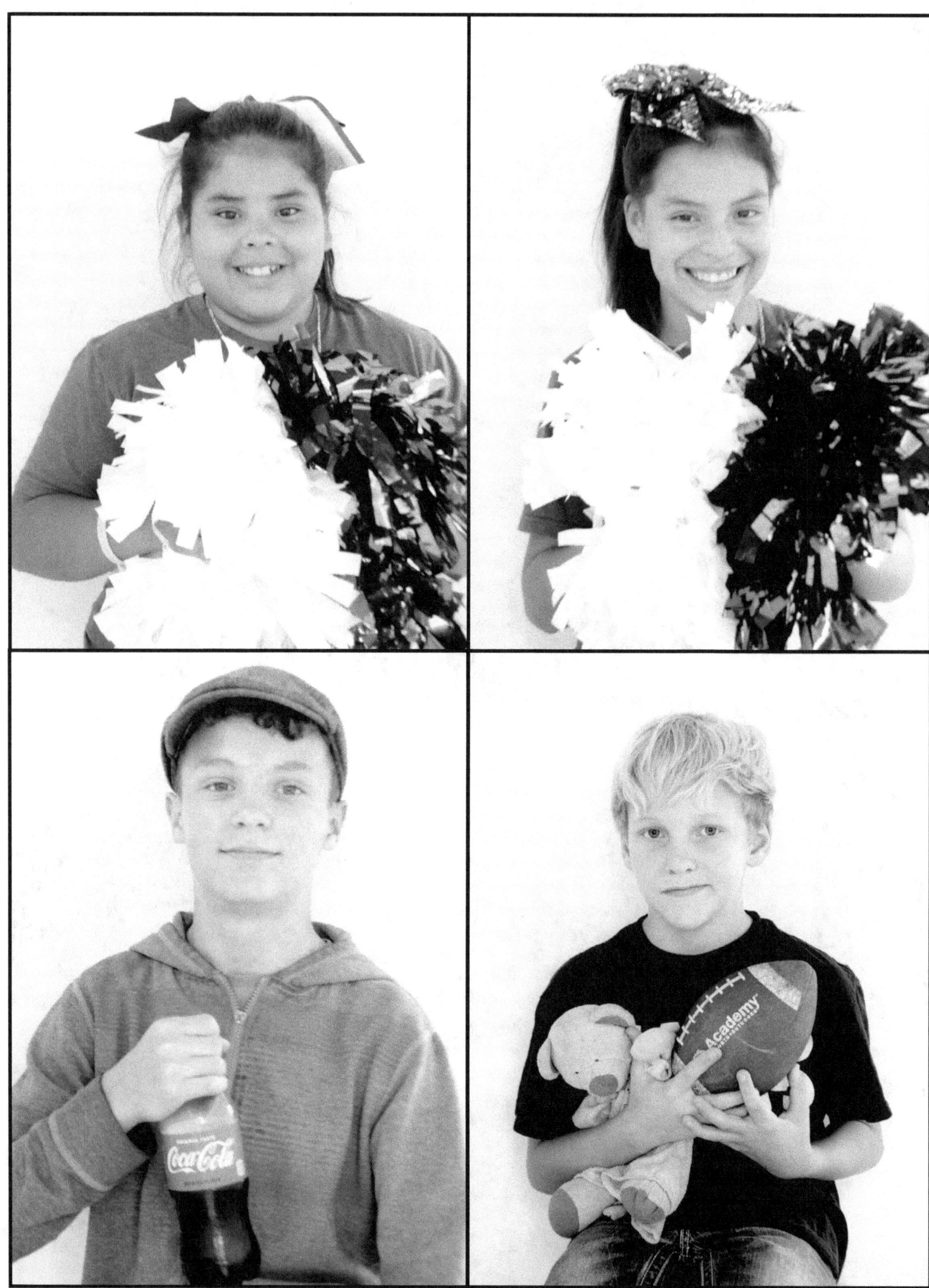

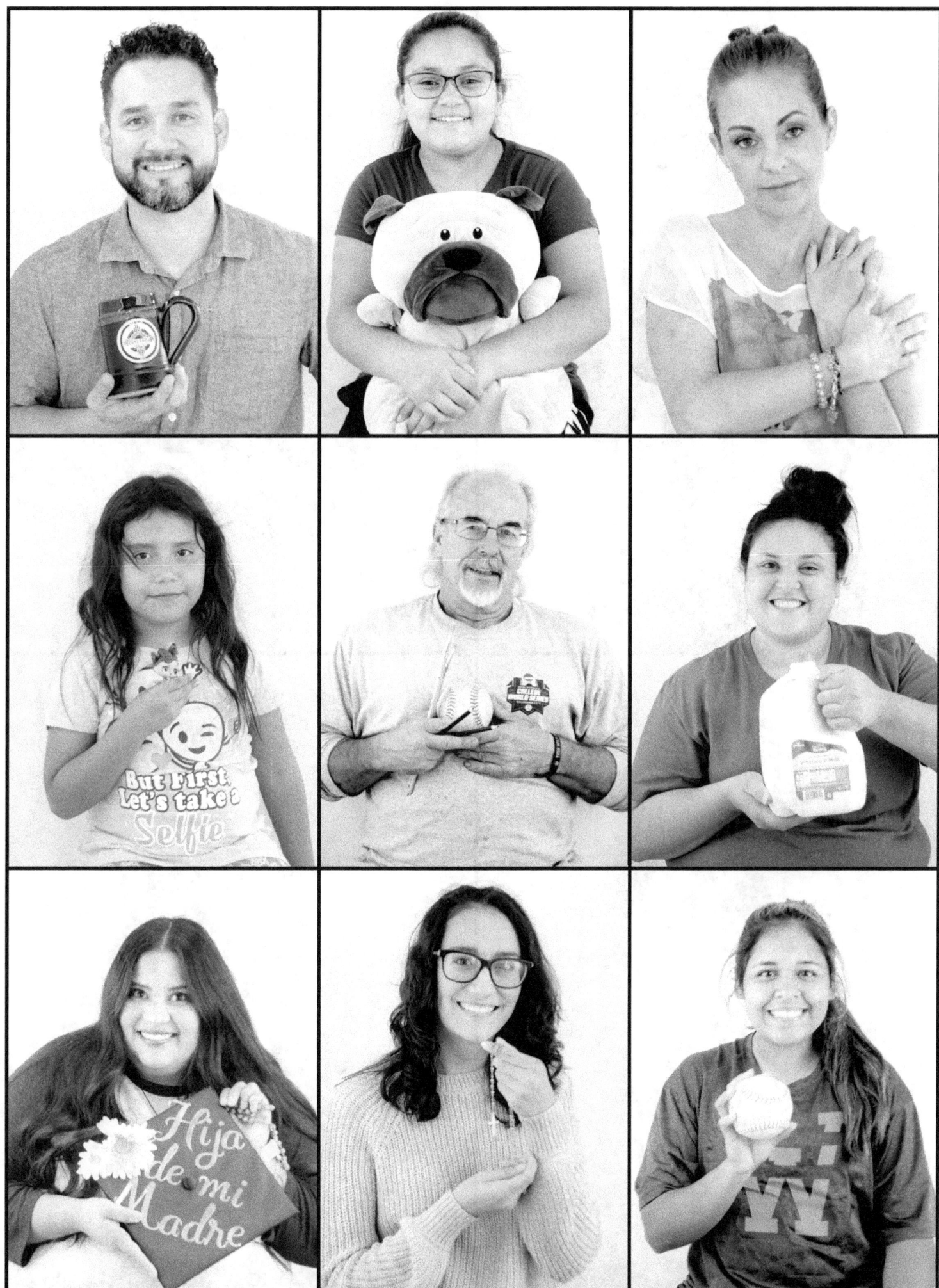

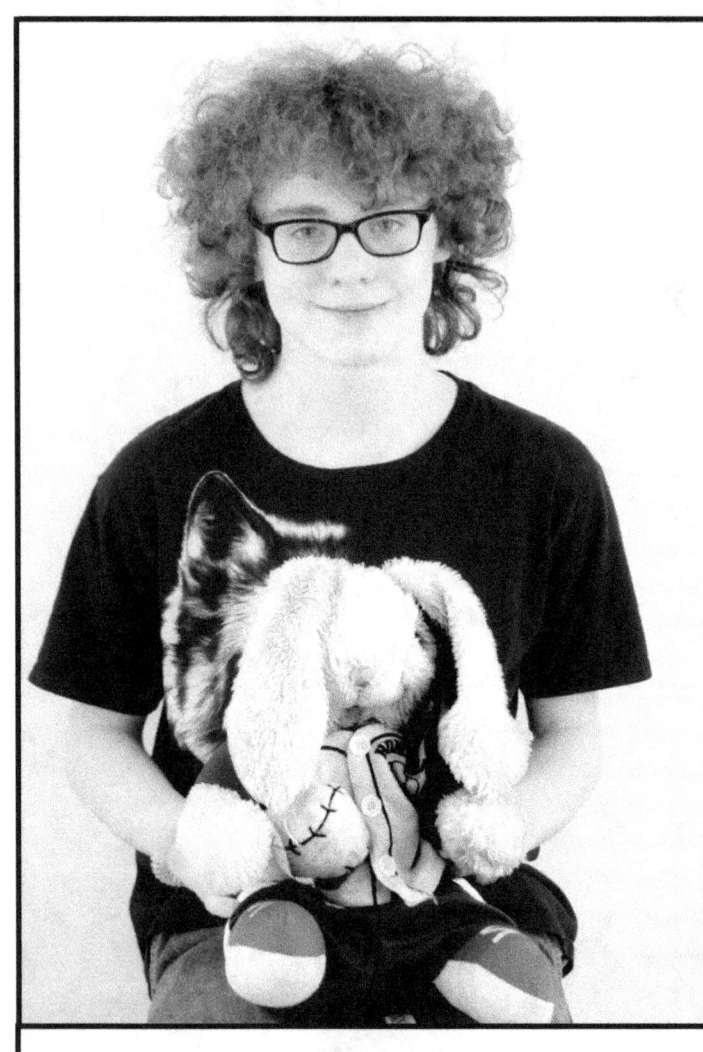

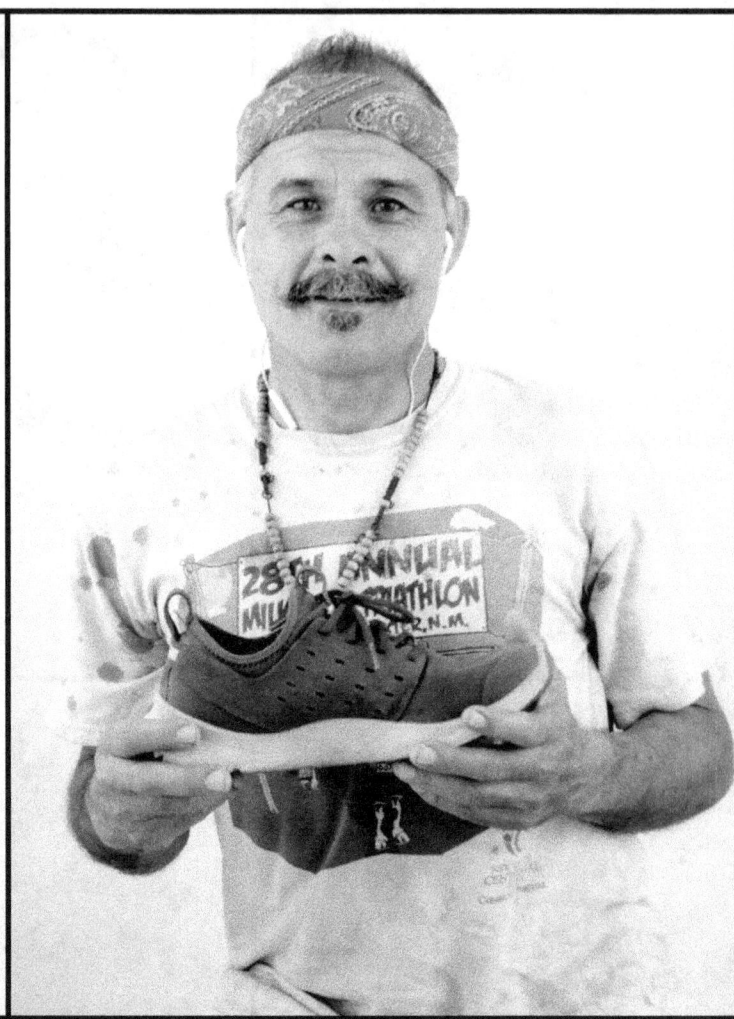

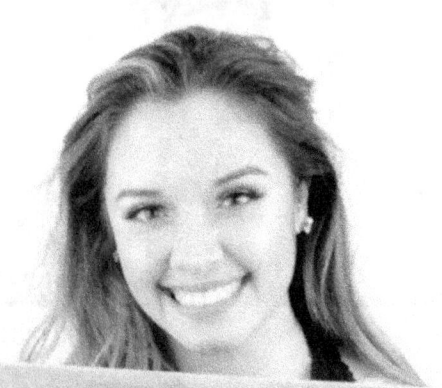

For I know the plans I have for you, plans to give you hope and a future.

Jeremiah 29:11

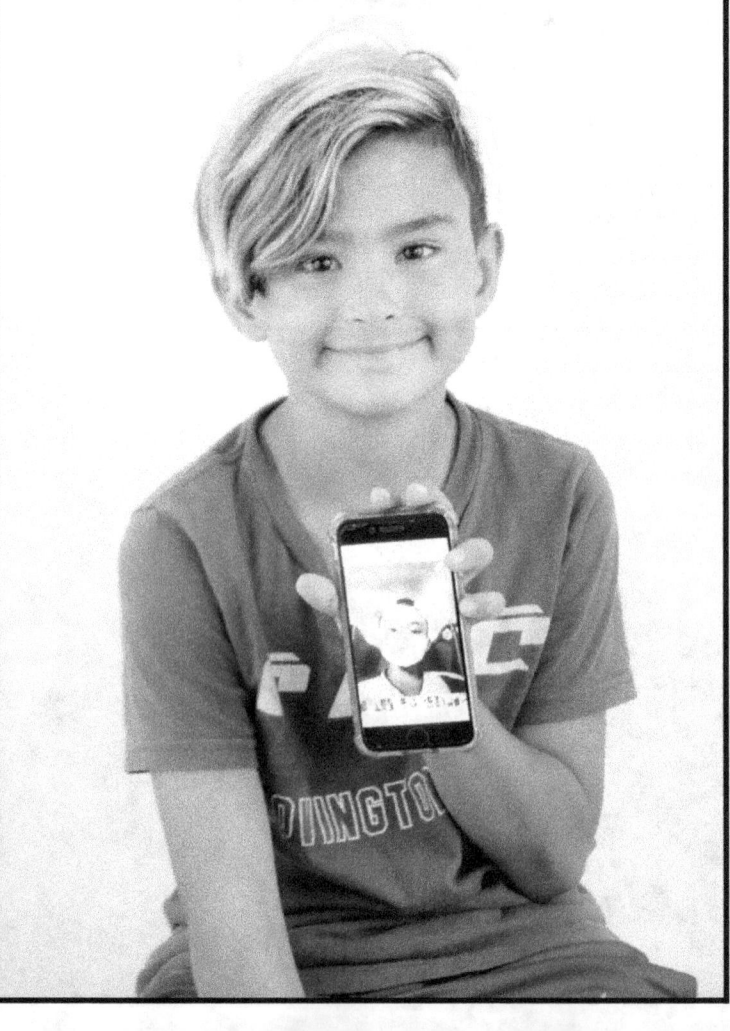

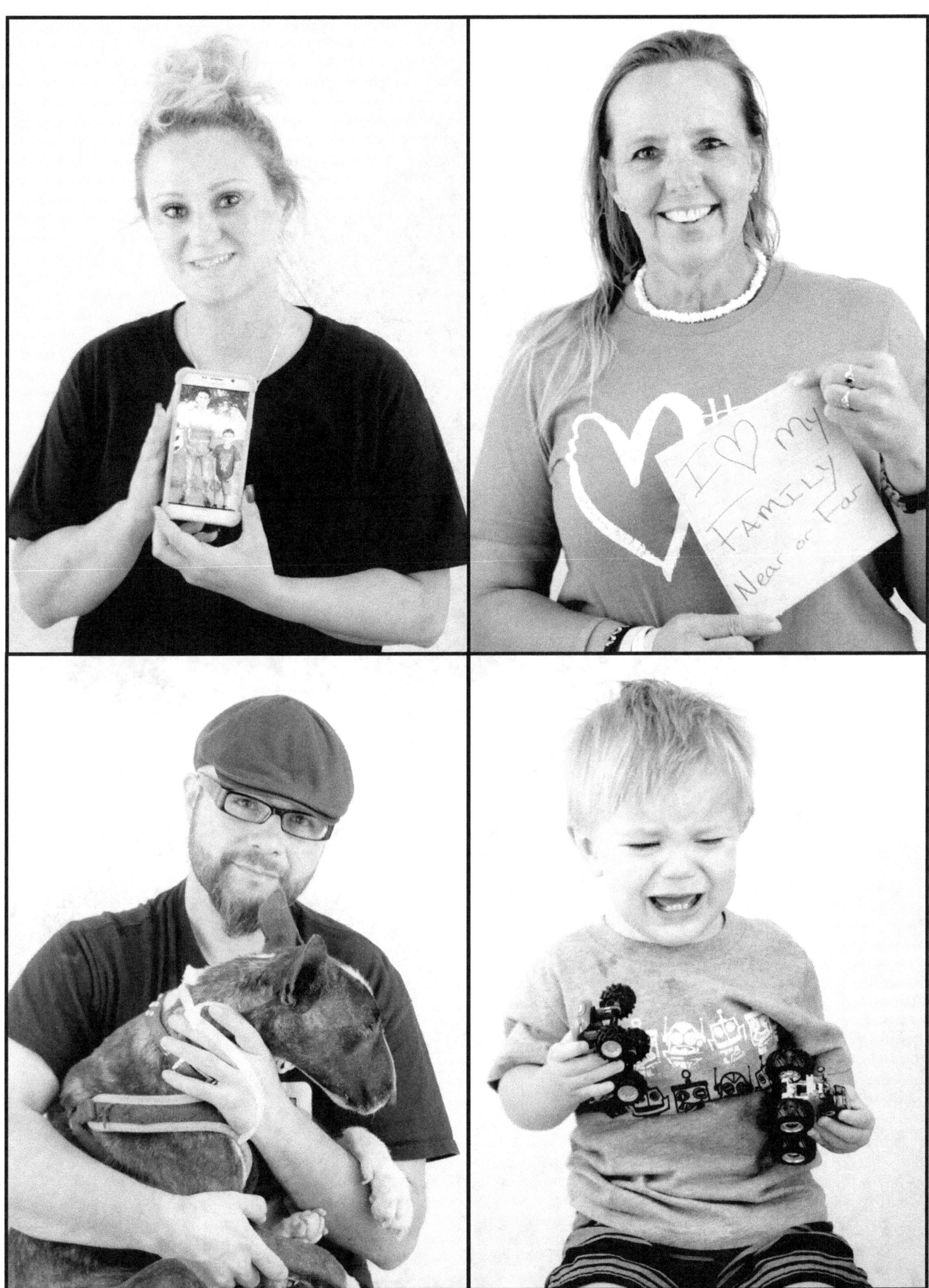

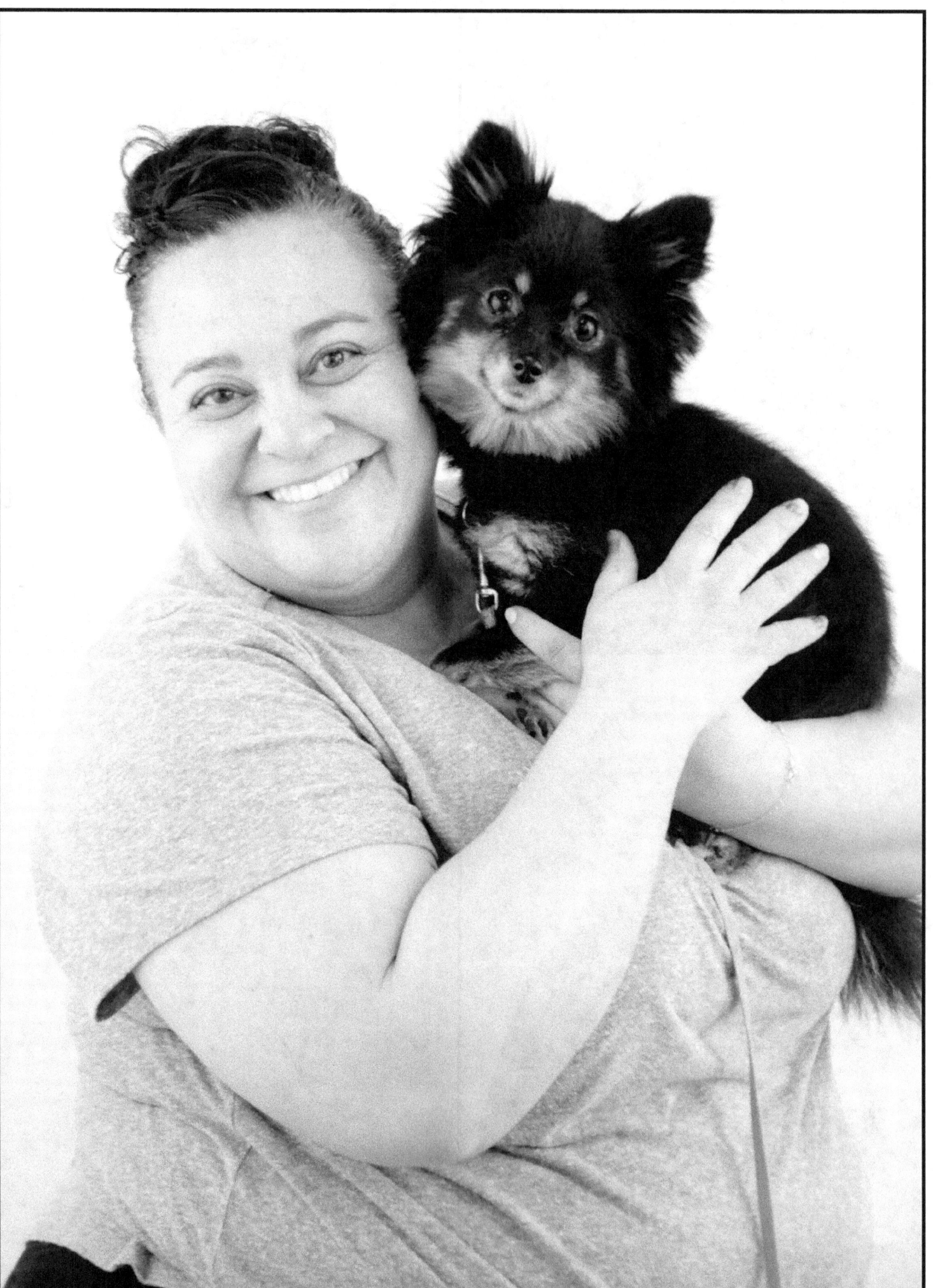

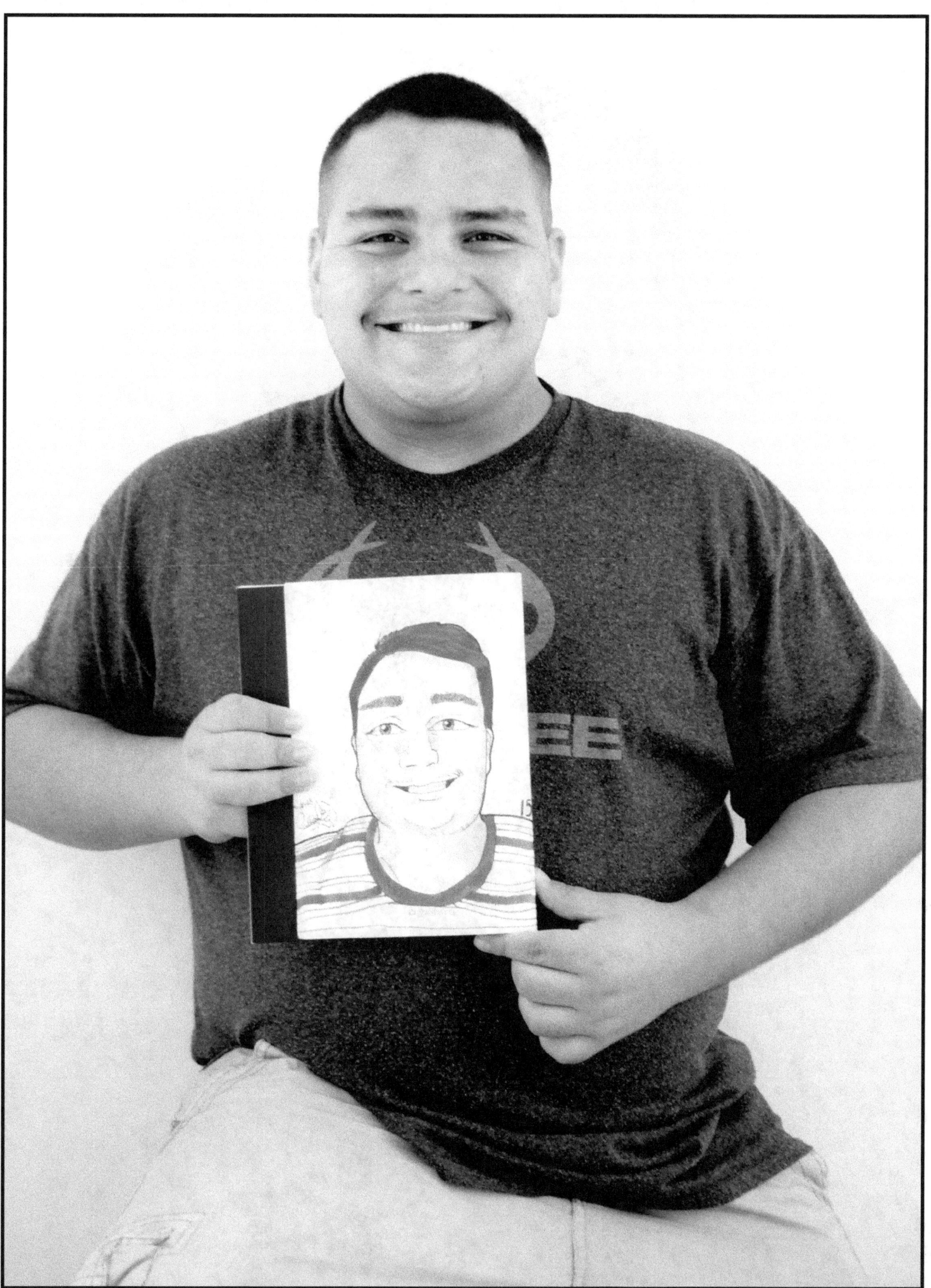

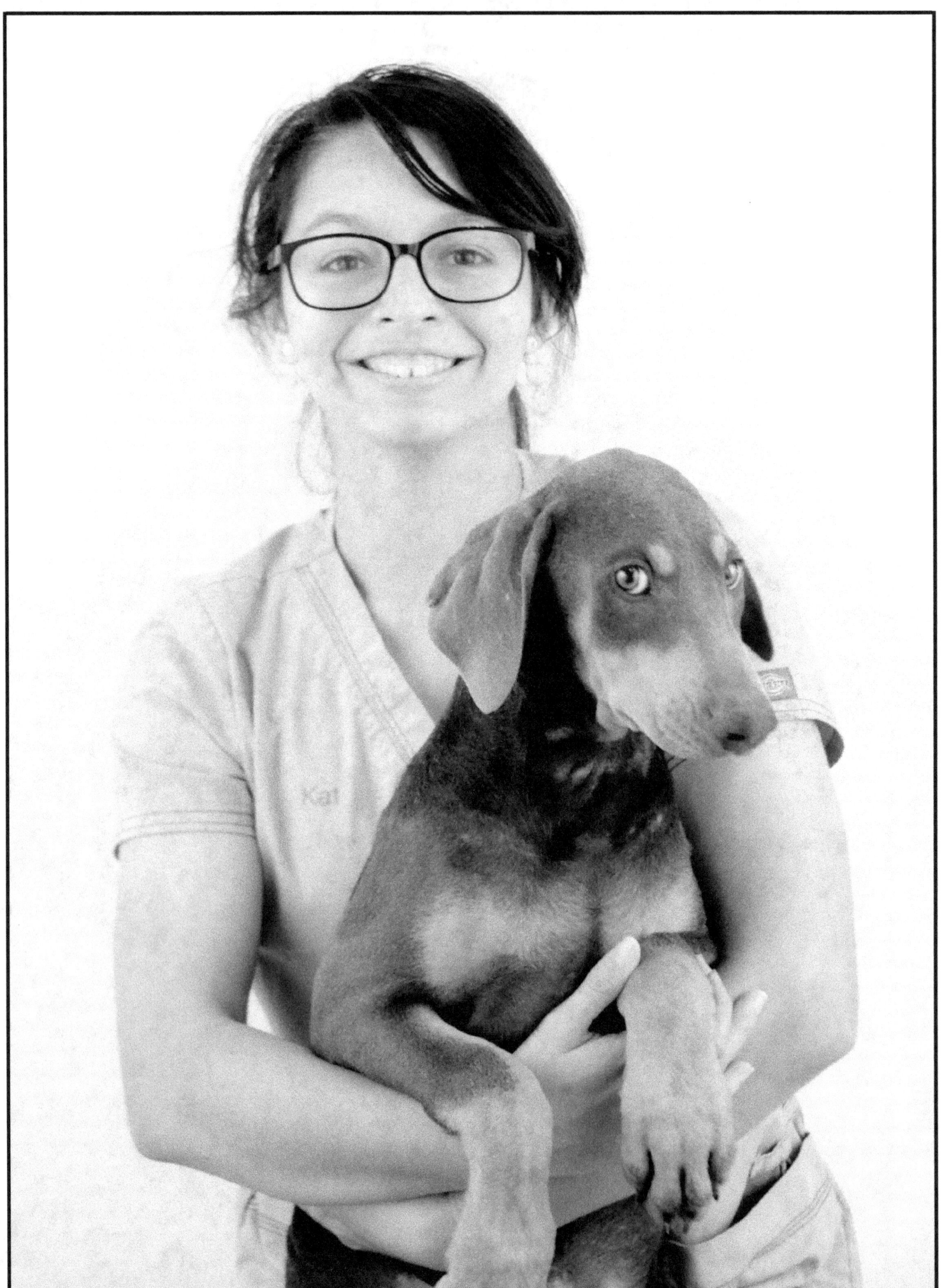

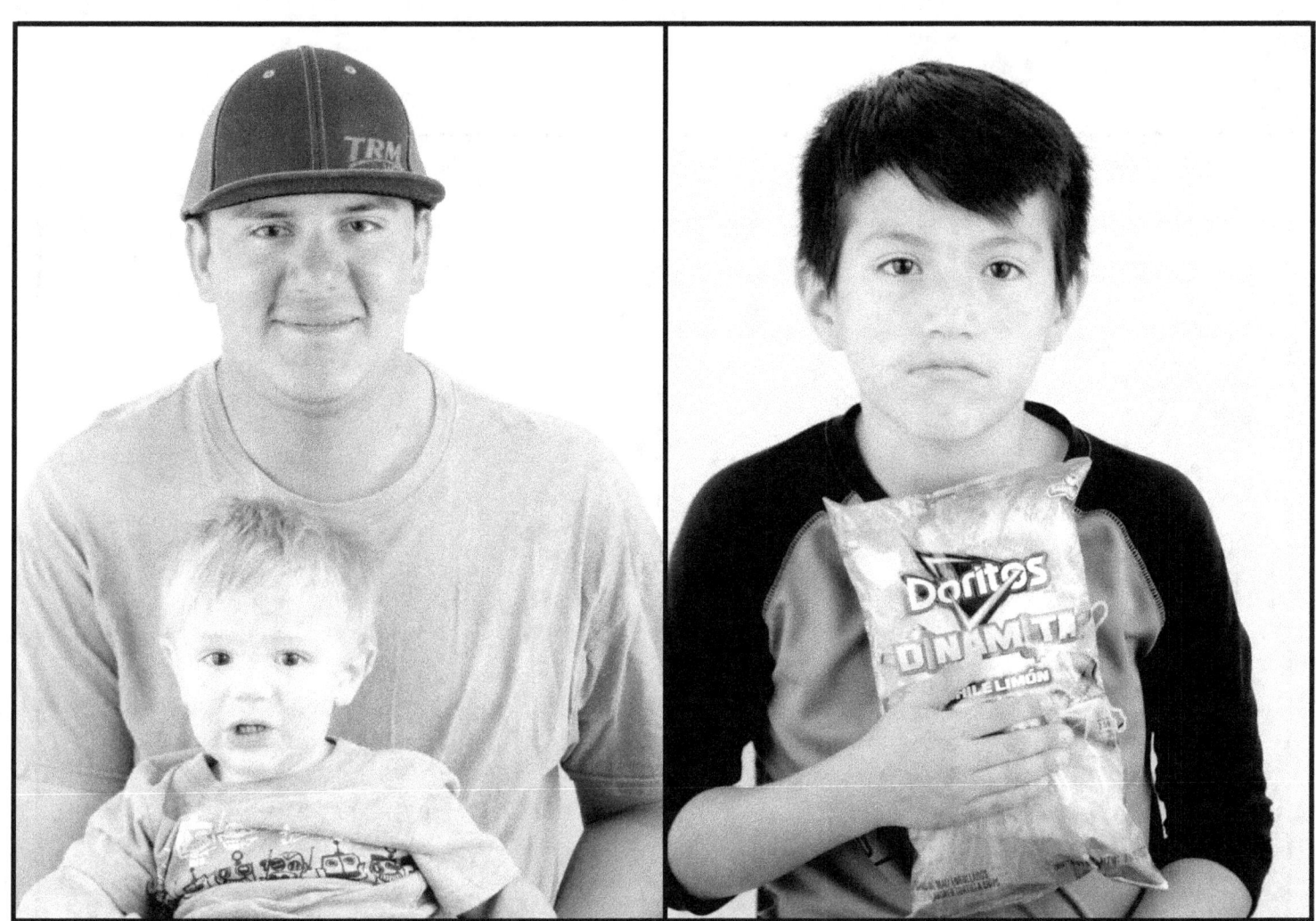

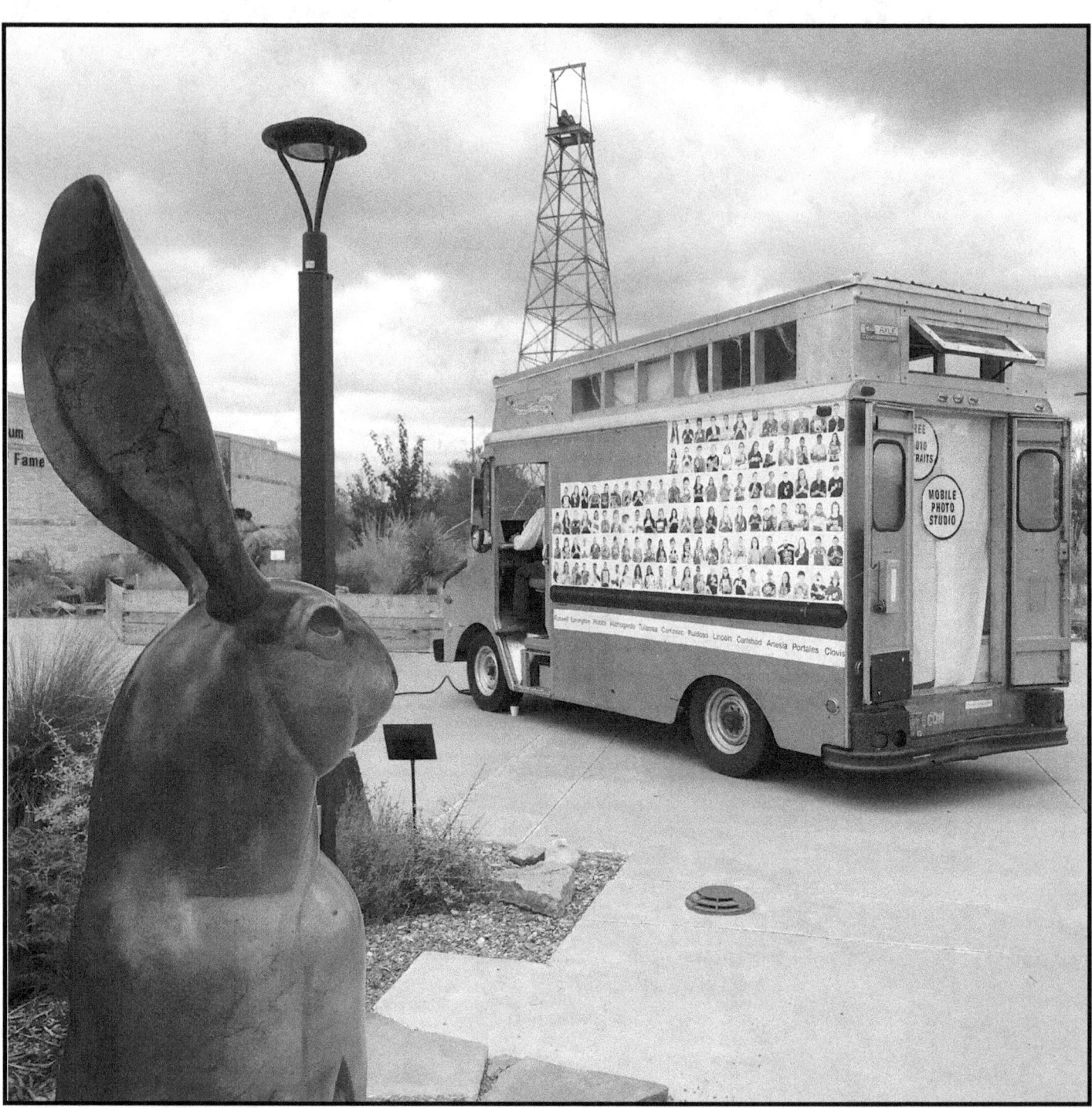

Hobbs

October 5-6, 2019

New Mexico Junior College

Center of Recreational Excellence

Western Heritage Museum & Lea County Cowboy Hall of Fame

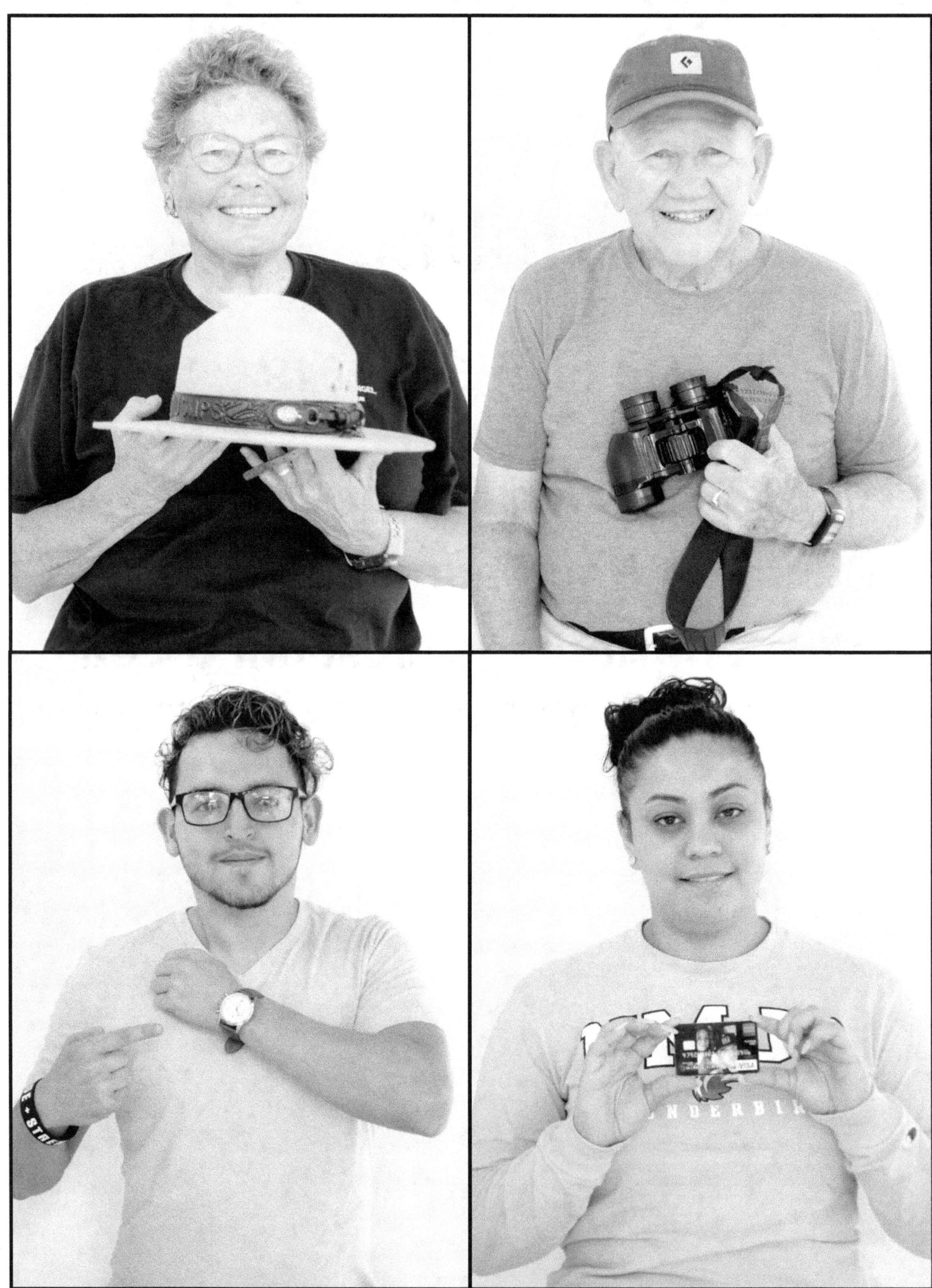

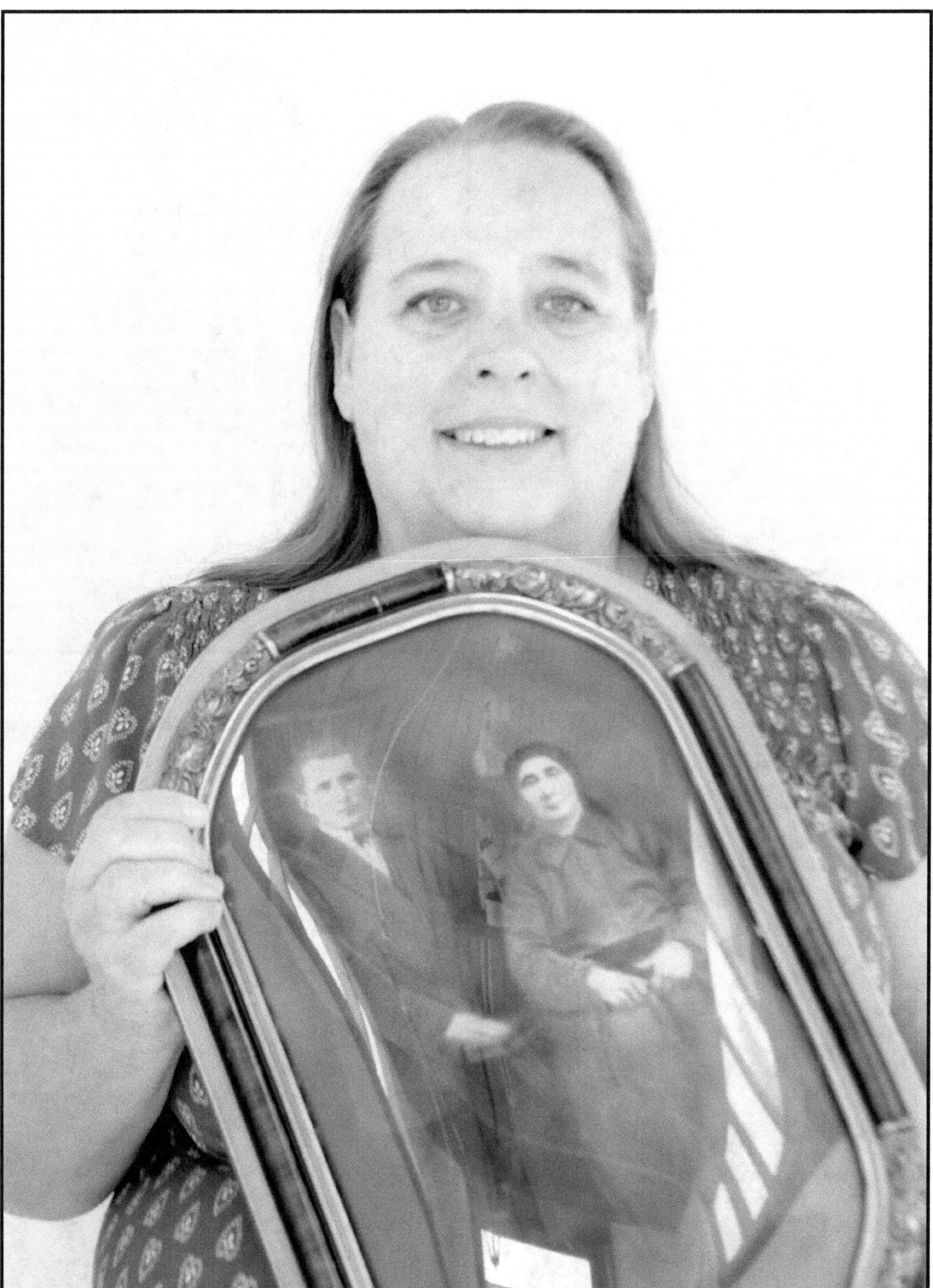

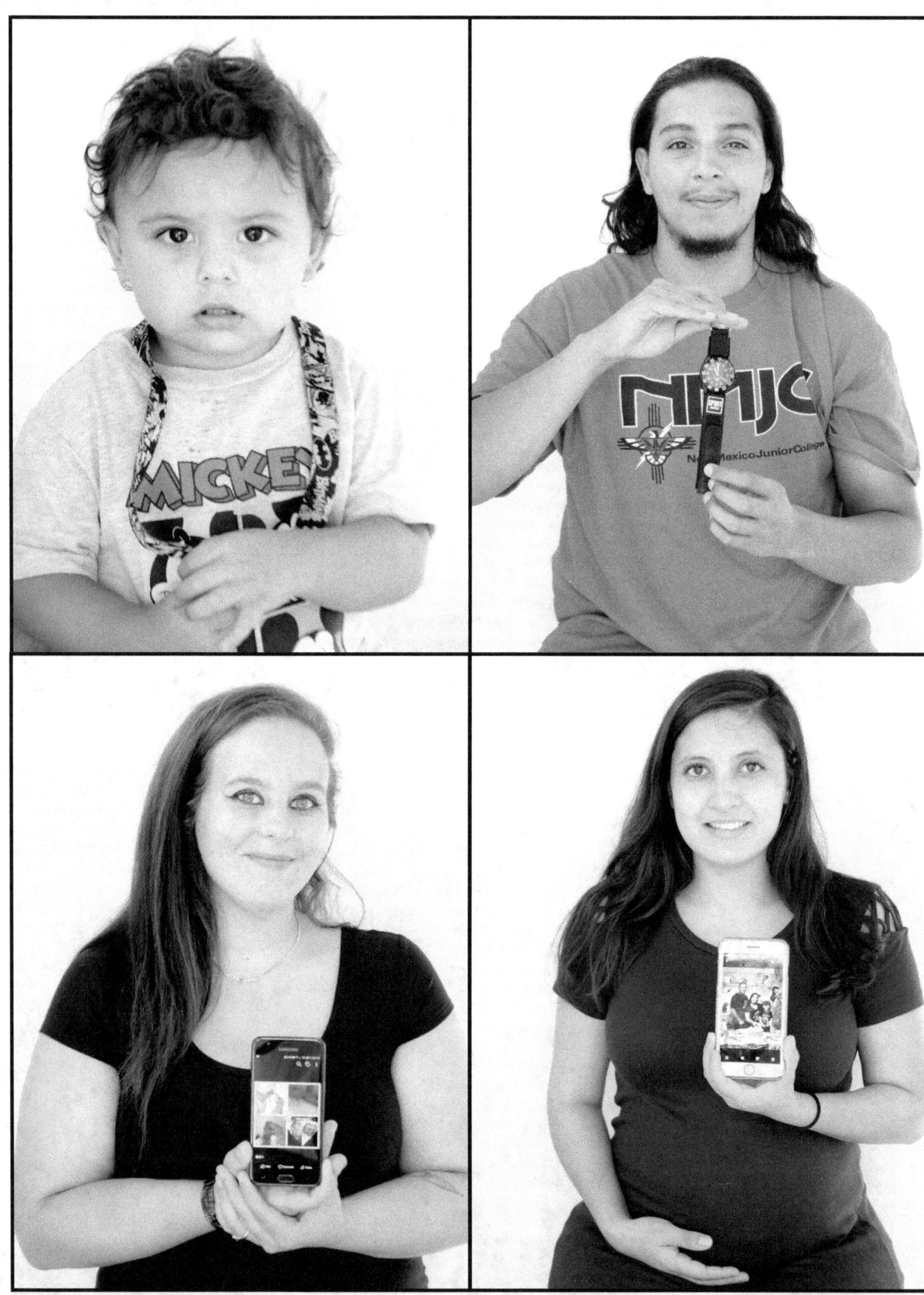

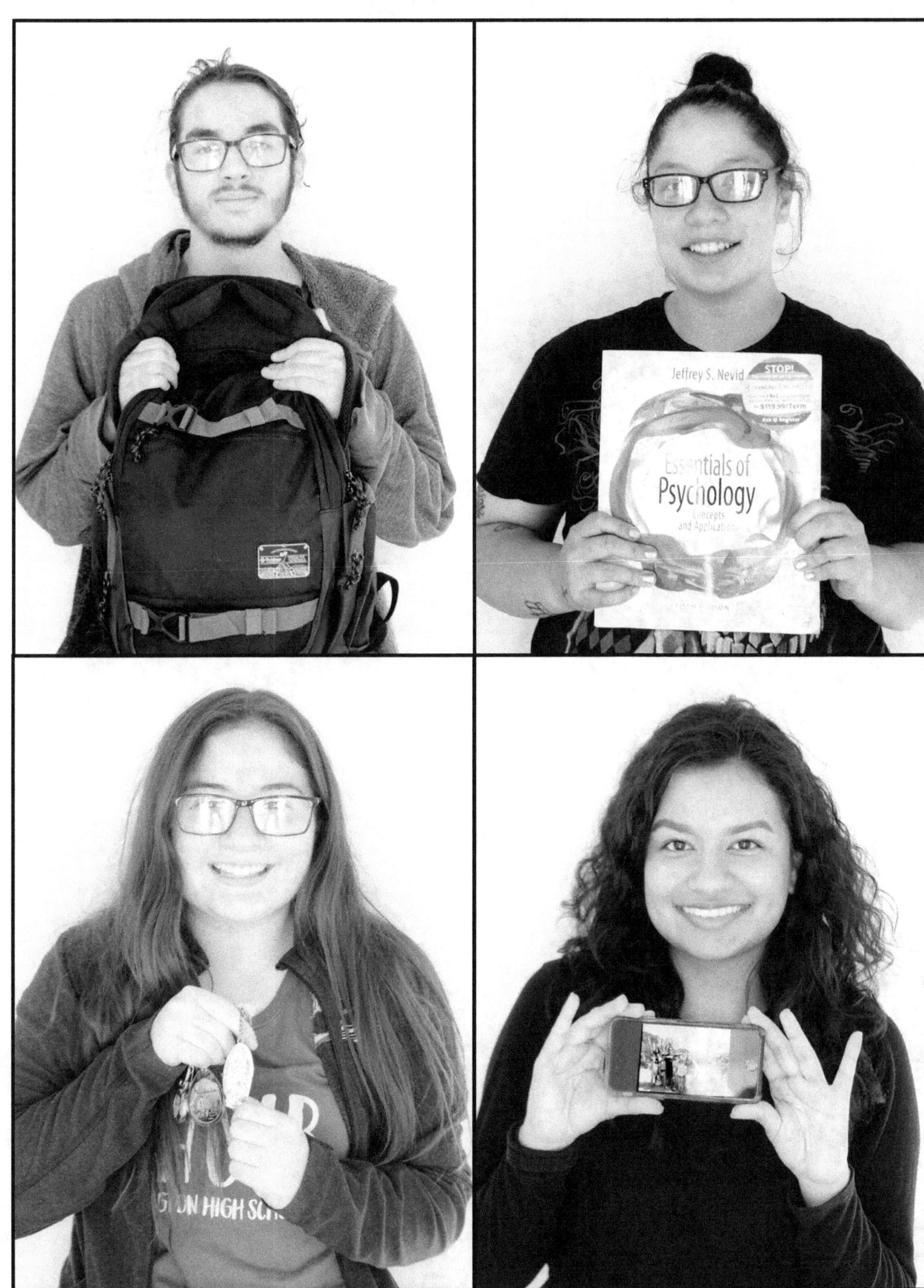

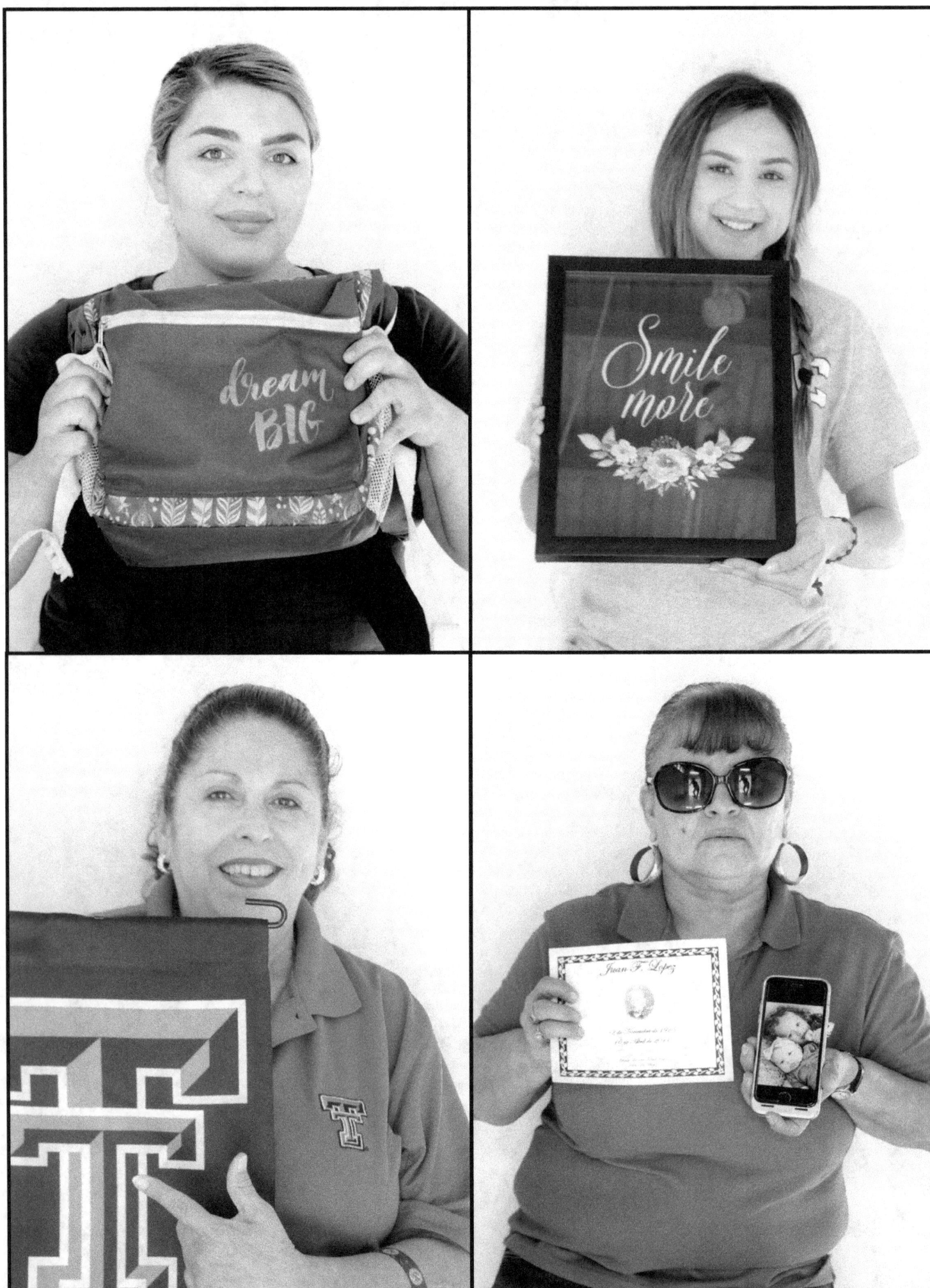

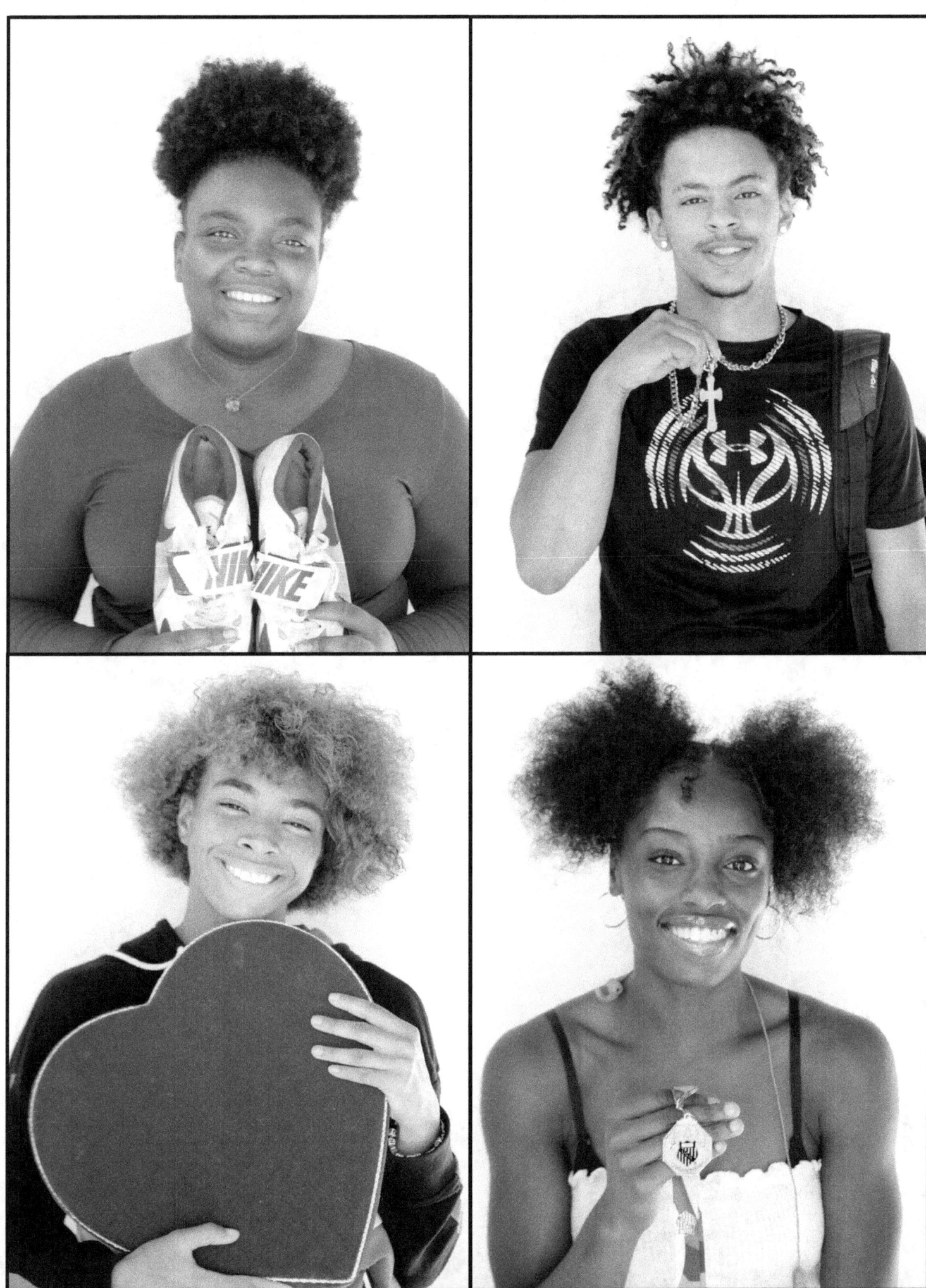

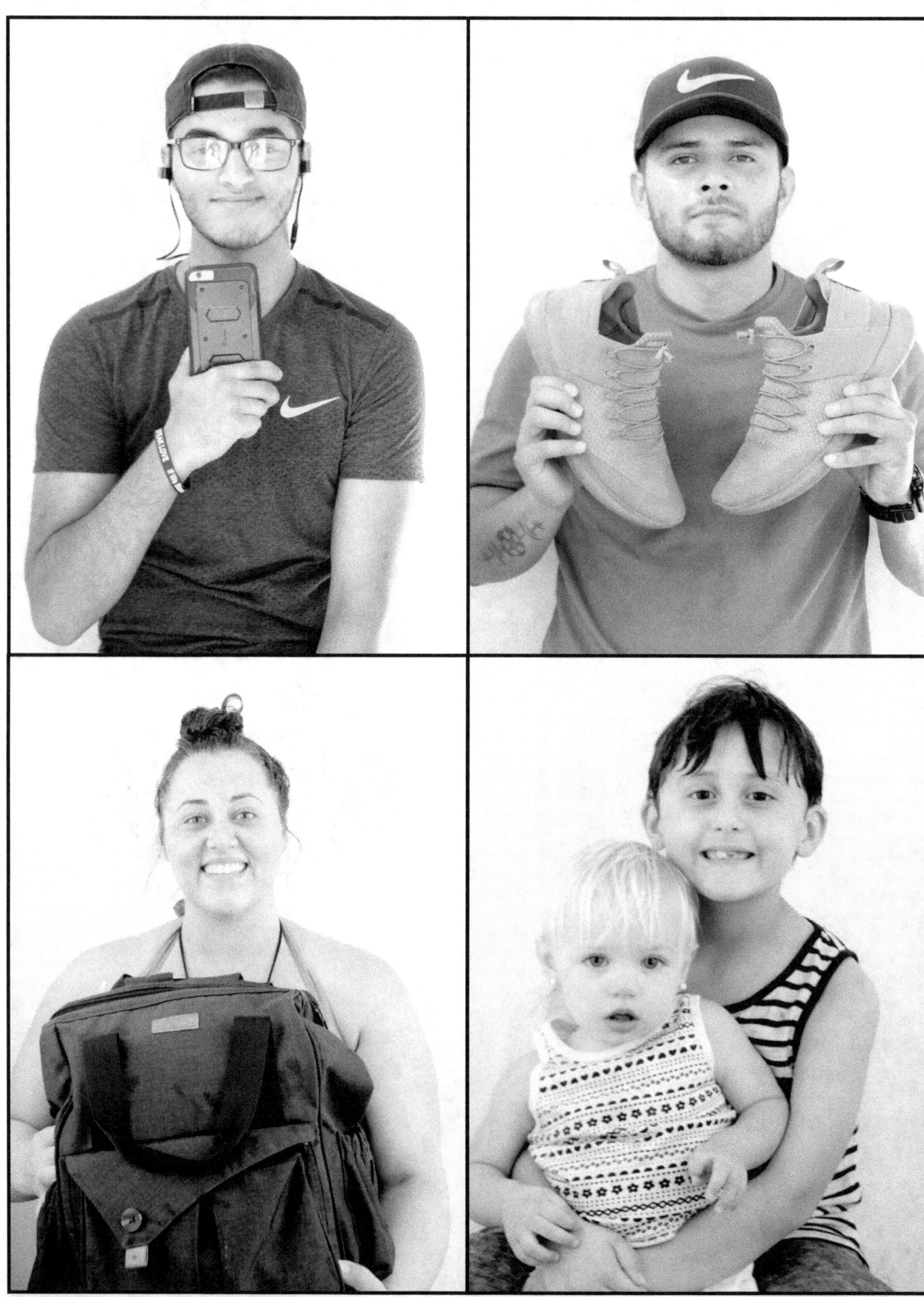

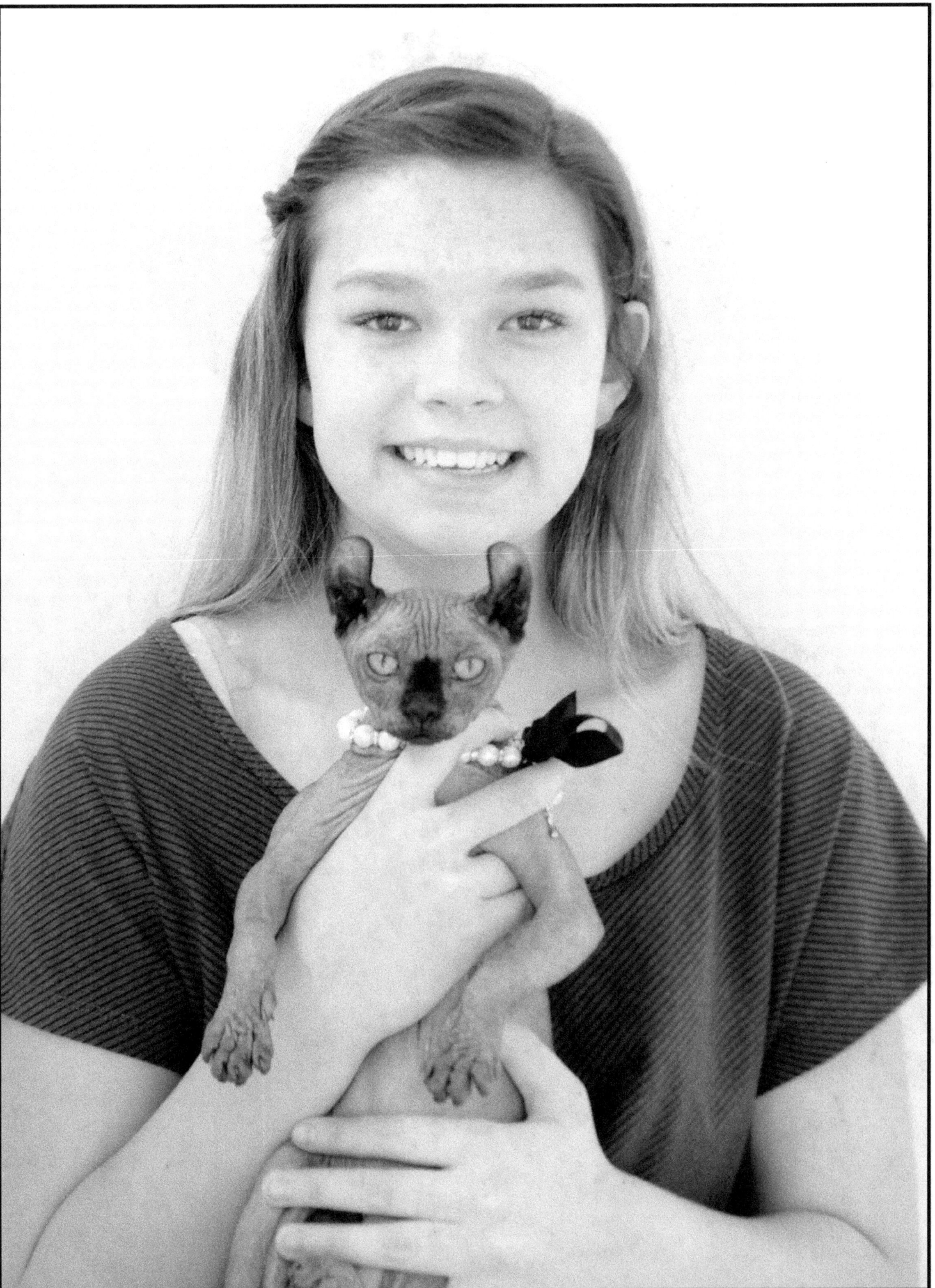

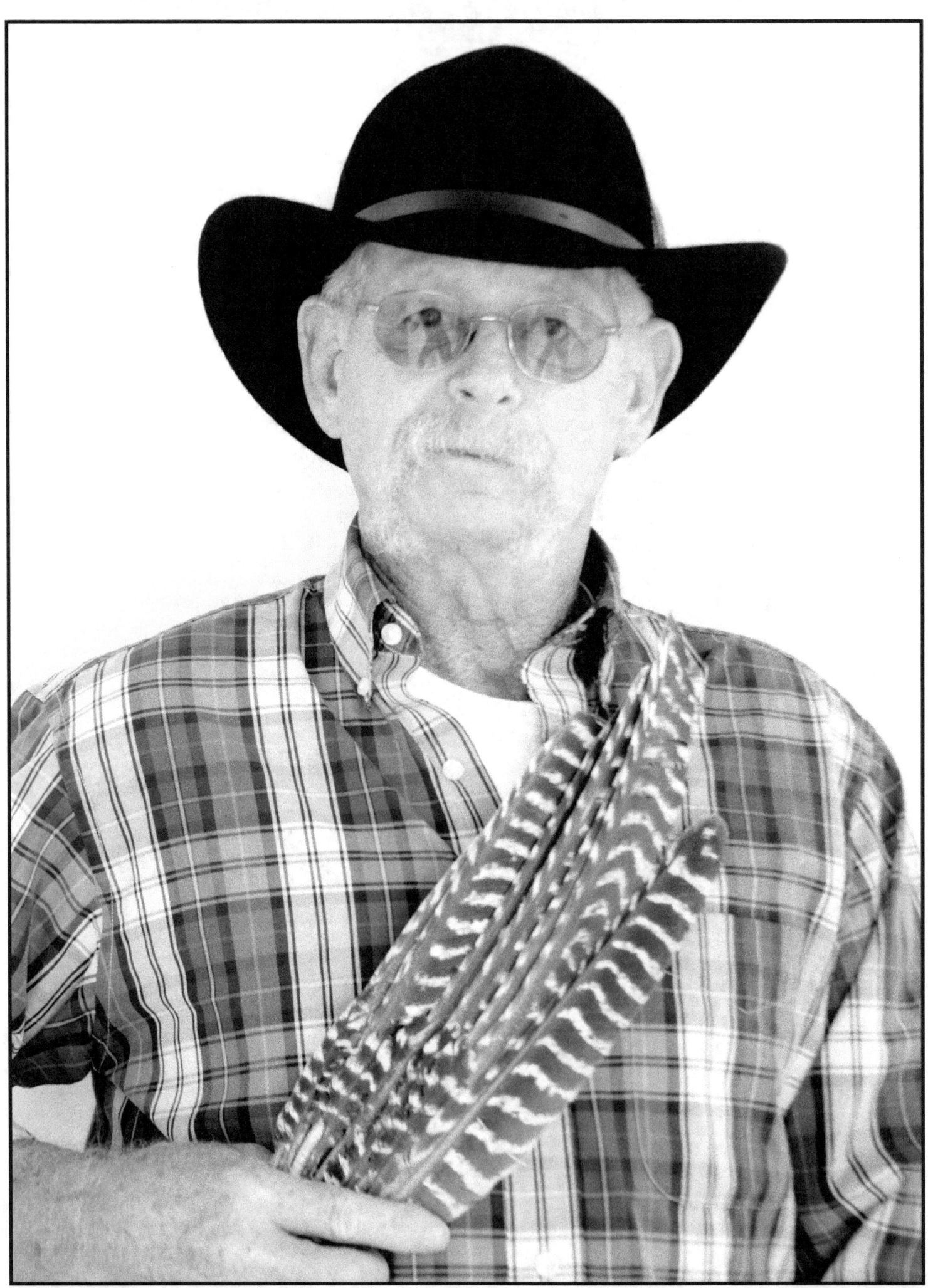

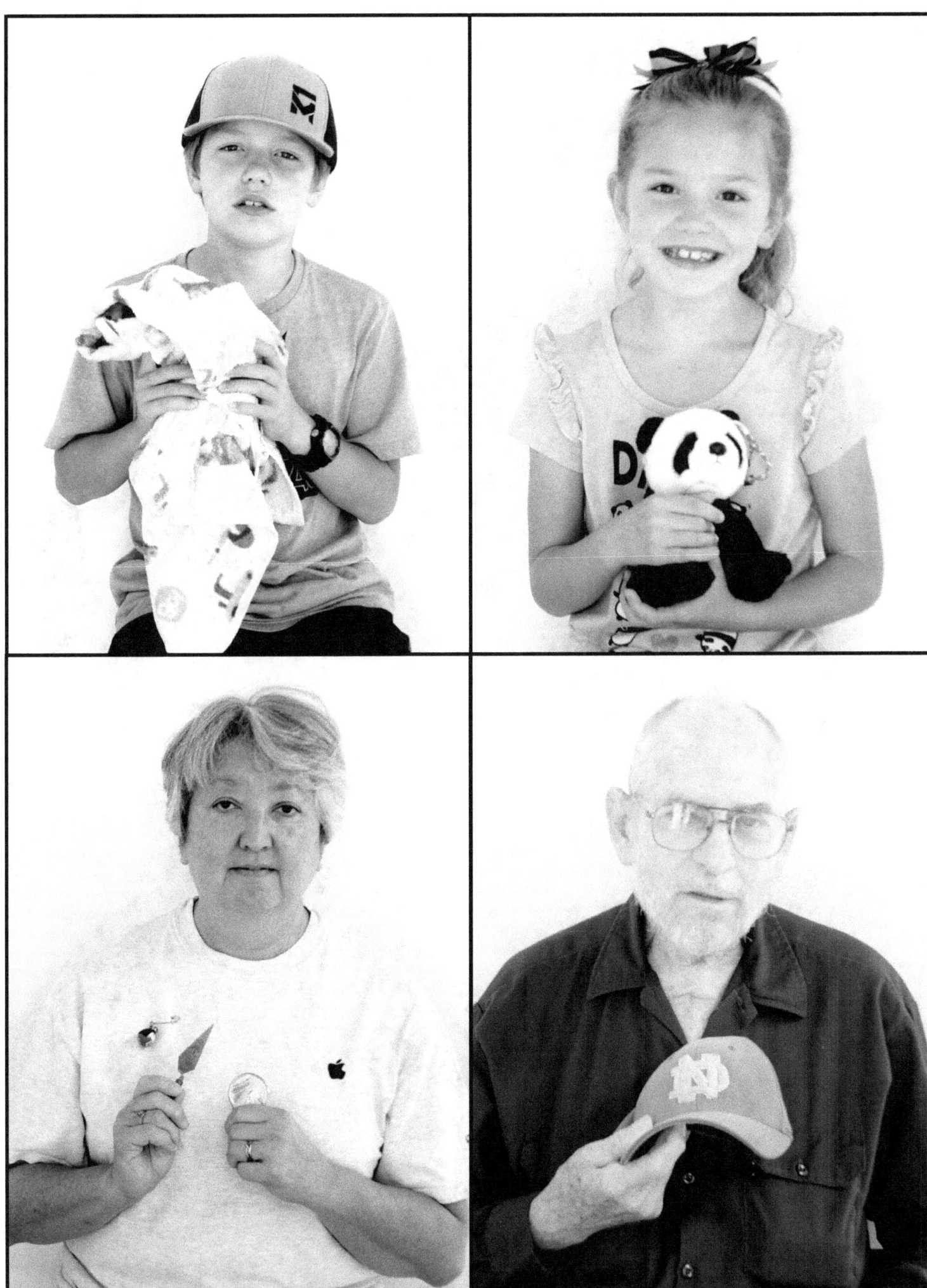

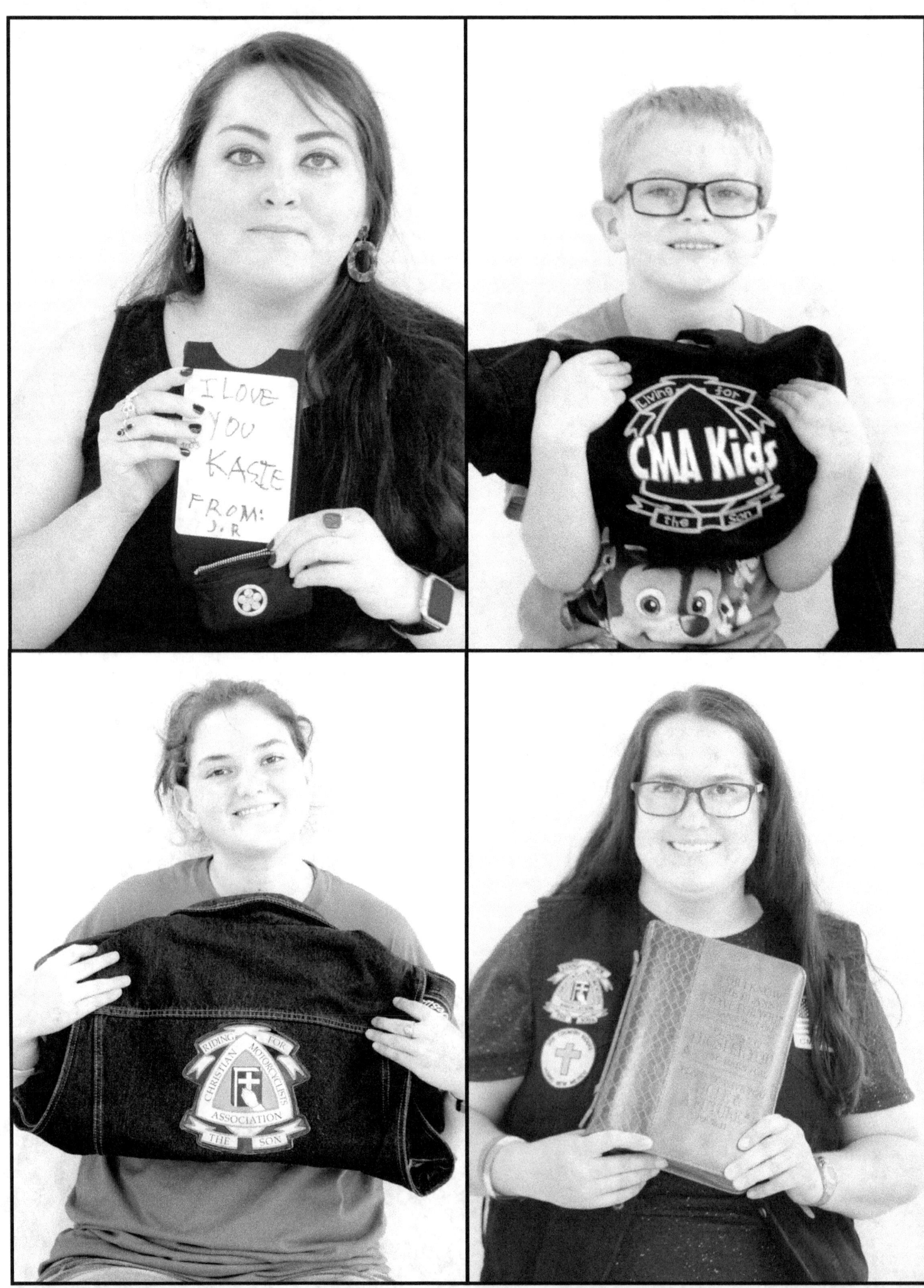

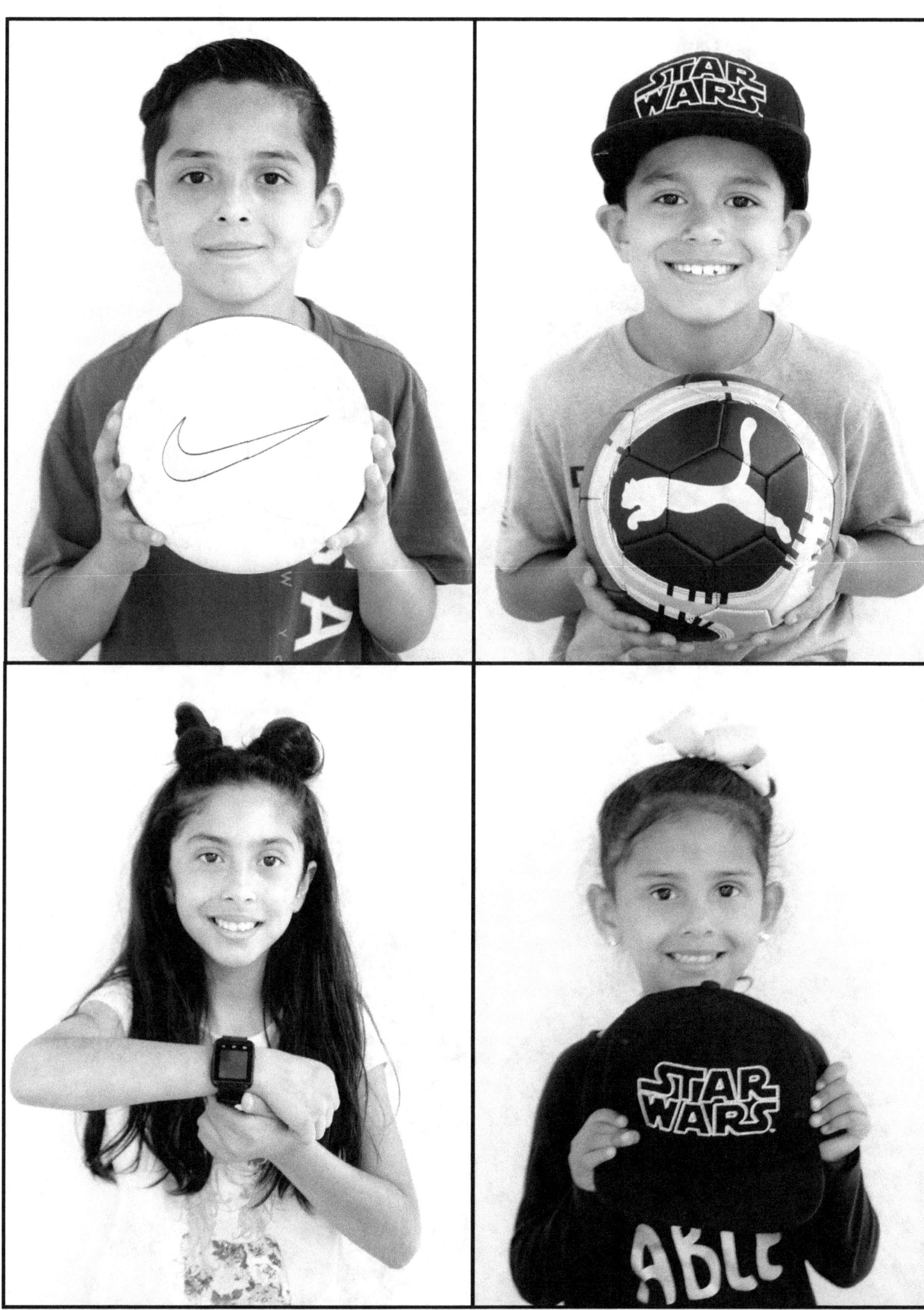

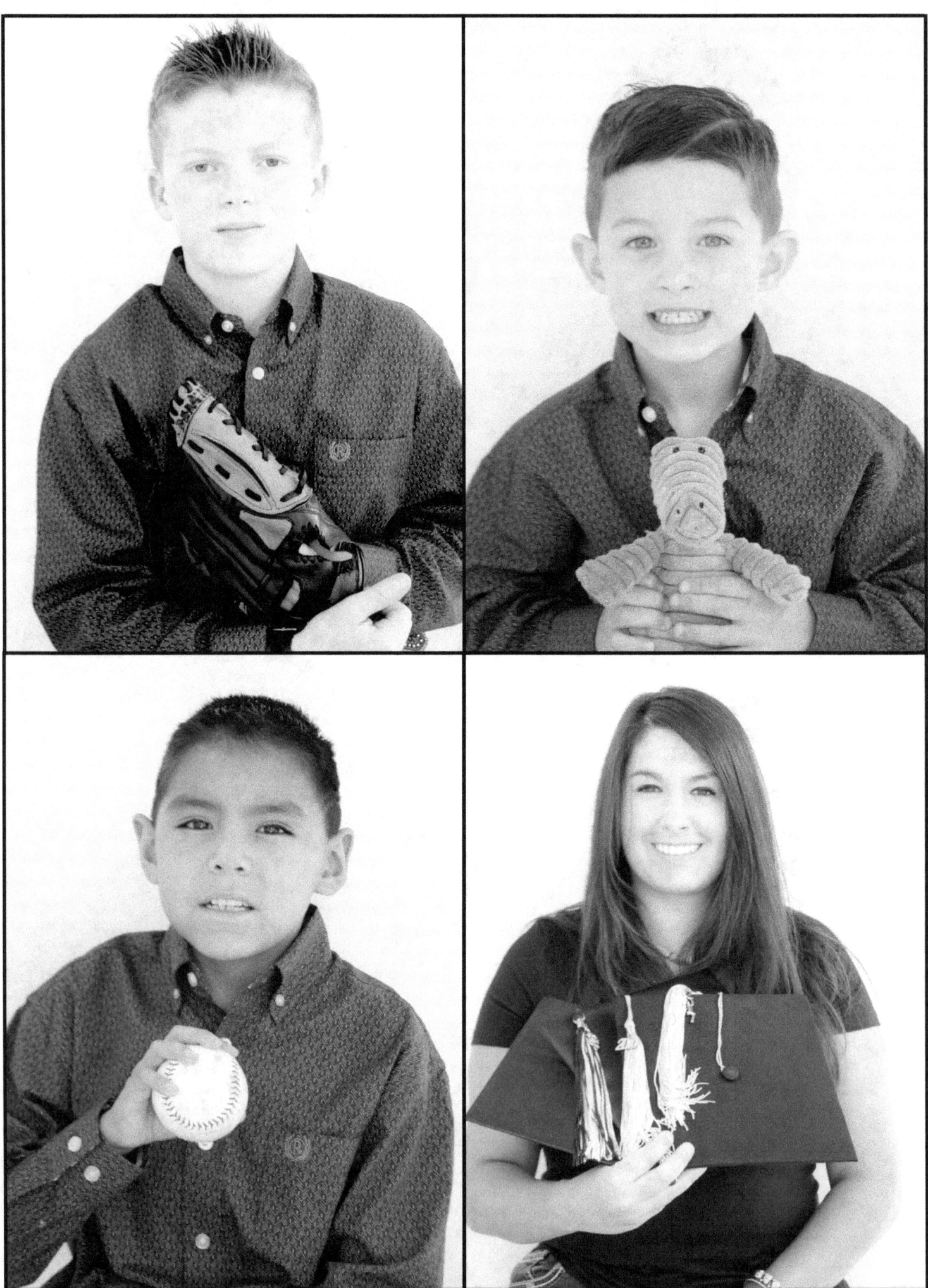

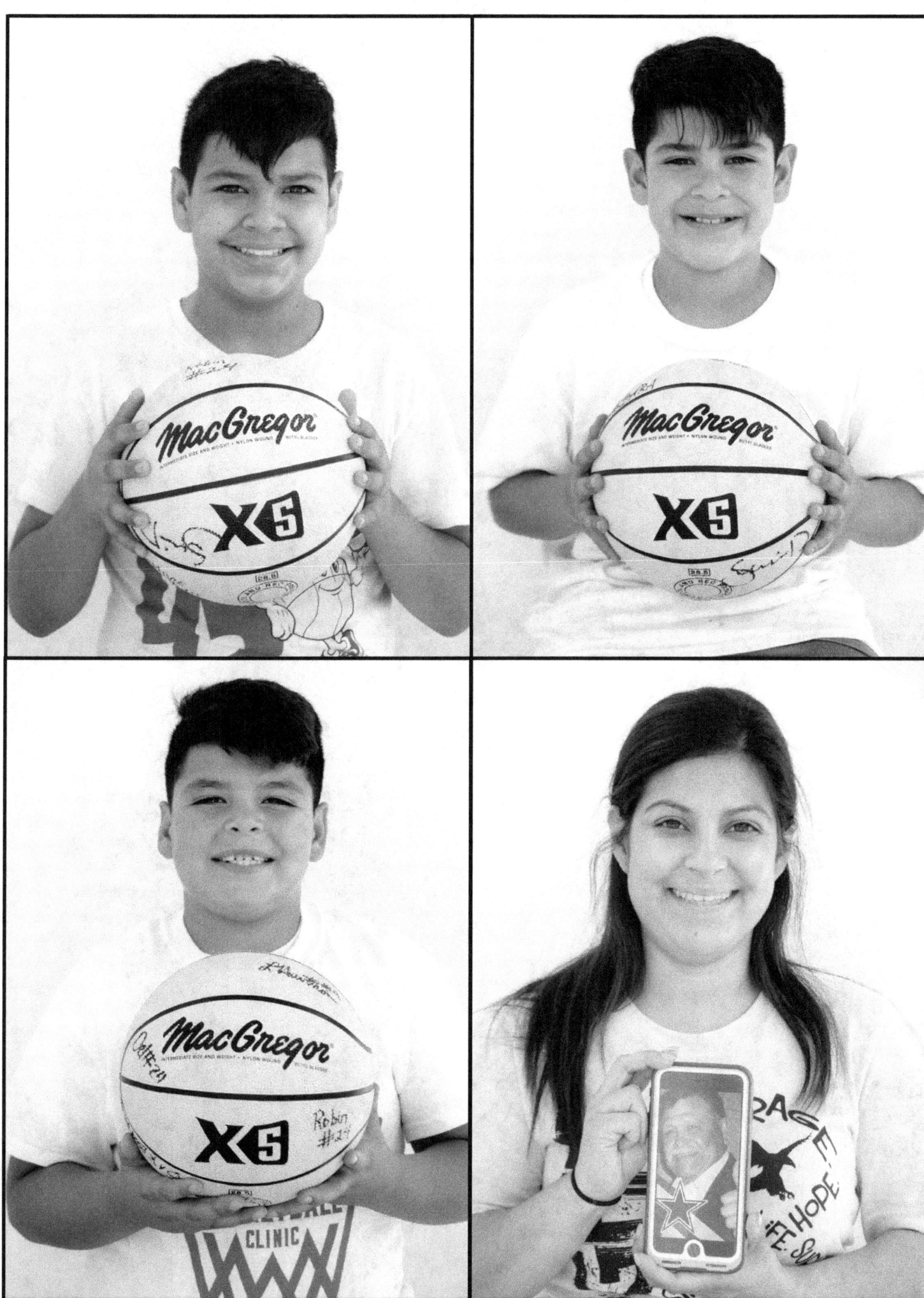

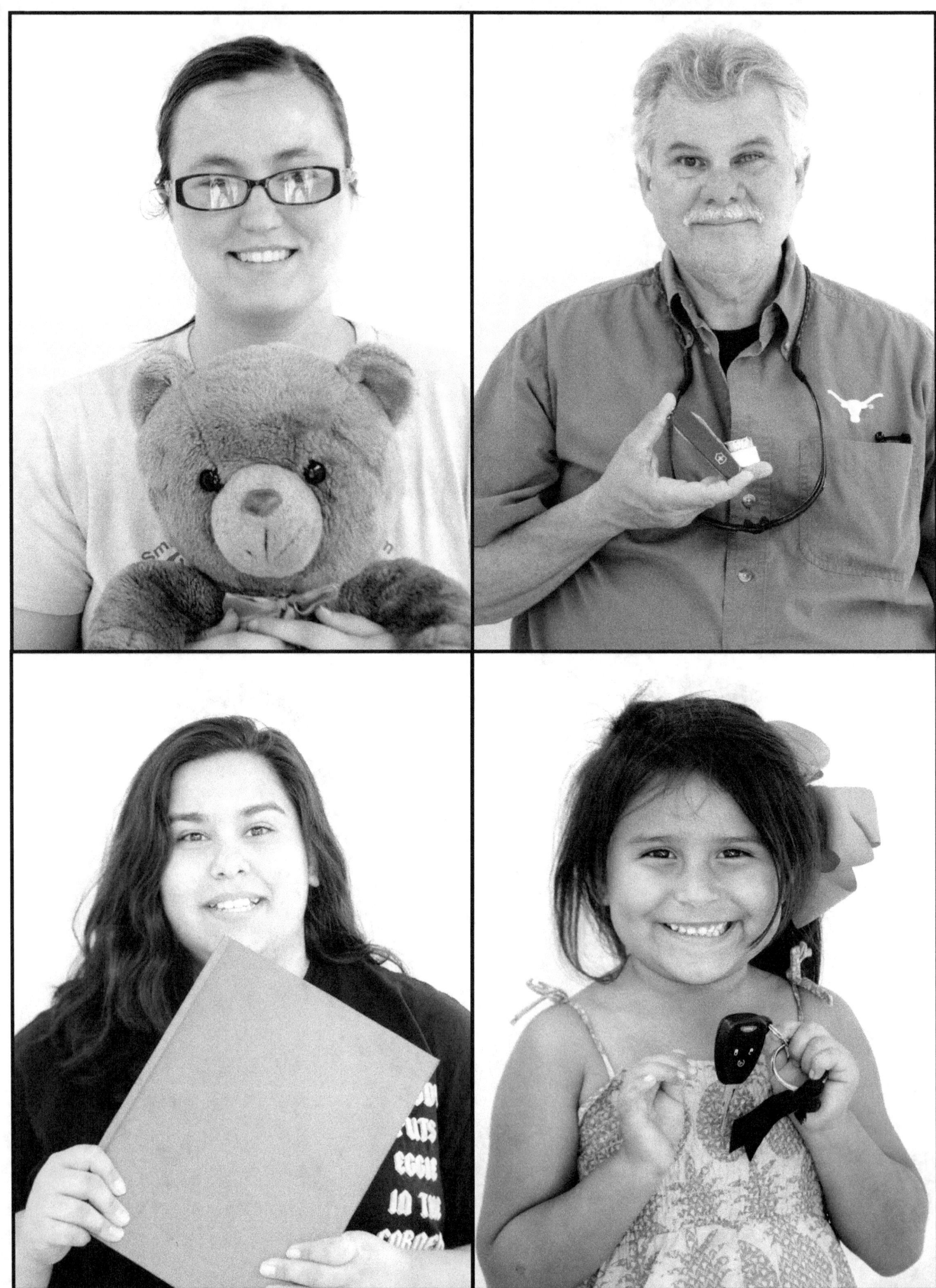

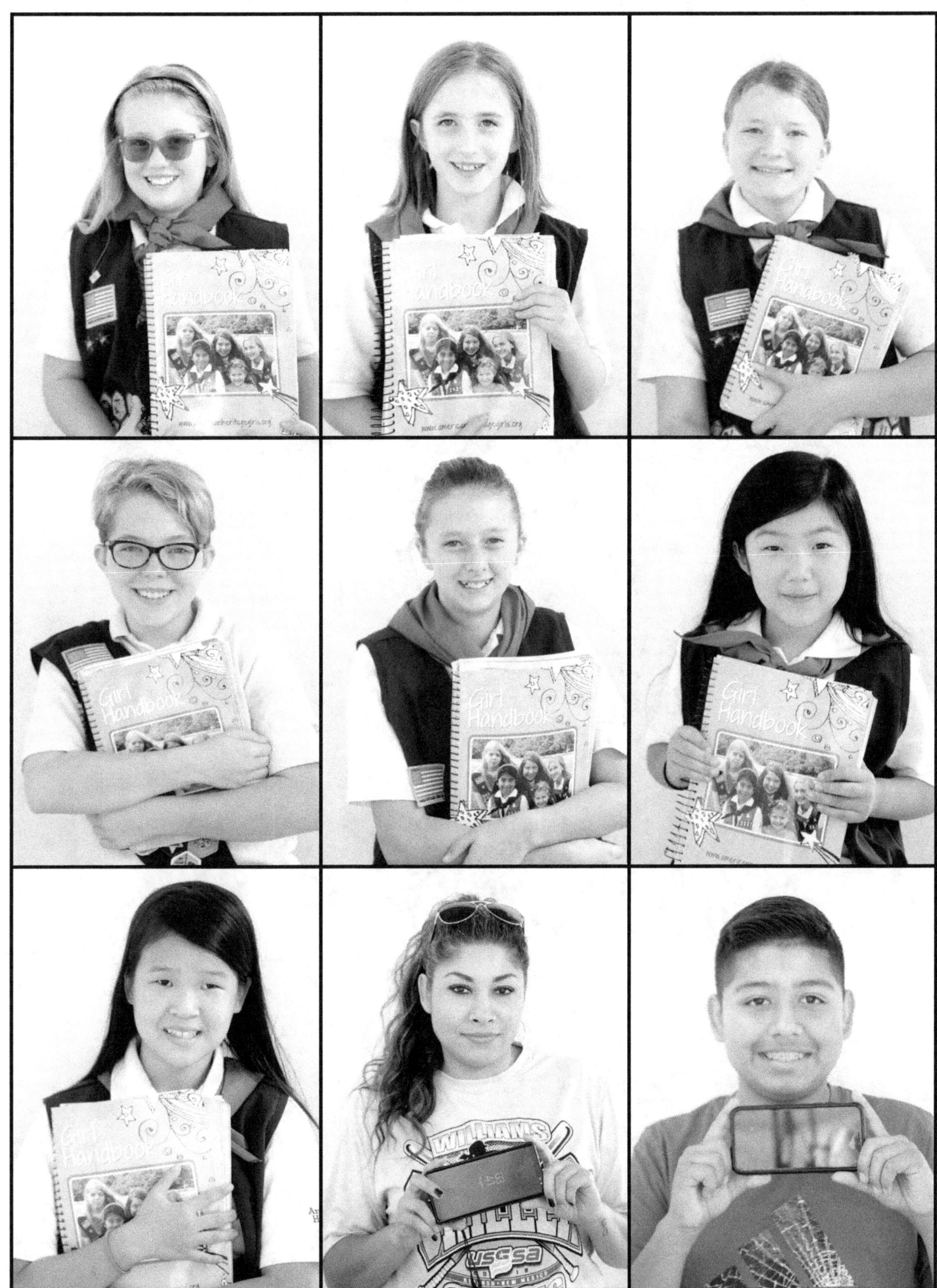

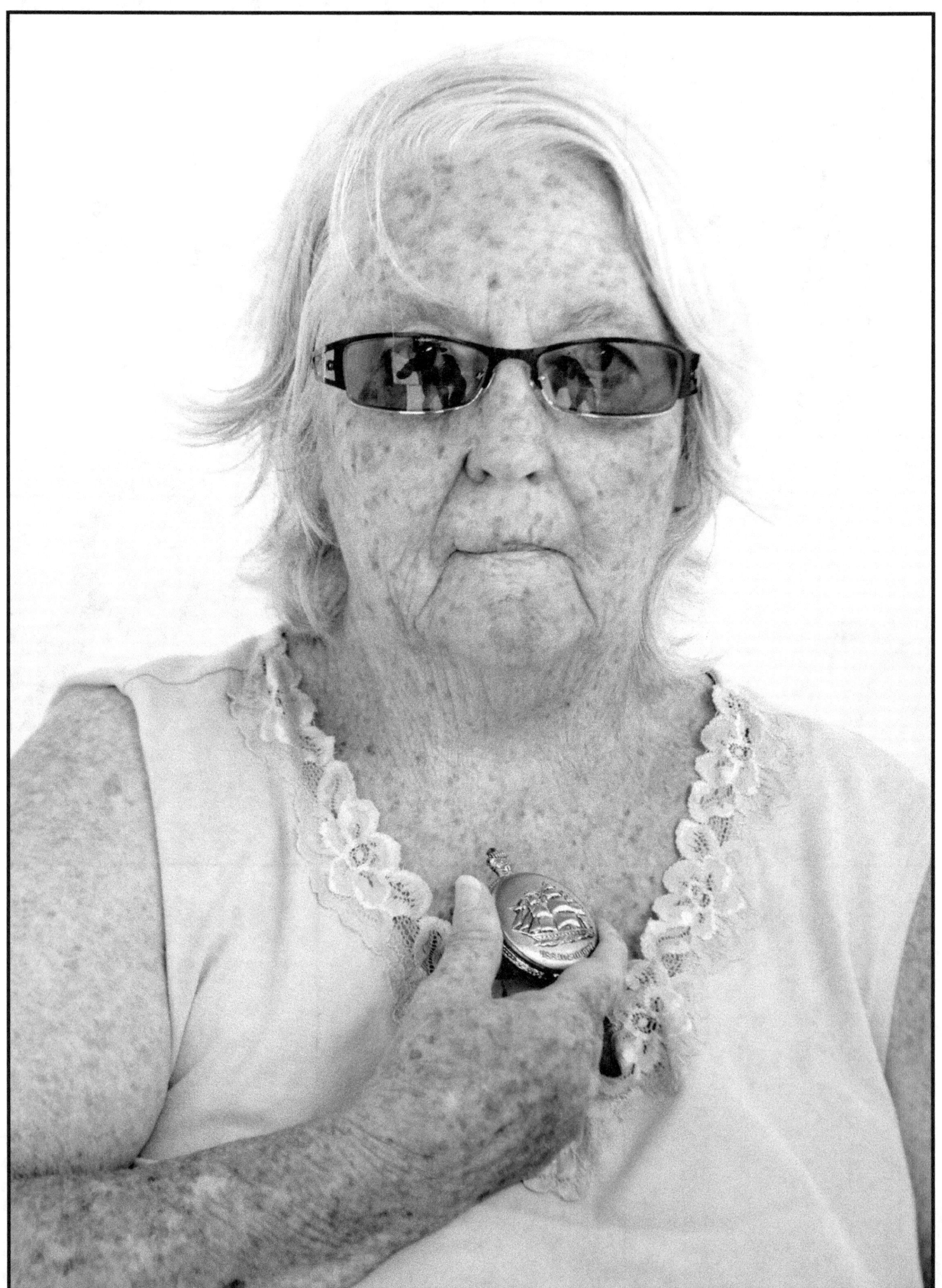

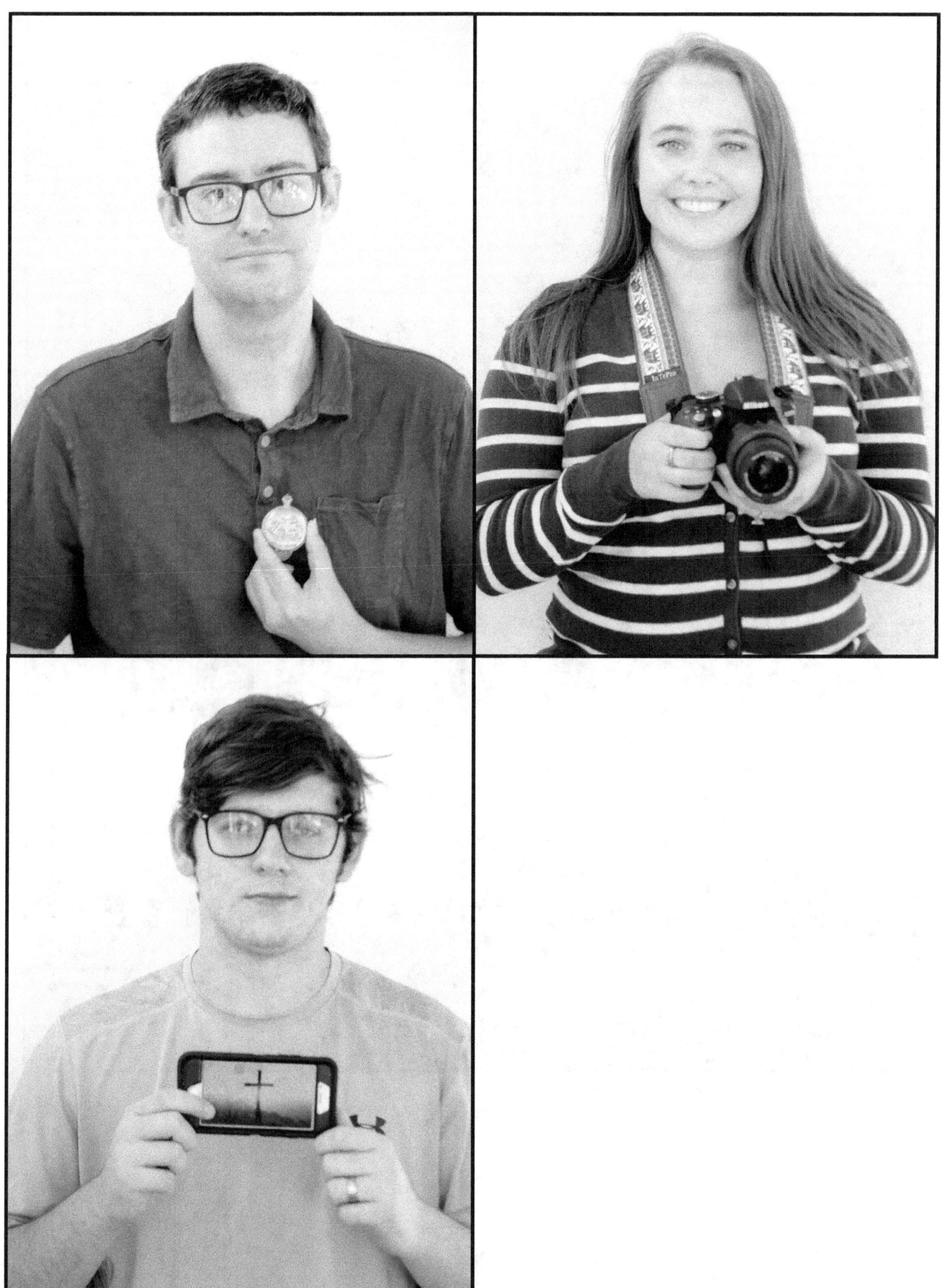

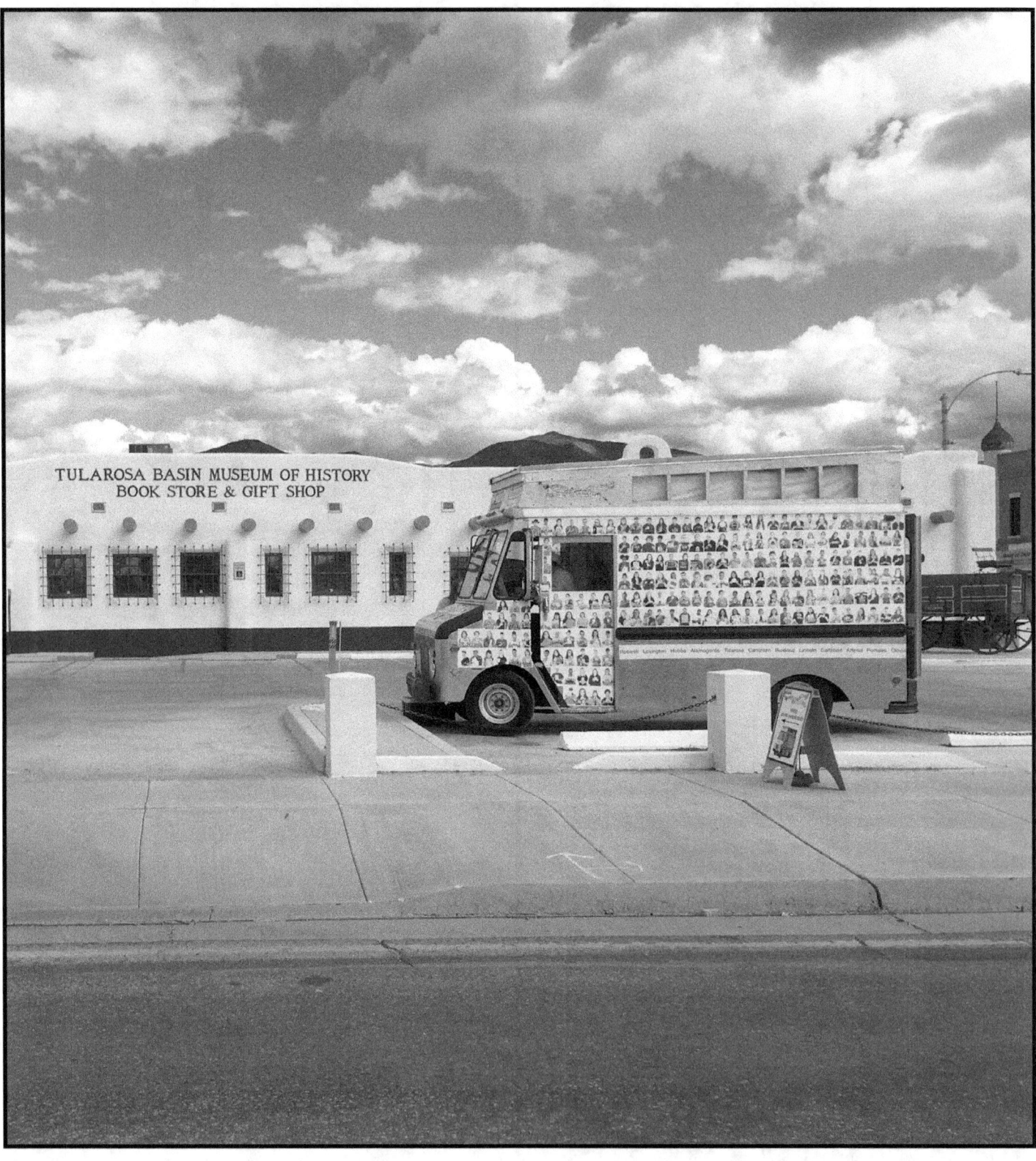

Alamogordo
October 14-15, 2019

Tularosa Basin Museum of History
New Mexico State University
Twice Blest Community Thrift Store

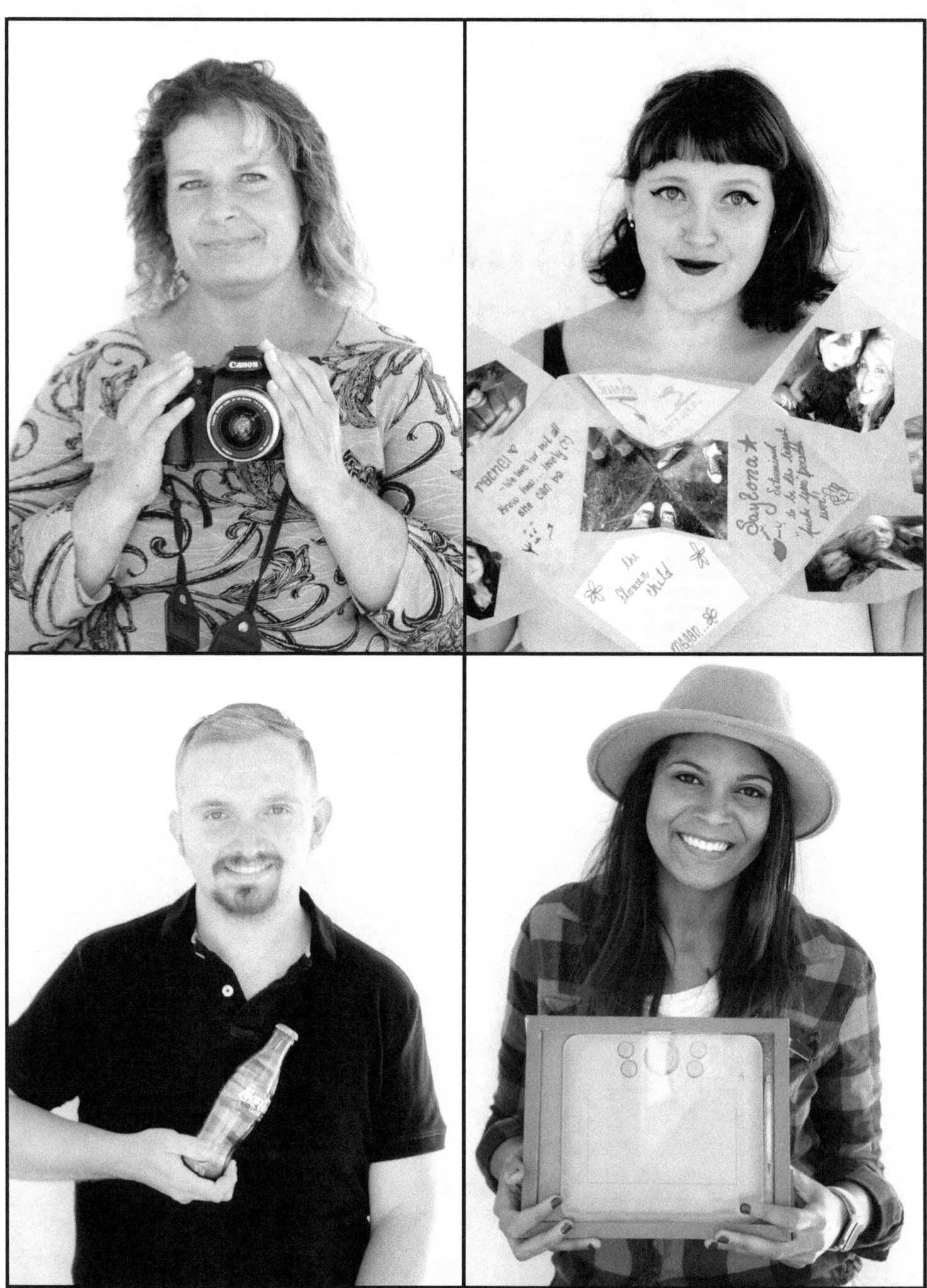

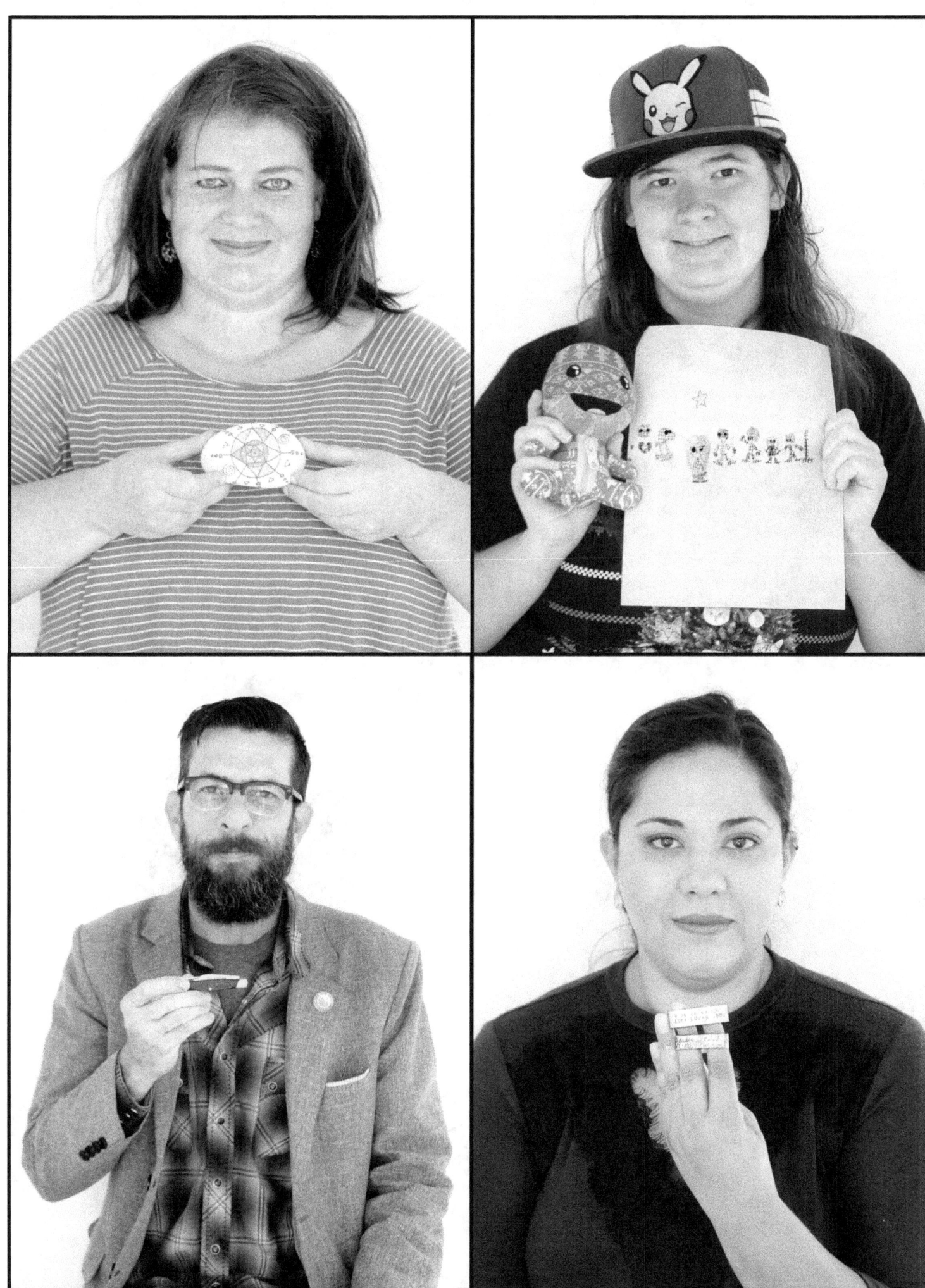

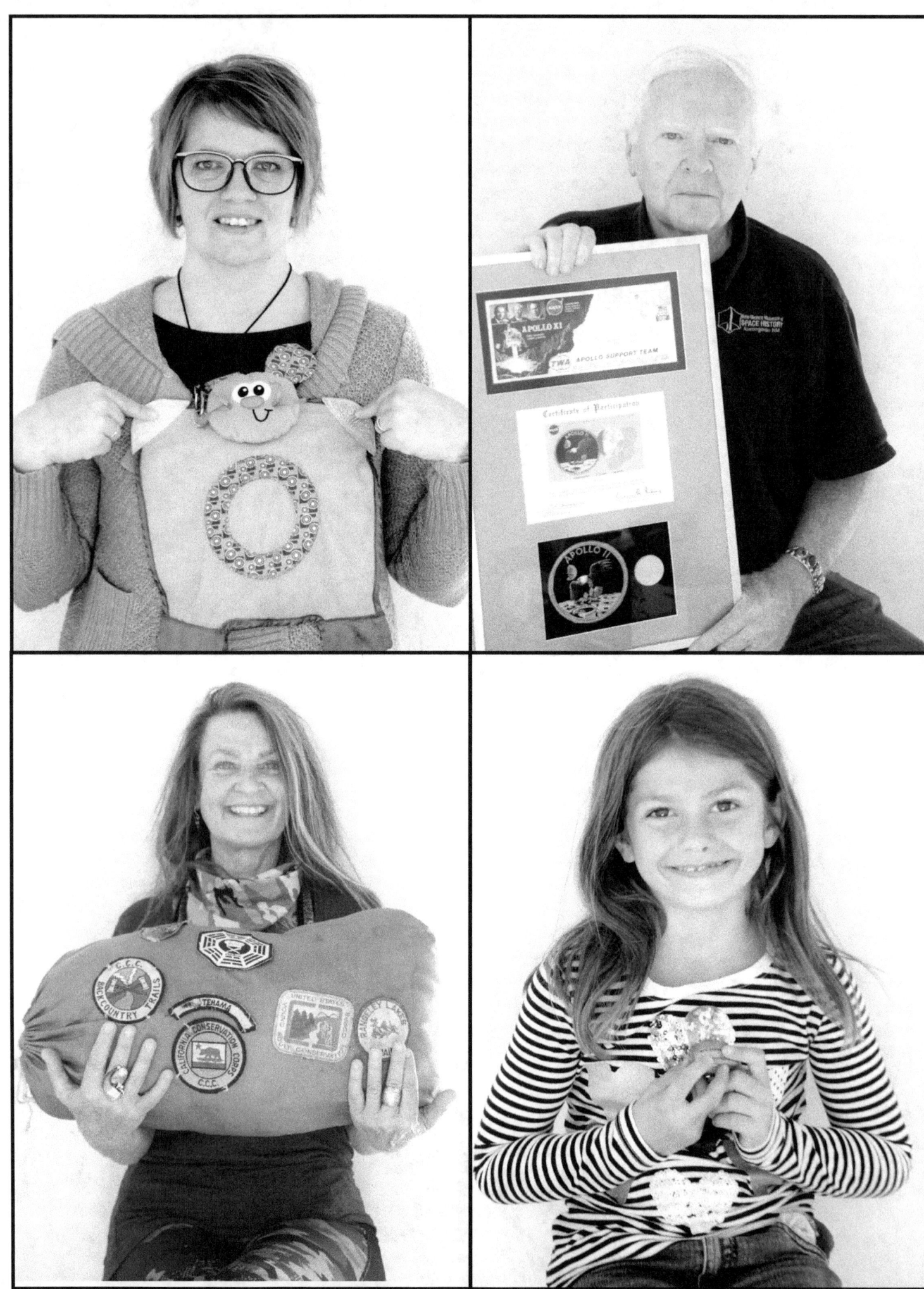

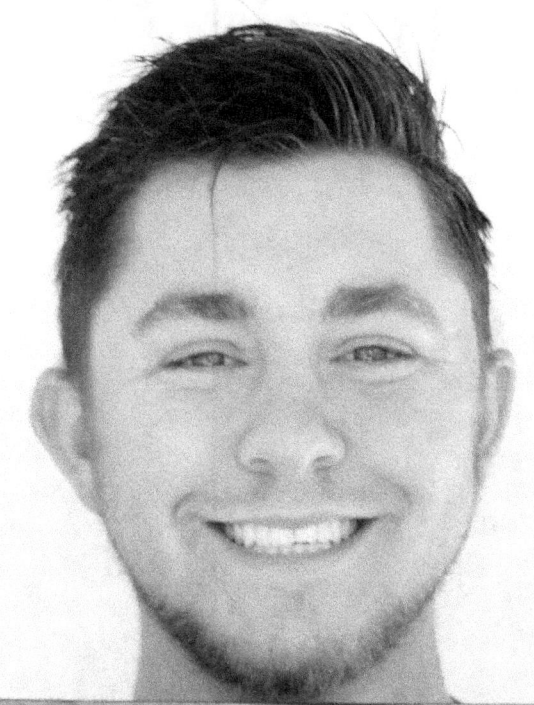
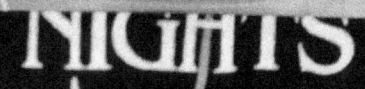

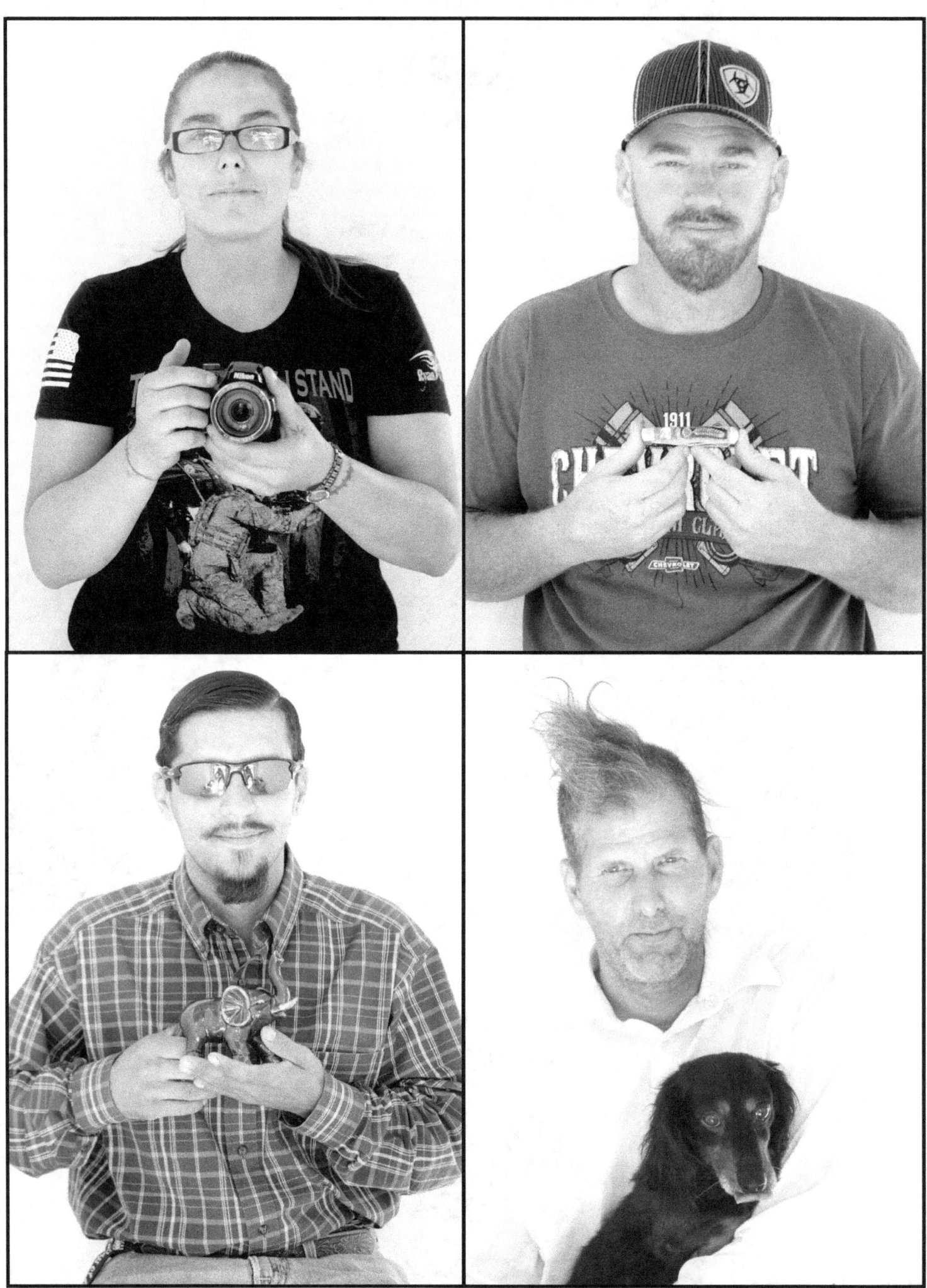

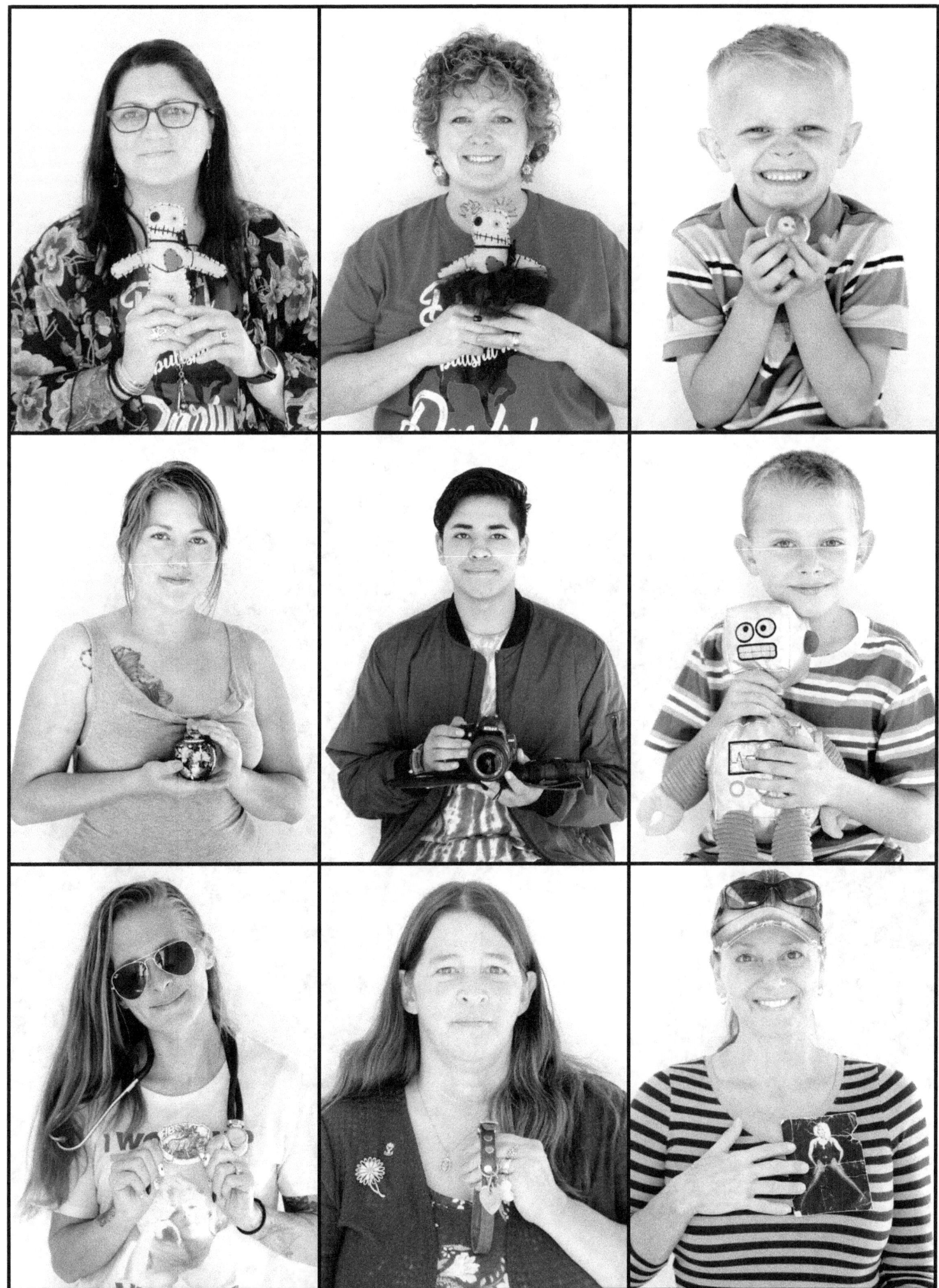

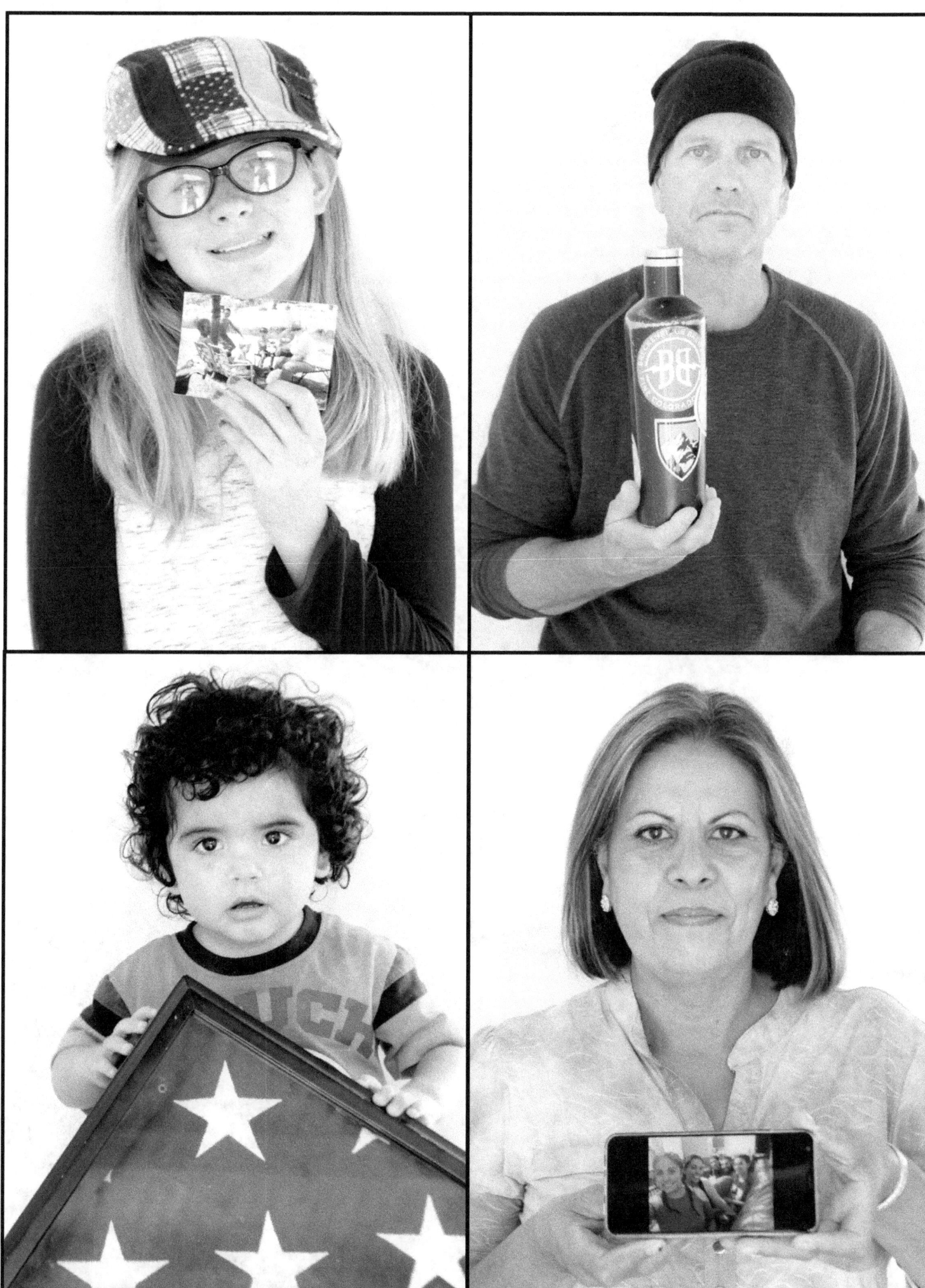

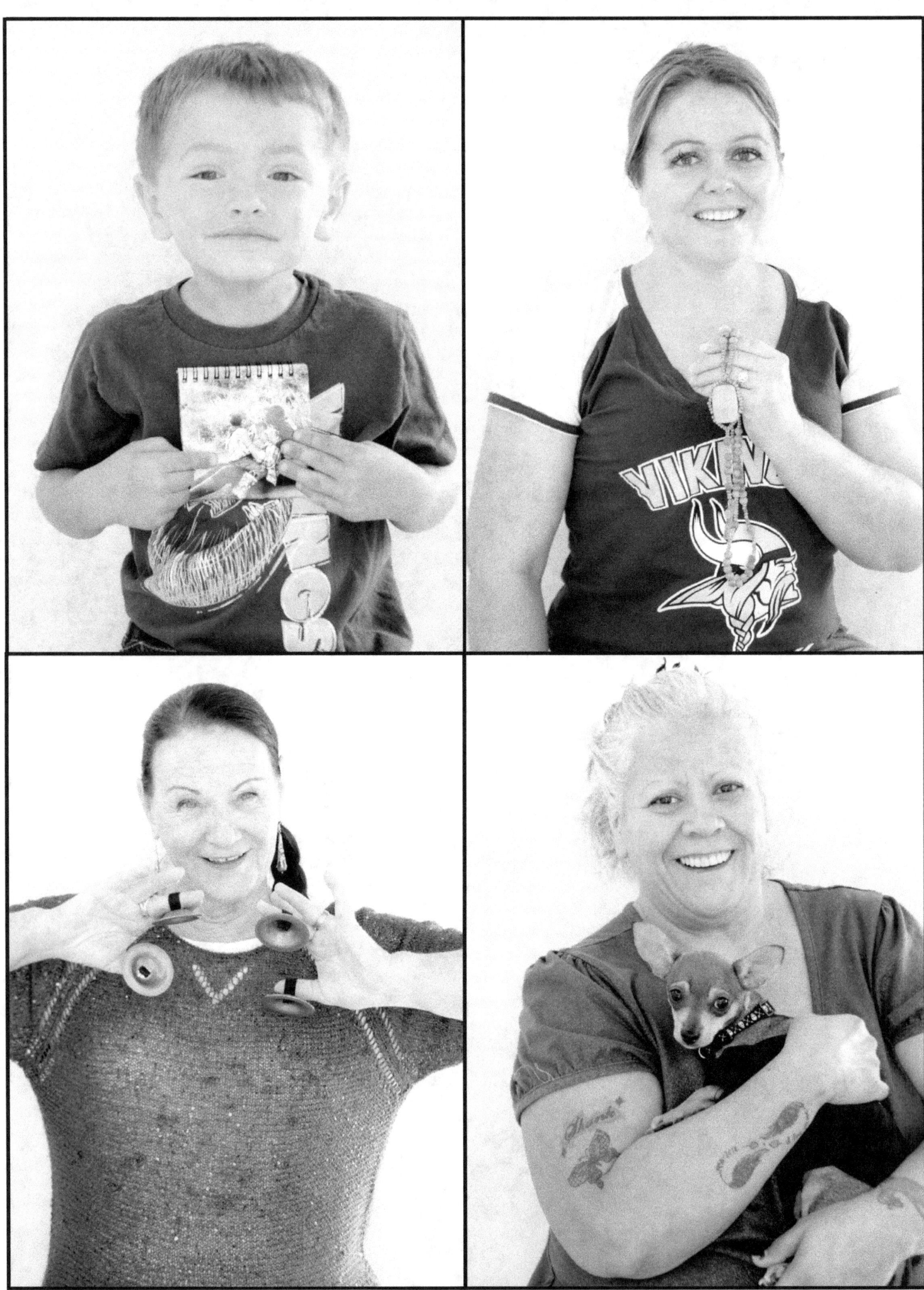

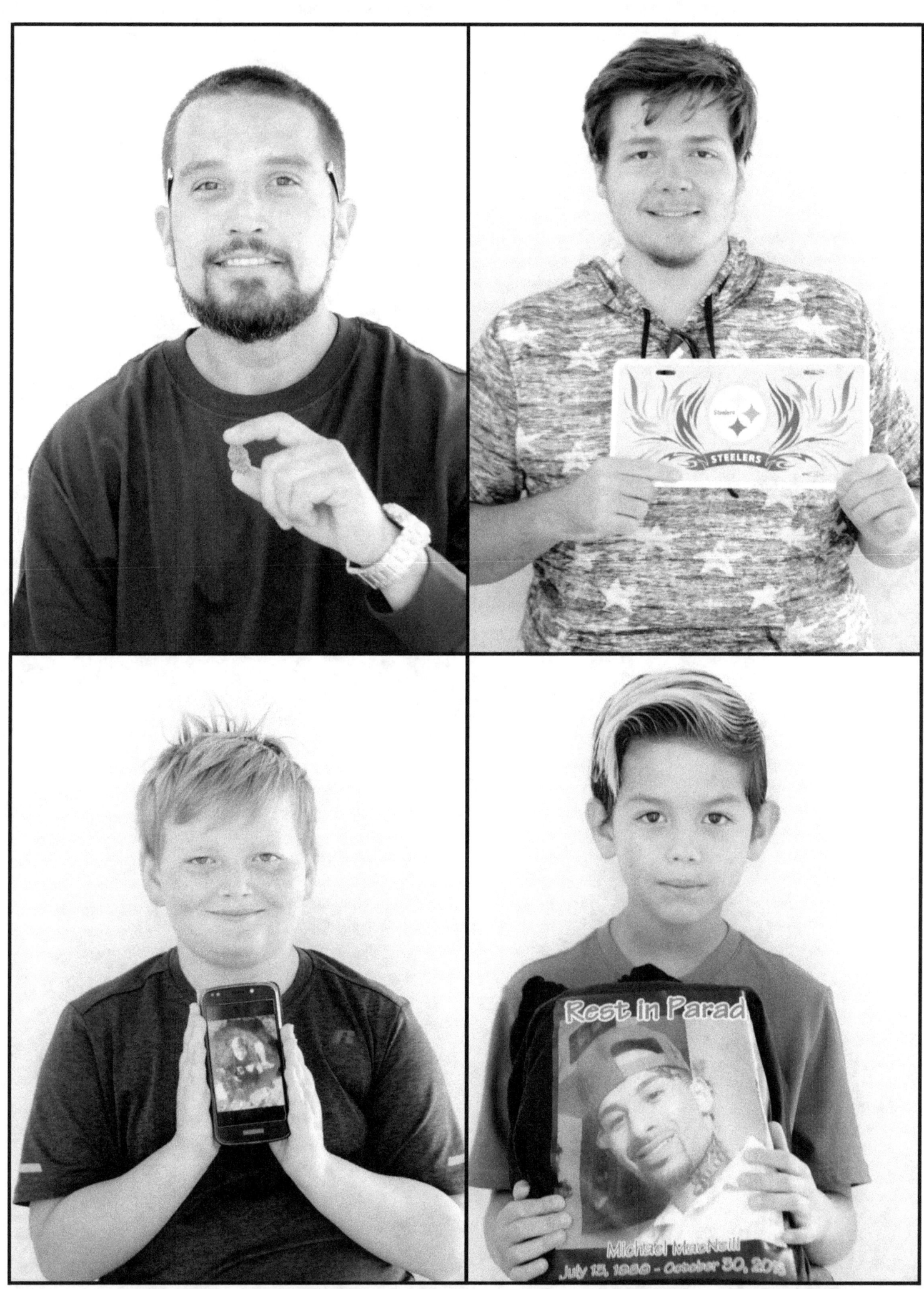

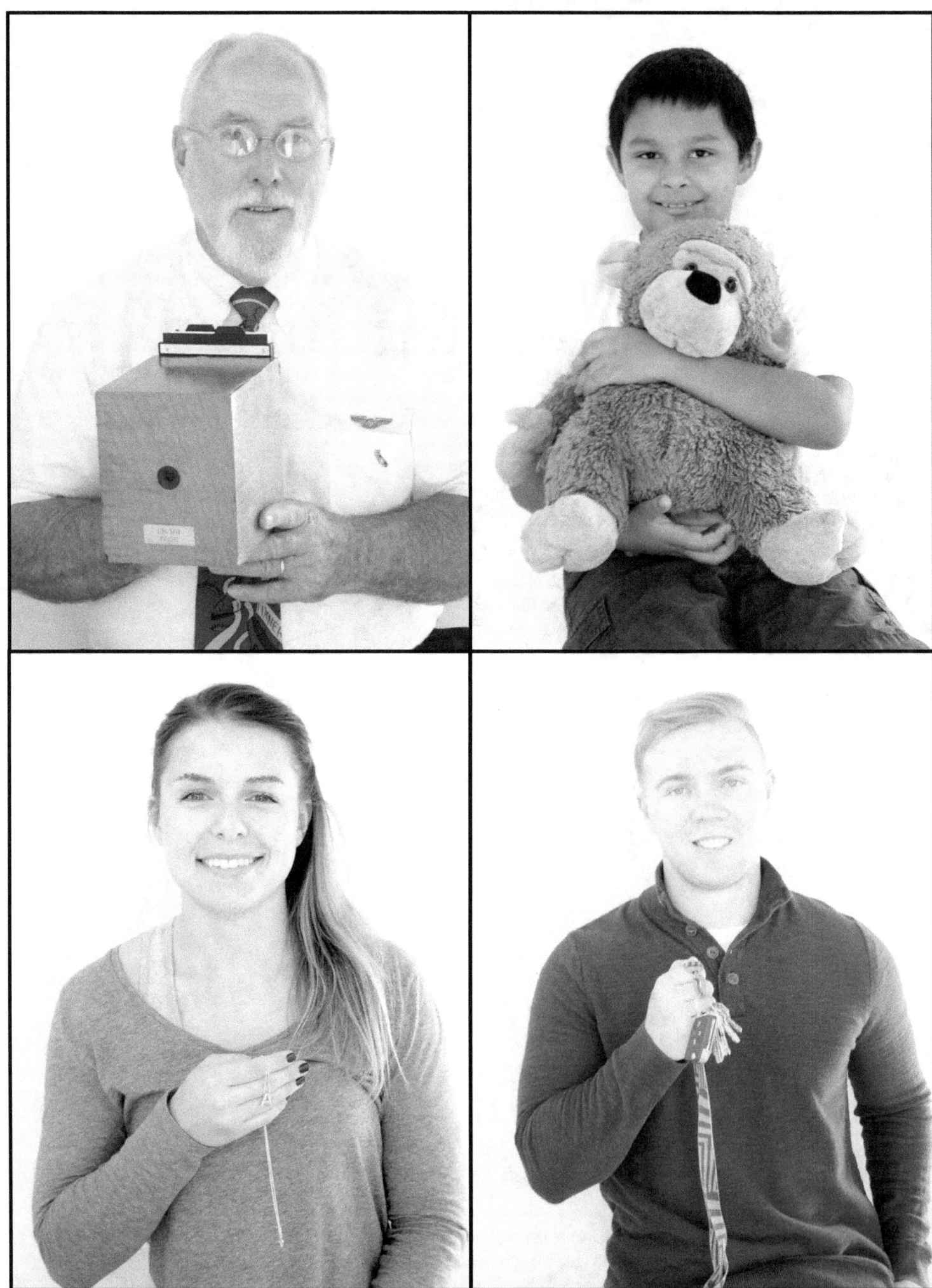

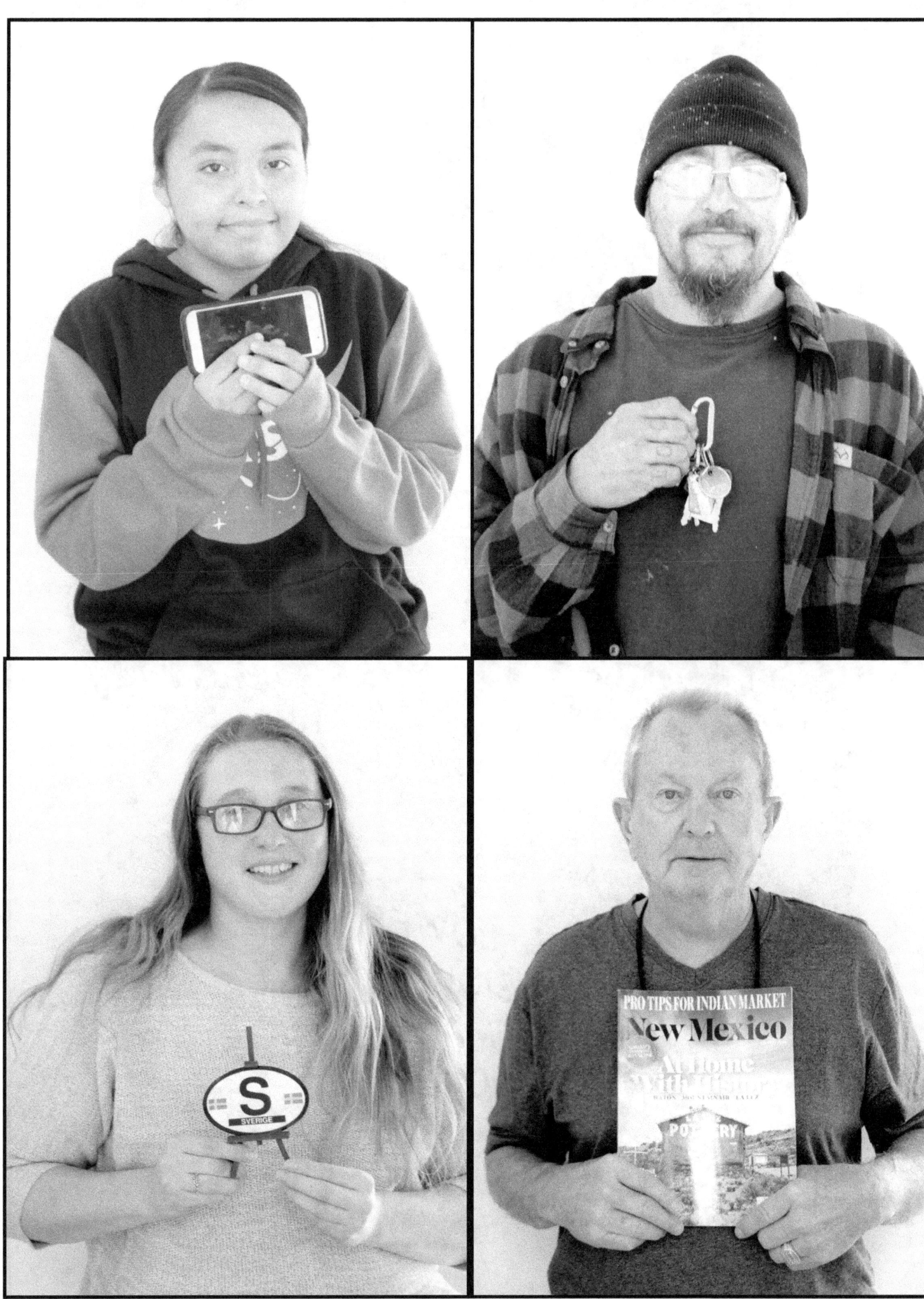

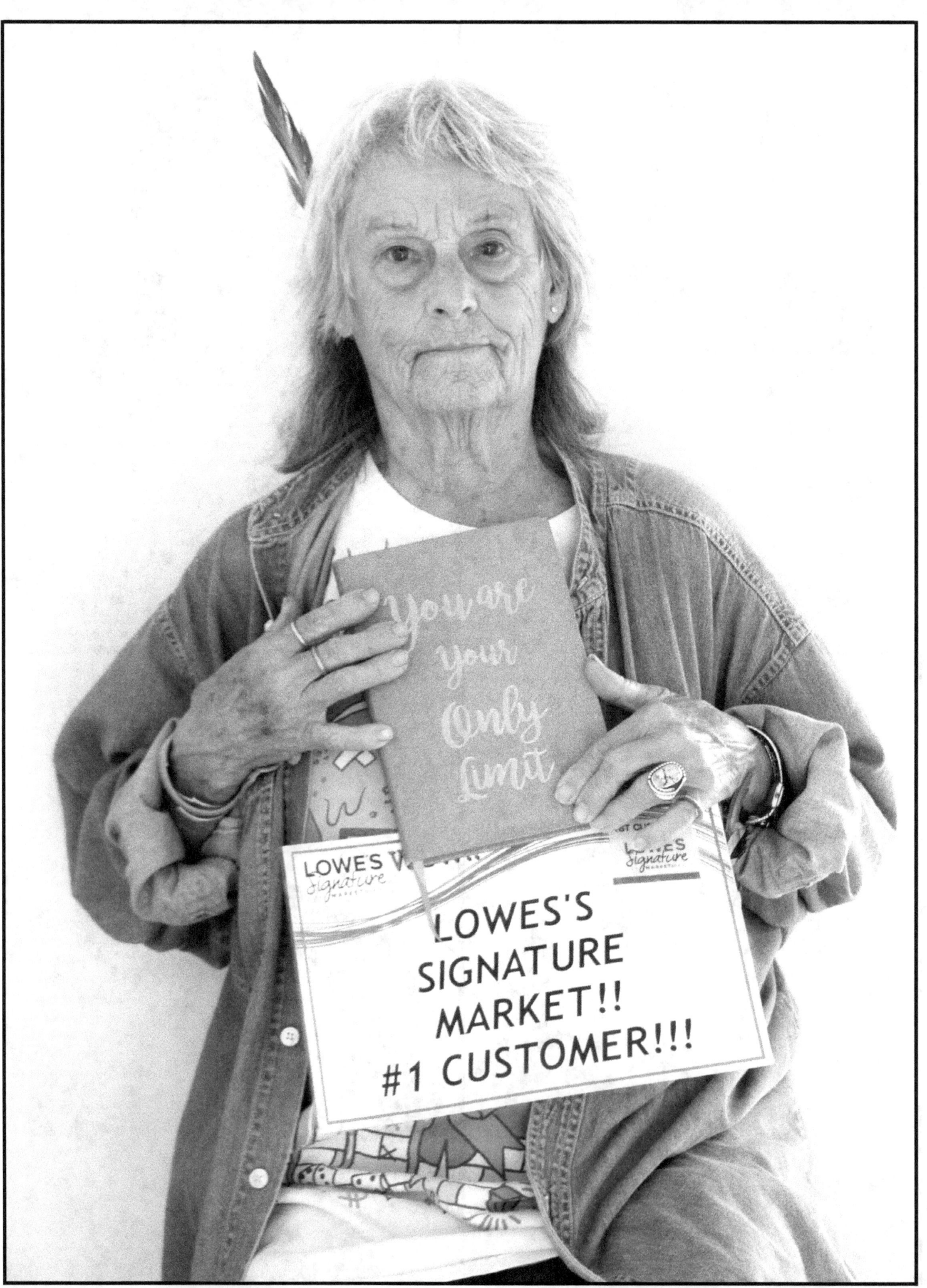

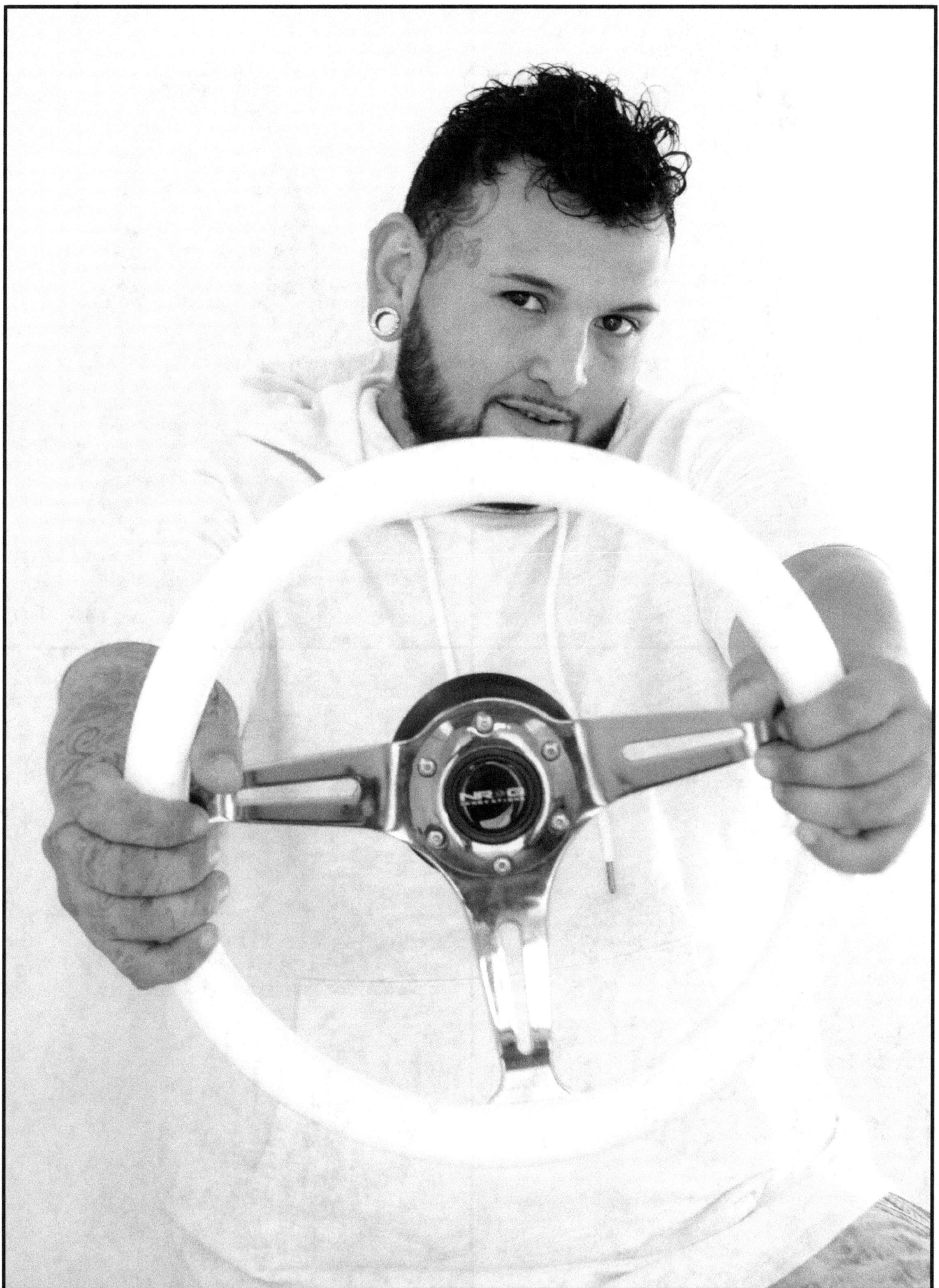

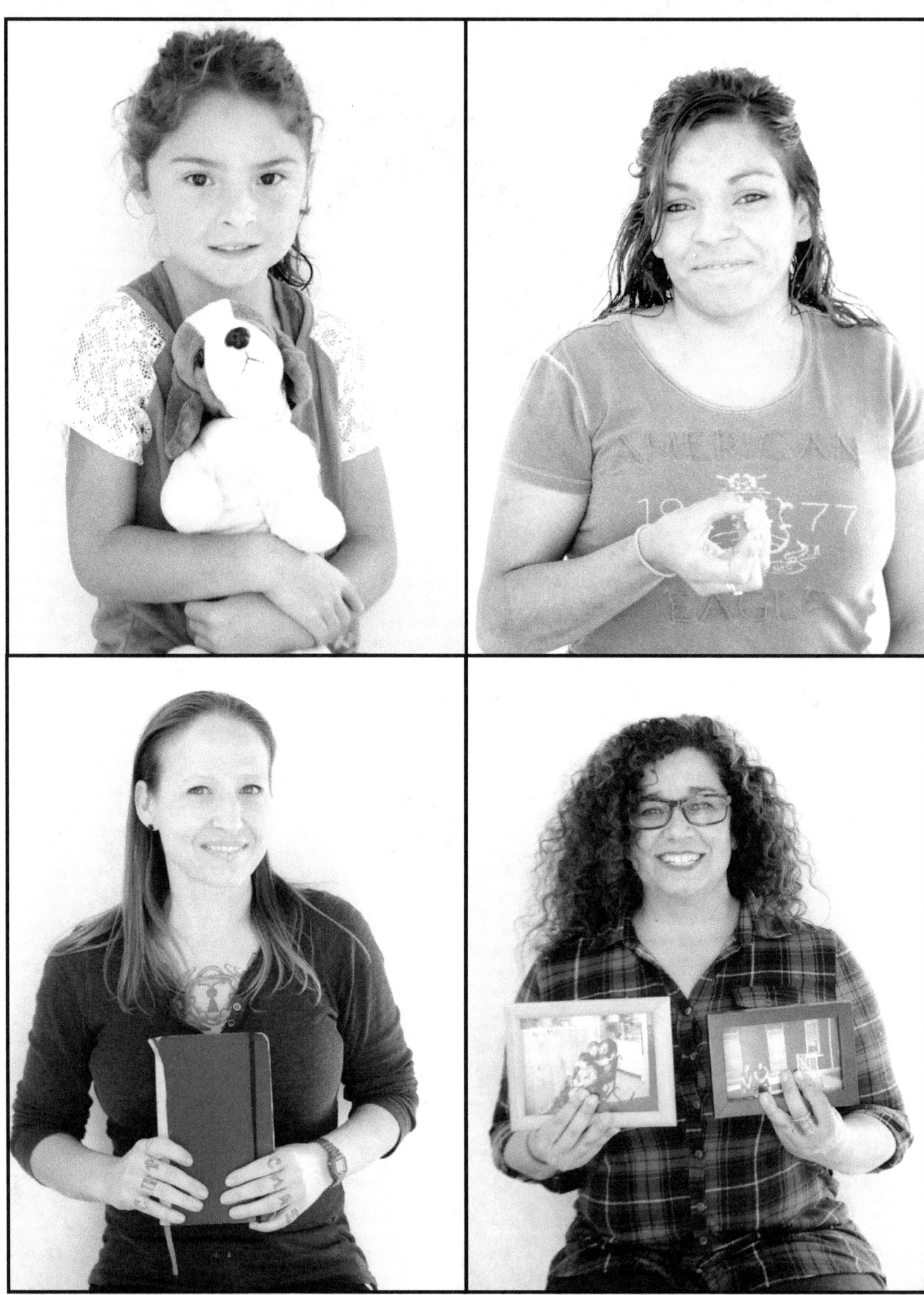

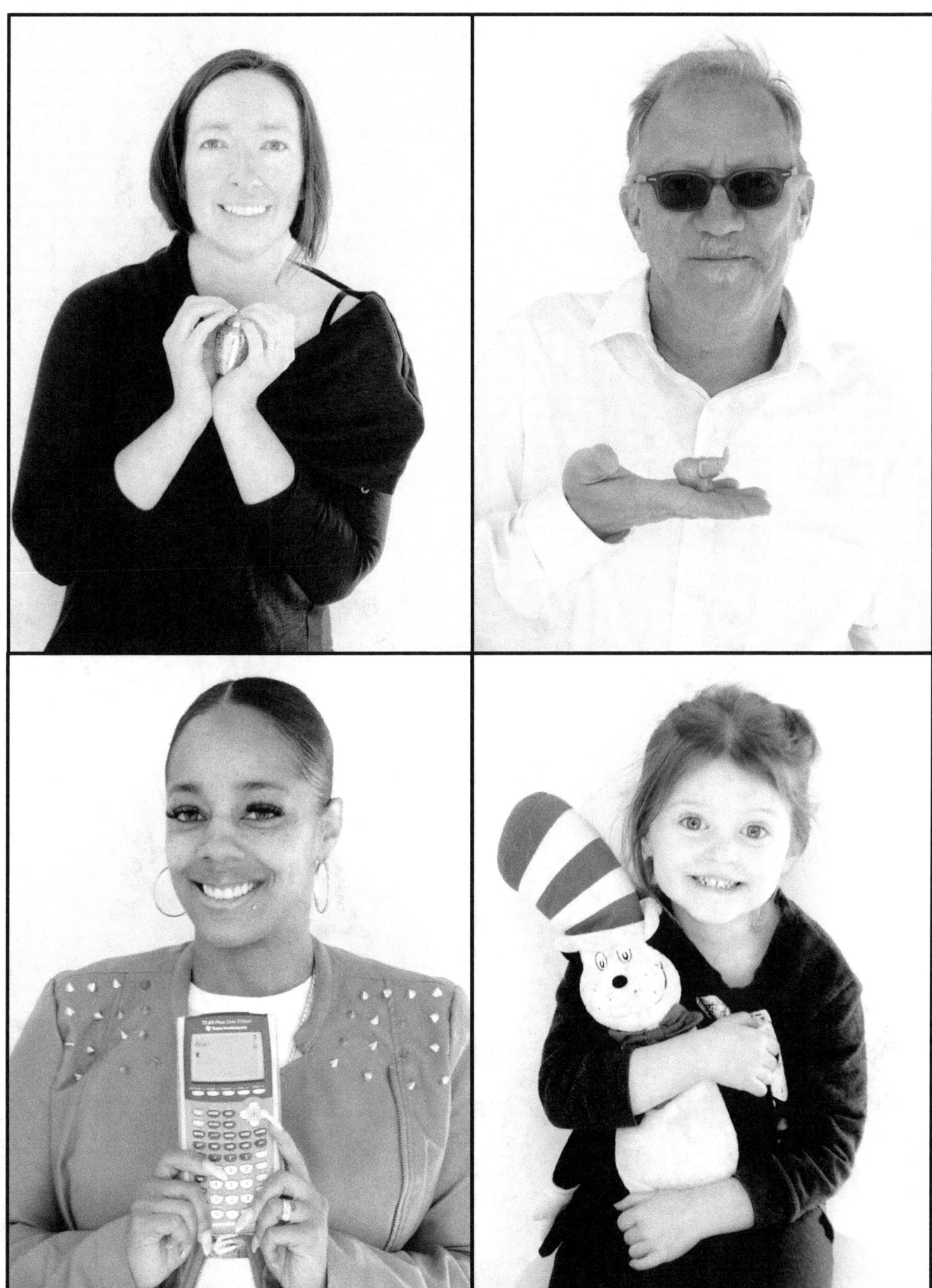

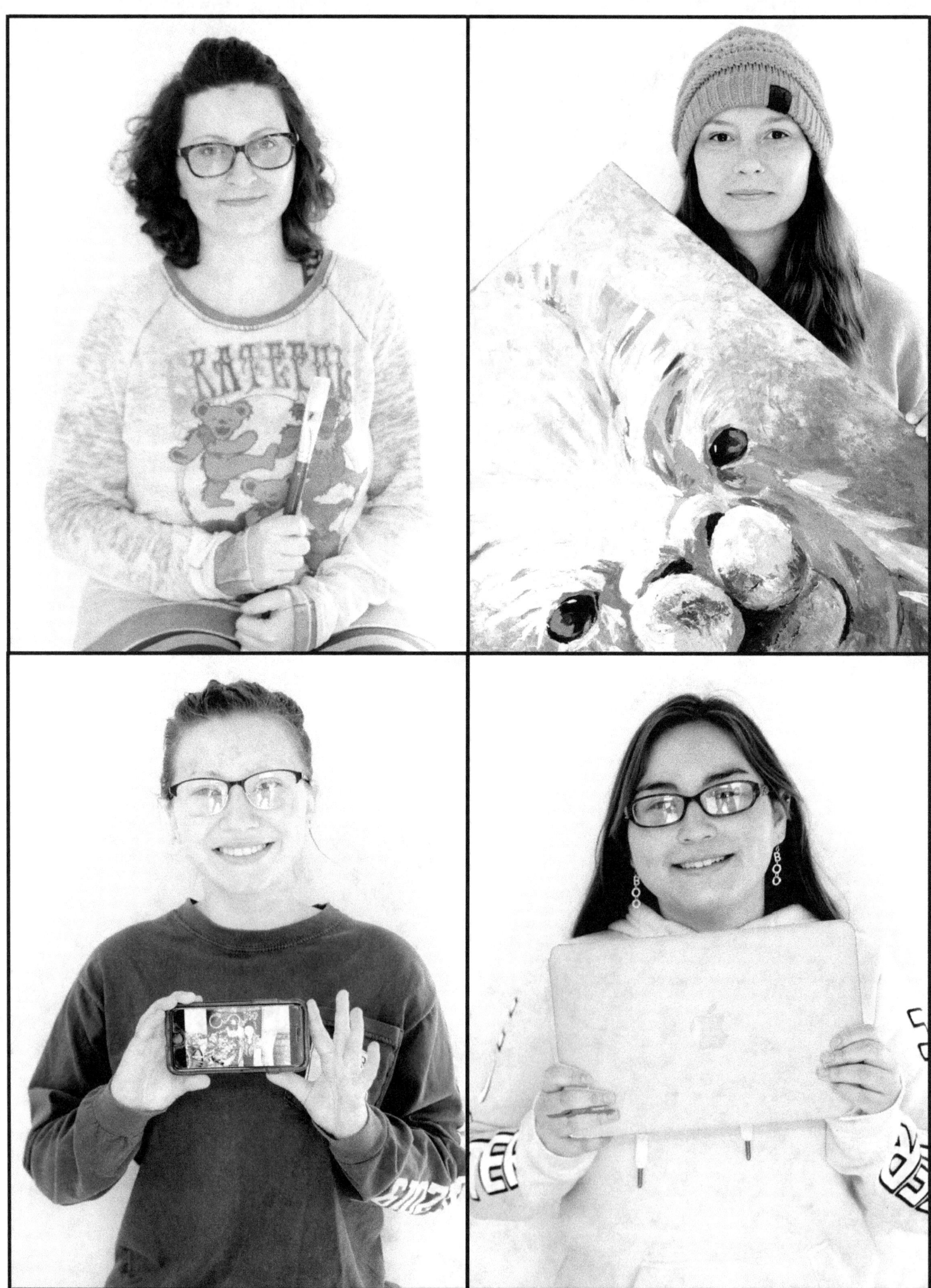

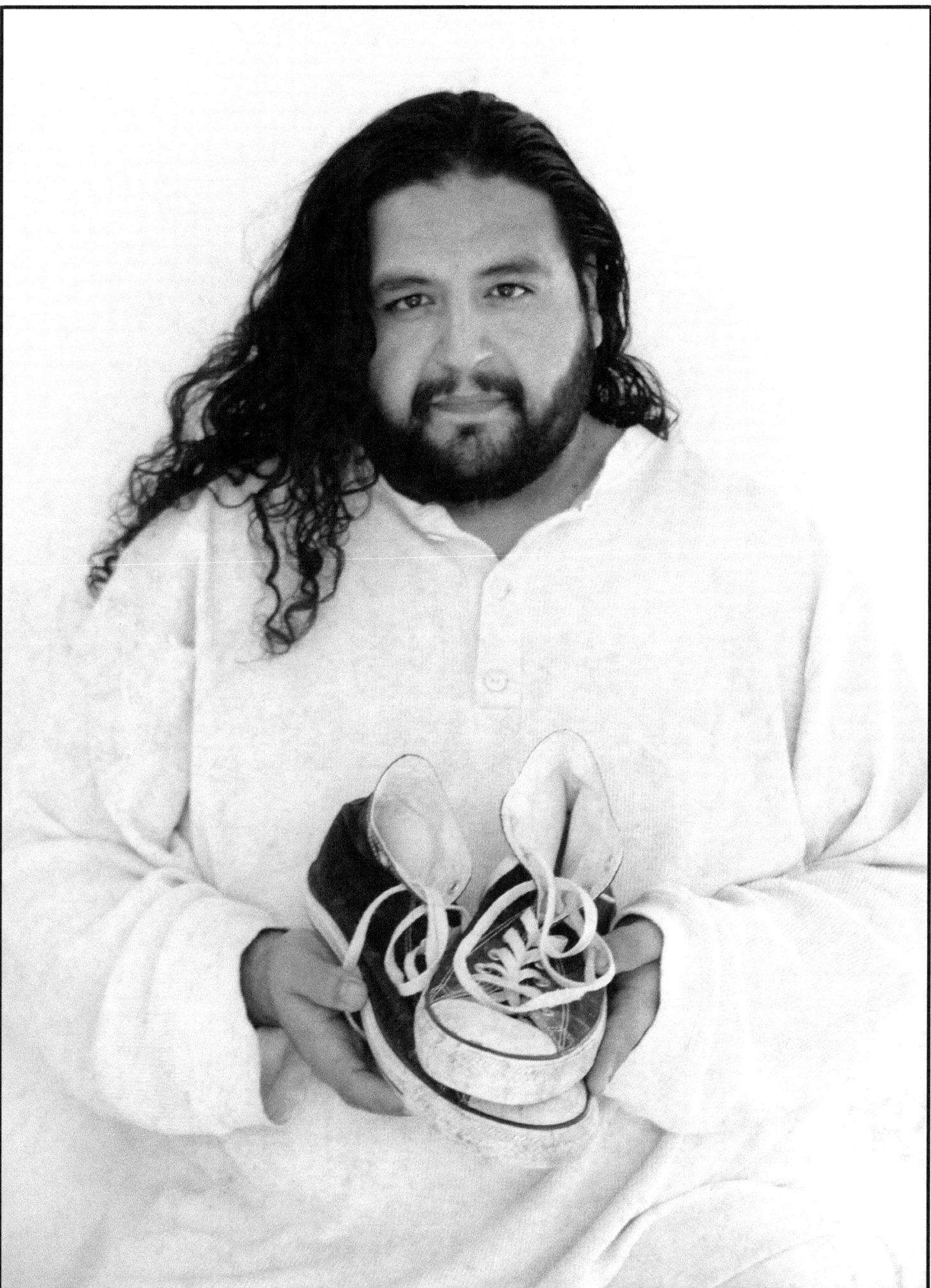

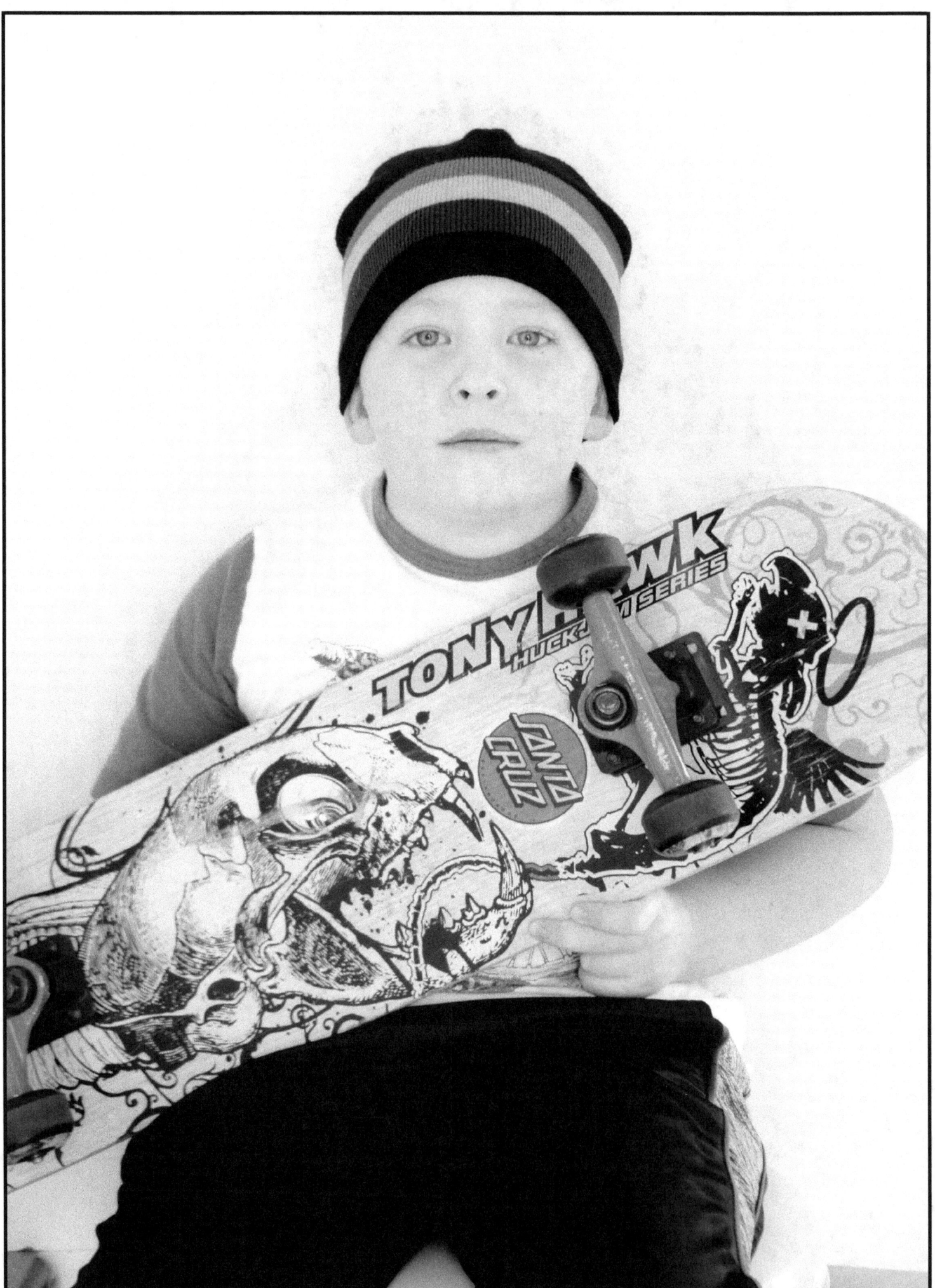

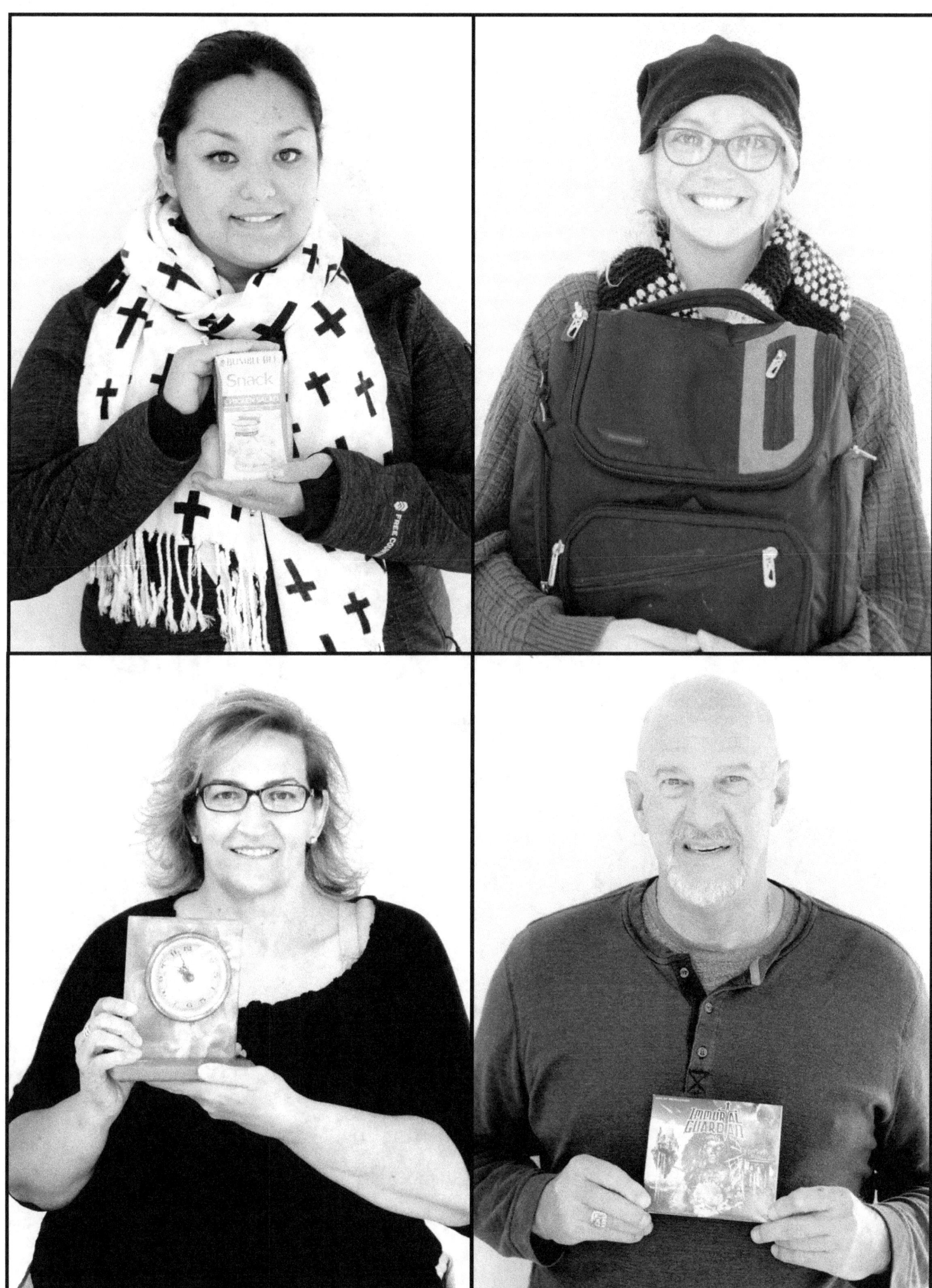

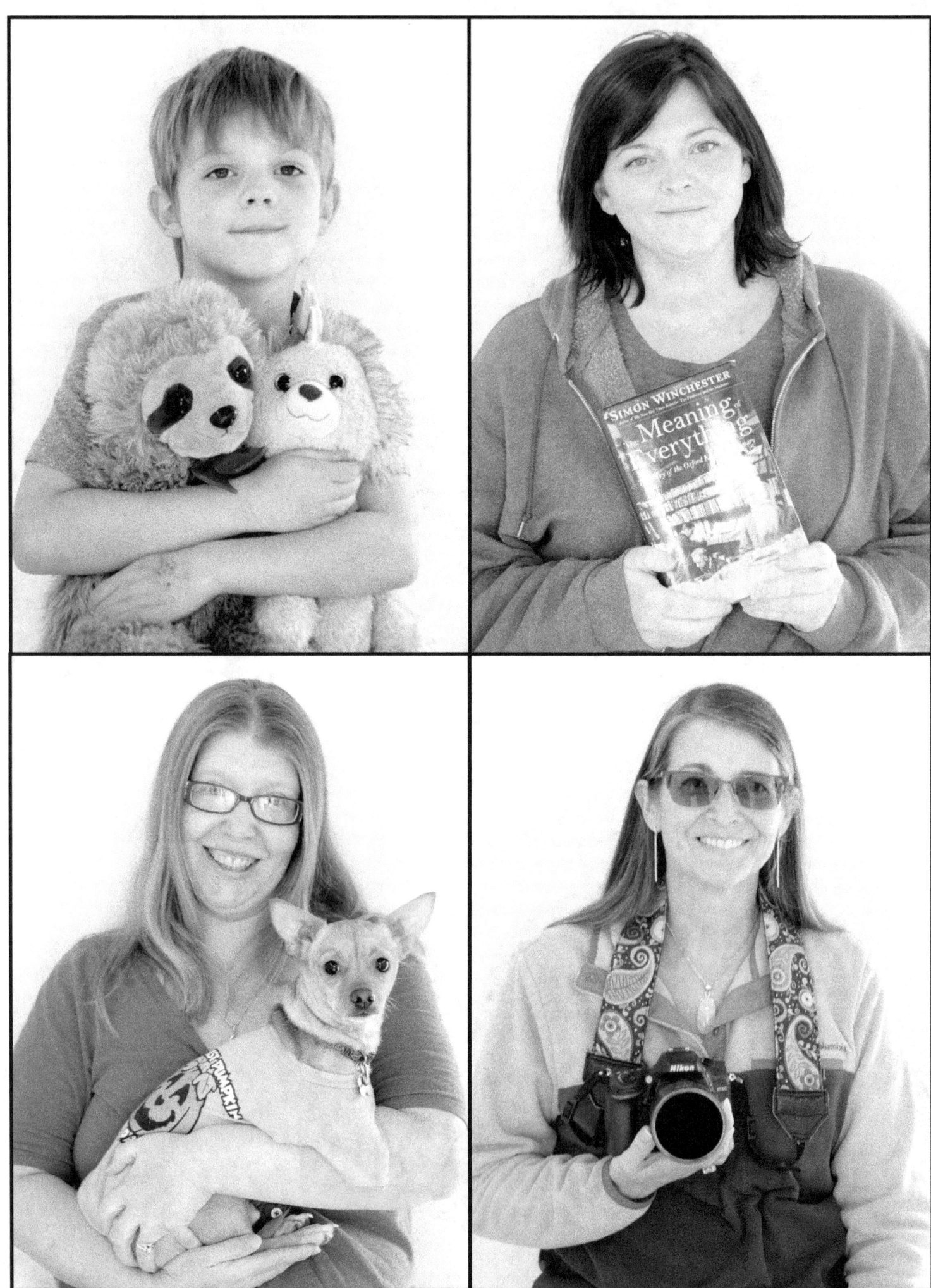

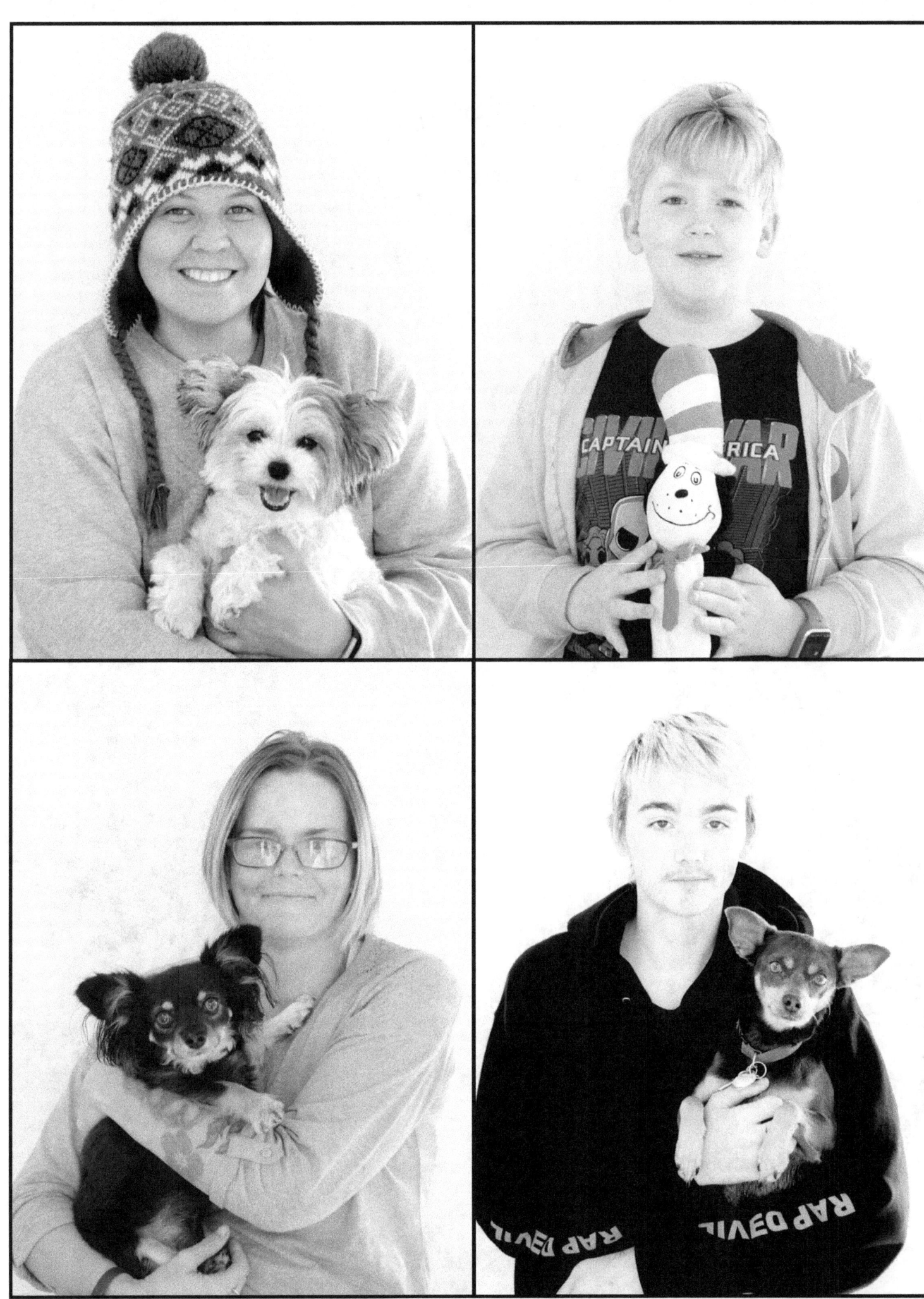

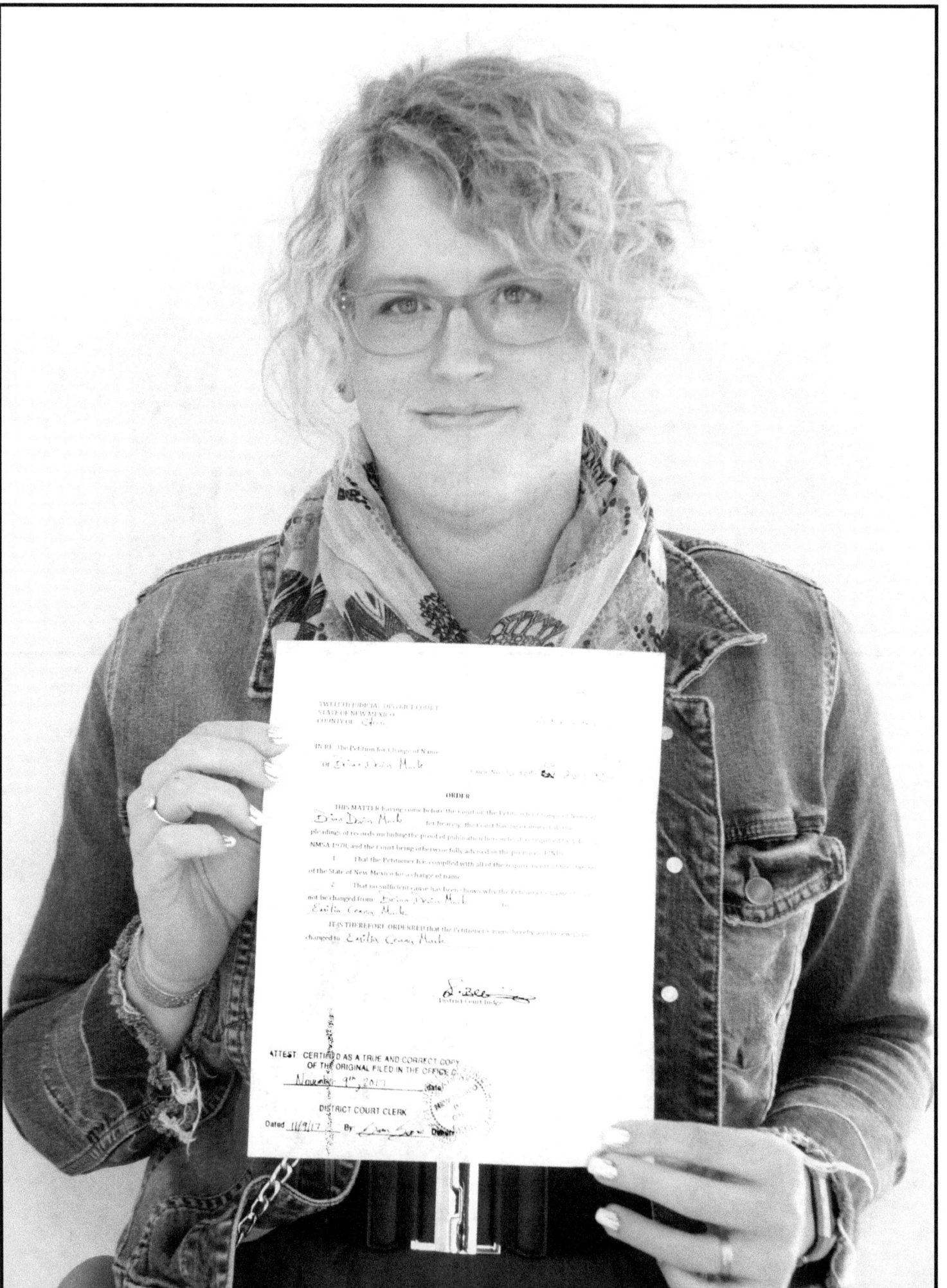

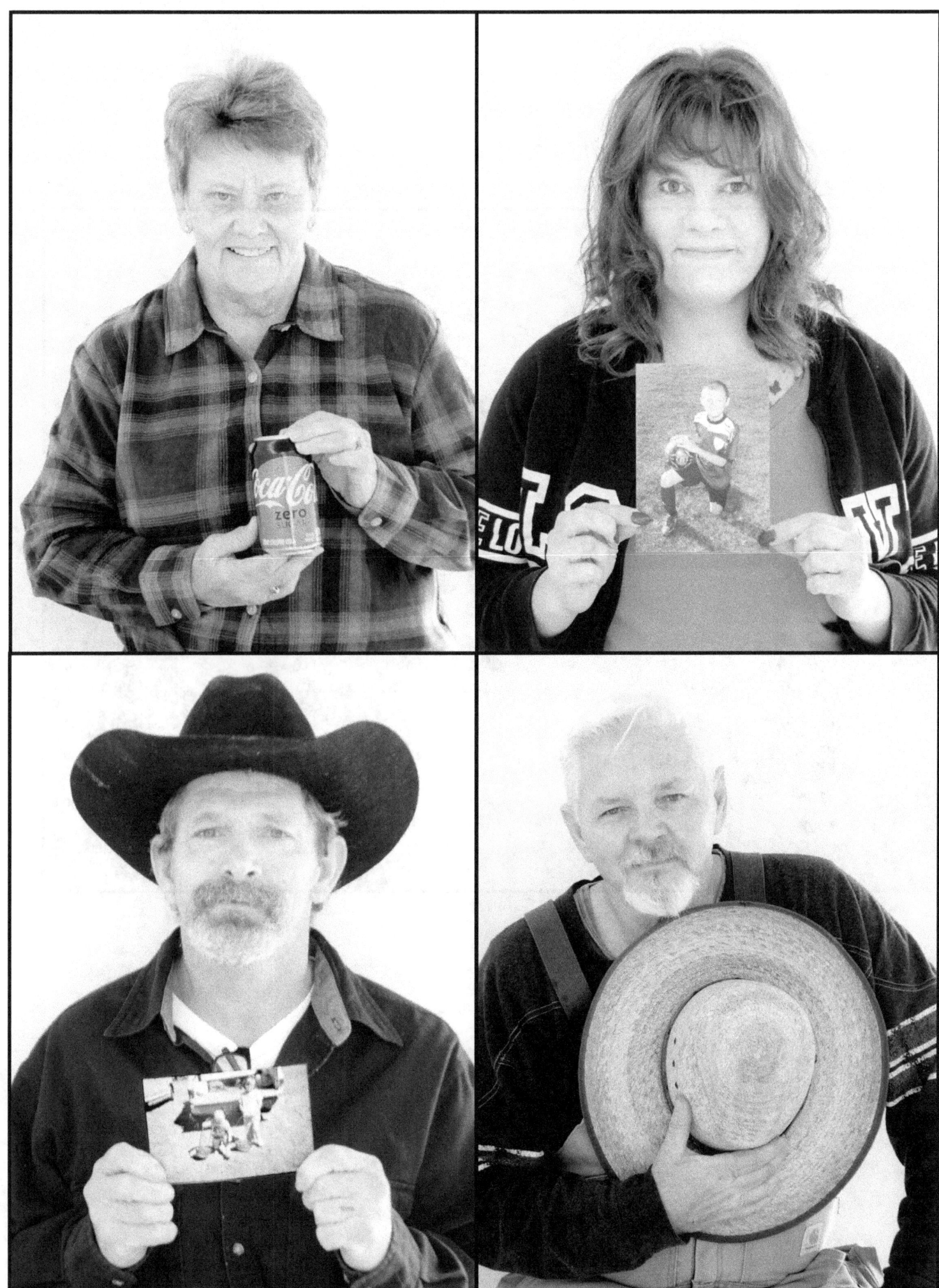

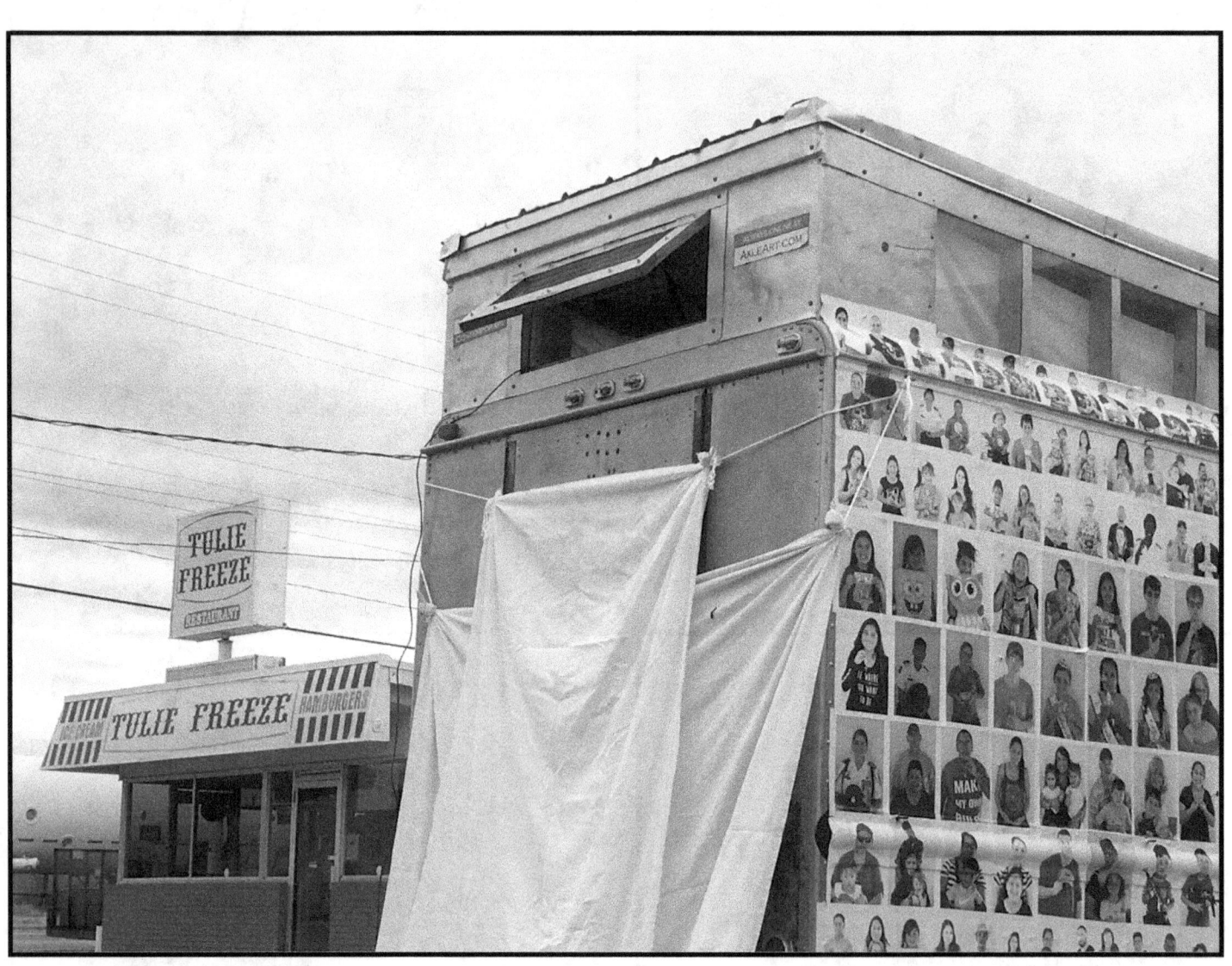

Tularosa
October 16, 2019

Tulie Freeze

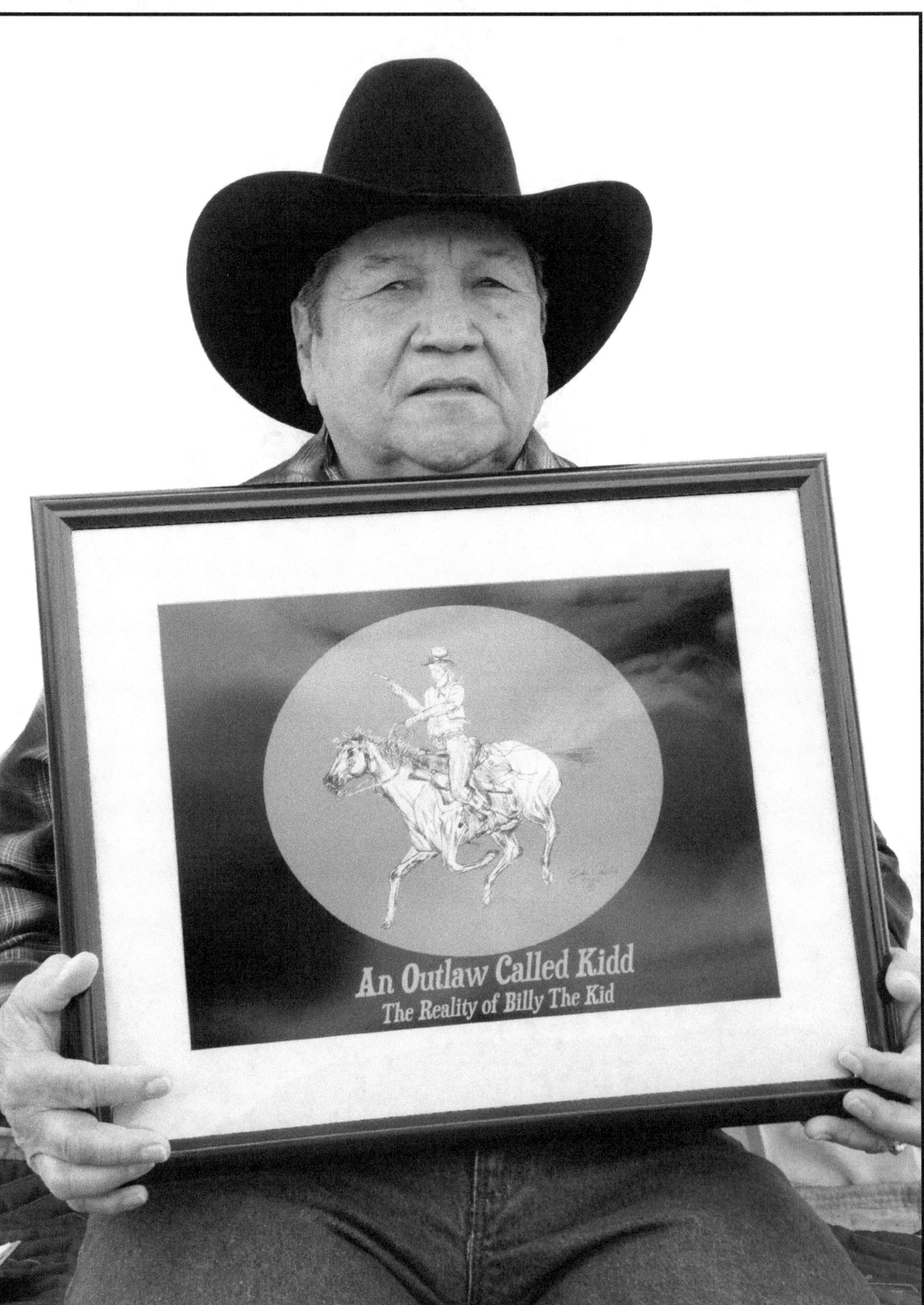

An Outlaw Called Kidd
The Reality of Billy The Kid

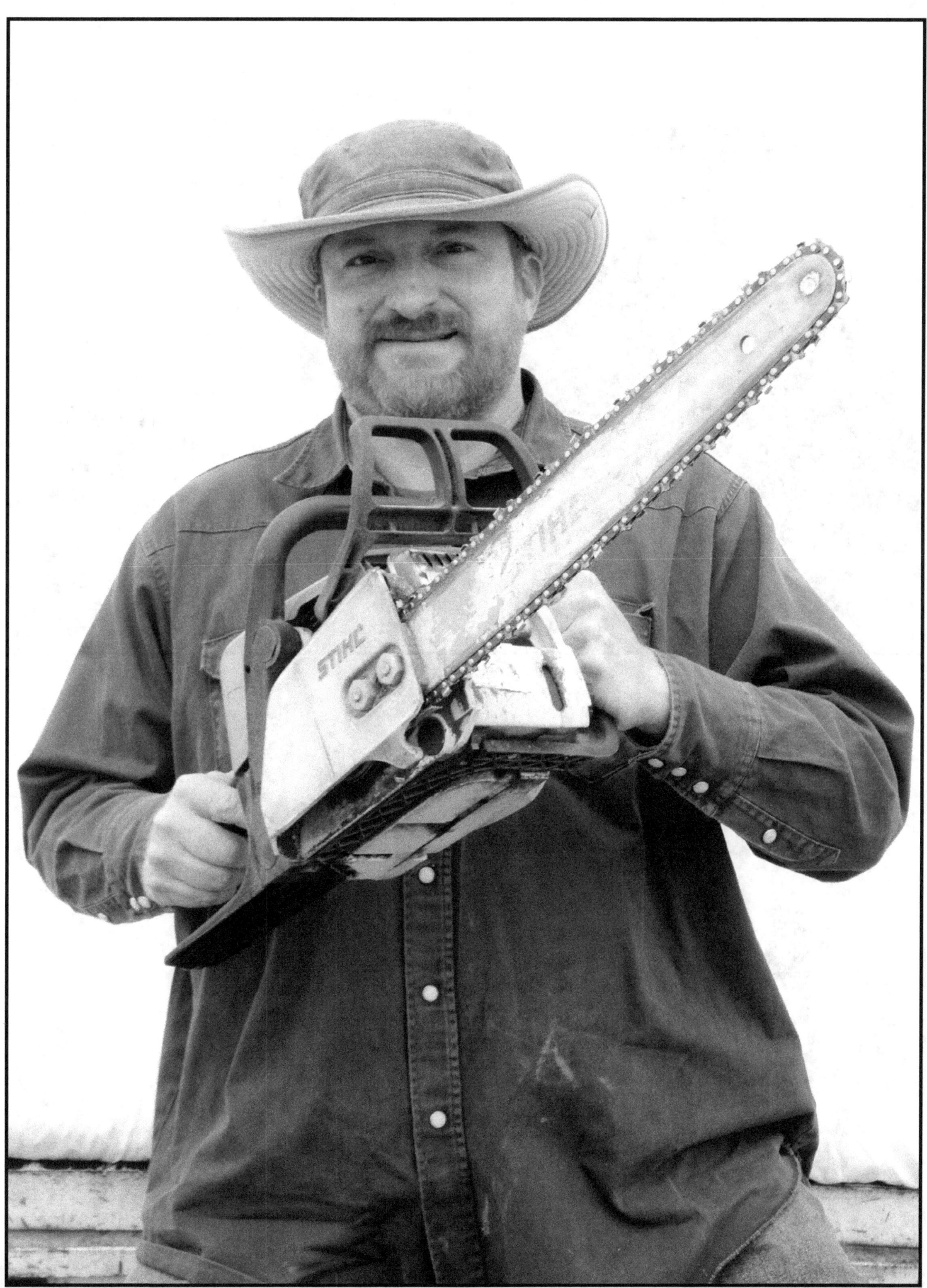

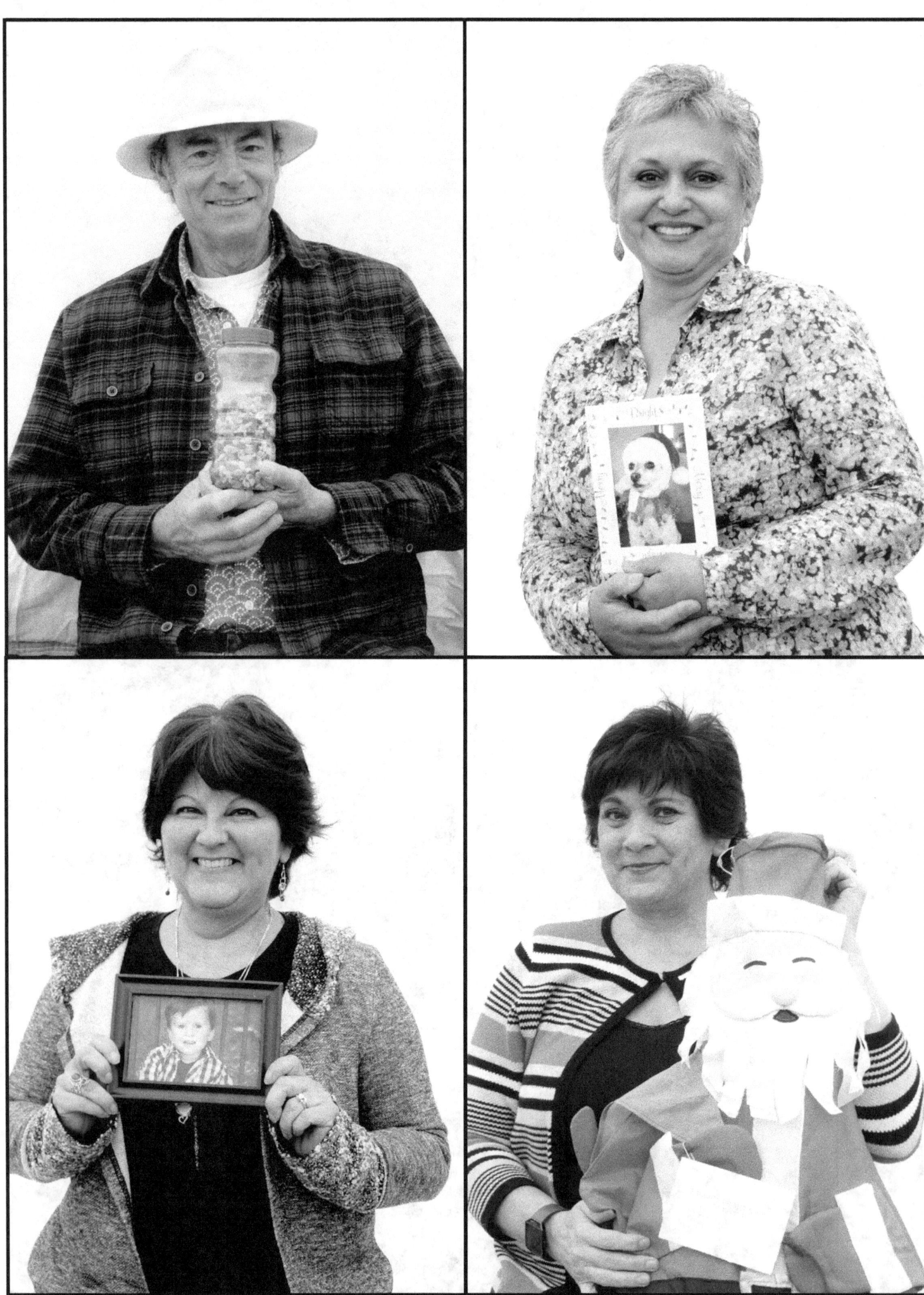

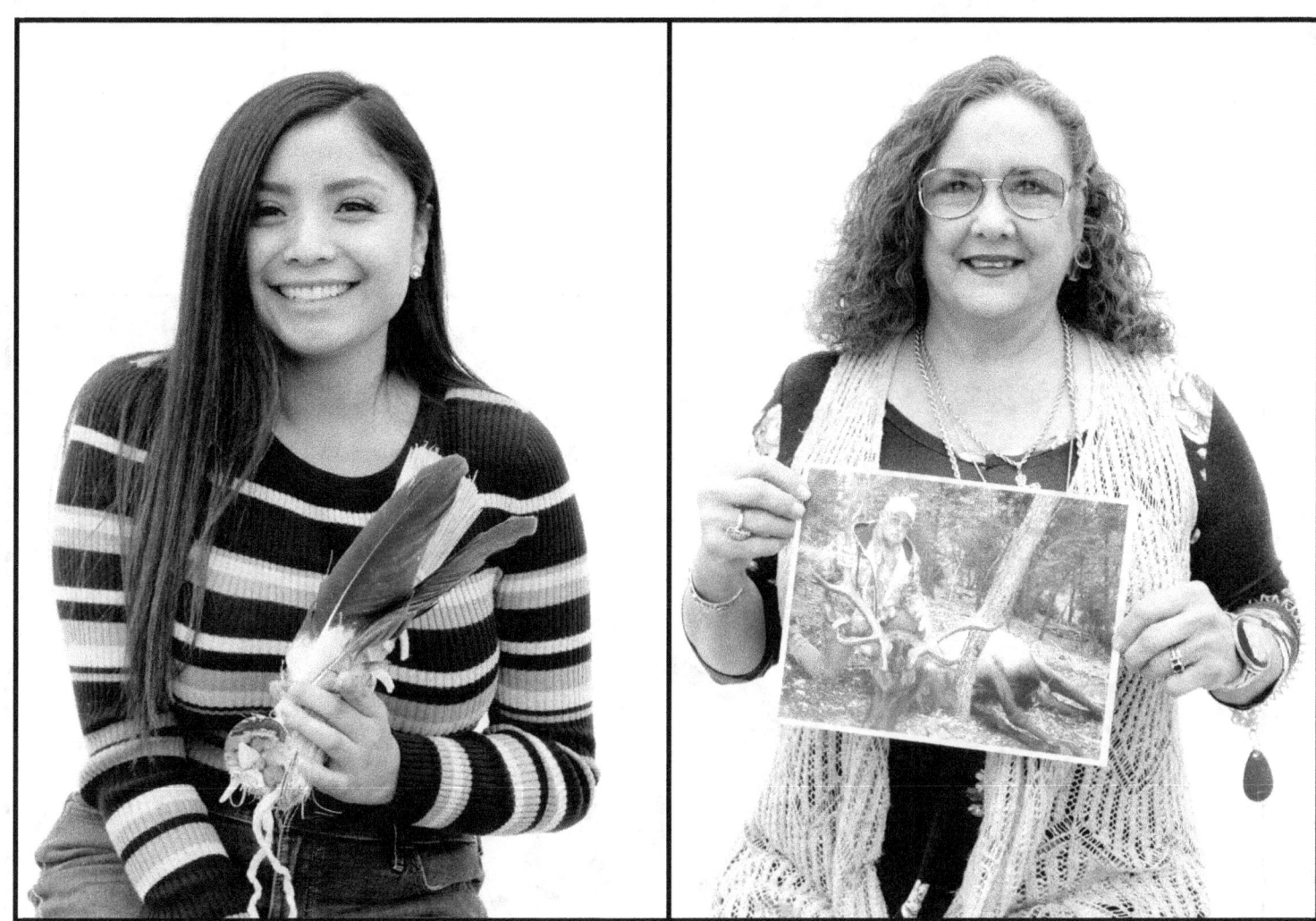

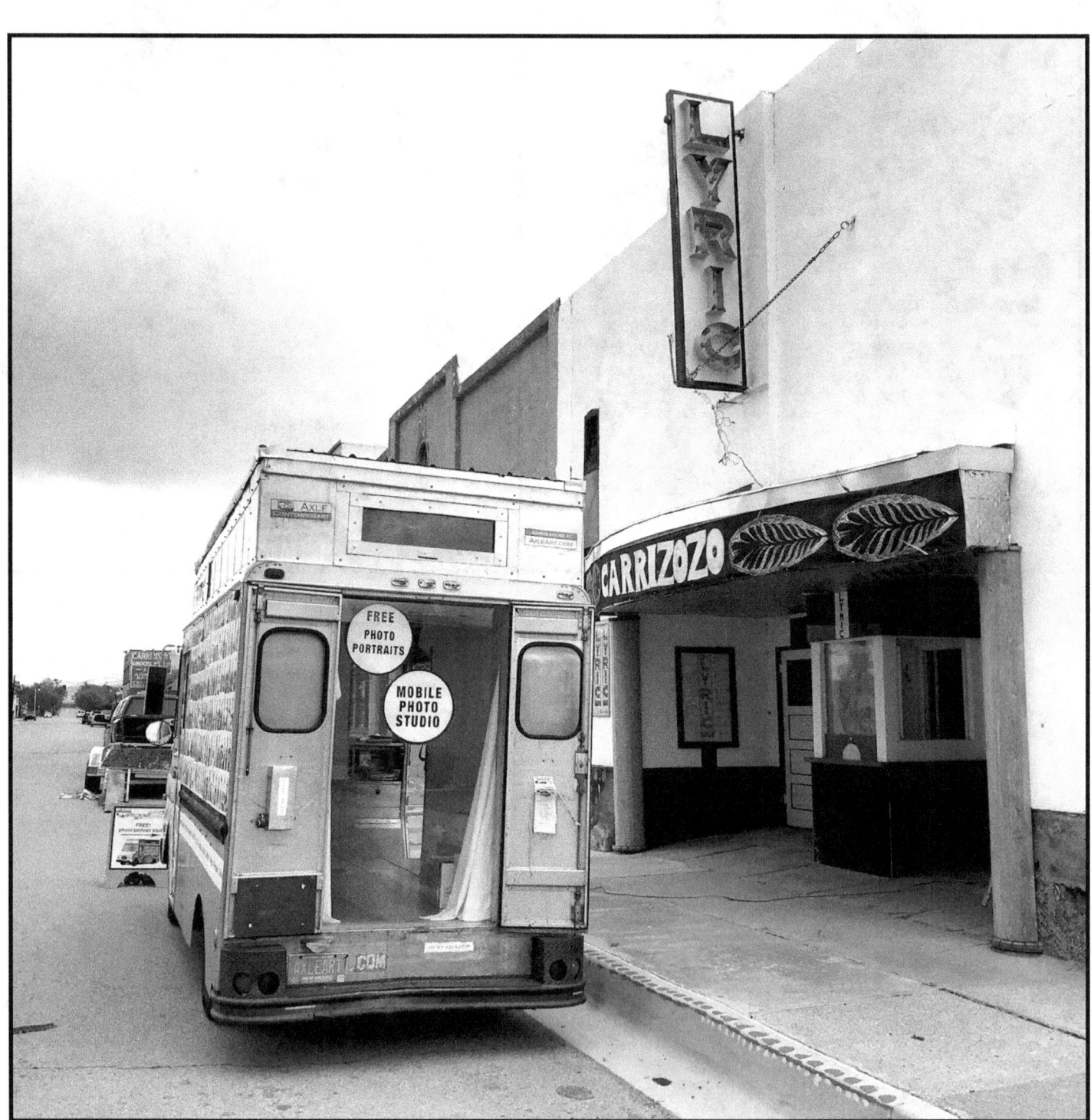

Carrizozo
October 16, 2019

MoMAZoZo

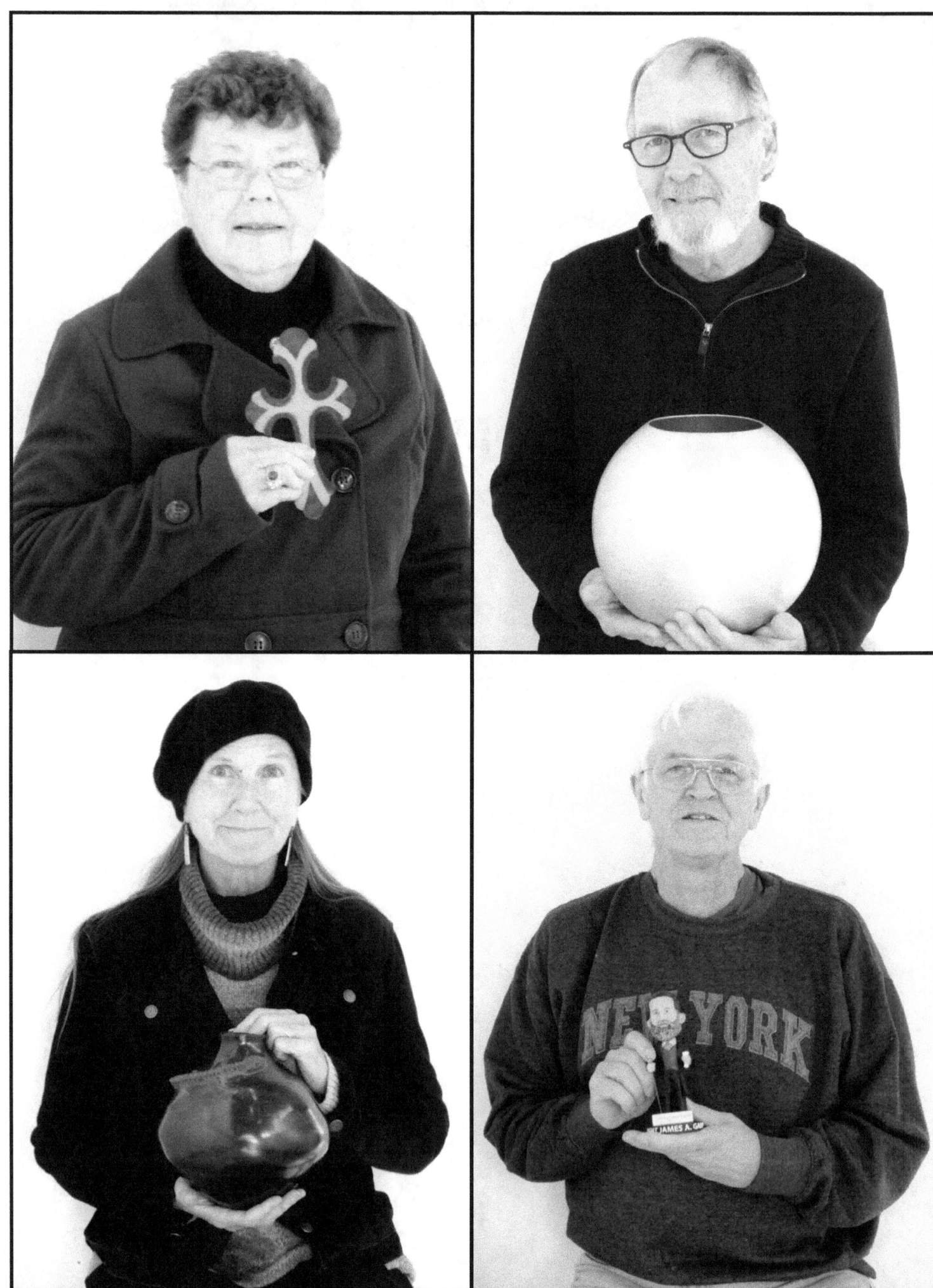

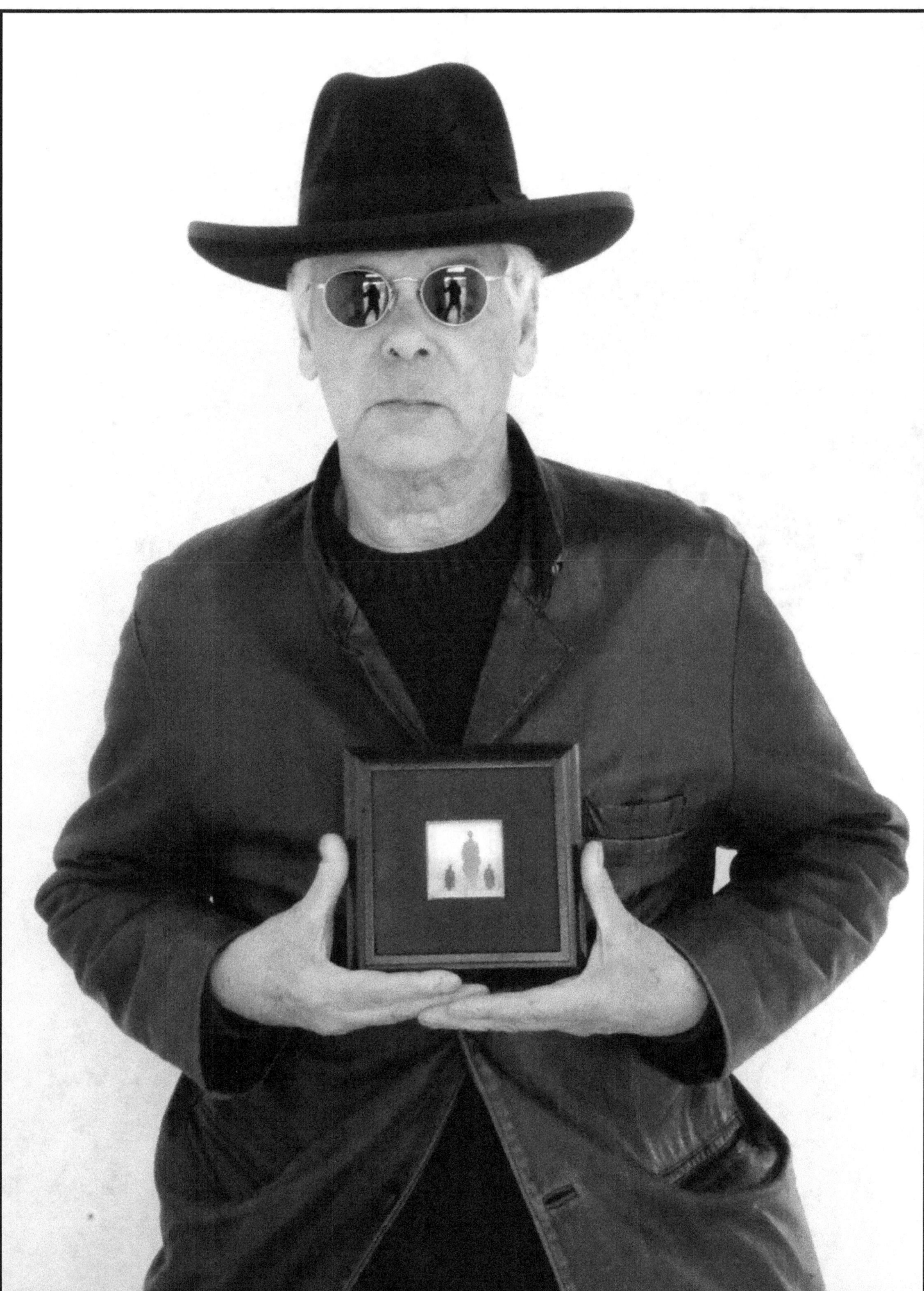

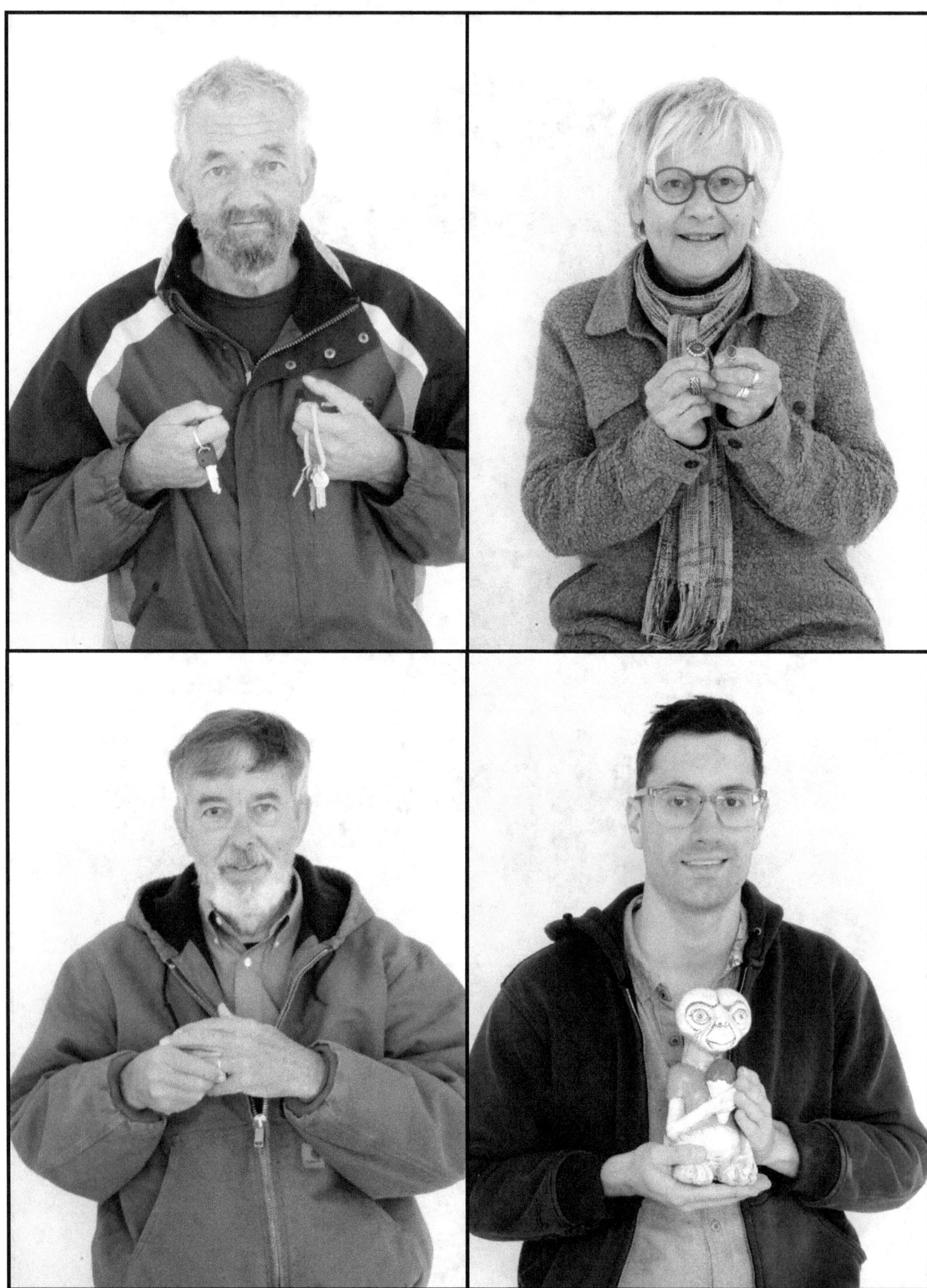

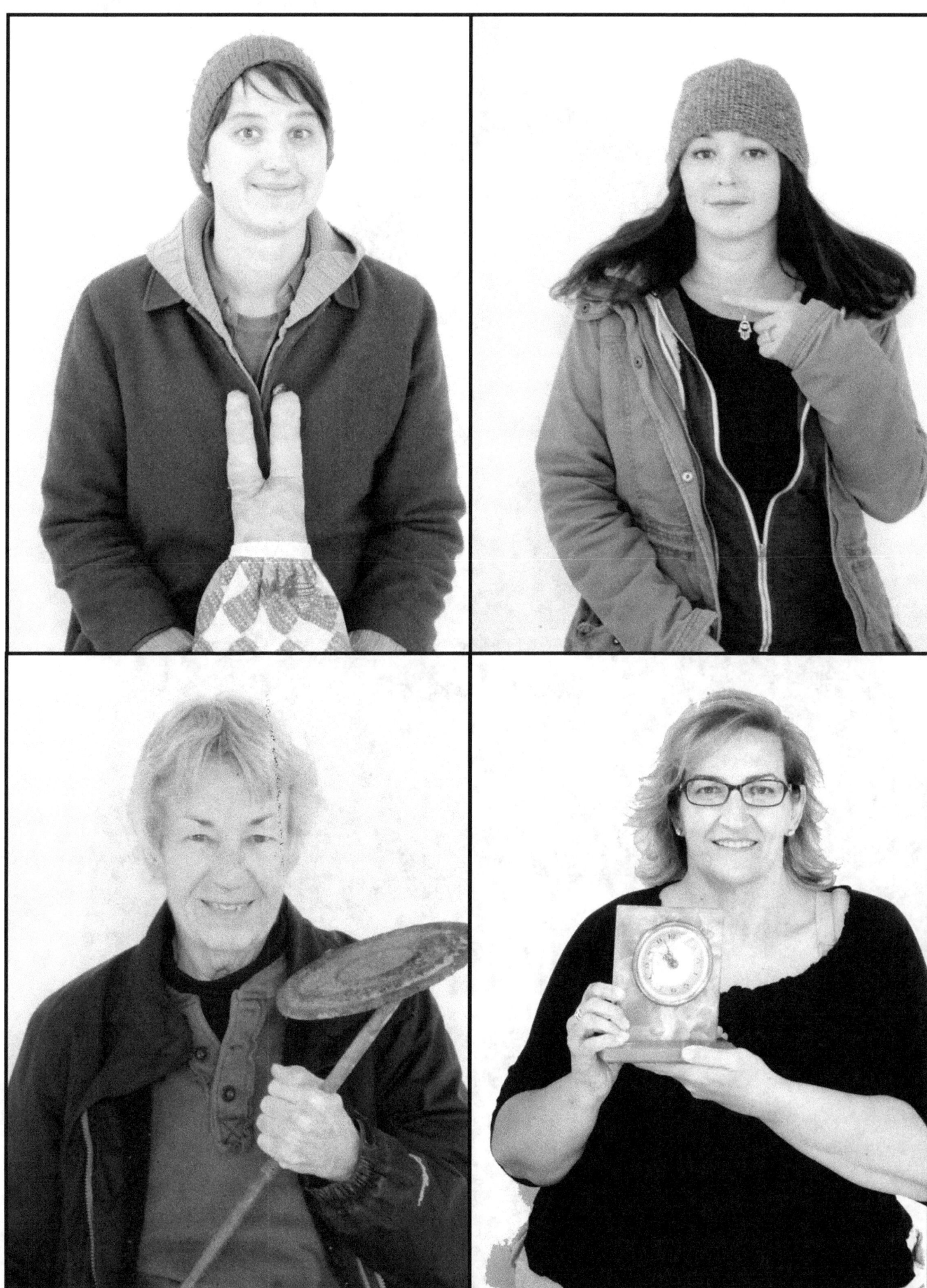

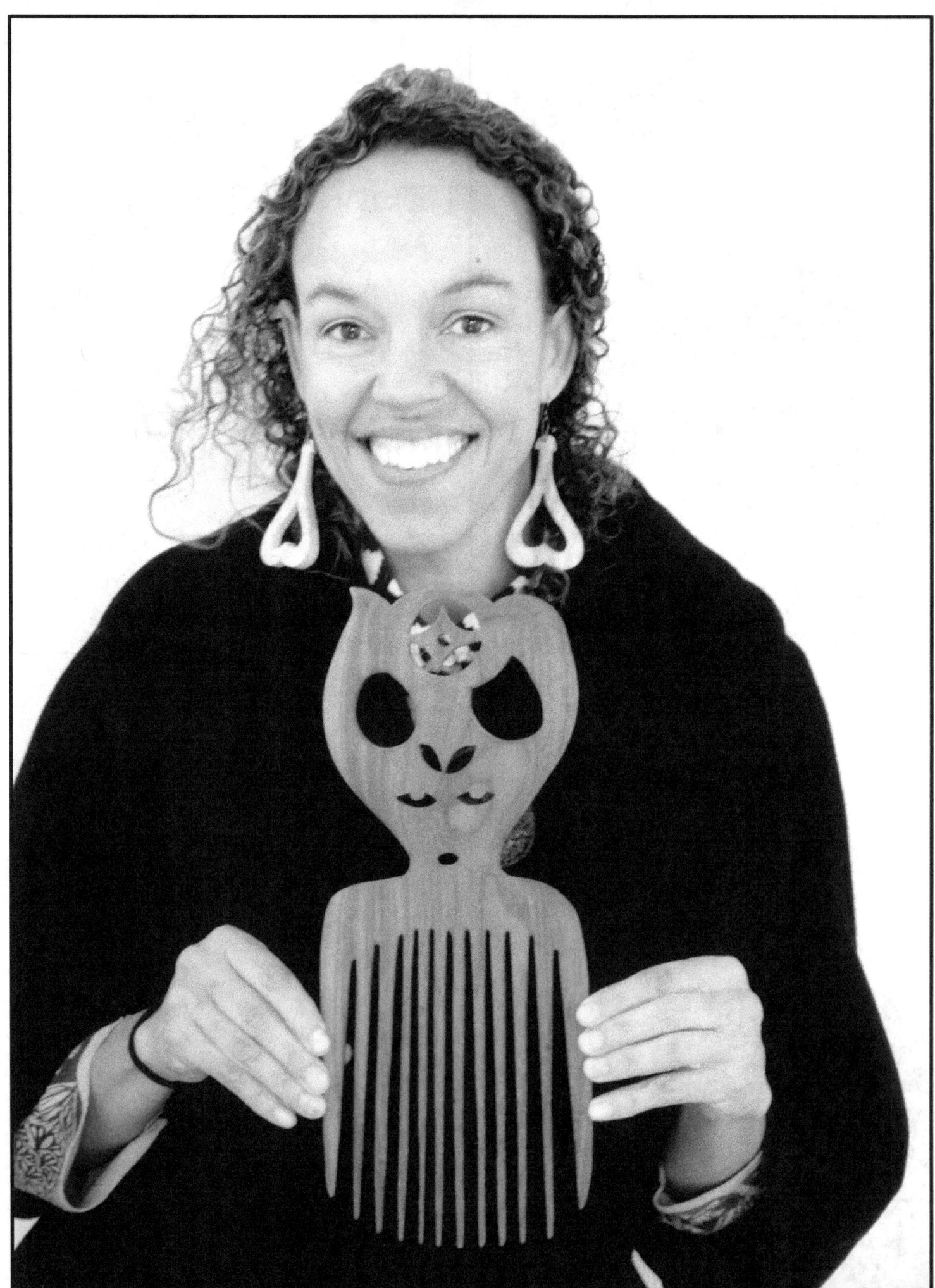

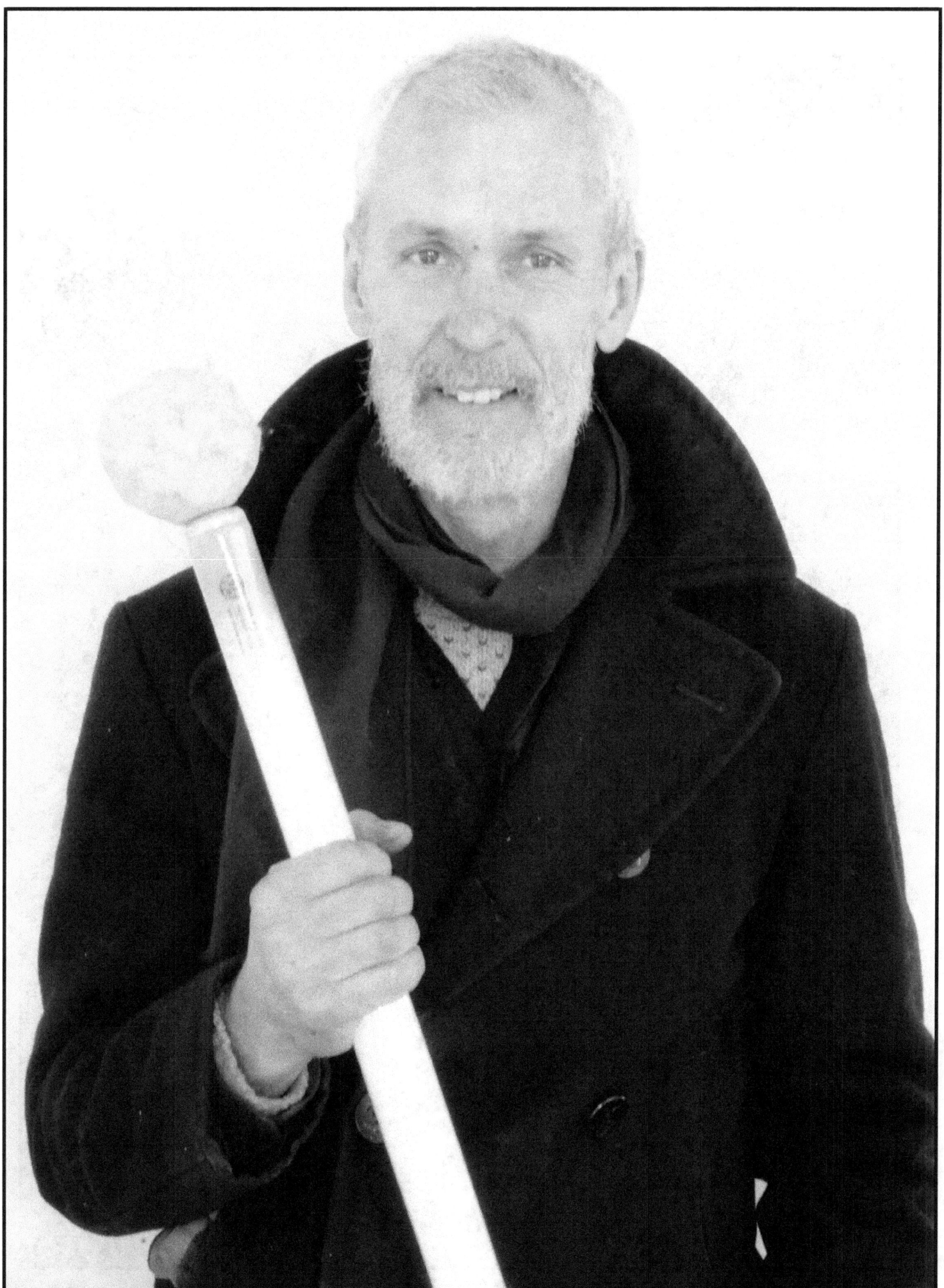

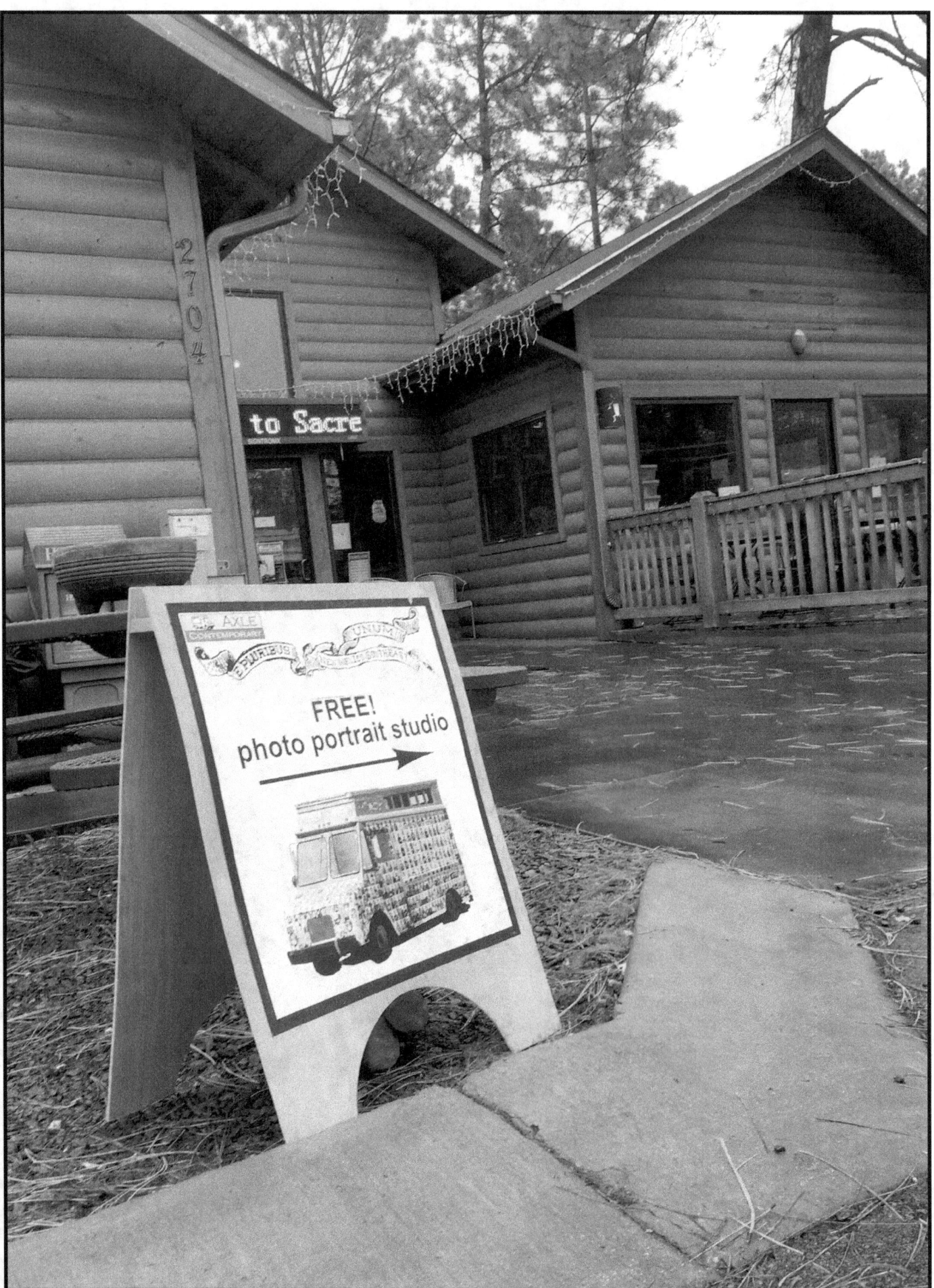

Ruidoso
October 17, 2019

Sacred Grounds Coffee & Tea House

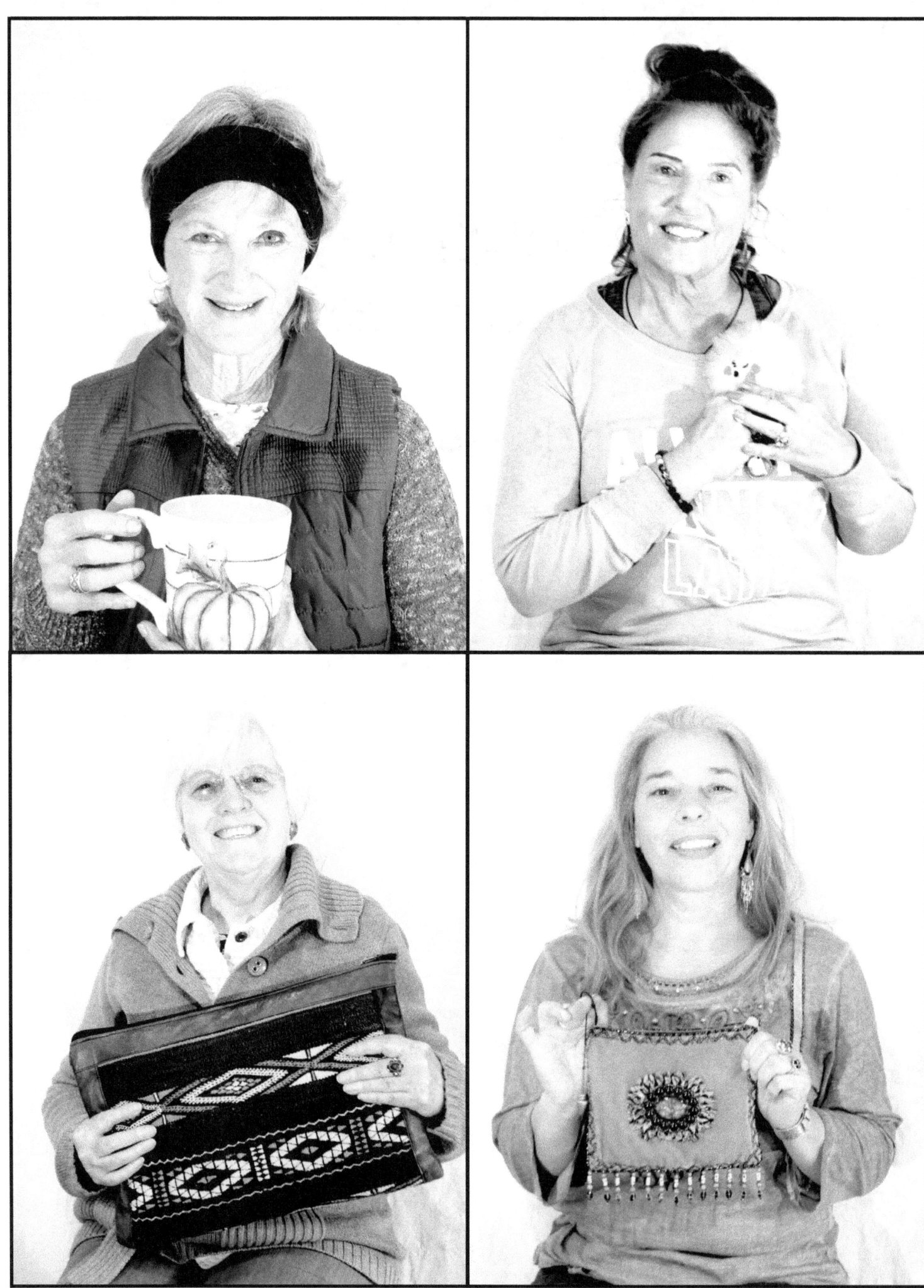

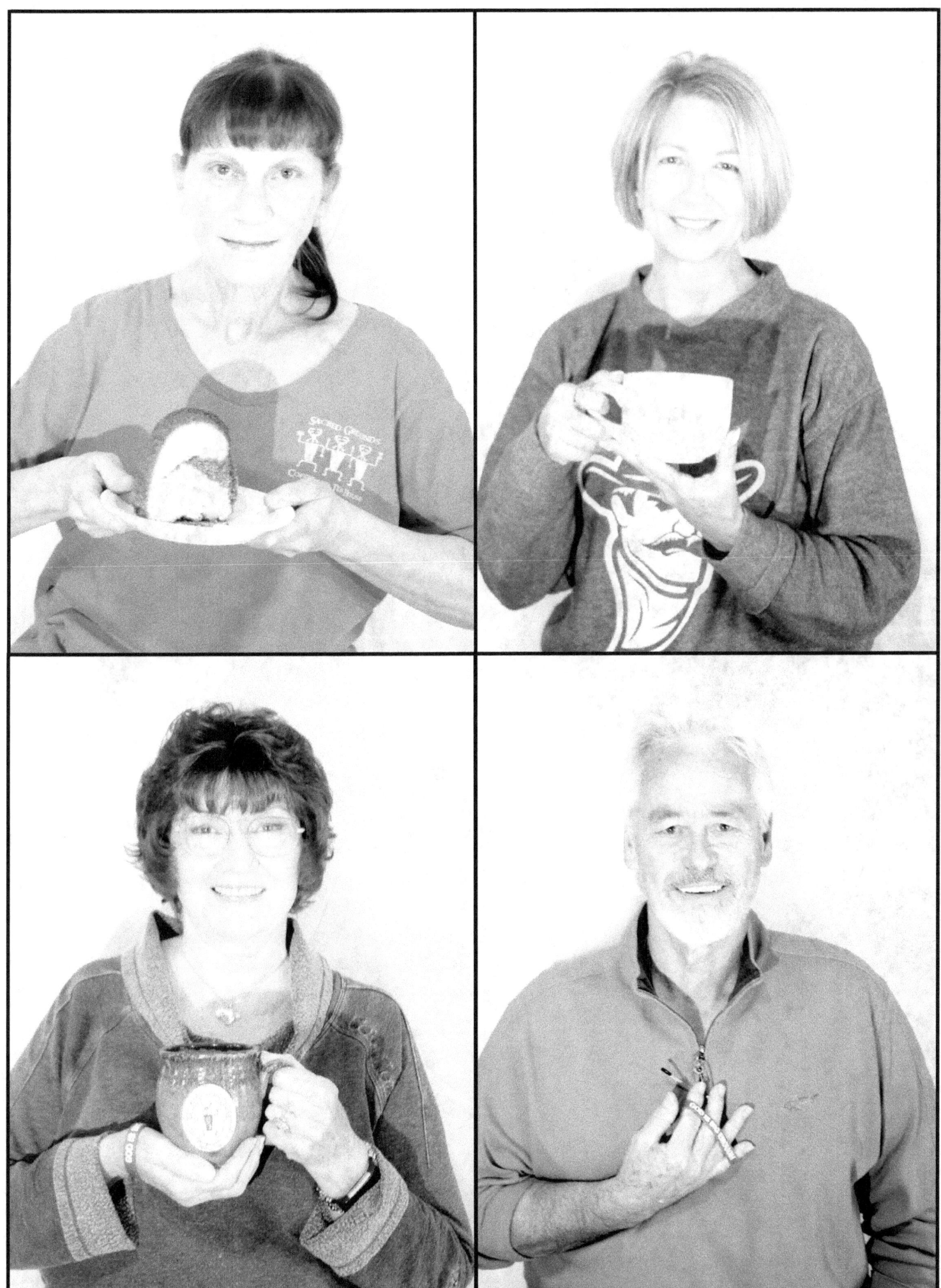

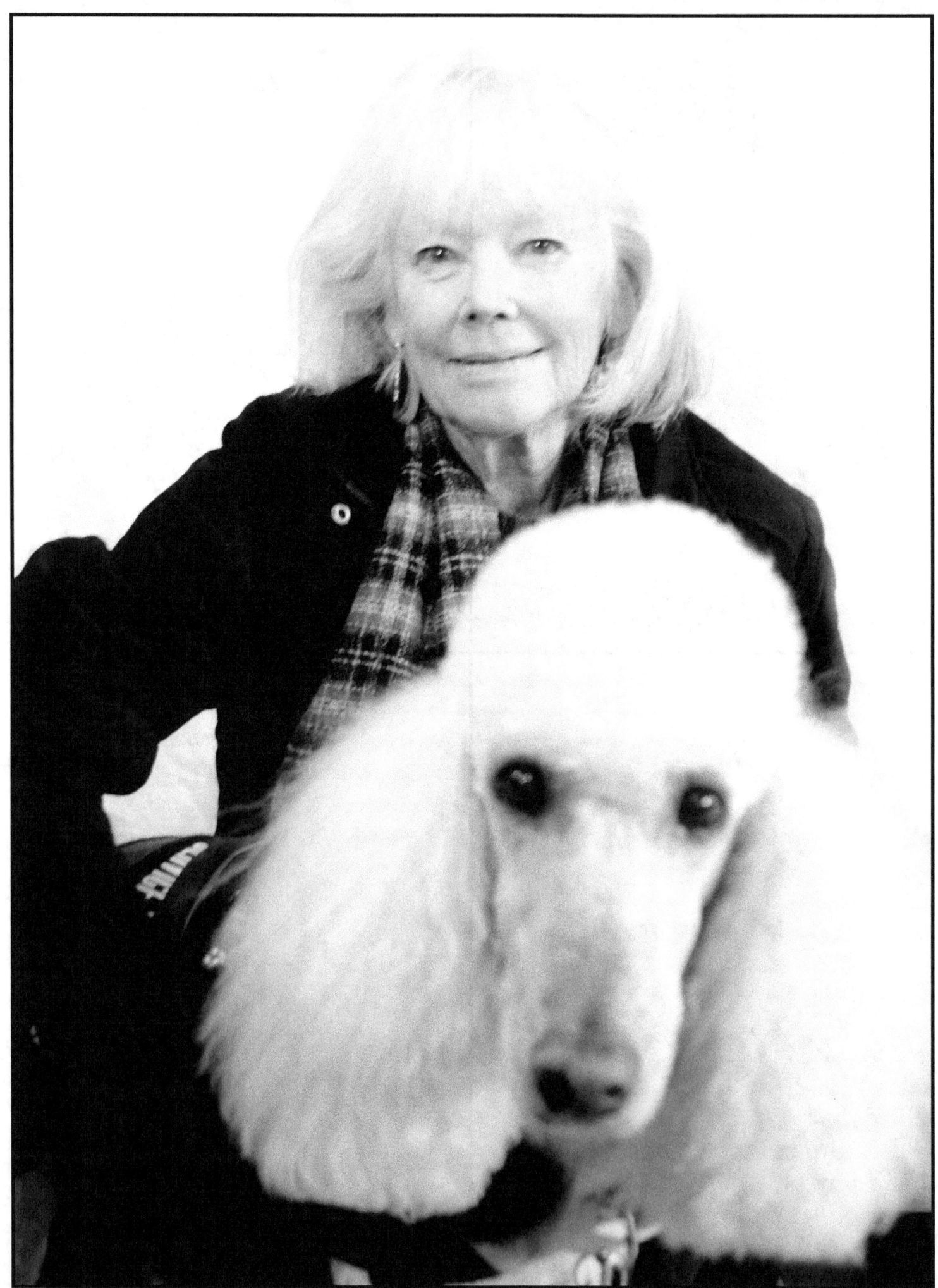

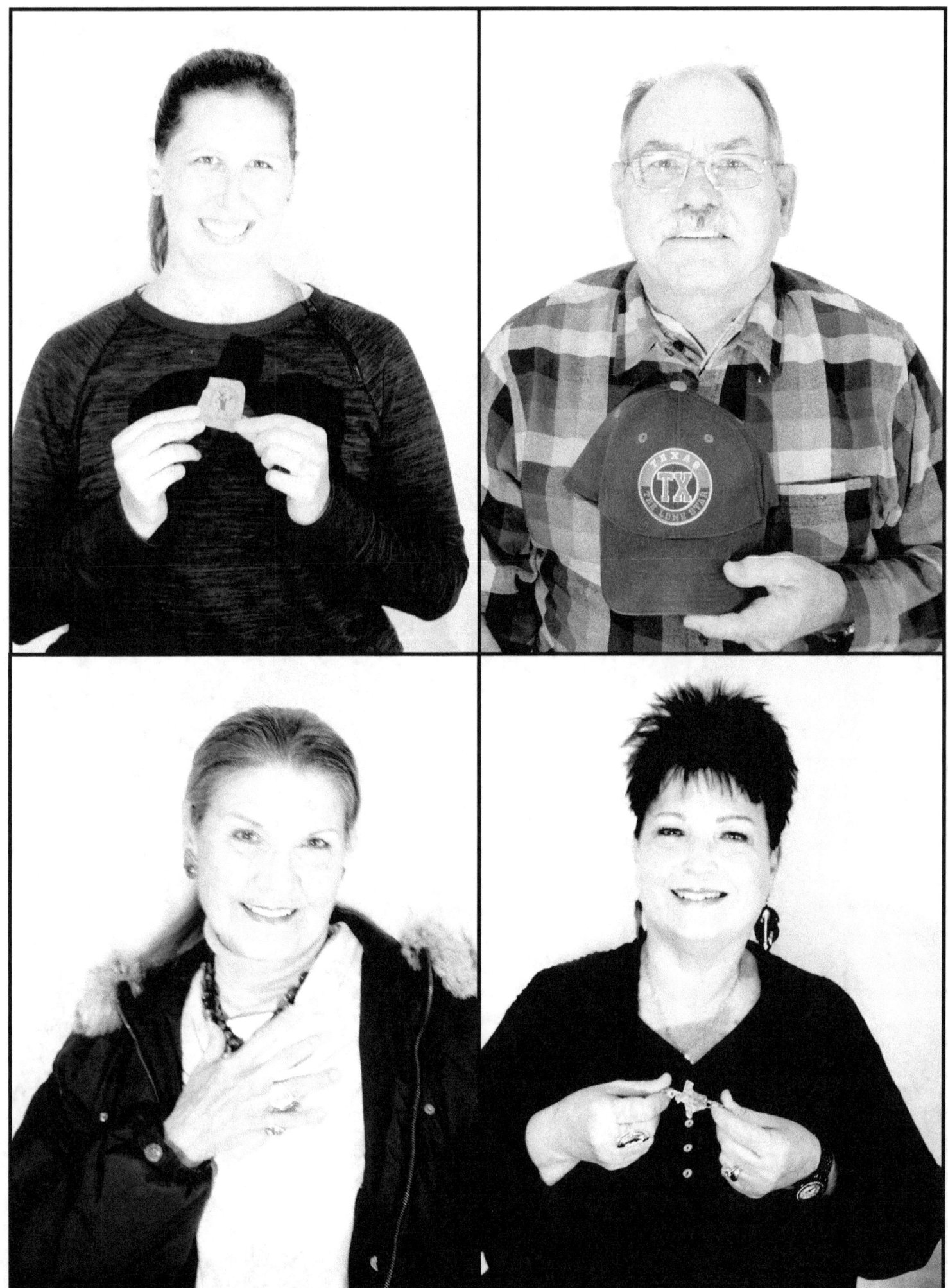

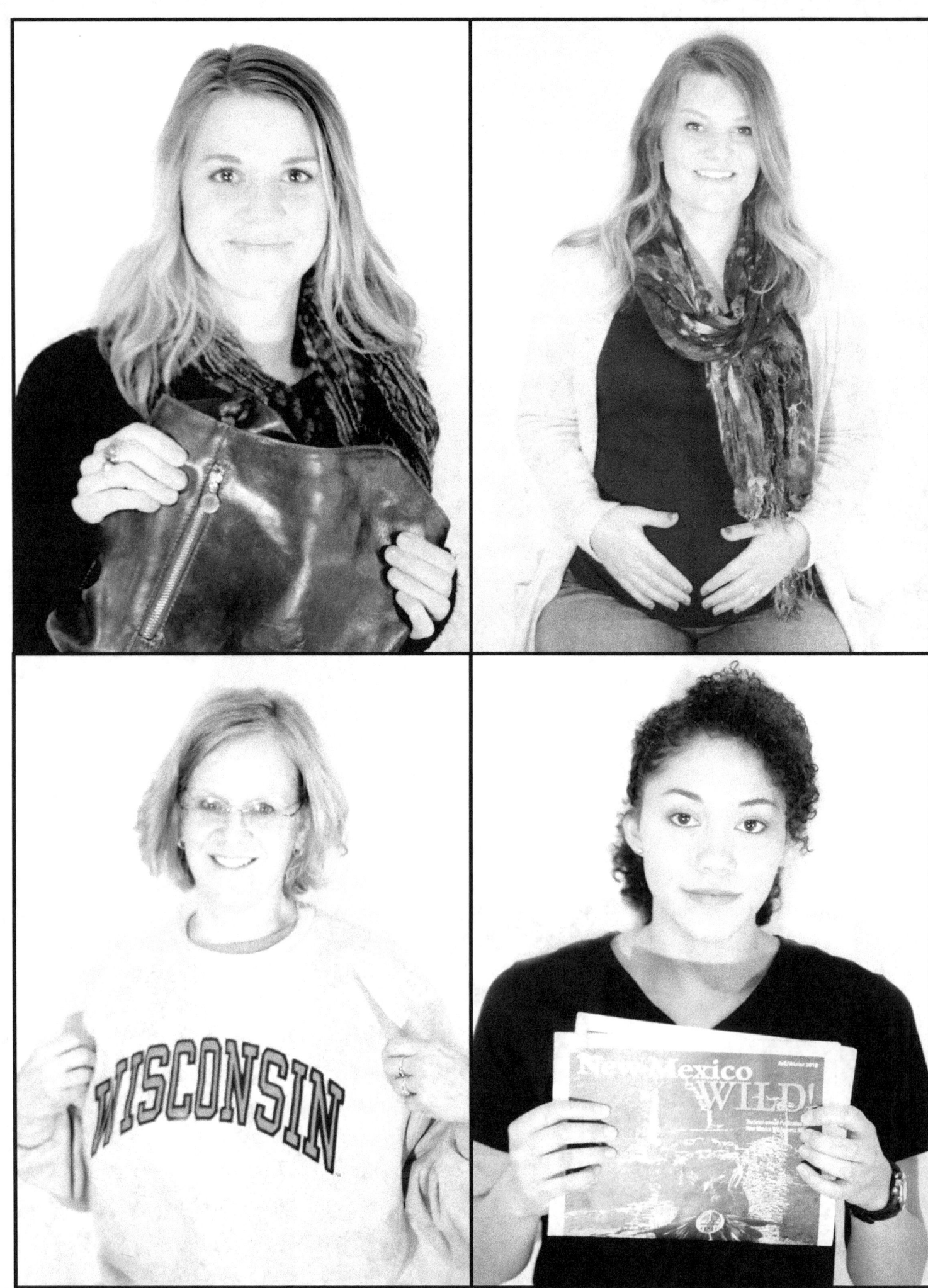

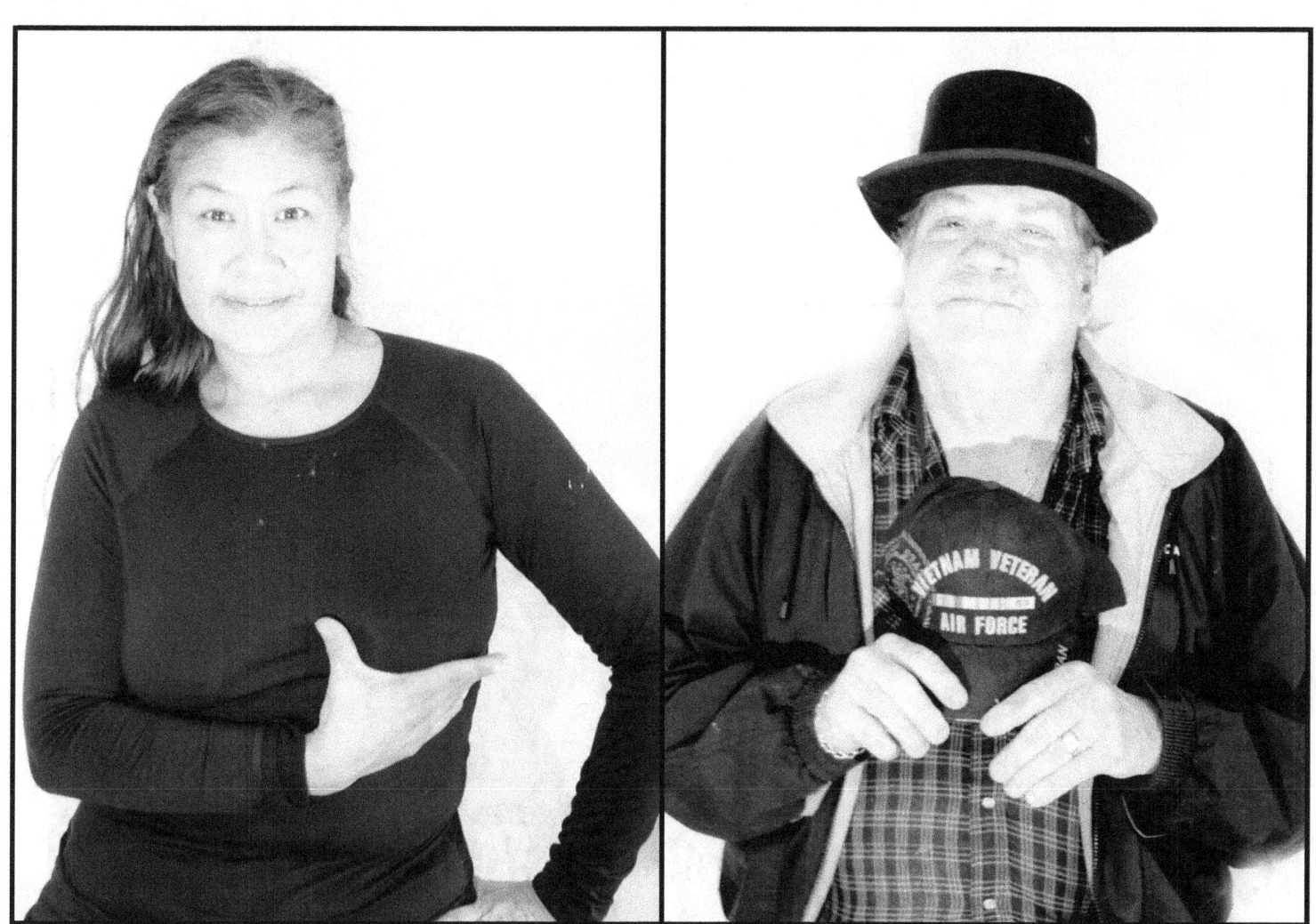

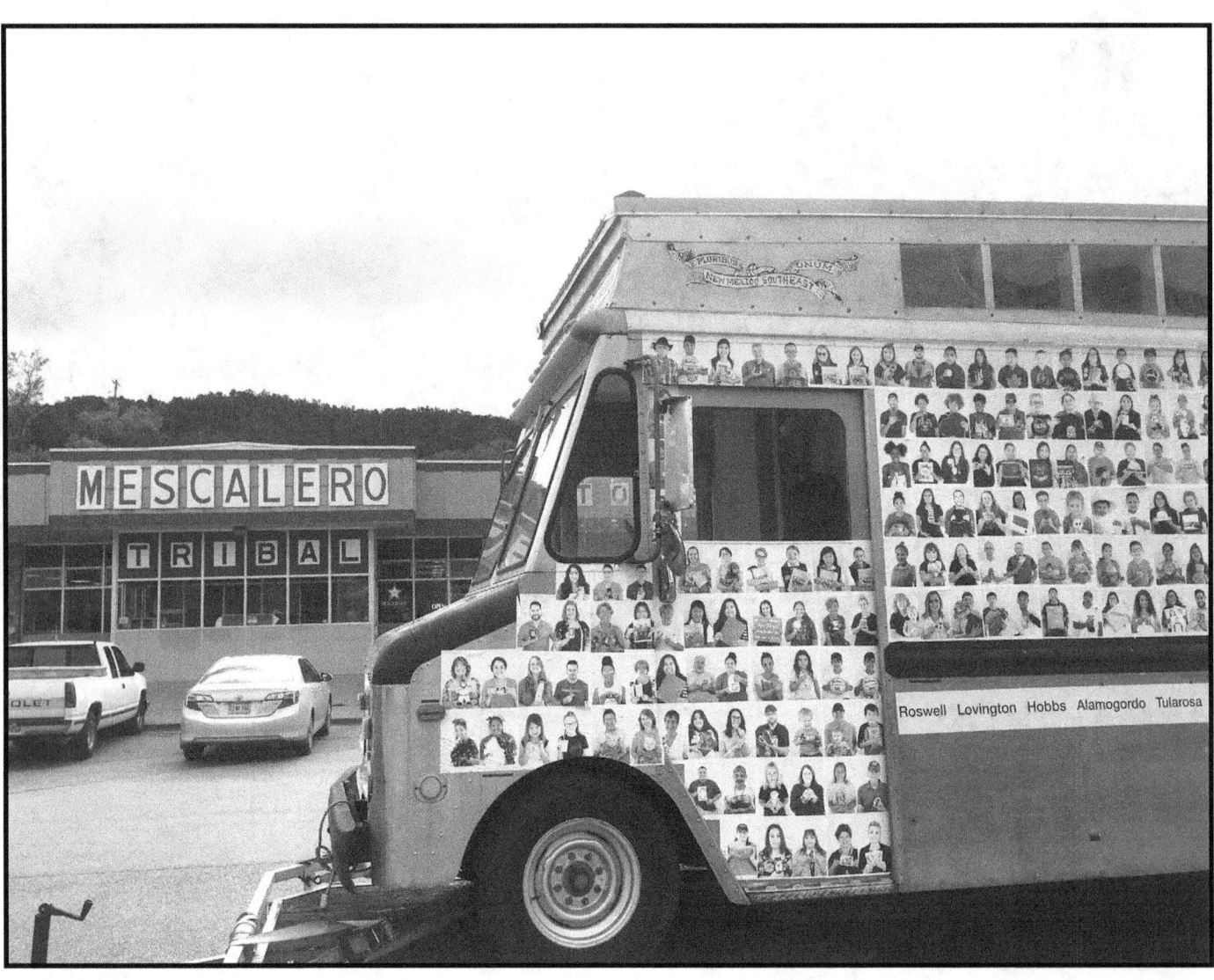

Mescalero
October 17, 2019

Mescalero Tribal Store

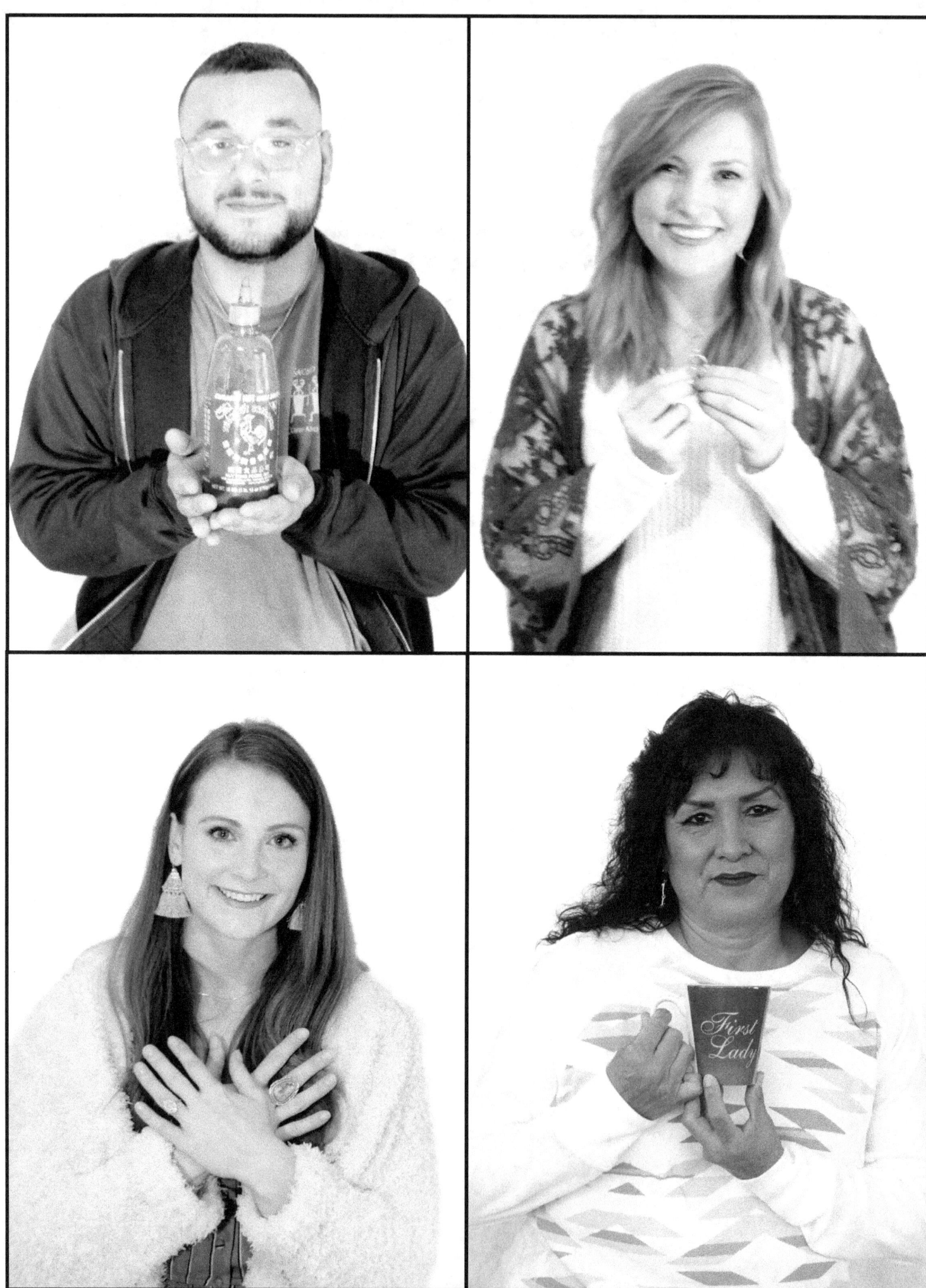

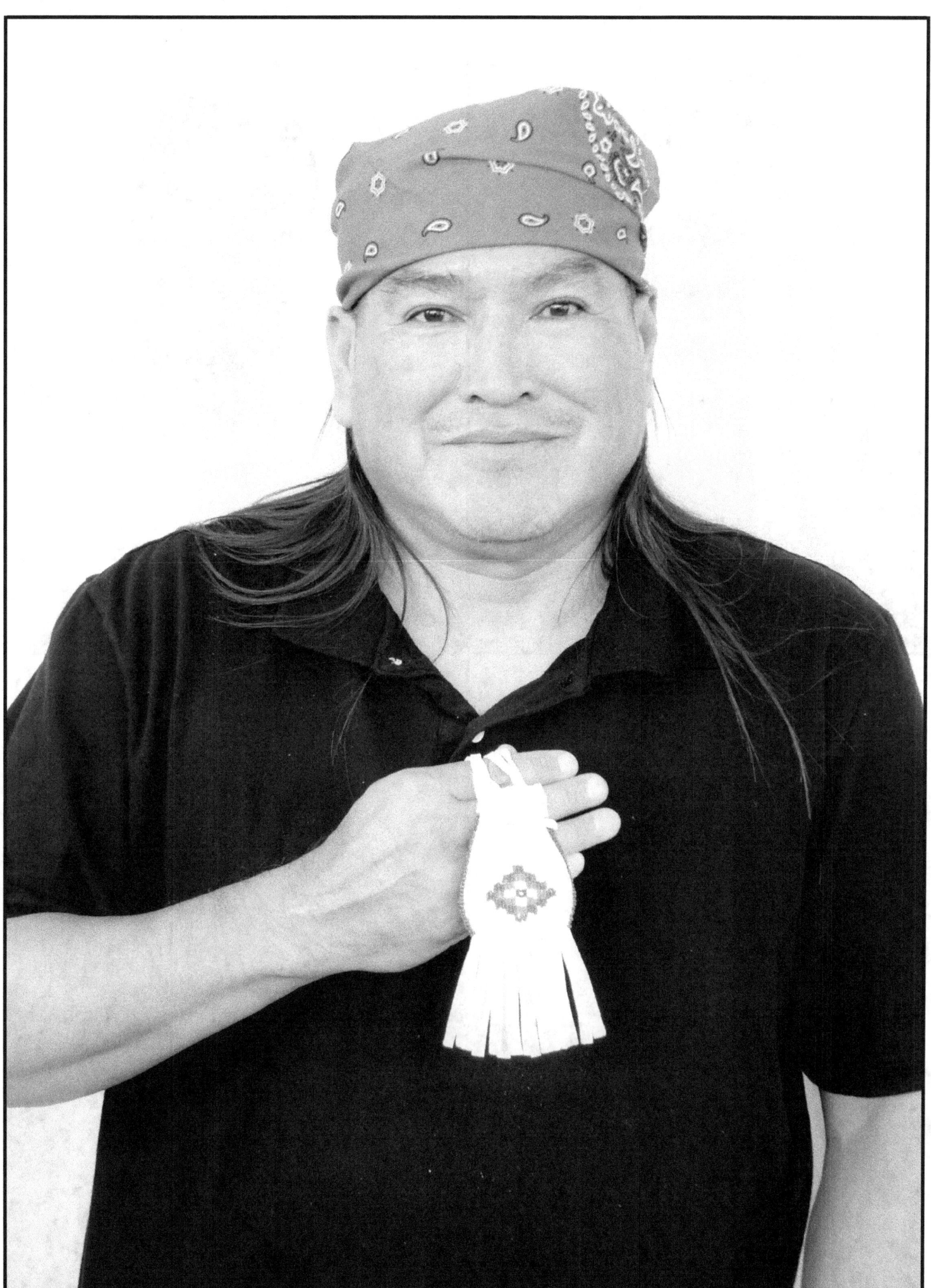

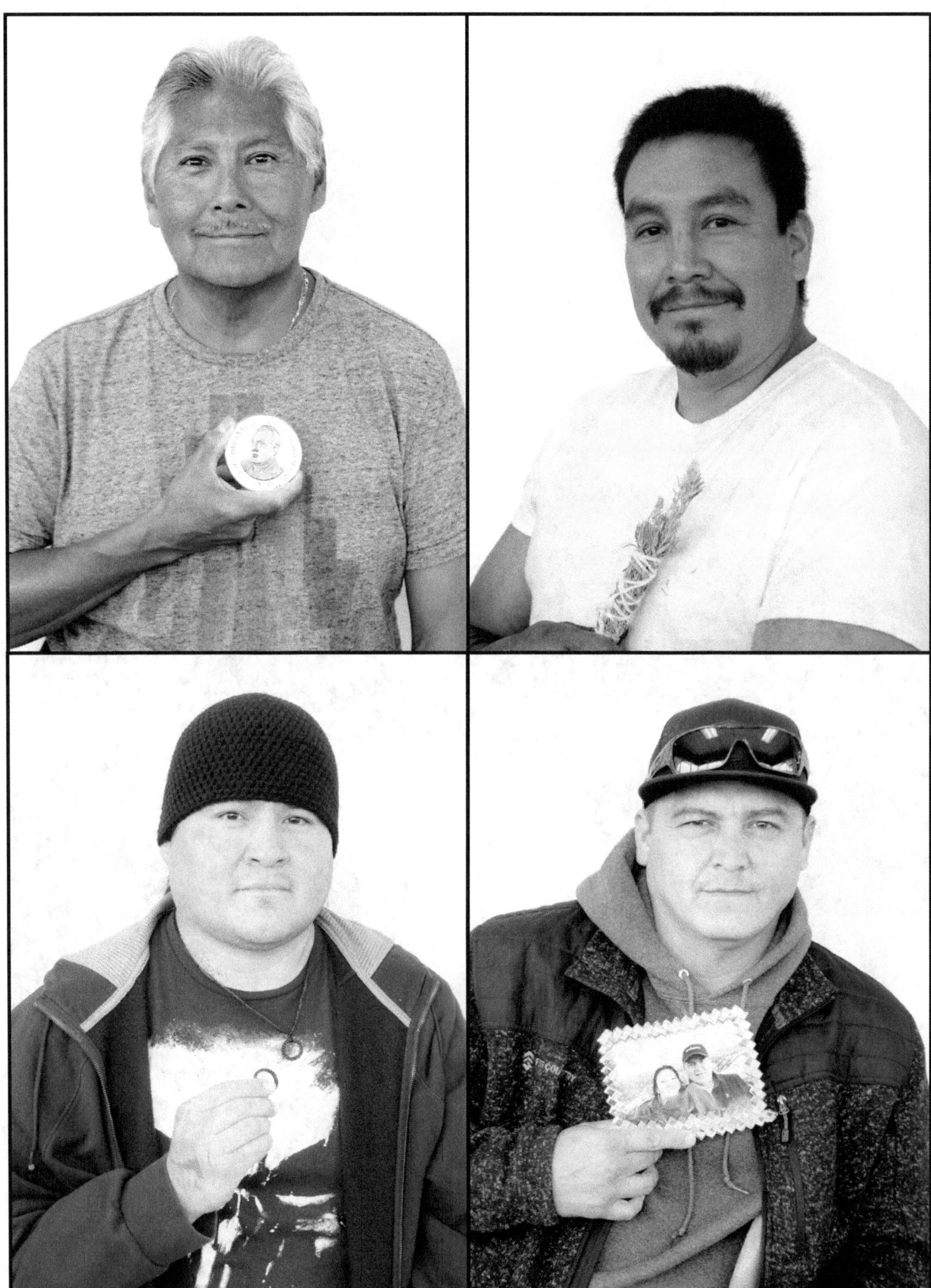

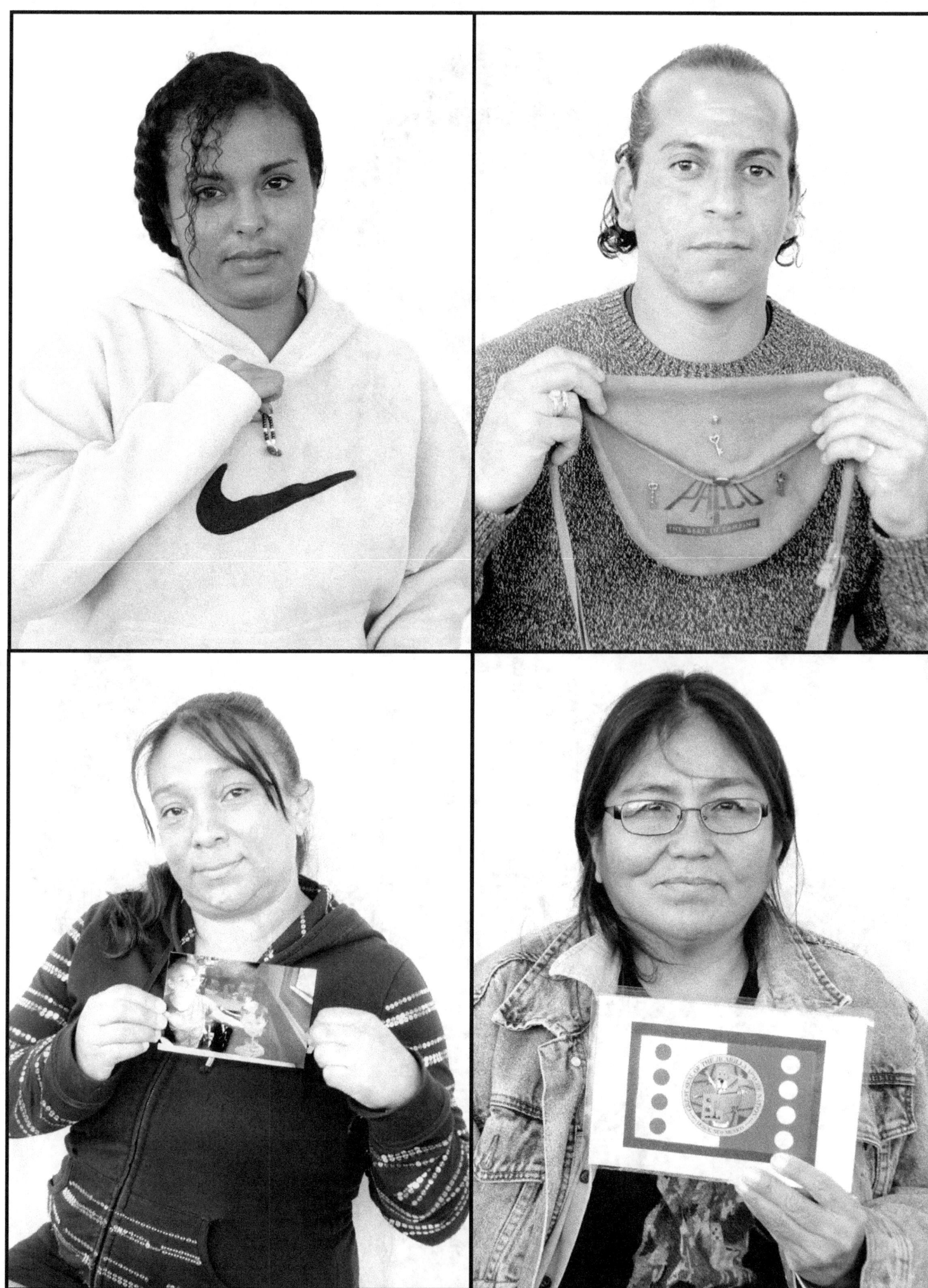

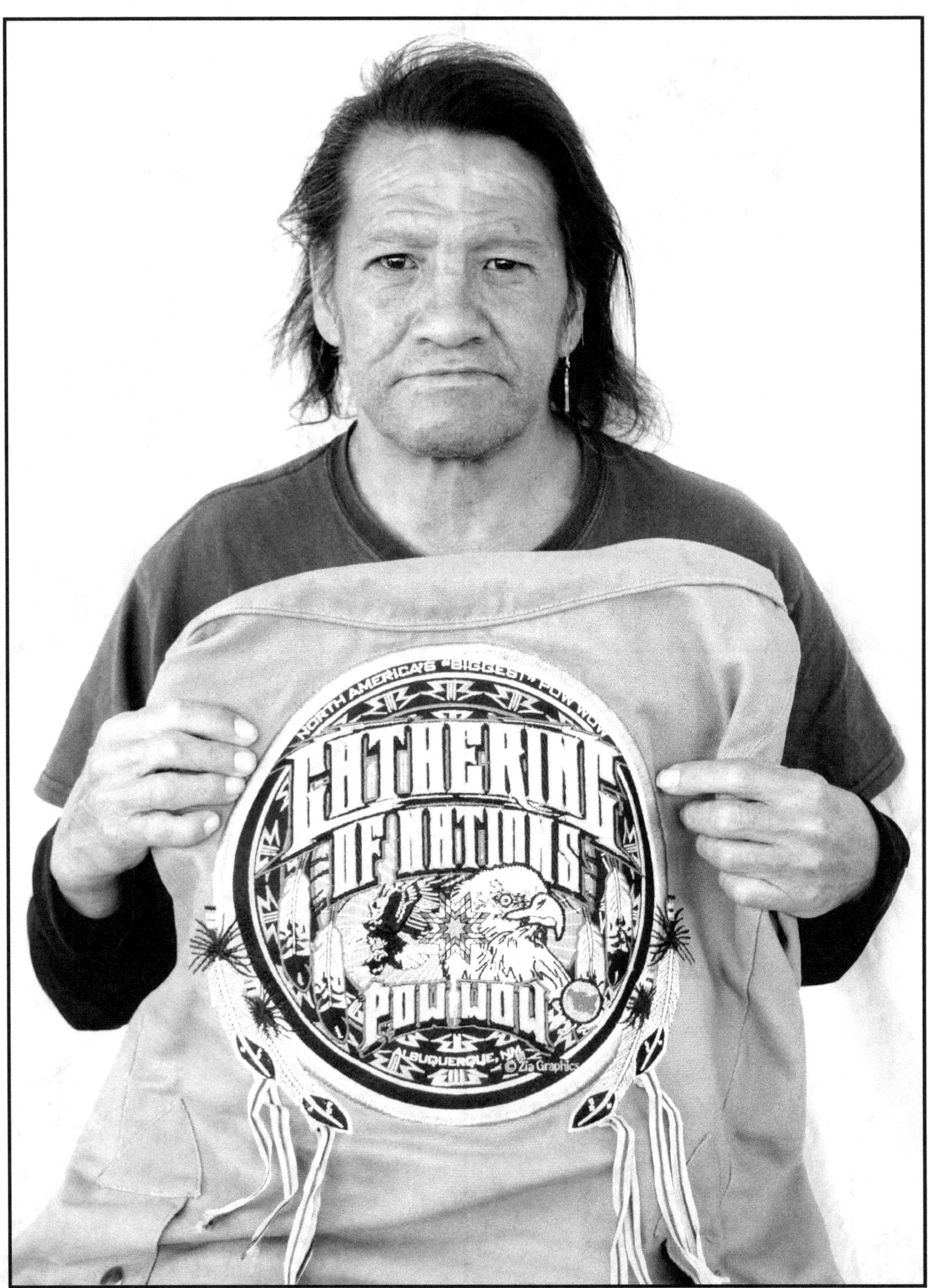

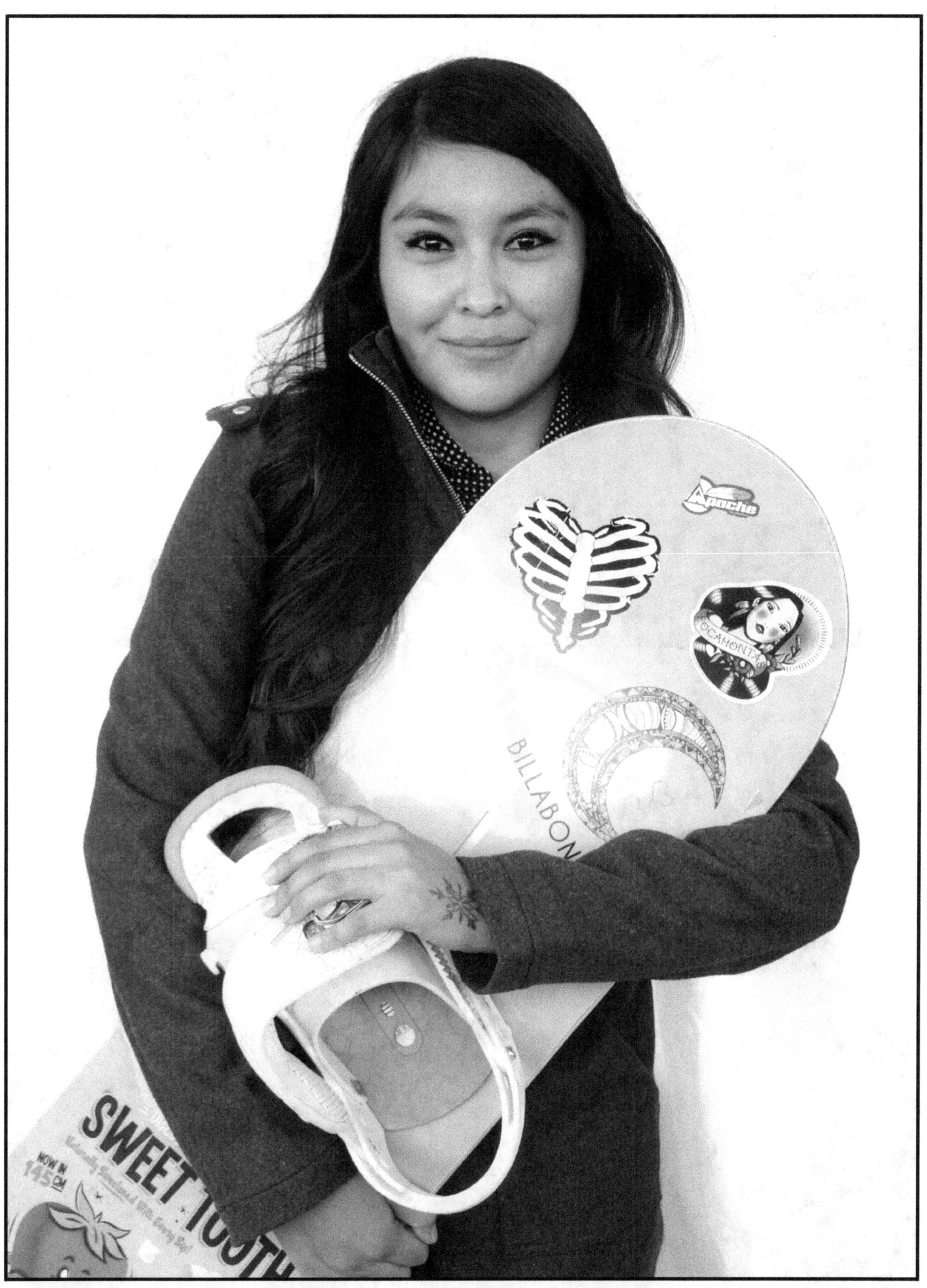

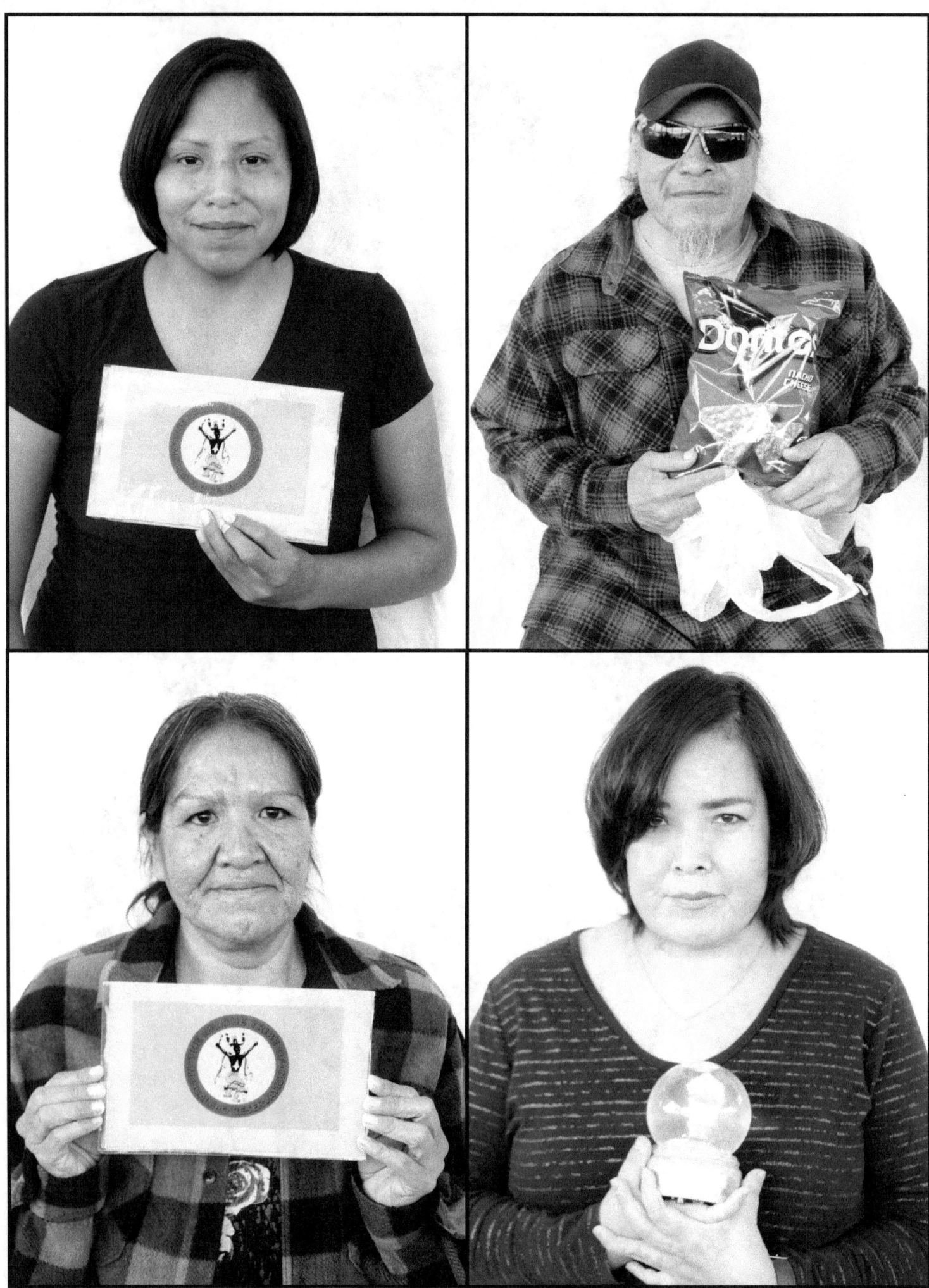

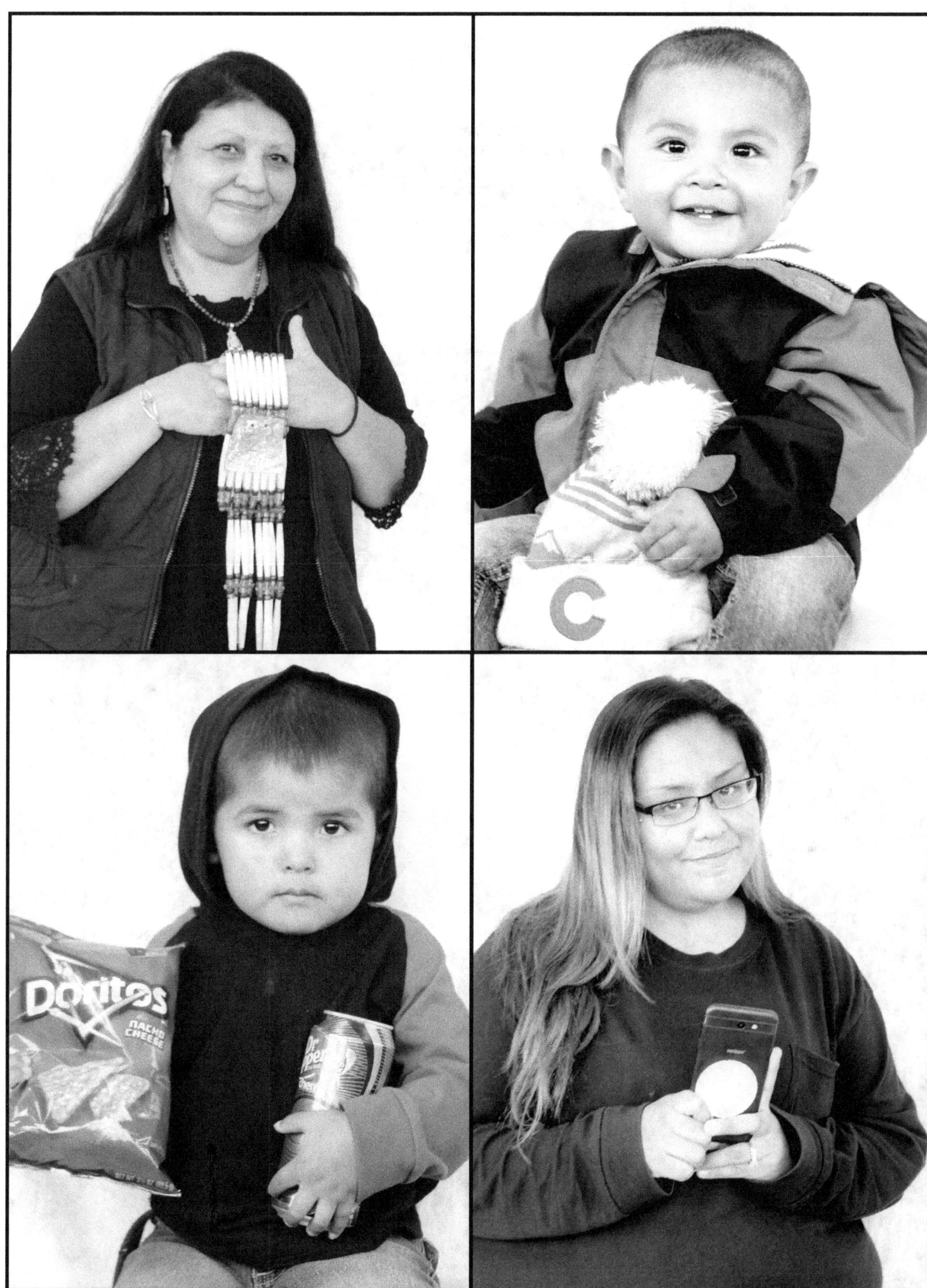

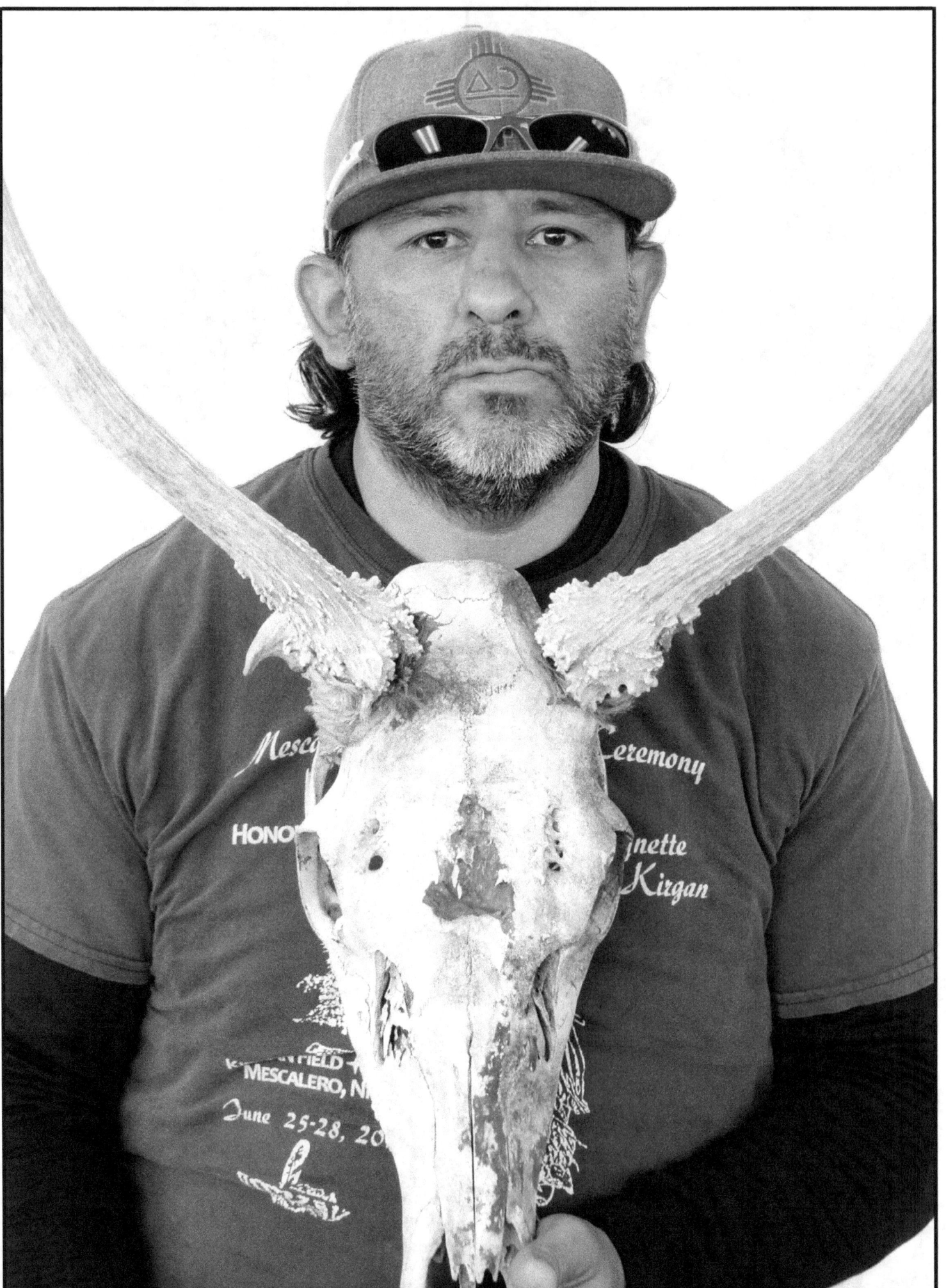

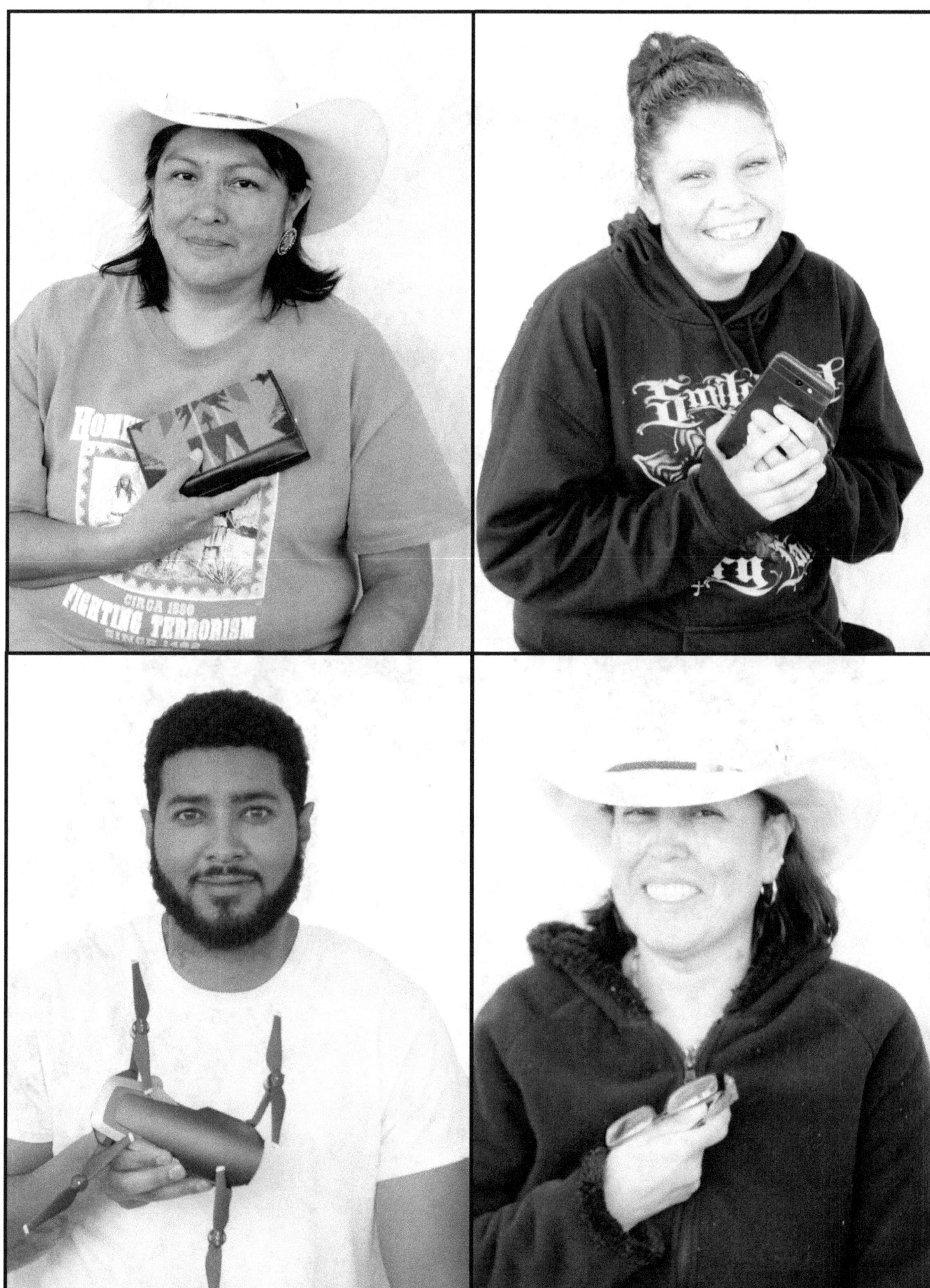

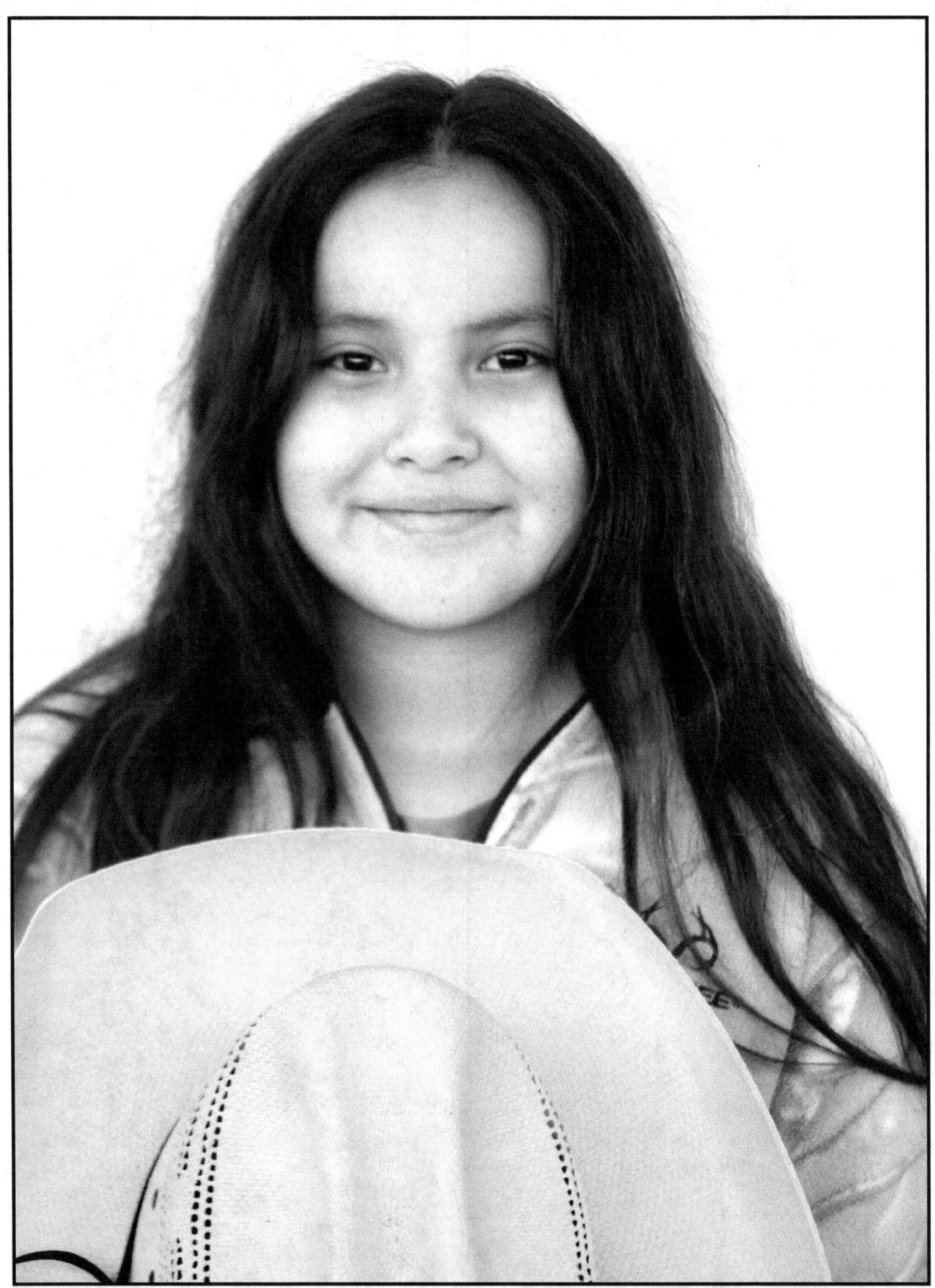

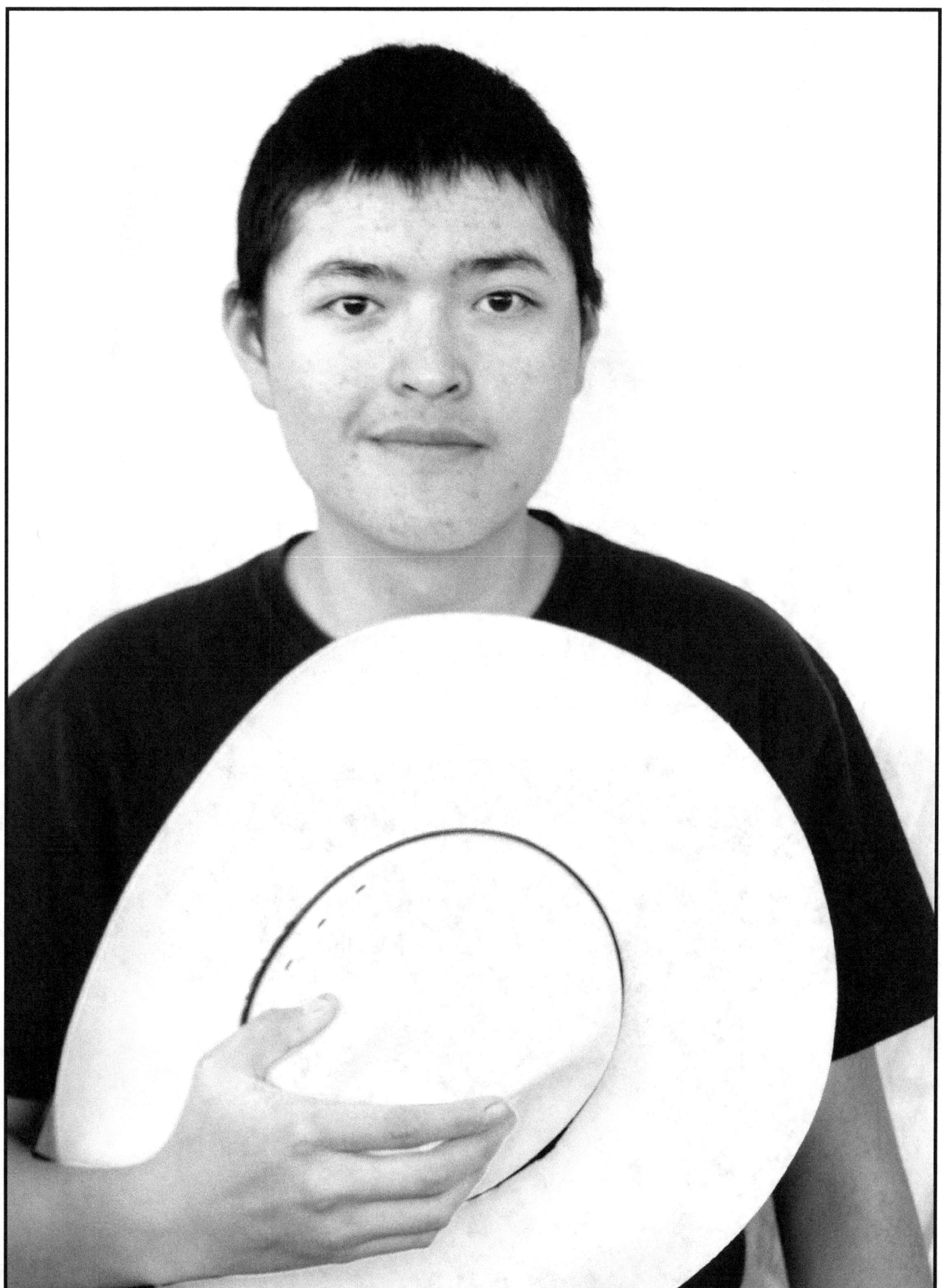

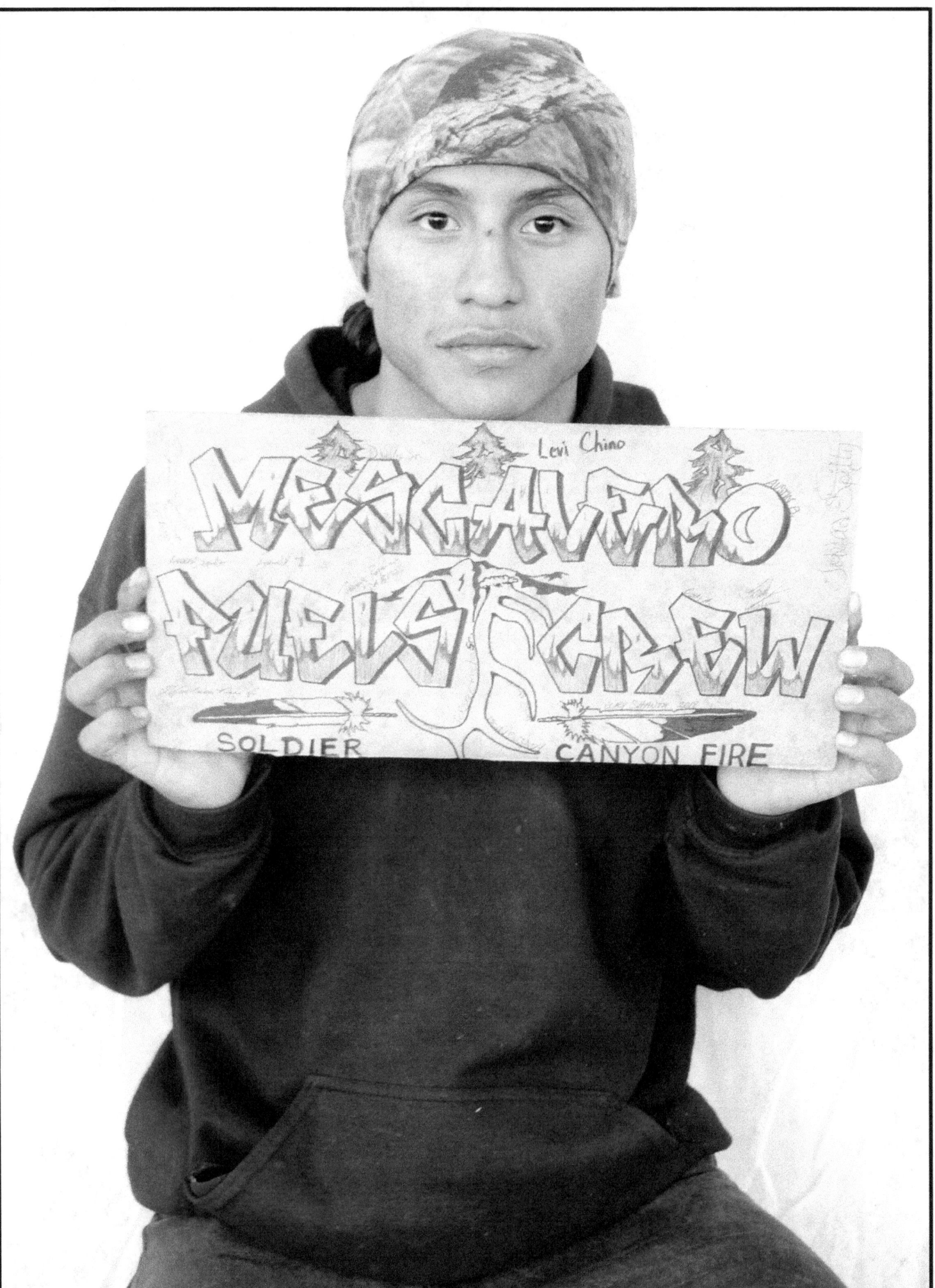

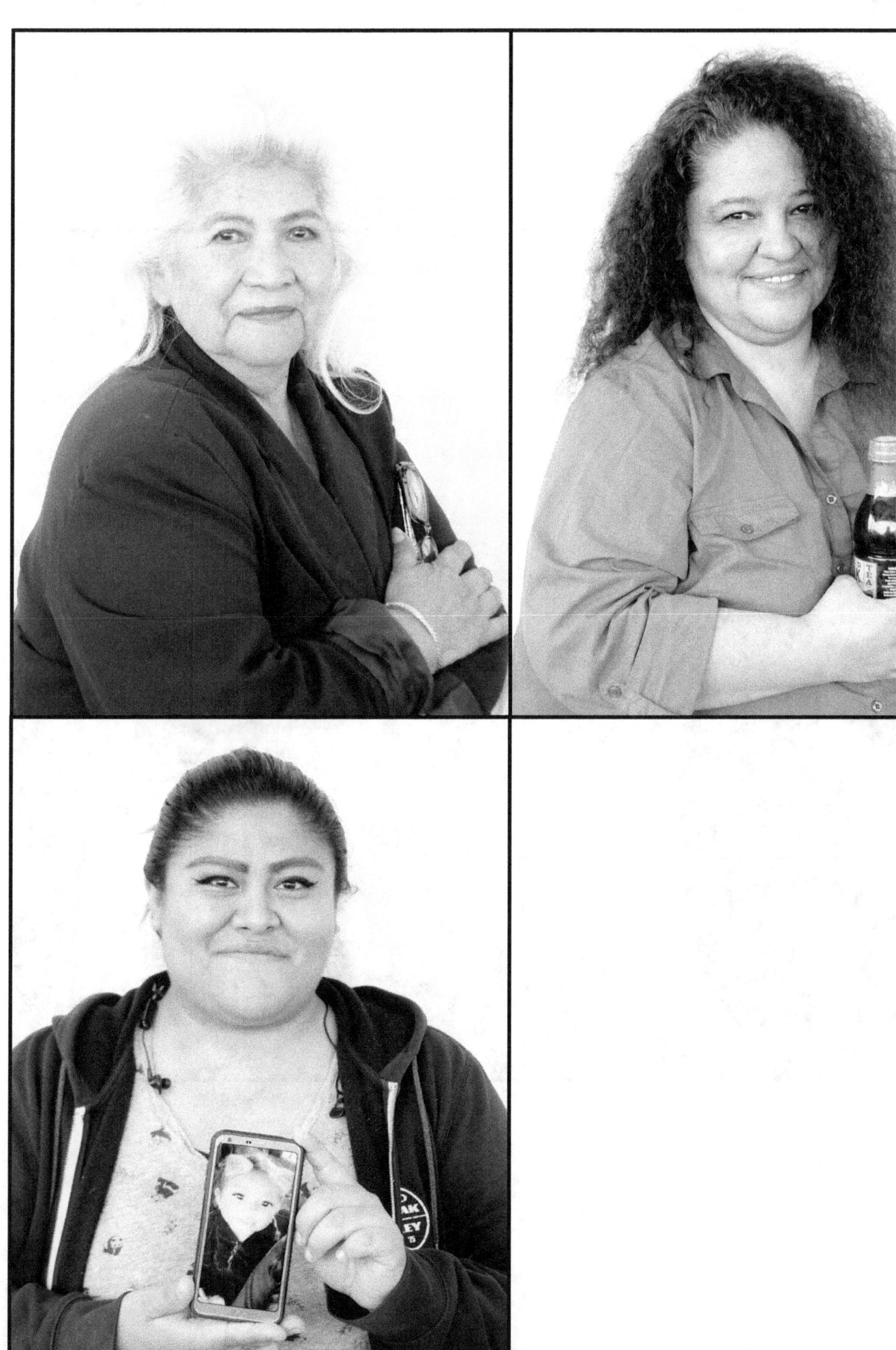

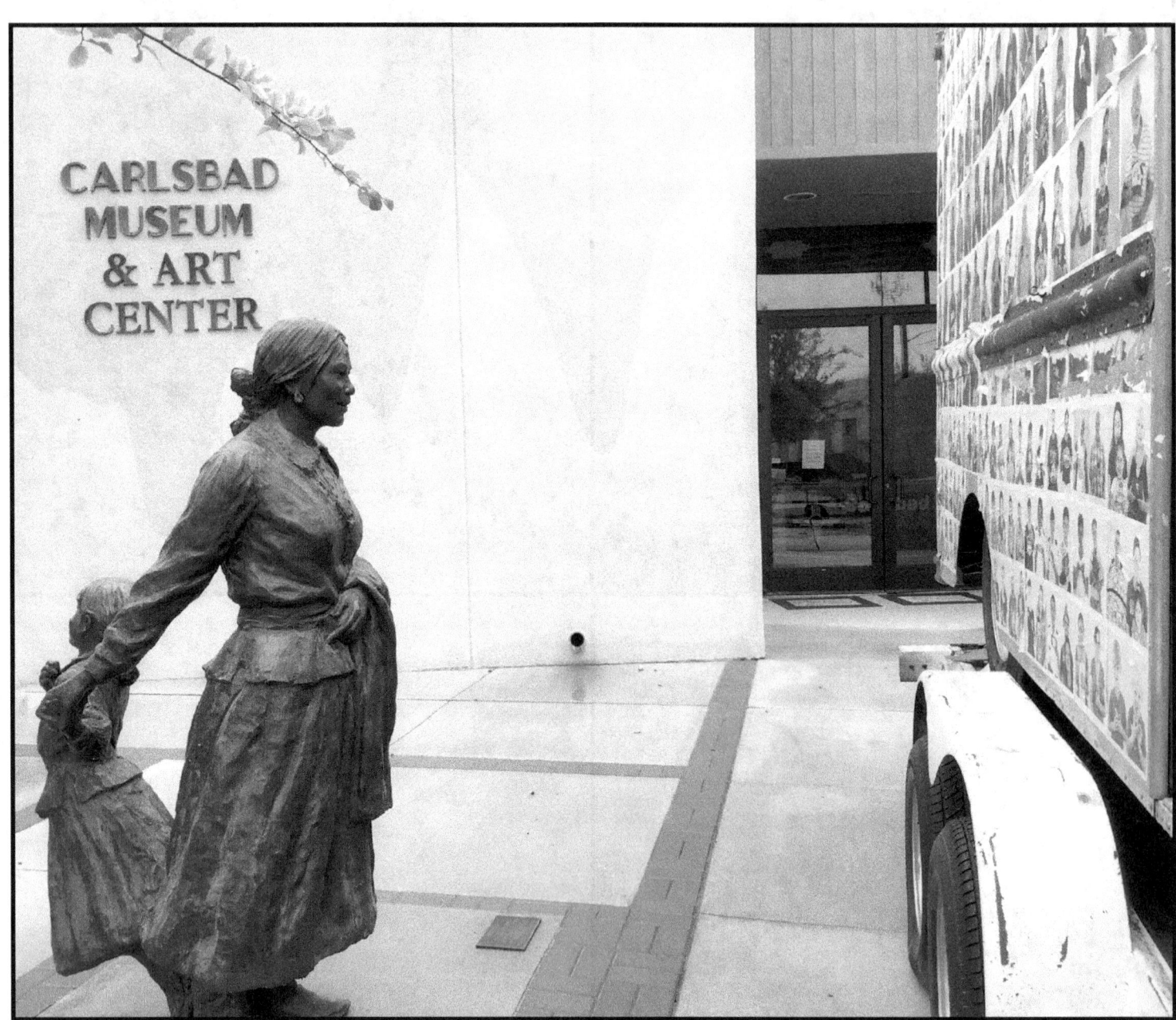

Carlsbad
October 18, 2019

New Mexico State University
Carlsbad Museum and Art Center

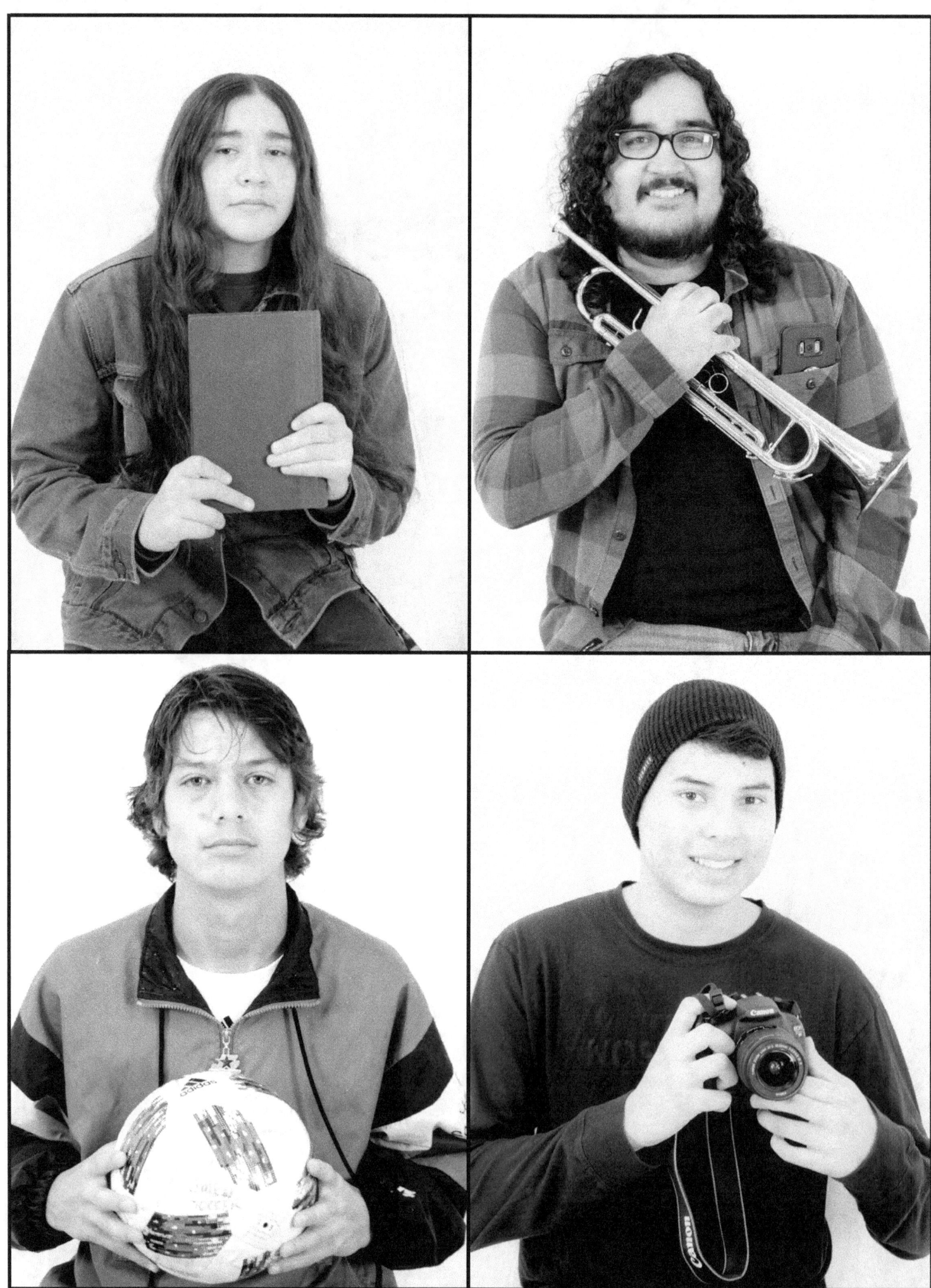

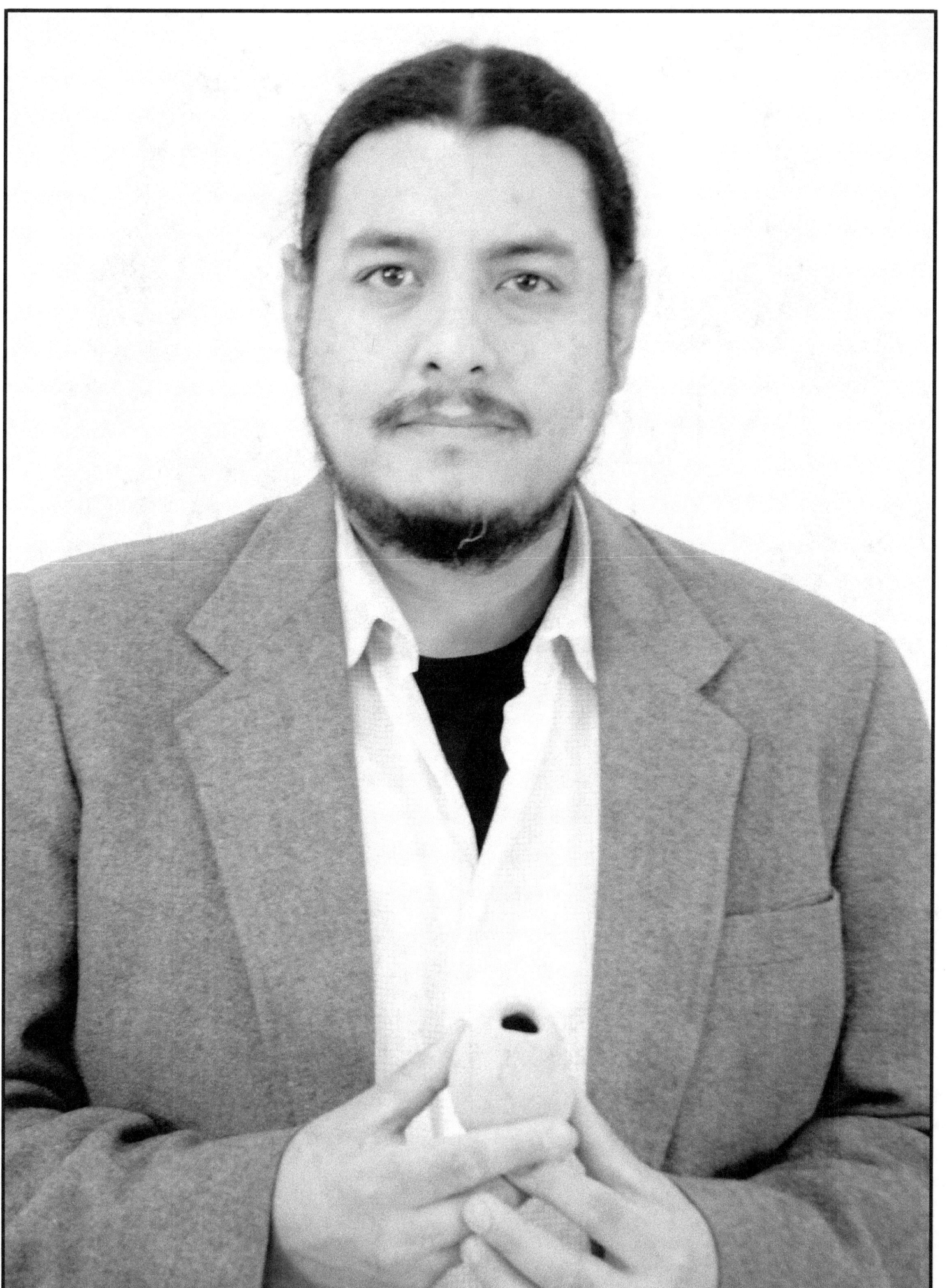

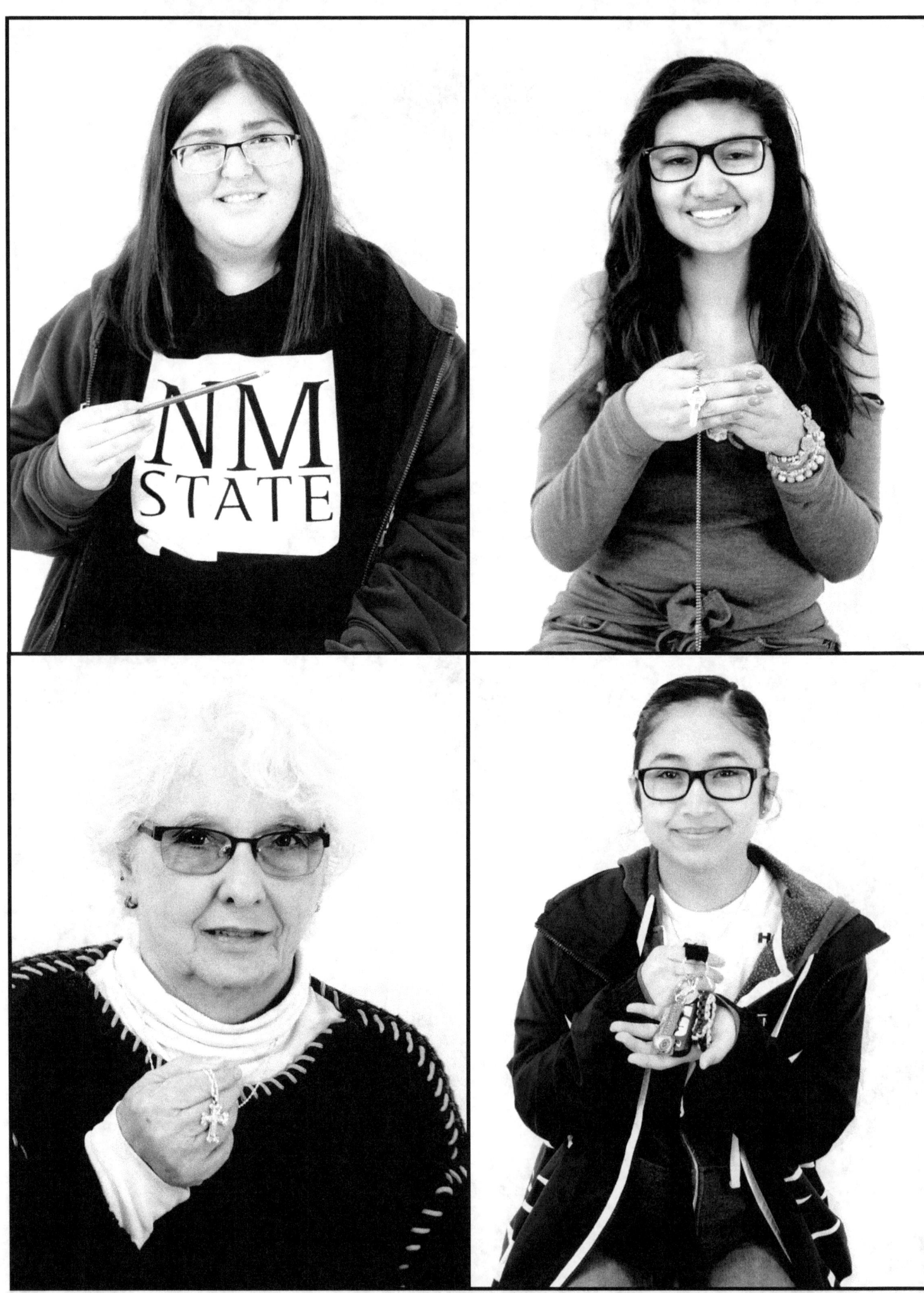

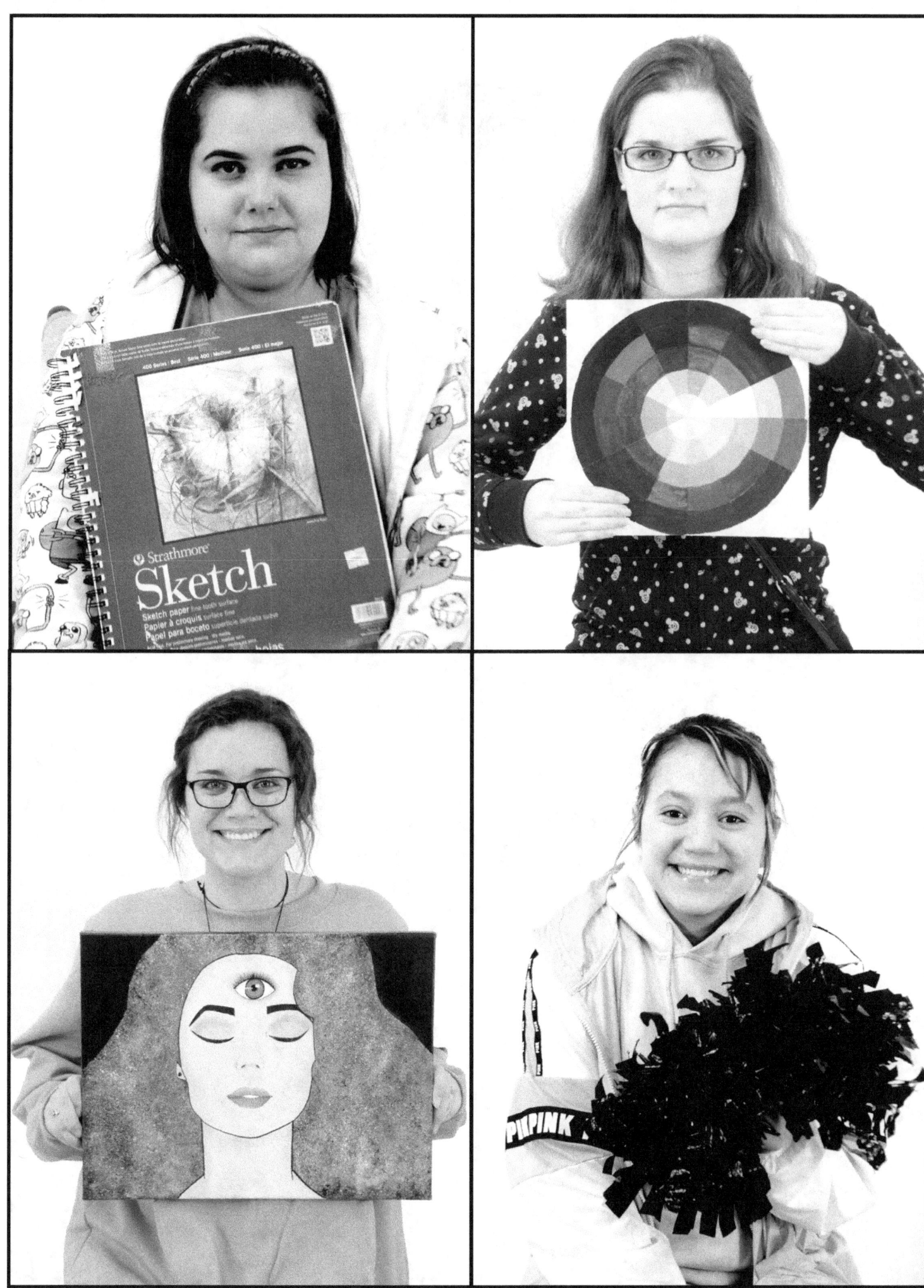

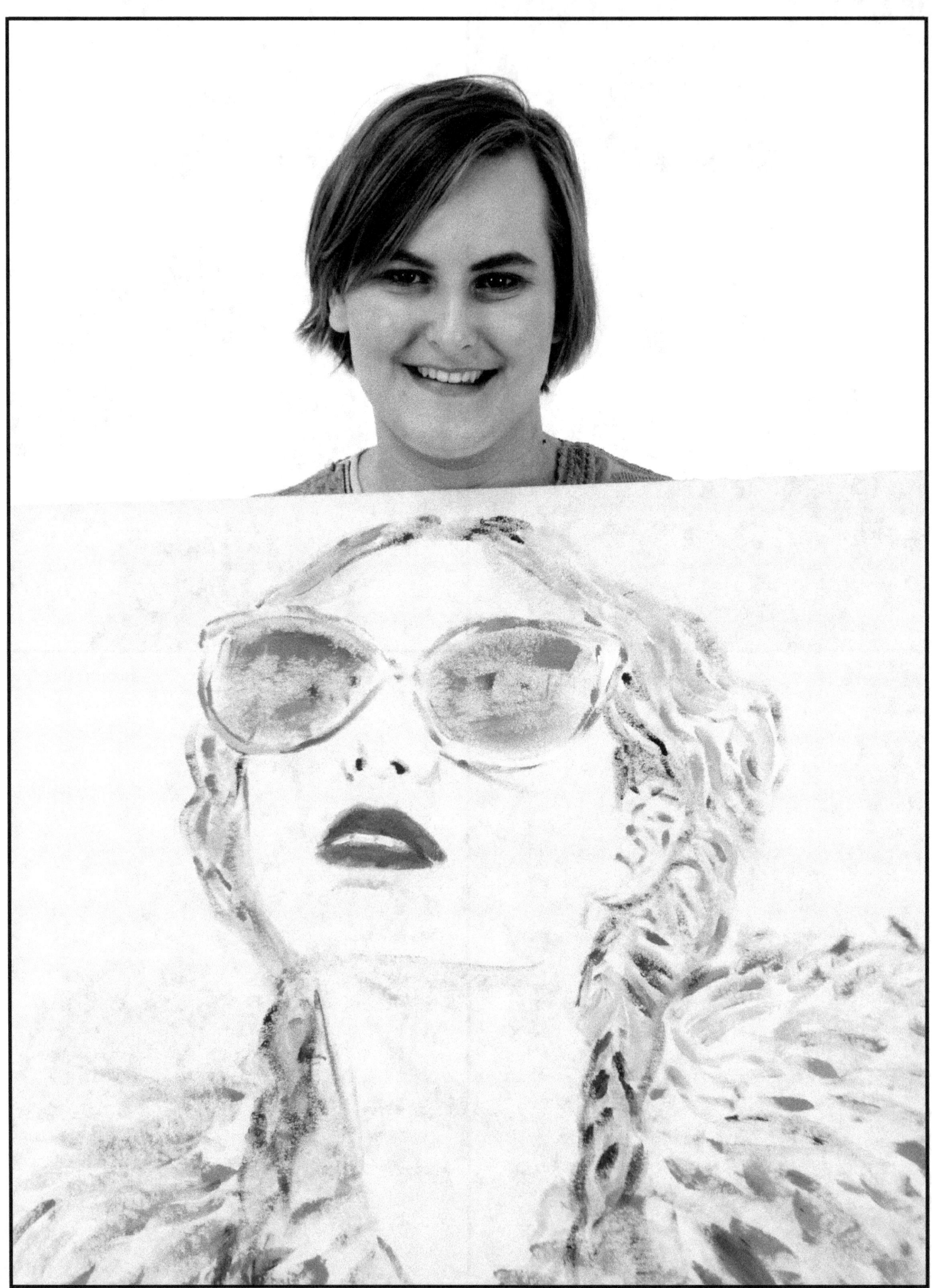

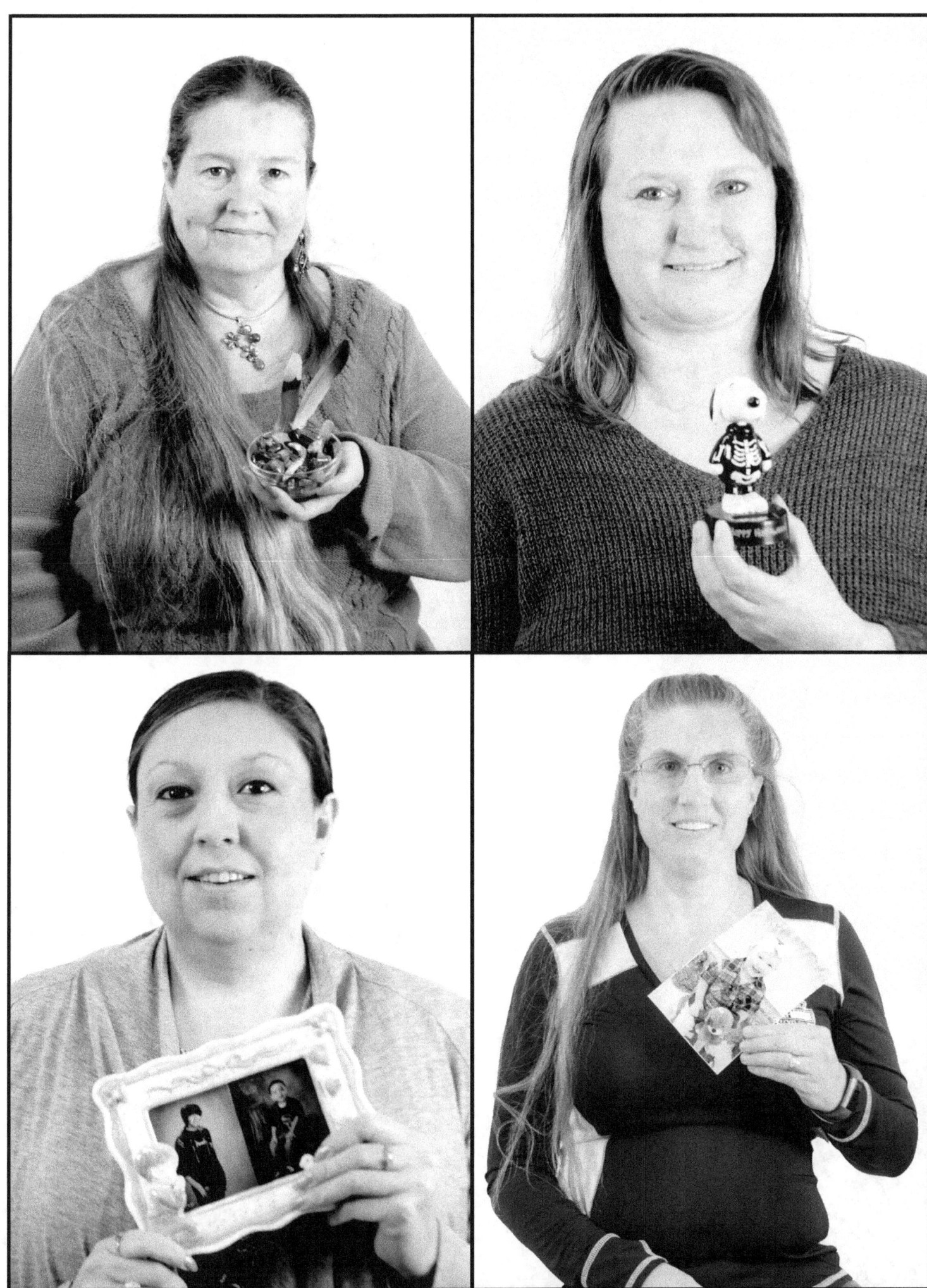

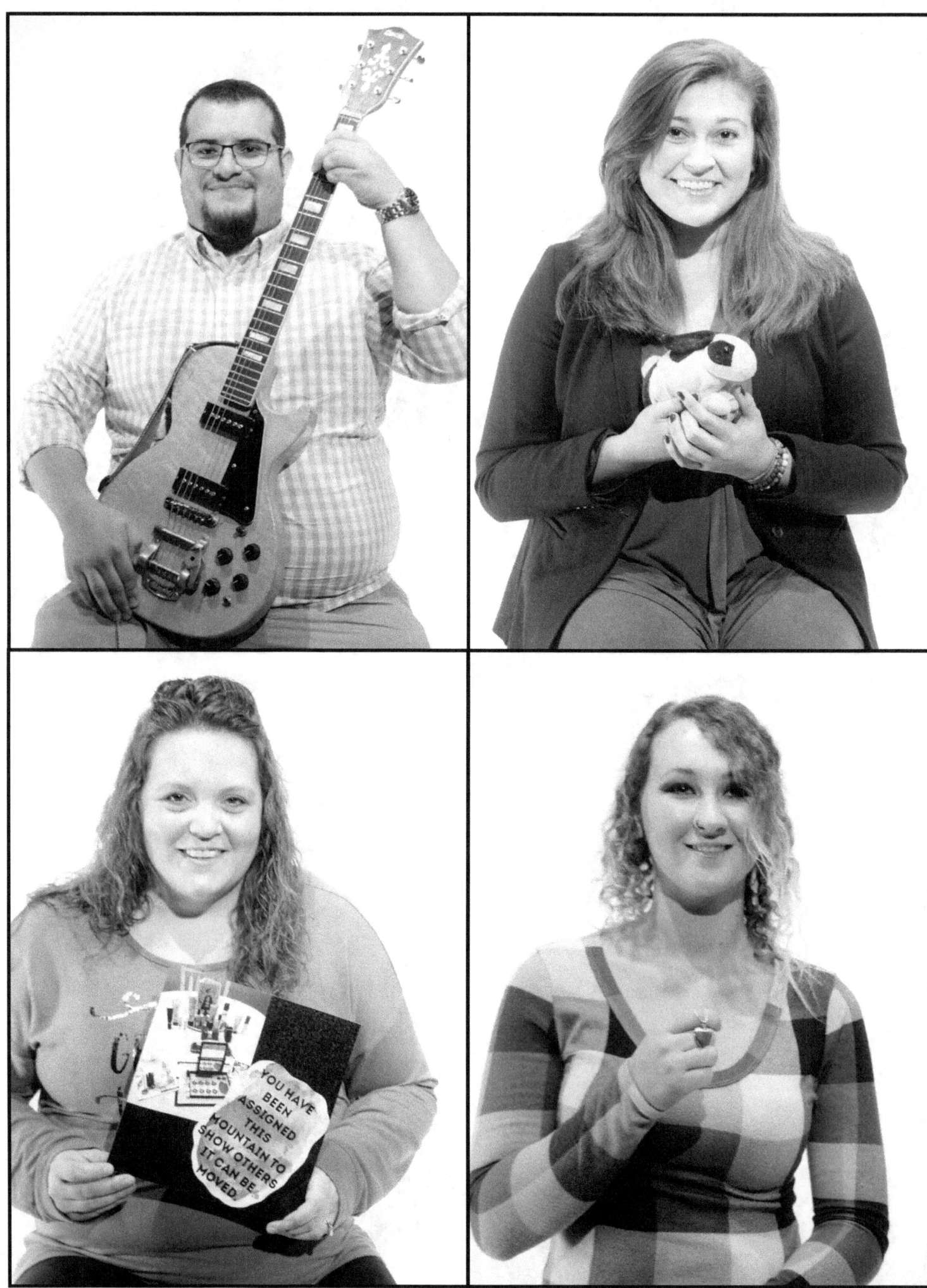

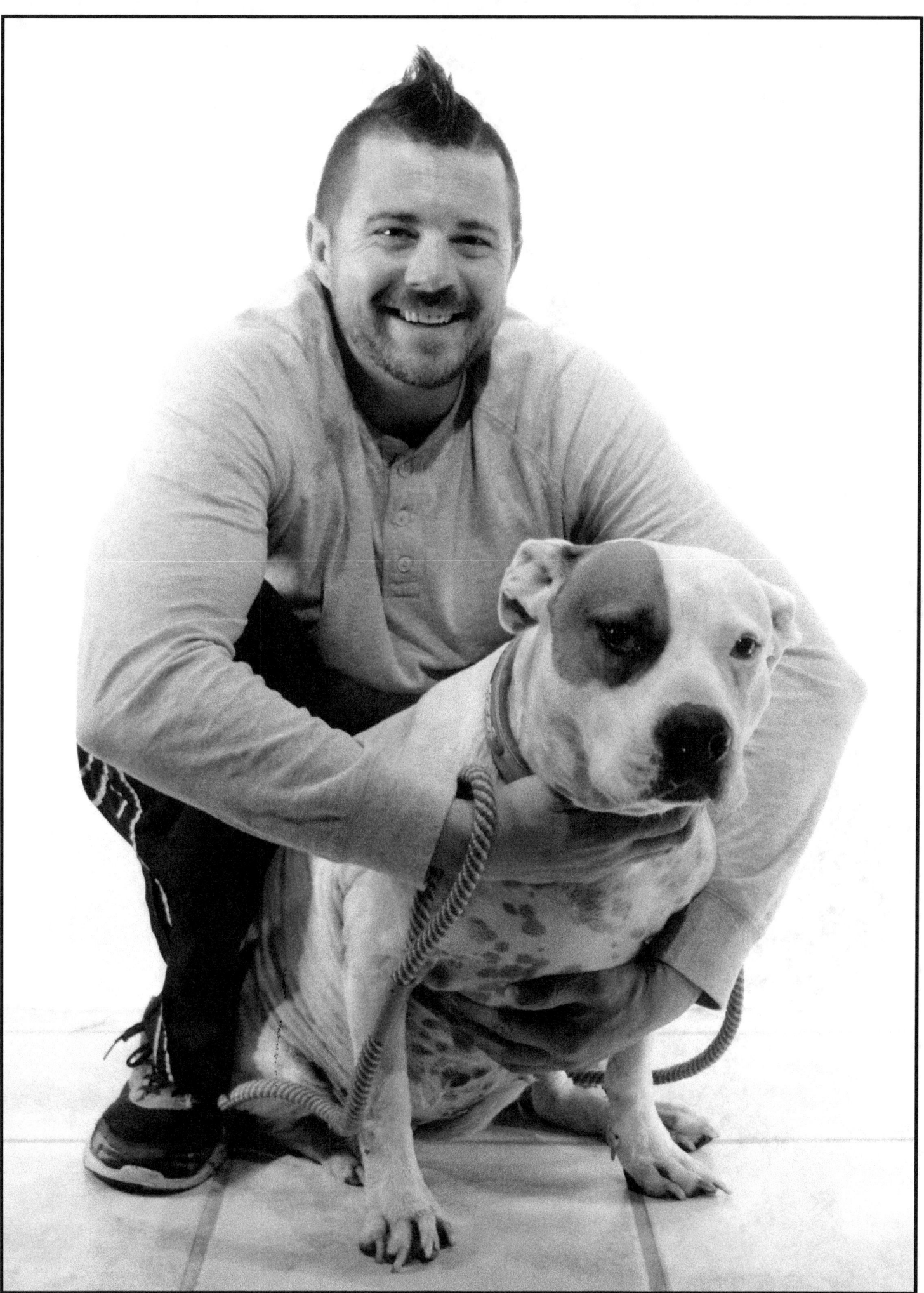

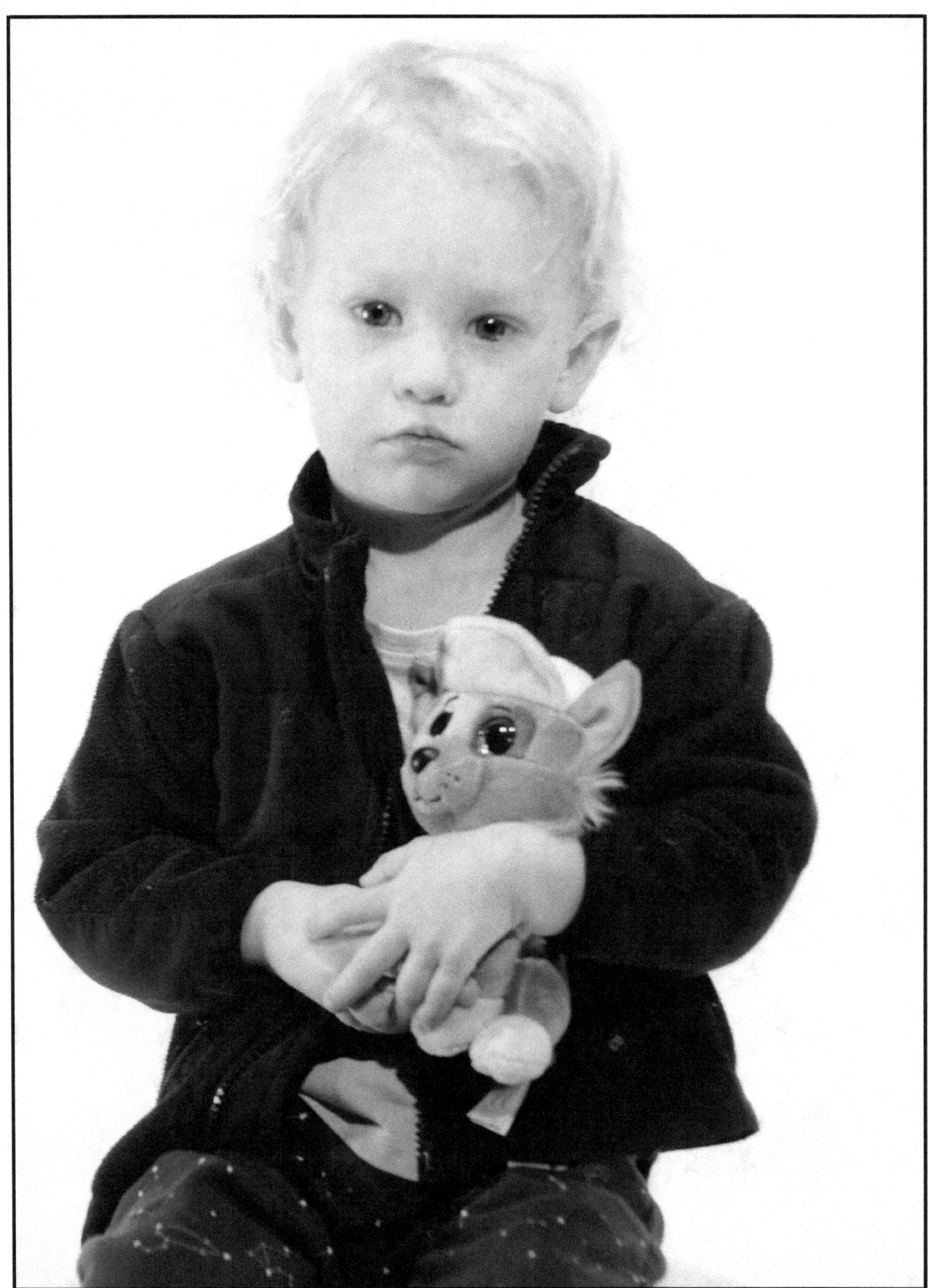

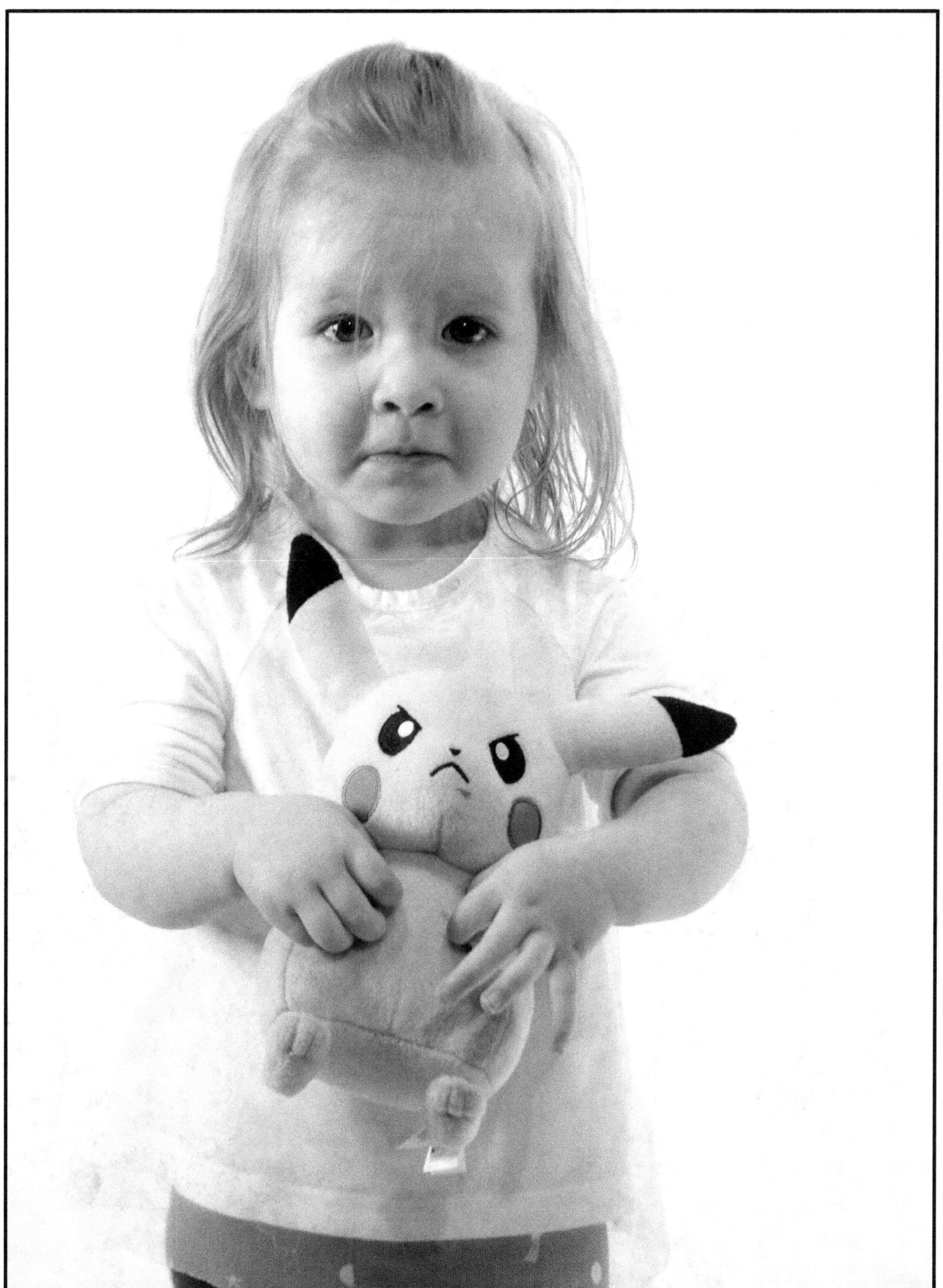

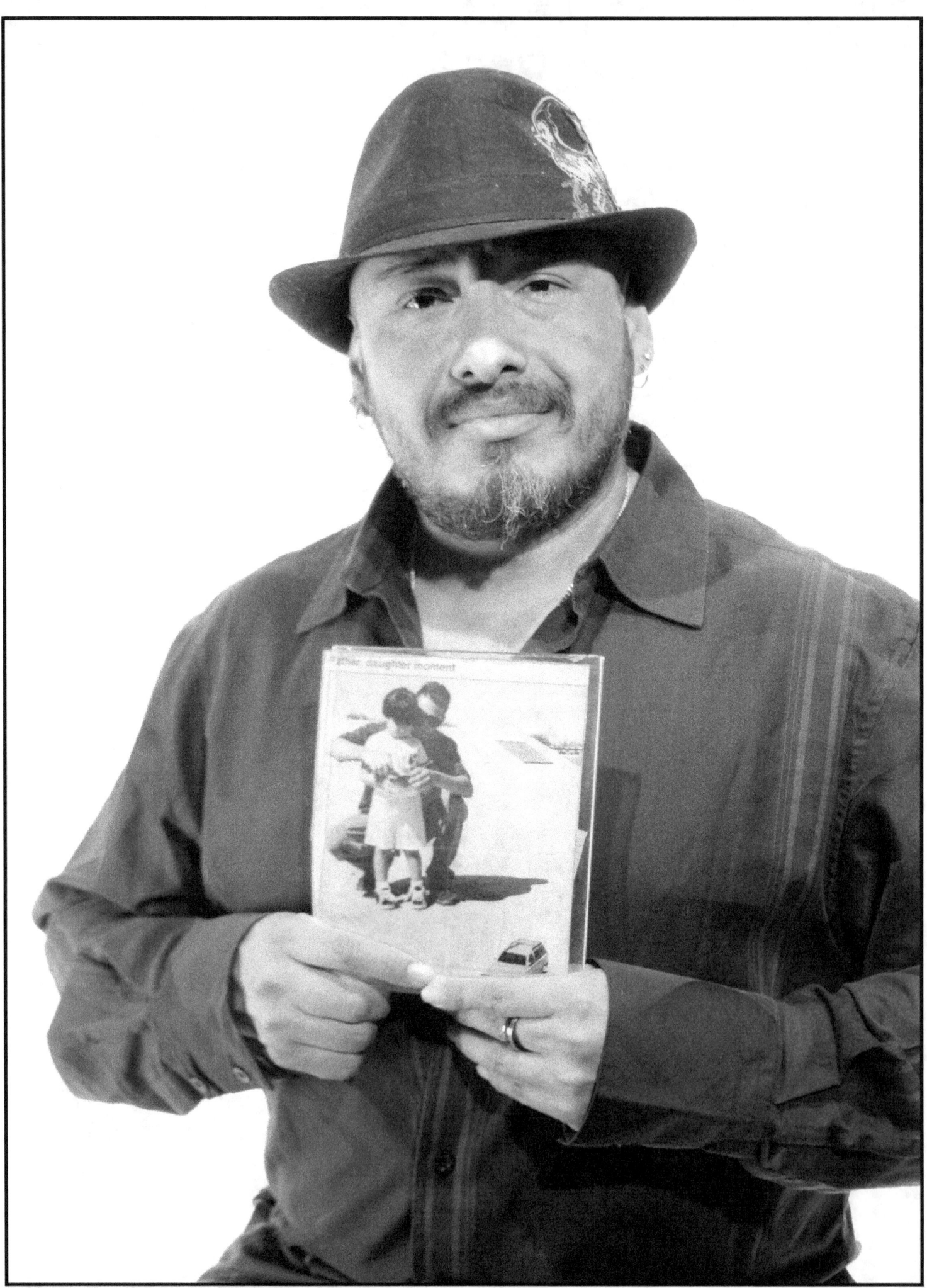

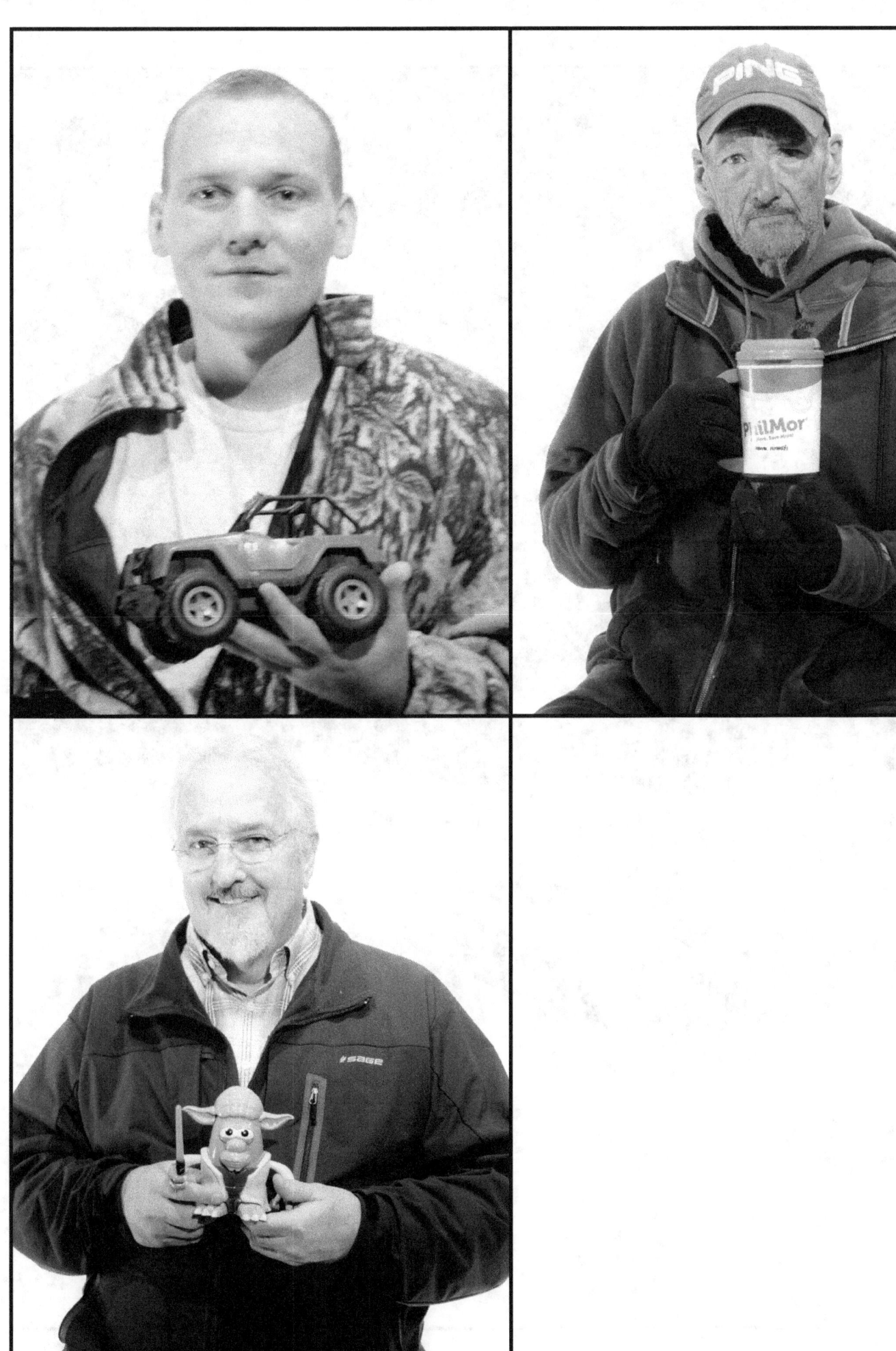

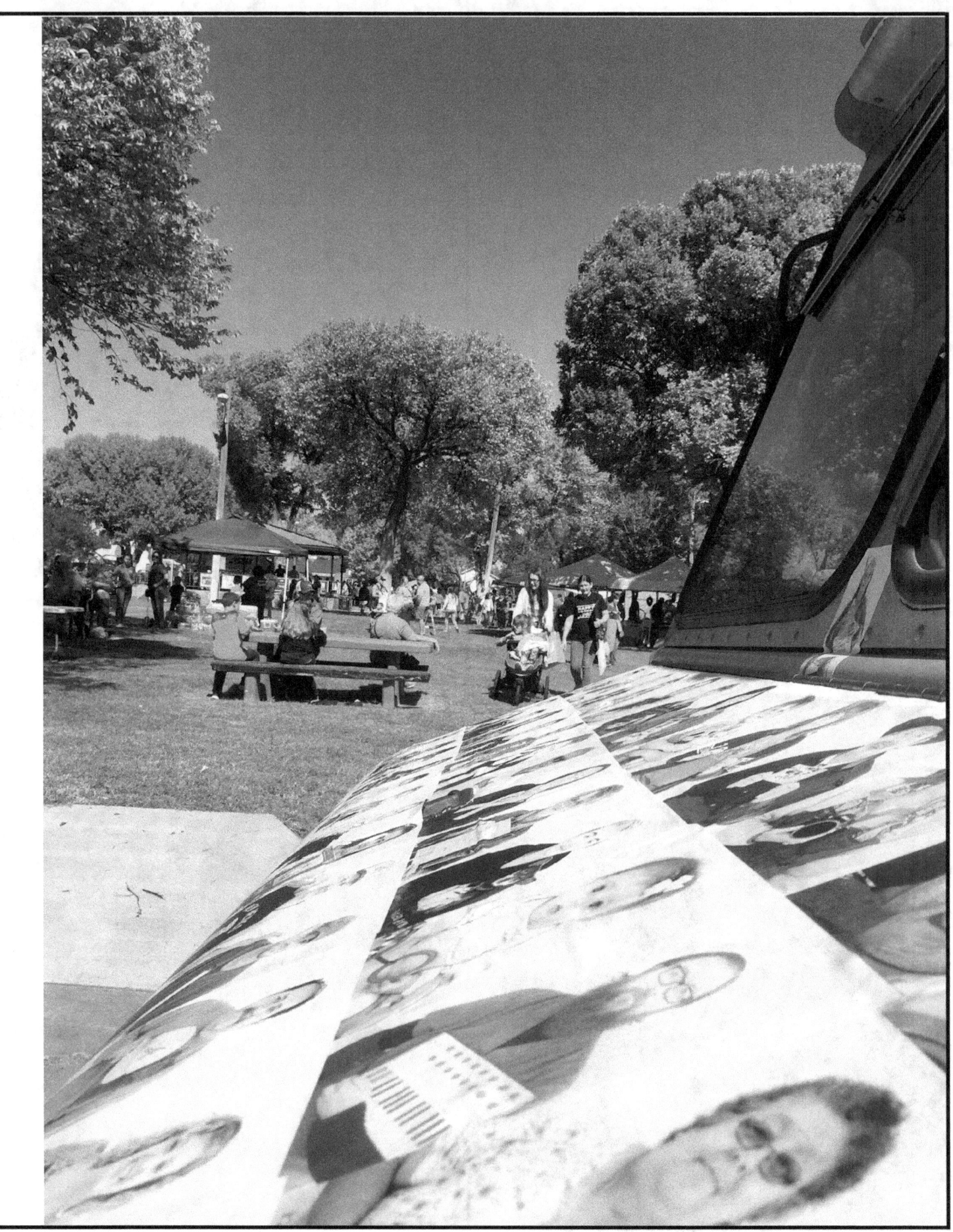

Artesia
October 19-20, 2019

Artesia Public Library
Art in the Park, Central Park

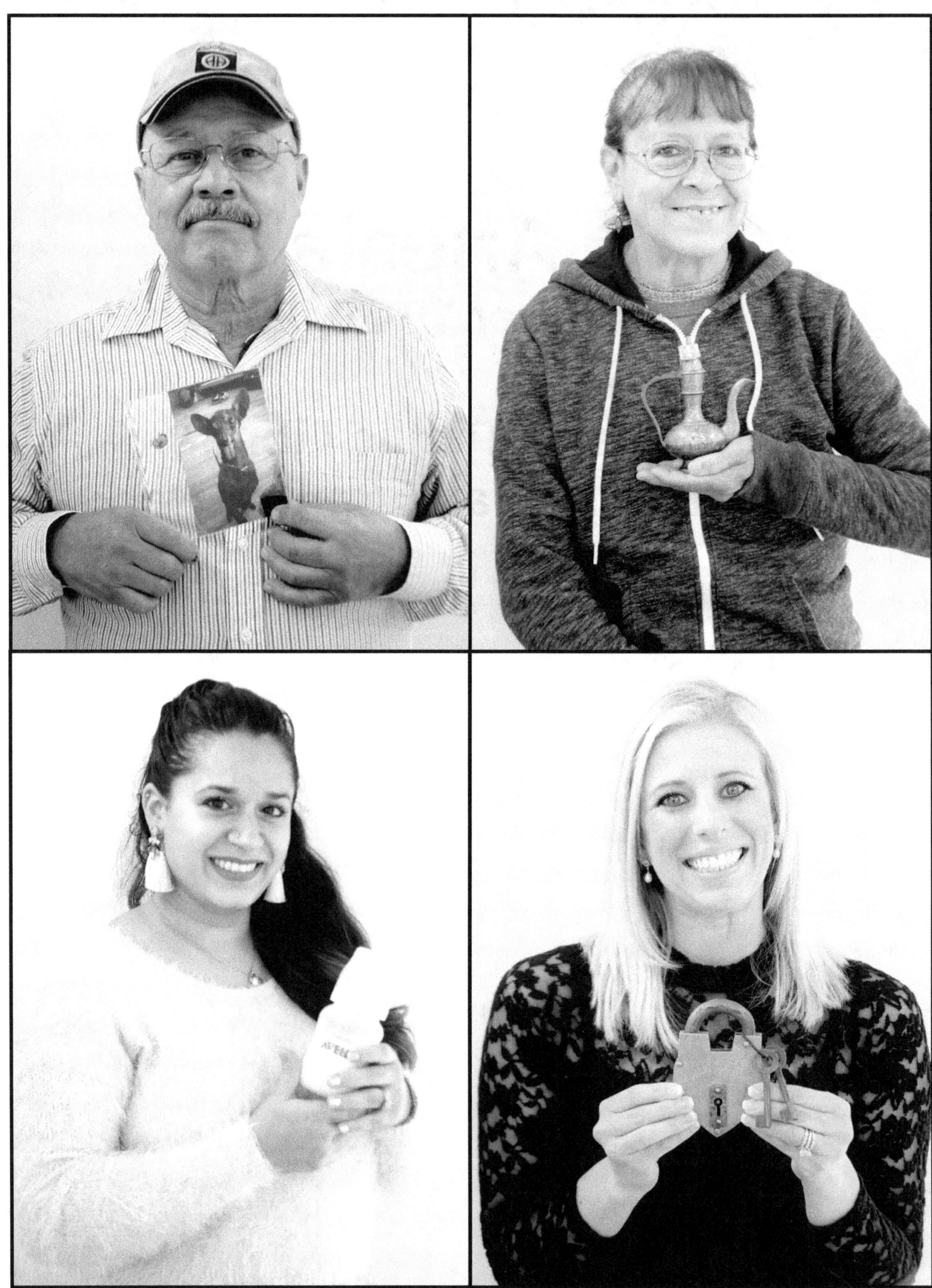

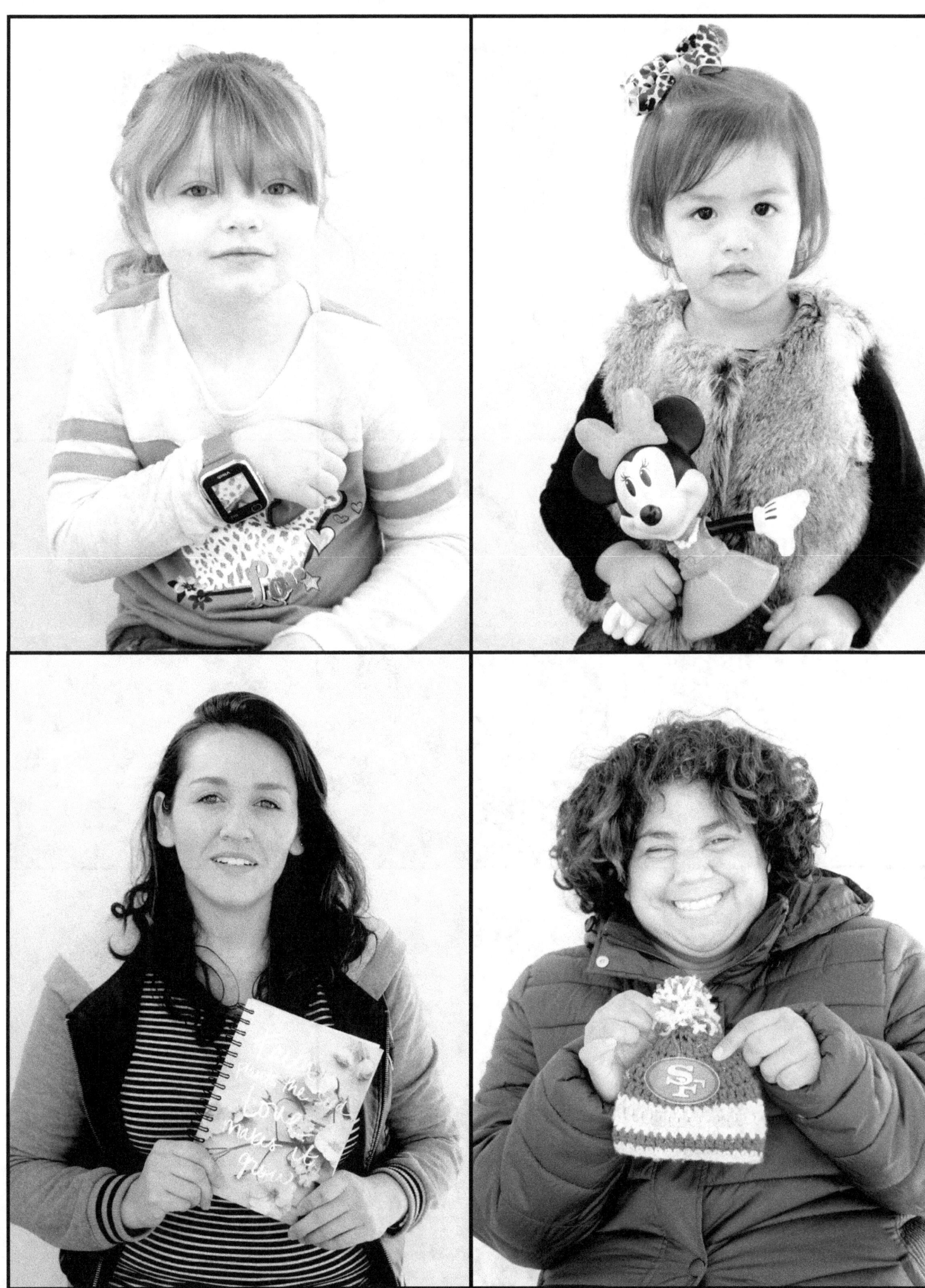

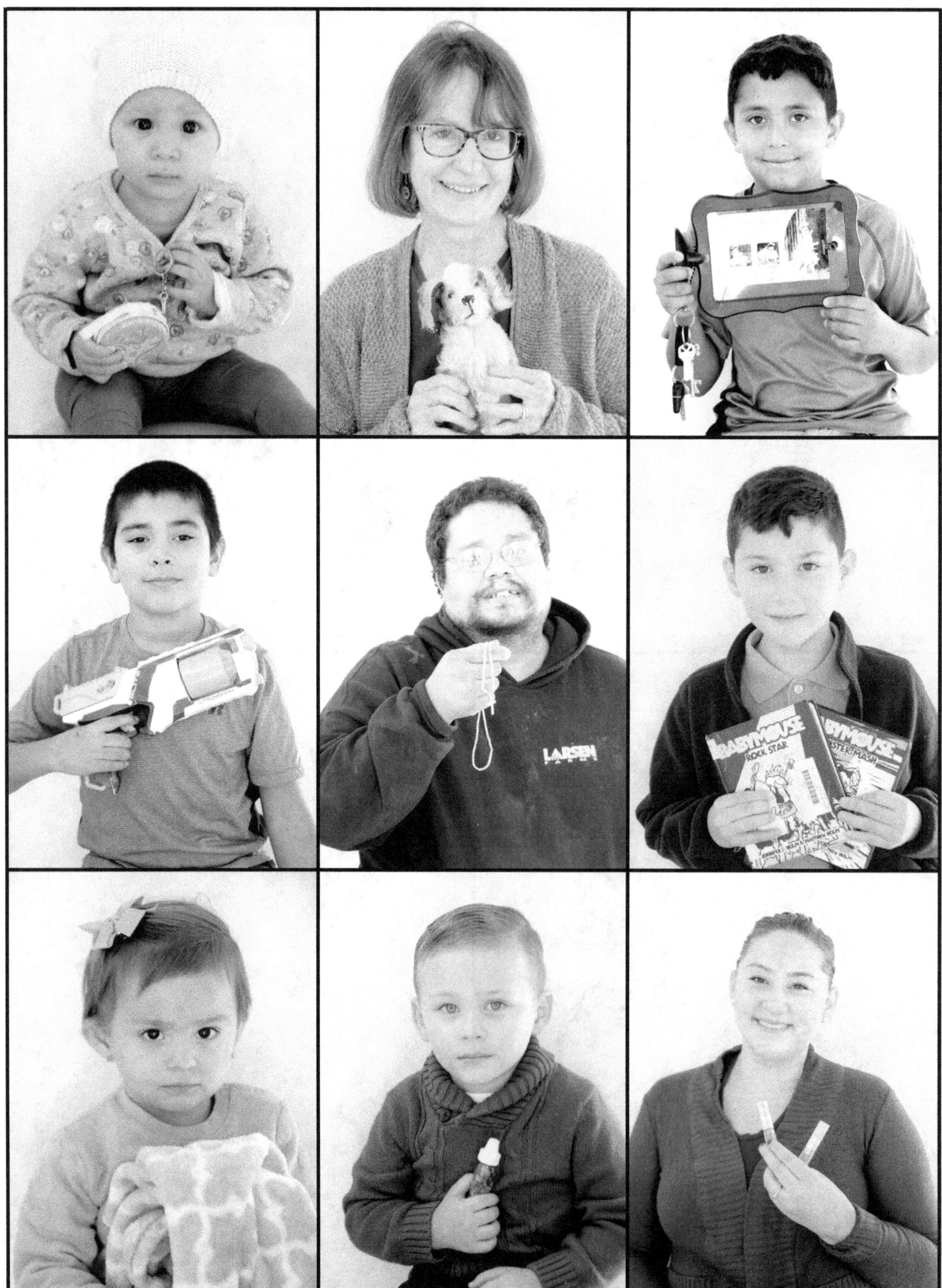

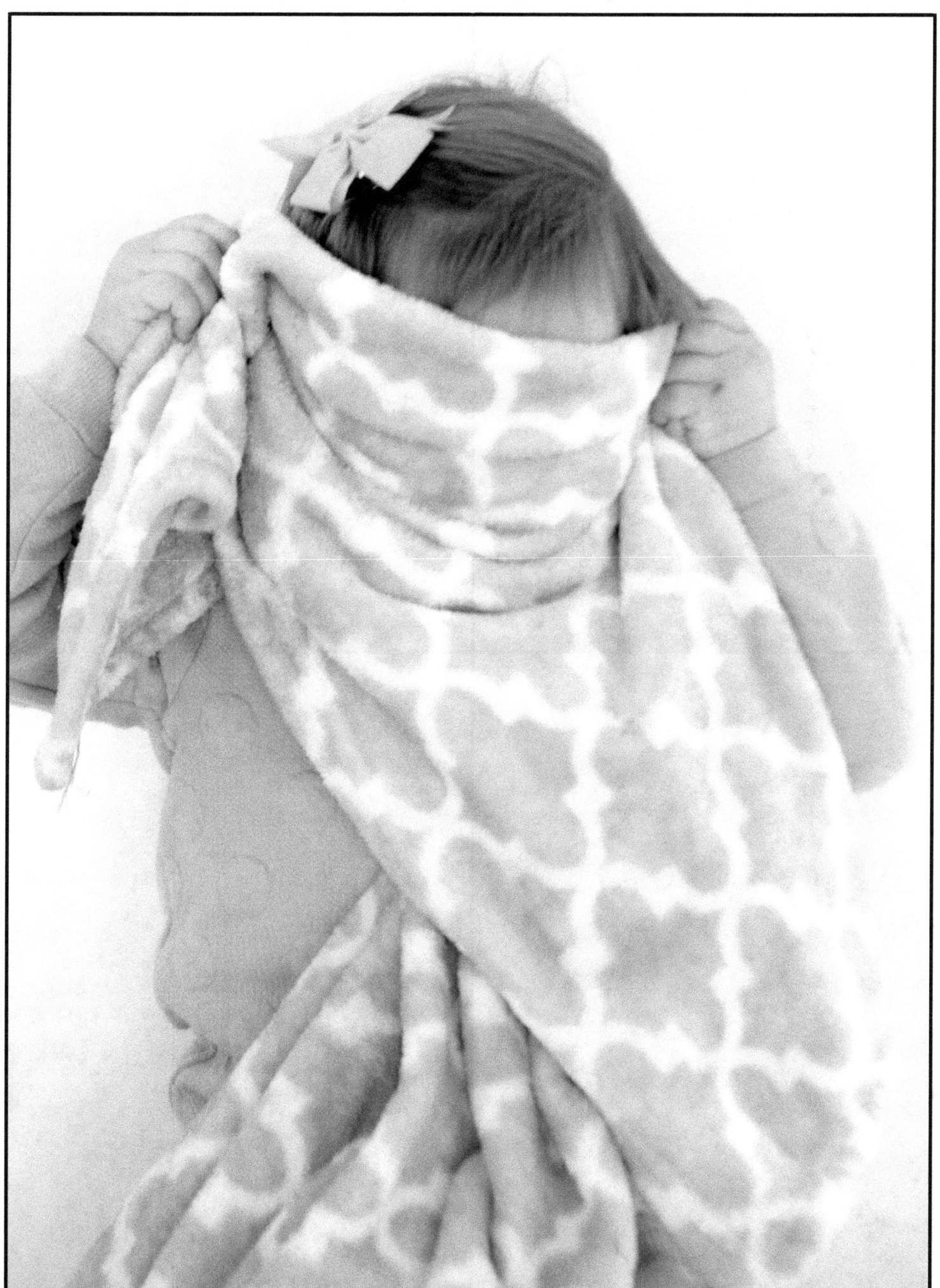

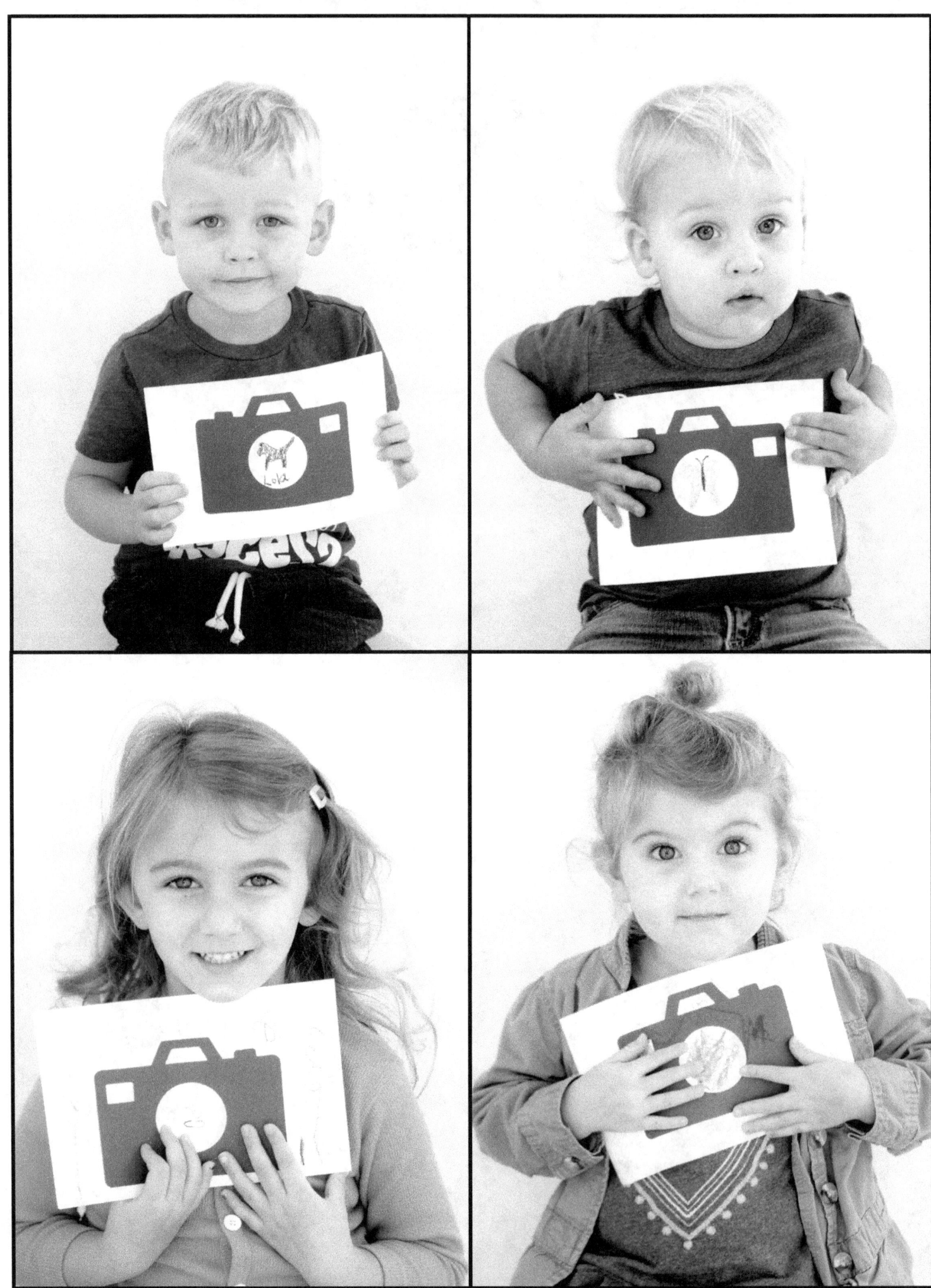

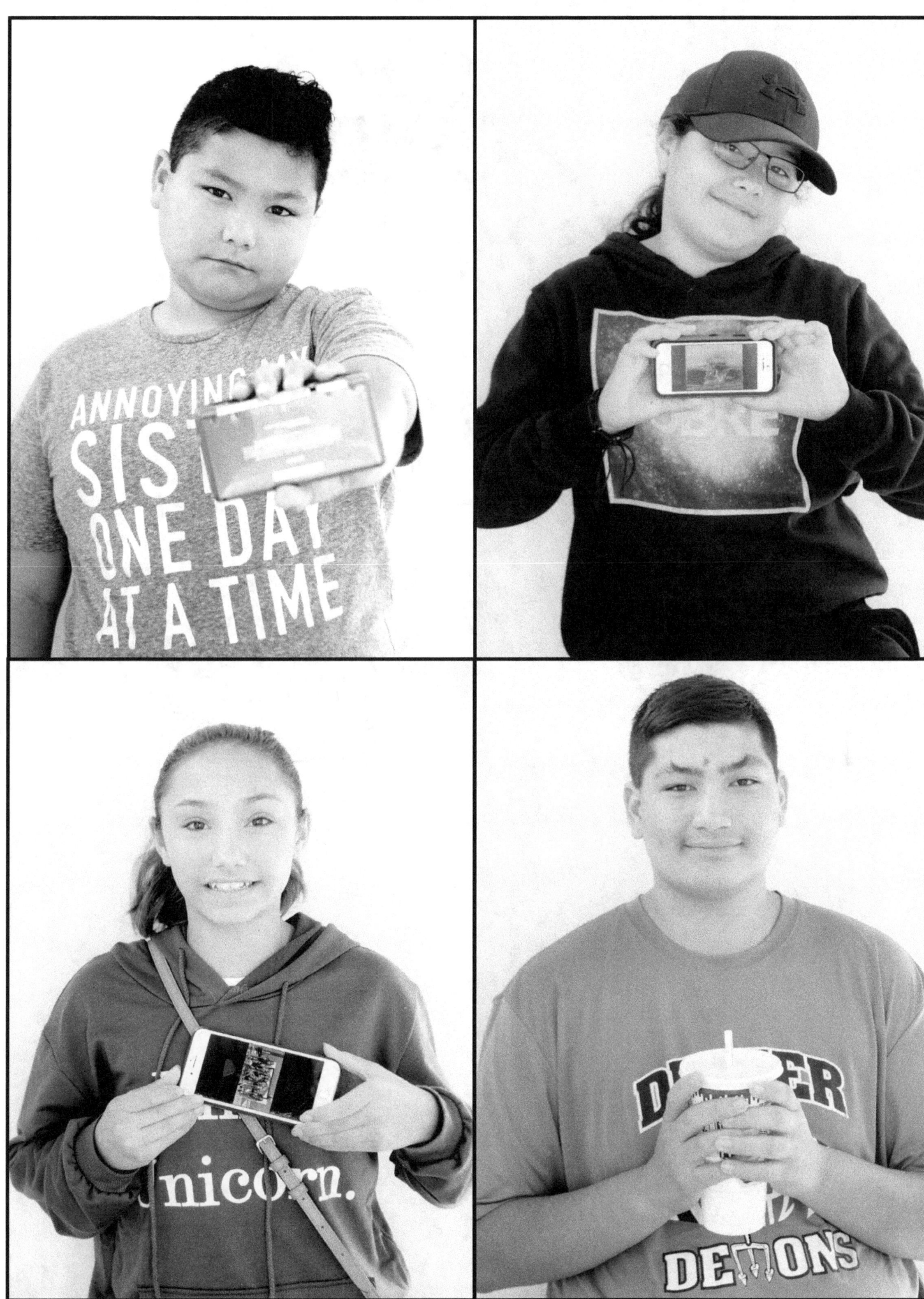

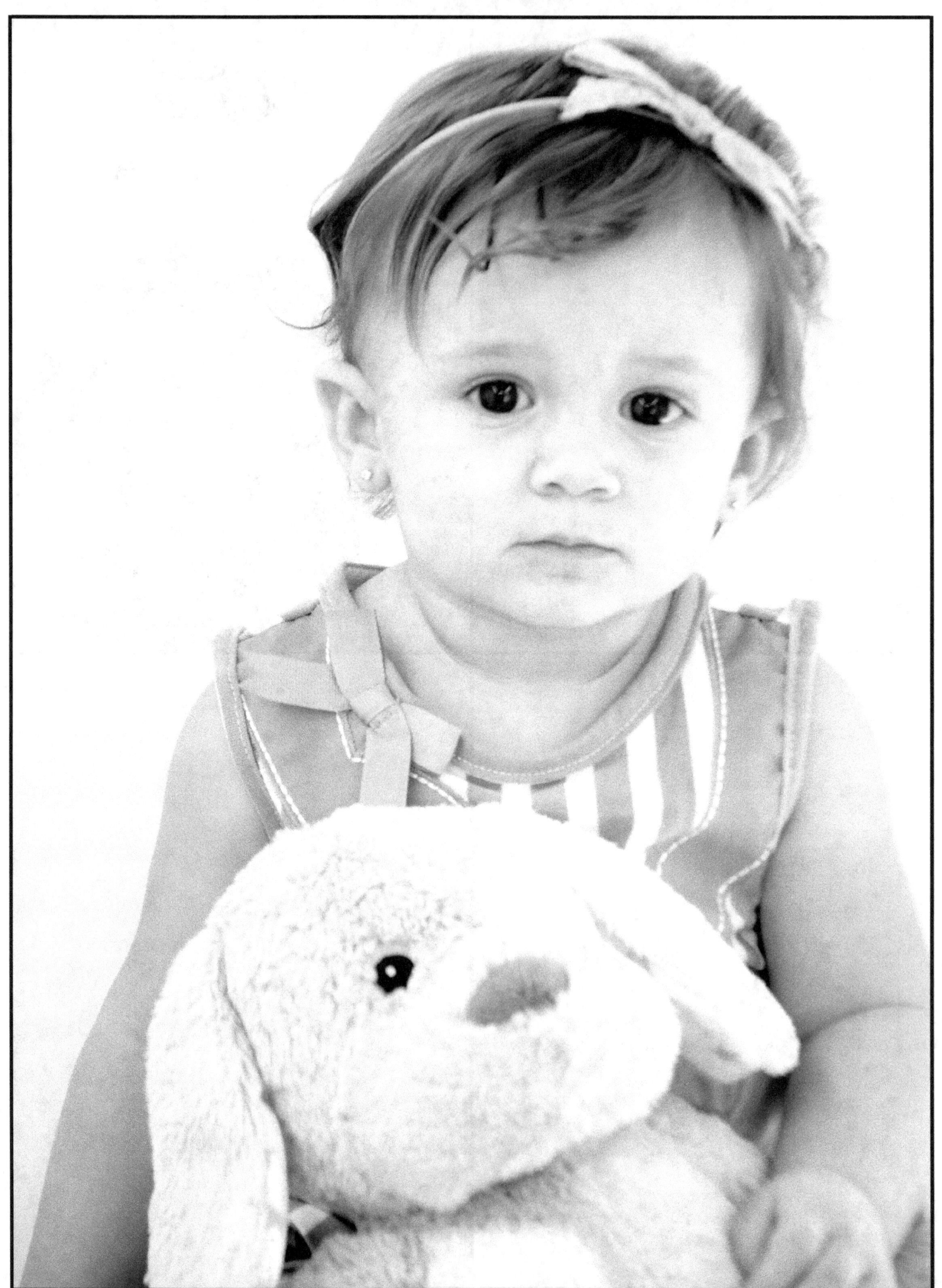

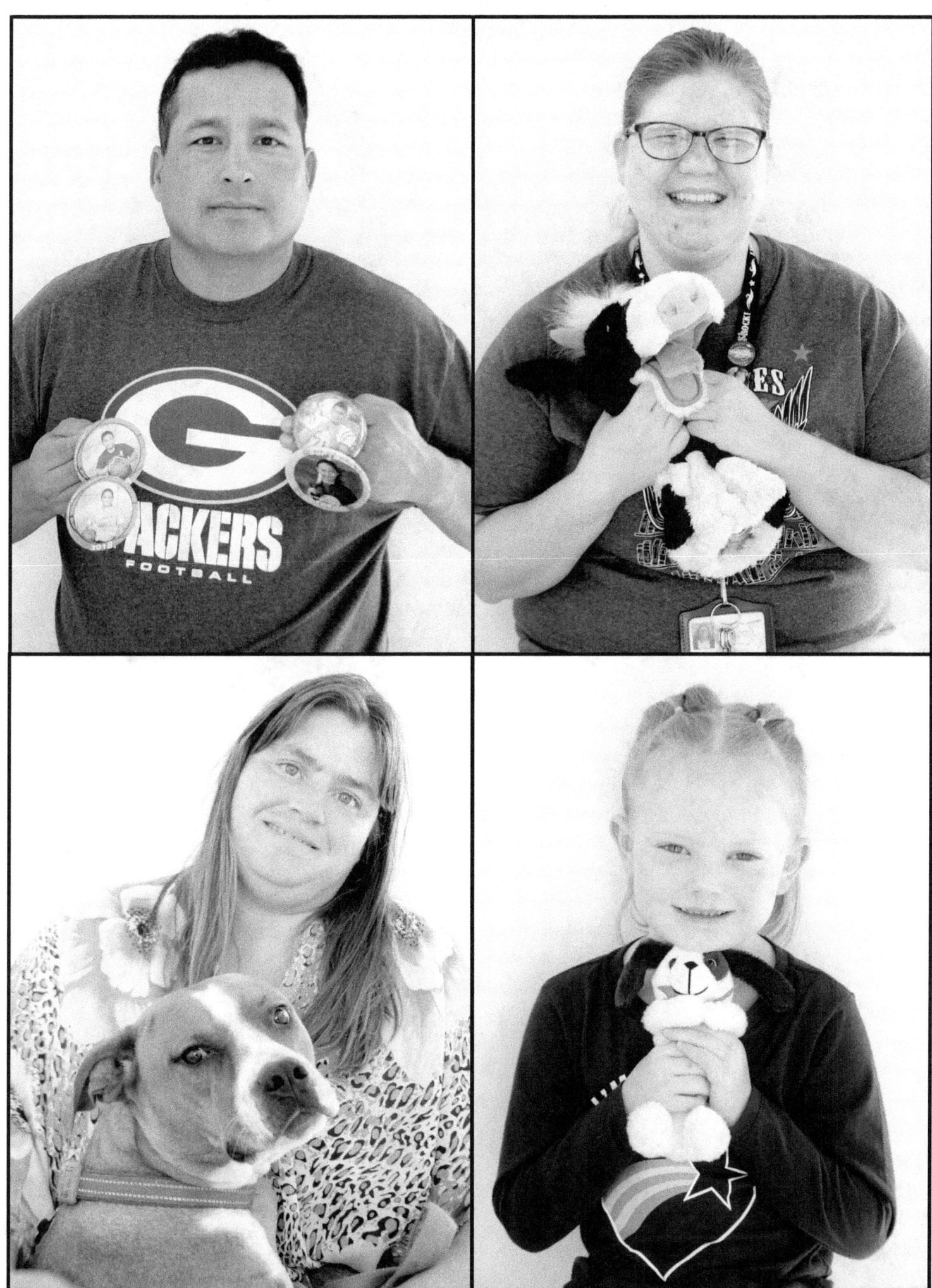

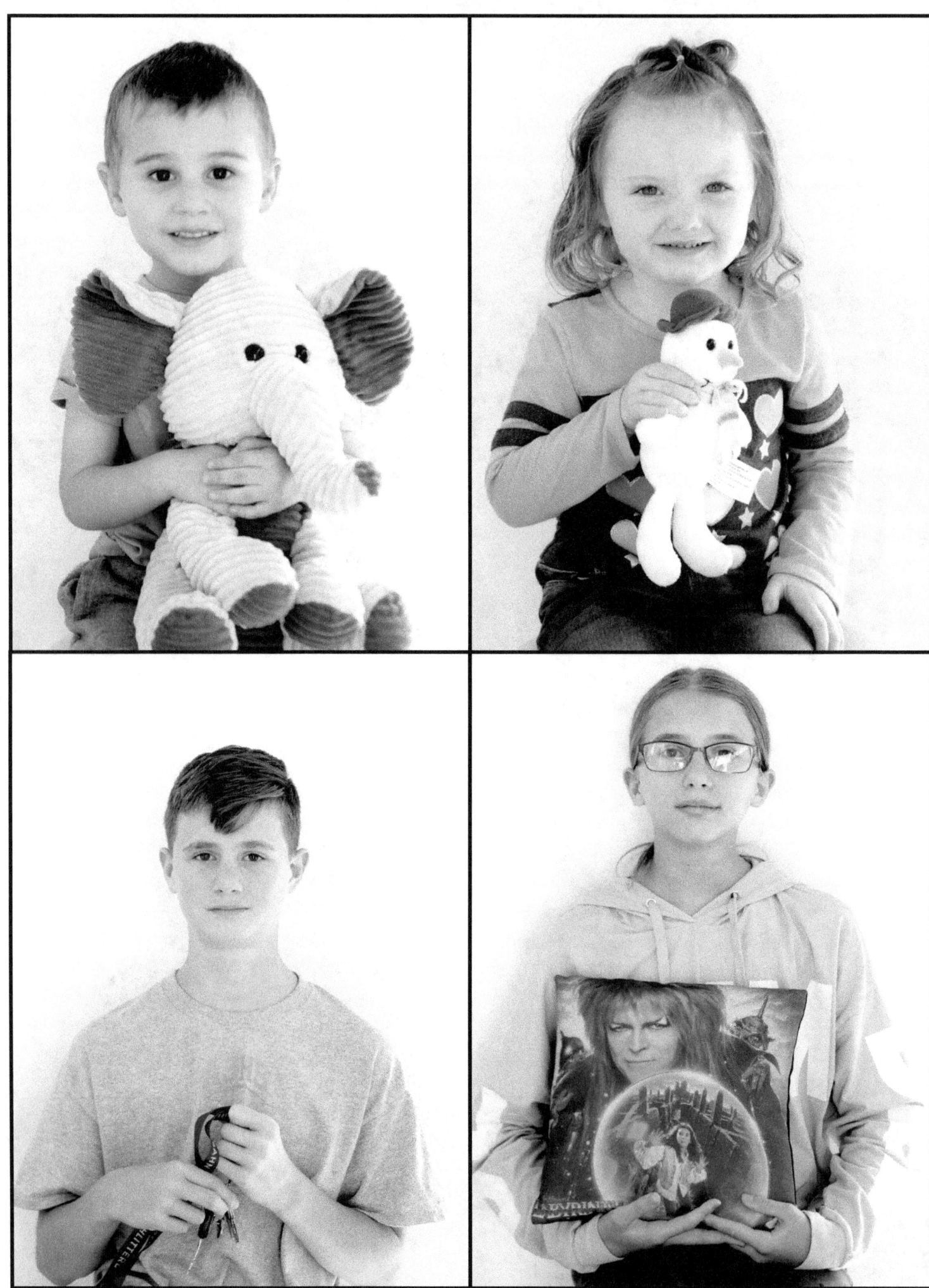

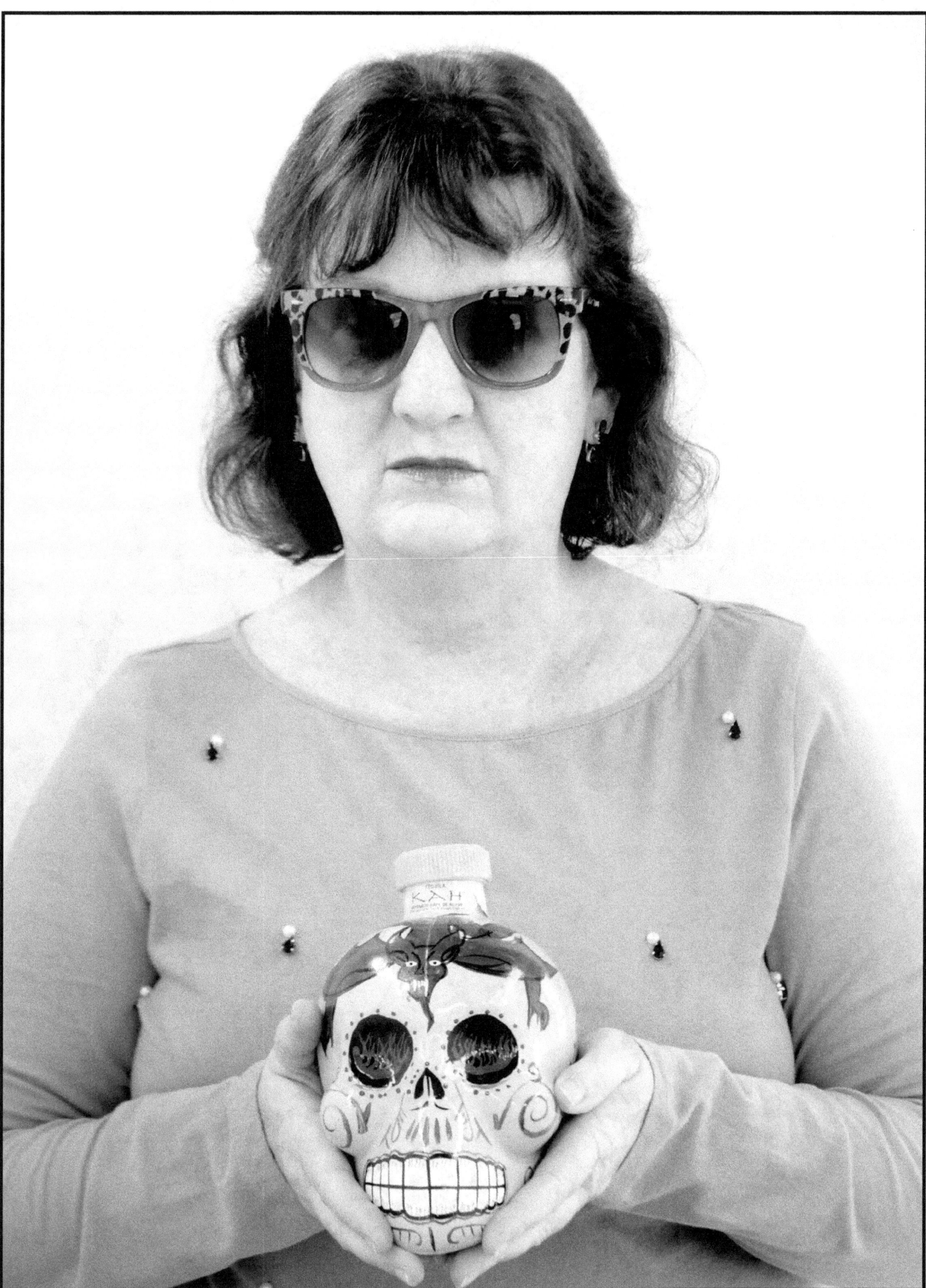

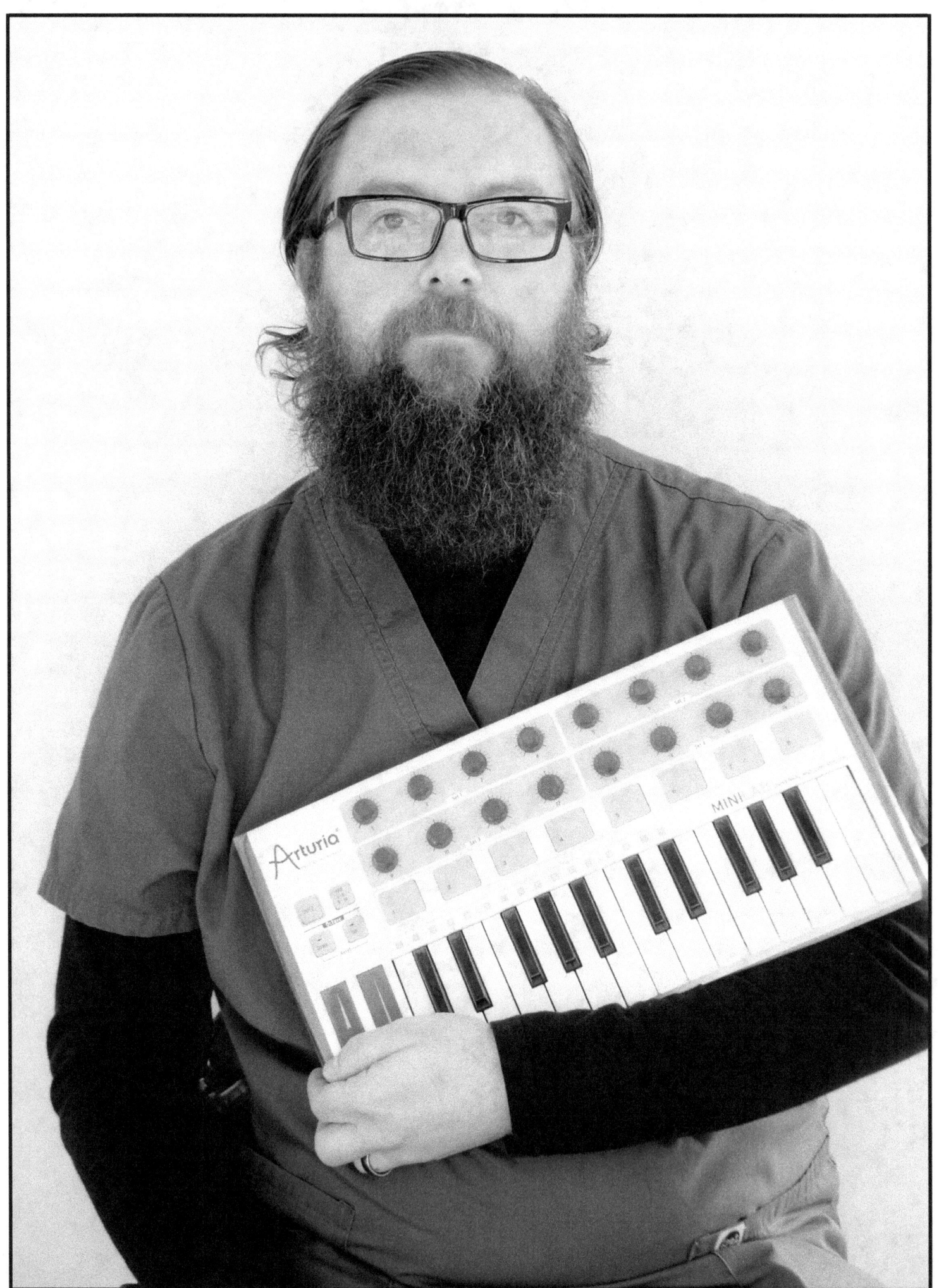

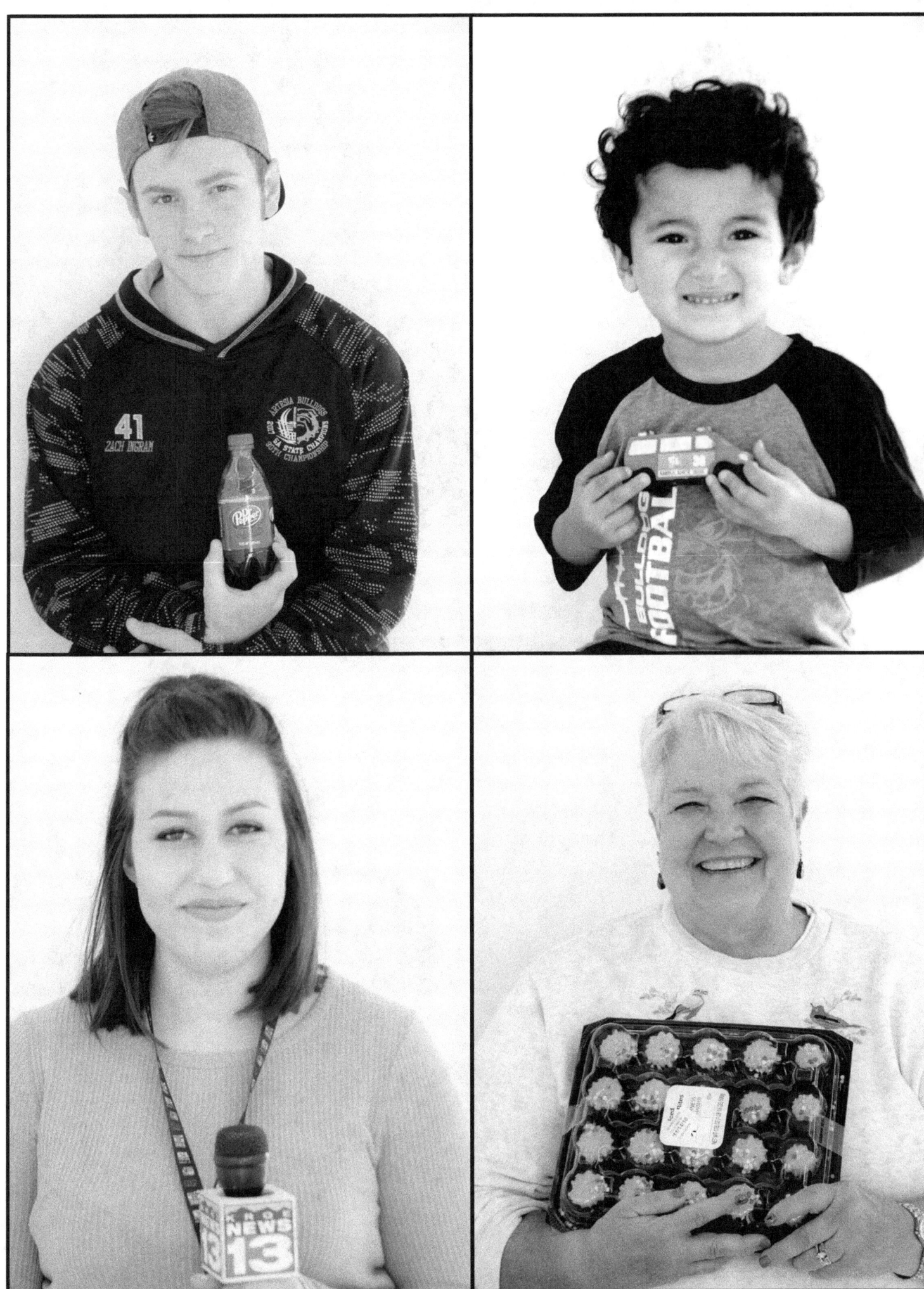

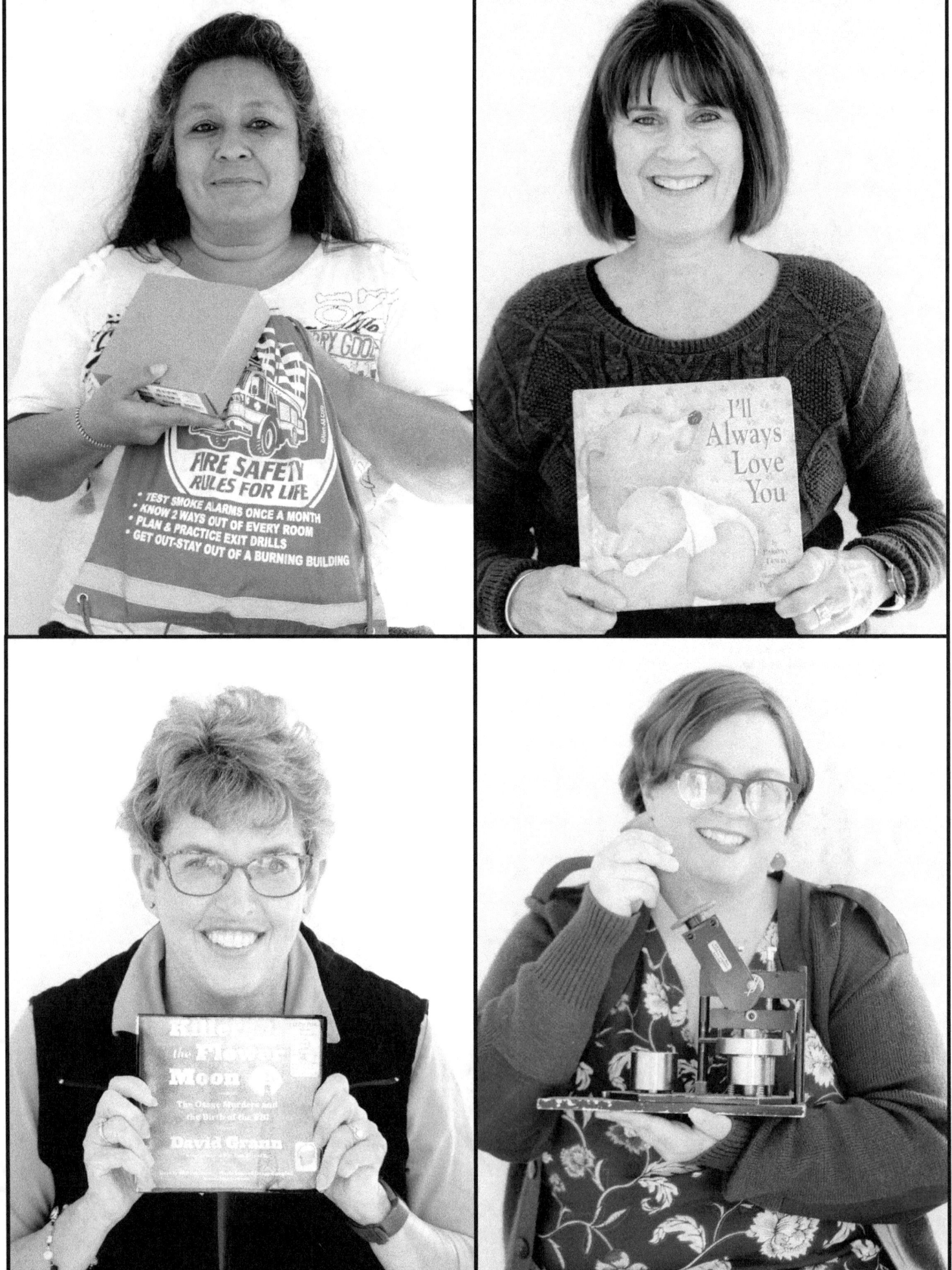

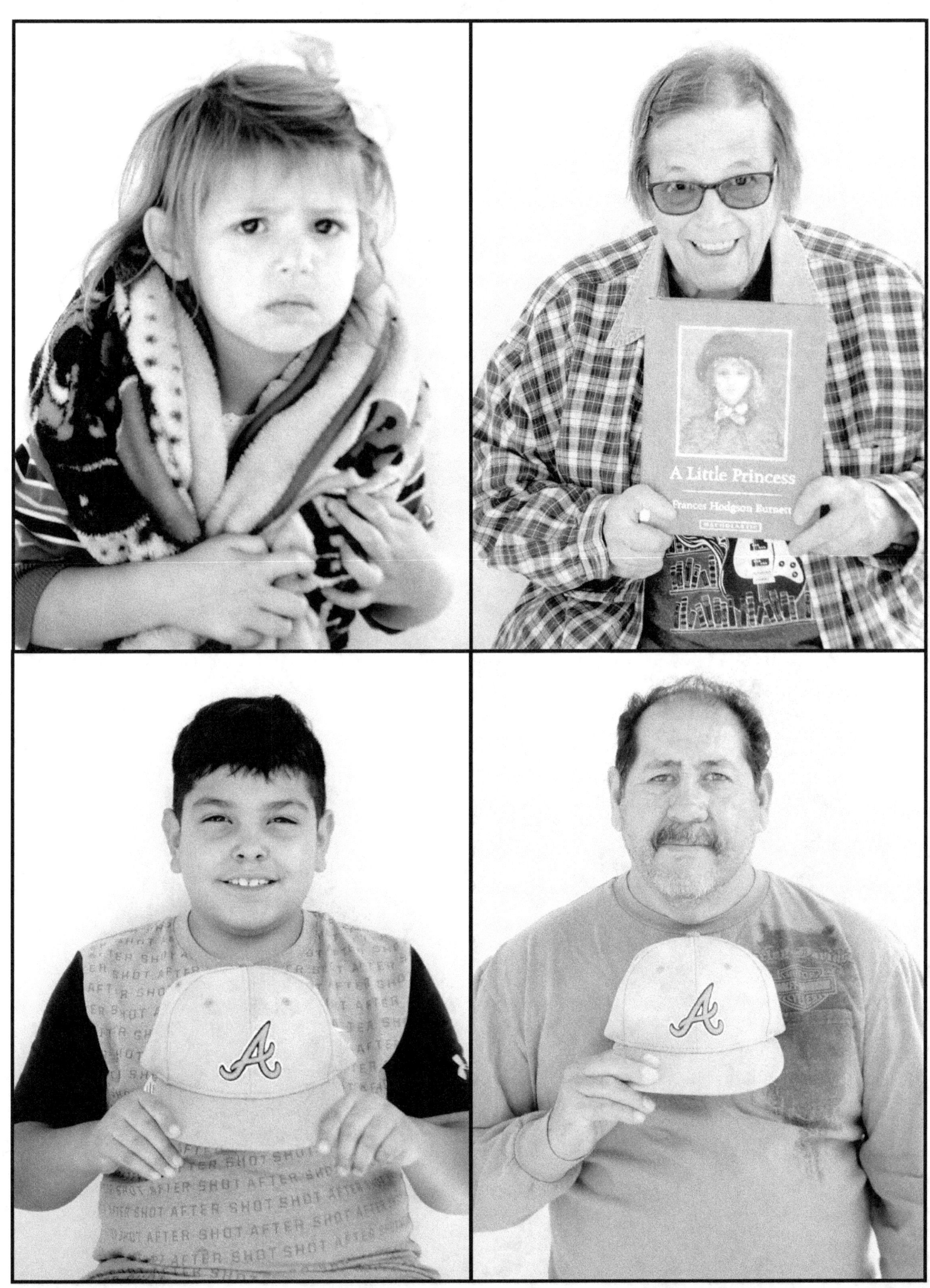

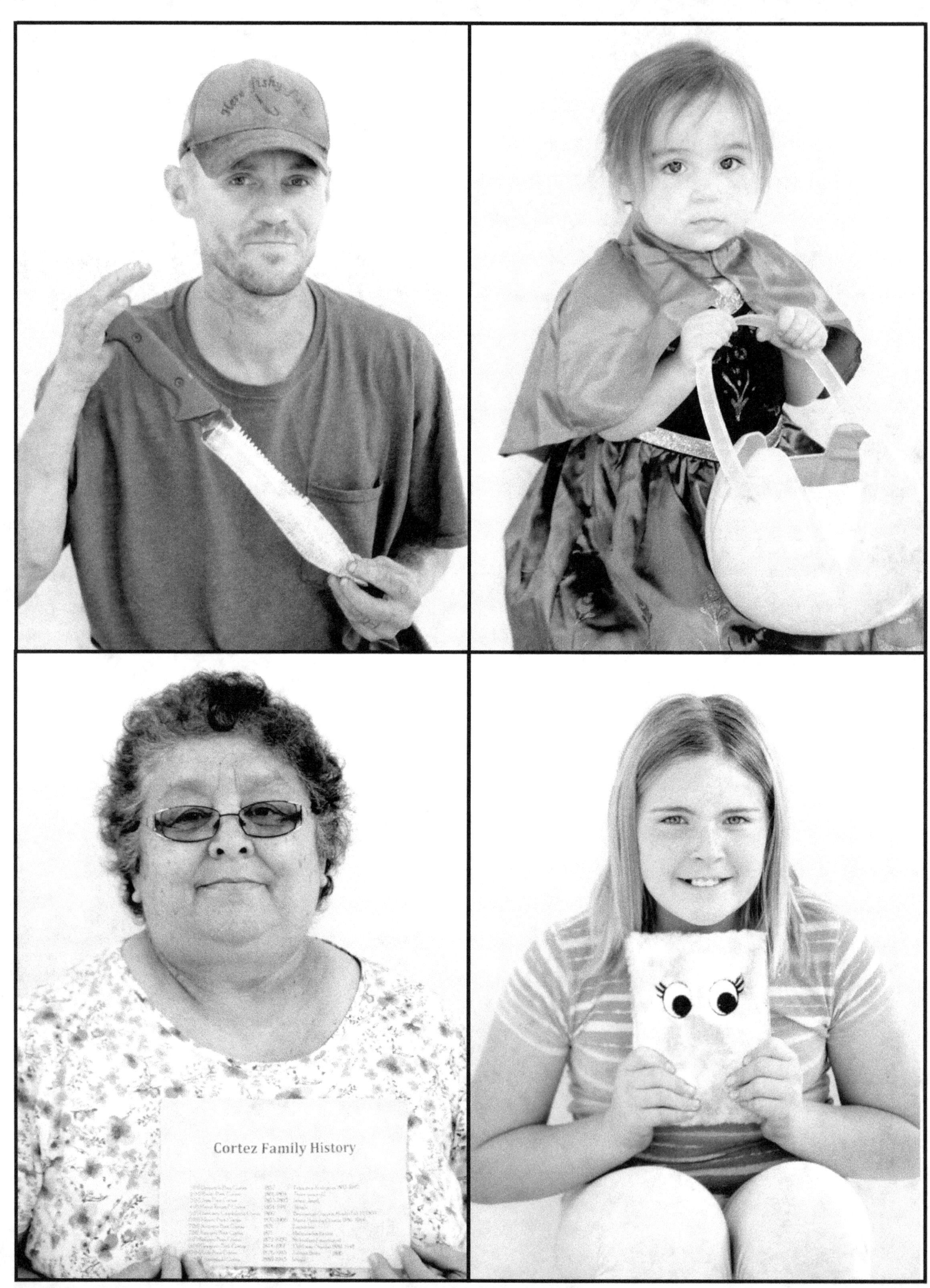

Cortez Family History

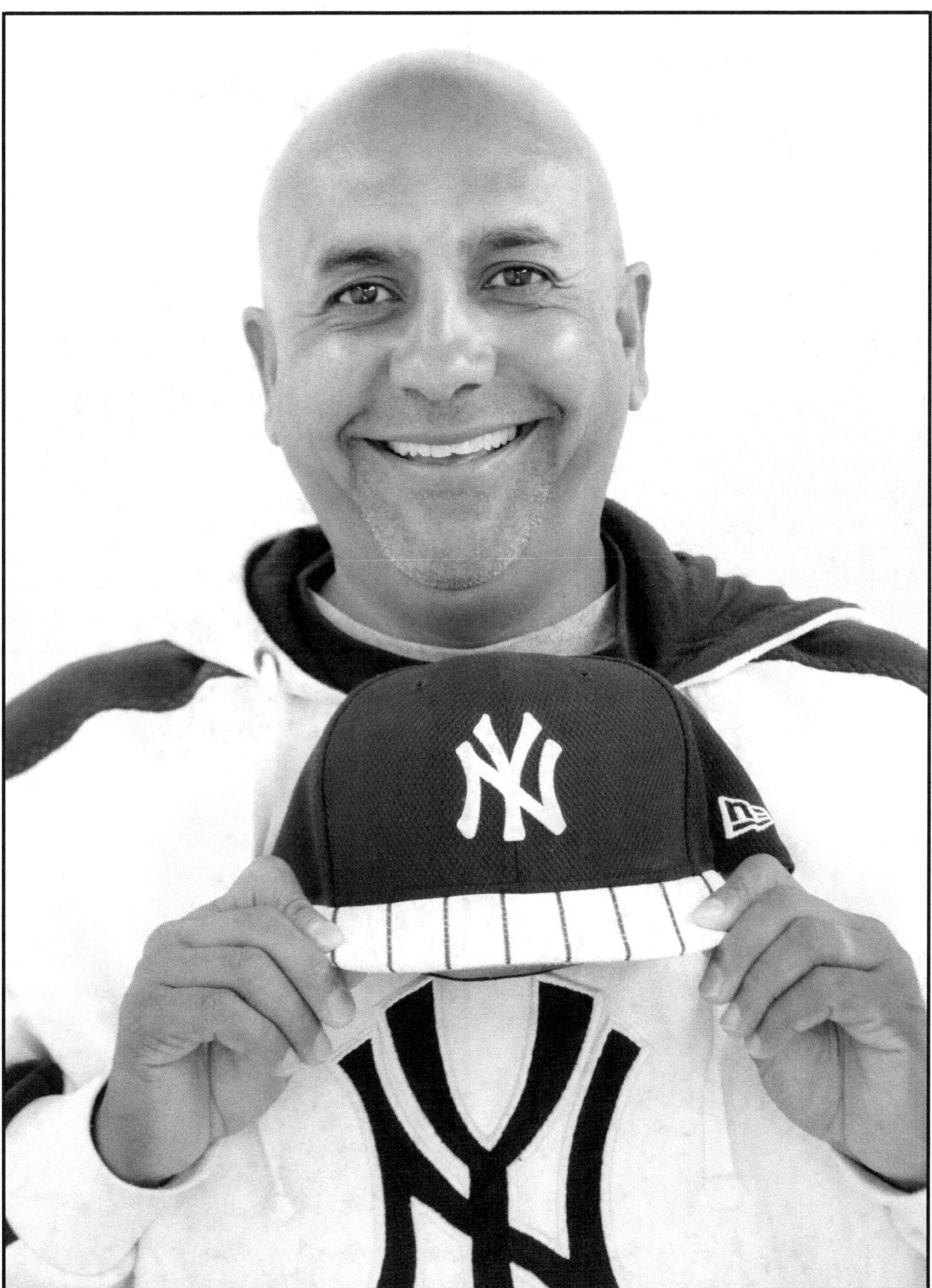

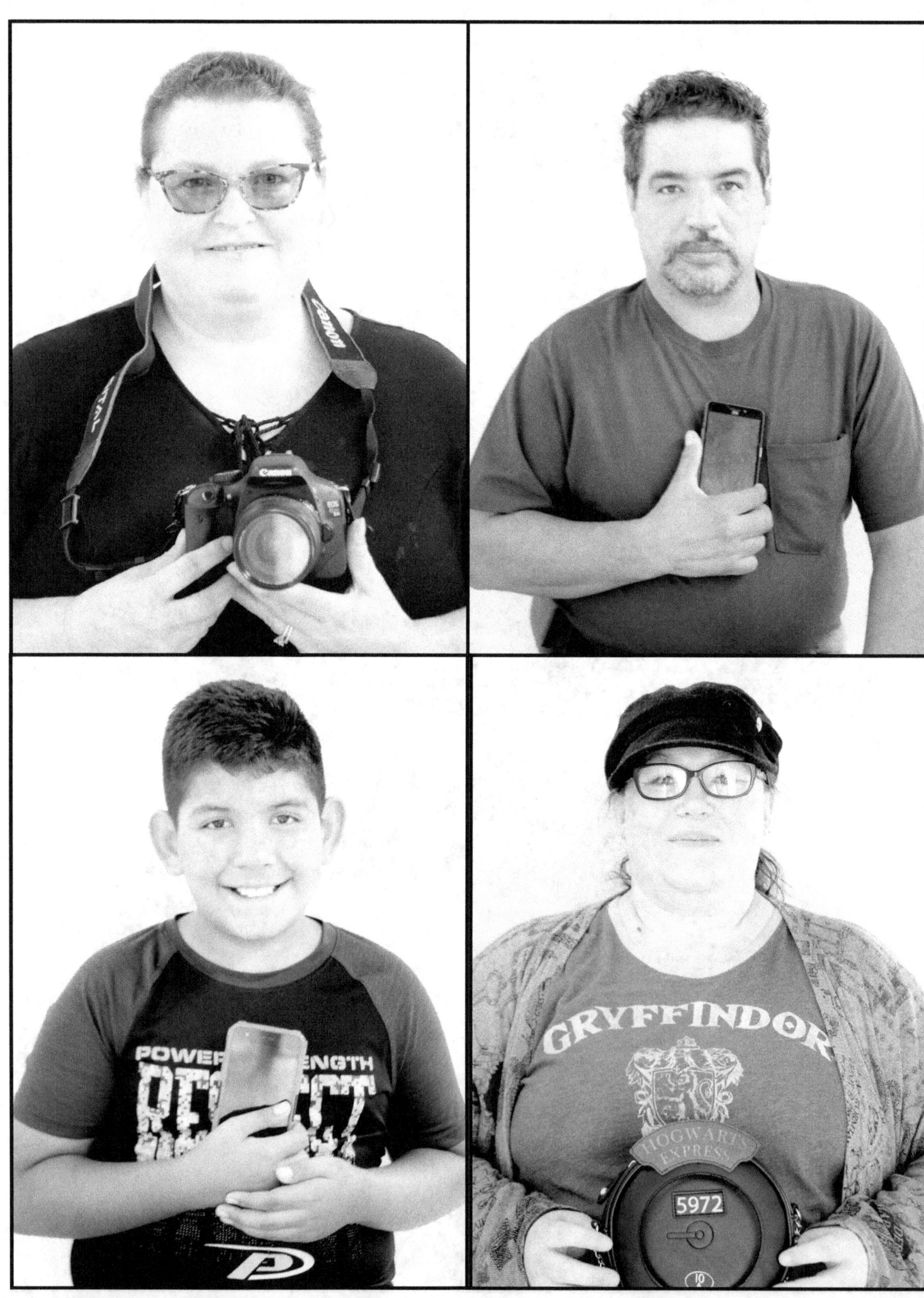

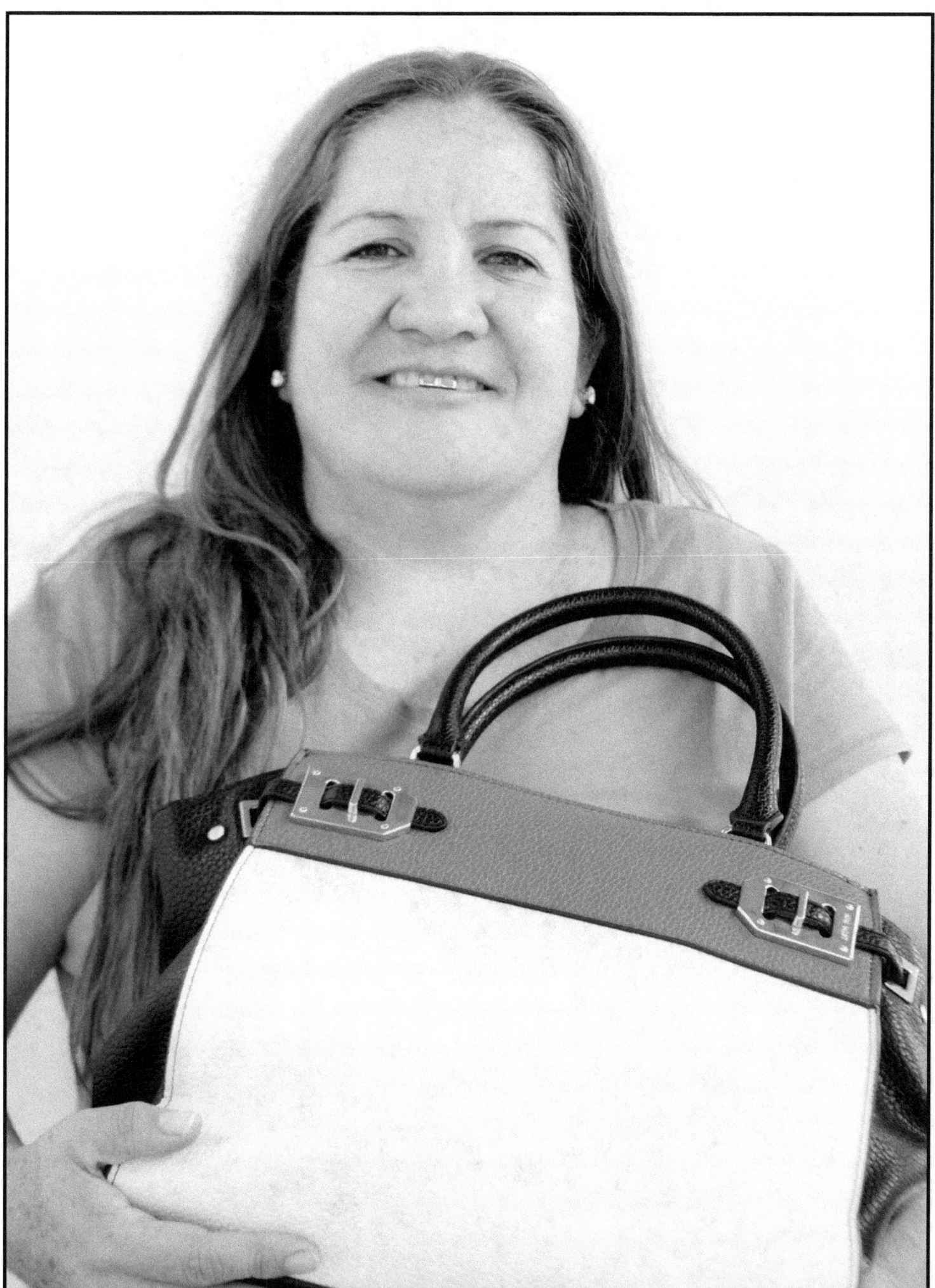

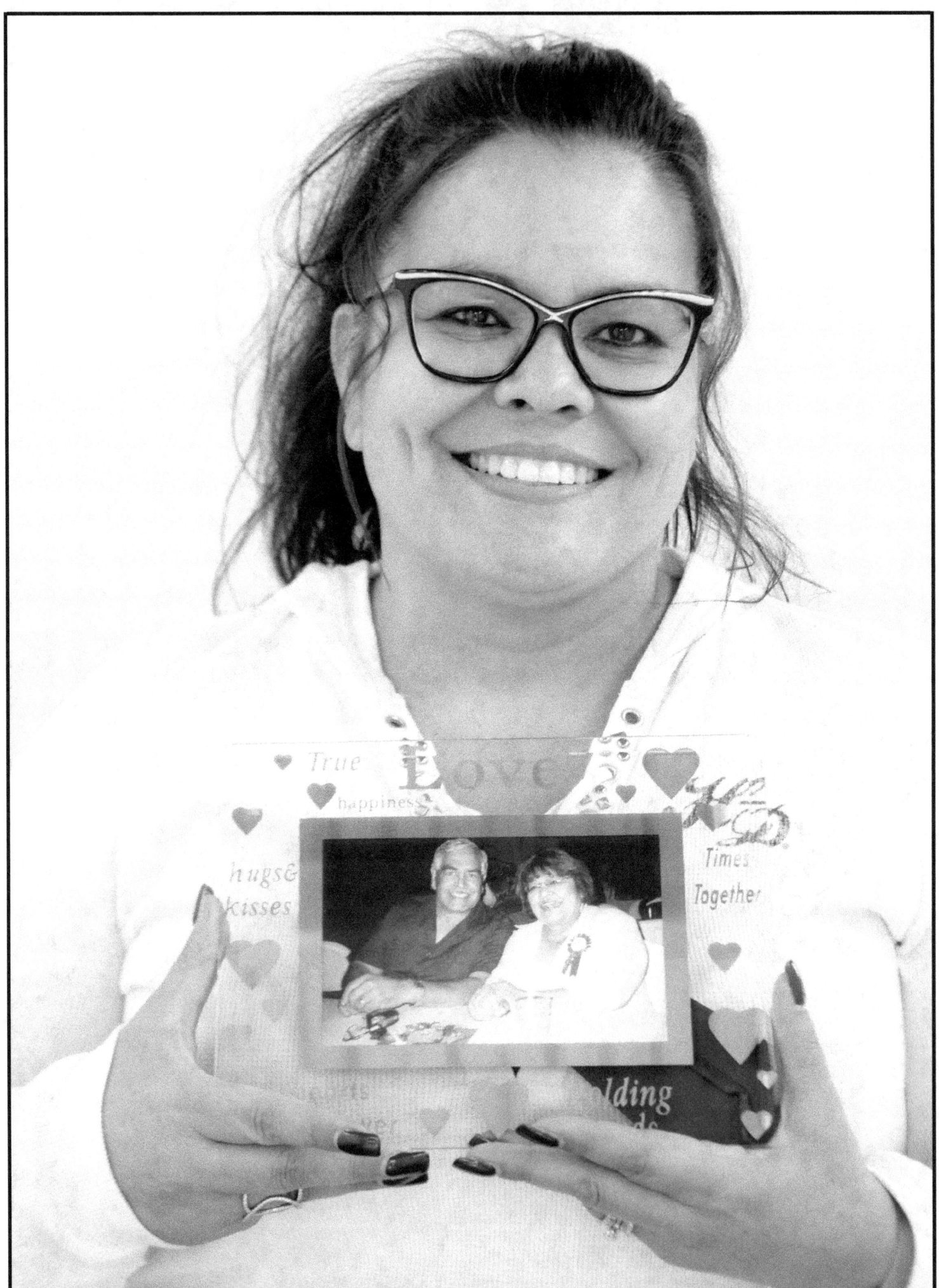

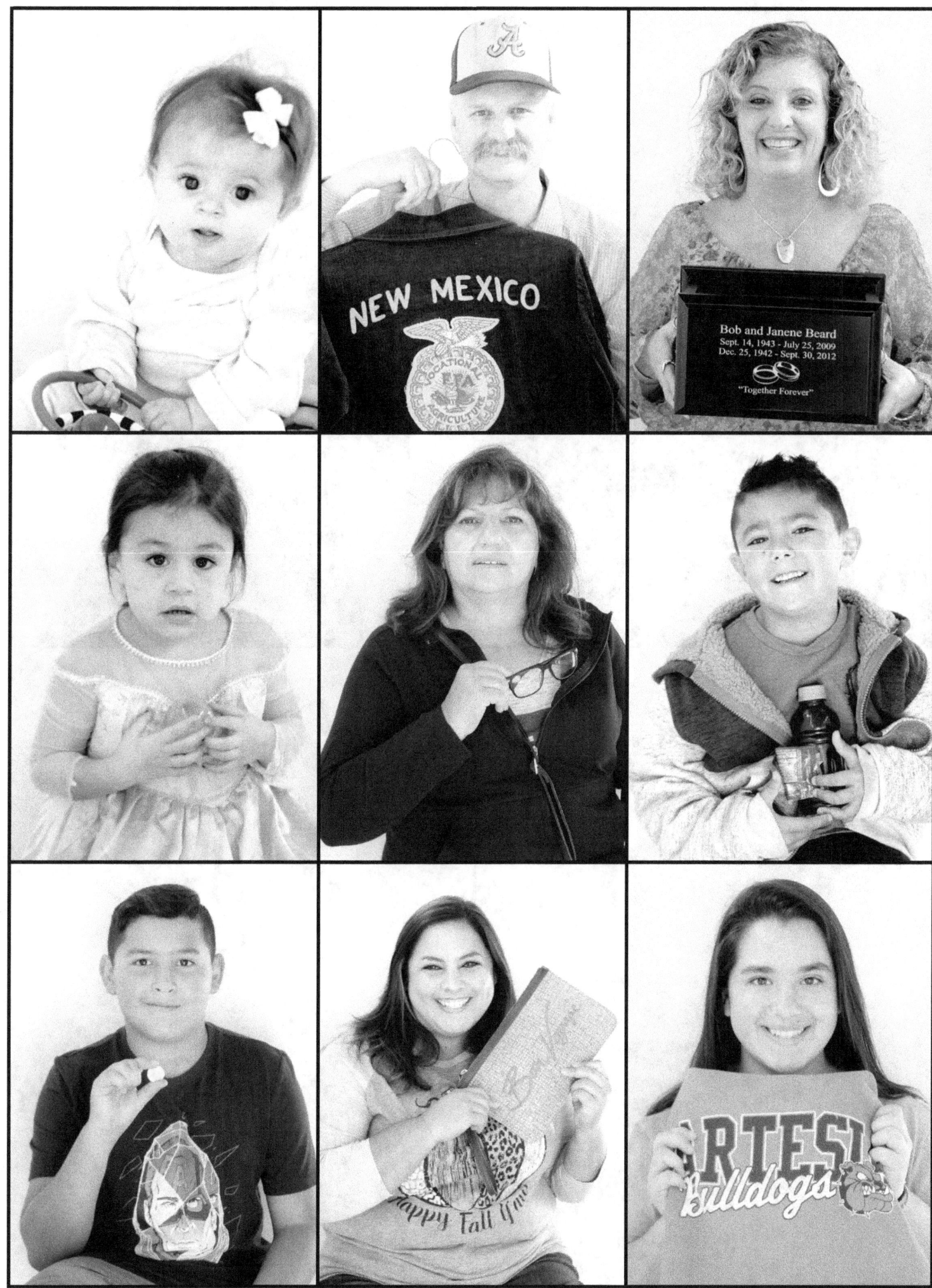

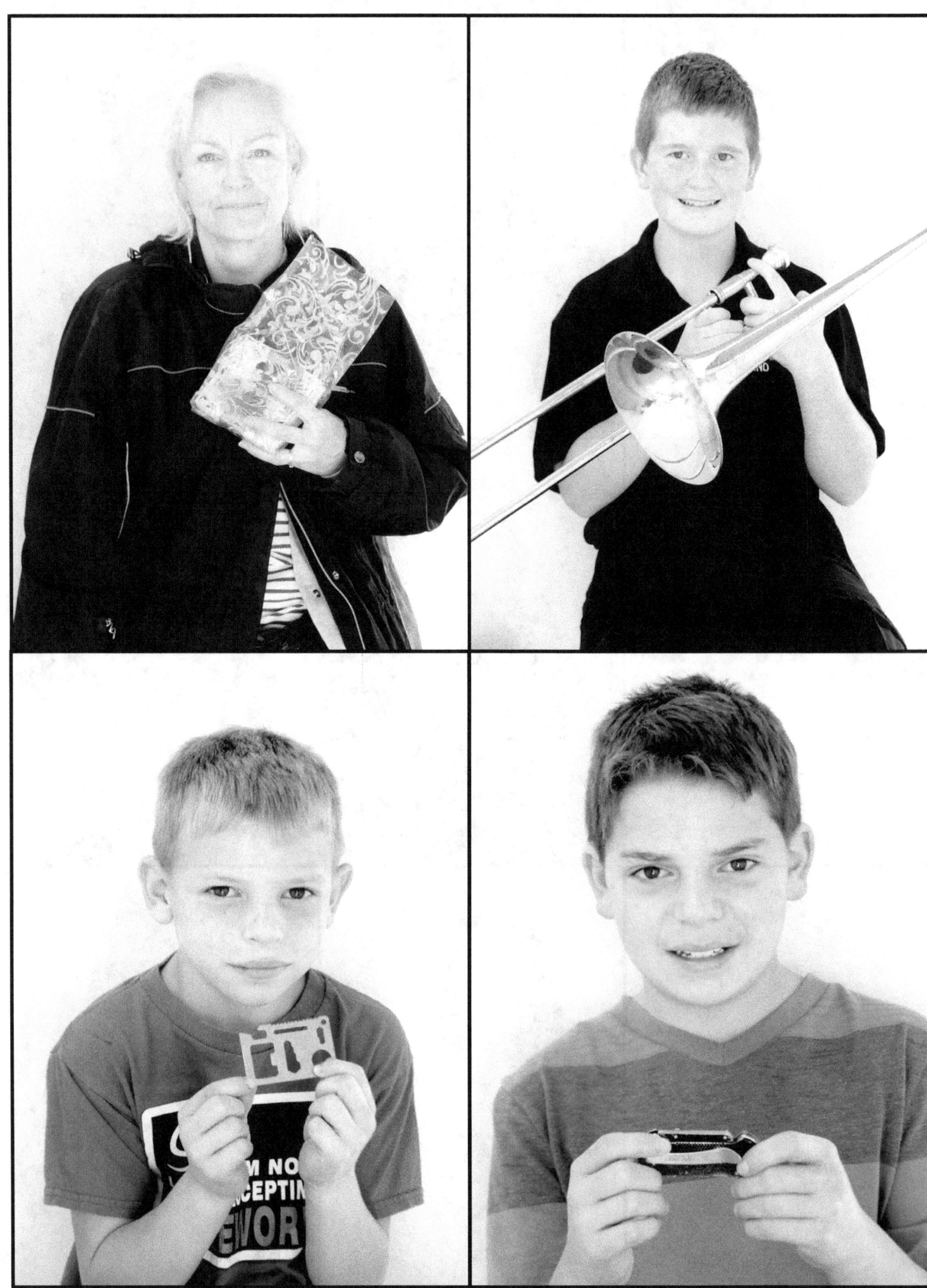

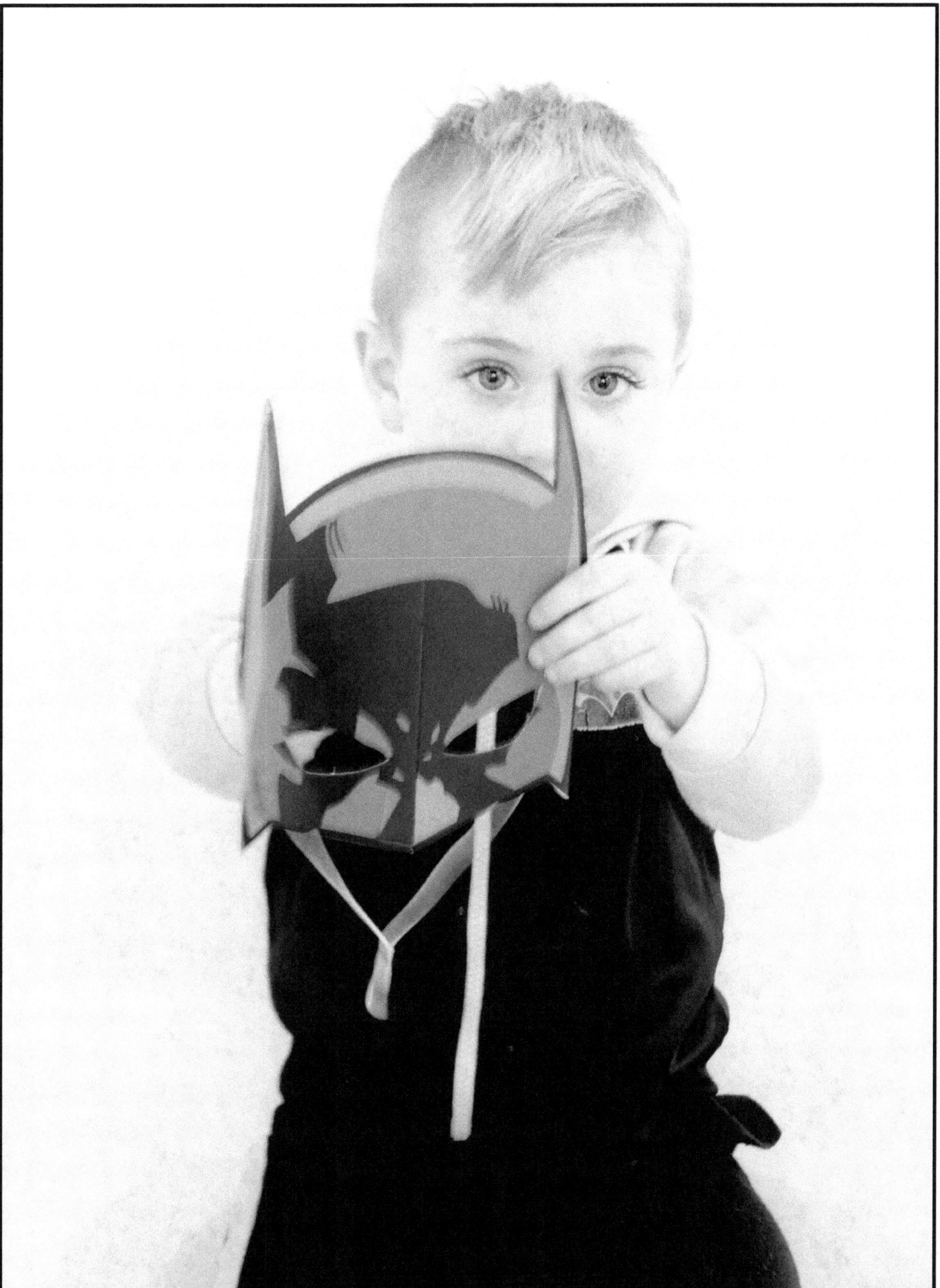

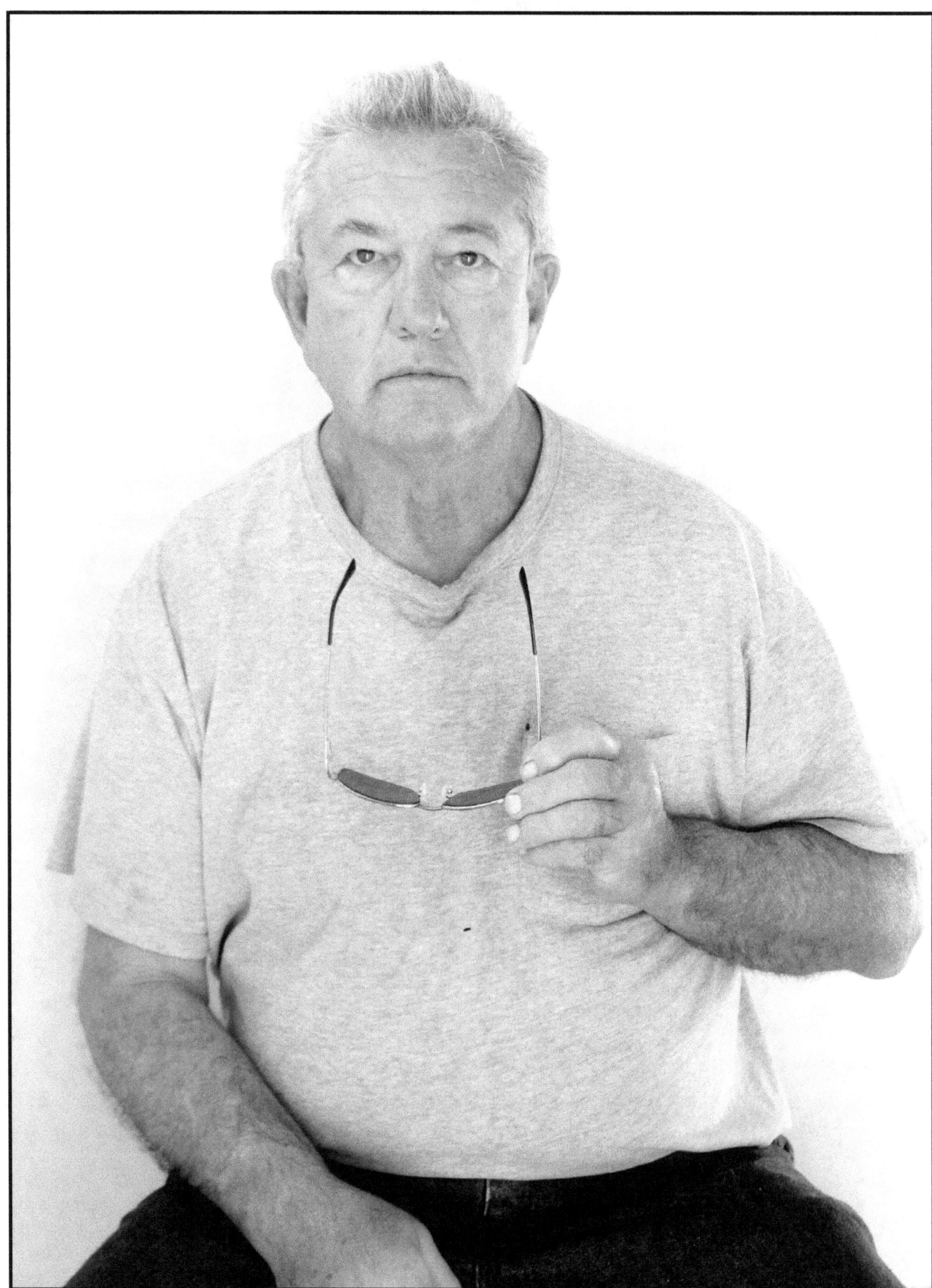

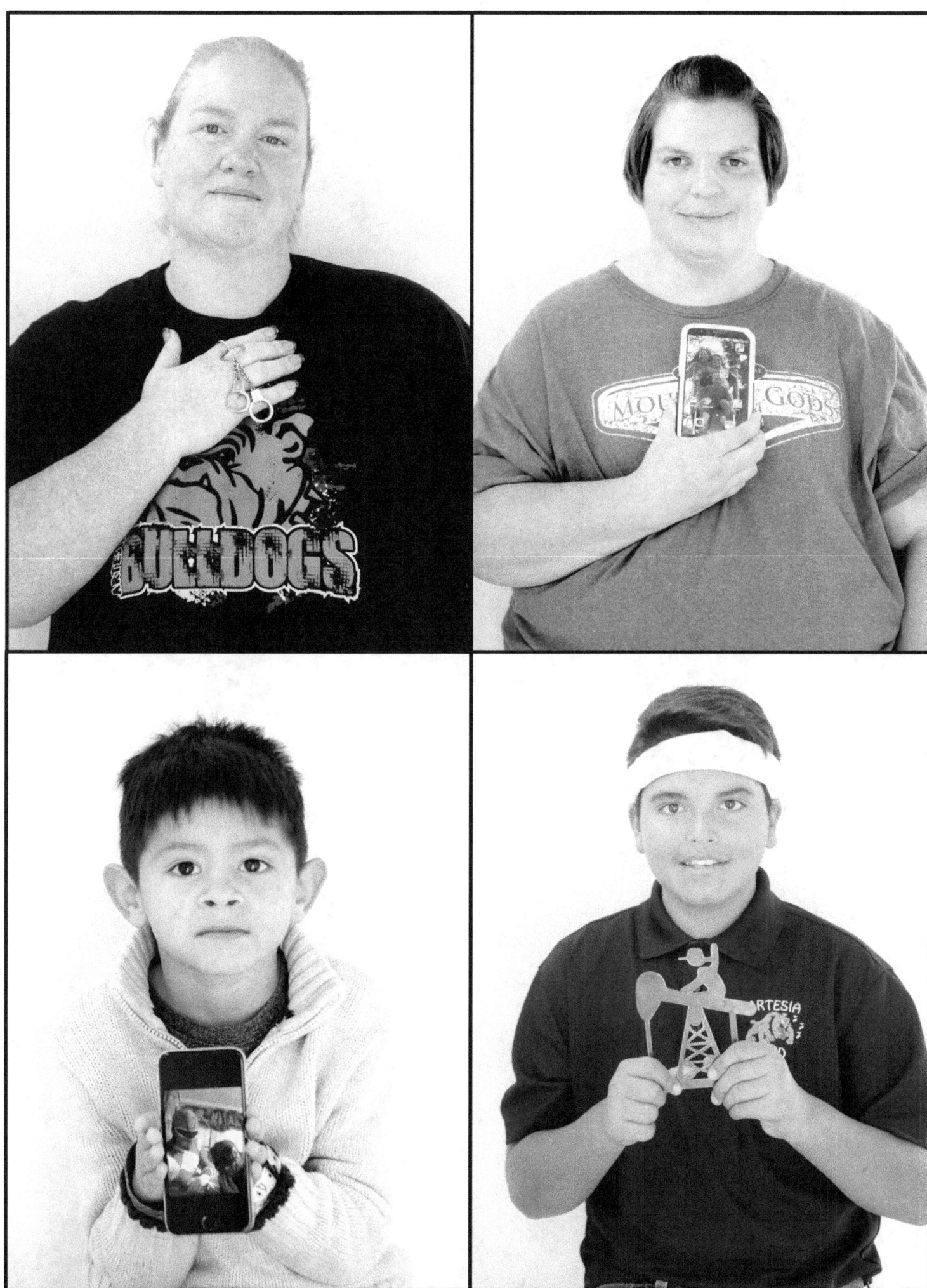

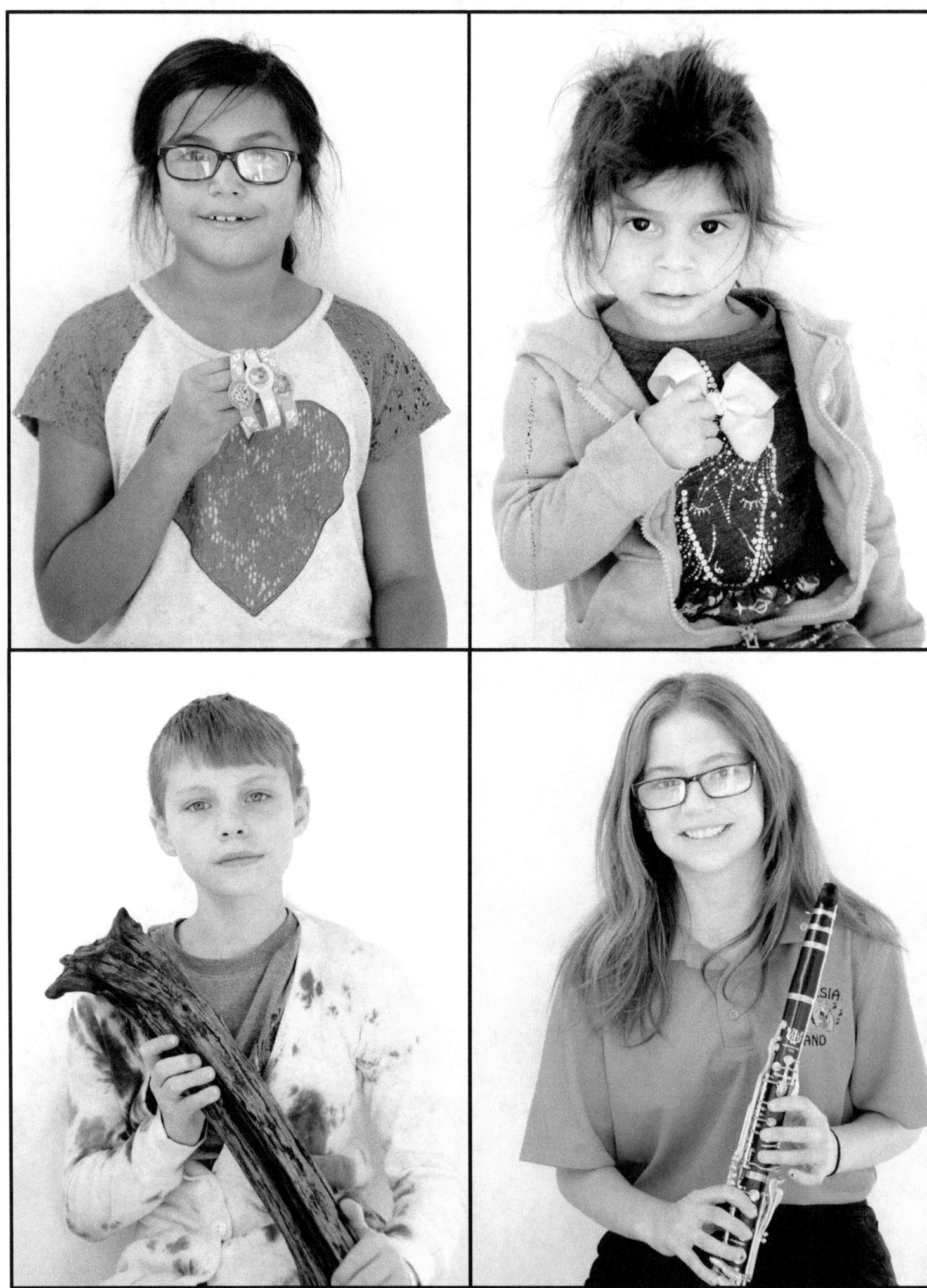

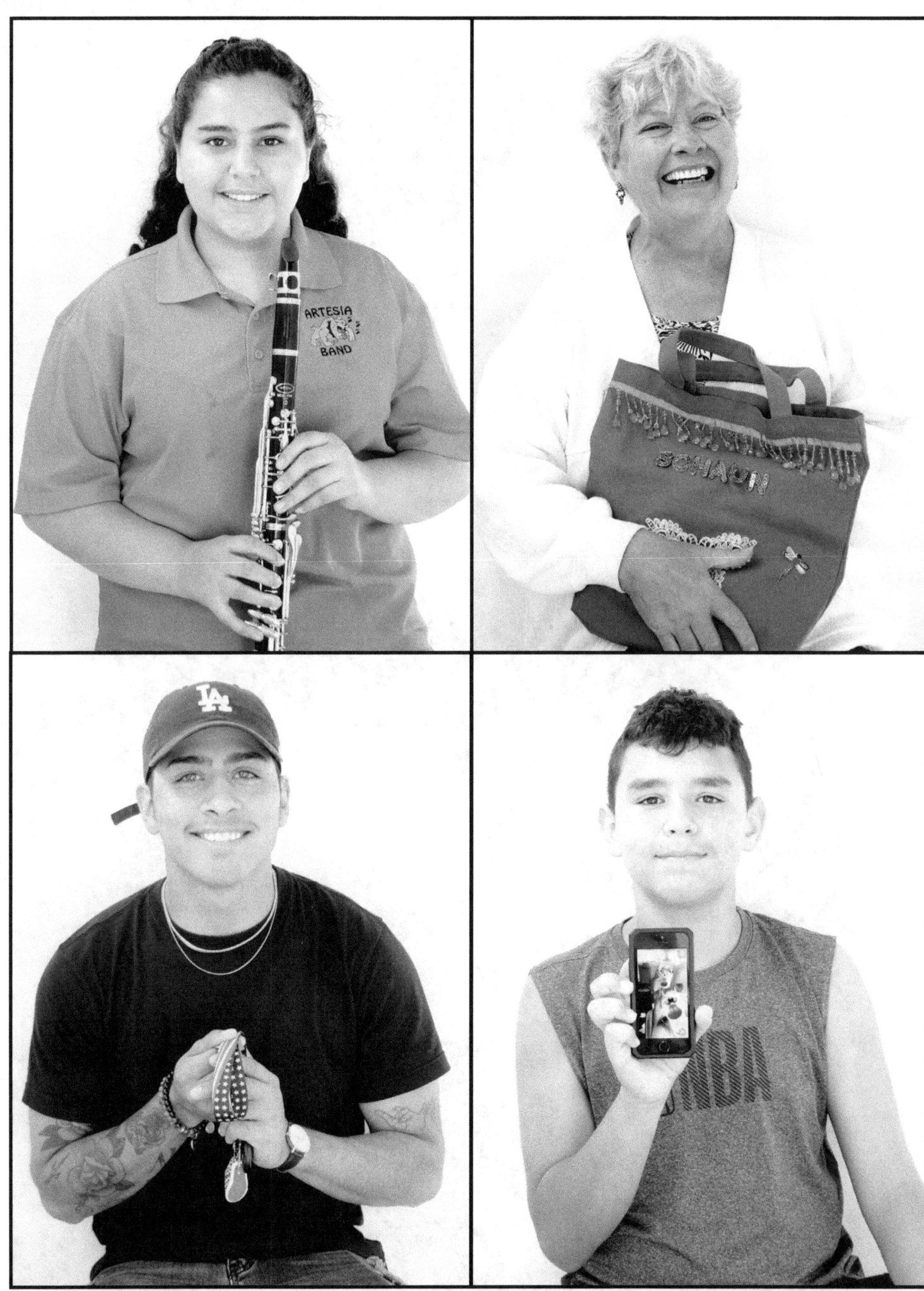

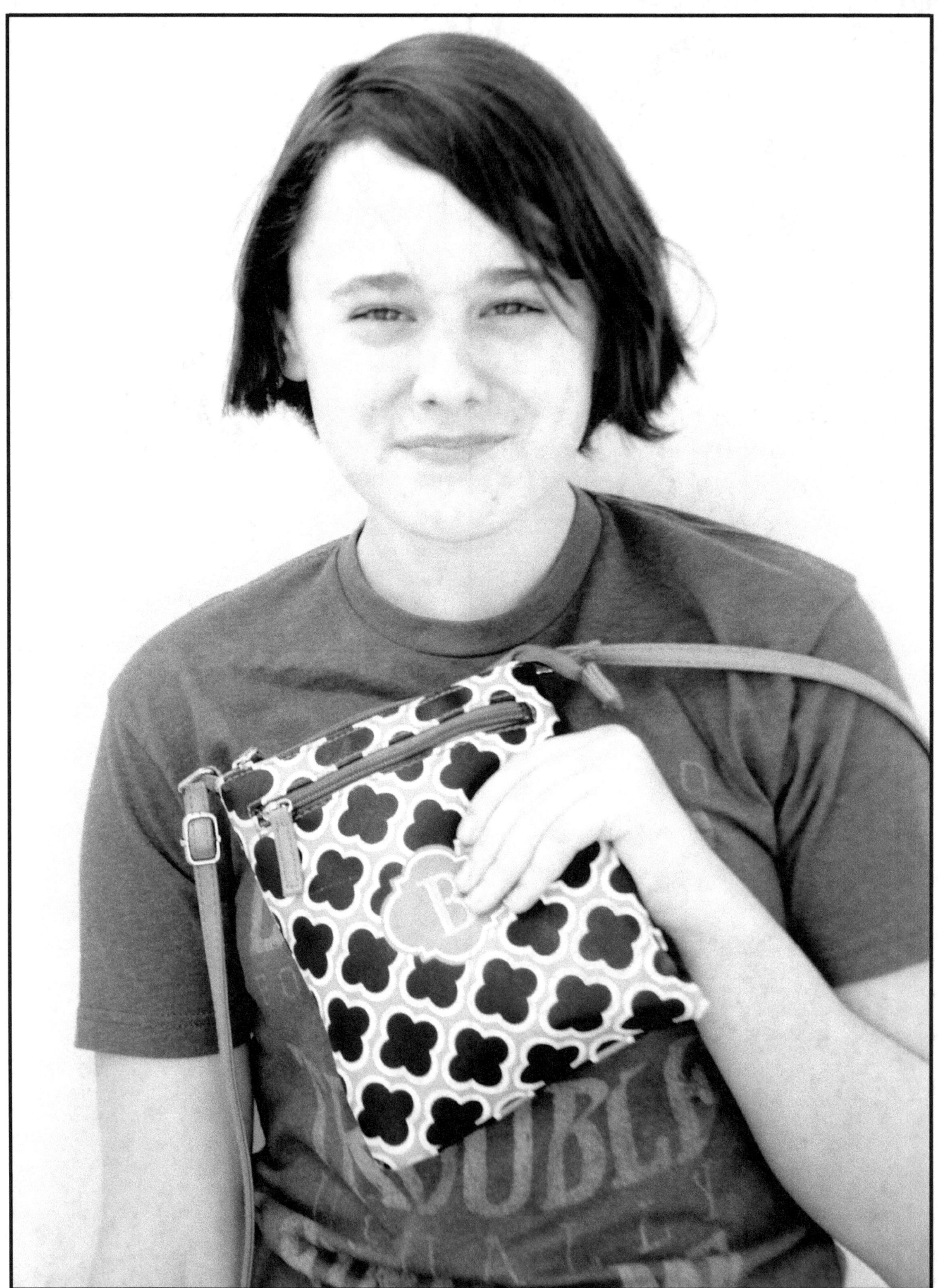

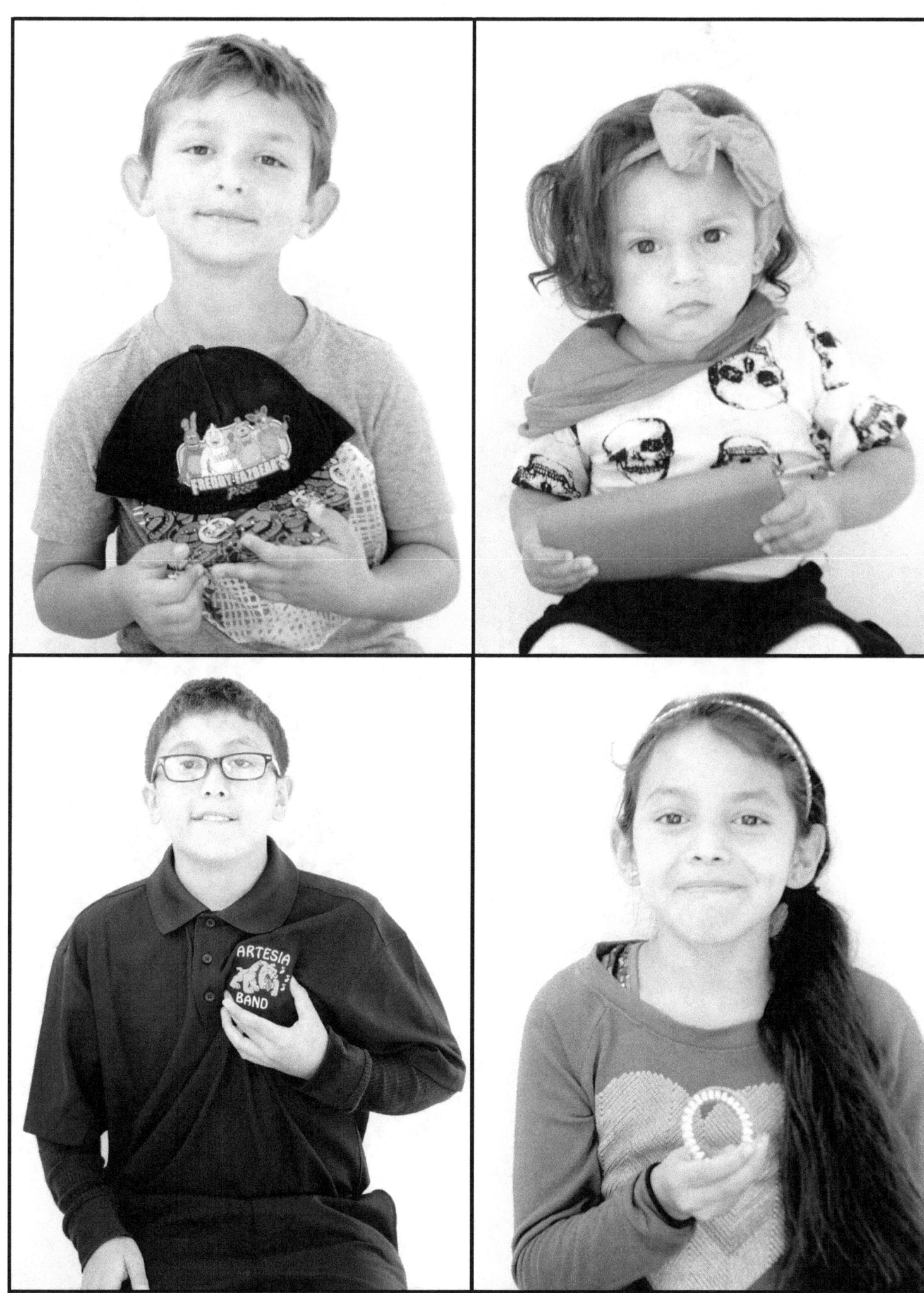

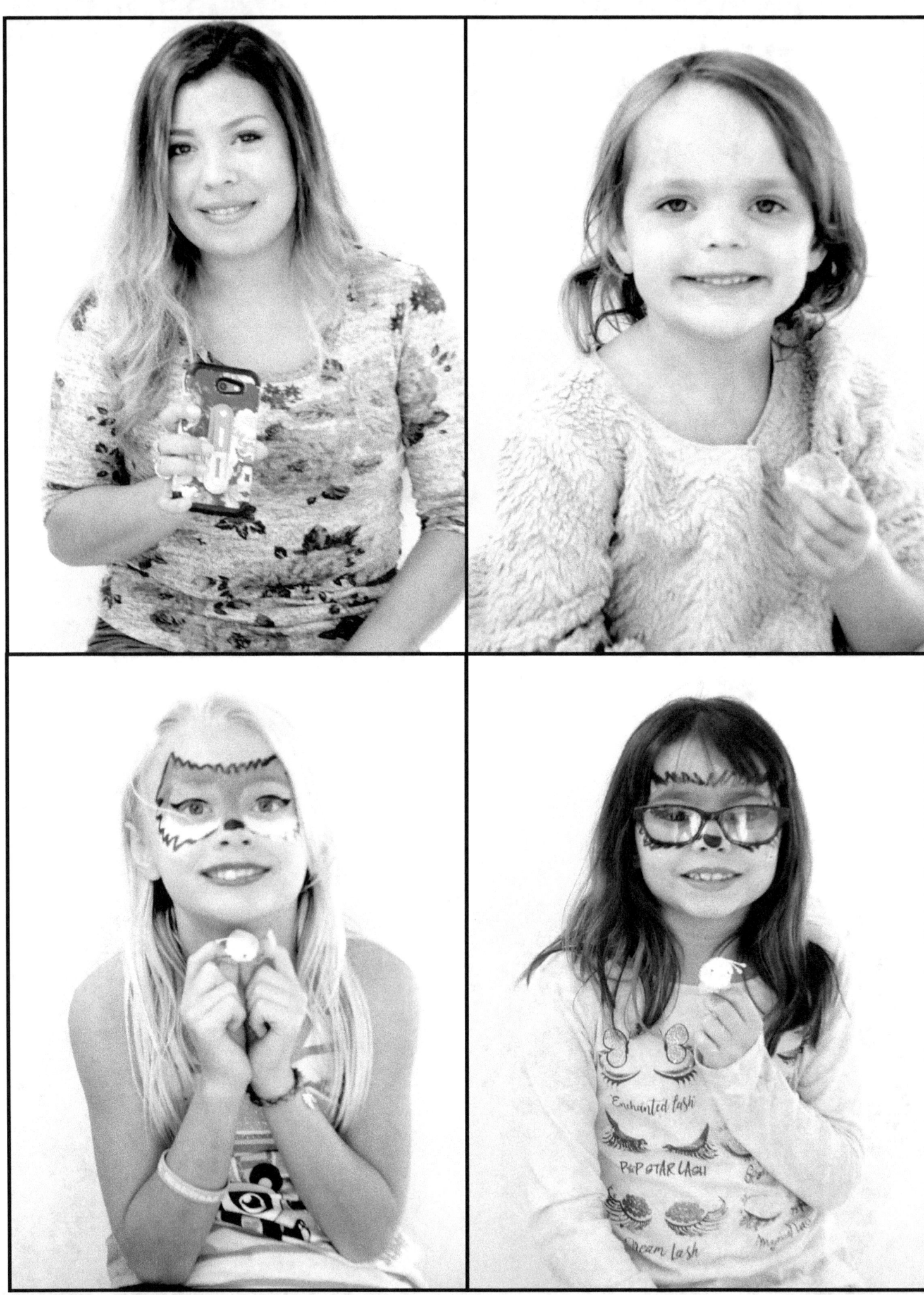

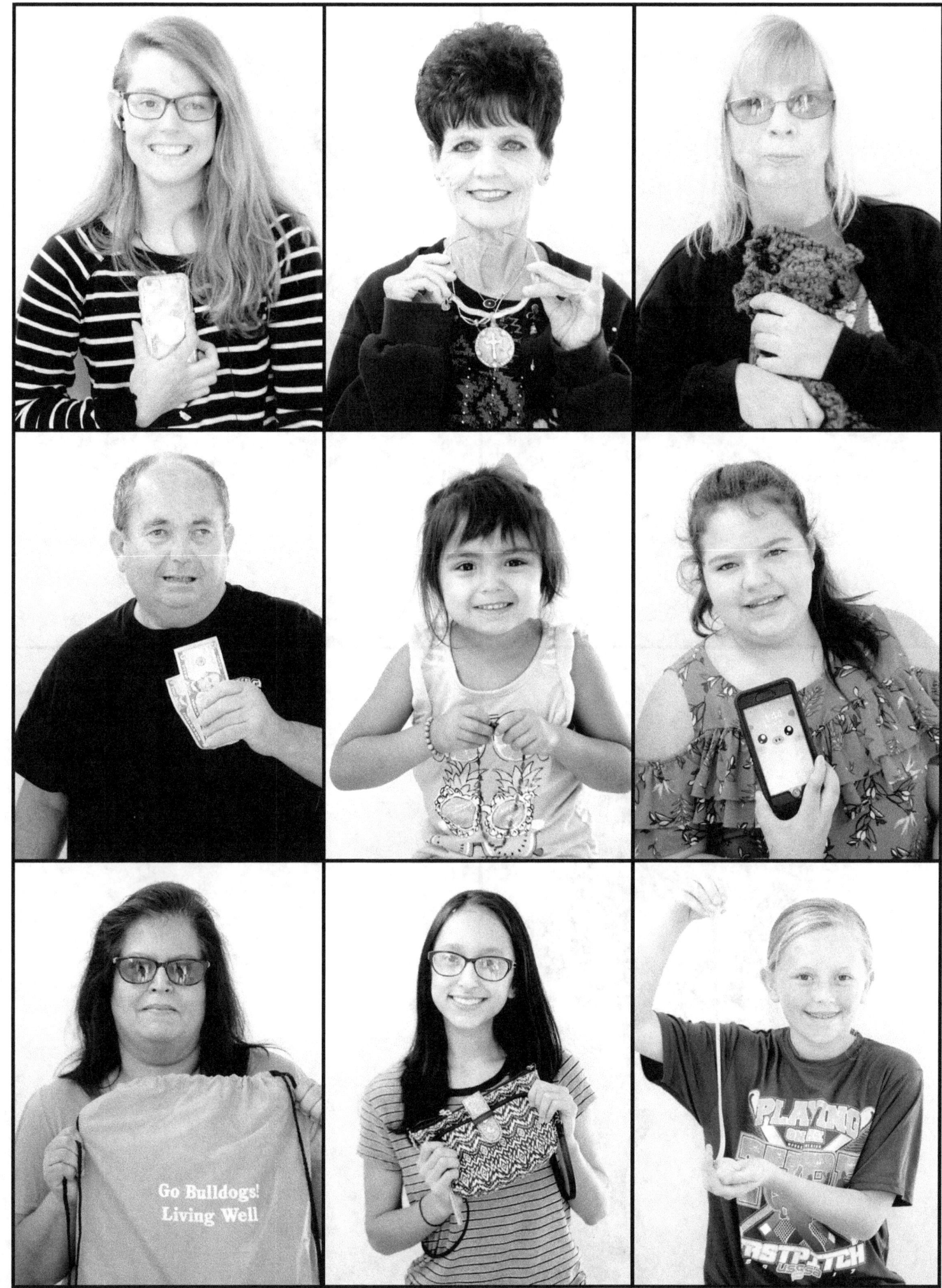

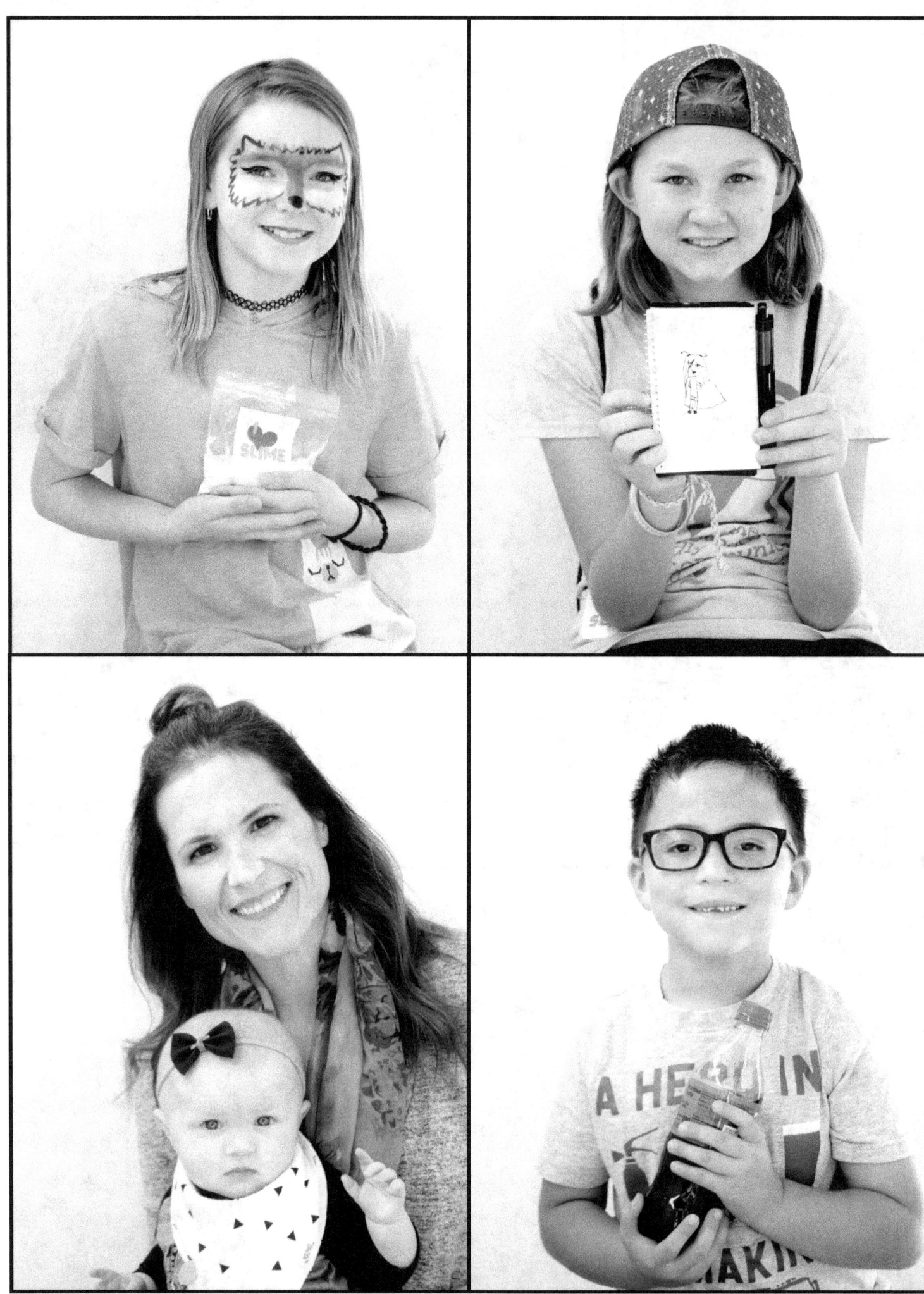

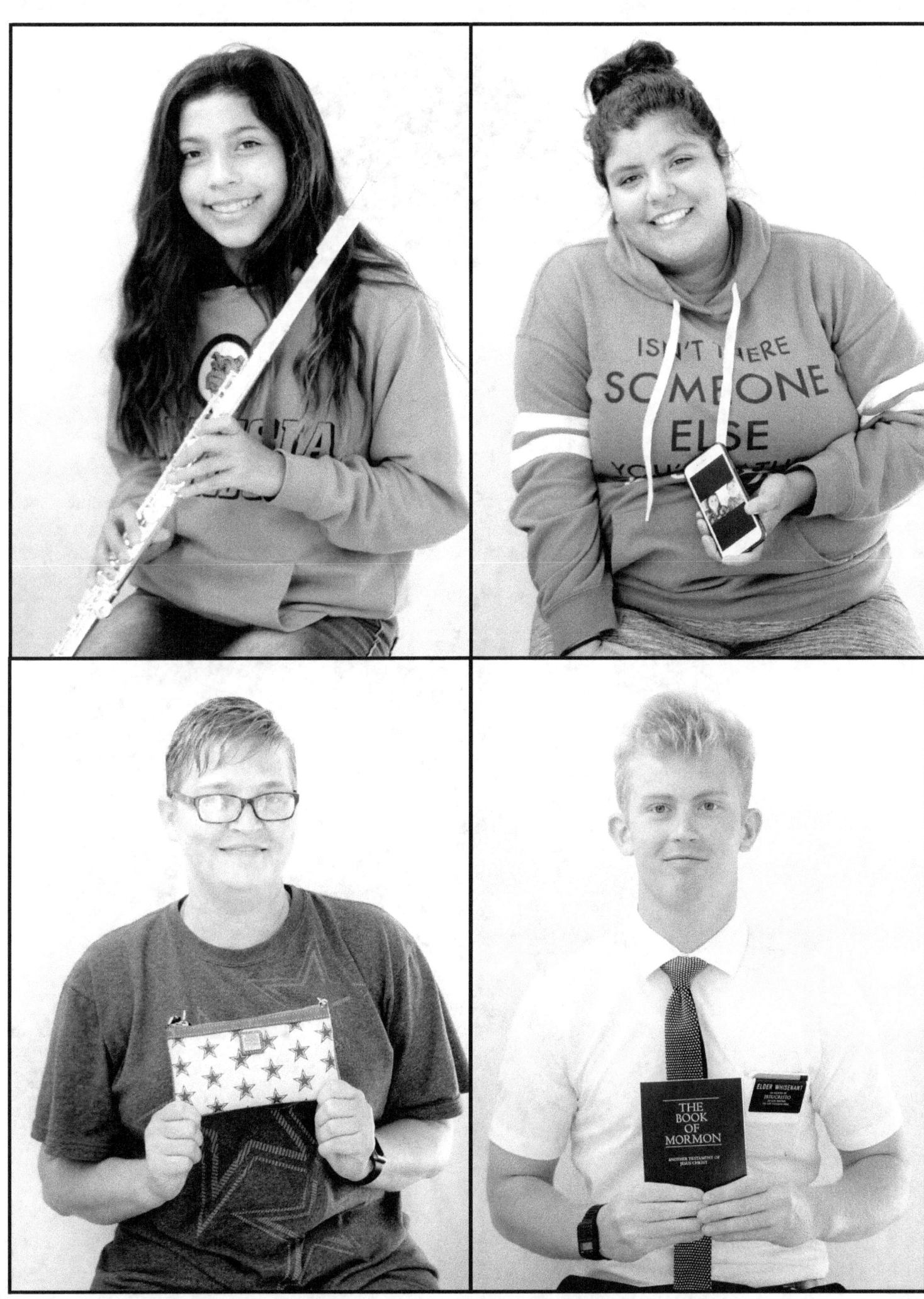

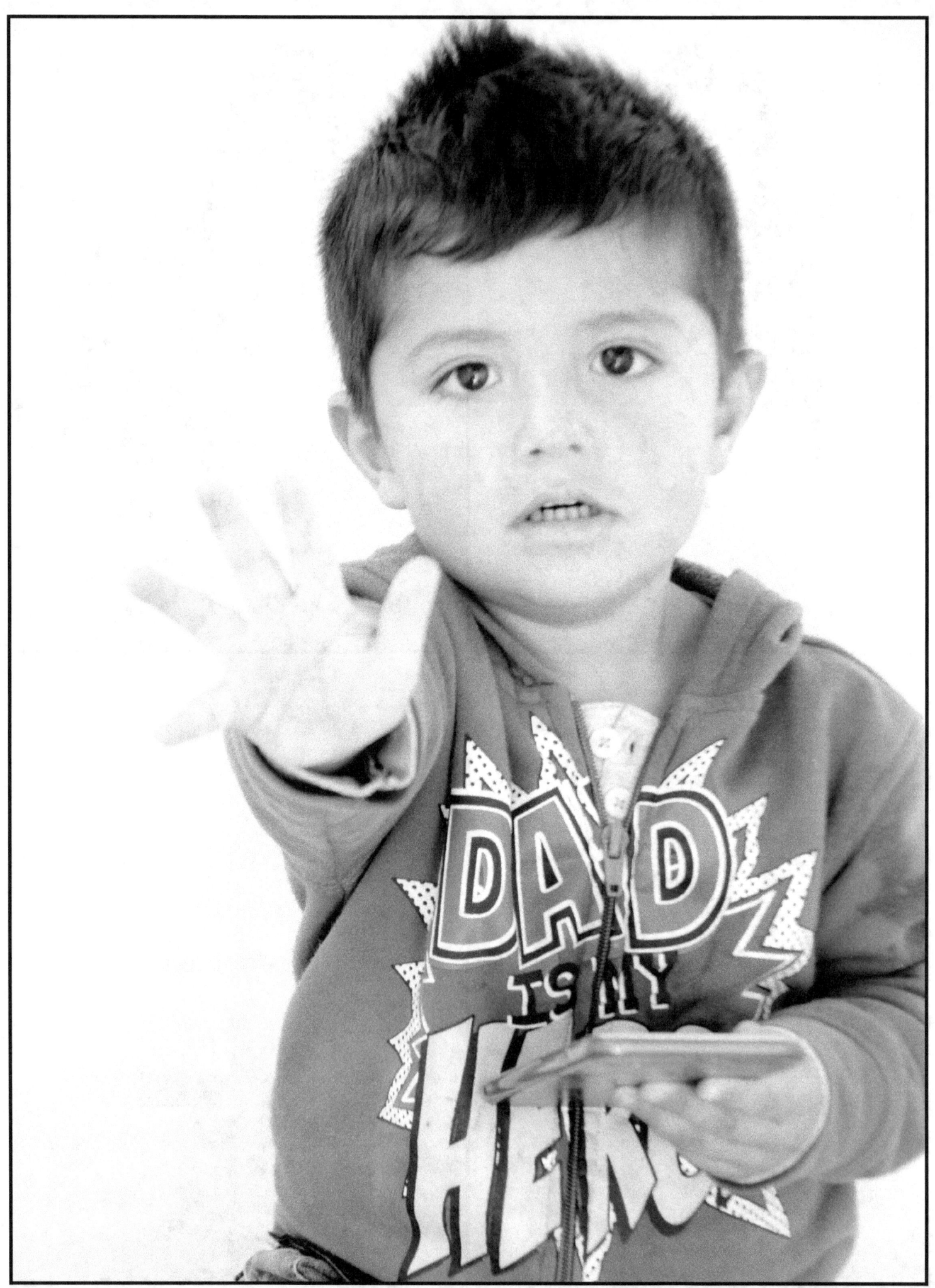

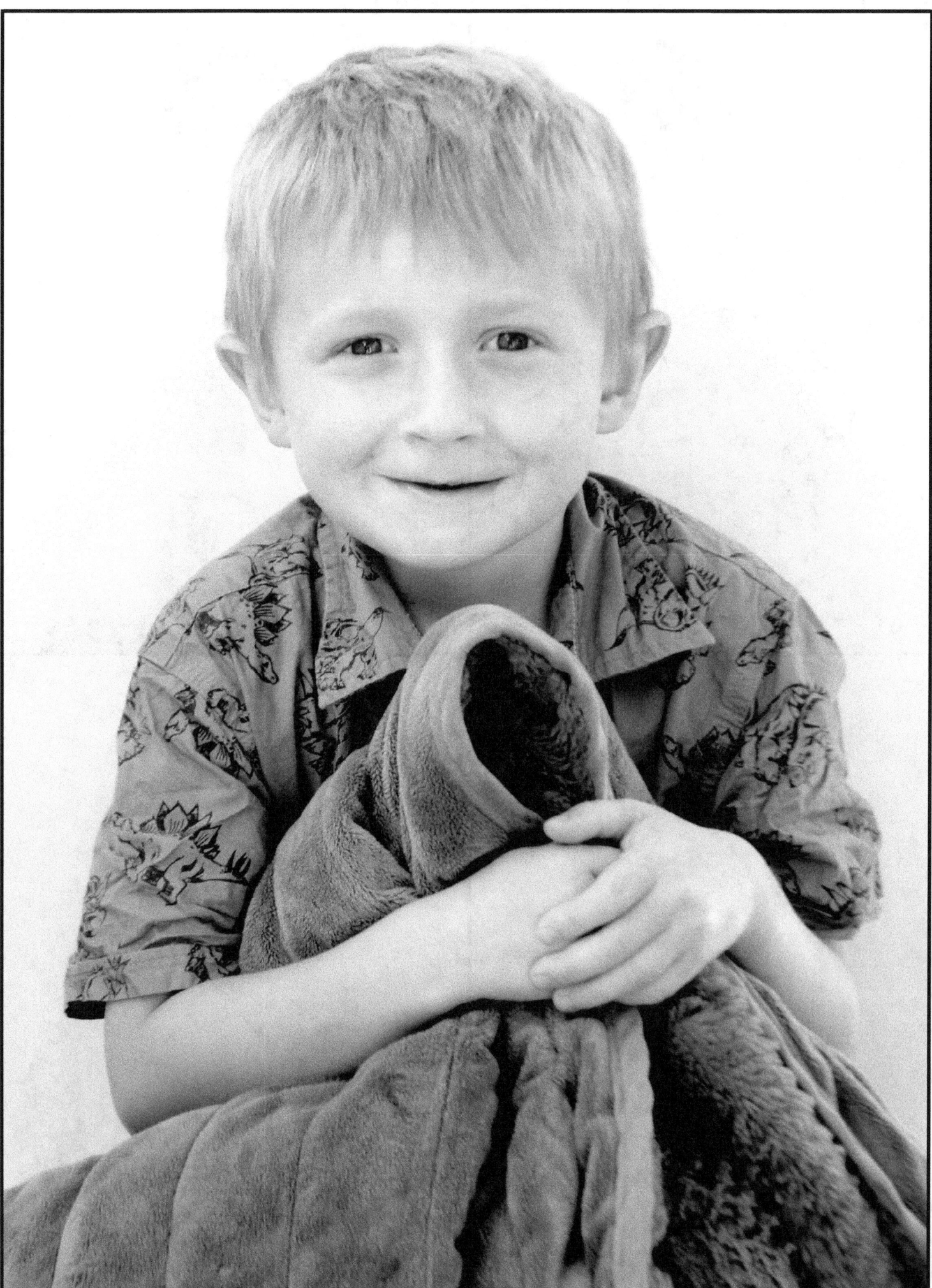

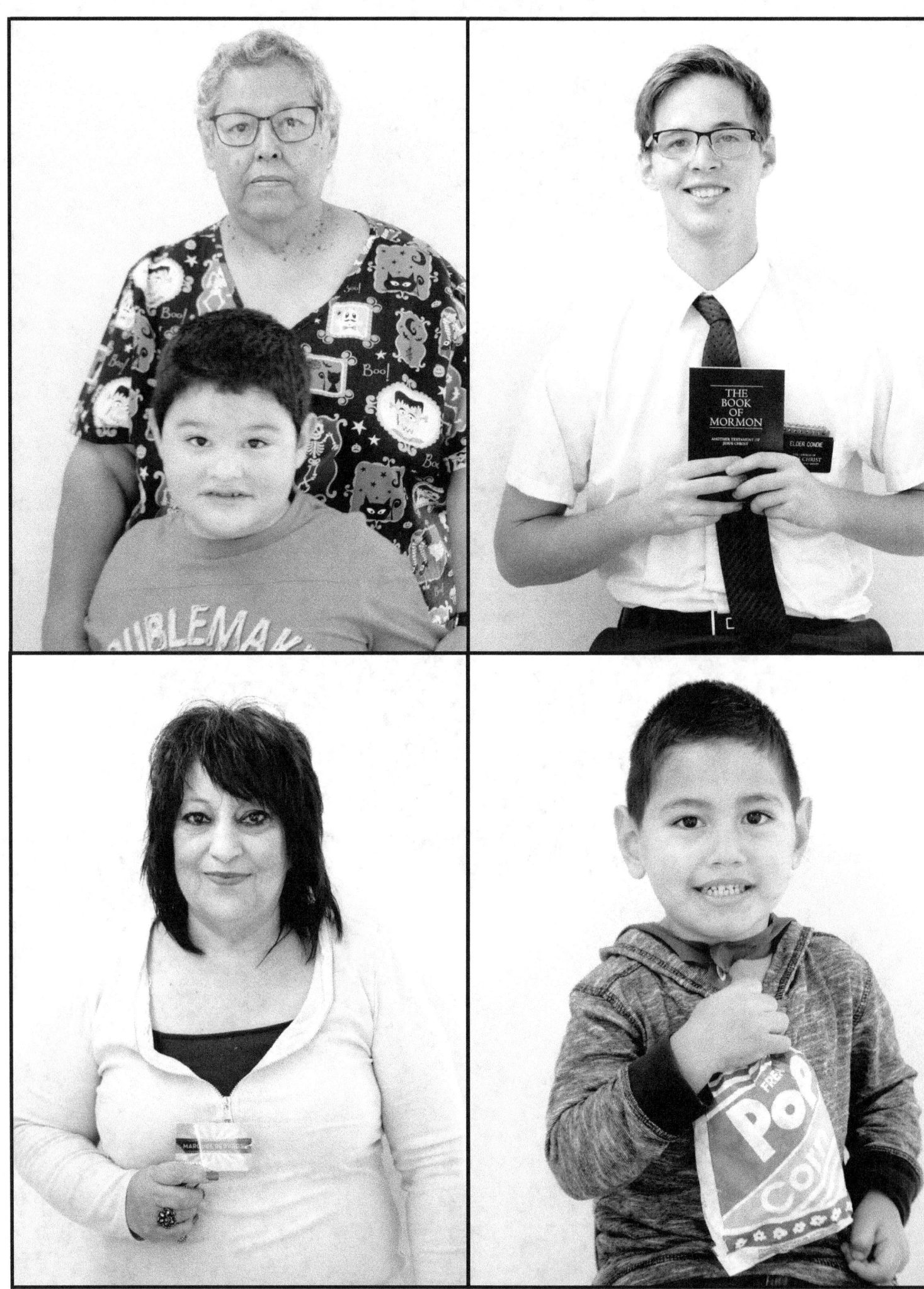

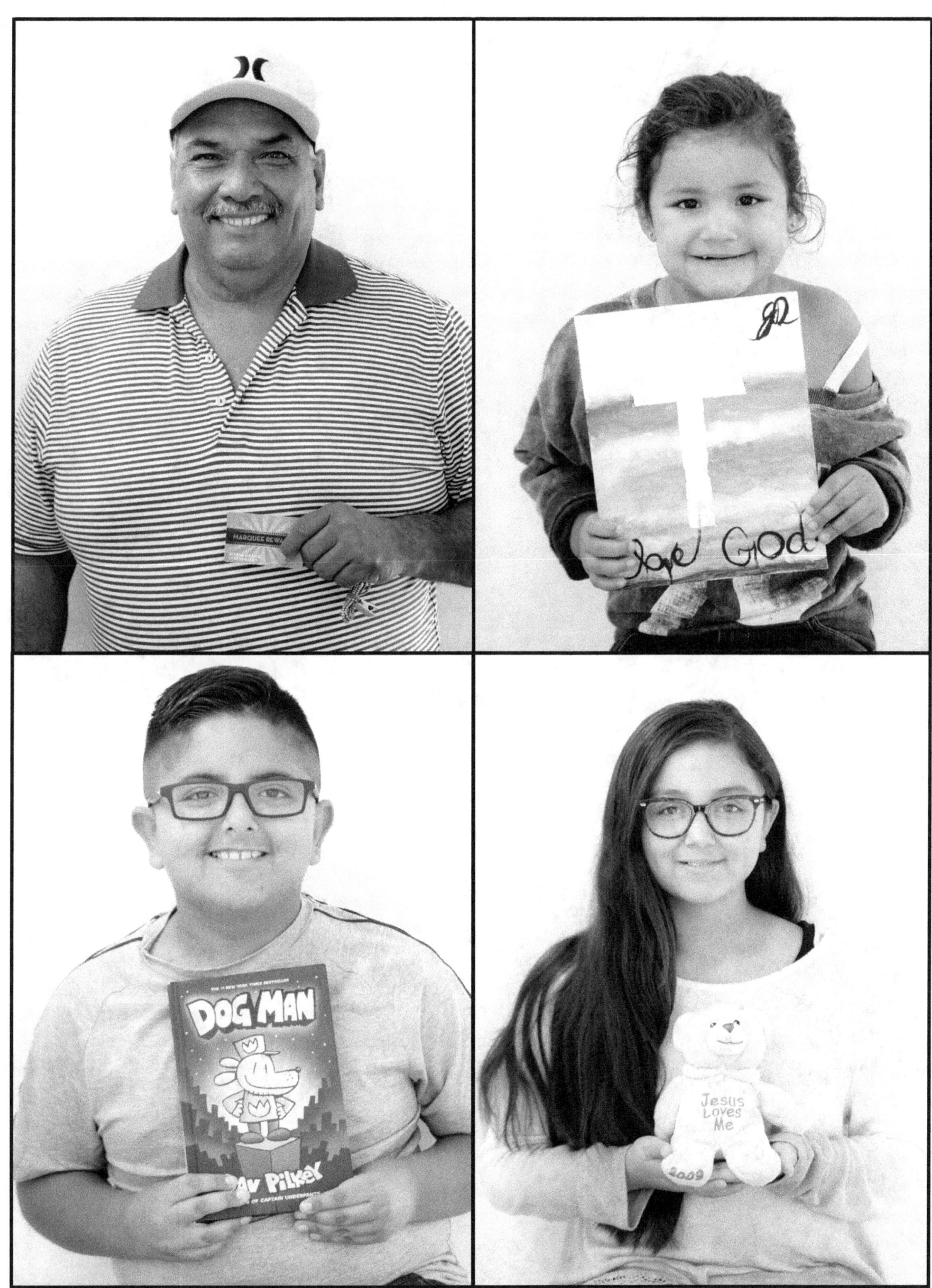

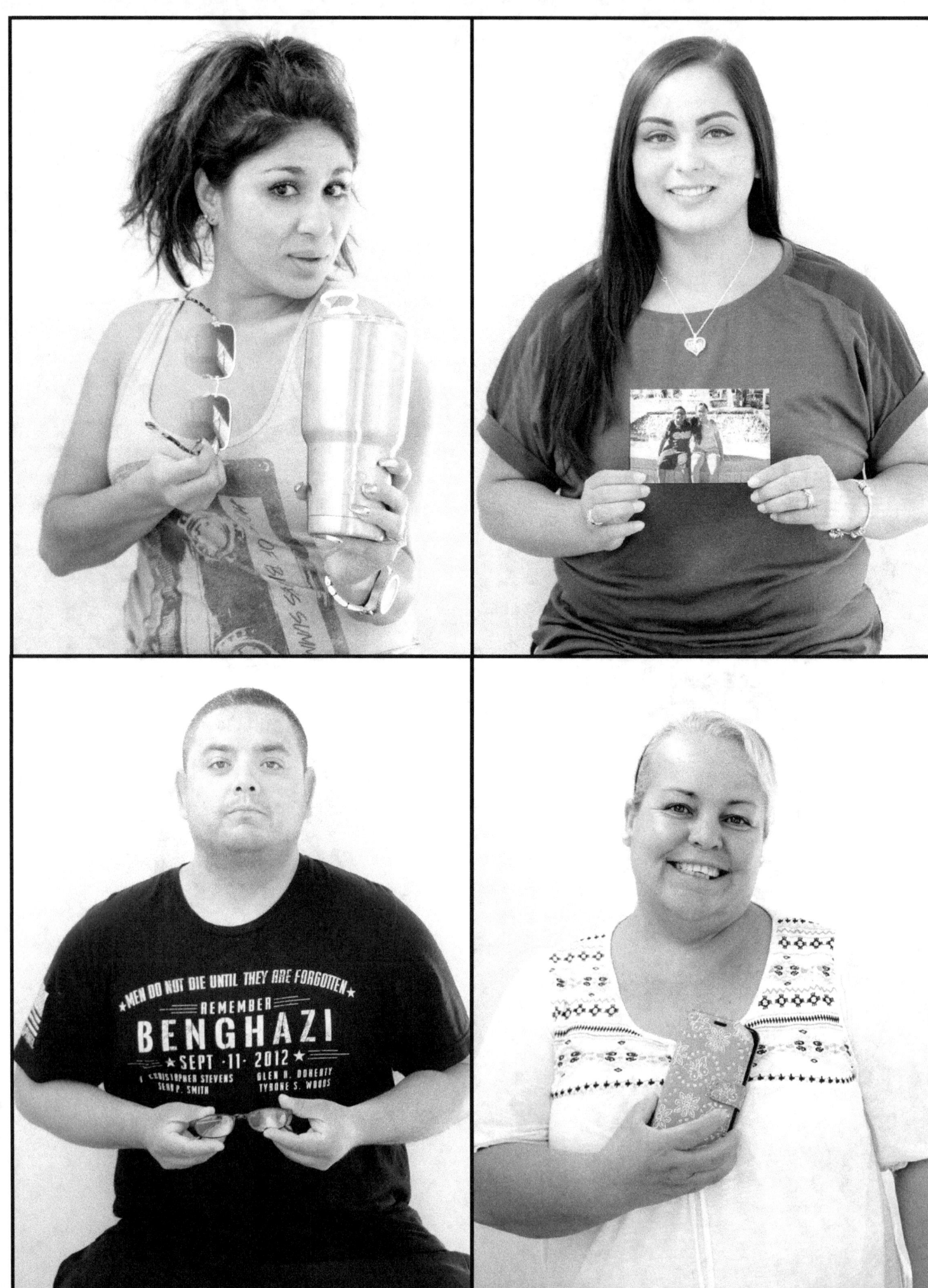

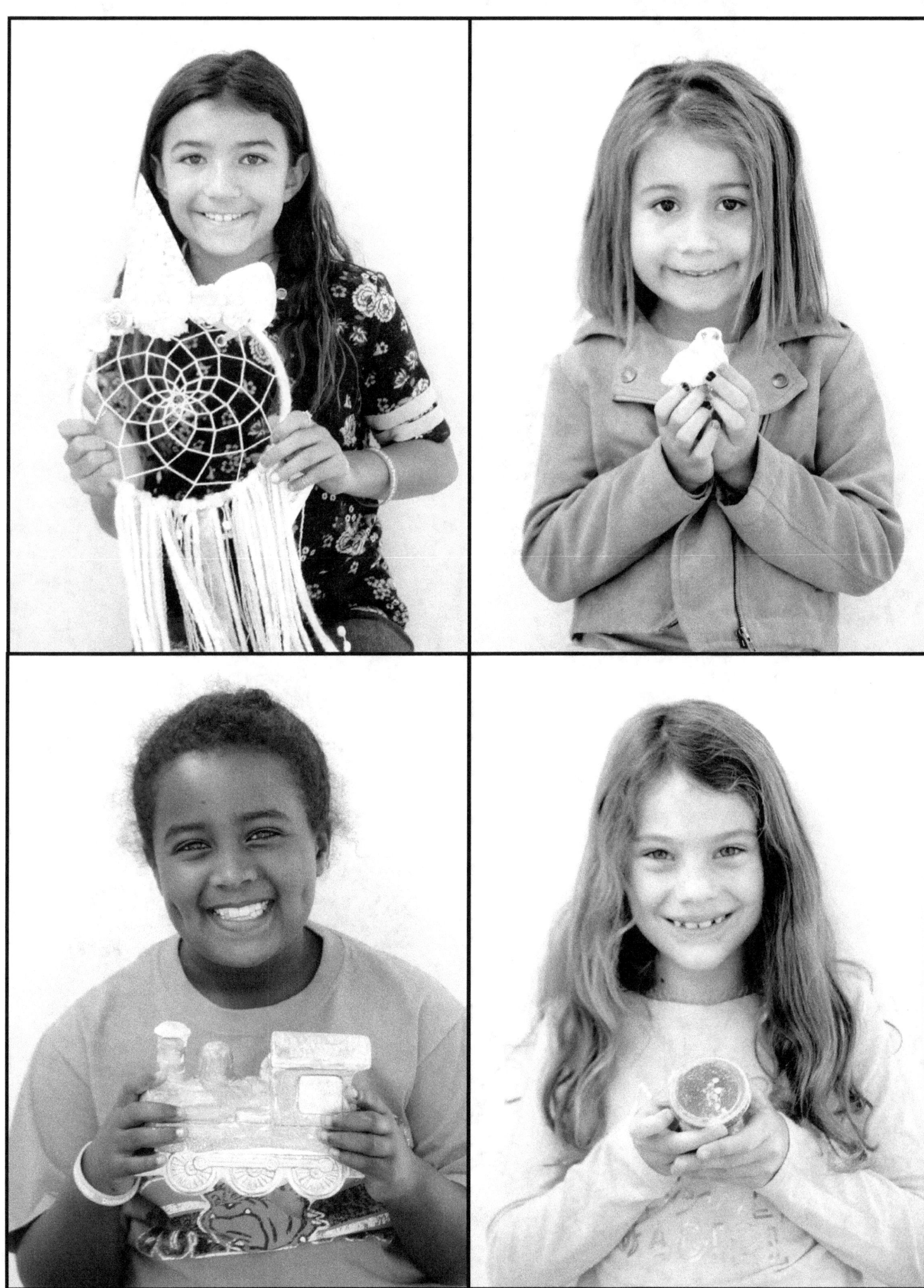

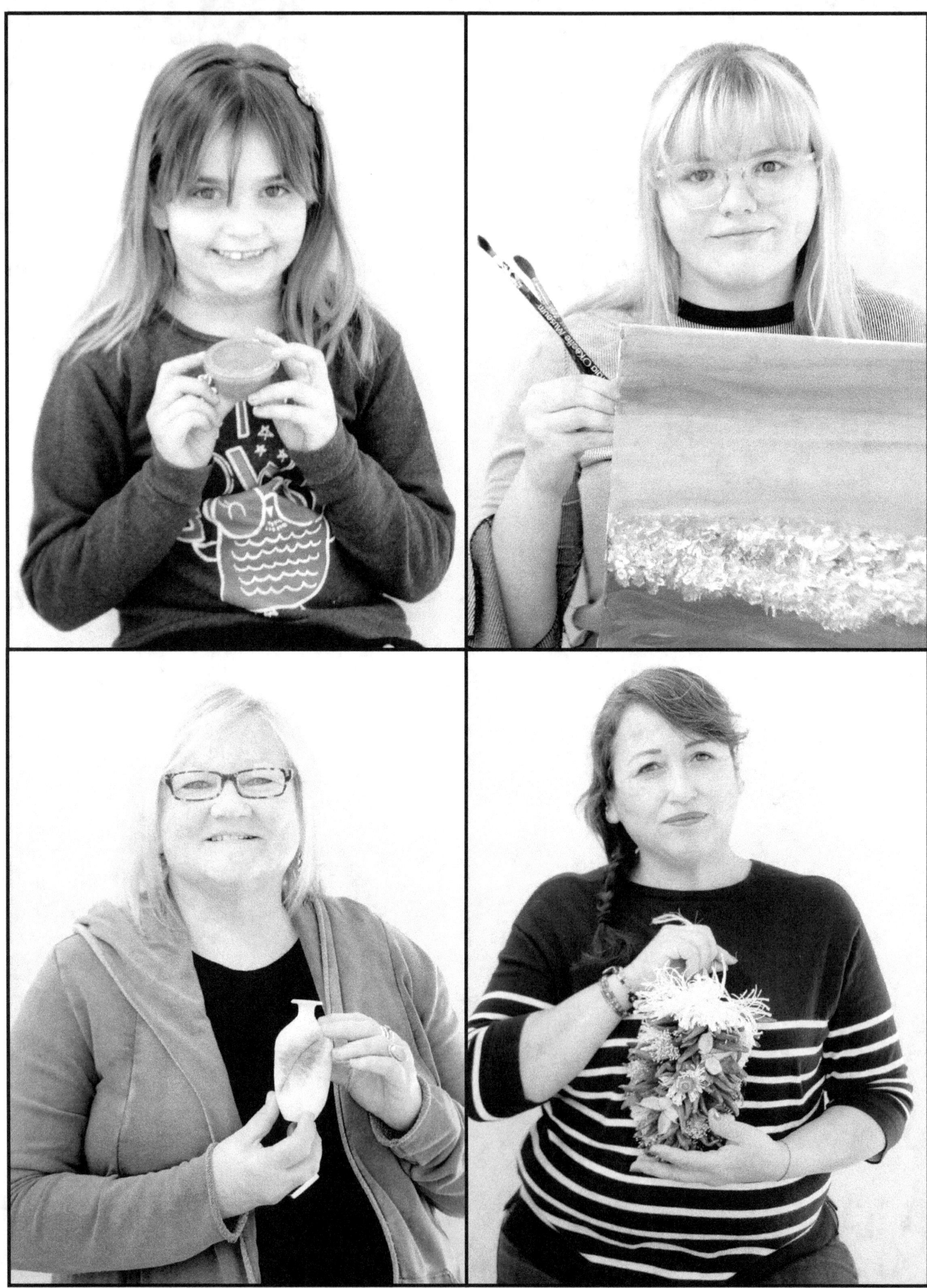

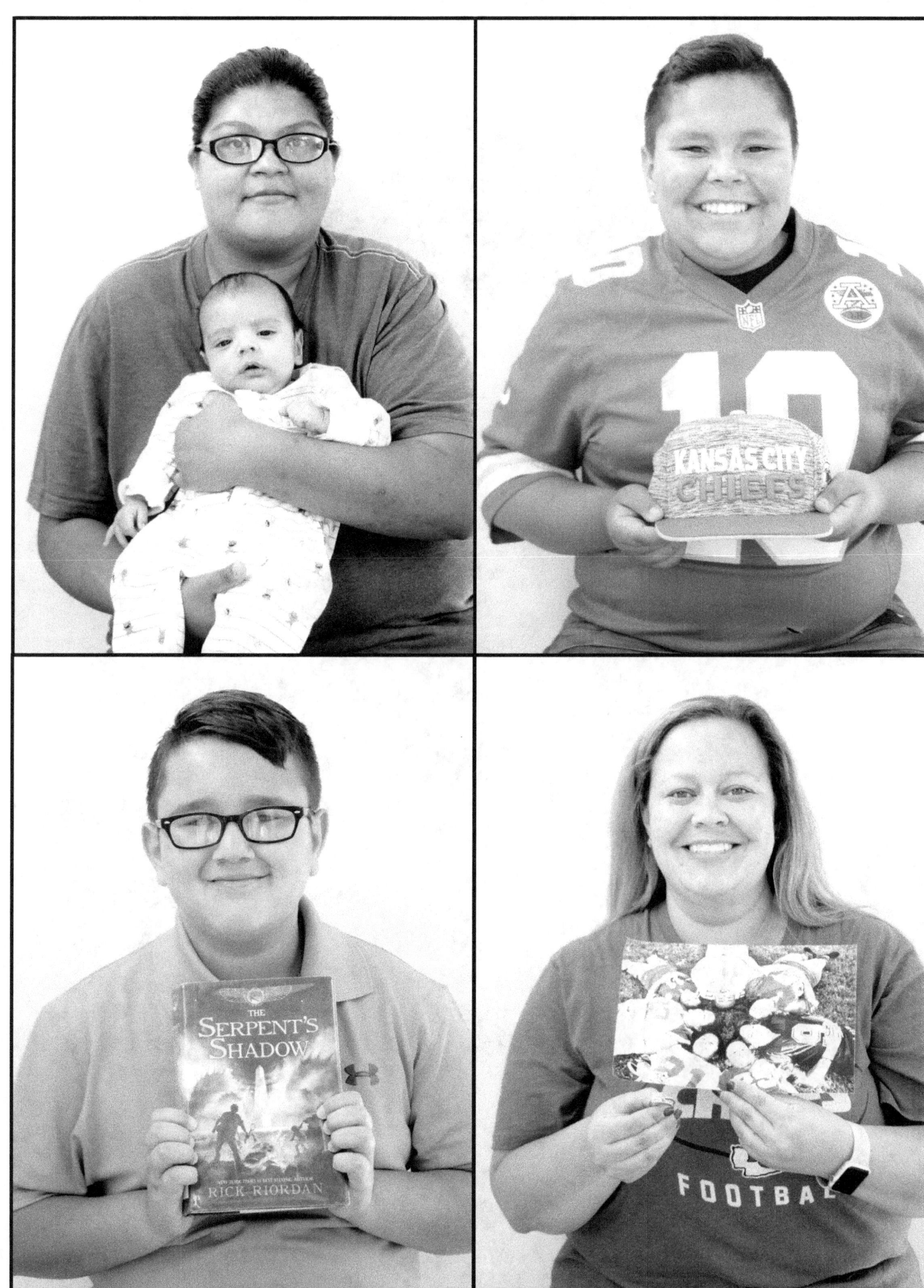

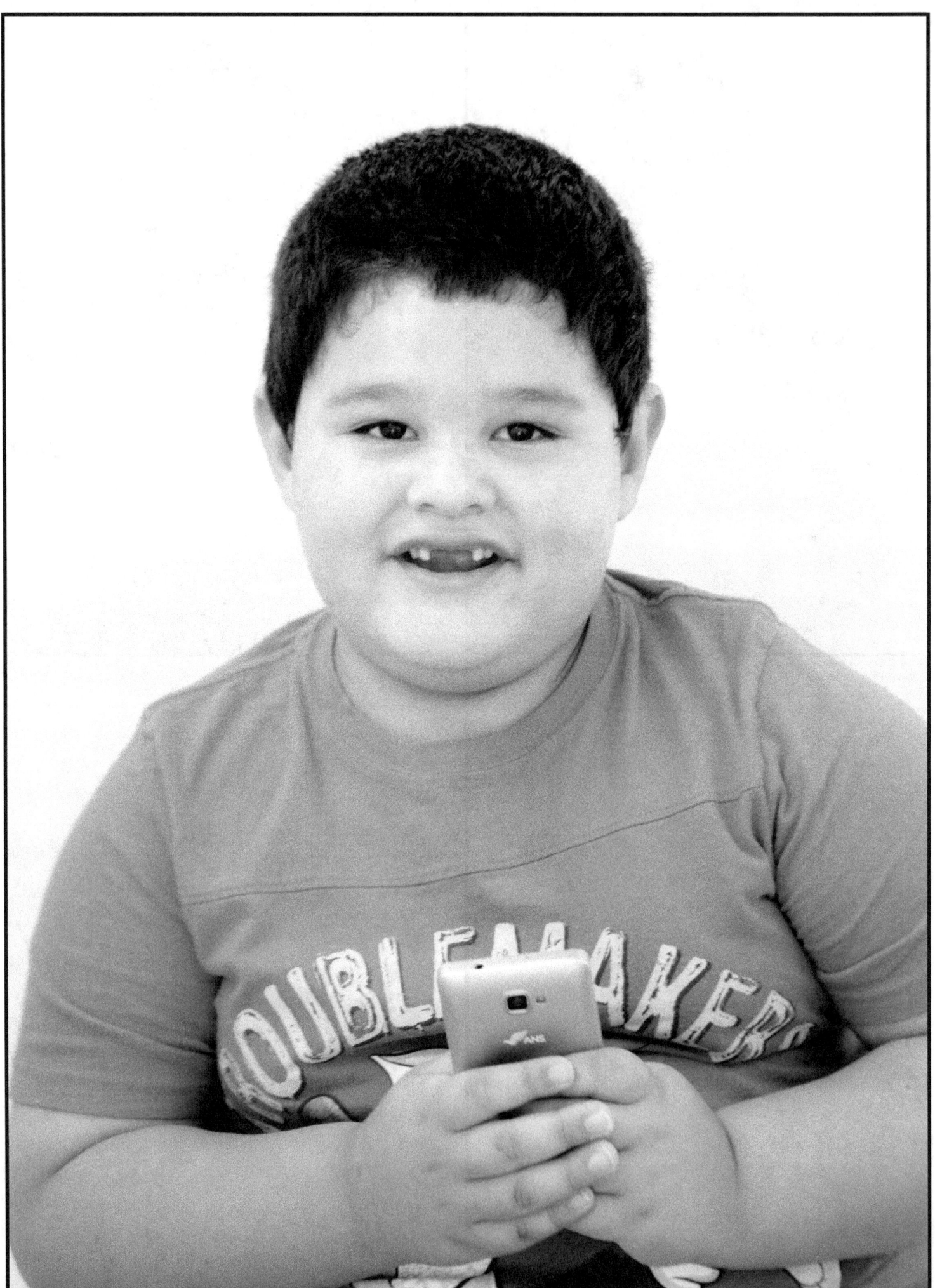

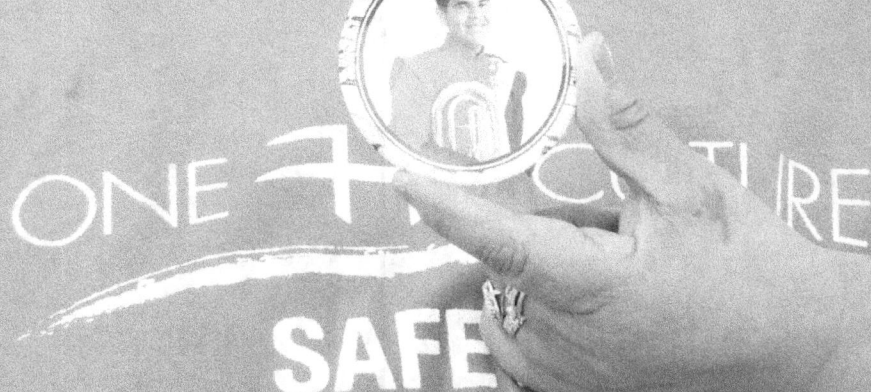

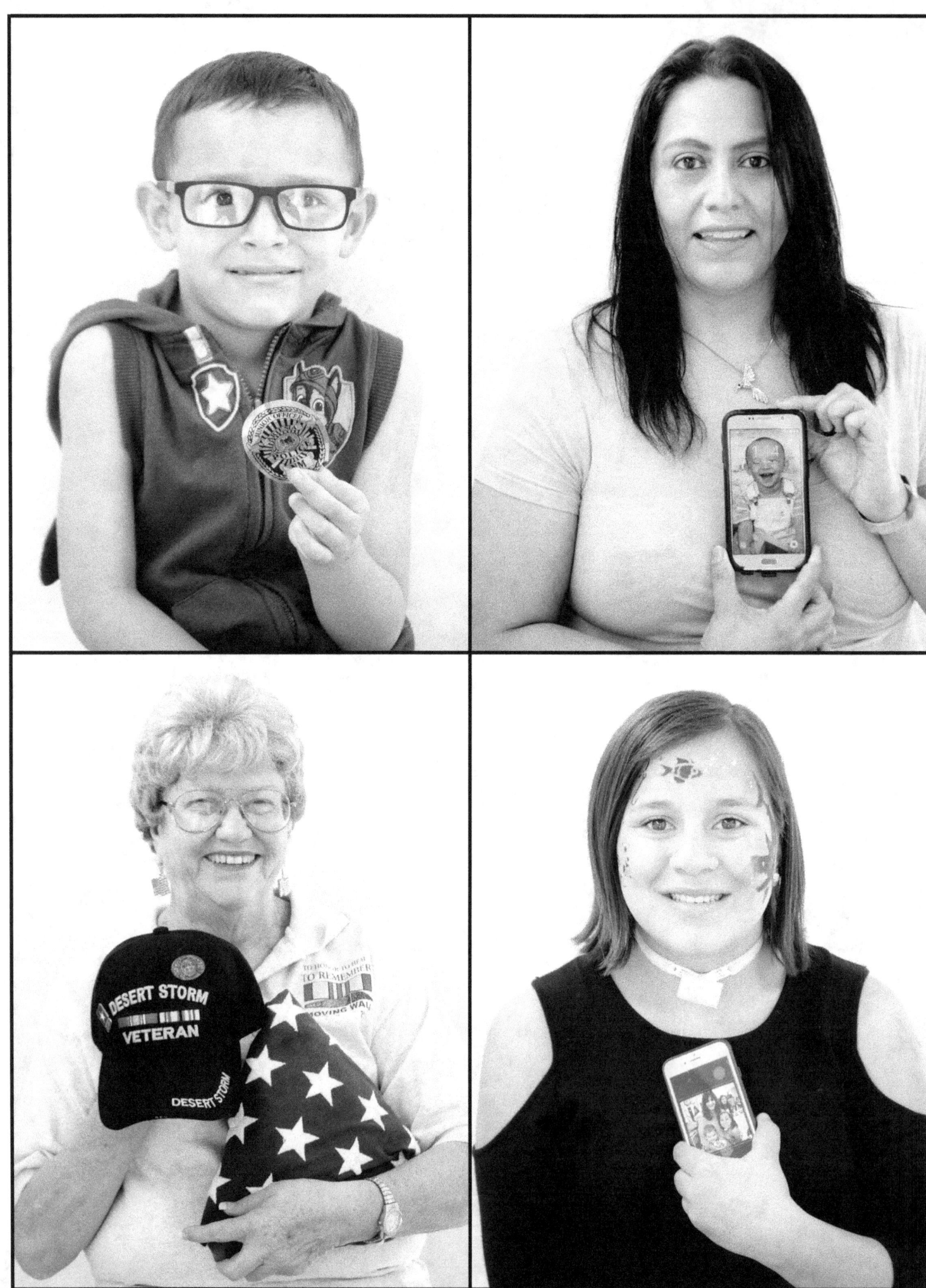

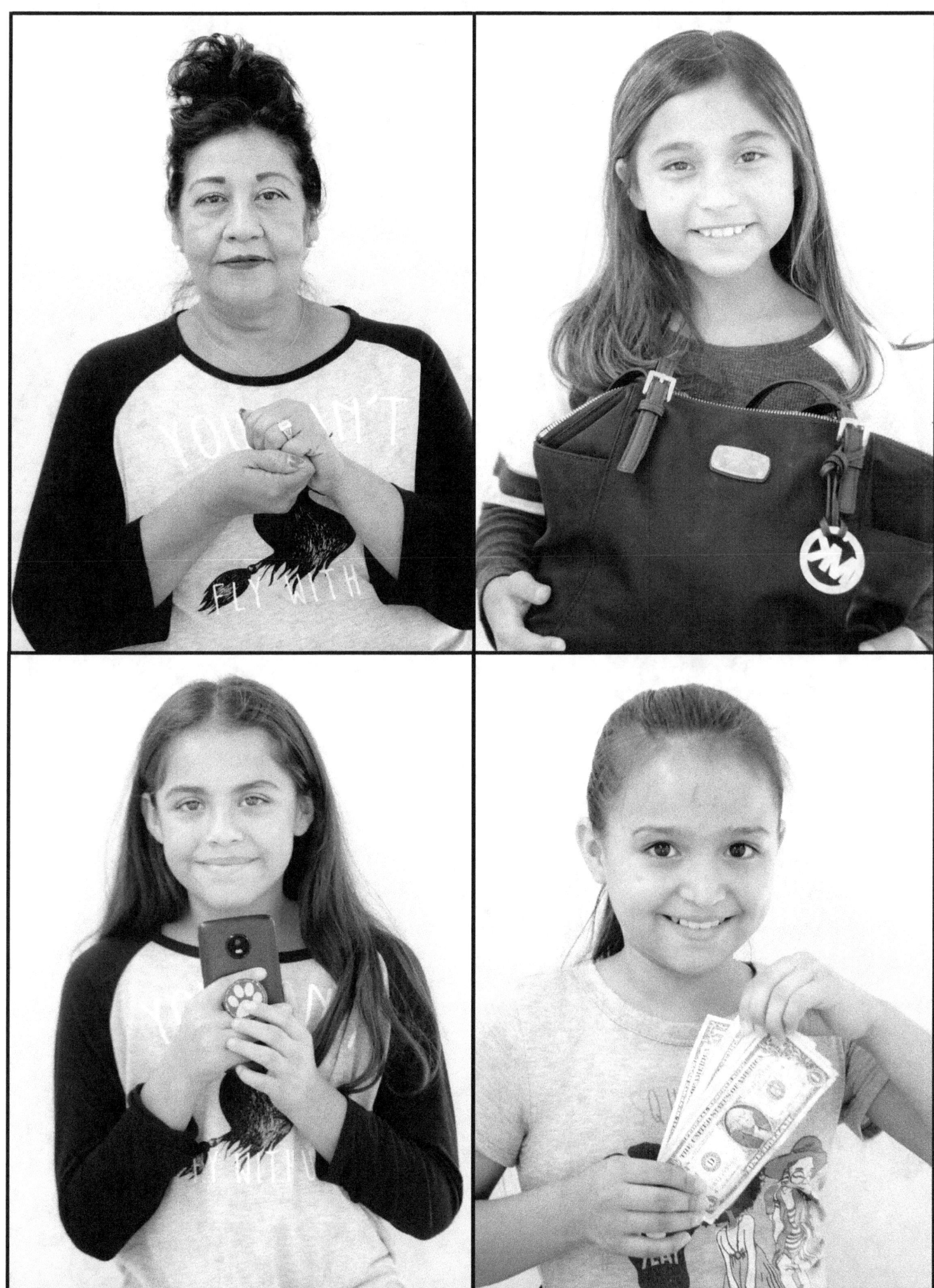

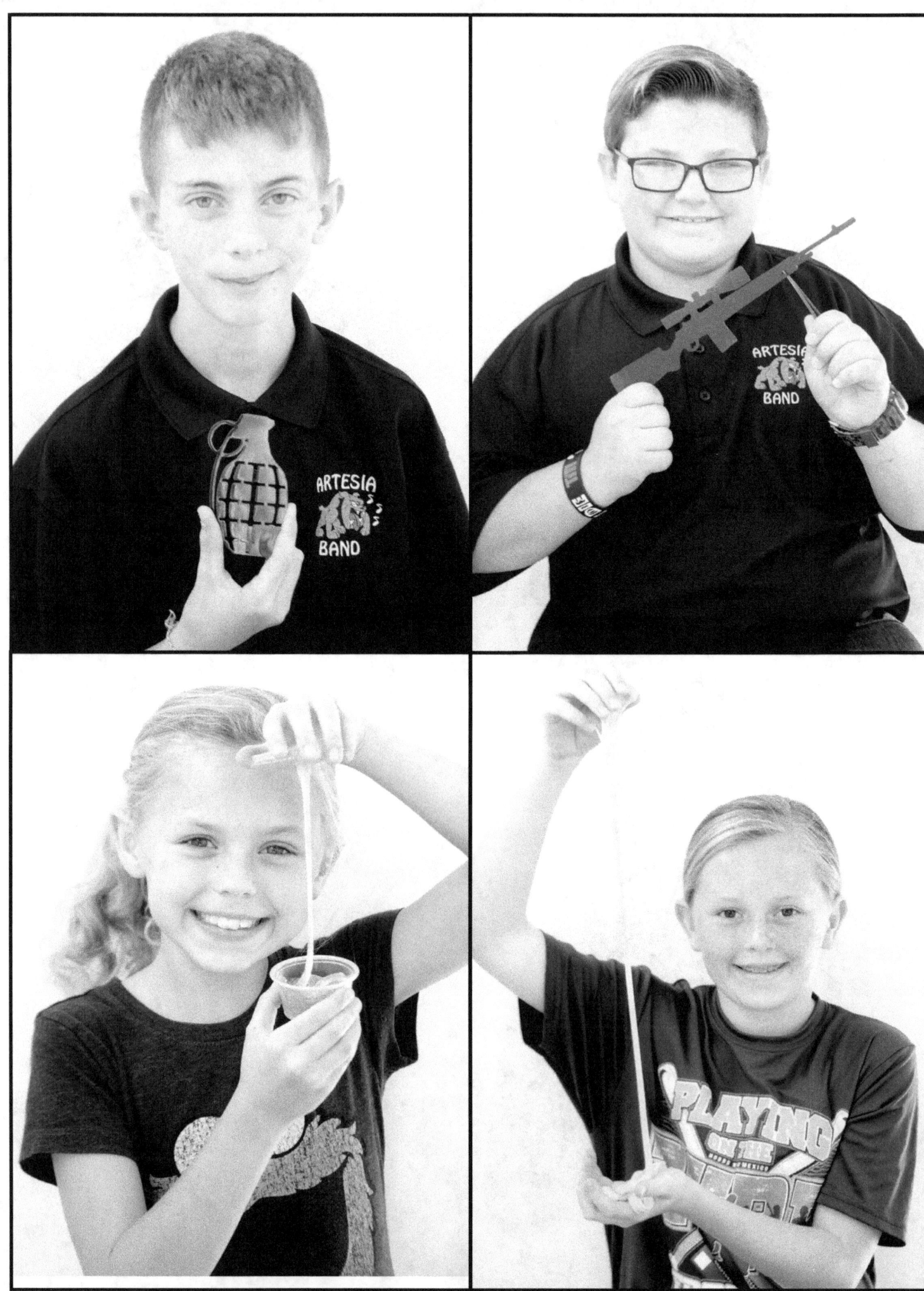

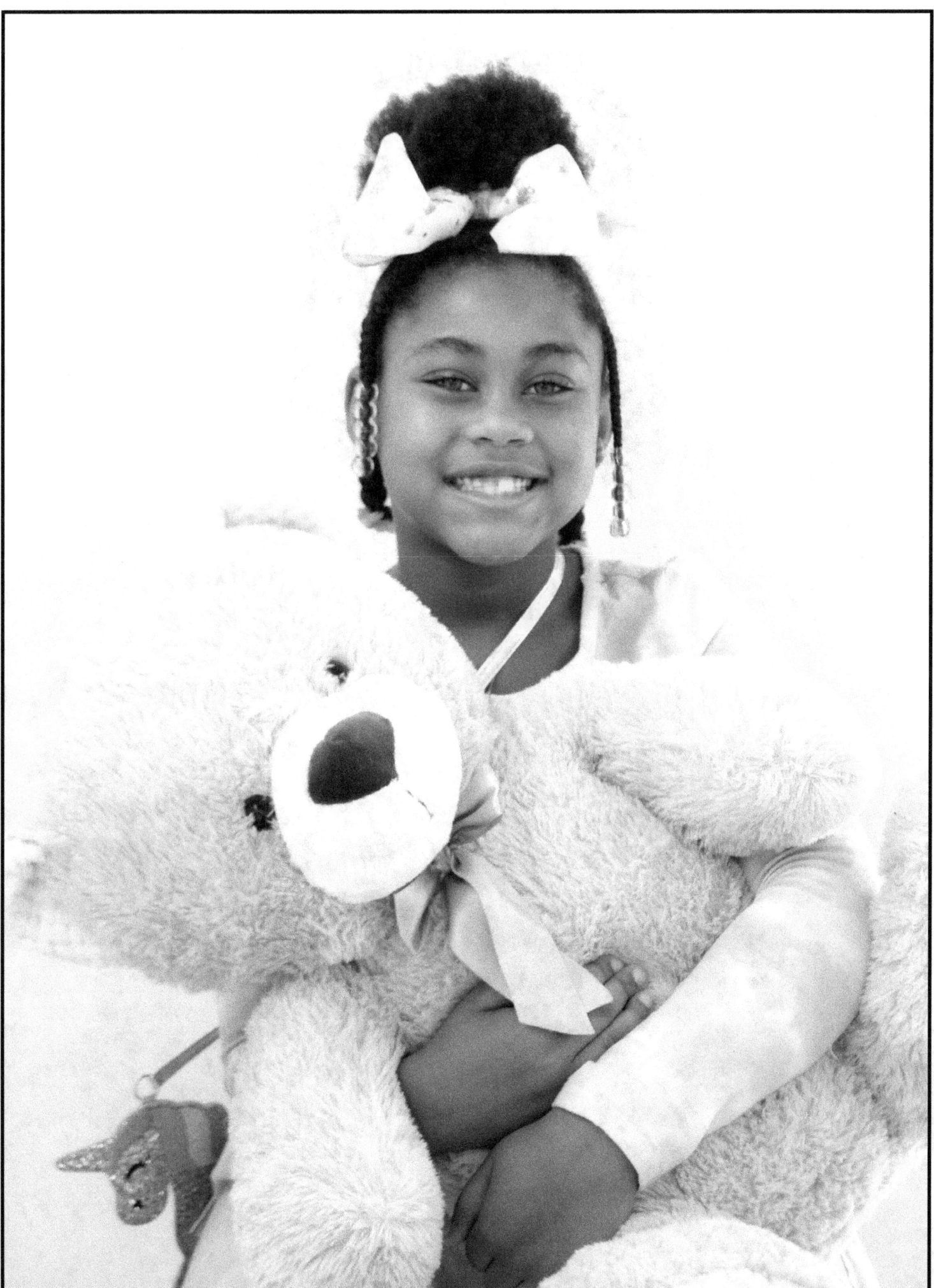

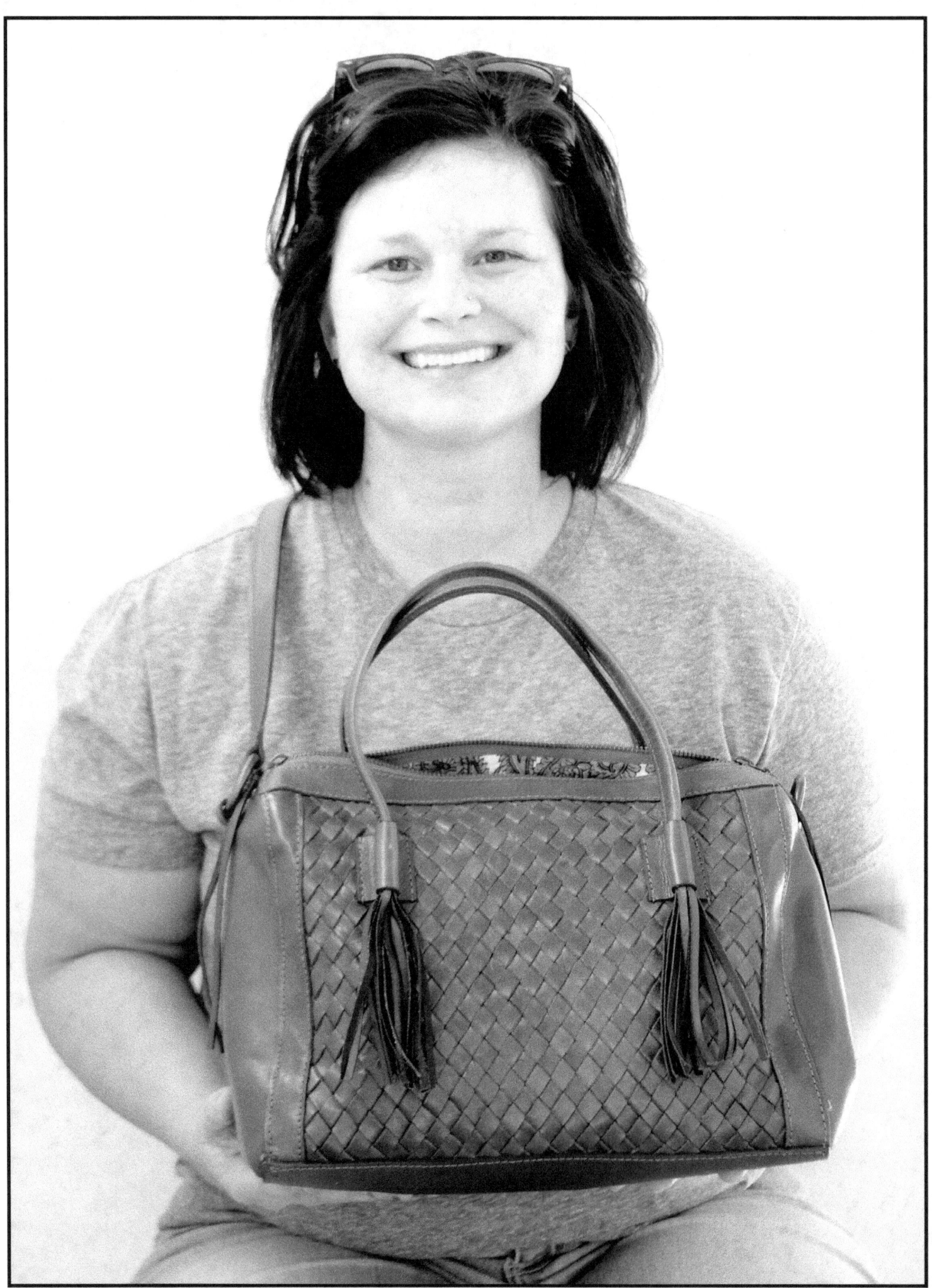

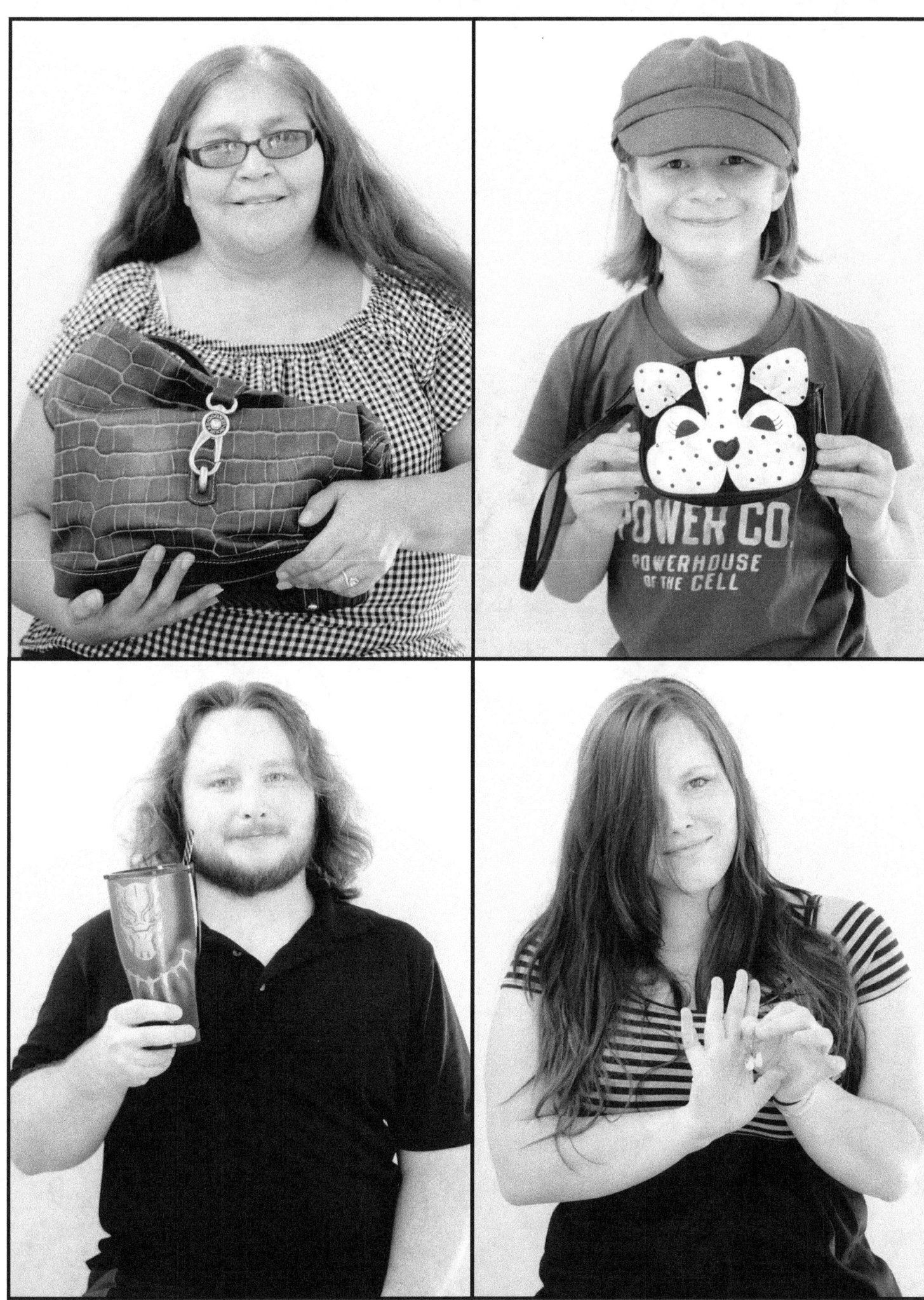

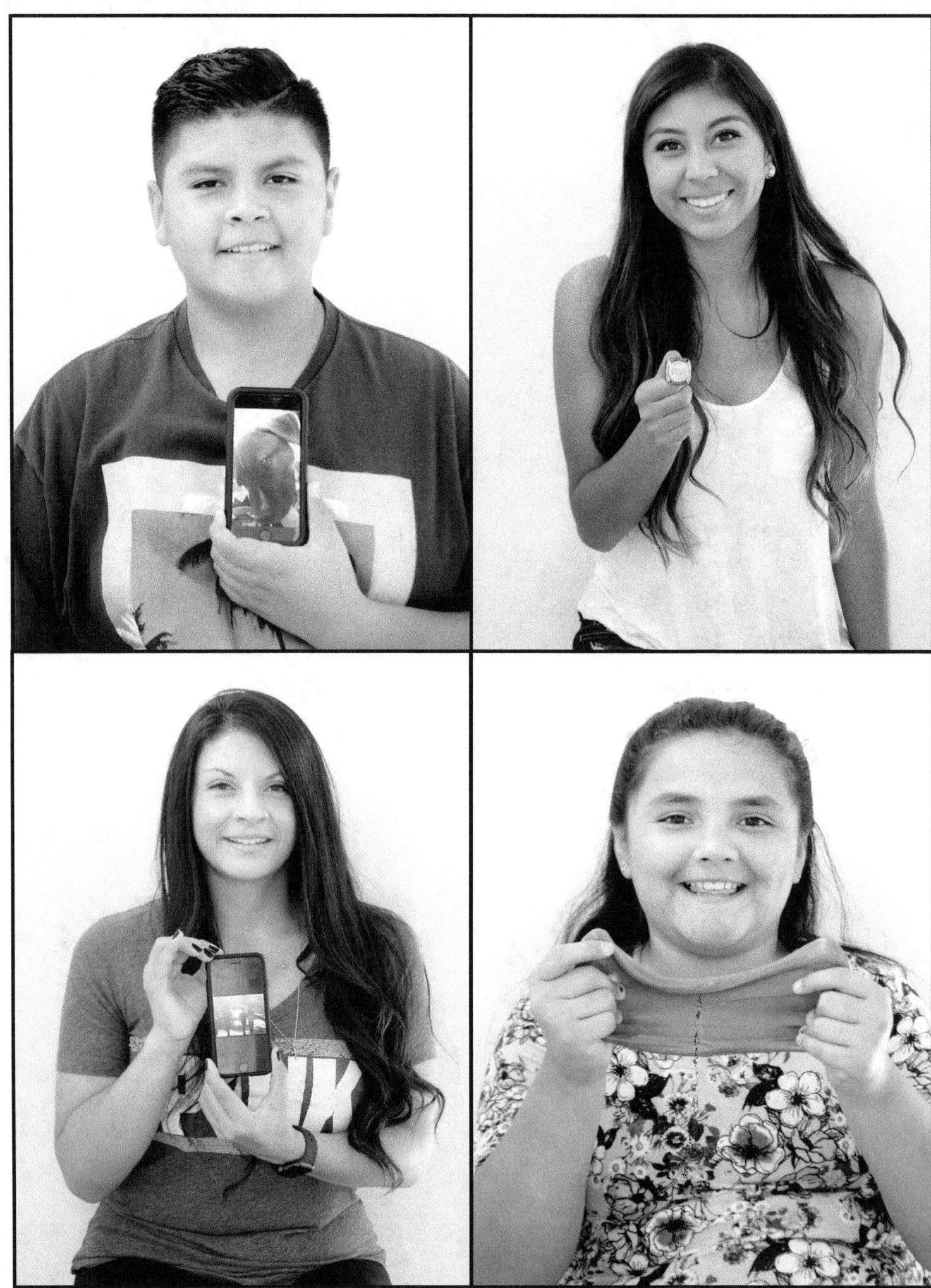

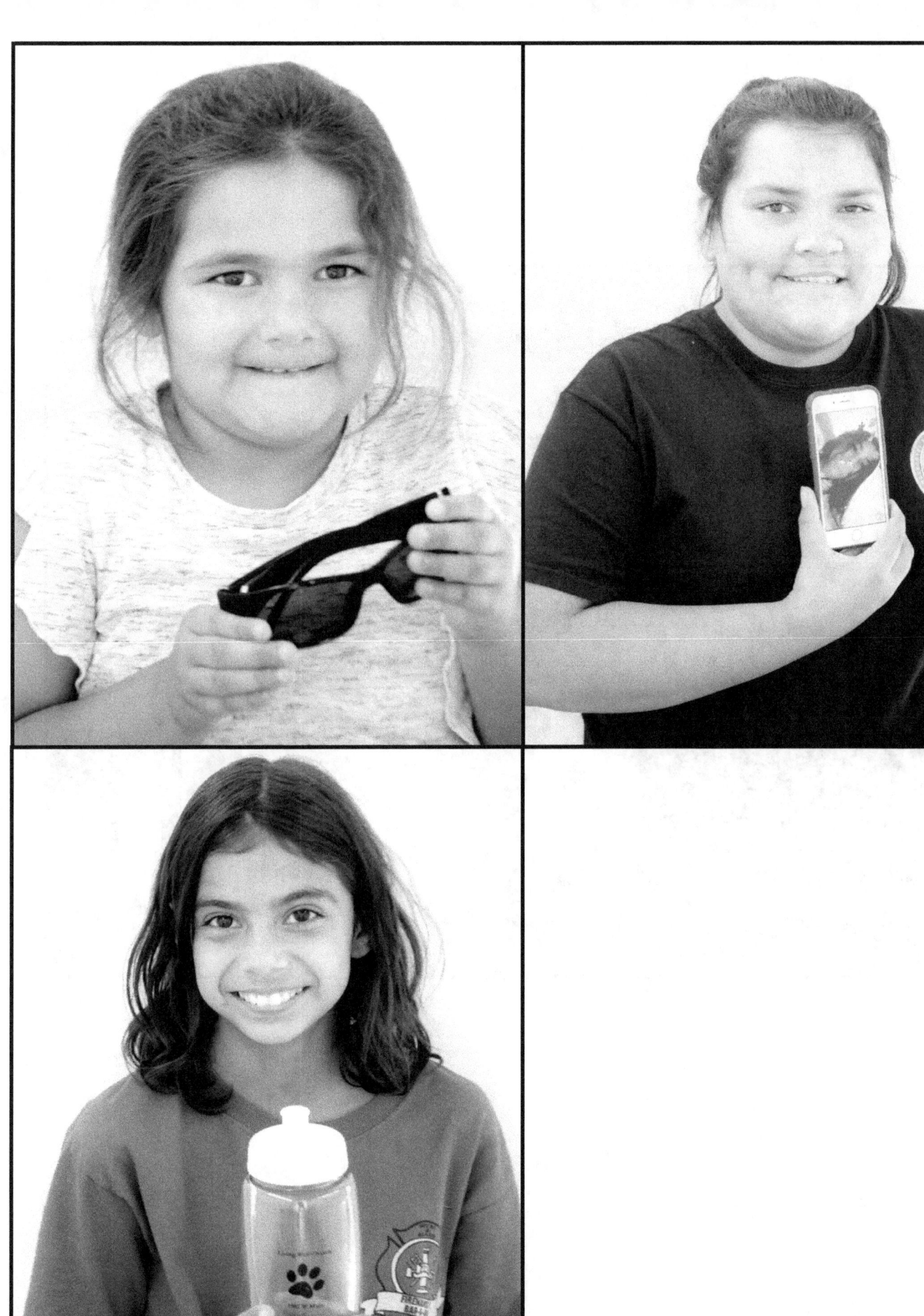

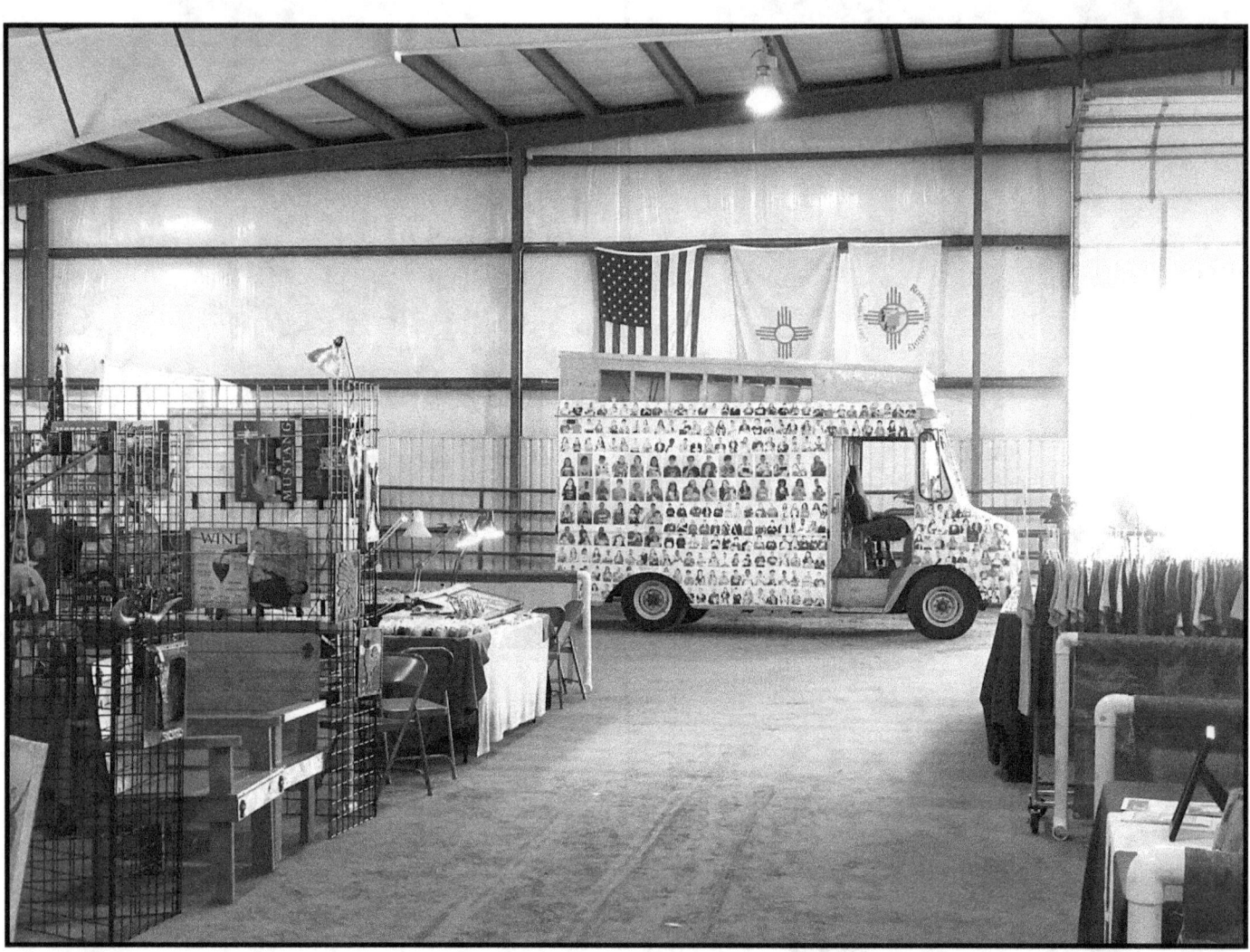

Portales
October 21-22, 2019

Peanut Valley Festival
Eastern New Mexico University
Courthouse Square

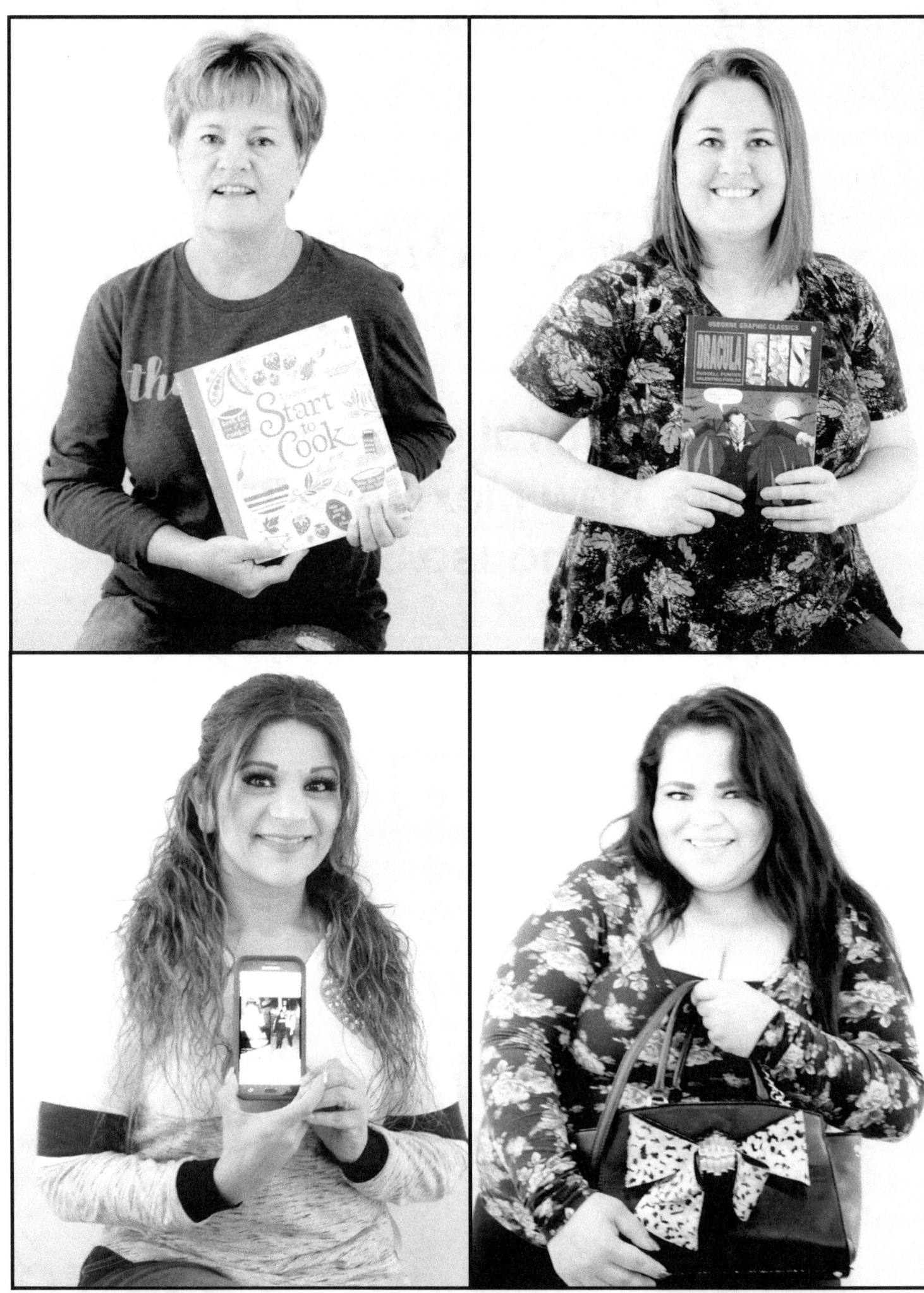

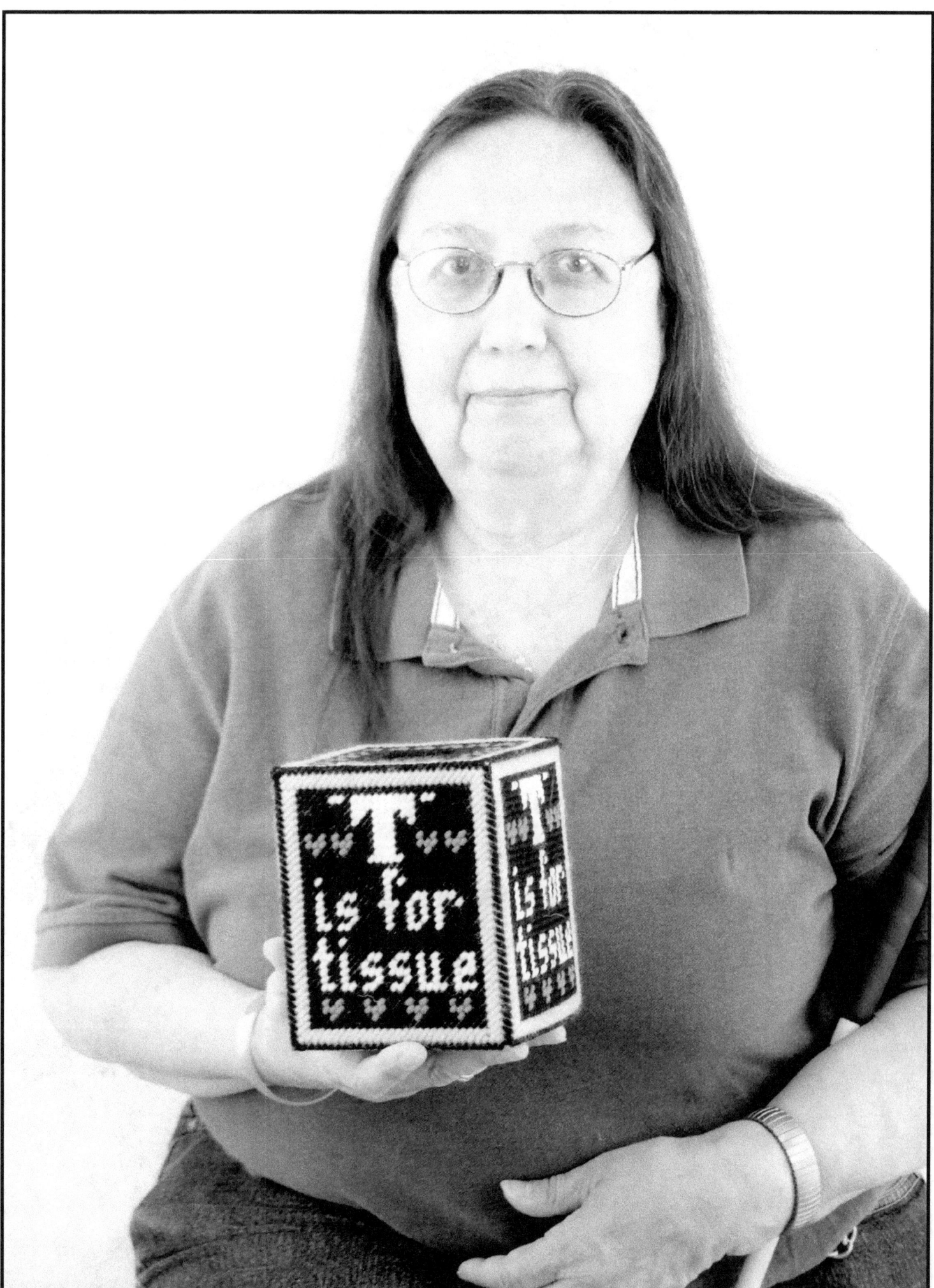

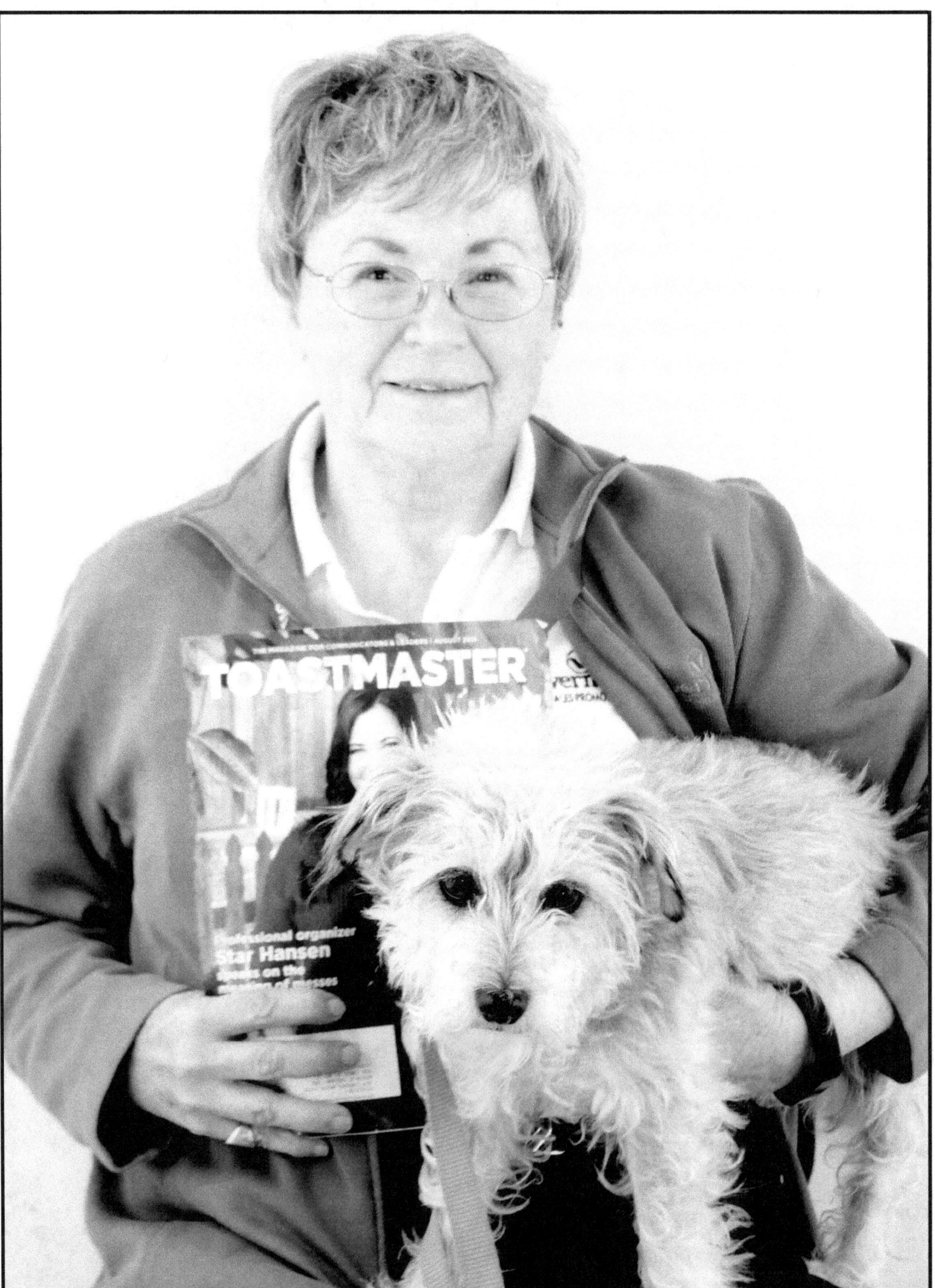

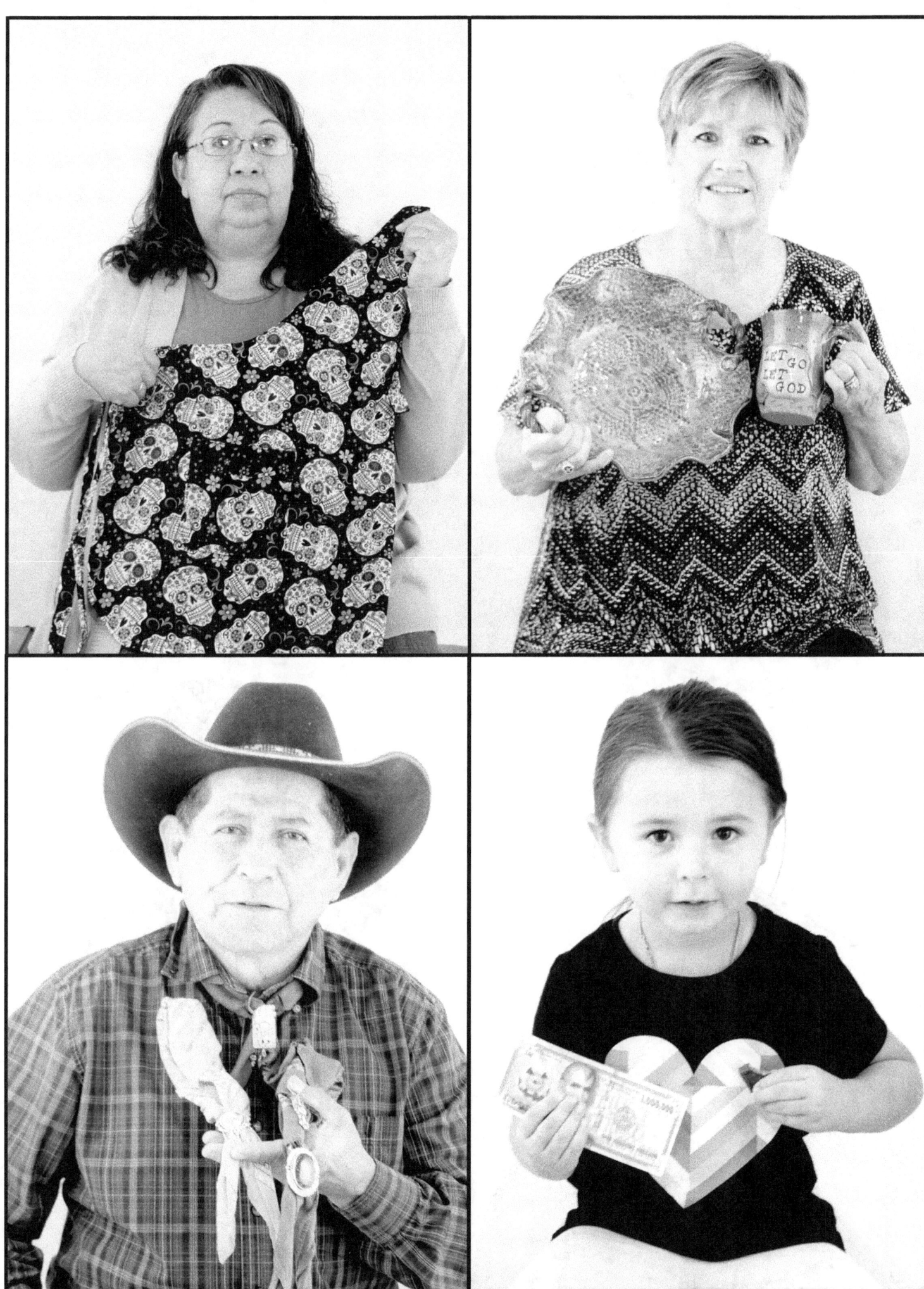

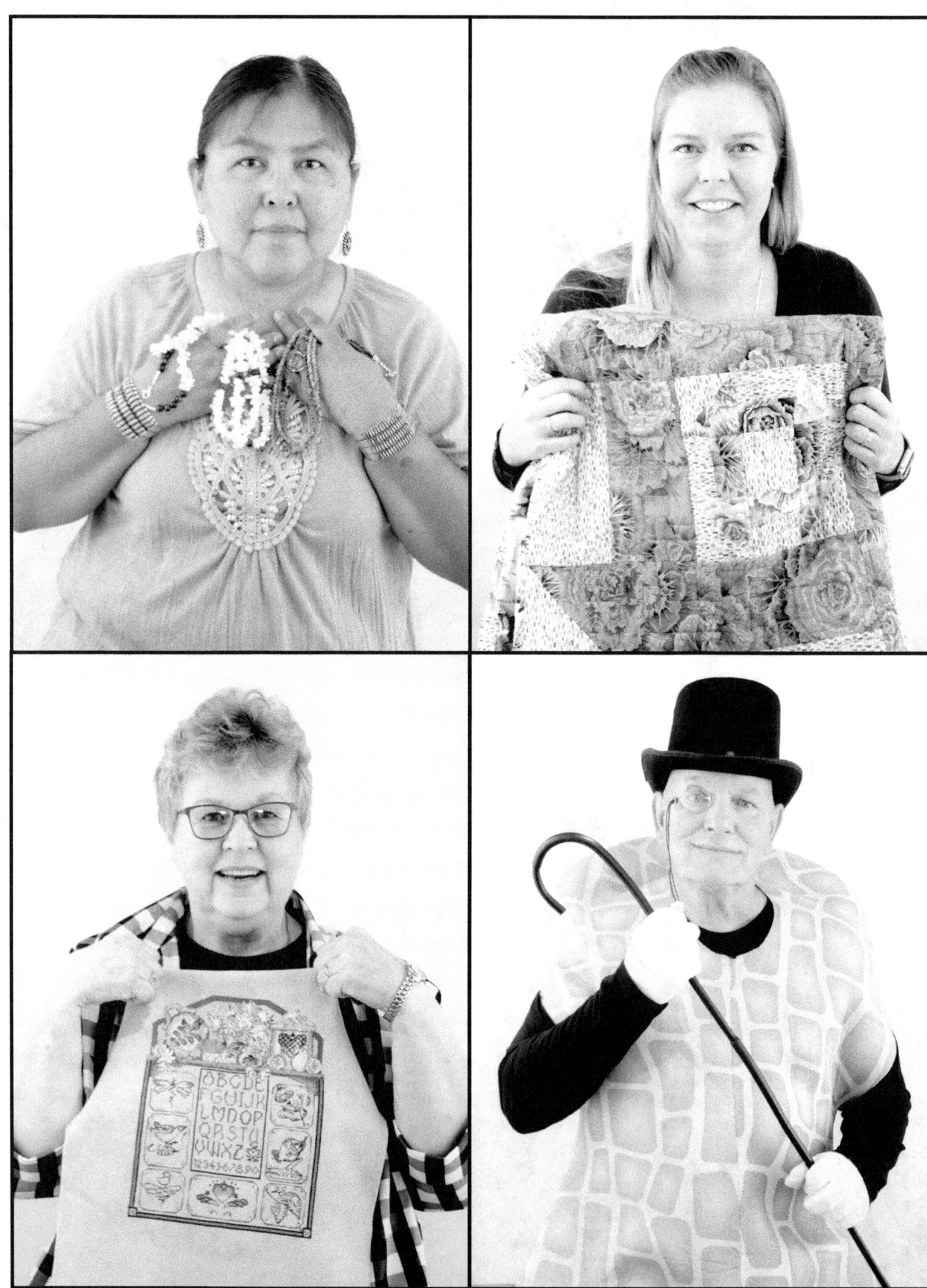

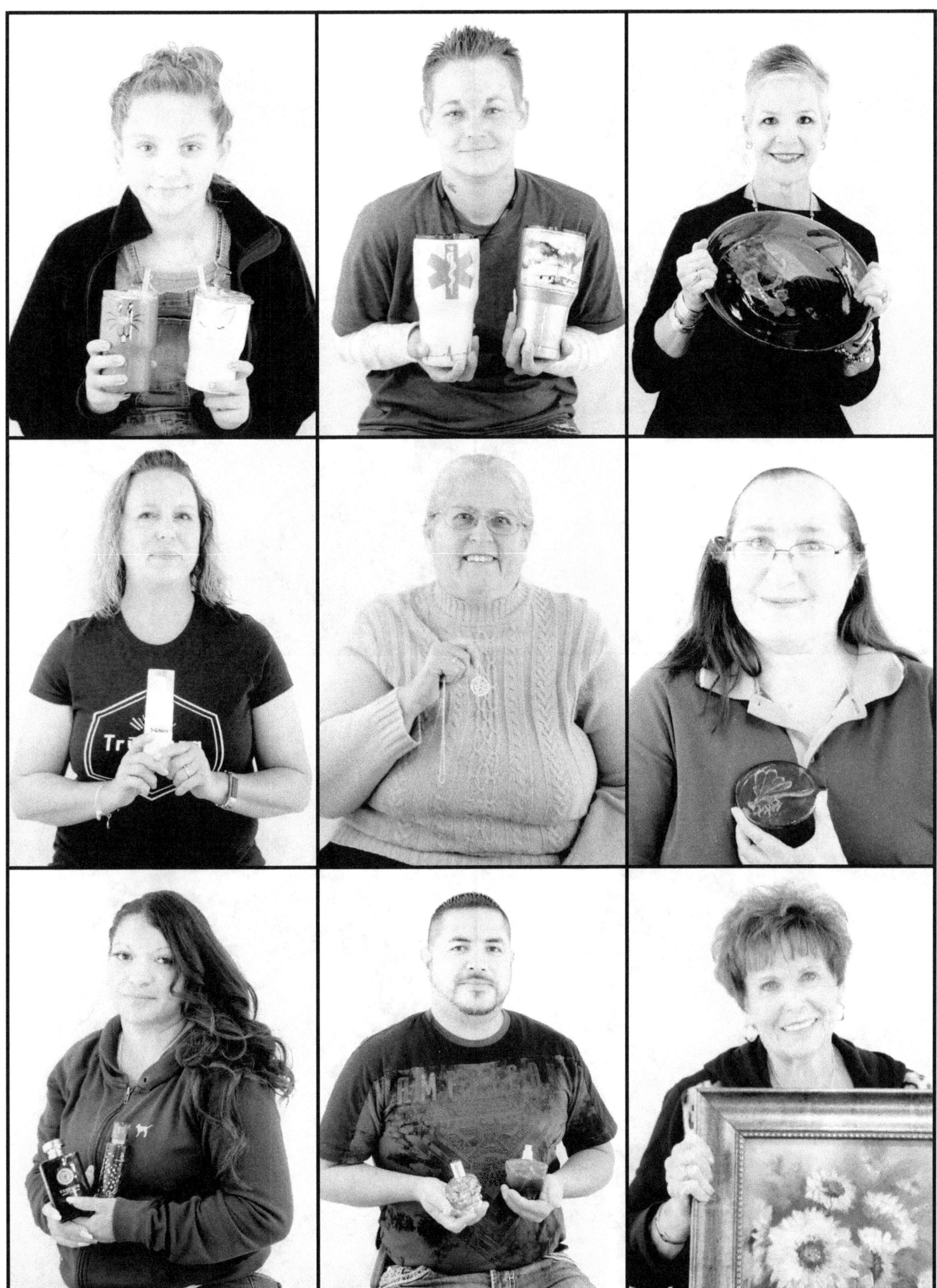

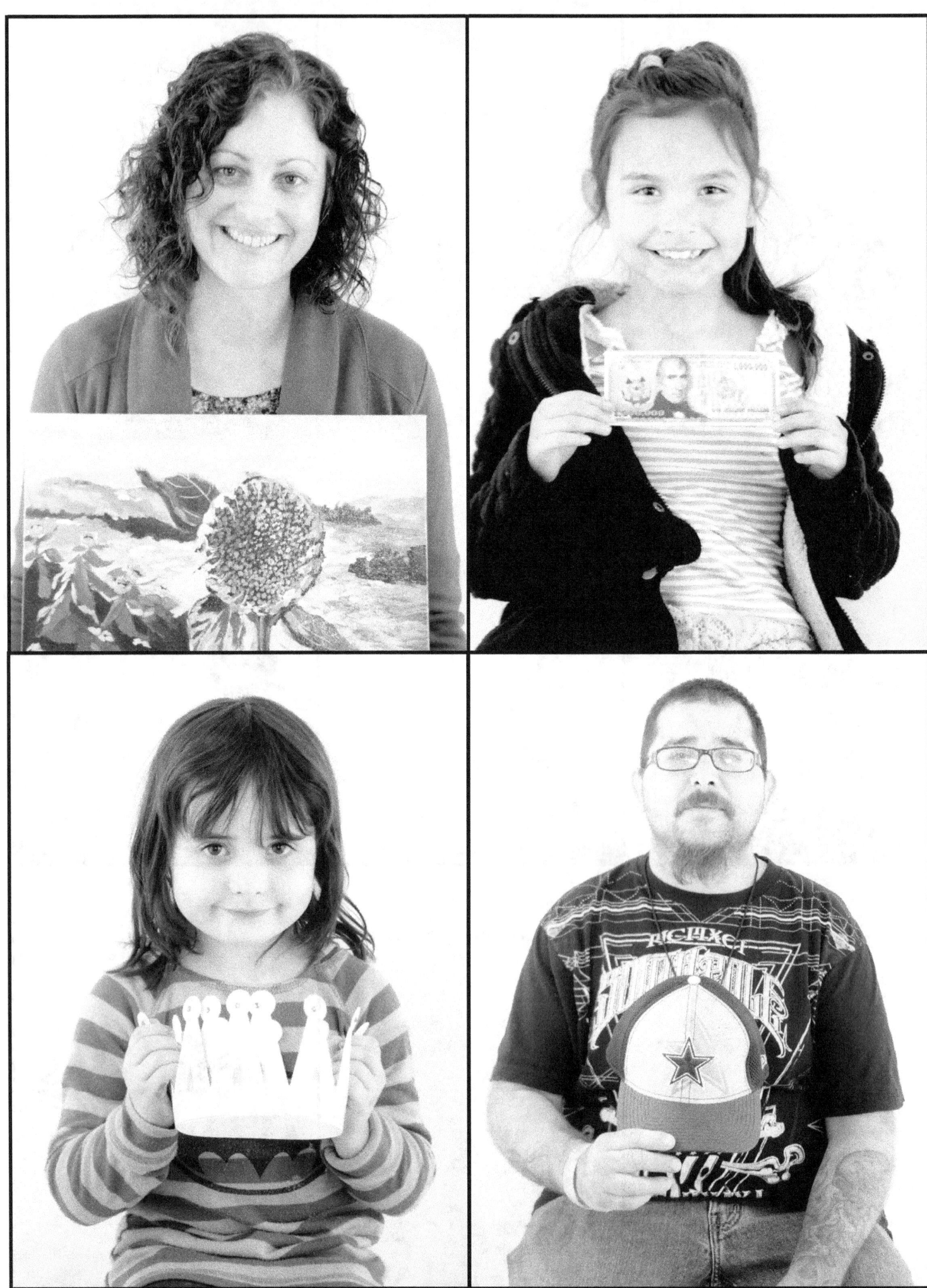

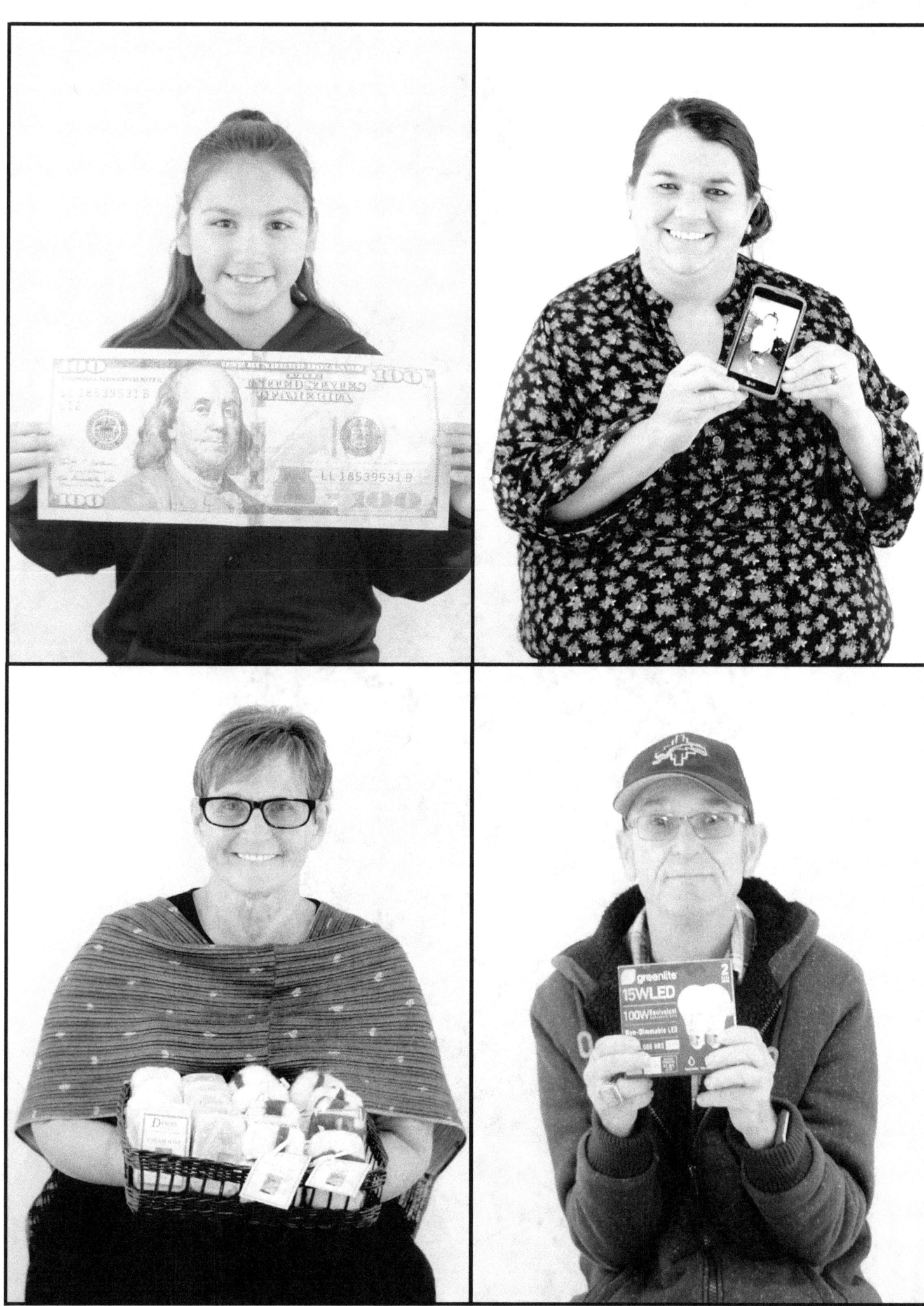

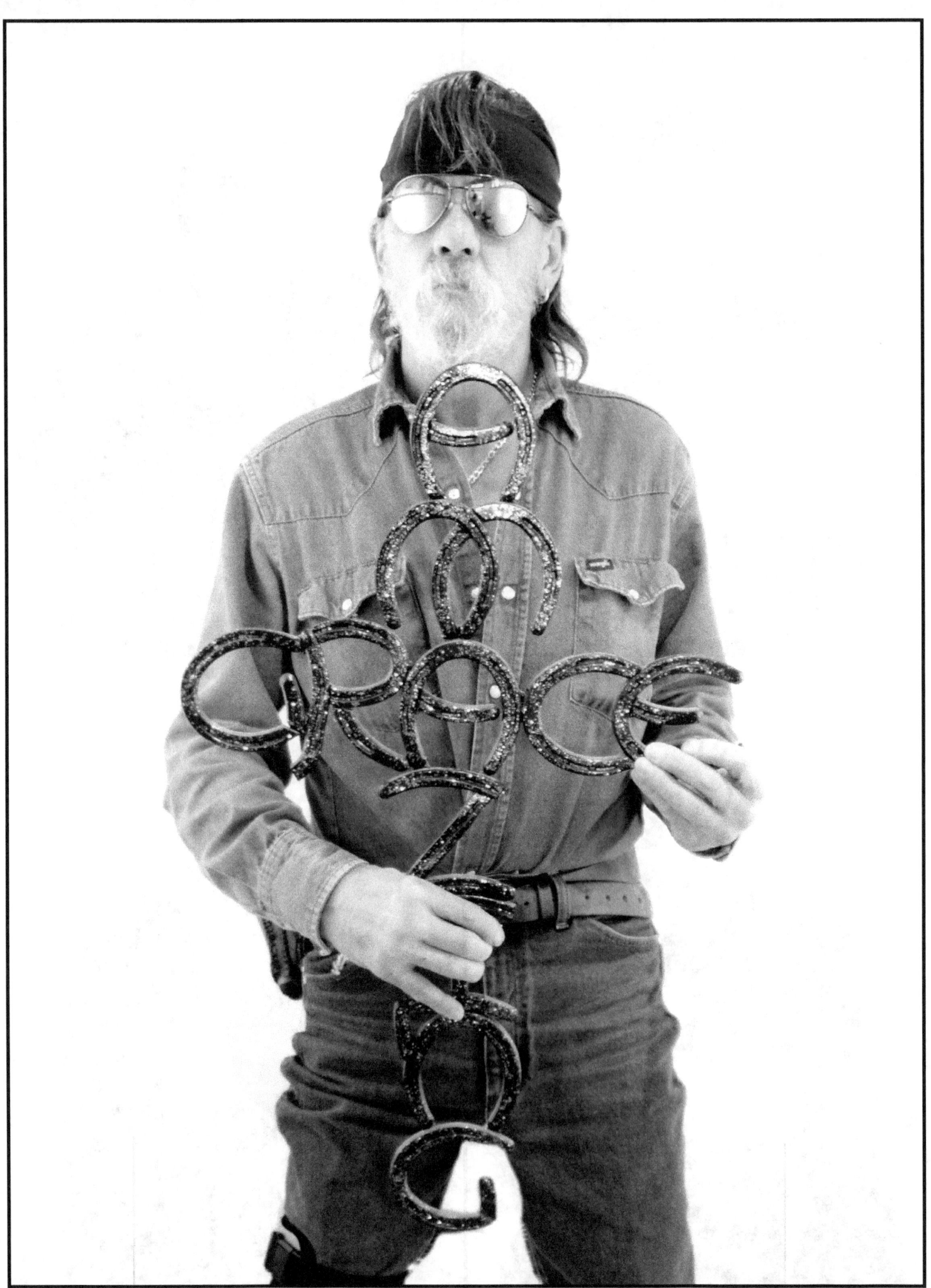

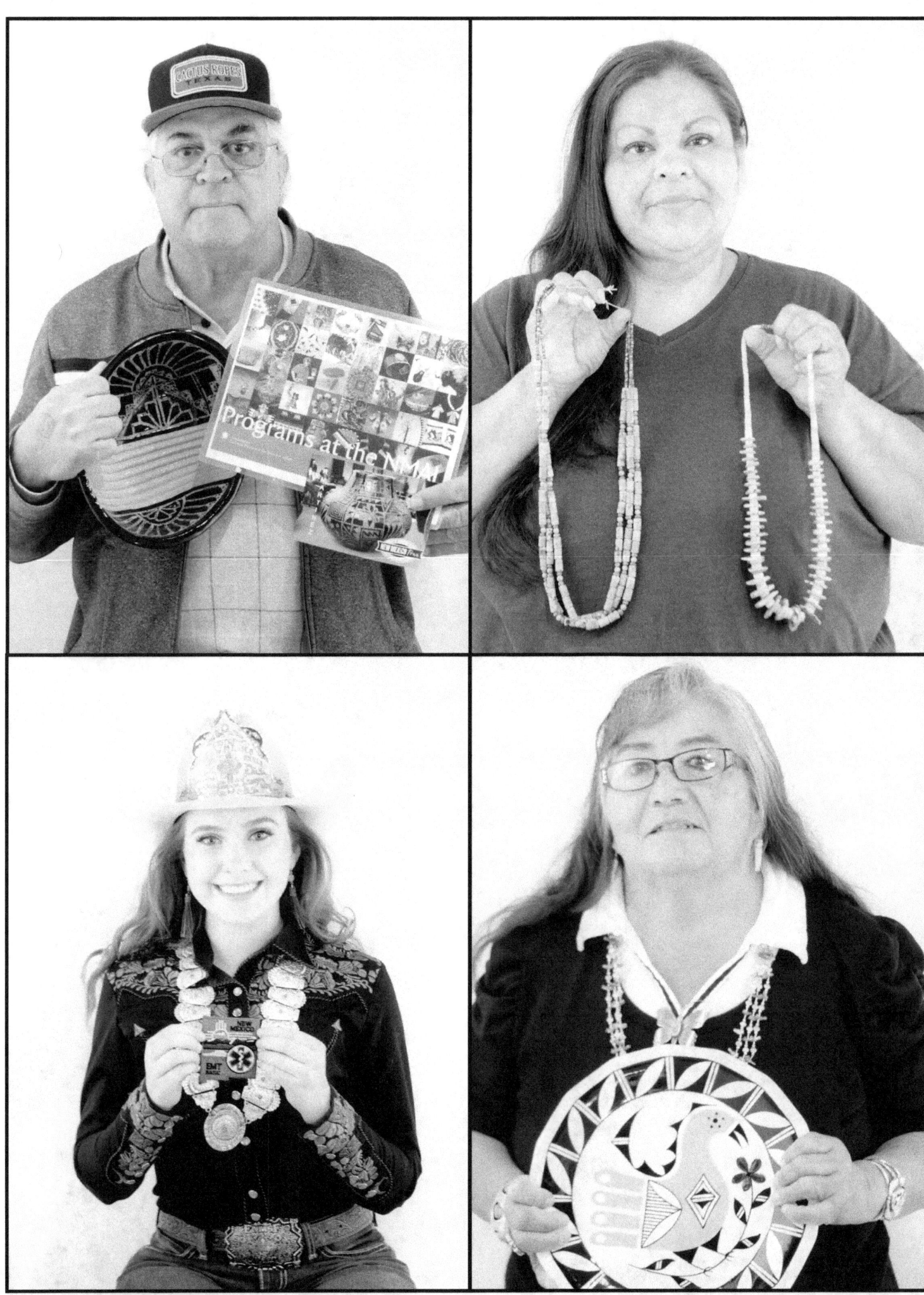

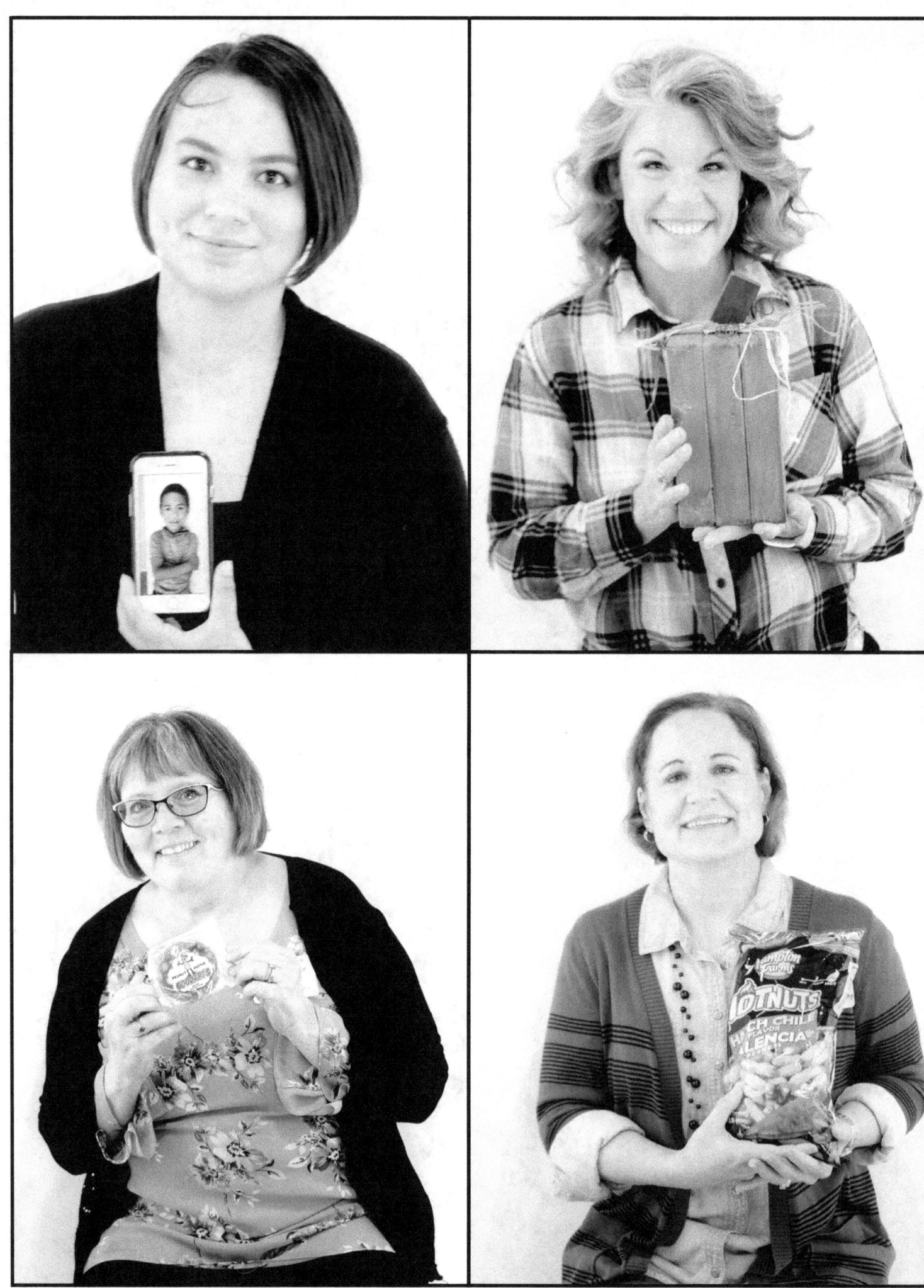

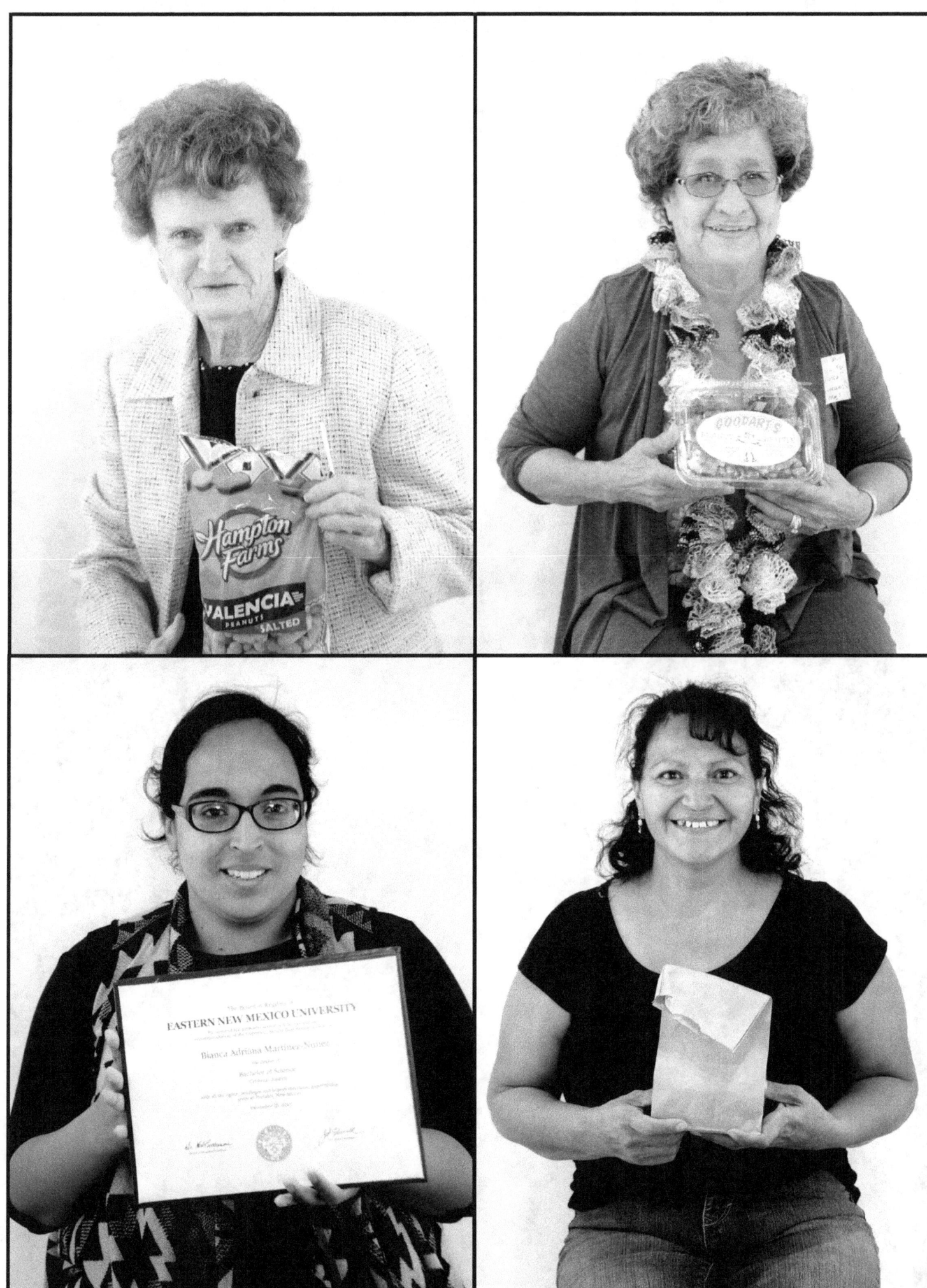

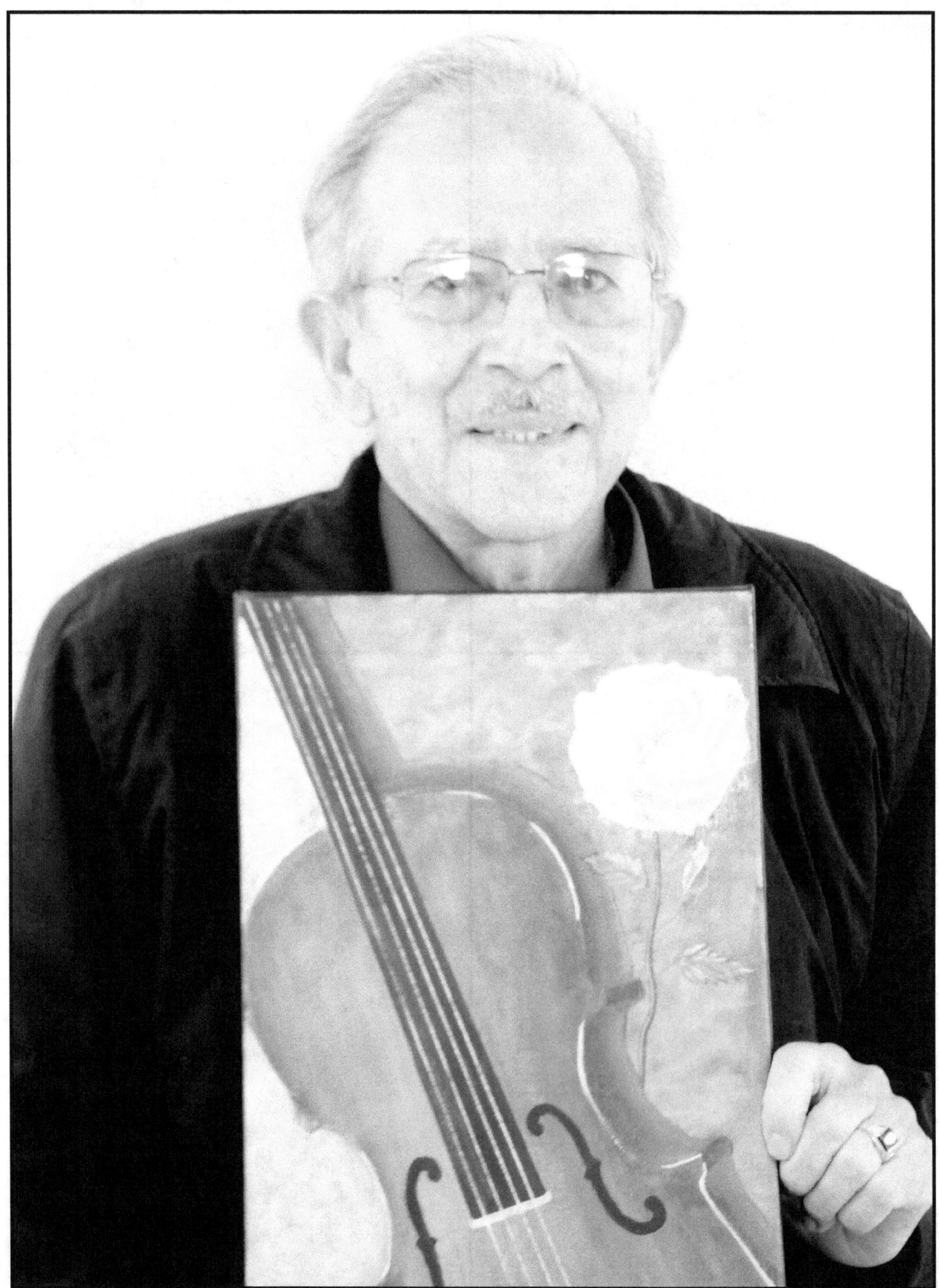

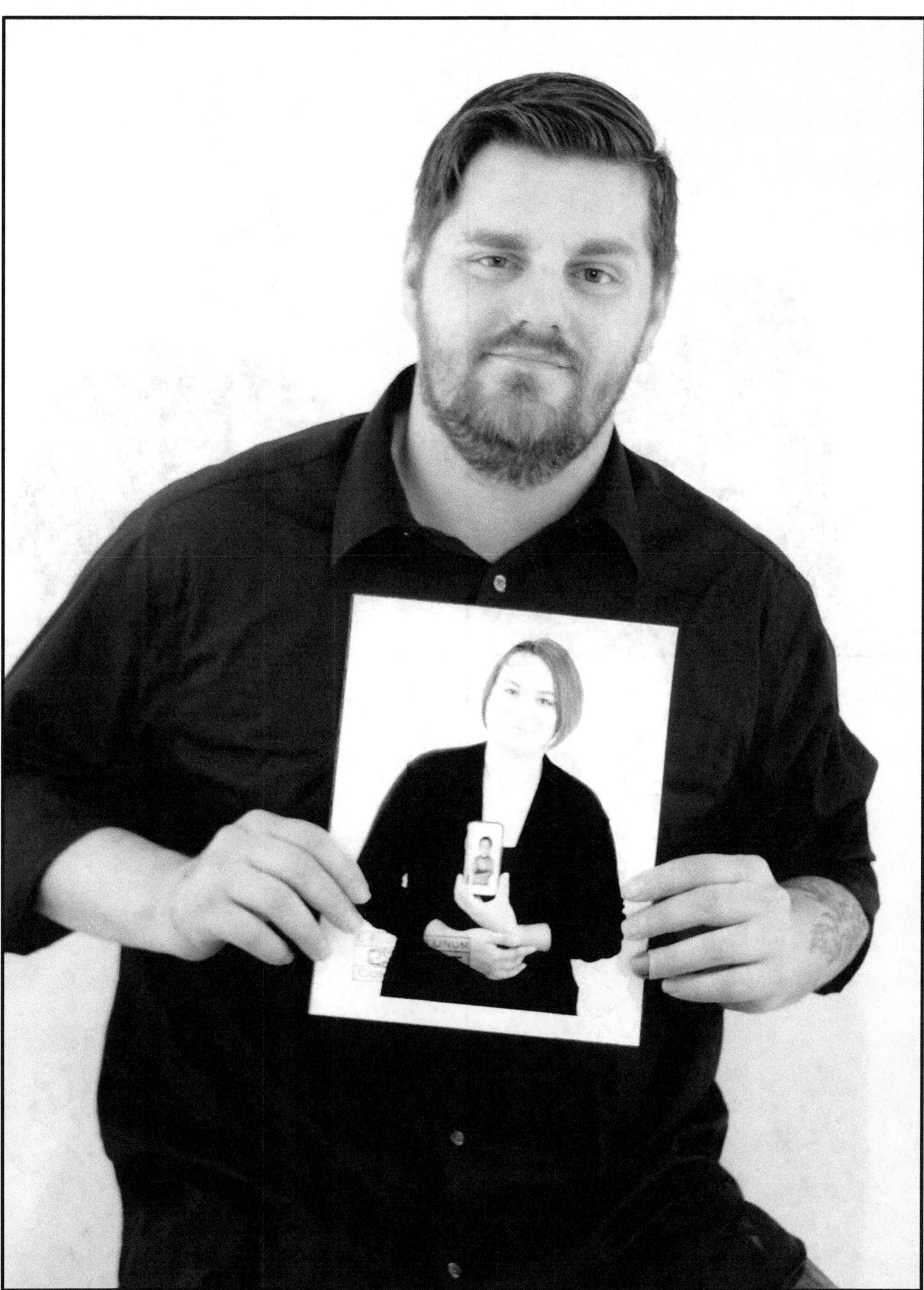

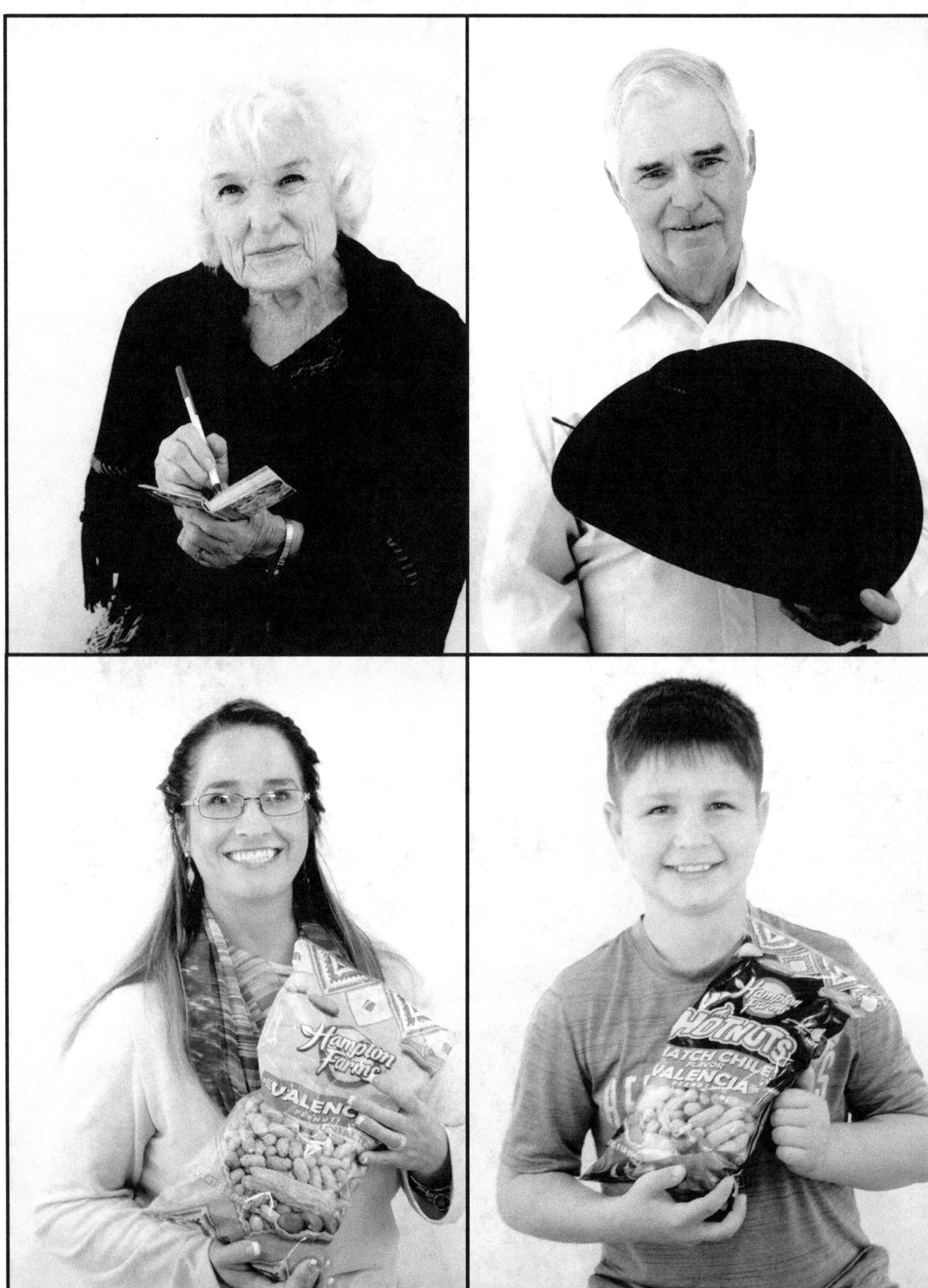

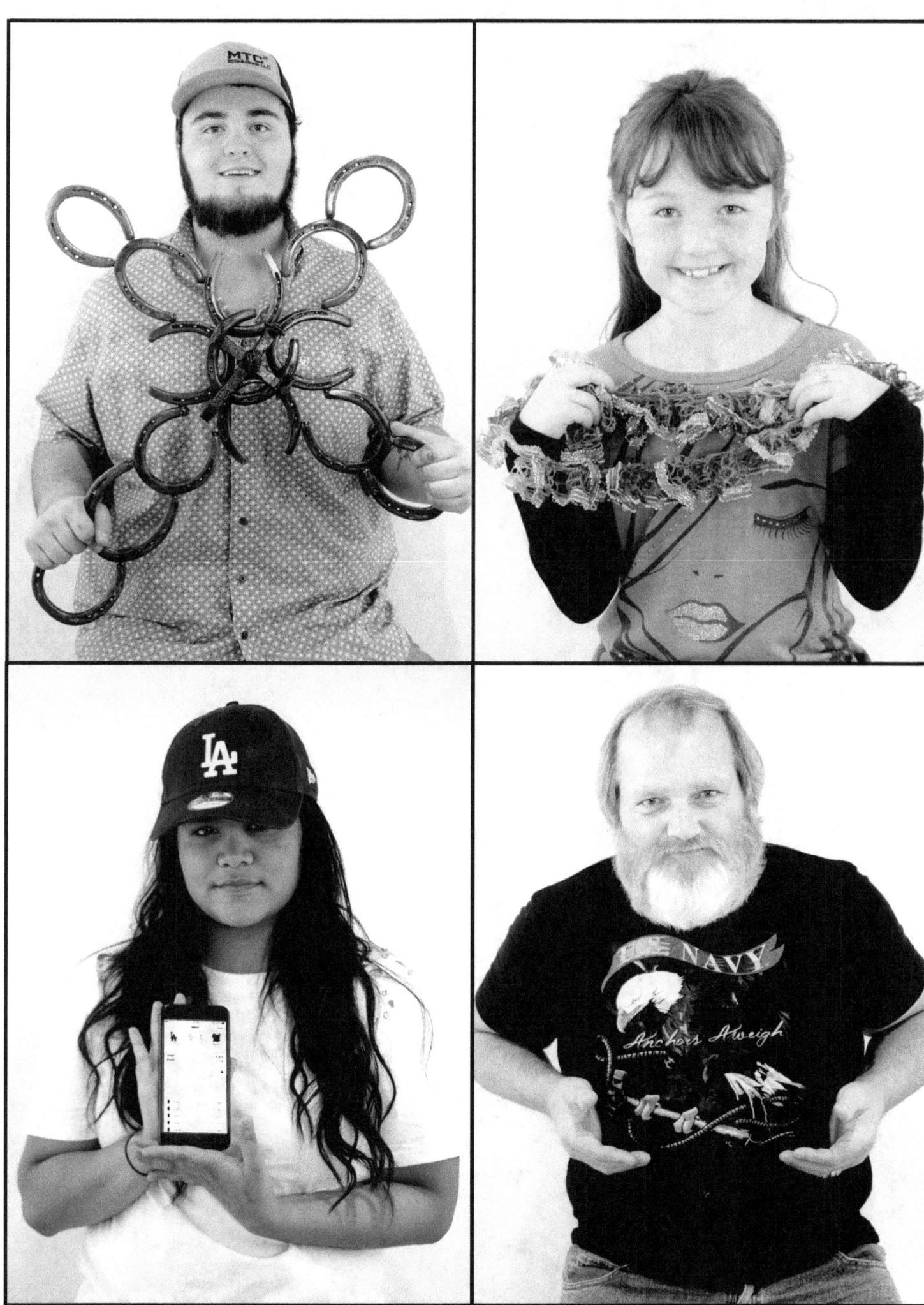

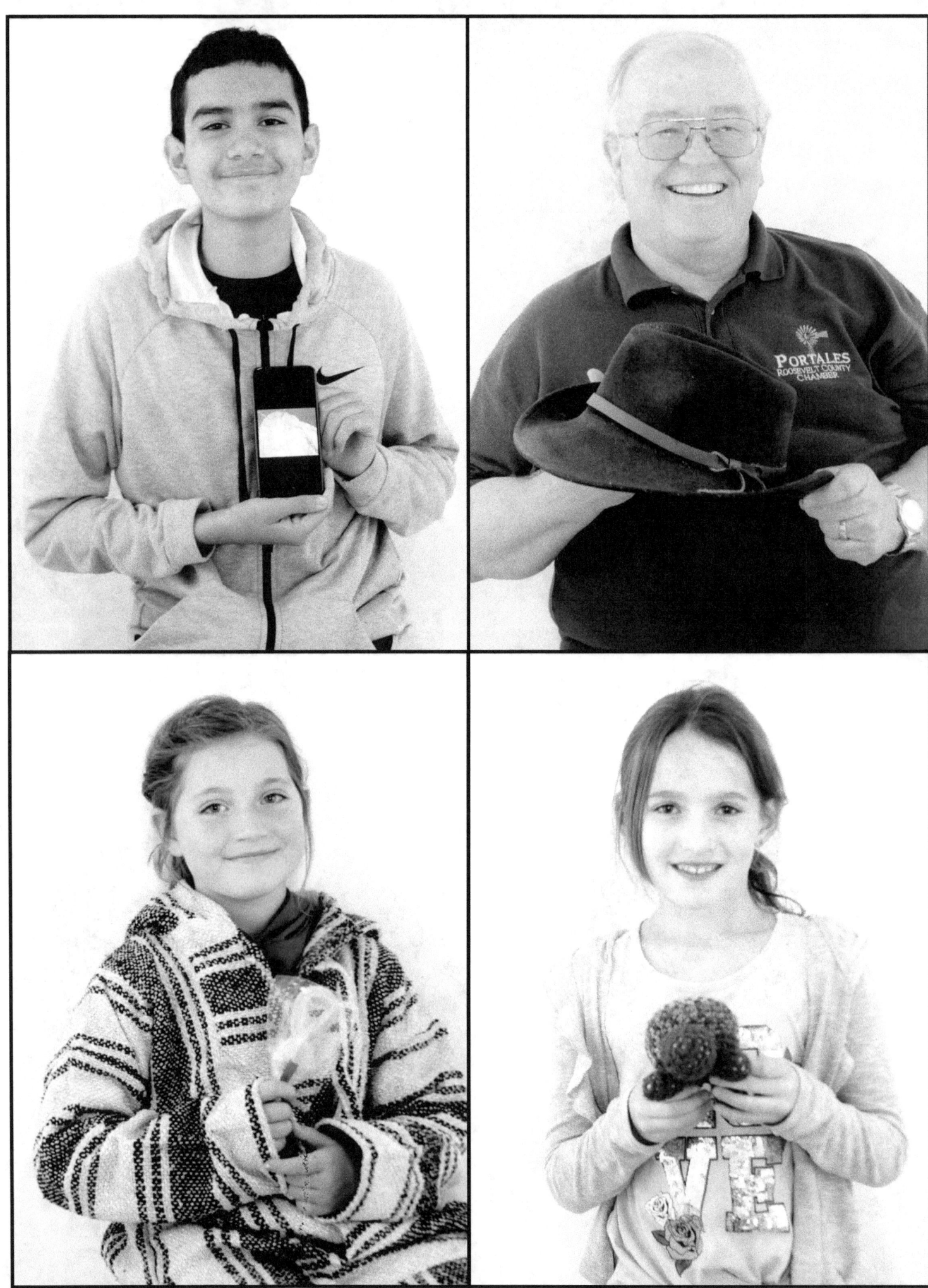

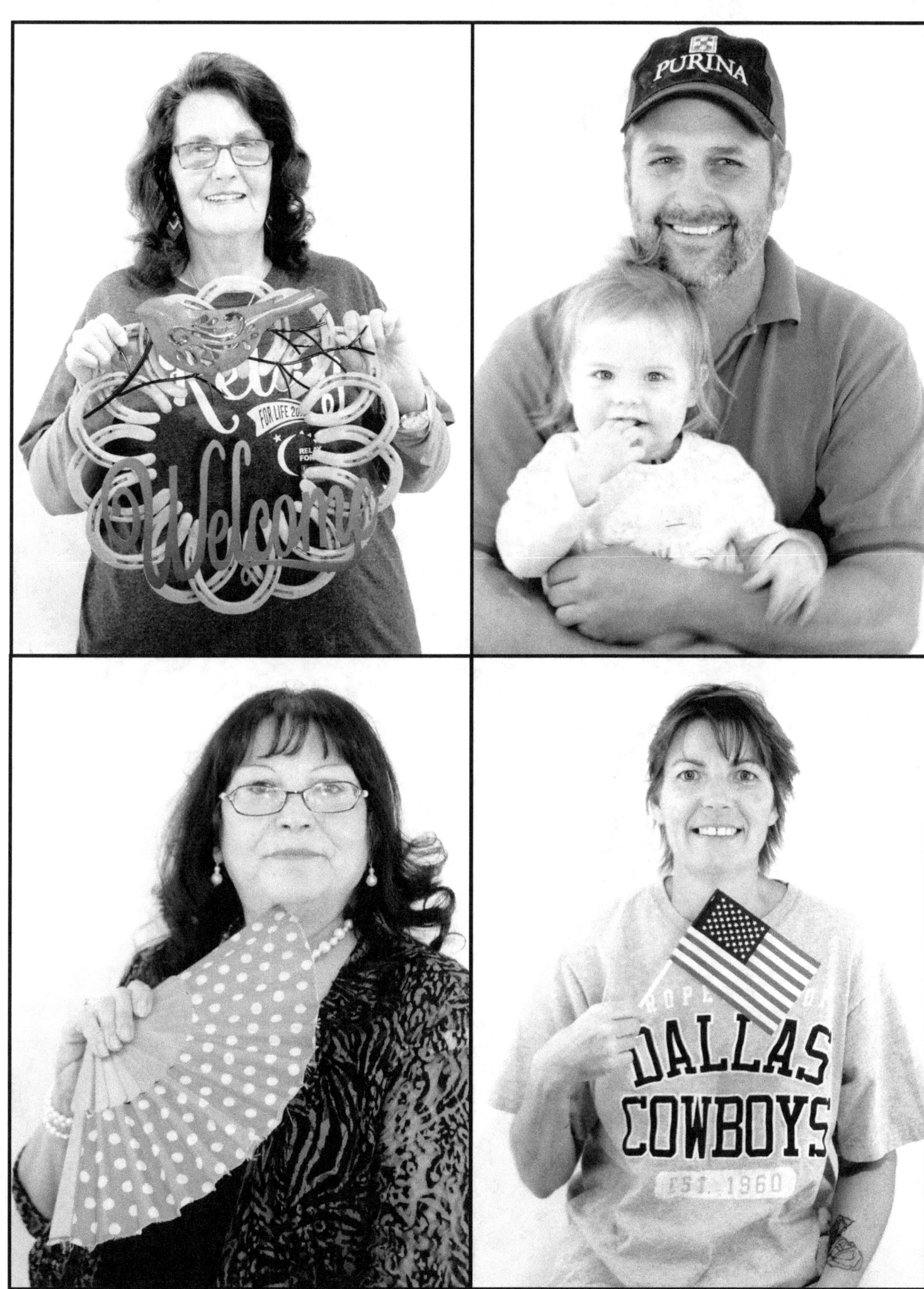

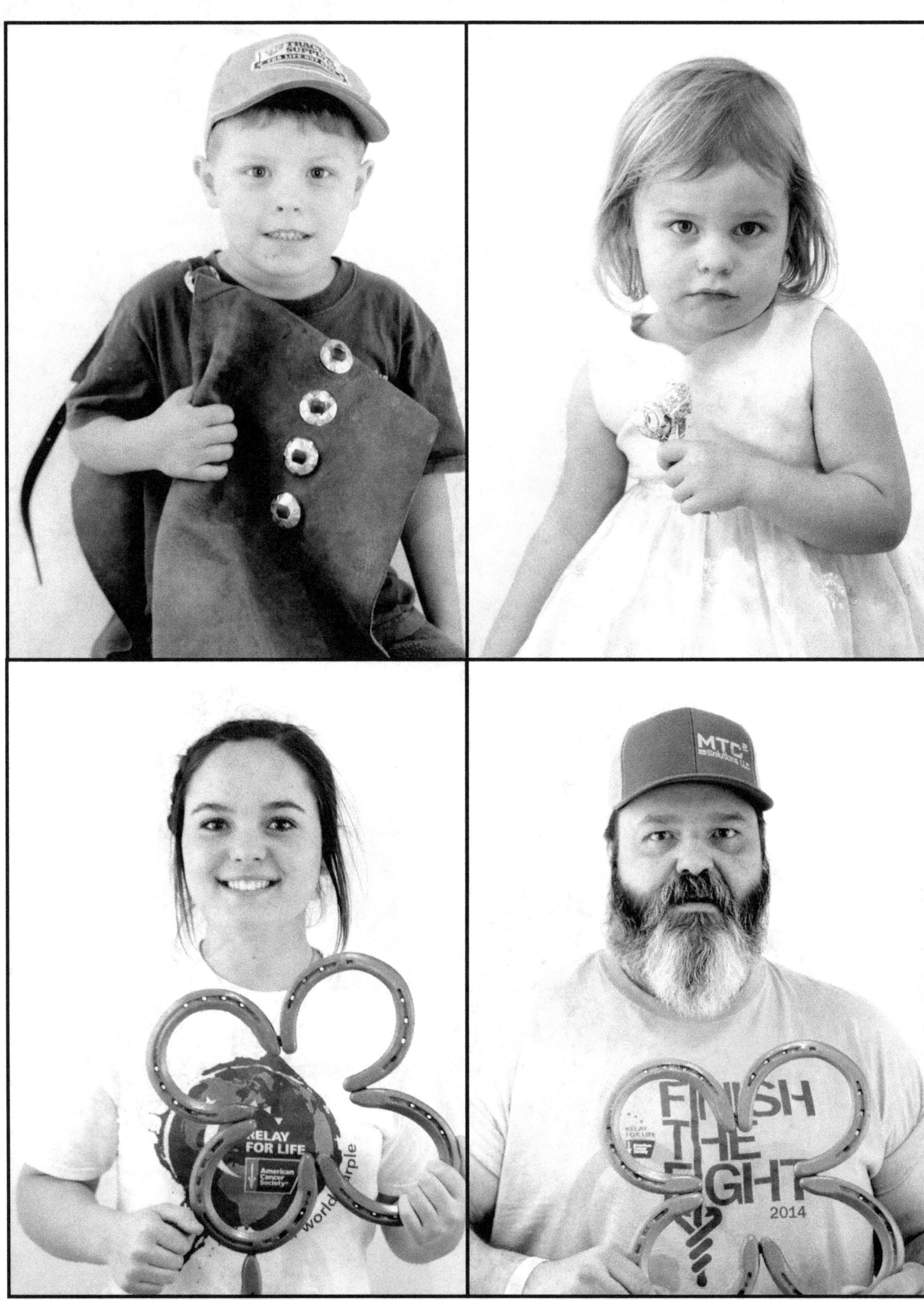

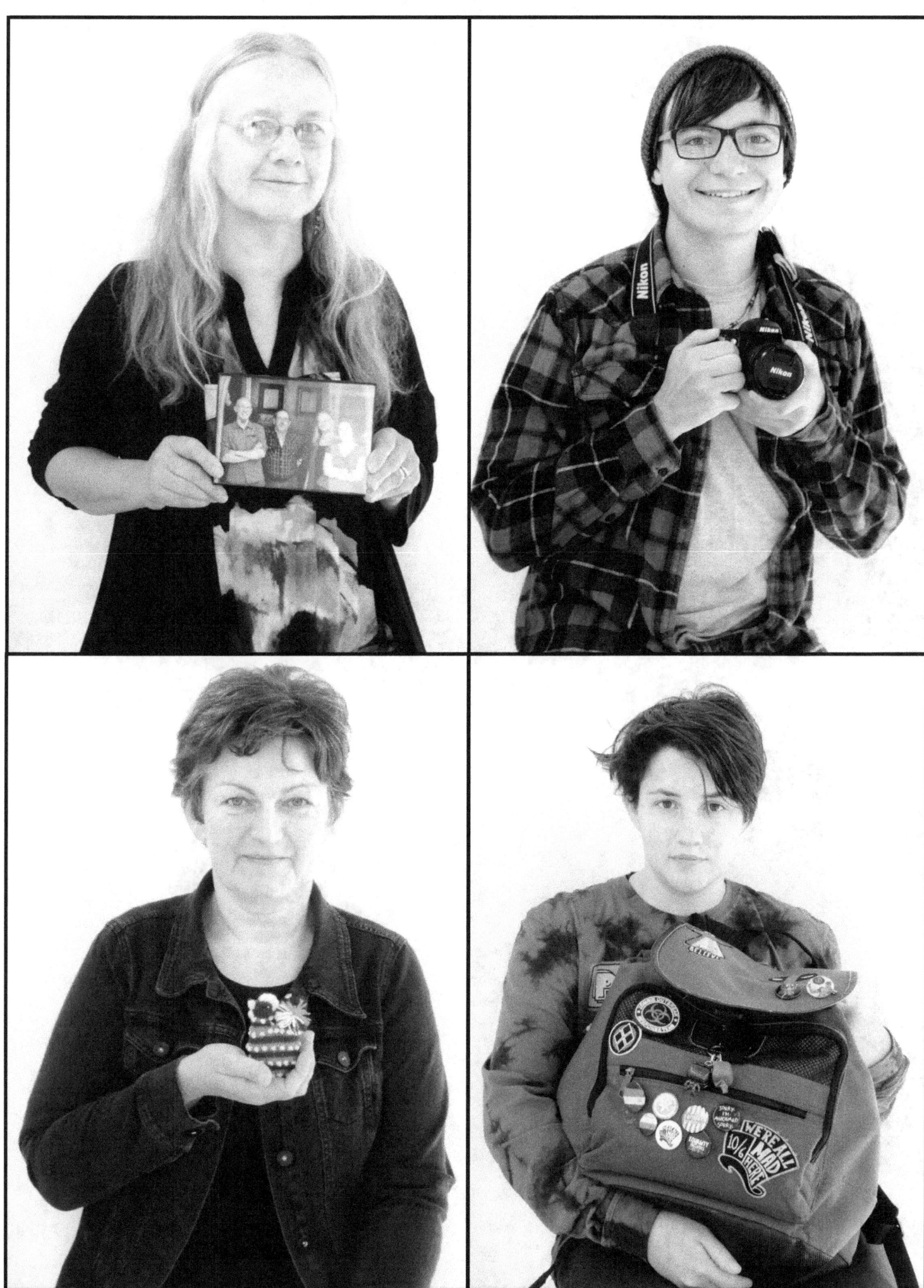

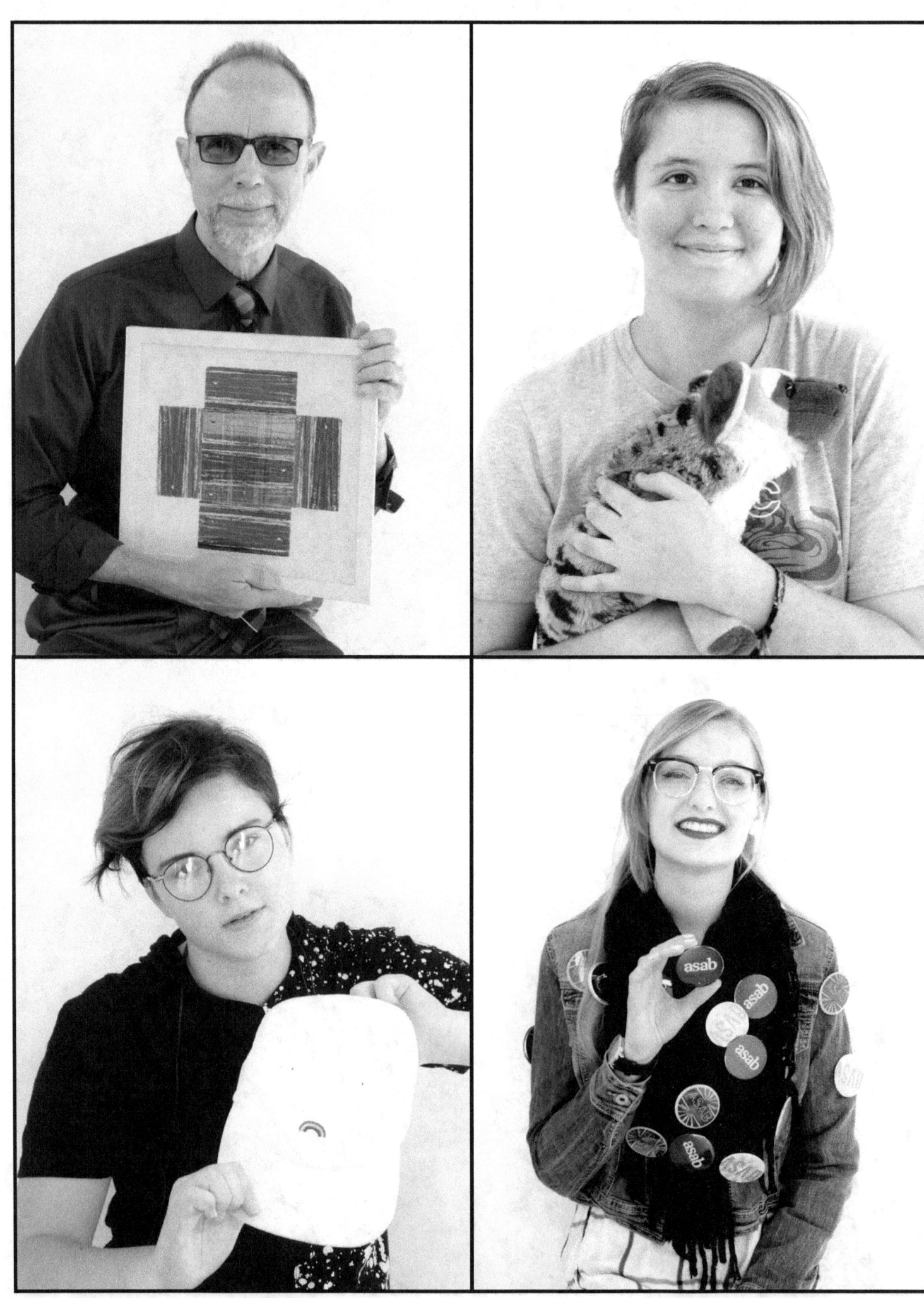

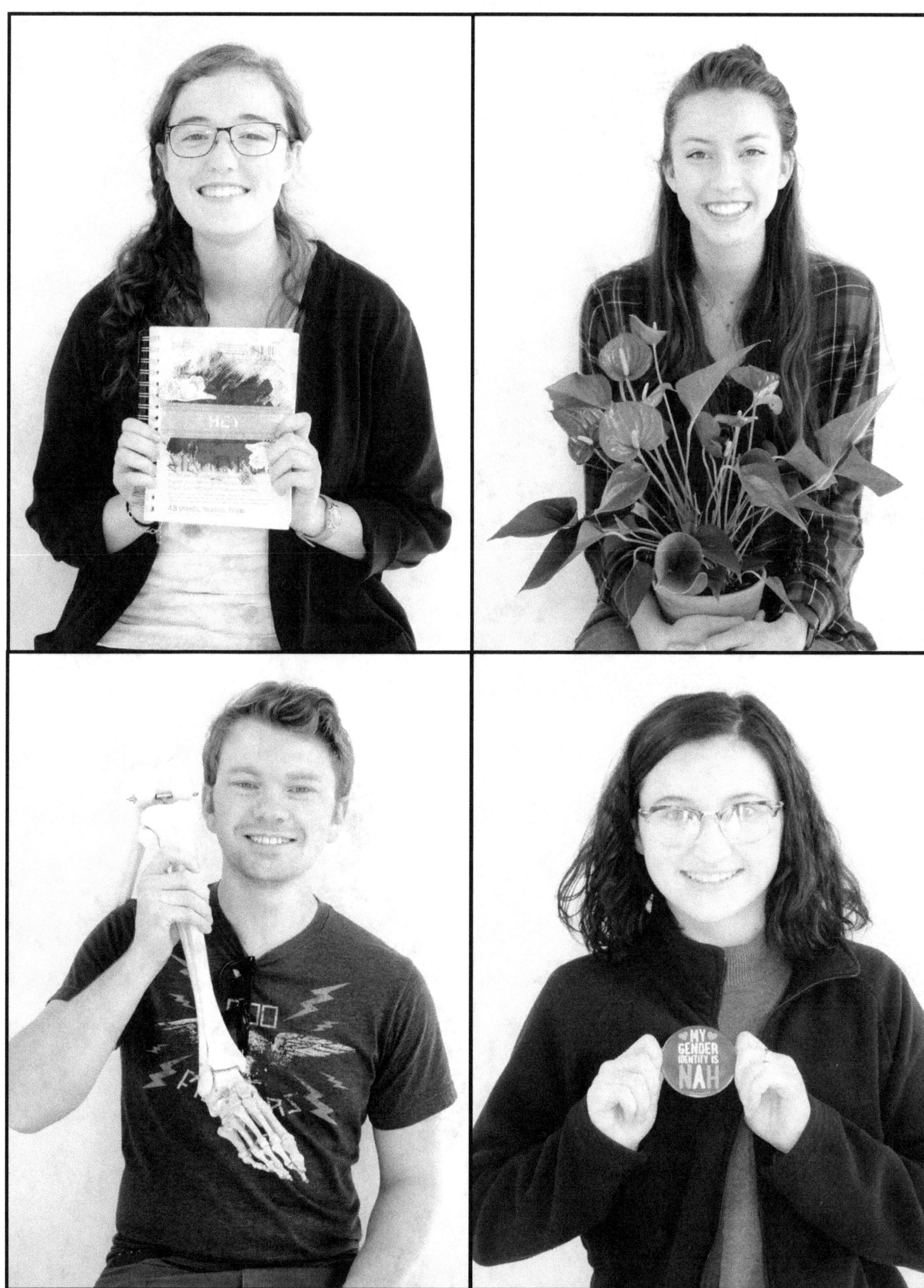

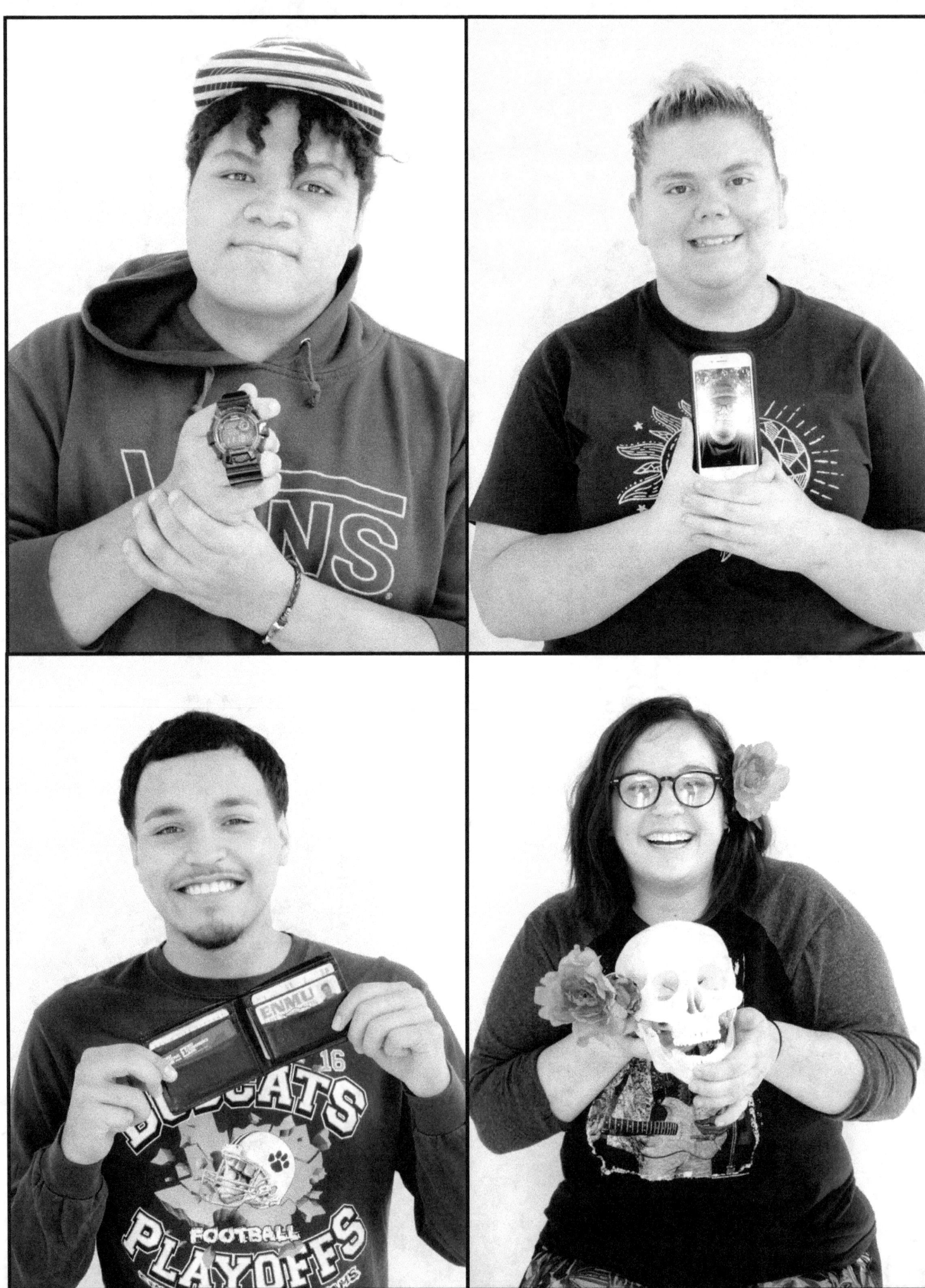

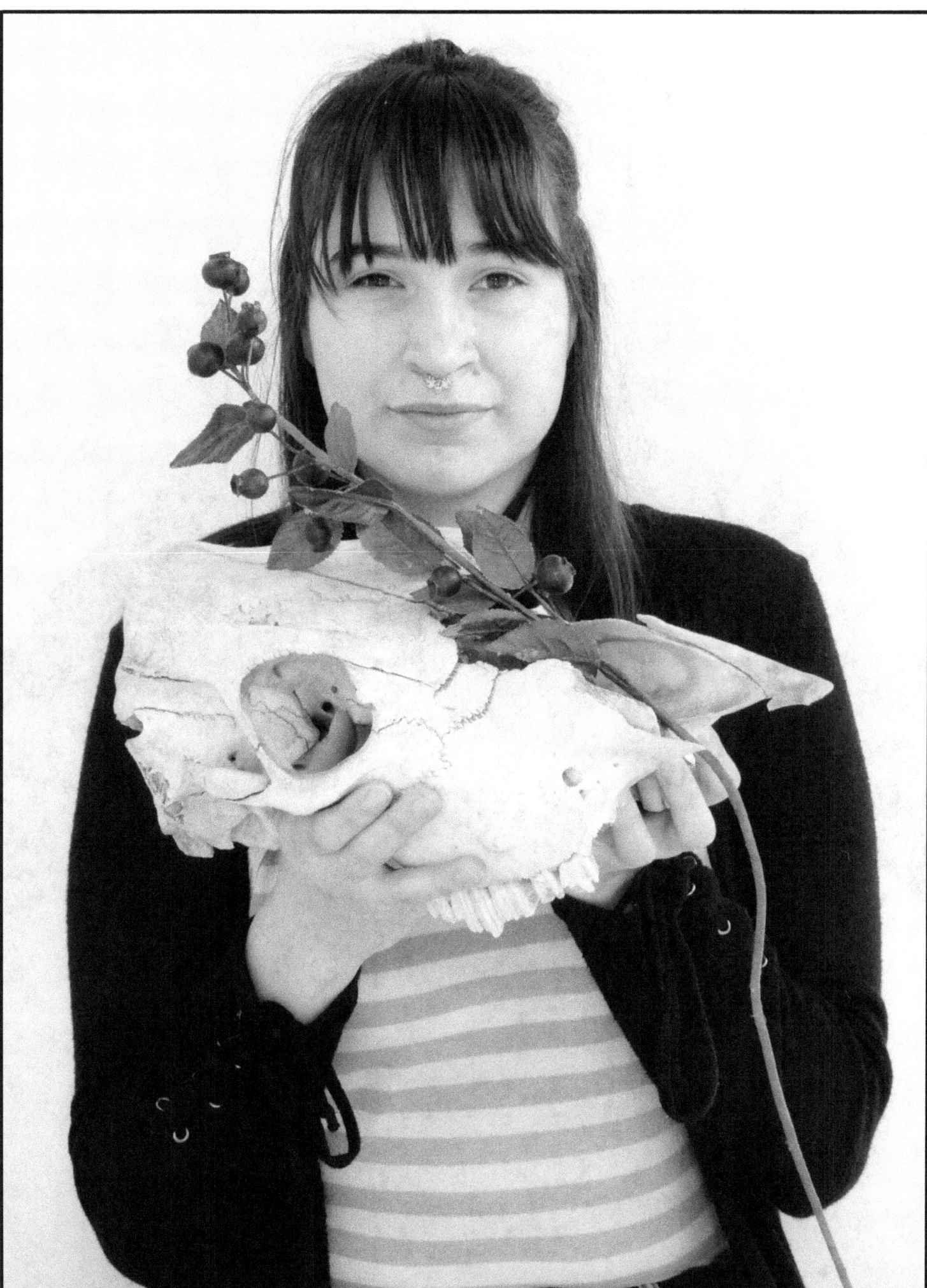

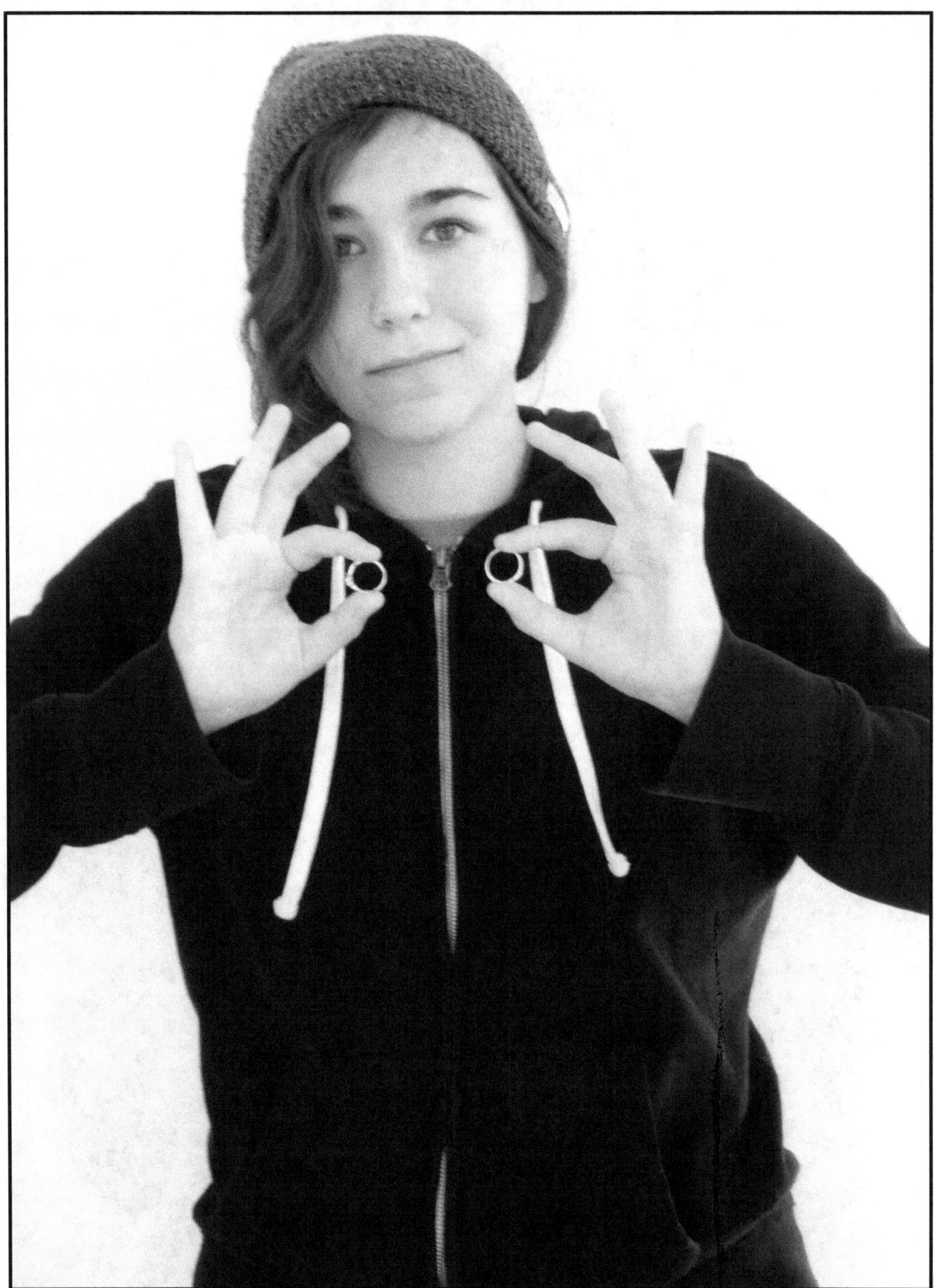

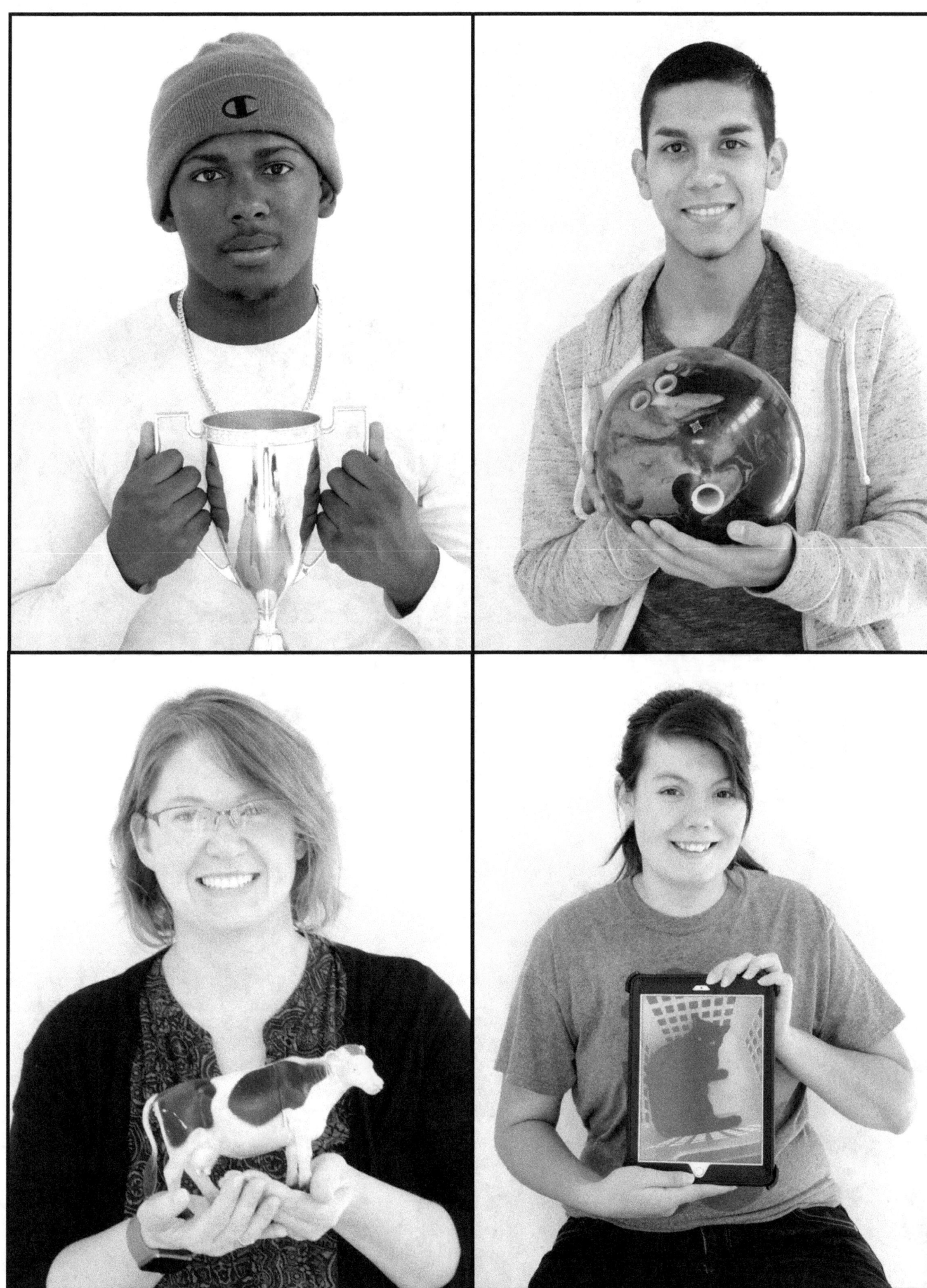

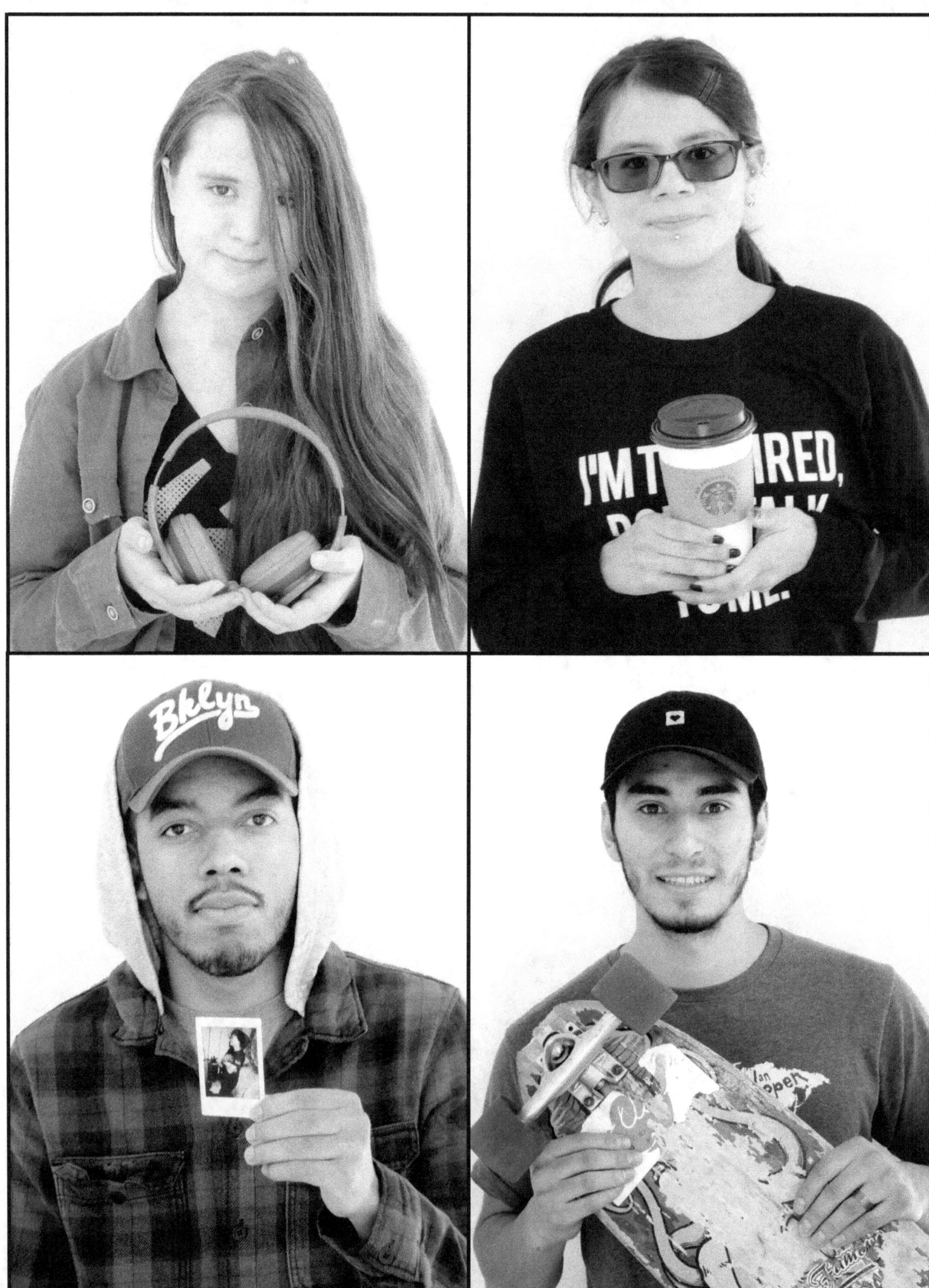

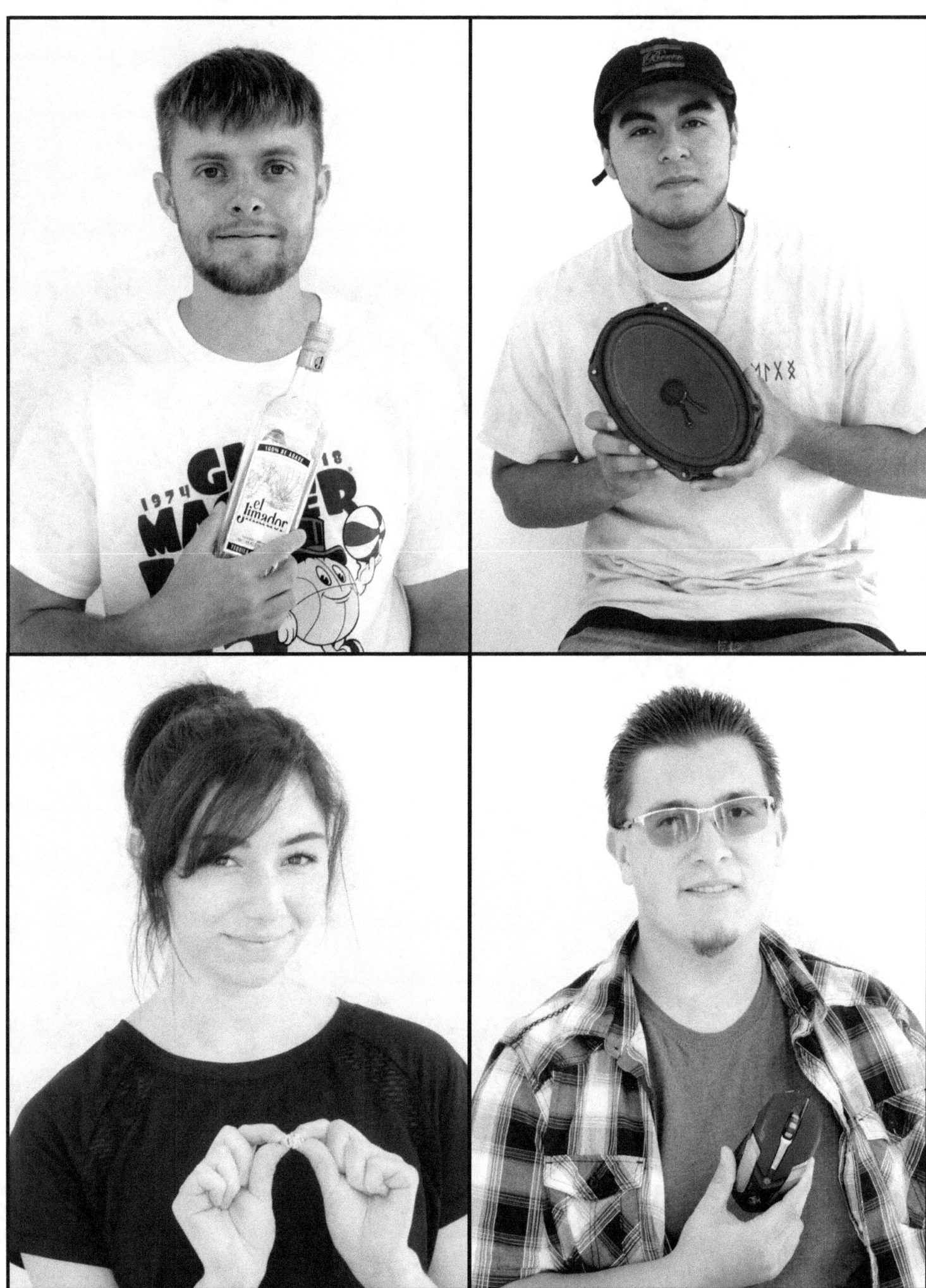

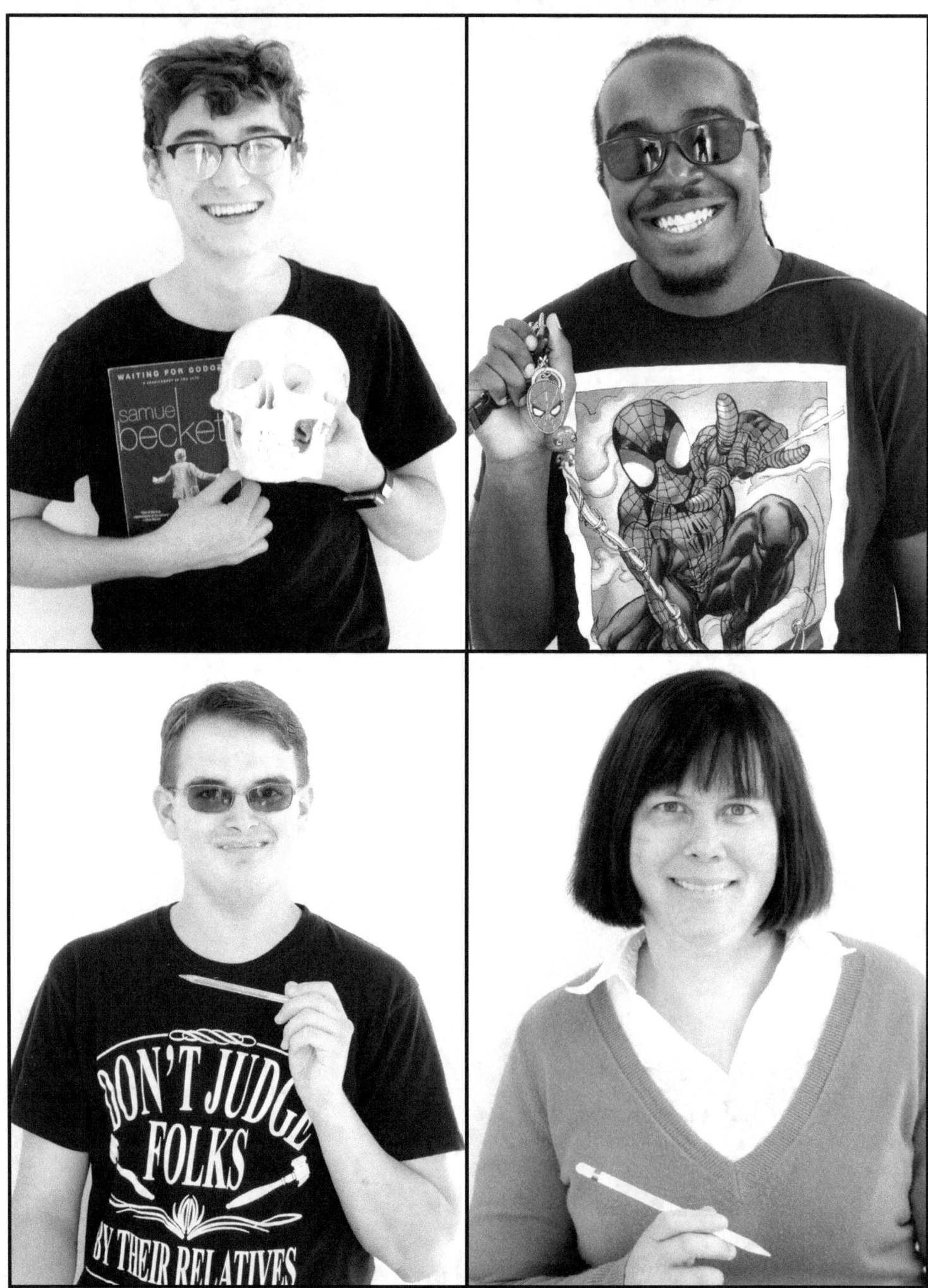

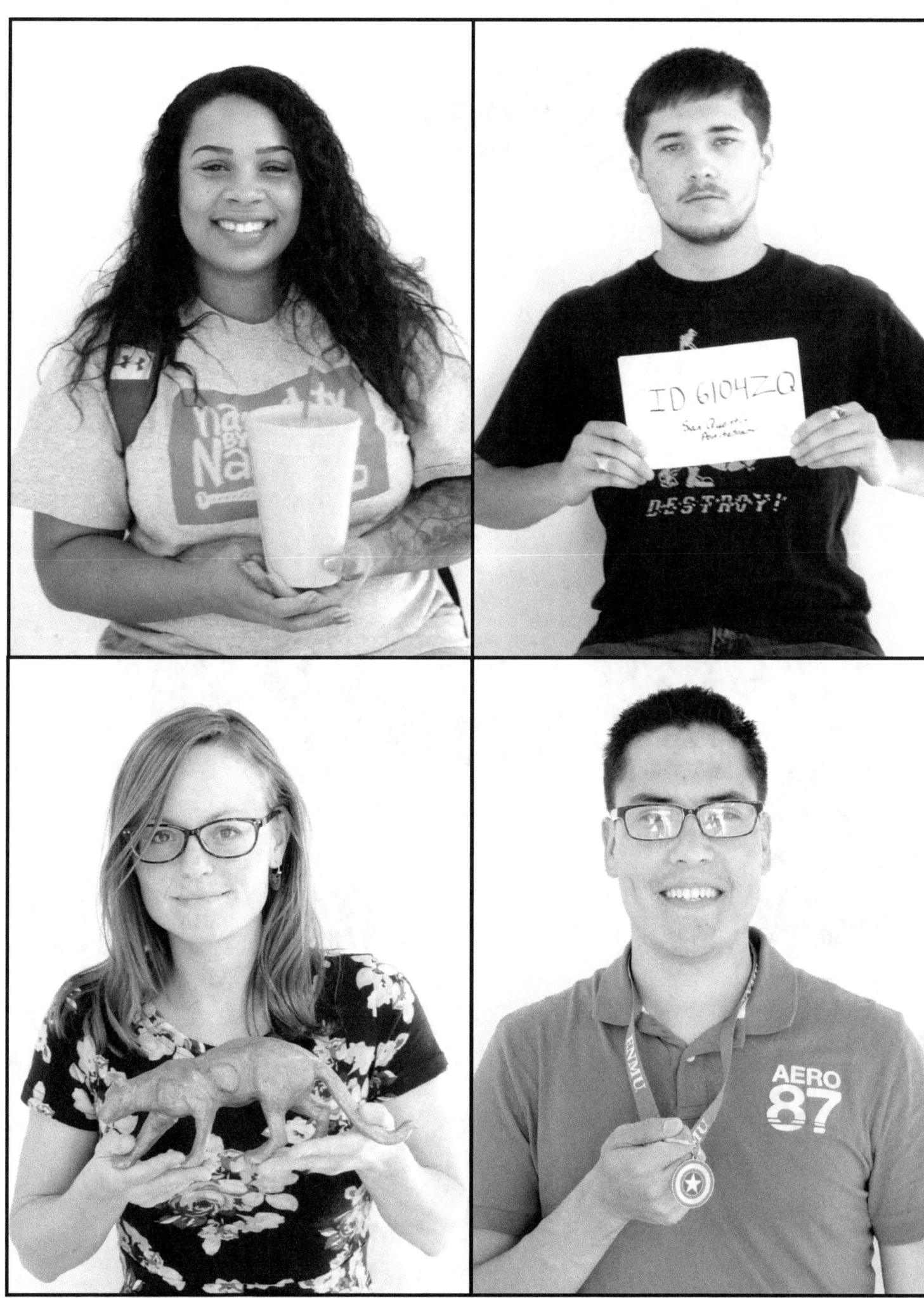

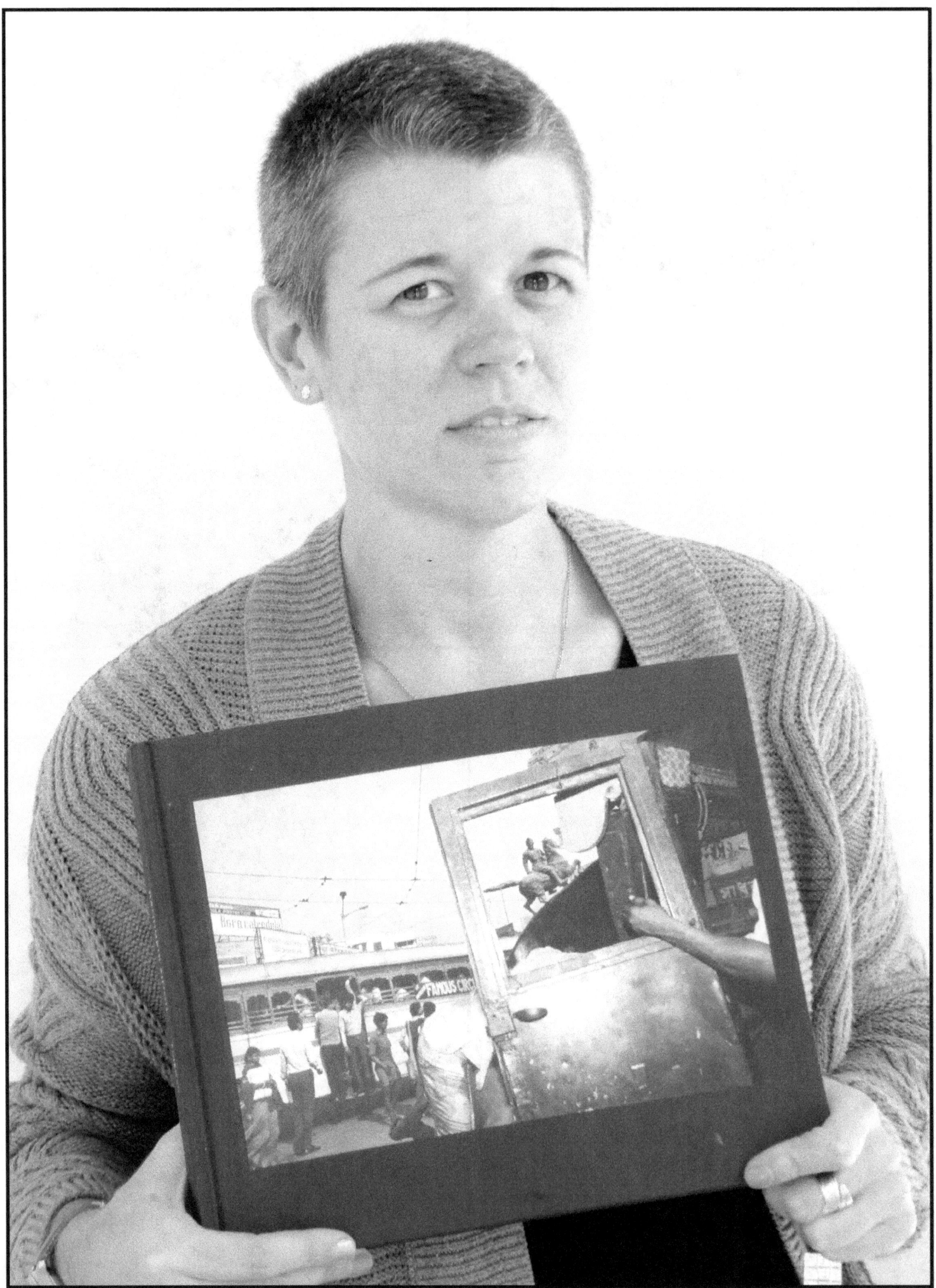

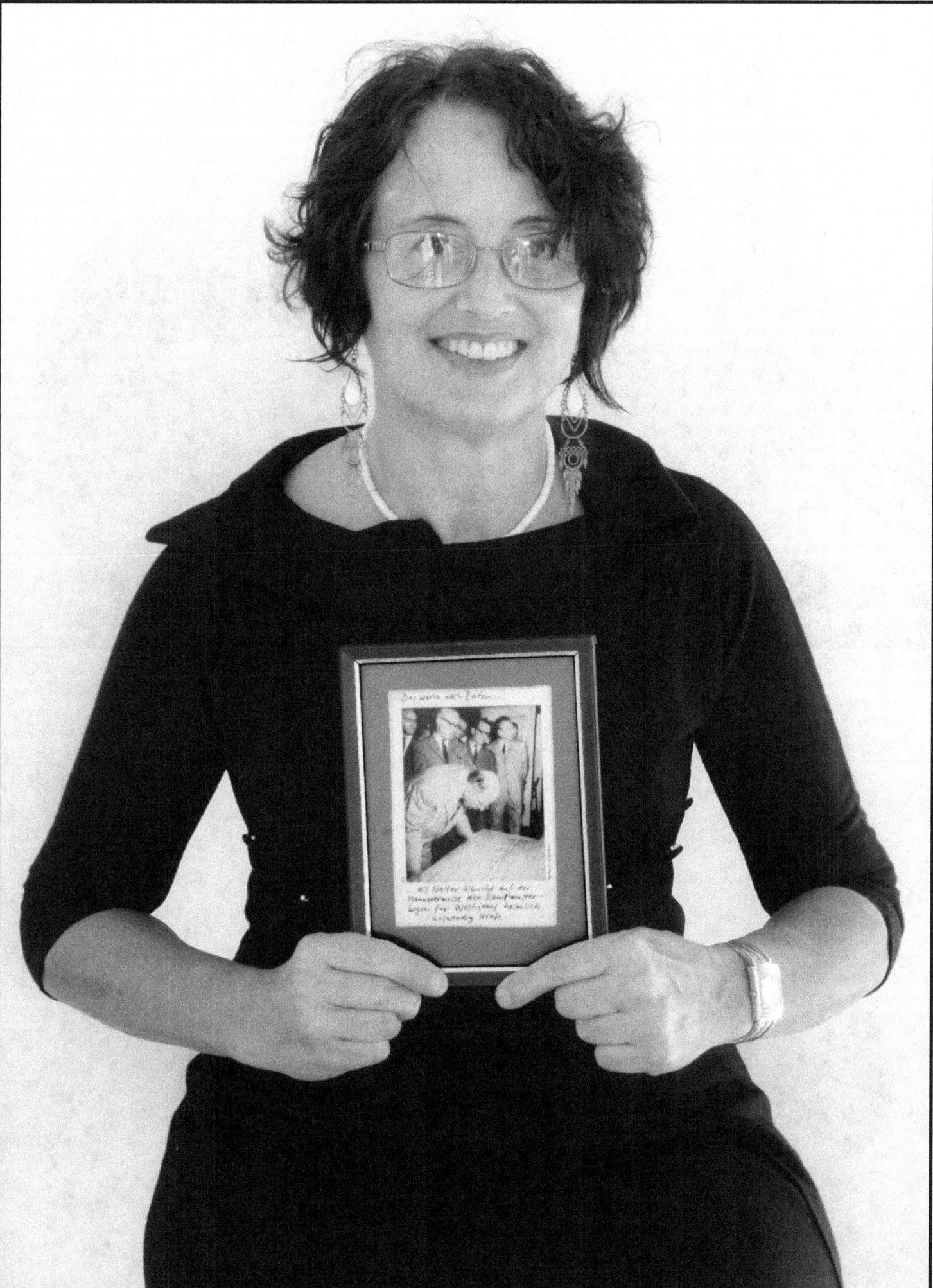

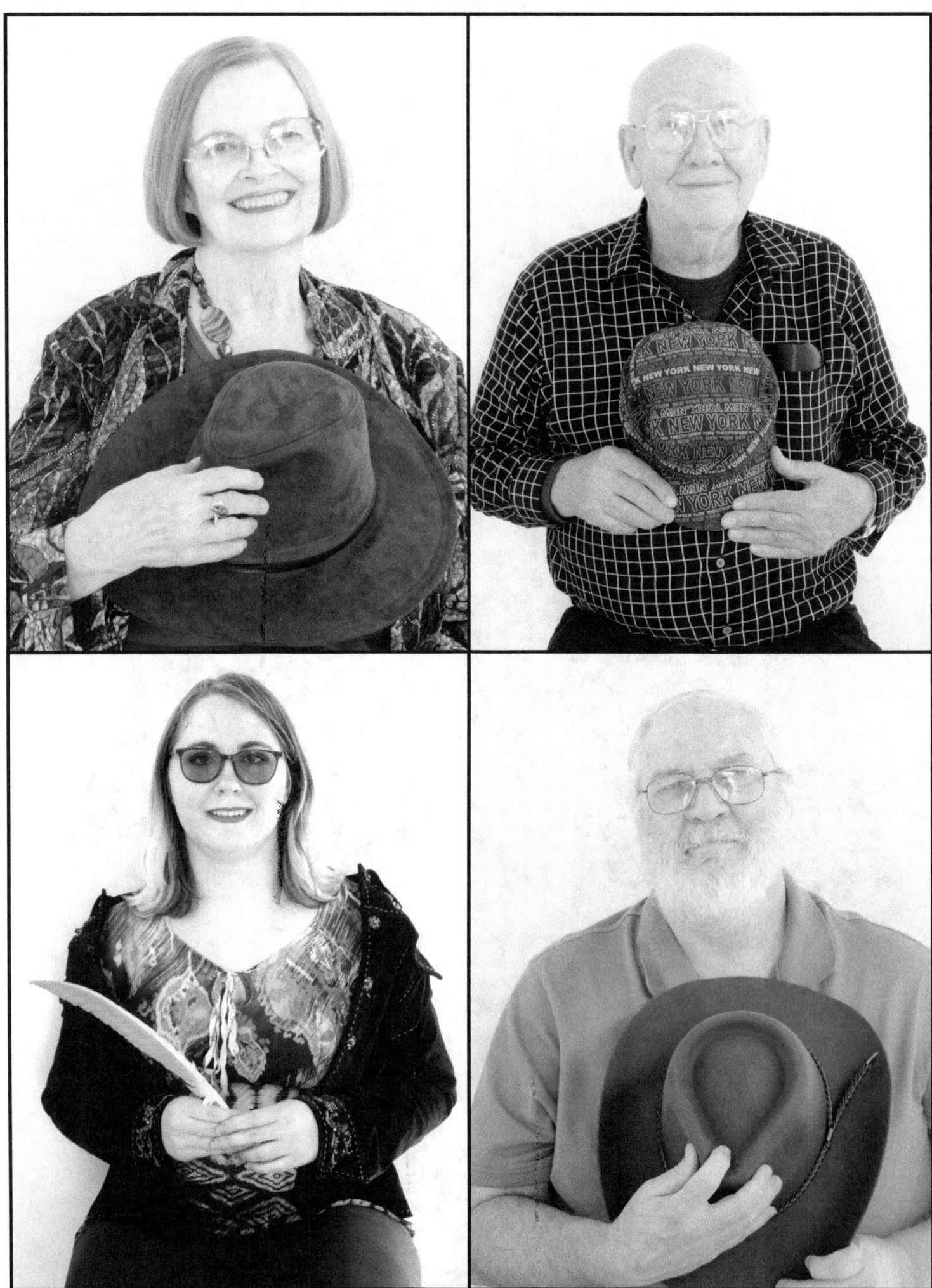

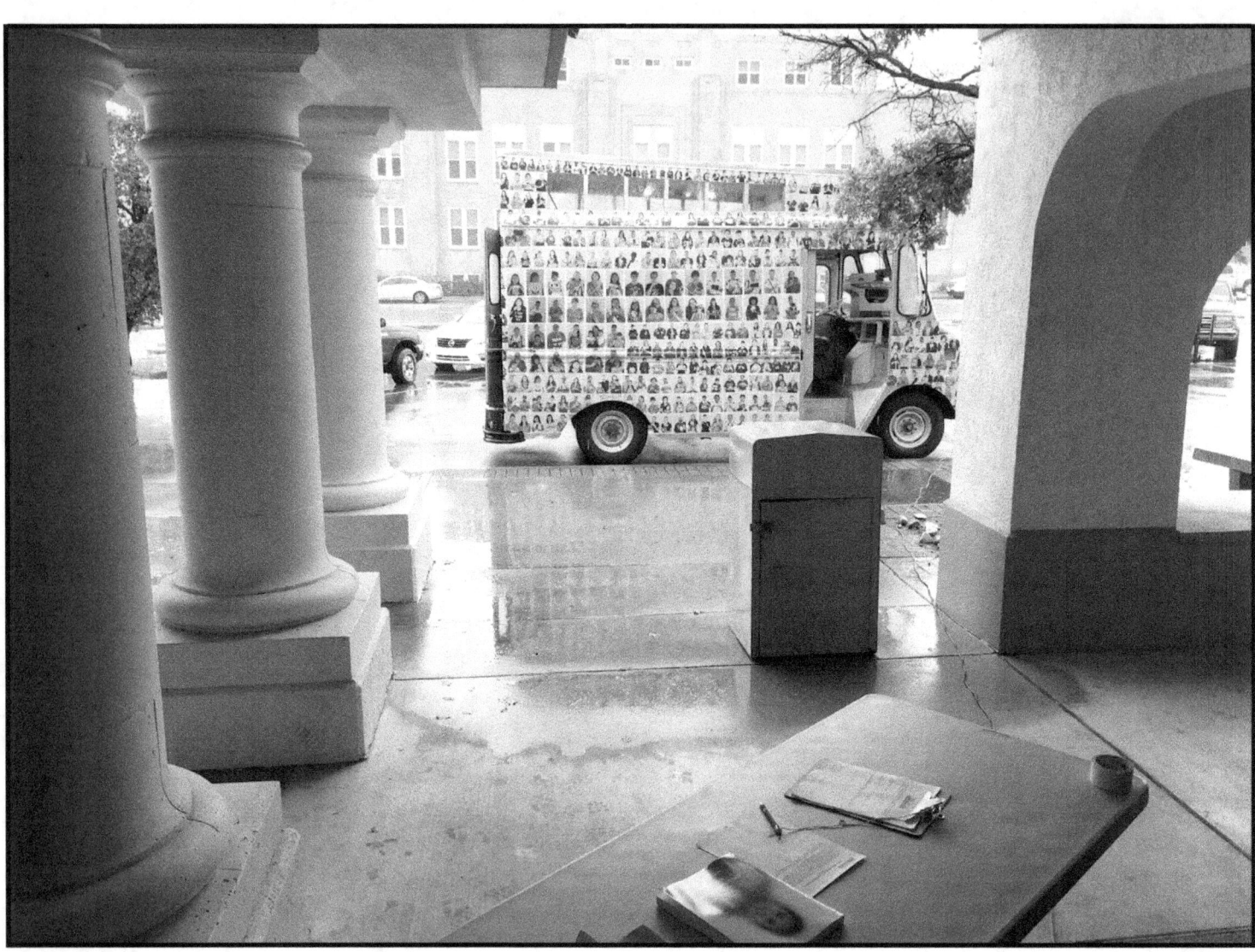

Clovis
October 17, 2019

Red Arrow
Eula Mae Edwards Museum
Clovis Carver Public Library

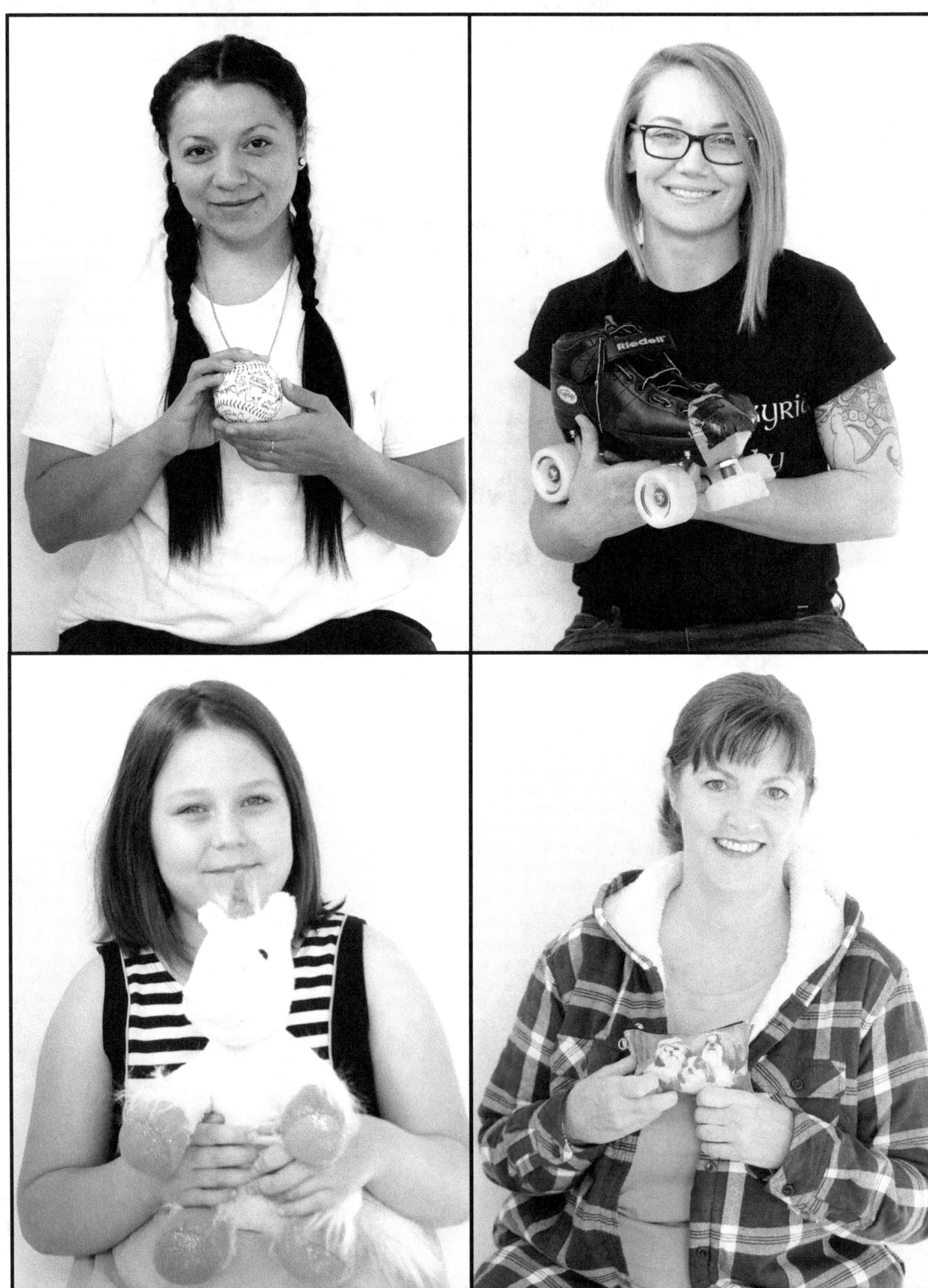

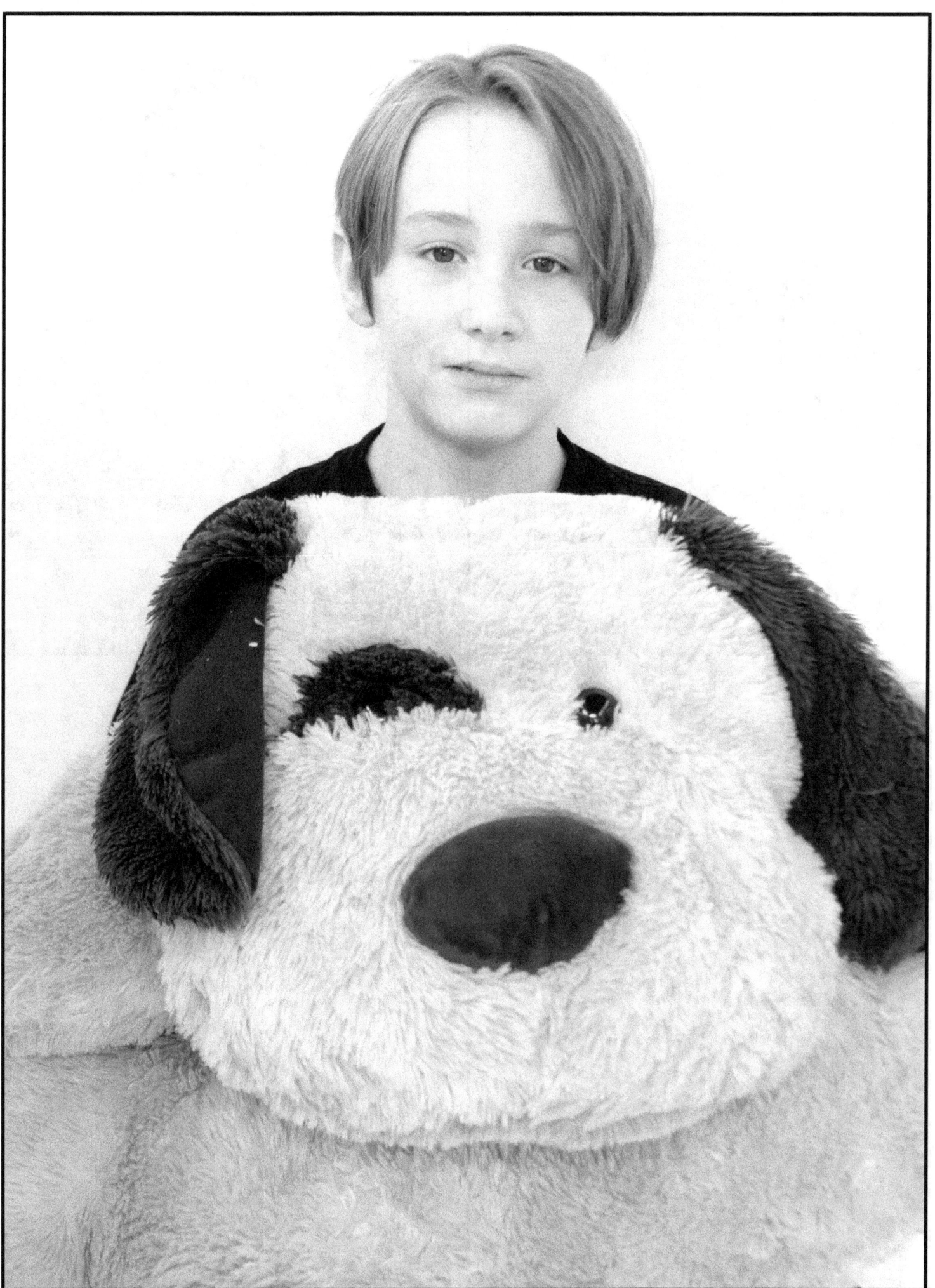

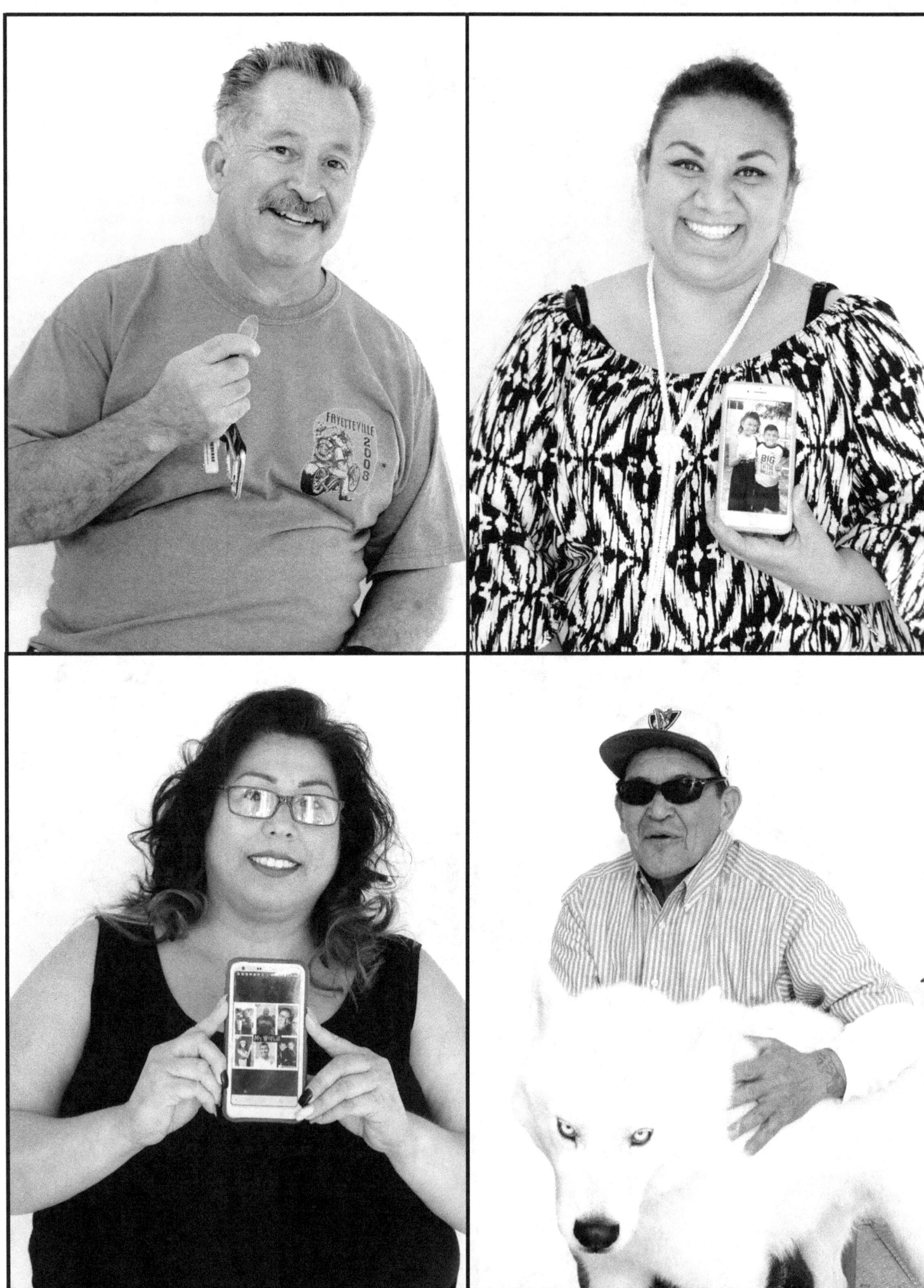

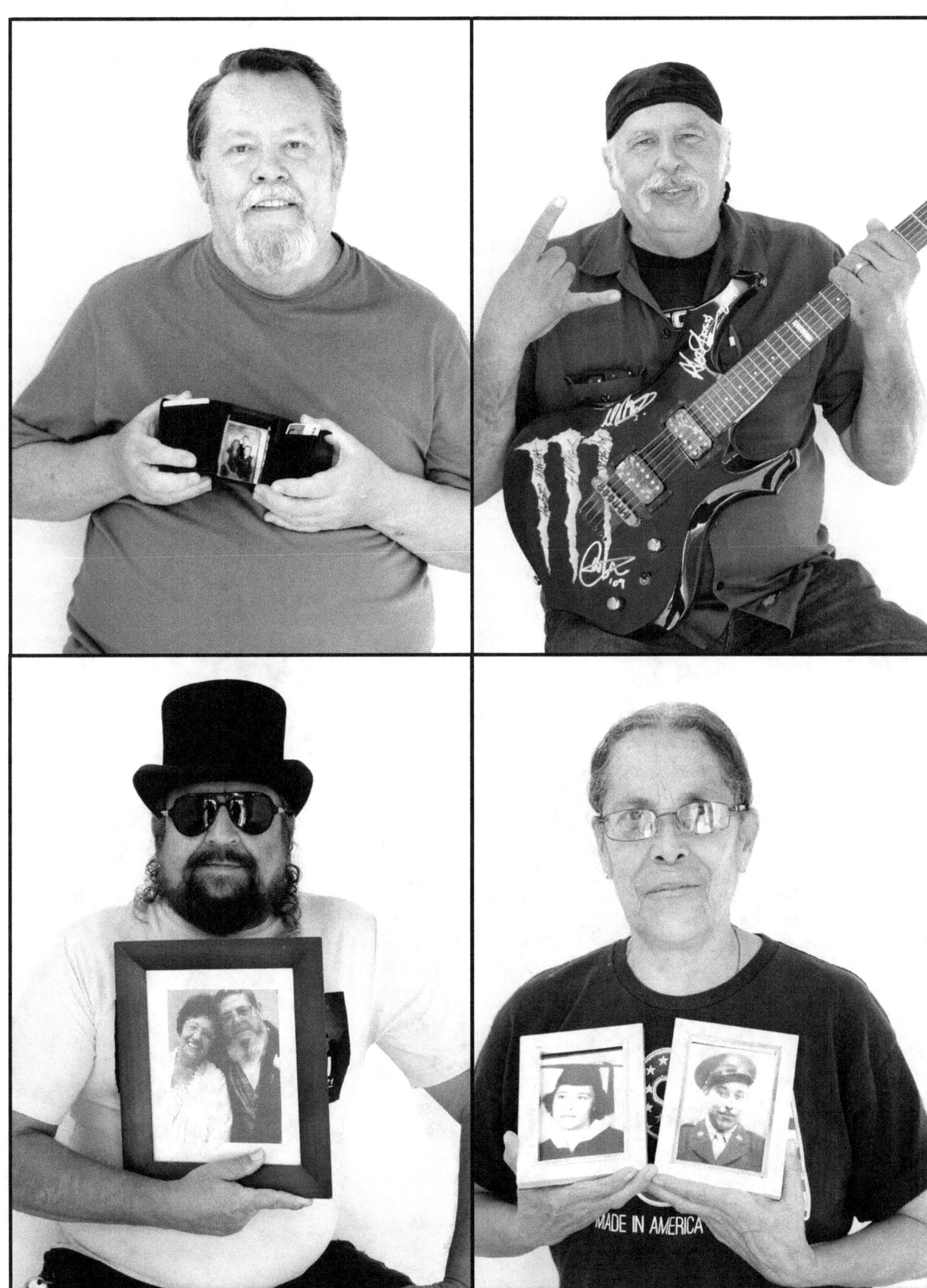

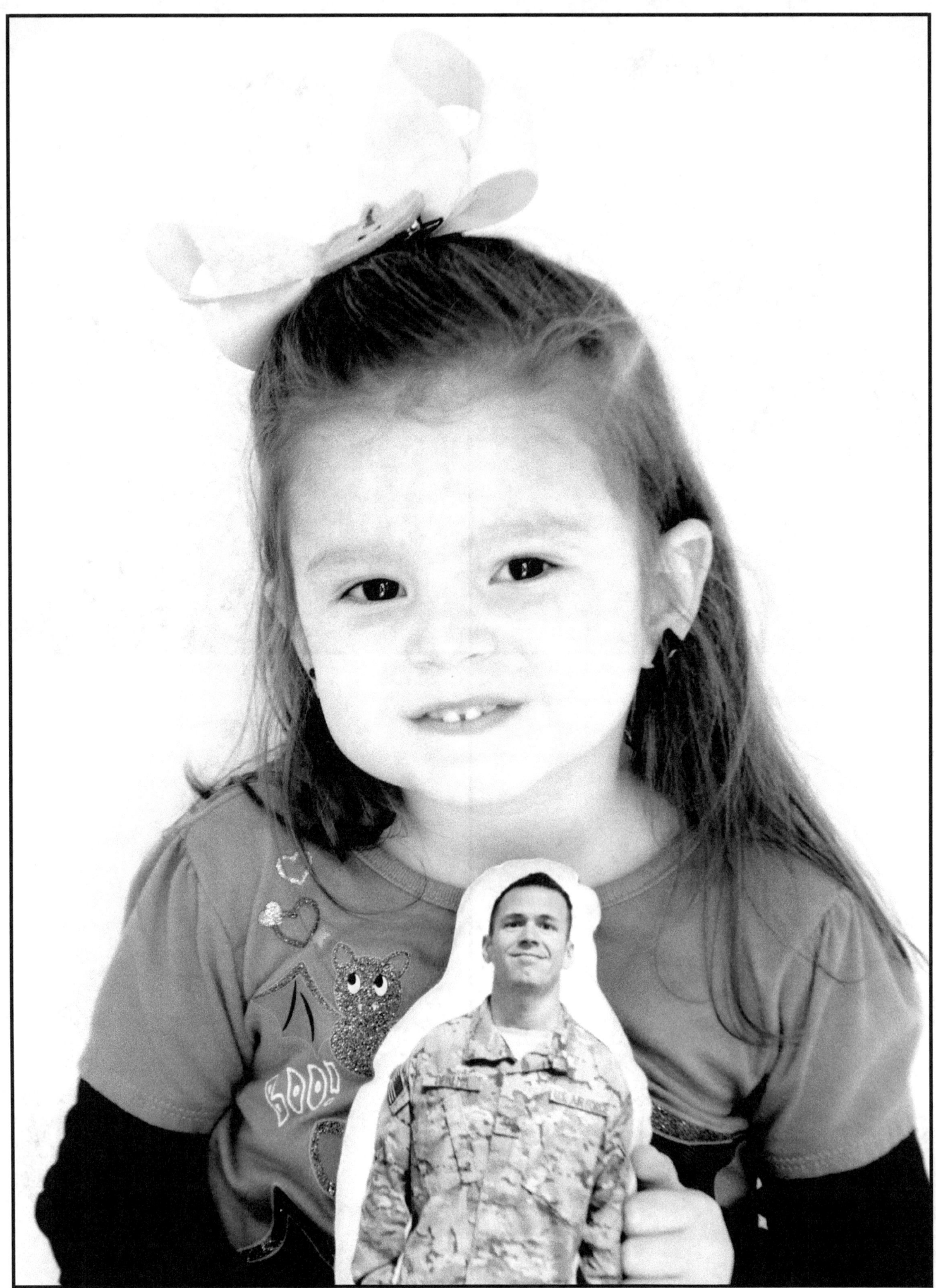

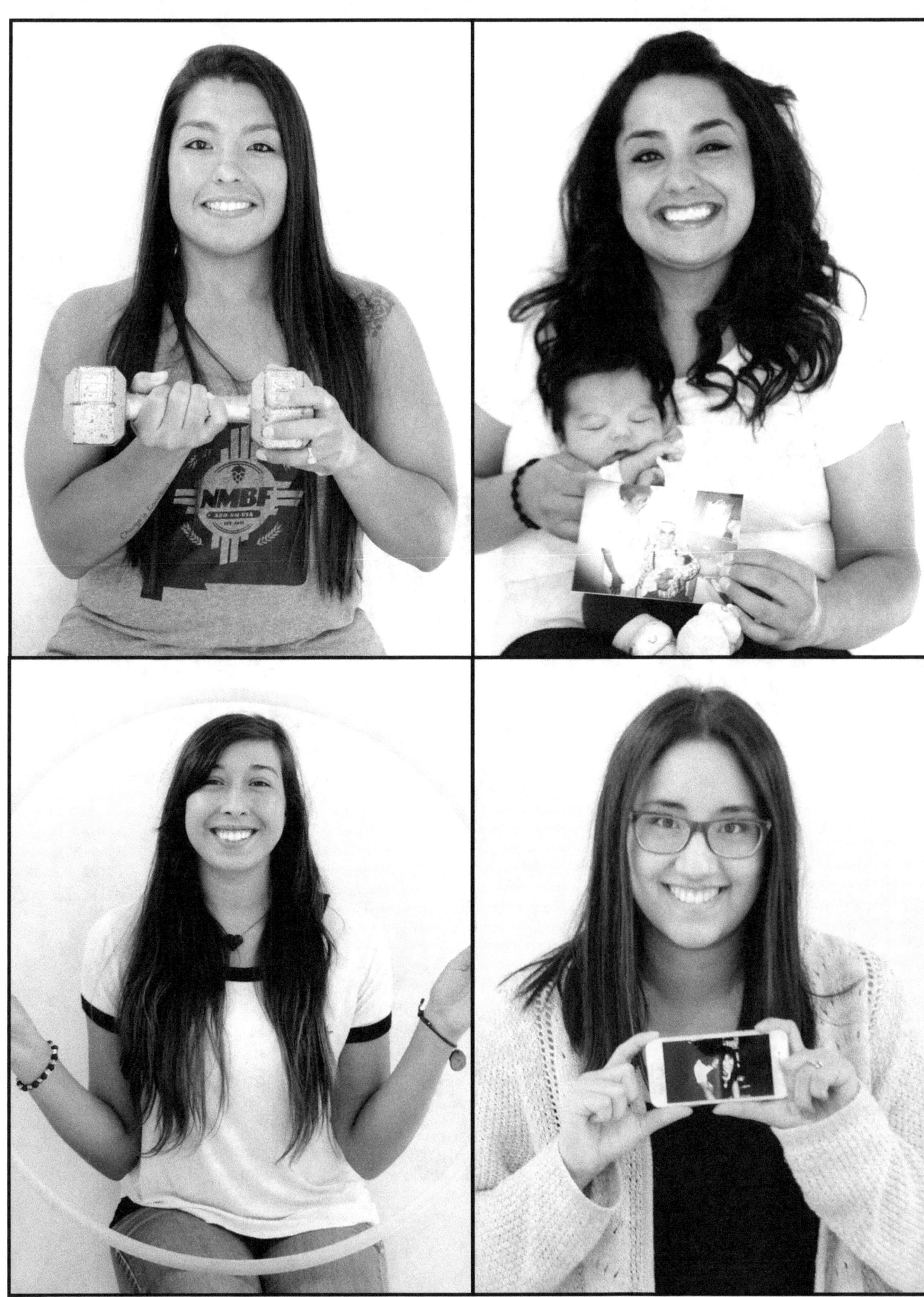

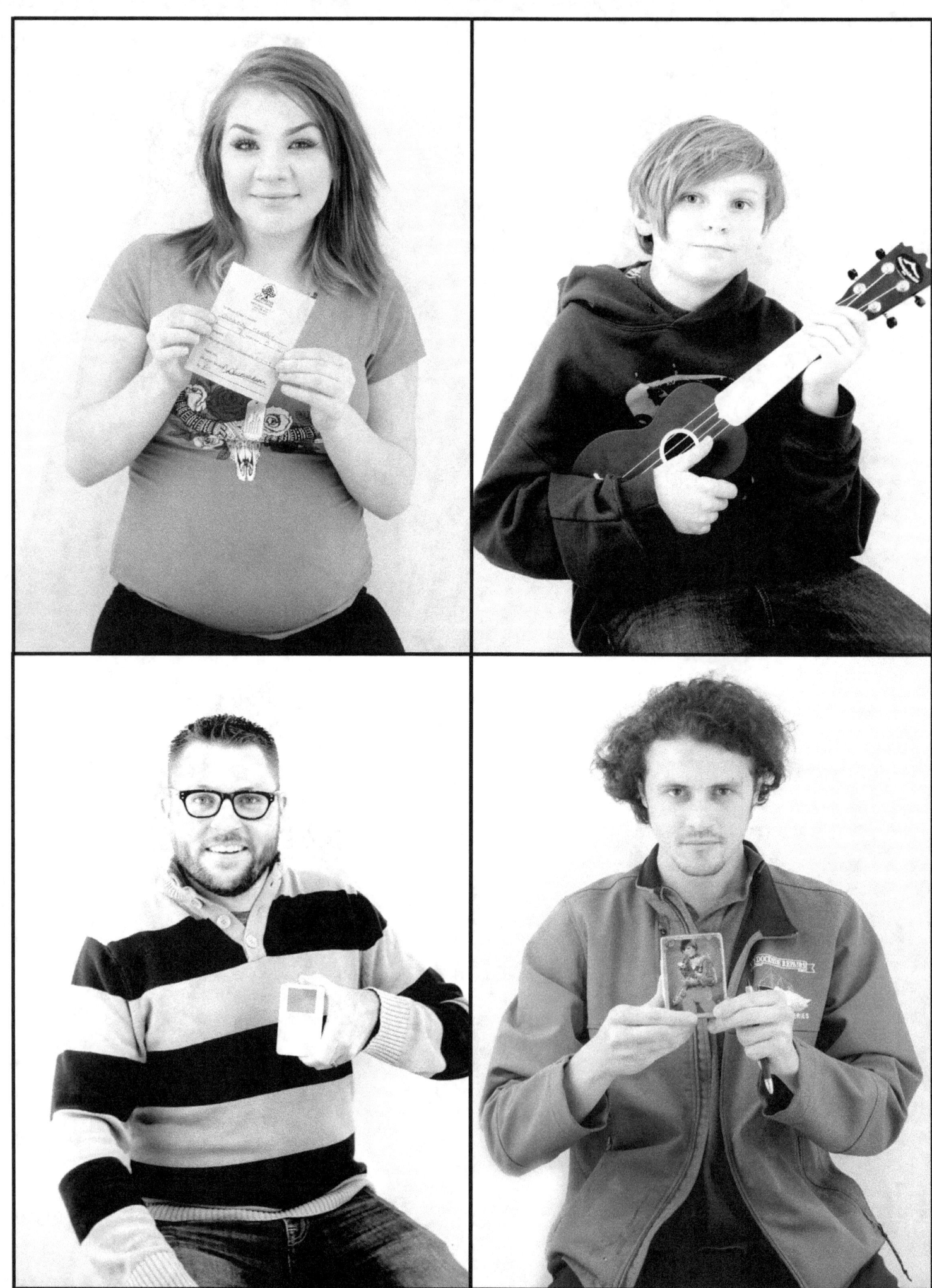

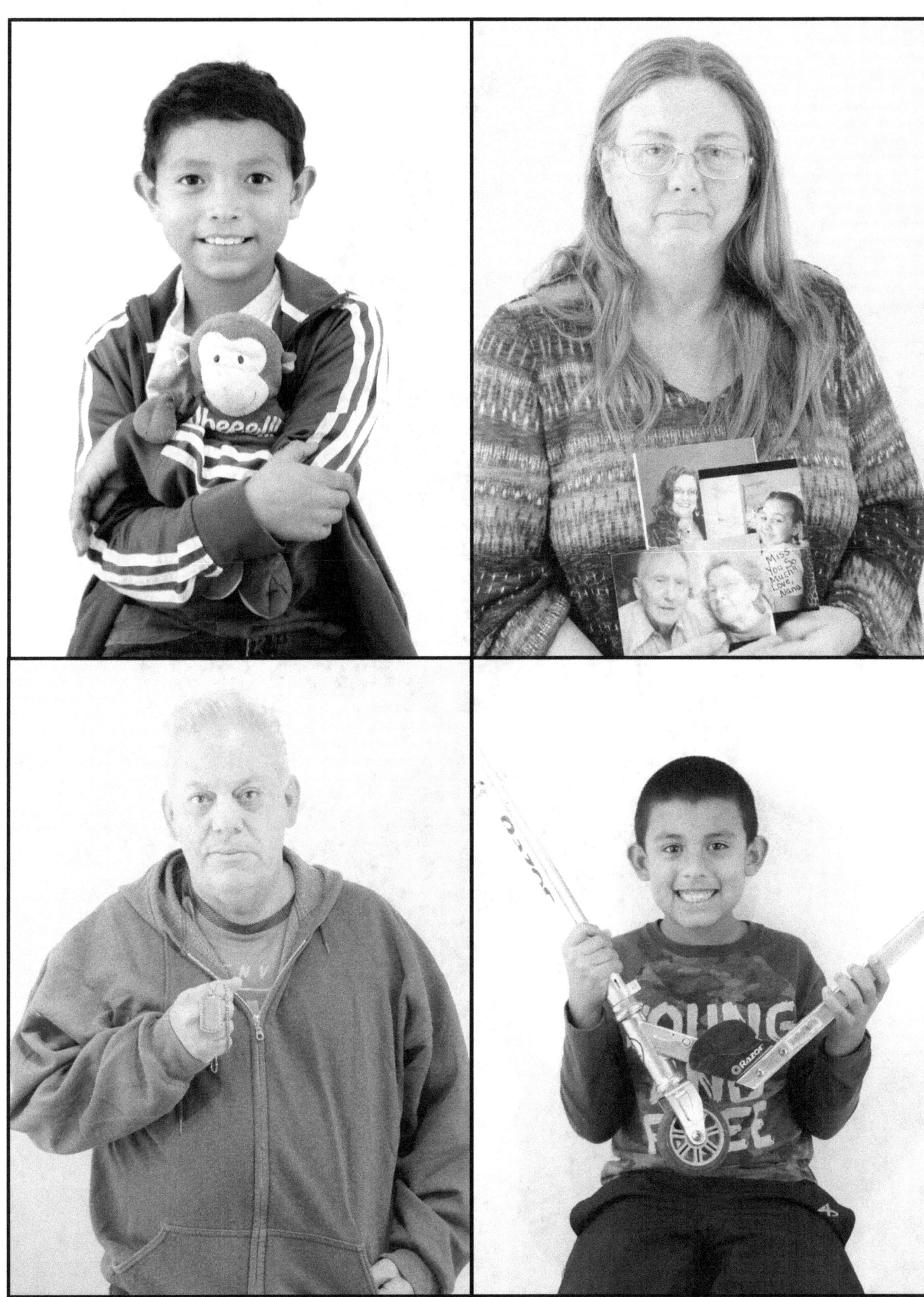

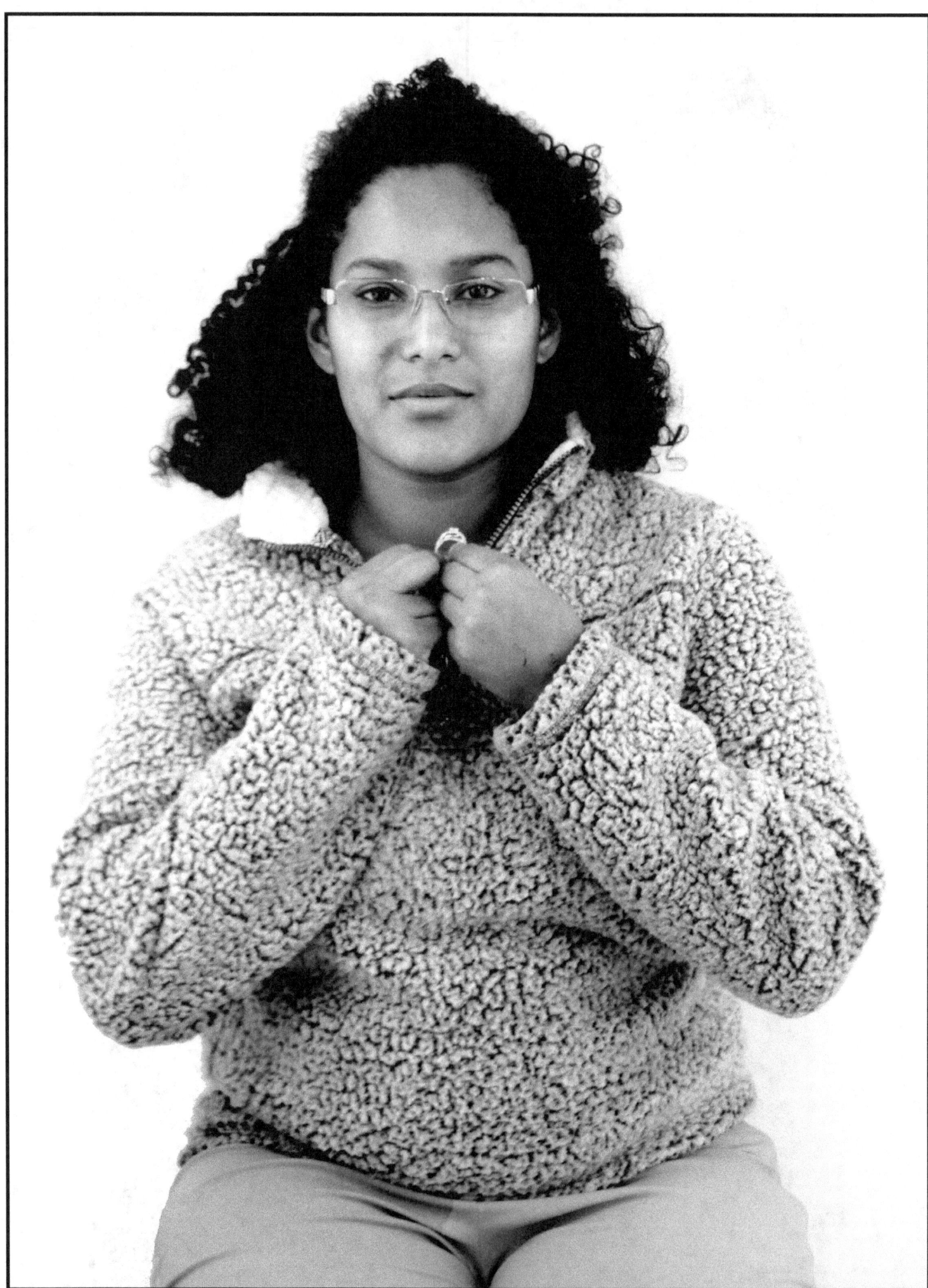

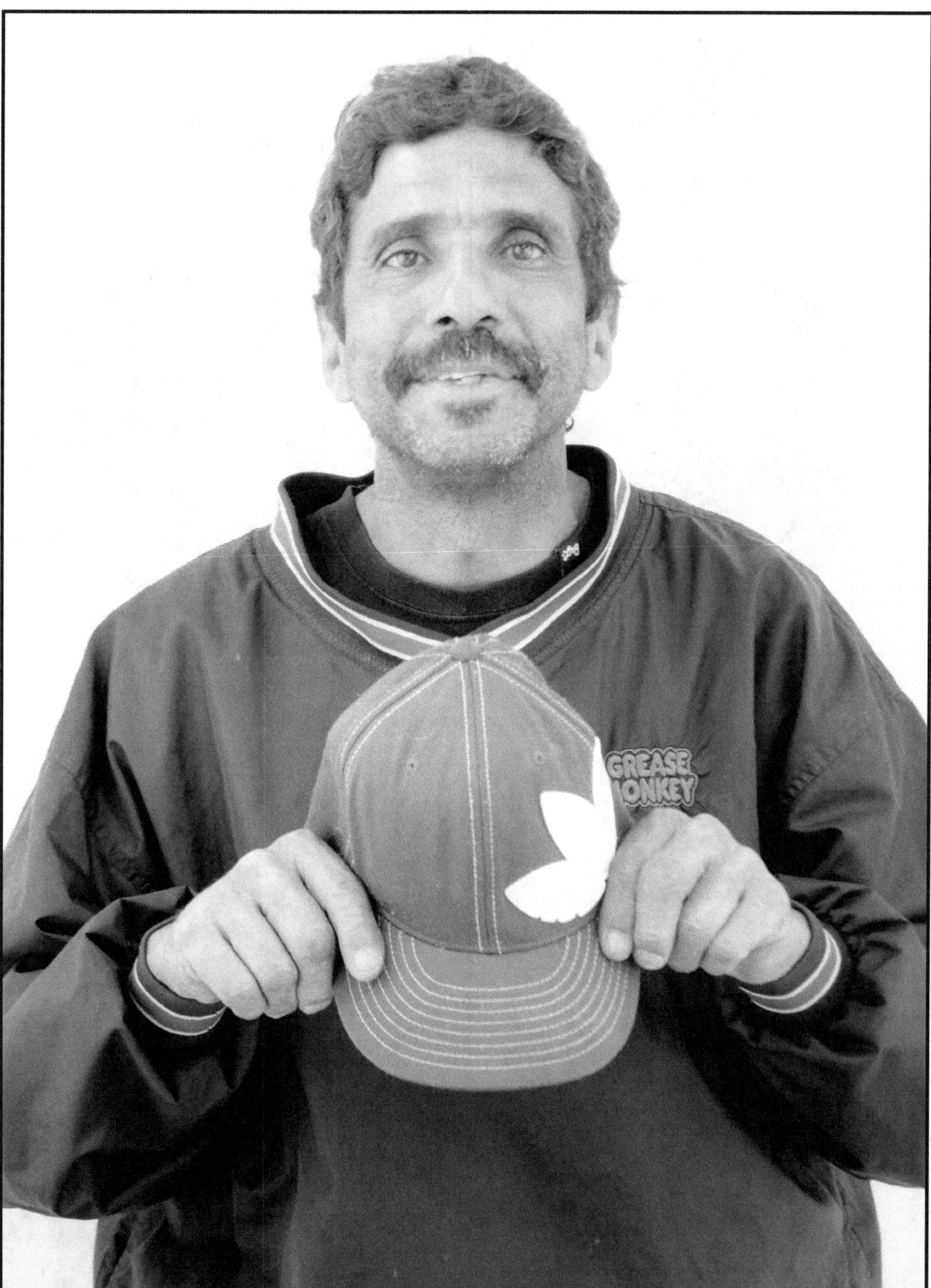

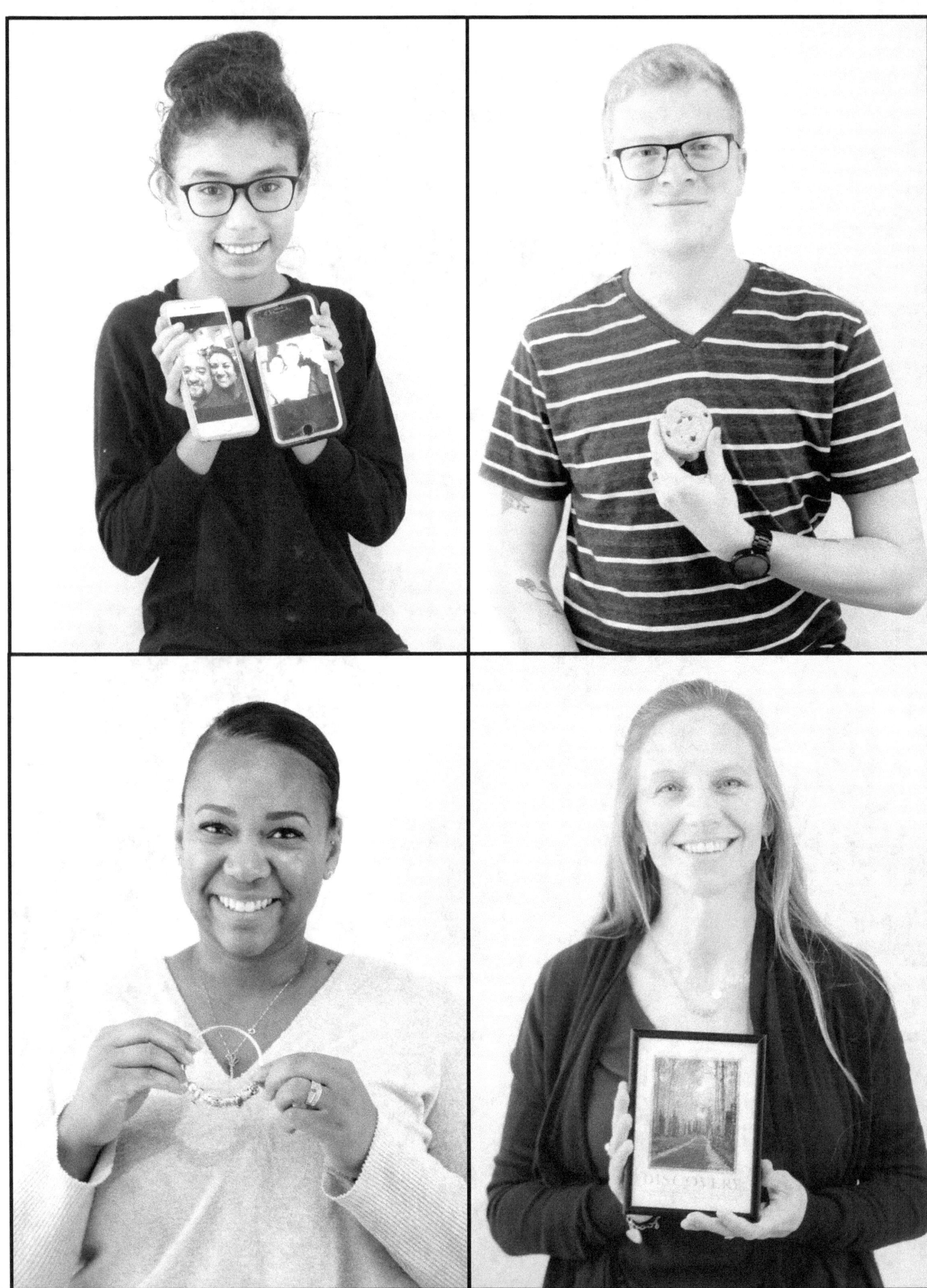

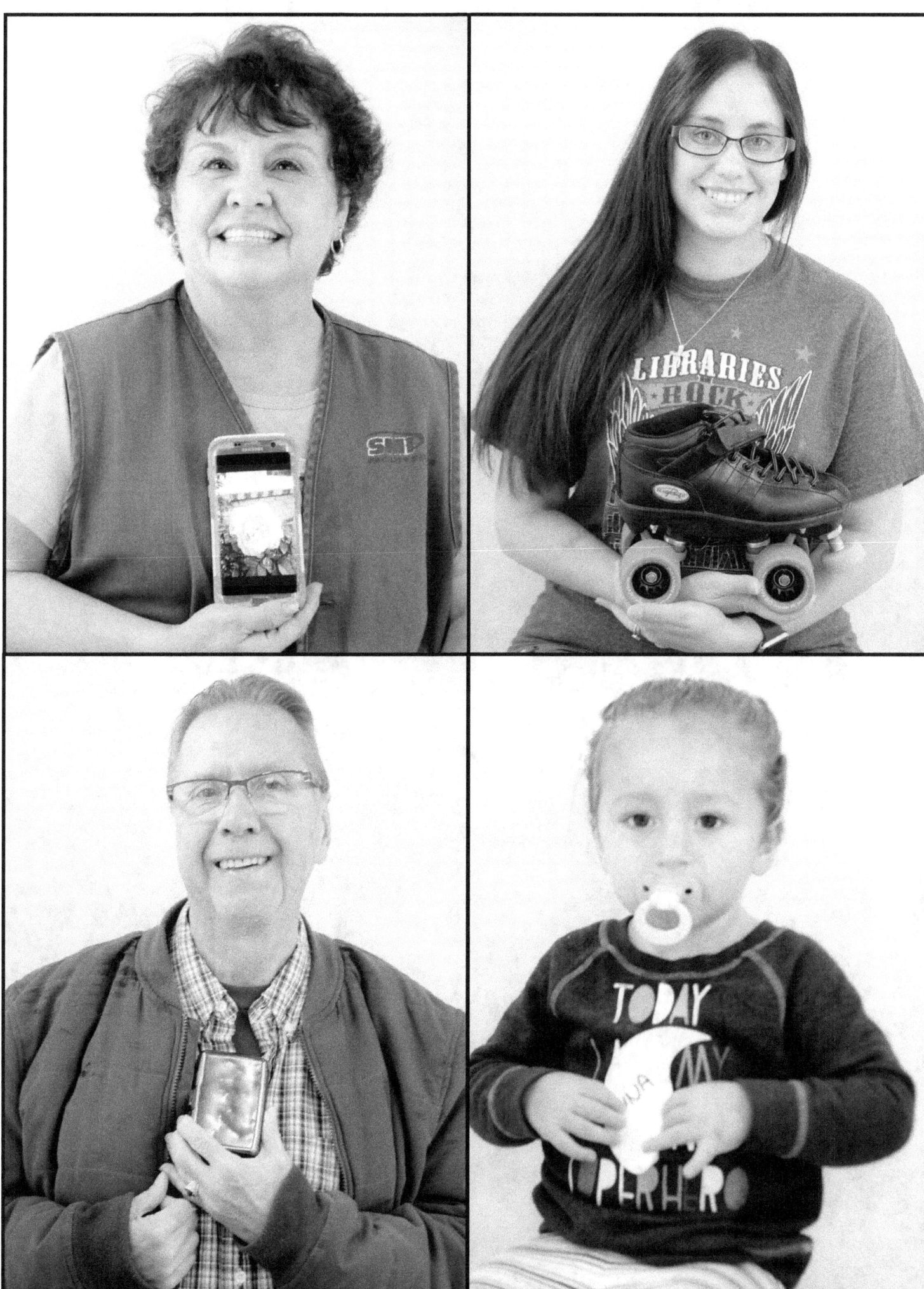

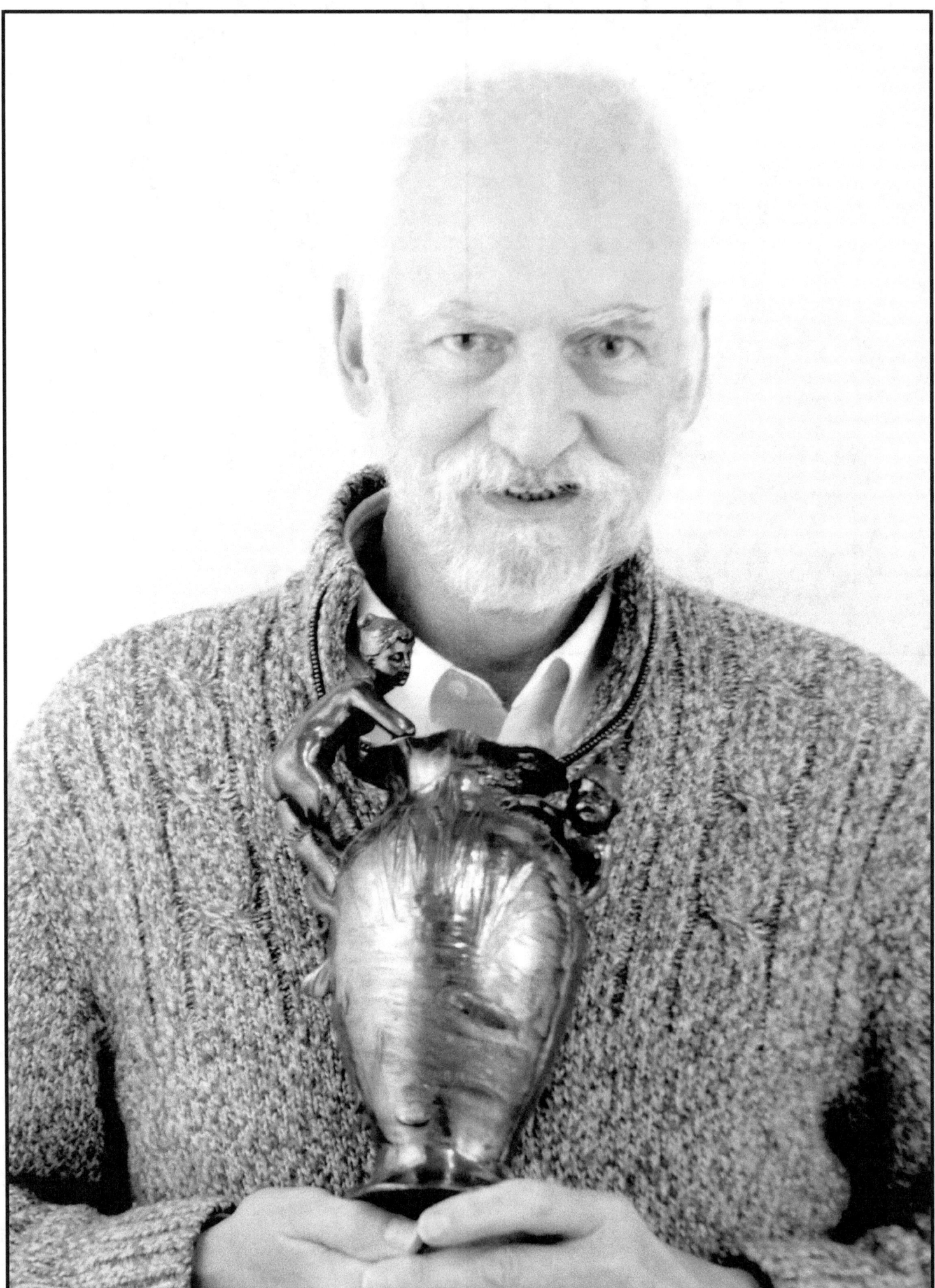

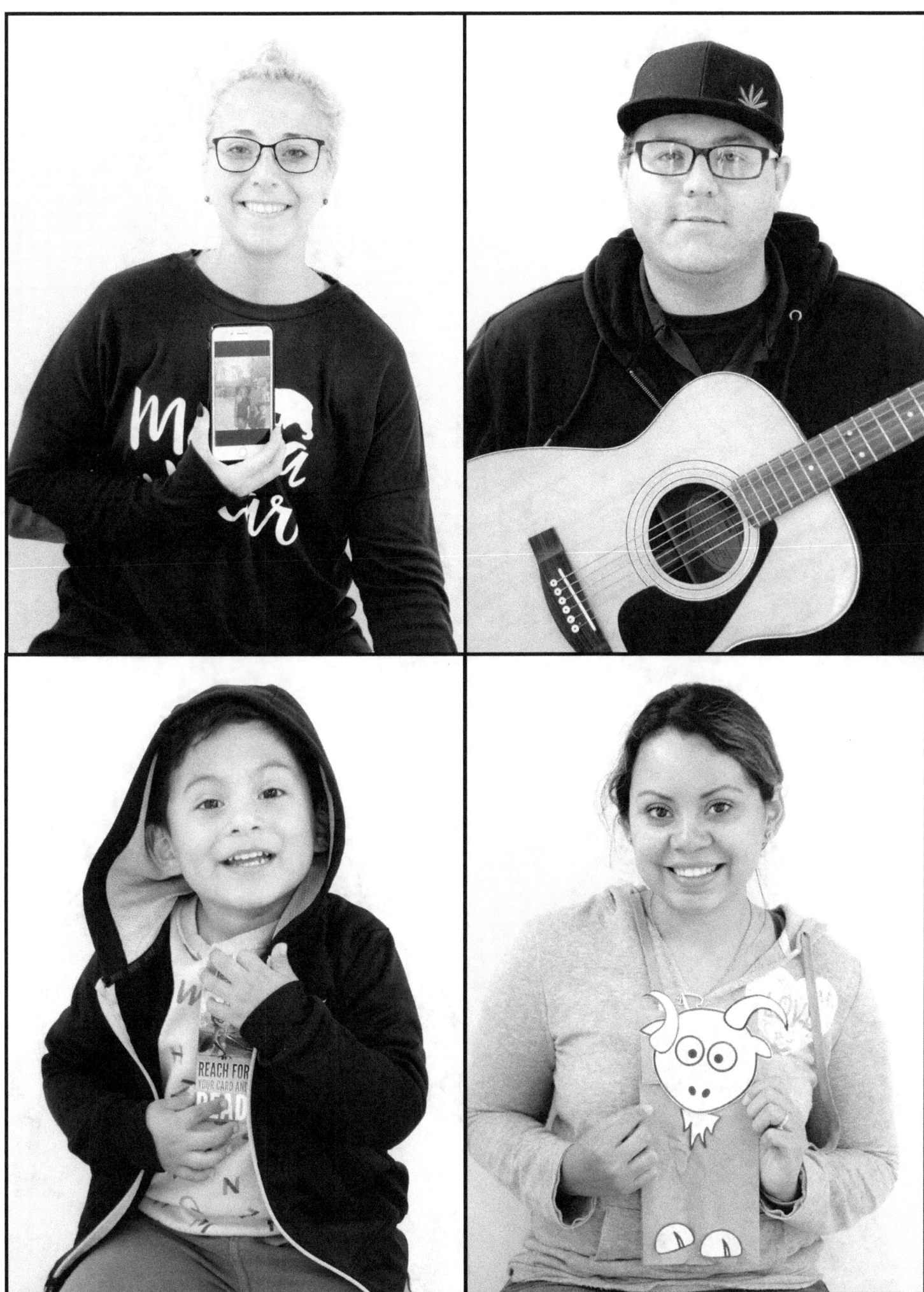

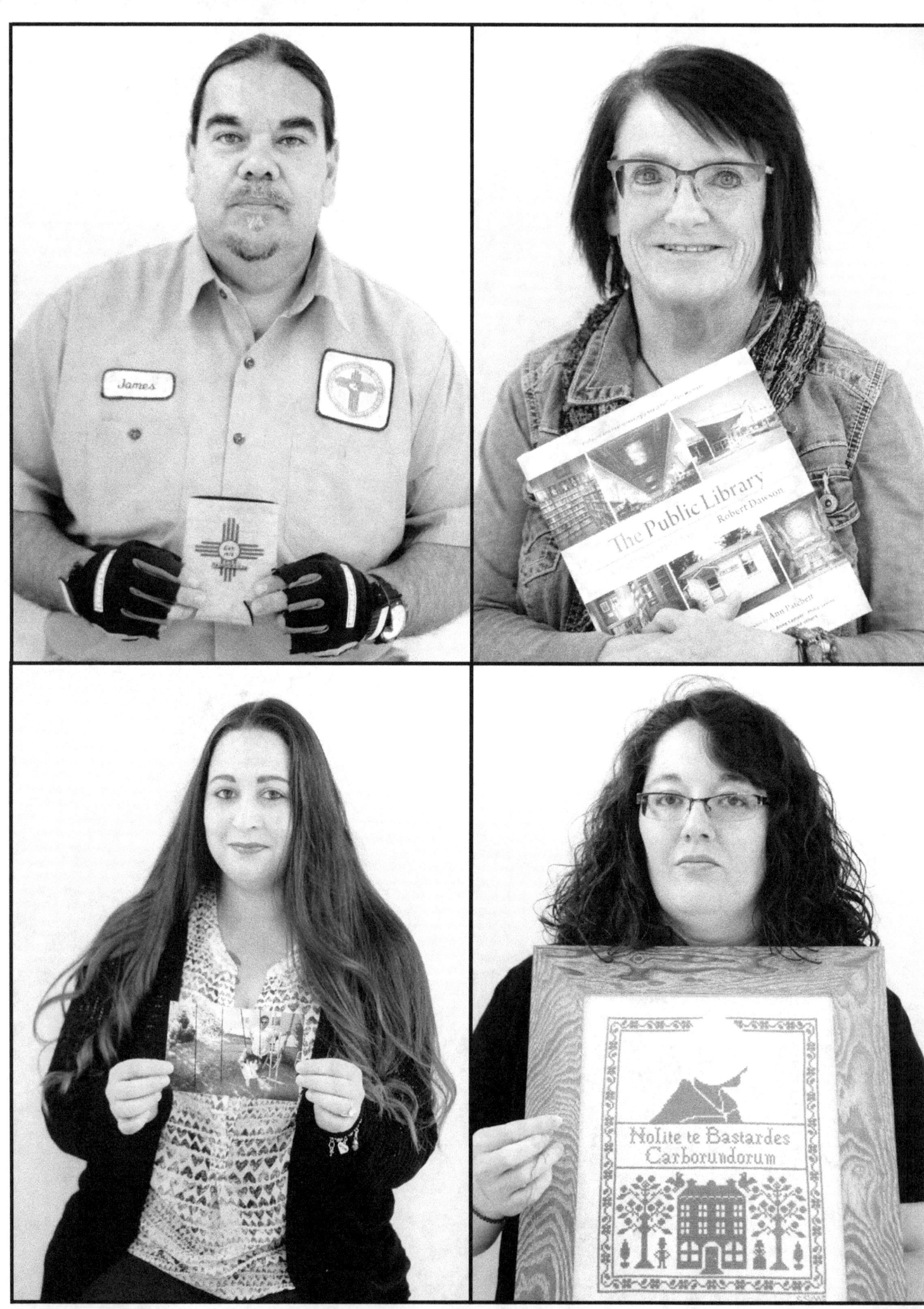

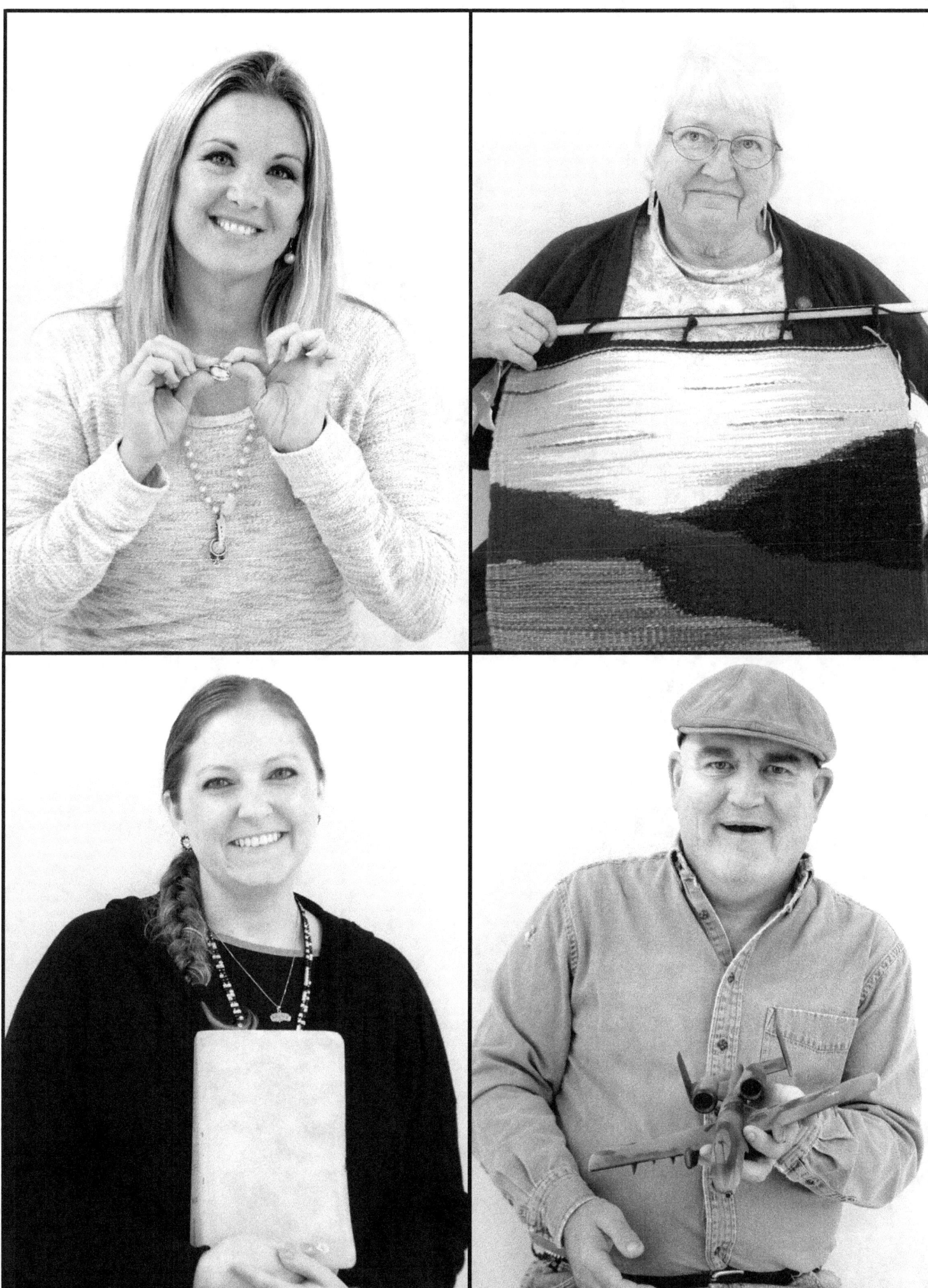

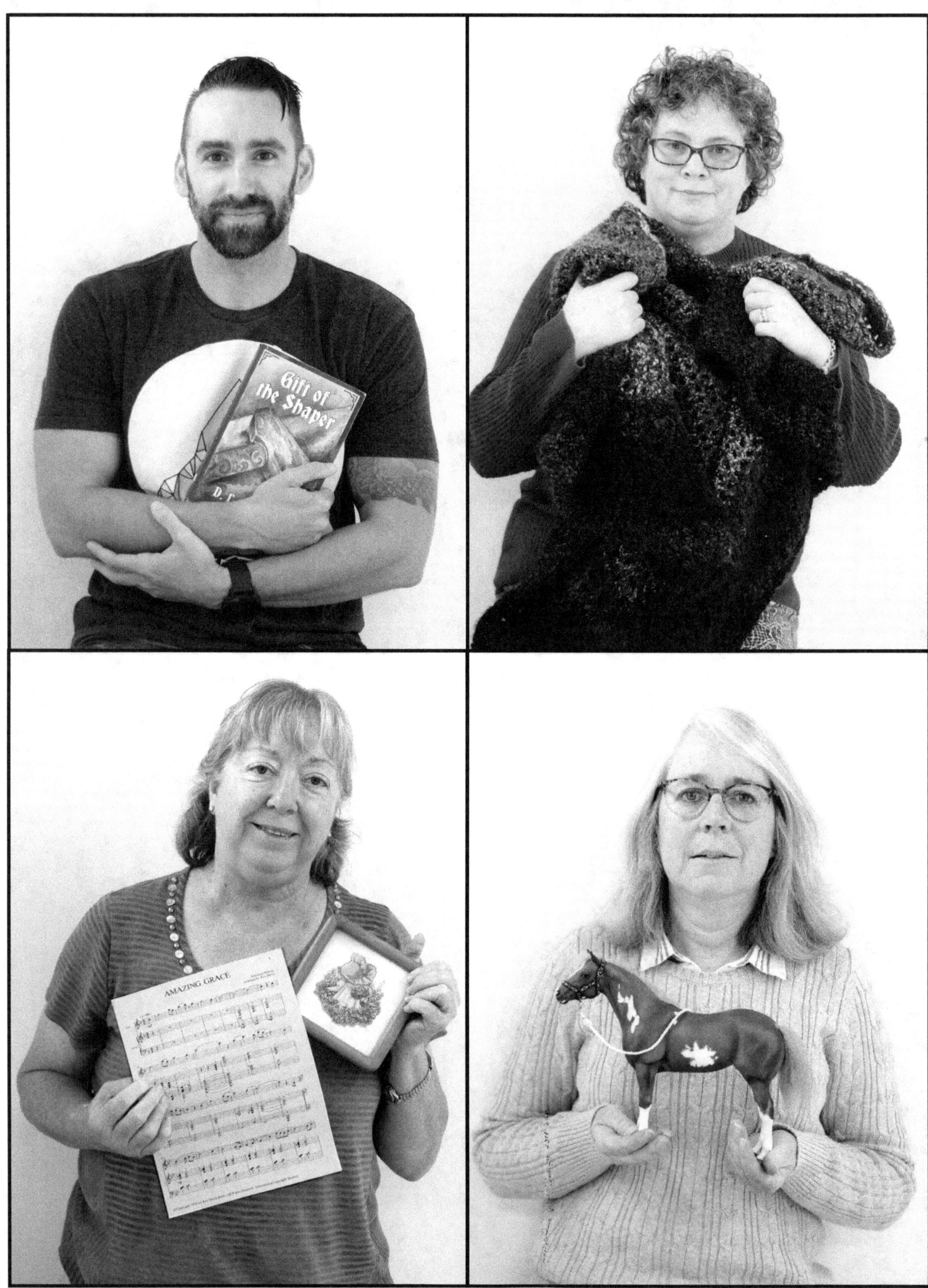

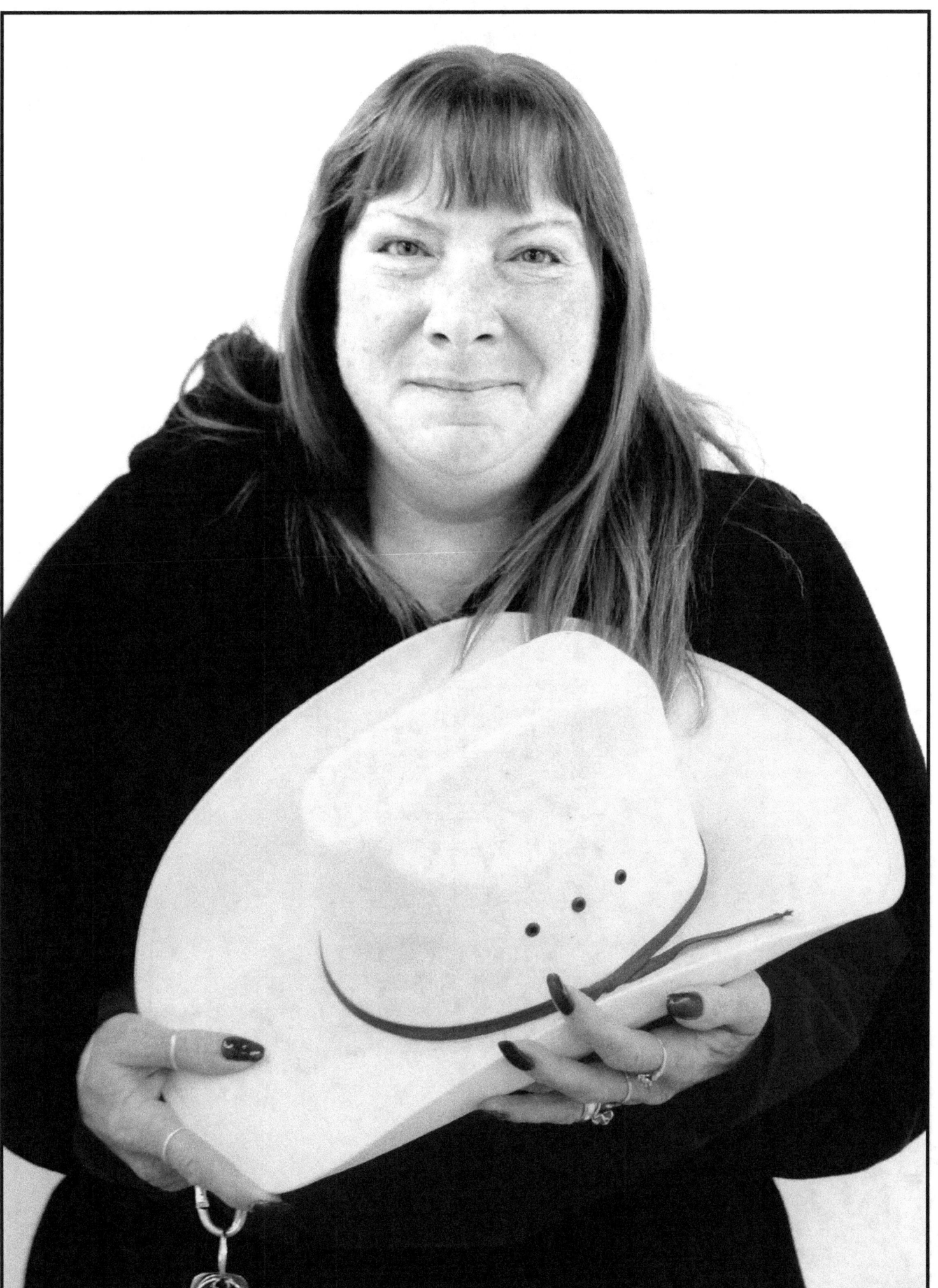

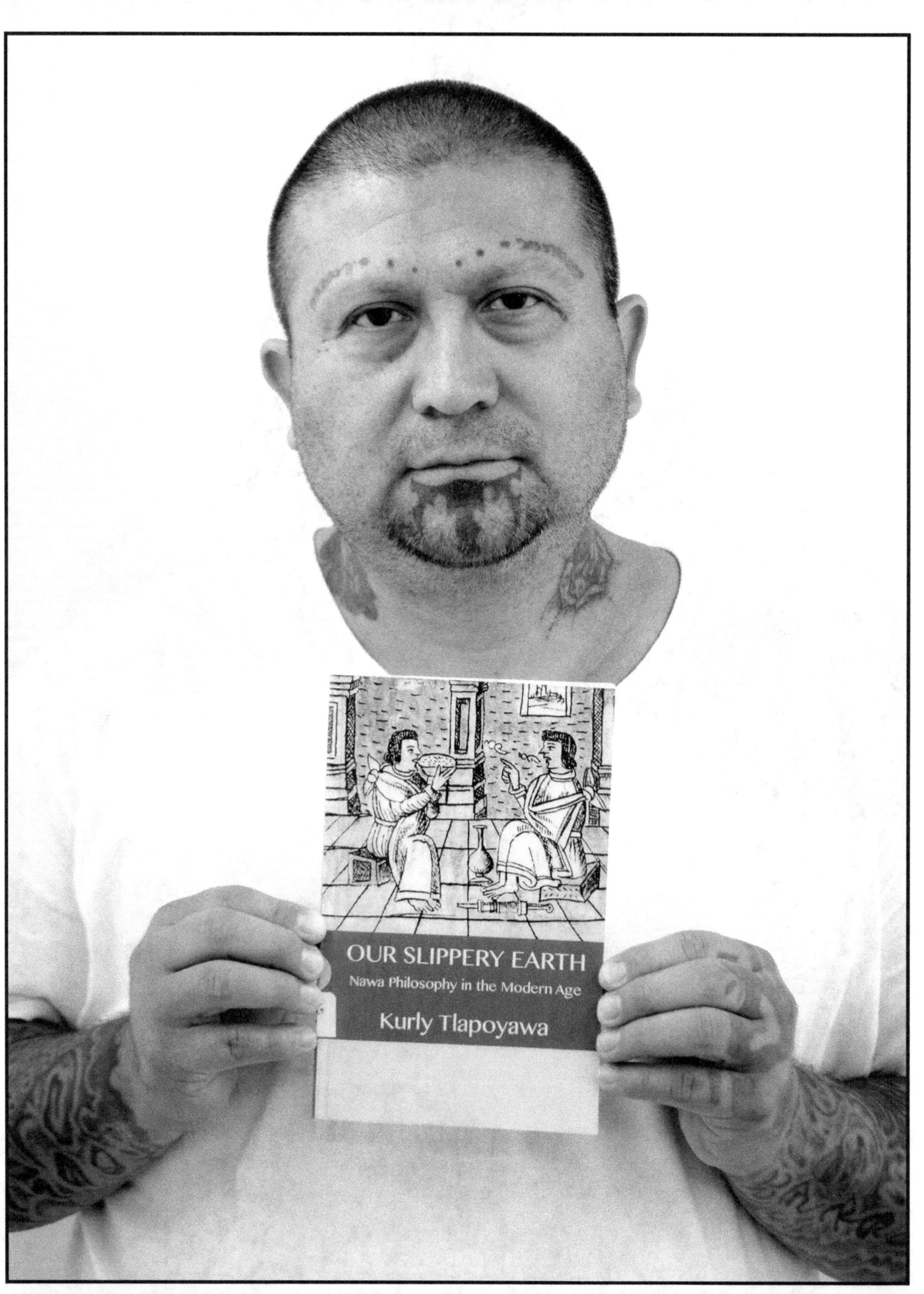

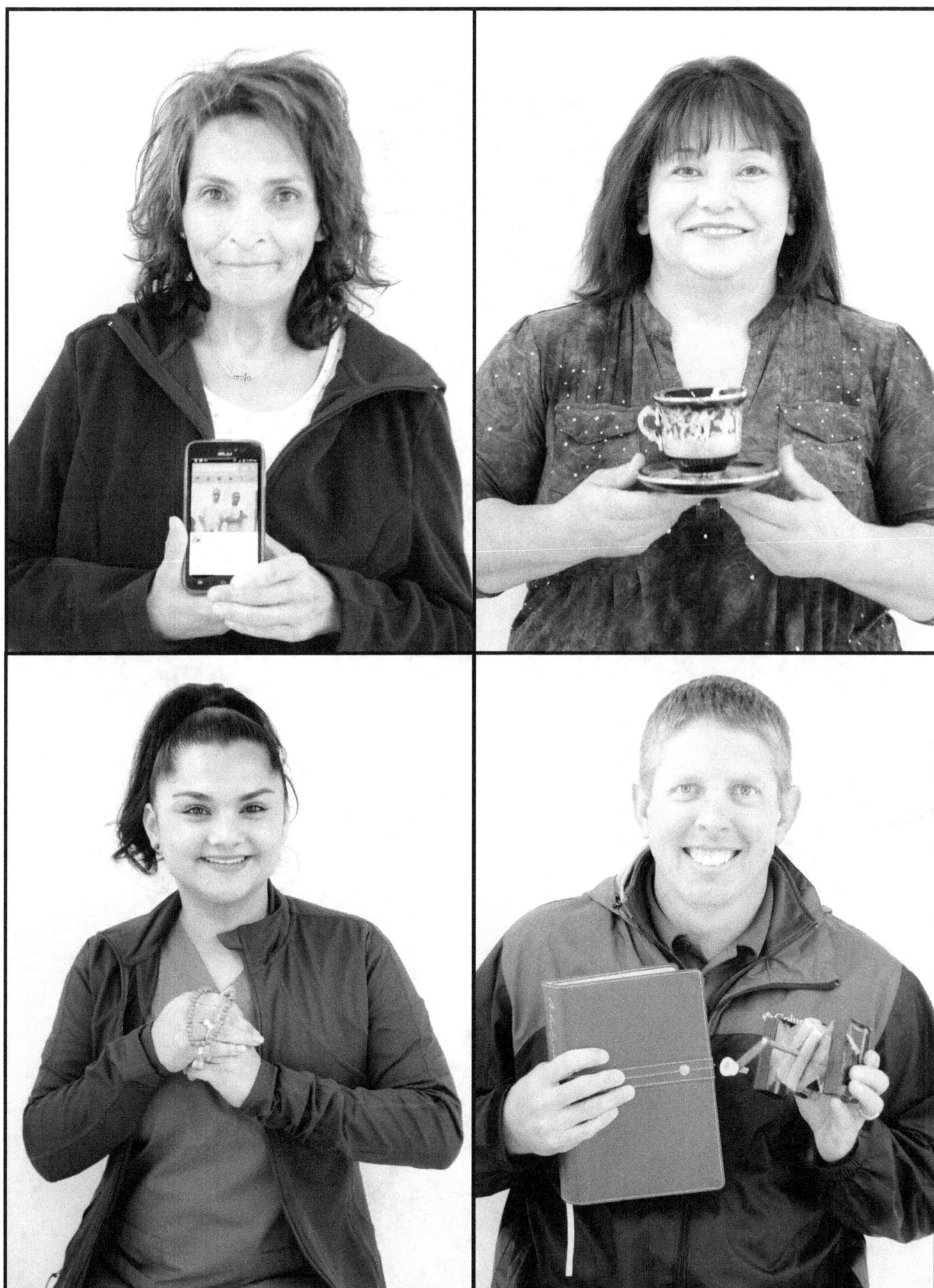

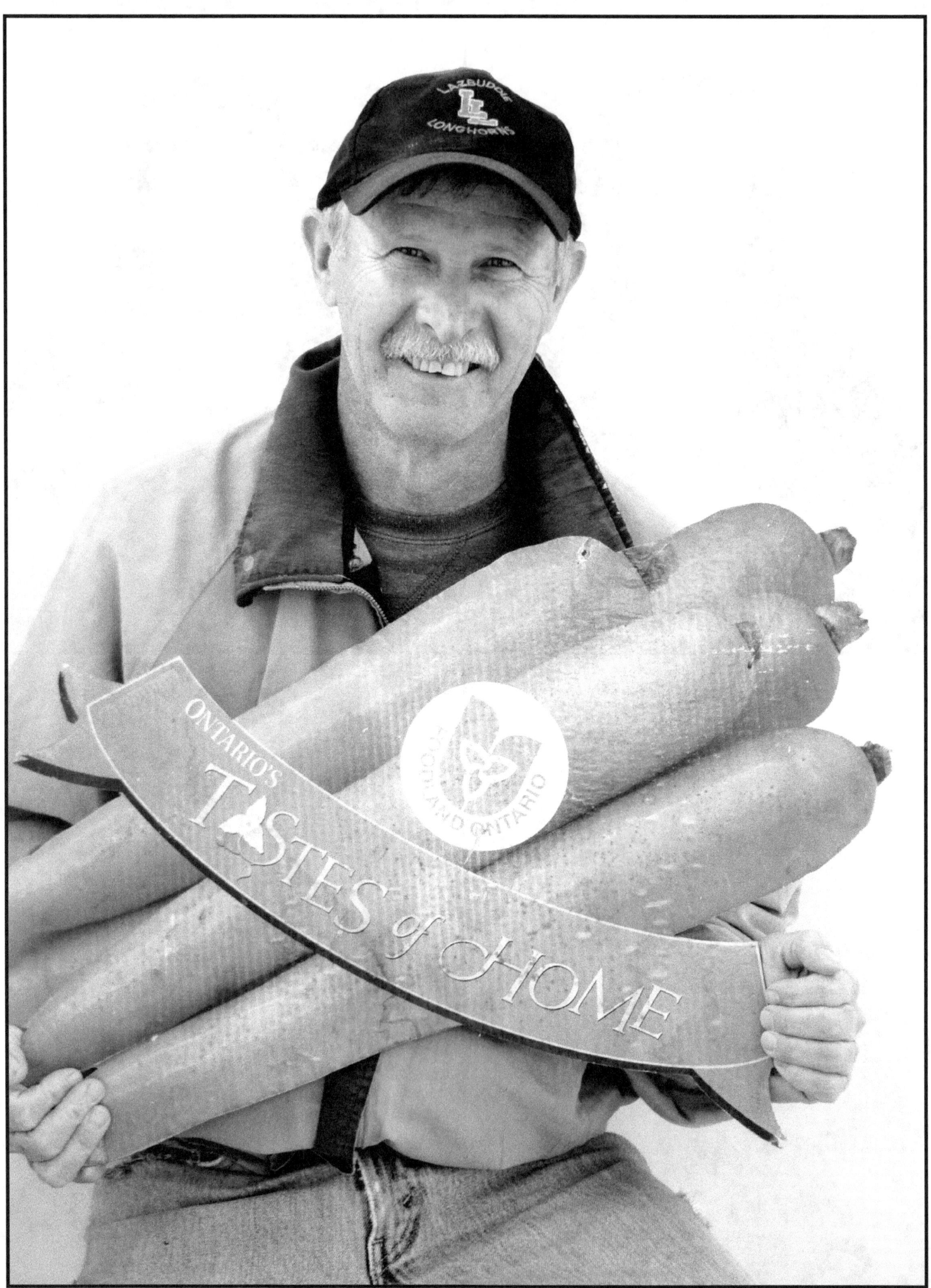

Participants were invited to reflect on the phrase "e pluribus unum."

In Roswell, the meaning of E Pluribus Unum (out of many, one) has been turned inside out to be: From one man, Donald B. Anderson, came an art community.

Don's philanthropy started in the 1940's with the Roswell Museum, then he founded the Roswell Artist-in-Residence Program in 1967 and the Anderson Museum of Contemporary Art in 1994. No other individual has affected the arts and culture in Roswell as much as Don; and I, having been a Roswellite all my life, am eternally grateful. In fact the painting I'm holding in my Axle picture is more than just a special object (an original painting by Don), it represents my connection to the arts community and my appreciation to Don for enticing artists to come here.

Brinkman Randle, Roswell

I think that "from many one" means that all people should be treated alike.

Mason Deen

I think that "from many one" means people should be treated kind.

Ryder Deen

E Pluribus Unum to me means: One World made up of Many Diversified Peoples.

Shelia Laws

During the past 5 years I have had many sorrows and many joys. But the one joy that came out of the 5 years was my move to New Mexico to start a new begining. And the one sorrow out of the many sorrows was the passing of my partner of 20 years.

Gerald Kedik

I have never considered myself as not one of the many. I have considered myself equal to the many but at the same time, an individual person in my own right. I still believe I have the same rights as others. I believe that each of us chooses to belong to the larger group, the people of our country. We all have these same rights. Not more, not less, but equal.
E pluribus unum

Kenneth I Dewey

The phrase "e pluribus unum" has, since childhood, filled me with feelings of warmth and gratitude for my country, comprised of diverse peoples from all parts of the world who share a common love for this place we call home. I appreciate the opportunity my ancestors had to be able to come to this wonderful land and to help care for and respect it and the people they encountered here. In turn they were respected and greatly helped by others. I have always been inspired by the mix of people, whether they have heritage that comes from lineage that predates any written history or whether they are recent arrivals. I believed that through our many internal trials and conflicts, the struggle for equal opportunities and recognition would prevail. I have often been thrilled by the energy and the ideas that newcomers brought to our country. Our country and our people seemed to me a living entity, always stretching and trying new ways and incorporating fresh backgrounds into our fluid culture. We were not stagnant. I thought that throughout our country there was great pride in and appreciation for the incorporation of new peoples and their traditions into what makes us all "Americans". What other country in the world was so alive, so elastic, and yet so grounded? All of us carried, I thought, this underlying idealism of we are ONE. But today with the inflammatory and divisive rhetoric to which our country has been subjected in the past two years, my faith in "e pluribus unum" has been greatly challenged. I hope passionately that our country shows its strength and unbroken belief in our ideals of unification with diversity. I am sadly conscious of how dangerously close we have come to the tyranny of "one" rather than holding fast the inspiration of "from MANY, one". E Pluribus Unum!

Sandra Waldo

The phrase "e pluribus unum" means that people, with all their wonderful differences, can stand and mesh together to create something greater than themselves. In my time at college I've been a part of many groups that enhanced my experiences there through interaction with people different than I, as well as hopefully doing the same in return. This system strengthens the organization as a whole and helps people to understand and consider different cultures, beliefs, and attitudes of various peoples.

Katherine Perelas

E pluribus unum
"From many one"
This phrase carries great power and speaks to me on many levels. It acknowledges the beauty and diversity of the collective. As American children we were taught that cultural differences form the melting pot which we called home or the United States. Little did we realize that this medley of such was unique to us and would offer a myriad of opportunities to experience the arts, culinary cuisine, languages, religion, and insight into ancient traditions. To live amongst such diversity was one of the greatest gifts an American parent could give to a child. We were truly blessed!

Here in The Hondo River Valley of Southeastern New Mexico we are strongly influenced by a collaboration of Mexican culture and the American Wild Wild West. At one time this area was very productive and accredited for the high quality and great quantities of produce from the orchards. It also had great fishing holes and lucrative cattle ranches.

Here in the valley, we are participants of the self-governed irrigation system or acequias which is unique to New Mexico and legally allows for the use of the rivers for the production of food. We work hard to produce apples, pears, pecans, peaches. and vegetable gardens, using mostly old traditional methods of farming.

I am proud to be an American food producer and choose this lifestyle and location over anywhere else in the world. I am also an Australian citizen and have traveled extensively throughout Europe, Southeast Asia, America, and Australia. I am committed to a life of freedom and am truly lucky to be an American.

Wendy Ansel

There is a very good reason that "E Pluribus Unum" was adopted as our country's original motto, and this reason is still relevant to all of us today: the concept of uniting together to achieve great things is one that still works. I would like to see more of it on a national scale, in today's troubled times!

Fortunately, on a local level, I am blessed to work with many wonderful people as partners to make our town a happy place to live.

E. Pluribus Unum: Out of Many, One
The unit, the family, that which binds us together

Jowanna Staump

E Pluribus Unum. It's a phrase I've grown up with but never really put much thought into it until recently. I am a living example of e pluribus unum as are most of us. The many I come from are almost exclusively European. I think about what those people went through to get to this country that has been rightfully described as a "melting pot." What they might say or do in today's climate of unwelcoming fear. I like to think that they, like so many others, would have kept on coming. If we are all ones from the many, then we must realize that down that dark, twisty branch of la familia tree are many more. I see myself as connected at my core to the human race. I do not hold myself higher or lower. I simply hold my hand out to the rest of the world. Like me, they are ones from many.

Arwen Lynch-Poe

This phrase "from many one" represents people in this community, this country, this world. The internet is making the world smaller. Some complain that it is erasing culture, but I see it as a wonderful avenue for cultural access. As we get in touch with more and more people in parts of the world with whom never would have had contact without the internet, we gain new things from them that we carry into our regular lives. Just in our small area, you can see the impact of so many cultures, Native American, African American, Asian, German, Hispanic, etc. It's beautiful. We all have a unique part of ourselves to give the world. All of our contributions affect all others in ways we may never know, all around the world, of all cultures and races. That is what e pluribus unum means to me.

Robyn McComb

Just to let you know that I reflected upon the Latin phrase and it means to me that all peoples no matter race or creed who reside in this state of New Mexico belong to the One United States of America.

Fran Gelineau

E Pluribus Unum
In the photo, I am holding a leather-trimmed Moroccan textile case purchased years ago at a garage sale. Inside the case is a black leather notebook embossed with "Linworth Publishing, Inc." The notebook was a gift to me from Linworth after the publication of my second book, Children's and Young Adult Literature by Latino Writers: A Guide for Librarians, Teachers, Parents, and Students.

After my retirement as an educator and librarian, I wrote and published six guide books on authentic multicultural literature for young readers. During my years of work with students from several cultures, I became aware that very few minority authors had been published in the U.S. Even fewer books by minority authors had ever been published for young readers. My minority students never got to see characters like themselves in library books.

As a librarian, I was frustrated because I could not purchase books that would represent the cultural backgrounds of my students. In the course of researching for my six books, I read hundreds and hundreds of books by authors and illustrators representing a variety of cultural and ethnic groups in the United States. Through my research, I discovered the richness of many cultures.

Because I grew up not knowing my mother, some of my personal family history and heritage remain a mystery, but by reading authentic multicultural literature, I have experienced life in a multitude of cultures. Through my reading, I have come to realize that in most ways, we are all the same. Regardless of our skin tones and hair colors, we all exist in human bodies. Our blood is red. We all feel pain. We are all capable of love. Our family backgrounds and histories simply add more dimensions to our life stories.

When I consider the cultural backgrounds of the circle of friends who enrich my life, I can identify Native American, African American, Jewish, and European ancestry. Some of my friends' ancestors immigrated from Ireland, England, Scotland, Czechoslovakia, Spain, France, Africa, Poland, Cambodia, Laos, and Mexico. I am blessed to be living in the United States, a country populated by American Indians and a variety of immigrants. My life is made richer by the blending of a multitude of cultures. Like the patterns and colors of the case I am holding in the photograph, my country is a rich tapestry of cultures and ethnicities.

Sherry York

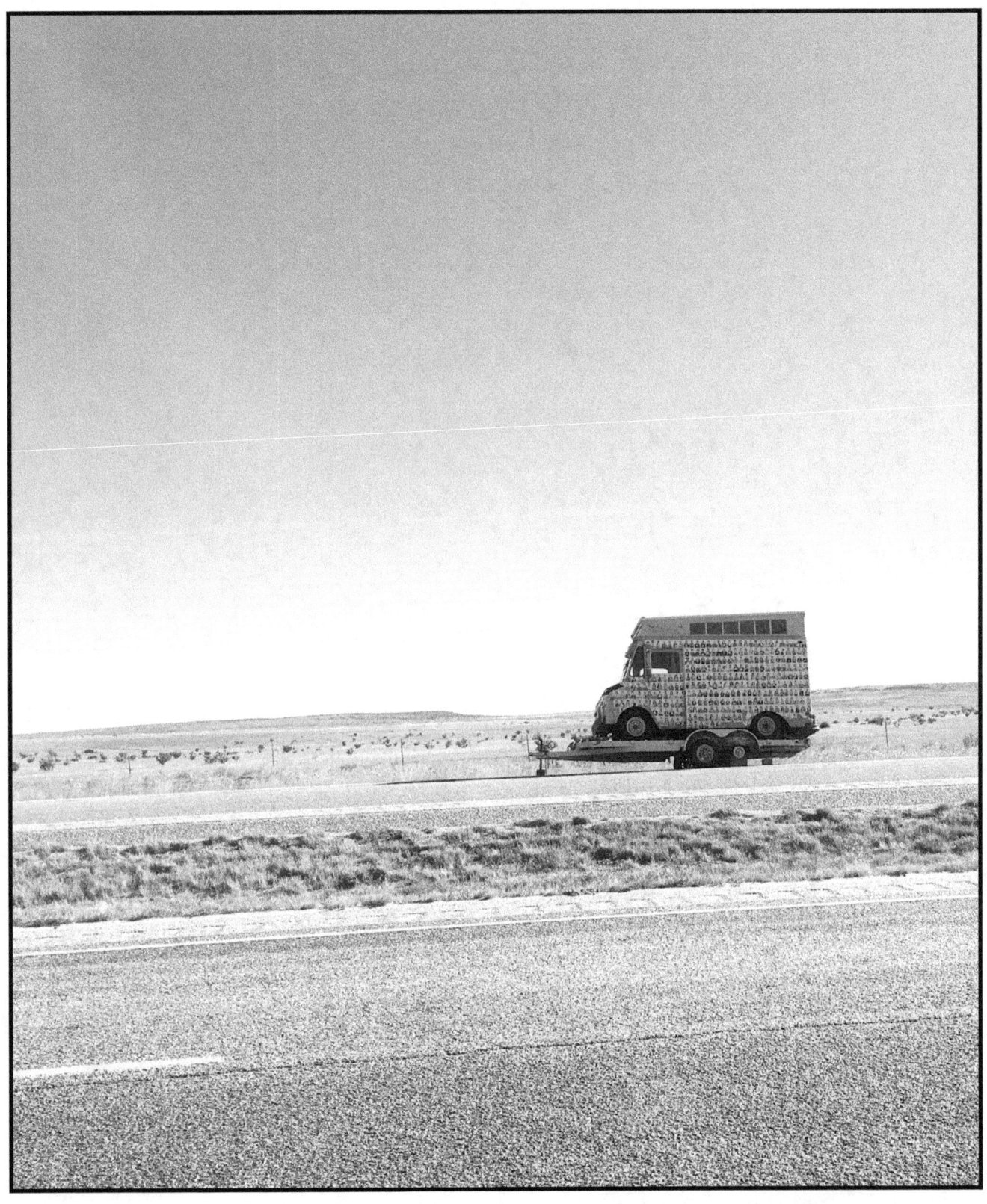

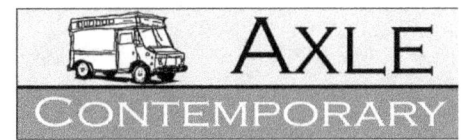

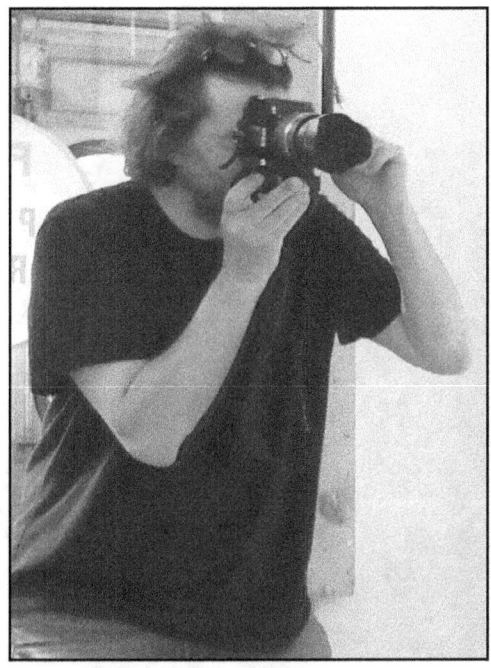

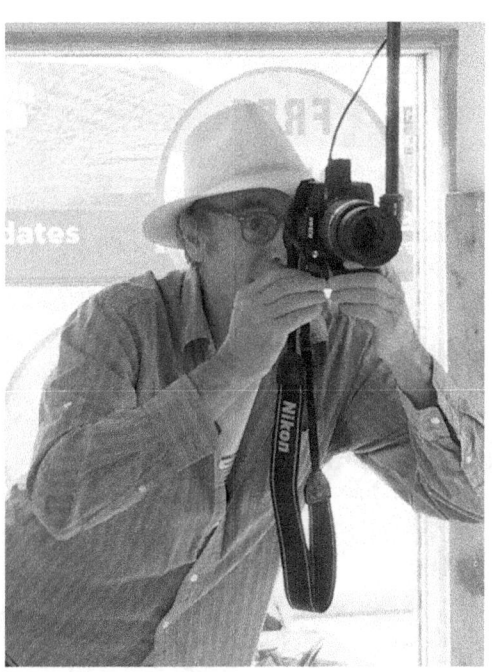

Matthew Chase-Daniel   Jerry Wellman

Axle Contemporary is a collaborative project by artists Matthew Chase-Daniel and Jerry Wellman. The mobile gallery is an innovative vehicle for arts distribution. Since 2010, it has grown beyond the confines of the van/gallery, and now includes book publishing, performance art, and alternative projects for socially engaged art creation and dissemination in the public sphere. Axle Contemporary has exhibited the work of over 300 New Mexico artists in over 100 exhibitions.

Matthew Chase-Daniel is a Santa Fe-based artist working primarily in photography and sculpture. His artwork has been exhibited across the U.S. and in Europe, and he has created numerous public art projects.

Jerry Wellman's paintings and drawings have been exhibited at various museums and galleries across the country, and his video animation work has been presented at national and international video festivals.

www.axleart.com